E DUE

SEXUAL DEVELOPMENT
IN CHILDHOOD

THE KINSEY INSTITUTE SERIES

John Bancroft, *General Editor*

SEXUAL DEVELOPMENT IN CHILDHOOD

Edited by John Bancroft

INDIANA
University Press
Bloomington & Indianapolis

This book is a publication of

Indiana University Press

601 North Morton Street

Bloomington, Indiana 47404-3797 USA

http://iupress.indiana.edu

Telephone orders	800-842-6796
Fax orders	812-855-7931
Orders by e-mail	iuporder@indiana.edu

Library of Congress Cataloging-in-Publication Data

Sexual development in childhood / edited by John Bancroft.

      p.   cm. — (The Kinsey Institute series ; v. 7)

      Includes bibliographical references and index.

      ISBN 0-253-34243-0 (alk. paper)

      1. Psychosexual development—Congresses. 2. Children—Sexual behavior—Congresses. 3. Teenagers—Sexual behavior—Congresses. I. Bancroft, John. II. Series.

BF723.S4S47 2003

306.7'083—dc21   2003001814

   2   3   4   5   08   07   06   05

Contents

Acknowledgments

This book and the workshop on which it is based were made possible by a grant from the W. T. Grant Foundation.

I would also like to express my gratitude to Sandra Ham for her editorial help.

Introduction

JOHN BANCROFT

Over the past 50 years we have seen a substantial change in the pattern of sexual activity among adolescents in the United States and many other parts of the world. During this time, sexual activity has started at progressively younger ages (Alan Guttmacher Institute, 1994). In the last few years, there has been a slowing or even reversal of some of these trends; the proportion of boys between the ages of 15 and 17 who have experienced sexual intercourse has decreased significantly, and teenage males are using condoms more frequently (Santelli, Lindberg, Abma, McNeely, & Resnick, 2000). However, in general we are dealing with a much more sexually active and aware adolescent population than was the case 50 years ago. While in some respects we can view this pattern positively—as reflecting a less sexually inhibited environment for young people to develop sexually in—there are substantial problems that ensue. Approximately one million teenagers become pregnant each year. Although there has been a decline in the proportion of sexually active teenagers who become pregnant, this has been counterbalanced by an increase in the proportion of teenage women who are sexually active (Alan Guttmacher Institute, 1994). Twenty-five percent of sexually active teenagers become infected with a sexually transmitted disease each year, and many of the cases of HIV infection diagnosed in adults in their twenties were contracted during adolescence. Sexual assault on teenagers is widespread, and 74% of women who had sexual intercourse before age 14 and 60% of those before age 15 were coerced (Alan Guttmacher Institute, 1994).

There are a number of factors influencing this picture. The rise of a youth culture (Hobsbawm, 1994), which allows relative independence of teenagers from the values and attitudes of their parents' generation, is important, combined with a massive commercial exploitation of sex, which fills the media and surrounds young people with sexual images and messages. The Internet is a new and important source of sexual stimulation as well as information which is basically outside of social control. The age of onset of puberty continues to decrease, with the earlier onset in African American girls becoming more marked (Herman-Giddens et al., 1997). Age at puberty has a considerable impact on the age of sexual debut (Rowe

& Rodgers, 1994) and may account for much of the racial differences in age of first sexual intercourse.

One obviously important aspect of adolescent sexual development is the influence of earlier childhood experiences. A substantial amount of evidence has been presented in recent years indicating a link between childhood sexual abuse and later problems, including premature onset of sexual activity in adolescence, multiple partners, and increased risk of STDs (Davis & Petretic-Jackson, 2000; Holmes & Slap, 1998; Kendall-Tackett, Williams, & Finkelhor, 1993; Wyatt, 1991).

The focus on childhood sexual abuse has, however, impeded any further understanding of the relevance of normal childhood sexuality and later development. The historian Philip Jenkins (1998) has recently documented the cycles of "moral panic" about child sexual abuse that recurred at strangely predictable intervals during the 20th century. We are in the midst of one such cycle right now, and one consequence of this is that rational debate and scientific inquiry into normal childhood sexual development are currently very difficult. Part of the "moral panic" phenomenon is the assumption that "normal" children are asexual, and any evidence of sexual behavior or interest in a child tends to be interpreted as evidence that the child has been sexually abused. This is not only potentially harmful to any such child who has not been abused, it also obscures our understanding of the impact of child sexual abuse when it does occur. It is also difficult, at the present time, for parents to know how best to react to signs of sexual interest or activity in their children.

A recent and disturbing episode in this story was the resolution, passed unanimously by the House of Representatives in Washington, D.C., on July 12, 1999, sponsored by Matt Salmon (R-Arizona), condemning a scientific paper (Rind, Tromovitch, & Bauserman, 1998) which, on the basis of a meta-analysis of 59 studies of college students, concluded that when other factors during childhood (e.g., negative family environment) were controlled for, the effect of childhood sexual abuse on later adjustment appeared to be small for the majority, especially boys. The paper was condemned as an endorsement of pedophilia. This paper is open to criticism on a number of counts, but it was a serious scientific study, and this rejection by the political establishment of a peer-reviewed scientific paper is probably without precedent. Since that time, a number of academics who have either supported Rind and his colleagues or in some other way questioned the assumption that the victims of childhood sexual abuse are invariably seriously traumatized have been accused in public of being pro-pedophile. This is the current social climate.

There is therefore a serious need for rational and scientific debate as well as research about childhood sexuality. In response to this need, The Kinsey Institute hosted a workshop on sexual development, bringing together an authoritative group of researchers into childhood and adolescent sexuality to work at establishing a consensus on a number of key issues.

This workshop was funded by a grant from the W. T. Grant Foundation. This book is based on the papers presented and the discussions held at this workshop.

This three-and-a-half day workshop was held from May 16 through 20, 2001. The usual Kinsey Institute workshop format was used; a number of participants were asked to prepare preworkshop papers, which were circulated to all the participants before the workshop, with the expectation that they would all be read before the workshop began. Each presenter then had a short time (usually 10 minutes) to present the main points of the paper. One or two participants were invited to open the discussion with prepared responses. They were usually given around 15 minutes each. There were a few participants who were not presenters or invited discussants, resulting in a total group of around 30 people. The majority of the program time was dedicated to group discussion. The whole meeting was audiotaped and transcribed for publication in this volume.

There were two exceptions to this general rule: Philip Jenkins, the historian, gave his talk at the opening reception. It was followed by a lively discussion which, regrettably, was not recorded, and therefore does not appear in this volume. Jack (John E.) Bates and his colleagues were scheduled to present a paper at the workshop on their longitudinal study of development. Due to unforeseen circumstances, they were unable to attend. They have, however, provided the paper that would have been presented, and it is included as a postconference paper in this volume. Once again, we regret that we have no discussion of this paper to present, particularly as the need for longitudinal studies, and the possibilities of "hooking in" some questions about sexual development into a longitudinal study with broader objectives, were much discussed at the meeting. But we are delighted to be able to include their paper in this volume.

In this meeting there was an additional objective. Because of the controversial nature of the topic and current difficulties in maintaining a rational public debate, a key objective of the workshop was to search for a reasonable and authoritative consensus which could then be disseminated more widely as a Consensus Document, helpful to health professionals, teachers, and parents. Some discussion related to this objective is included in the general discussion in the final section of the book "Toward a Consensus." The themes and counter themes of this discussion give some indication of how difficult a task this will be at this time. Maybe reaction to this book will aid the process.

References

Alan Guttmacher Institute. (1994). *Sex and America's teenagers.* New York: Author.
Davis, J. L., & Petretic-Jackson, P. A. (2000). The impact of child sexual abuse on

interpersonal functioning: A review and synthesis of the empirical literature. *Aggression and Violent Behavior, 5,* 291–328.

Herman-Giddens, M. E., Slora, E. J., Wasserman, R. C., Bourdony, C. J., Bhapkar, M. V., Koch, C. G., et al. (1997). Secondary sexual characteristics and menses in young girls seen in office practice: A study from the Pediatric Research in Office Settings Network. *Pediatrics, 99,* 505–512.

Hobsbawm, E. (1994). *Age of extremes: The short twentieth century, 1914–1991.* London: Michael Joseph.

Holmes, W. C., & Slap, G. B. (1998). Sexual abuse of boys: Definition, prevalence, correlates, sequelae, and management. *Journal of the American Medical Association, 280,* 1855–1862.

Jenkins, P. (1998). *Moral Panic.* New Haven, CT: Yale University Press.

Kendall-Tackett, K. A., Williams, L. M., & Finkelhor, D. (1993). Impact of sexual abuse on children: A review and synthesis of recent empirical studies. *Psychological Bulletin, 113,* 164–180.

Rind, B., Tromovitch, P., & Bauserman, R. (1998). A meta-analytic examination of assumed properties of child sexual abuse using college samples. *Psychological Bulletin, 124,* 22–53.

Rowe, D. C., & Rodgers, J. L. (1994). A social contagion model of adolescent sexual behavior: Exploring race differences. *Social Biology, 41,* 1–18.

Santelli, J. S., Lindberg, L. D., Abma, J., McNeely, C. S., & Resnick, M. (2000). Adolescent sexual behavior: Estimates and trends from four nationally representative surveys. *Family Planning Perspectives, 32,* 156–165, 194.

Wyatt, G. (1991). Child sexual abuse and its effects on sexual functioning. *Annual Review of Sex Research, 2,* 249–266.

SEXUAL DEVELOPMENT
IN CHILDHOOD

Part 1.

The Historical Context

Watching the Research Pendulum

PHILIP JENKINS

Briefly, the answer is No. The question, in case you were wondering, is the one posed by John Bancroft when he was suggesting the theme of my presentation, namely, is it possible for researchers to avoid being influenced by the extreme terms in which debates over childhood sexuality are so often presented? "Can we avoid this pendulum-swinging in our approach to this subject?" As we look at the study of childhood sexuality over the last century or so, the enormous variation in public attitudes over time initially seems to have little relation to the real threat posed to children's health or safety at any given point. I hope to show that the degree of variation is not quite as random as this might suggest, and that it might be possible to predict how attitudes will change over the next decade or so. But initially, what we see appears to be no more than a random walk between the extremes of indifference and panic.

To illustrate what I mean by these extremes, let me take two episodes. In 1931 an 11-year-old girl was brought before a juvenile court for her sex delinquency following repeated intercourse with a 60-year-old "boyfriend" who picked her up in a park. The man himself was acquitted, as the jury refused to send a man to prison "for a girl like that." She was the offender, she had caused the distressing incident, and any possible harm that she might have suffered was of trivial concern when set beside her moral depravity (Jenkins, 1998, p. 32). At another extreme, we will recall the overwhelming—if not surprising—reaction that greeted the 1998 study by Rind, Tromovitch, and Bauserman in the *Psychological Bulletin*. This was the now-notorious "meta-analytic examination" which dared to cast doubt upon the prevailing public orthodoxy that holds that any adult-child contact whatever, any type of child sexual abuse, must inevitably have catastrophic and life-ruining consequences for the younger partner—who in every instance must be termed "the victim" (Rind, Tromovitch, & Bauserman, 1998; Rind, Bauserman, & Tromovitch, 2000, 2001; see also Rind & Tromovitch, 1997). The 1931 incident occurred at a time of complacence about or indifference toward adult-child sexual contacts; the 1998 affair was a manifestation of a quite different period, at the opposite end of the pendulum swing.

Cycles of Concern

I wish to make several points in this presentation, but my first, and perhaps most important, is that such a cycle of public reactions has occurred over time—which is not obvious. There are still child protection activists who accept a far more simplistic view, namely that through much of history, child exploitation was virtually ignored as a social problem, presumably due to the patriarchal assumptions of government and the medical profession. Research in the past was restricted by cultural taboos, by prejudice and obscurantism. Only in modern times, since the 1960s or 1970s, have we discovered child abuse in all its horror, and this revelation is a paradigm shift comparable to the insights of Darwin, Freud, or Pavlov.

Today, it is claimed, we know facts unknown to previous generations, namely that children face a grave sexual danger in the form of abuse and molestation. Sexual abuse is a pervasive problem of vast scope; molesters or abusers are compulsive individuals whose crimes are repeated frequently with little hope of deterrence or cure; the behavior all too easily escalates to violence or murder. Sexual relations between adults and children invariably cause lasting damage to the child involved: a battery of psychological explanations exists to account for any failure by the victim to perceive harm from abuse, or to recognize its severity. Equally well established is the cycle of abuse, the notion that molestation so disturbs the victim that he or she will in later life repeat the same acts against a new generation of children.

Any or all of these ideas may be objectively correct, but it is striking how very recently they have been established and popularized: These were not social facts as recently as 25 years ago. In a sizable literature from the 1950s through the 1970s, one can easily find writers then regarded as leading experts making statements diametrically opposed to current beliefs. These older views were so at variance with contemporary opinion that they could scarcely be published today, and if repeated in a modern context could destroy the reputations of the individuals concerned. A book from the 1960s might state what was then the current orthodoxy, that molestation was a very infrequent offense unlikely to cause significant harm to the vast majority of subjects (the word "victim" seemed too harsh), and the molester was a confused inadequate unlikely to repeat his offense. Children could often be regarded as seducers who provoked such offenses for their own psychological reasons. This perception of child molestation was as innocuous as the modern image is threatening. (This account is drawn from Jenkins, 1998; see also Kincaid, 1998).

In turn, the benevolent view of these years was in sharp contrast to the more sinister notions of the 1940s and early 1950s, when a vast social threat to children was conceived of in terms of dangerous predators, who killed their victims or scarred them for life. And the cycles can be pushed back further. The modern discovery of a child abuse problem has its roots in the Progressive Era, between about 1890 and 1920, but this era of discovery was itself followed by years of apathy or indifference. And in each era, the prevailing opinion was supported by what appeared at the time to be convincing objective research. One reality, one orthodoxy, prevailed until it was succeeded by another.

Concern has fluctuated wildly over the last century, both in the degree of fear apparent at any given time, and in the direction from which threats are believed to come. The problem of sexual threats to children was perceived quite differently in 1915 from how it was in 1930; the child abuse issue of 1984 had a very different cast from what it would acquire in 2001. In eras of concern, the common assumption is that adult-child contacts scar for life; in eras of indifference, the sense is that such contacts are merely passing phenomena. To a disturbing extent, these perceptions shape what scientists study. And the Rind affair suggests that these attitudes establish limits for what experts are encouraged or permitted to say.

The Experts Speak

Looking back over the scholarly discussions of these issues, it really is remarkable how little new has been learned. Of course, excellent and sophisticated modern studies have advanced our knowledge of sexual issues, but in terms of the broad shape of perceptions, I am repeatedly struck by the high quality of largely forgotten studies from 50 or 100 years ago. Above all, I stress forgotten pioneers like Travis Gibb in the 1890s, apparently the first American to delineate a child sexual abuse problem. He was the one who first noted that "there is little or nothing in the medico-legal literature pertaining directly to the crime of indecent assault upon children." The acts "occur much more frequently than is generally supposed," and are "usually committed in secret and without witnesses" (Gibb, 1894). I think of feminist activists like Sophonisba Breckinridge and Edith Abbott, who have left us so much evidence about the state of adult-child sexual contacts in the cities of the Progressive Era, and of Jacob and Rosamond Goldberg, who, in their 1935 book *Girls on City Streets,* gave a wonderful overview of sexual threats to children. We must get a powerful sense of déjà vu when we look through the pages of the journal *Social Hygiene* from the 1910s through the 1950s, with its wonderfully shrewd case studies of child abuse and childhood sexuality. How often social scientists assume that little of use is to be found in the older journal literature, and there is little need to cite literature more than 10 or 15 years old. What treasures we are missing (Goldberg & Goldberg, 1935; Jenkins, 1998, pp. 20–48).

We have had the data for a very long time, but what we do with it has very much been subject to the political ideologies of the time. And, all too often, experts have stated their arguments in the strongest possible terms in order to combat the exaggerated orthodoxies of the day. When the popular nightmare imagines sex fiends on every street, scientists often go too far in presenting adult-child contacts as mild and even benevolent in nature. When these views triumph, and adult-child sex seems almost respectable, a new generation of activists comes along to make overstated claims of a precisely contrary nature.

In retrospect, neither type of claim can be read today without some embarrassment. We are all familiar with the wild overstatements and excessive claims made by child protection activists since the mid-1970s, the successive waves of lunacy arguing for the massive prevalence of incest, organized pedophile rings, recovered memories of cult abuse, and the rest of it. It is simply too easy a target. But in understanding these arguments, it is helpful to appreciate what they were reacting against, the complacency of a previous generation.

Let us just take the issue of harm. We today "know" the parlous effects of abuse, and how any challenge to this doctrine is simply "denial." In the 1940s and 1950s, liberal-minded scholars "knew" exactly the reverse, that childhood sexual contacts caused little harm. The sacred writ for this view was the 1937 article by Lauretta Bender and Abram Blau, "The Reaction of Children to Sexual Relations with Adults" (Bender & Blau, 1937).

Based on this absolute knowledge, the greatest scholars of the time made statements that today look outrageous. Typically, Paul Tappan rejected the view "That the victims of sex attack are 'ruined for life'" as one of the pernicious myths diverting social policy. He argued that little lasting harm need be caused by the experience of "rape, carnal abuse, defloration, incest, homosexuality or indecent exposure."

> In some instances the individual does carry psychic scars after such an experience. Characteristically the damage is done far more, however, by the well-intentioned associates of the victim or by public authorities than by the aggressor. This is not to condone the offense, but merely to emphasize that its implicit danger has been grossly exaggerated, and that the possible traumatizing of the individual is almost always a product of cultural and individual responses to the experience rather than because of the intrinsic value of that experience itself. . . . the young individual in our own society who has not been exposed to an excess of parental and community hysteria about sex can absorb the experience of a socially disapproved sexual assault without untoward consequences. (Cohen, 1980, pp. 669–670)

The Kinsey researchers agreed: "The emotional reactions of parents, police officers and other adults who discover that the child has had such a contact may disturb the child more seriously than the sexual contacts themselves"

(Kinsey, Pomeroy, Martin, & Gebhard, 1953, p. 121), and the danger was all the worse given "the current hysteria over sex offenders" (Jenkins, 1998, pp. 98–106).

There were even doubts about the potential harm arising from incest. In 1955, Weinberg's standard account stated that "incest is very rare in all types of societies," and the few cases that did occur were believed to be largely confined to bizarre and isolated subcultures (Weinberg, 1955). As to the question of harm, Wardell Pomeroy argued that incest between adults and children could be "a satisfying and enriching experience," giving rise to "many beautifully and mutually satisfying relationships between fathers and daughters. . . . they have no harmful effects" (Russell, 1986). Though molested children might seem disturbed, this condition preceded and even contributed to the molestation, rather than being its visible consequence. In 1964, Mohr, Turner, and Jerry remarked of the effects of molestation that "If one excludes cases of violence or force which are fortunately rare, the amount of damage—if any—would depend primarily on the child's emotional status and his security in his environment" (pp. 3, 8). Excessive official intervention could provoke evil consequences, and interrogation and cross-examination in court could wreak more harm than the actual offense.

This tradition dominated the professional literature as recently as the mid-1970s. A text co-authored by C. Henry Kempe argued in 1978 that "A single molestation by a stranger, particularly of a nonviolent kind, appears to do little harm to normal children living with secure and reassuring parents" (Kempe & Kempe, 1978, p. 55). This was powerful testimony, as Kempe was one of the principal authorities in constructing modern concepts of child abuse. Another standard text stated that "Early sexual contacts do not appear to have harmful effects on many children unless the family, legal authorities or society reacts negatively" (McCary & McCary, 1984). The implication is that balanced and mature families have a duty to raise children who are sufficiently well informed not to be disturbed by sexual assault. Responsible parents know better than to risk their child's well-being by dragging the incident to the attention of police and courts: The danger lay in making an issue of mere molestation. "Irrationality about sex led to the original offense; it is important that parents and other adults keep their own irrationalities from doing any further damage to the child" (Gagnon & Simon, 1970, p. 6).

In 1960, David Abrahamsen wrote of rape that "The victim herself unconsciously also may tempt the offender. . . . Often a woman unconsciously wishes to be taken by force. . . . We sometimes find this seductive inclination even in young girls, in their being flirtatious or seeking out rather dangerous or unusual spots where they can be picked up, thus exposing themselves more or less unconsciously to sexual attacks" (Abrahamsen, 1960, p. 161). Writing of underage victims, Karpman opined that "Generally the fact that a particular girl is the victim is no accident; there is something in her background, personality or family situation that predisposes her to participation. Frequently victims are victims in the legal sense only; the attitude that the child is an unwilling victim is not always true; in some cases the child is the aggressor. In some cases parents have abnormally stimulated sex urges. . . . Certain children, even at early ages, incite elders to sex experience even as elders incite them," and deliberate incitements by wayward girls constituted a "widespread problem" (Karpman, 1954, pp. 72–73). In 1974, a psychiatric textbook cited the "well-known" fact that "a nine year old girl may be capable of seduction" (Russell, 1986, p. 172).

Reality and Perception

Why, then, do these tectonic shifts in opinion occur? I am struck by the lack of relationship between the objective realities of childhood sexuality in a given society and the public response, as shaped by legislators, scientists, and mass media. To take a minor but obvious example, how is the age of sexual consent decided in various societies? The prohibition on sex between adults and minors is neither absolute nor universal. A basic biological instinct mandates the protection of the young, which explains the common taboo against intercourse with very small children. Having said this, many societies both past and present are far more tolerant of sexual play with children than modern Western standards would permit. In addition, the definition of childhood varies greatly according to time and location. "Minority" is a legal concept profoundly shaped by political pressures and interactions in any given society. While virtually all societies define a 5-year-old as a child, only in relatively recent times would a 15-year-old be placed in a comparable category and subjected to the same kind of legal restraints and protections. The concept of "adolescence" is less than a century old, dating as it does to G. Stanley Hall's book of that name, published in 1904 (Hall, 1904/1969).

In most traditional societies, the transition from girlhood to womanhood is linked to puberty, and the assumption is that at this point the young woman is able to participate legally in sexual activity, subject to the moral codes of the community in question. Nor is even puberty necessarily a hard and fast line. In the United States, the age of sexual consent for girls stood at 10 years from colonial times until the 1880s, when it was raised in response to heightened sensitivity to the dangers facing both children and women. Over the next century, the American age of legal consent rose steadily, commonly to 16 or 18, while at the same time, the age of sexual maturity fell equally dramatically, from 15 to 12 or 13. During the 20th century, therefore, young teenage girls were far more likely to be sexually active than their predecessors, though virtually all such behaviors were newly defined as seriously illegal. Only as recently as 1984 was the age at which individuals could legally be depicted in a sexual or pornographic context raised from 16 to 18. The notion that a 17-year-old girl is legally a "child" has thus been legislated within very recent memory, and would have astounded most previous societies. I think of the recent Michigan case in which a 24-year-old man was federally convicted of taking and possessing such illegal images of his 17-year-old girlfriend, who consented to the photographs' being taken. Regardless, the man faced a five-year prison sentence. Childhood, self-evidently, is a historically contingent concept (Higonnet, 1998; Jenkins, 2001).

I also venture into really perilous turf when I suggest that there is little or no correlation between the actual rate of childhood abuse or exploitation and the amount that is observed or recorded; indeed, that there may be an inverse relationship between the prevalence of abuse and its recognition as a social problem. Historically, I would argue that the society most perfectly designed to facilitate childhood exploitation was urban America of the late 19th and early 20th centuries, the society that largely perished with slum clearances and the move to the suburbs following World War II. Between about 1880 and 1930, both social investigators and moral crusaders cited sexual abuse as one of the principal evils arising from catastrophic poverty, poor education, and slum housing. In 1913, an attack on "inhuman herding in the tenements" remarked that "cases growing out of the defilement of innocent children by lodgers are common in the Children's Court," with attendant problems of pregnancy and syphilis. "In many of the houses were lodgers who came in tipsy at night, and there were young girls groping their way up those dark stairs too" (Coulter, 1913). Poor families depended for their economic survival on taking in lodgers, who would generally share a room with children. In 1911, a committee on congestion in New York City advised that lodgers should not share rooms with children of the opposite sex over the age of 12, though it saw no dangers to younger children, or to others of the same gender. This is too extensive an issue to argue in any detail here, but I would suggest that the rate of actual child abuse in our society has been steadily declining for some 70 or 80 years. The concern soared in the 1970s and 1980s, but this had nothing whatever to do with the objective problem under consideration. Arguably, the less frequently it occurs, the more we see it, and the very fact that we are counting it means it is declining.

Nor are changes in the amount of concern, rises or declines, a natural or rational response to new social scientific findings, like the abundant evidence that suddenly became available in the late 1970s for the prevalence of child sexual abuse and incest. Victimization surveys certainly contributed to the child abuse revolution, but they were neither the only nor the necessary cause of this transformation. After all, the scale of the abuse problem was laid out in remarkably modern-sounding terms by the Gold-bergs in 1935, while Kinsey's 1953 study of sexuality and the human female (Kinsey et al., 1953) suggested that abusive experiences befell a quarter of American girls. Still, the idea of mass molestation by intimates and neighbors was all but ignored because it could not be fitted into prevailing social ideologies, and the Goldbergs' work was little noticed or cited until the 1970s. Nor did neglect of the Kinsey findings arise from well-founded doubts about the validity of his samples: No such qualms prevented immediate acceptance of his estimates for the prevalence of male homosexual behavior a few years before. In the mid-1960s, similarly, books seeking to prove an "epidemic" of rape and sexual violence made no impact on policy-makers, because they did not meet the needs or expectations of their audience. Similar events and discoveries provoked panic responses in one era but not in another.

New Markets for Claims

What changes is neither the amount of evidence for claims, nor the skill with which they are framed, but the nature of the audience to whom claims are marketed. Demographic factors play a critical role here. Indeed, the history of sex offender laws can almost be traced in terms of the shifting demographic balance of the population, in terms of age and ethnicity. At the start of the 20th century, there was a major movement toward child protection and restricting childhood sexuality. This must partially be explained in terms of contemporary demographic trends, as mass immigration on a scale unprecedented in world history contributed to the mushroom growth of cities like New York and Chicago. The high fertility of the mainly young migrants portended a transformation of the American population. Between 1900 and 1920, American birth rates stood at a remarkable 30 or so per thousand, almost double the modern figure, and national population grew at a faster rate between 1890 and 1915 than in any subsequent era. Fears of a shifting ethnic balance galvanized old-stock Americans to launch a social reform movement to civilize this new and mainly urban class by "saving" their teeming young, while ethnic fears boosted eugenic notions. The end of mass immigration in 1924 was followed by a sharp decline in birth rates and the proportion of children in the total population, a fall accelerated by the economic catastrophe of the early 1930s. By 1935, the birth rate was under 19 per thousand, and the median age of the U.S. population rose from 25 in 1920 to 29 by 1940. This was an era of "apathy" toward abuse issues.

Demographic history since mid-century has been dominated by the vast cohort of the baby boom generation: Birth rates between 1946 and 1957 were usually around 25 per thousand and the proportion of children in the national population reached a higher level than for many years before or since. Parental concerns led to demands for laws to protect this group from molestation, so that the emphasis of the sex menace moved away from attacks against women and toward the threat to young children. But as those children came of age, their demands for personal and sexual freedom placed intolerable burdens upon sexually restrictive laws and specifically on the age of sexual consent, creating the relaxed attitudes of the 1960s and 1970s. Those teenagers became parents and grandparents in the following decades, as the median age of the U.S. population rose sharply from 28 in 1970 to 33 in 1990. However, the new families grew up under domestic circumstances very different from those which boomers themselves had known, and with less direct supervision over their own children. These trends created the potential for the new abuse panics of the 1980s and 1990s. Meanwhile, youngsters themselves had less of a voice: Americans aged 14 through 17 represented almost 8% of the population in 1970, but only 5.3% by 1990. In each epoch, the audience for claims was substantially different, and problems were conceived differently.

The demographic cycle described here has wider relevance. Concern about sex crimes was at its lowest during periods of relatively high tolerance for sexual experimentation, like the 1920s and especially the sexual revolution under way by the early 1960s. Though influenced by new reproductive technologies like the contraceptive pill, this latter movement was strongly correlated to the sexual maturing of the baby boom generation. The revolution was in retreat by the early 1980s, under the assault of diseases like herpes and later AIDS, and a new conservatism became evident. The cycle also helps explain why waves of concern about social dangers like drugs are often correlated with sex crime fears. Later, the baby boom generation was as sympathetic to illicit drugs as to sexual experimentation, and drug use enjoyed broad middle-class acceptability from the late 1960s through the early 1980s. The 1980s saw a simultaneous reaction against youth sexuality and drugs. While child abuse advocates concentrated their ire on rings of pedophiles and molesters, drug warriors showed a like zeal in demonizing drug kingpins, foreign and domestic, with crack cocaine playing the same role as "ultimate evil" that child pornography did in sexual matters. Both movements were part of a general determination to purge Sixties decadence from American life. Both sought to reassert mechanisms of law and control that had all but collapsed in those libertarian years; both appealed successfully to an aging audience of baby boomers. And both movements were powerfully symbolic in nature.

The apparently simple phrase "child protection" is multilayered, with complex rhetorical implications for family control and individual responsibility. Superficially, "protection" implies that children are endangered, and need safeguarding over and above what they would normally receive from the family and traditional support networks. But in addition, *to protect is also to assert control;* and to declare that young people are "children" is to state that they are and should be limited in their proper scope of independent action. By definition, it is to deny such a person the full rights of choice appropriate for an adult. Where the subject is 4 or 7 years old, that decision seems thoroughly reasonable, but what of an older teenager? At what age does childhood give way to autonomy? (For changing notions of dangers to children, see Best, 1990; Fass, 1997.)

Desexualizing the Young

Campaigns to protect children often involve the reassertion of a control that has been forfeited in some way, due perhaps to political or social upheaval, and this is done by expanding the terminology of "childhood" to cover adolescents and young adults. I stress this point: Preventing sexual acts *against* the young can be a way of regulating acts *by* that population. The market for claims in a given era is conditioned by perceptions of how far young people have strayed from proper discipline, and the threat they pose to social and sexual order.

Remarks that young people have lost respect for their elders can be found in any era, and should not necessarily be taken to reflect a change in mores, but generational relationships genuinely do undergo transformation at certain times, and these trends coincide with fluctuations in the child protection ideology. This is most obviously true with the end of the "youth revolution" in the 1970s, which was followed so shortly by the morality campaigns of 1977, but similar sequences had occurred before in American history. Traditional family controls carried over poorly into the new megalopolis during the years of mass immigration, and the first decade of the 20th century was marked by a desperate literature about the fate of the uncontrollable rising generation, with its gang culture and pervasive immorality. A panicked middle class responded to this phenomenon by creating juvenile justice and social welfare agencies that would impose proper WASP standards of discipline upon the polyglot invaders. The sex crime threat reinforced the child saving movement by providing the strongest ideological justification for discretionary and rehabilitative devices in the justice system, as well as for eugenic controls. Threats to women and children proved the need to restore proper family control and supervision, to bring children back from the streets to the hearth. (For shifting concepts of childhood, see Fass & Mason, 2000.)

The demand for protection was marked in the 1940s, with the disruption of family life caused by the Second World War, and to a lesser extent the Korean conflict. The social upheavals of these years inevitably changed sexual mores, with a greater occurrence of extramarital and premarital sexual contacts, as well as new opportunities for both genders to discover or express homosexual impulses. For the young, the removal of parental controls presented new opportunities for precocious experimentation that was remarked upon with prurient horror in books and magazines. The war years witnessed the "unprecedented" discovery of mass juvenile delinquency, which in reality was similar to conditions of 30 or so years previously. Delinquency statistics soared, most scandalously among girls. The sexual predator threat of the 1940s assisted in reimposing family discipline and curbing the sexual activities of the young. Emphasizing the uniquely horrible character of illegal sexual acts against children and teenagers reinforced the fundamental message that the age of consent was sacrosanct, and should not be transgressed, whether forcibly or voluntarily.

More recently, too, the threat from sexual outsiders has circumscribed the behaviors appropriate to the young. The movement against child pornography reasserted sexual boundaries that had crumbled so dramatically over the previous decade, and reimposed an ideology of social discipline. This found expression in the emerging definition of child pornography as the depiction of persons under 16 (later 18), with the implication that youngsters had no business being involved or portrayed in any sexual context. Defining adolescents as children implied that they were or should be subject to appropriate parental and social discipline, notably in sexual matters. This corpus of law has succeeded beyond the wildest dreams of decency campaigners in creating a perilous environment in which eroticism involving a person under 18 is automatically criminal.

Abuse rhetoric has also expanded medicalized and deviant labels over juvenile sexual behaviors that until very recently were commonly regarded as harmless play. Since the late 1980s, a school of therapists has popularized the idea of the danger from "children who molest children," pubescent or younger children identified as abusers on the grounds of sexual behaviors with their peers. That these acts might be mild by most standards is suggested by the case of the 9-year-old boy whose career of crime involved looking up girls' skirts and sexually touching his sister, but mandatory abuse reporting demands that such behavior be related to authorities. Schools were also hypersensitive to cases that could lead to expensive litigation, and some attracted media derision when they imposed severe penalties on small children whose depredations extended to kissing classmates. An increasing number of youngsters find themselves before juvenile courts as sex offenders, "sexualized children," requiring lengthy and expensive behavioral therapy: Several hundred programs now offer treatment for offenders under age 12. (The phrase "sexualized children" is a wondrous notion in its own right, in its implication that any sexual interest by the young must be a form of pathology!) Therapeutic trends are reinforced by conservative moralist demands that schools teach total abstinence as the only acceptable form of juvenile sexuality. The whole phenomenon recalls mid-century accounts of young sex delinquents and sex offenders, guilty of nothing more than intimate experimentation; and more distantly, the 19th-century doctors who made careers from advising families how to stop children masturbating. In each instance, the ideal of childhood proffered wholly excludes a sexual dimension: The only good child is a non-"sexualized" one.

Shifting gender expectations were as important as issues of generational control in conditioning receptivity to claims. Protecting and nurturing children has always been a central component of the traditional role of women, so that if children were exposed to abuse, this implied that women had failed in their responsibilities, and should move proactively to defend their young. Activists promoted concern for political or moralistic reasons, but their dramatic success shows they were able to build upon existing and ill-defined feelings of malaise and guilt among women who felt that they were not fulfilling familiar gender expectations. This sense would be all the greater when women's movement into the workplace occurred quite suddenly and involved a reversal of long-standing roles, as occurred in the 1940s and 1970s. In the decade after 1945, psychiatric experts portrayed sexual deviancy as the result of departures from the ideal of the nuclear family, in which both genders knew and respected appropriate roles, and mothers did not "domineer" in the home. The return to postwar "normality" demanded swift restoration of the gender hierarchy. Nor could women abandon their children to day care as in the war years, as failure to supervise and protect youngsters could lead to consequences of the bloody sort regularly portrayed in the news media. The psychopath provided a vital rationale for the assertion that a woman's place was in the home, and not in the no-woman's-land of the streets.

The indices gauging women's independence accelerated once again during the early 1970s, and this goes far toward explaining the rediscovery of sex crime shortly afterward. The proportion of women working outside the home now increased as rapidly as it had in the Second World War. In 1970, about 43% of women aged 16 or over were in the labor force, a figure that grew to 52% by 1980 and approached 60% in the early 1990s. A new independence coincided with the aspirations inspired by the feminist movement, and these factors contributed to the upsurge of divorce from the early 1970s. In 1958, there were roughly four marriages for every divorce in the United States: By 1970, the ratio was three to one, and by 1976, it reached the level of about two to one that it maintained for the next two decades. Married couples with children represented over 40% of all American households in 1970, but only 26% by 1990. Day care was much more commonly used, and for younger children; and for all the rhetoric of independence, a confusion of cultural messages ensured that many women felt ambiguous about "abandoning" children to the kindness of strangers. This offered fertile ground for the new panics, which so closely echoed the concern of the previous generation. In the 1980s, the public was all too ready to accept the reality of threats emanating from abductors and child pornographers, lurking in caregiver settings like play-schools and churches.

The Permanent Problem

To speak of waves or cycles of American concern about sex crime implies a regular and even predictable process, and at first sight, this model seems to work well. Successive peaks of interest appear to be separated by an interval of about 35 years, so that legislation to regulate molesters and perverts is most evident in roughly 1915, 1950, and 1985, and troughs of interest follow in the late 1920s and again in the early 1960s; but there the pattern breaks down. Far from 1995 marking a new era of indifference, that year was characterized by the furor over sex predator statutes and the fear of cyber-stalkers. The cycle has been broken in the modern era, when child abuse has become part of our enduring cultural landscape, a meta-narrative potentially explaining all social and personal ills.

The durable quality of the modern child abuse concept is linked to the irreversible social change which has brought women in unprecedented numbers into the economy and into public life, and not merely, as in the 1940s, for the duration of the national emergency. A growing literature is examining the many-sided effects of the feminization of American culture and politics. Women voters increasingly decide national elections, and retailers and advertisers gear their products to the presumed tastes of women consumers. A similar trend affects perceptions of social problems, so that society in the last decade has become far more sensitive to sexual violence and exploitation. In this context, the sexual threat to children will remain a central social issue, however reconceived: Even in 1993–94, when the recovered memory movement was being denounced, the response was not to abandon the abuse threat but to redirect attention to the stranger predator. When the media attacked errant therapists, they usually did so by stressing the harm done to women retractors and their families, inviting a female audience to sympathize with these "victims of memory." Any movement that can survive a fiasco as total as the ritual abuse affair must be all but indestructible.

Social change is reinforced by the institutionalization of the child protection idea in many aspects of social life, not least in the expanded social welfare agencies. Though these might come under attack for occasional abuses of power, it is unthinkable that any federal or state government in the foreseeable future might trim the child protection machinery back to its levels in the 1950s or 1960s, as this would attract politically lethal charges of being soft on child molestation. Another focus can be found in the academic world, where themes of incest and abuse are a mainstay of scholarship in departments of social and behavioral science, but are also in different ways found in the humanities, in units studying literature, social theory, cultural studies, or women's studies.

Another factor is the vast expansion of the health care industry over the last two decades, so that therapeutic care and counseling represents one of the swiftest growing forms of employment in the contemporary economy. A myriad of clinics and treatment programs exist to treat all manner of personal problems which would once have been regarded as moral or legal issues, including drug abuse, alcoholism, eating disorders, and, of course, child abuse. Whereas analysis and counseling were once reserved for those with private means, a democratization of therapy has followed the extension of insurance coverage throughout the middle class. Moral issues have been medicalized and institutionalized, producing a huge constituency with an overwhelming interest in keeping these issues at the center of public concern. The therapeutic establishment has a powerful interest in ensuring that "their" problems continue to be viewed as serious, threatening, and likely to respond only to the medical solutions which they market, and in continuing to bring other issues into their orbit. This does much to explain the constant generation of new syndromes and diagnoses, from recovered memory and multiple personalities through "sexualized children."

Current concerns also differ from their predecessors in that this child protection movement is the first to emphasize the experience of victims, beyond merely using the images of faceless children to excite pathos. Since the antirape movement of the 1970s, victims of sexual assault have responded enthusiastically to calls for self-assertion and mobilization in successive survivor movements, a trend that reached its height with the incest survivors of the early 1990s. For the first time in history, perhaps millions of people, mainly but not exclusively women, have constructed their self-identity in terms of the experience of sexual victimization. Networks of survivors became a powerful interest group protesting any weakening in society's vigilance against abuse, launching virulent attacks on therapists or writers who dared to speak of "false memory." The mass media accorded "survivor" groups the respect and authority due to anyone who had passed through a traumatic ordeal. It became difficult to contest their views without seeming callous or naive, any more than one could decently criticize proposals or figures set forth by the parent of a murdered child. Support from survivor movements immeasurably strengthens the claims of therapists and counselors, with whom they form a solid front.

This discussion of recent trends might have predictive value. We have seen that the current construction of the child abuse issue now has firm social roots. It remains to be seen how it will be affected by current changes in our nation's demographic structure. Within a decade or so, America will be facing a major expansion in the number of people aged 15 through 25, and this could conceivably lead to a repetition of the libertarianism of the 1960s and 1970s. The clash between this social upsurge and the entrenched institutions of child protection will be fascinating to watch.

The Language Trap

When I was writing my book *Moral Panic,* it very soon became obvious to me that issues of language were going to be exceedingly important, so delicate in fact that I almost needed to place quotation marks around every other word. I pass on this experience because it may be very relevant to the proceedings of this workshop. Basically, every time we speak of issues of childhood or adolescent sexuality, we need to think very carefully about the ideological meanings of the words we use. In this matter more than any other—except perhaps race—we realize the force of the postmodern critique of language, and the sheer impossibility of speaking or writing without venturing into the realm of ideology.

Put simply, just how, for instance, are we to discuss sexual contacts between an adult and a younger person? The English language lacks an accepted and value-neutral vocabulary for adults who engage in sexual acts with minors, and the commonly available terms make little distinction depending on whether the young person in question is a small child or an older teenager. This is important because public opinion draws a sharp distinction in the blame that can be attributed when the younger party is 15 rather than 5, and very different personality types are involved in each instance. What exactly should we call a man sexually interested in younger teenagers? The favored medical word, "ephebophilia," is utterly obscure, and the archaic "pederast" has virtually dropped out of common usage. Moreover, "pederast" applied only to man-boy interactions: No equivalent term existed for heterosexual behavior because not until the 20th century was this regarded as pathological or illegal. Though, correctly, a pedophile is someone sexually interested "in a prepubescent child (generally age 13 years or younger)" (American Psychiatric Association, 2000), the word is popularly extended to a man who carries out a sexual act with an adolescent, making that person a "molester," a "baby-raper." Legal proceedings often assume a similar identity of villainy. Nor, critically, can we properly use terms like "boy-love," "intergenerational intimacy," and even "relationship," which suggest elements of consent and mutuality unacceptable to the vast majority of observers.

No signifier used to describe sexual acts between adults and children represents a neutral consensus view, and most either are metaphors or reflect a discredited science. An adult man who has sex with a 12-year-old girl or a 14-year-old boy is not literally a fiend or a predator, which are figurative terms designed to express horror at actions considered despicable or dangerous. In panic eras, the terminology of "objective" science is used, with the act being attributed to perverts, degenerates, defectives, and sex psychopaths, but in each case the word represents a scientific or medical worldview that is now obsolete. When technical terms enter general discourse and the mass media, they become vastly aggravated through frequent retellings, and come to imply compulsive violence and monstrous perversion, directed against the youngest and most vulnerable victims. There is a constant cycle whereby experts introduce new and more objective words to describe sexual criminals, but in each case, that term itself acquires the worst connotations: Successively, this fate has befallen "sex offender," "molester," and "pedophile."

And what of the sexual contact itself, or the minor concerned? Even the word "abuse" is controversial. Originally it was a technical prosecutor's word, in the form "carnal abuse," implying sexual acts with a child under 10 years old. It owes its modern-day meaning to one person, feminist Florence Rush, who in 1971 galvanized the new feminist movement against childhood exploitation. Clearly, it is in no sense a neutral or scientific word, since the very word "abuse" signifies improper and presumably harmful treatment. Since the mid-1970s, moreover, it has acquired vast present cultural and ideological significance, with all its connotations of betrayal of trust, hidden trauma, and denial. Florence Rush herself wrote, famously, "The sexual abuse of female children is a process of education that prepares them to become the wives and mothers of America" (Rush, 1974). Even where the reality of abuse itself is not in serious doubt, must we always use the word "victim," or even "survivor," which carries all the cultural freight of the modern "incest survivor" movement? If neither victims nor survivors, might we describe the children involved as "partners"? Surely not. One is a "partner" in a "relationship." I hope you will note all the qualifying quotation marks.

Briefly, it seems literally impossible to write on this topic without using language that virtually accepts the ideological interpretations of a particular school of thought, and in so doing forecloses the exploration of other avenues of interpretation. I suppose I am telling researchers that they can say or write nothing on this topic that is not thoroughly value-laden, culturally bound, or actively offensive. The solution is clear: Just find a way to avoid the use of language altogether.

References

Abrahamsen, D. (1960). *The psychology of crime.* New York: Columbia University Press.

American Psychiatric Association. (2000). *Diagnostic and statistical manual of mental disorders.* Washington, DC: Author.

Bender, L., & Blau, A. (1937). The reaction of children to sexual relations with adults. *American Journal of Orthopsychiatry, 7,* 500–518.

Best, J. (1990). *Threatened children.* Chicago: University of Chicago Press.

Cohen, F. (Ed.). (1980). *Law of deprivation of liberty.* St. Paul, MN: West.

Coulter, E. K. (1913). *The children in the shadow.* New York: McBride and Nast.

Fass, P. S. (1997). *Kidnapped: Child abduction in America.* New York: Oxford University Press.

Fass, P. S., & Mason, M. A. (Eds.). (2000). *Childhood in America.* New York: New York University Press.

Gagnon, J. H., & Simon, W. (1970). *Sexual encounters between adults and children.* New York: Sex Information and Education Council of the U.S.

Gibb, W. T. (1894). Indecent assault upon children. In A. M. Hamilton & L. Godkin (Eds.), *A system of legal medicine* (Vol. 1, pp. 649–652). New York: E. B. Treat.

Goldberg, J. A., & Goldberg, R. W. (1935). *Girls on city streets.* New York: American Social Hygiene Association.

Hall, G. S. (1969). *Adolescence.* New York: Arno. (Originally published 1904.)

Higonnet, A. (1998). *Pictures of innocence: The history and crisis of ideal childhood.* New York: Thames and Hudson.

Jenkins, P. (1998). *Moral panic.* New Haven, CT: Yale University Press.

Jenkins, P. (2001). *Beyond tolerance: Child pornography on the Internet.* New York: New York University Press.

Karpman, B. (1954). *The sexual offender and his offenses.* New York: Julian.

Kempe, R. S., & Kempe, C. H. (1978). *Child abuse.* London: Fontana/Open University.

Kincaid, J. R. (1998). *Erotic innocence: The culture of child molesting.* Durham, NC: Duke University Press.

Kinsey, A. C., Pomeroy, W. B., Martin, C. E., & Gebhard, P. H. (1953). *Sexual behavior in the human female.* Philadelphia: W. B. Saunders.

McCary, S. P., & McCary, J. L. (1984). *Human sexuality (3rd ed.).* Monterey, CA: Wadsworth.

Mohr, J. W., Turner, R. E., & Jerry, M. B. (1964). *Pedophilia and exhibitionism: A handbook.* Toronto, Ontario: University of Toronto Press.

Rind, B., Bauserman, R., & Tromovitch, P. (2000). Science versus orthodoxy: Anatomy of the congressional condemnation of a scientific article and reflections on remedies for future ideological attacks. *Applied and Preventive Psychology, 9,* 211–225.

Rind, B., Bauserman, R., & Tromovitch, P. (2001). The condemned meta-analysis on child sexual abuse: Good science and long-overdue skepticism. *Skeptical Inquirer, 25*(4), 68–72.

Rind, B., & Tromovitch, P. (1997). A meta-analytic review of findings from national samples on psychological correlates of child sexual abuse. *Journal of Sex Research, 34,* 237–255.

Rind, B., Tromovitch, P., & Bauserman, R. (1998). A meta-analytic examination of assumed properties of child sexual abuse using college samples. *Psychological Bulletin, 124,* 22–53.

Rush, F. (1974). The sexual abuse of children. In N. Connell & C. Wilson (Eds.), *Rape: The first sourcebook for women.* New York: New American Library.

Russell, D. E. H. (1986). *The secret trauma: Incest in the lives of girls and women.* New York: Basic.

Weinberg, S. K. (1955). *Incest behavior.* Secaucus: Citadel.

Part 2.

Methodological Aspects

Methodological Issues Associated with Studies of Child Sexual Behavior

LUCIA F. O'SULLIVAN

The empirical study of child sexual behavior has been seriously hampered by a number of sociocultural obstacles inherent to such research. Most notably, concerns of various gatekeepers, including parents, school authorities, and granting and community agents, have hindered research progress in this area. Their concerns often center on beliefs that involving children in studies of sexual behavior will cause distress or spur sexual curiosity and experimentation (Goldman & Goldman, 1982; Lenderyou, 1994; Thomson, 1994). Although there is no obvious empirical evidence to support these concerns, few researchers effectively overcome these objections and obstacles to launch studies of normal child sexual behavior. Instead, researchers tend to limit their inquiry to more socially condoned topics of sexual science, such as variations in pubertal development (e.g., Udry, 1994), child sexual abuse (e.g., Finkelhor & Berliner, 1995), or the development of "problem behaviors" (e.g., Fortenberry, Costa, Jessor, & Donovan, 1997; Jessor & Jessor, 1977). These studies frequently employ clinic populations, or describe atypical experiences or outcomes, and as such, they may ultimately serve to perpetuate the perspective that children's sexual behavior is essentially aberrant.

It is important to note, however, that studies of child sexual behavior are likely to be obstructed much earlier in the research process than the data collection phase. Institutional review boards (IRBs), which oversee the proposal of formal studies, view research about personal matters as particularly distressing for participants (Nolan, 1992). For example, in a survey of 78 chairs of IRBs, research on illegal activities, research involving children, "socially sensitive research" (research with notable political and moral implications), and research on AIDS were listed as the topics requiring the greatest degree of IRB scrutiny (Sieber & Baluyot, 1992). In fact, proposals addressing "socially sensitive topics," such as child sexuality, were twice as likely to be rejected by institutional review boards as those involving less sensitive topics (Ceci, Peters, & Plotkin, 1985). In one study, researchers found that IRB decisions regarding a protocol involving HIV-positive early adolescents were based more on institutional risk aversion or precedent than a consistent assessment of participant risk or level of adherence to a standard of protection (Rogers, Schwartz, Weissmann, & English,

1999). In this light, research proposals outlining methods involving the direct survey or observation of children with regard to sexual behavior understandably cause alarm among those responsible for providing institutional approval for such work to go forward.

This paper reviews what is known about the consequences for children of their involvement in research addressing child sexuality, in particular by drawing on a recent study of children's reactions to their participation in a study requiring sexual information. In addition, this paper addresses a range of methodological issues associated with direct and indirect methods of assessment of child sexual behavior, and suggests a number of ways to overcome common obstacles.

Children's Reactions to Participation in Studies of Child Sexual Behavior

Countering concerns about the well-being of child participants in studies of sexual behavior is a critical first step toward advancing this field of study. There is substantial evidence that *educating* children about sexuality matters does not produce adverse consequences, such as prompting early onset of sexual behavior (see Visser & van Bilsen, 1994, for a review), although this evidence has hardly eliminated concerns about exposing children to sexual information. However, it is possible that some of the obstacles to this type of research can be overcome with findings demonstrating that children are not distressed by direct inquiry regarding sexual matters.

To this end, informal observations during audiotaped individual sex interviews and a survey of reactions to the interviews were used to investigate boys' personal evaluations and feelings about their participation in a larger study of the development of disruptive behaviors (O'Sullivan, Meyer-Bahlburg, & Wasserman, 2000). Participants were 98 boys between the ages of 7 and 13 years. All boys were brothers of adjudicated youths in New York City, and came from primarily minority families. The boys completed an interviewer-administered battery of questionnaires which included a range of gender, heterosocial experience (including kissing experiences, girlfriends), and AIDS-related measures. In addition, the battery included a few sexuality knowledge items: (a) "How can anyone know that a newborn baby is a boy or a girl?" (b) "Do the bodies of boys and girls grow differently as they grow older?" and (c) "How are babies made?" (Goldman & Goldman, 1982, pp. 192, 217).

The boys easily answered questions regarding their heterosocial experiences, such as whether they had ever kissed a girl romantically and whether they had ever had a girlfriend. Interviewing the boys about their sexual knowledge proved unexpectedly long and tedious. In contrast to the heterosocial sections of the protocol, boys became markedly reticent and responded slowly with long silences. The interviewers found it difficult to help them to overcome internalized prohibitions and assure them that no repercussions would follow. Boys who reported being unwilling to participate again generally had taken longer to complete the sex knowledge portion of the protocol than those who reported being willing. The boys' reluctance was attributed in part to a lack of information (e.g., details regarding conception), and in part to lack of a vocabulary for the sexual anatomy, so that they resorted eventually to slang terms typical of young children (e.g., "dick" for penis).

A number of techniques were used to facilitate boys' responses in this study: The interviewers explained to the boys that they could say anything without repercussion and that all responses were kept confidential (stressing that, in particular, nothing would be reported to the mothers). Interviewers also acknowledged the boys' difficulty, but explained that other boys had overcome this difficulty in answering questions. Sometimes boys were instructed to write or draw the word instead of saying it aloud, spell the word instead of saying it, or whisper the word into the tape recorder after the interviewer left the room. Boys were rewarded for their cooperation with candy and access to games throughout the interview, all of which appeared to mitigate any uneasiness on behalf of the participants.

Of particular importance here is that almost all boys reported feeling positively about their participation in the study despite obvious discomfort in talking about sexual matters. In particular, they reported liking the rewards that they received for participation and interacting with the staff. Those boys who reported disliking something about the study tended to cite discomfort with sex questions and the long duration of the study. Difficulty answering sex questions and maintaining attention throughout the interview were not necessarily related to reports of a negative interviewing experience. Moreover, the majority of boys reported being willing to participate again, which supports the finding of positive reactions to the study overall. Of the unwilling participants, only one boy attributed reluctance explicitly to the sexual aspects of the interview. The others were more likely to attribute reluctance to the duration of the study or else did not elaborate. No strong adverse emotional reactions were noted, and there was no need for on-the-spot counseling for emotional problems or interview-related referrals to mental-health services. None of the mothers contacted us after the study about any adverse reactions of their sons. In sum, even though some boys commented about their discomfort with or dislike of some of the sexual questions, these reactions did not have a clinically significant degree of severity. Thus, we do not have any reason to assume that the sex knowledge interview exposes children to significant emotional risk.

We assumed at the time that the reticence noted in this sample of boys when asked questions about sex may be attributable, in part, to characteristics of the sample itself. These boys lived in economically depressed inner-city areas of New York and came from families with generally low educational and economic attainment. They also would not have received formal sex education in their schools until they were older. However, some of our more recent work with young girls with similar backgrounds has challenged this assumption. Focus groups with girls 6–17 years of age required girls to discuss age-related sexual norms, including their opinions about influences on their thinking with regard to relationships with boys (e.g., parents, peers, media, church, school), issues related to parent-child communication (about reproduction, physical maturation, "boy-girl relationships"), and community-endorsed norms about romantic relationships for girls in their age group (O'Sullivan, Meyer-Bahlburg, & Watkins, 2000, 2001).

The facilitator first asked easier, unrelated questions (e.g., about TV shows they like to watch and games they like to play, and their favorite course at school) to ease the girls further into the discussion about boys and romantic relationships. All girls were asked to respond to these early questions to practice using their voice in the group. For the most part, the sessions produced useful and relevant information: Girls provided detailed responses to the series of questions put forth by the facilitator, but also tended to veer to other topics easily or delve into lengthy, often unrelated, monologues. Some girls did not actively participate in the group discussion, or only supported the discussion by indicating agreement with the opinions of others. Groups with older girls were more successful because the participants were better able to focus on the leading question despite the open-ended format for responding. Focus groups would not be an appropriate method for asking for more detailed personal sexual information, but proved successful in eliciting perceptions of peer sexual norms.

We are now conducting a series of structured individual interviews with girls 12–14 years of age, also residents of impoverished inner-city neighborhoods of New York City. These girls are able to complete a large number of sex-related measures, all of which ask their attitudes, opinions, and beliefs regarding various norms and standards of sexual behavior. In the interview portion, girls are required to complete a long, detailed sexual interview assessing pubertal development, developmental milestones of sexual behavior, and, for sexually experienced children only, a detailed history covering all sexual partners, significant sexual practices, and condom use (PDI-RISK-C-F; Meyer-Bahlburg, Dugan, & Ehrhardt, 1998). The administration of this instrument is arranged in such a way that the interviewer reads aloud the questions and related instructions, while the child reads along with her copy of the interview and points to the answers without speaking to the interviewer. The measure incorporates a shorter "gateway" version using core sexual milestones as screen items so that those girls without lower levels of sexual experience are not asked detailed questions about more intimate levels of sexual experience. Although some girls are not enthusiastic about completing the sexual history, most complaints relate to the length of the questionnaire rather than to the sexual nature of the questions.

Direct Methods of Assessment

Asking children directly about their sexual experiences and behaviors is fraught with methodological problems, even though it is often assumed that interviews or surveys of children provide the most valid information about child sexual behavior. In the past, sexuality researchers have used these direct methods to assess children's sexual knowledge about age-appropriate issues, such as conception, pregnancy, and birth (Goldman & Goldman, 1982, 1983), genital differences (Gordon, Schroeder, & Abrams, 1990), and names of body parts (Fraley, Nelson, Wolf, & Lozoff, 1991), rather than inquiring about their sexual behavior or experiences. Children often lack the cognitive abilities required to reflect on past behavior, and the language to report these experiences to another (Blair, 2000; Rademakers, Laan, & Straver, 2000). Moreover, children learn quickly that there is something shameful about admitting to or discussing sexual matters. Children's experience of parental disapproval with regard to communication about sex in Western cultures and particularly the United States is well known (e.g., Gadpaille, 1975; Gagnon & Simon, 1973; Goldman & Goldman, 1982).

Children develop social desirability constraints and respond to the power differential of adult interviewers relatively early (Blair, 2000). Researchers can avoid prompting children's suggestibility by choosing neutral probes as much as possible. Children have been found to report less the more frequently they are questioned, and they provide less elaborated responses to later questions than to earlier ones, possibly in response to a test-like rather than conversation-like atmosphere (Wood & Wood, 1983). Blair (2000) cautions against imposing a structure on a protocol, such as a restricted reporting period, as it may make responding more difficult for children given their less structured sense of memory. Providing a relevant logical structure, such as referring to the children's normal routines, may aid recall and keep the children focused.

Researchers need to be creative in their direct approach to the study of child sexual behavior. Questions must be age-appropriate, in language familiar to the children, and tailored in ways that are most likely to facilitate children's disclosure. Piloting all measures to solicit feedback regarding the acceptability, interpretability, and appropriateness of the measures and items chosen goes far toward assuring the collection of useful information. Incentives should be chosen that children like and can understand (Blair, 2000). Use of visual techniques, such as cartoons, film clips, drawings, or puzzles, may help children to become more comfortable with the topic. If an adolescent discussion group is a useful guide, conducting initial interviews with two or more children may diminish children's inhibitions, especially if the group includes a child who can model comfort in responding to questions about sex. Taking the time to develop a relationship with the child, perhaps interviewing the child on multiple occasions, can ease inhibitions about discussing taboo topics with an adult.

The utility of interactive computer or video programs is being explored (e.g., Gribble, Miller, Rogers, & Turner, 1999), but research on the characteristics of interpersonal interactions most conducive to disclosure for these ages is needed. In one study, children were interviewed about a neutral topic by a trained adult either face-to-face or across a live video link (Doherty-Sneddon & McAuley, 2000). These conditions did not differ in terms of total correct information provided, but significantly more incorrect information was provided in face-to-face interviews, and younger children were notably more reluctant to respond in the video conditions.

Little is known about the best means of asking sensitive questions of children, or about the impact of the data collection mode, question formats, or contexts. Moreover, there is little information available about the types of protocols that have worked best with children, how they compare to each other, the development of the protocols as instruments for child respondents, the pretesting methodology, the relative advantages of multimethod assessment, and the overall performance of children as respondents.

Indirect Methods of Assessment

Obstacles thwarting many researchers' attempts to conduct sound research on child sexuality have not stymied all researchers; there are notable exceptions of those who have produced good work in this area (e.g., Broderick, 1966, Elias & Gebhard, 1969; Paikoff, 1995; Paikoff et al., 1997; Stanton et al., 1994). However, most of what is known about child sexual behavior is derived from indirect sources, such as retrospective reports from adolescent and adult samples (e.g., Kinsey, Pomeroy, & Martin, 1948; Kinsey, Pomeroy, Martin, & Gebhard, 1953; Rotheram-Borus et al., 1992a, 1992b), and surveys of parents regarding their children's sexual behavior (e.g., Achenbach, 1991; Friedrich, Grambsch, Broughton, Kuiper, & Beilke, 1991), rather than more direct sources.

There is clearly a range of problems associated with reliance on these methods. Retrospective reports are subject to biases in recall and other problems of faulty memory.

For decades, psychologists have argued that remembering is a creative process, typically designed to enhance one's current self-views (Ross & Newby-Clark, 1998). People invoke implicit theories to reconstruct the past when memories fade or are difficult to access, revising their accounts of the past in response to current knowledge, circumstances, and goals (Ross, 1989). Cognition research demonstrates how the dating of autobiographical memories steadily declines in accuracy over time (Wagenaar, 1988). The autobiographical memories of younger adults show the greatest variability across successive recalls, apparently because younger people's memories are dynamically reconstructed on each occasion of recall (Anderson, Cohen, & Taylor, 2000). Those of older people, on the other hand, are relatively consistent on each occasion of recall, but only because they are constructed from a fixed representation of personal memories earlier in their lives. Neither group should be considered exceptionally reliable sources of information about childhood sexual experiences.

Cognition research has also established the problem of "childhood amnesia," in which retention of autobiographical memories for ages 10 and younger is found to be most poor (Rubin, Wetzler, & Nebes, 1986). Children may be able to recall significant levels of detail regarding events that occurred even in very early childhood, but they are paradoxically unable to maintain such memories across time (Fivush & Schwarzmueller, 1998). In a longitudinal study of autobiographical memory concerning events and relationships that occurred during adolescence, 73 males were interviewed at the age of 14 about their family relationships, dating, sexuality, and other personal topics, and reinterviewed at age 48 (Offer, Kaiz, Howard, & Bennett, 2000). Accurate memories of key events in adolescence were no better than expected by chance. These findings clearly have important implications for the reliability of retrospective data about childhood sexual behavior; our earliest years are commonly shrouded from us as adults. Of related significance are findings and debates concerning repressed memory and false memory syndrome (Trian, 1997).

As always, researchers relying on retrospective reports should make great efforts to improve the accuracy of participants' recall by contextualizing the events via the elicitation of a range of associated cues. Moreover, there is a growing body of evidence that adult recall of childhood events is greatly improved when using cues, such as photographs, that do not require verbal or linguistic representation (Fivush, Haden, & Adam, 1995).

Researchers often have to rely on secondary sources of information about child sexual behavior. Surveys of parents or other mediators are also plagued with methodological problems. These methods rely on observers' vigilance, motivation to provide accurate information, and freedom from motivations guiding the public presentation of the children's conduct. Parents do not accurately report on their children's past and present academic achievements (Gilger, 1992), for instance, although they tend to provide more valid reports of less value-laden areas, such as linguistic development (Camaioni, Castelli, Longobardi, & Volterra, 1991). In addition, Sandfort and Cohen-Kettenis (2000) argue that there may be a critical discrepancy between the meaning attached to the behavior by parent and child; parents may label behavior sexual and attribute sexual motivations that are not necessarily present. Along this line, researchers have noted significant discrepancy in children's and parents' reports of parent-child sex communication (Jaccard, Dittus, & Gordon, 1998; O'Sullivan, Jaramillo, Moreau, & Meyer-Bahlburg, 2000; Pick & Palos, 1995), with parents reporting higher levels and better quality of communication.

Studies employing secondary sources are also based on the possibly erroneous assumption that the parents or caretakers interact frequently with the children, enough to witness, note, accurately perceive, record, and report the children's sexual behaviors. Intensive interviewing and training of observers may improve the validity of the findings to the extent it is possible to witness what may remain a private, hidden activity. Parents can be desensitized to issues of sexuality and trained to closely monitor a child's behavior. Researchers need to find ways of increasing parents' investment in the collection of accurate information.

Conclusion

Overcoming the obstacles to conducting studies of normal child sexual behavior is an ambitious goal. Acknowledging and substantiating children's sexuality clearly requires the dissolution of a well-endorsed, indeed cherished, sociocultural belief in children's fundamental asexuality or sexual "innocence" (Craft, 1994; Jackson, 1990). However, studies employing more direct methods have had notable success in collecting useful information. Child participants generally react positively overall, with some discomfort noted when more explicit responses are required. Findings from our research program involving children and early adolescents challenge concerns about unduly stressing children who participate in such investigations. It is hoped that these findings will encourage other researchers to further investigations in this area.

References

Achenbach, T. M. (1991). *Manual for the Child Behavior Checklist/4–18 and 1991 Profile*. Burlington: University of Vermont, Department of Psychiatry.

Anderson, S. J., Cohen, G., & Taylor. S. (2000). Rewriting the past: Some factors affecting the variability of personal memories. *Applied Cognitive Psychology, 14*, 435–454.

Blair, J. (2000). Assessing protocols for child interviews. In A. A. Stone, J. S. Turkkan, C. A. Bachrach, J. B. Jobe, H. S. Kurtzman, & V. S. Cain (Eds.), *The science of self-report: Implications for research and practice* (pp. 161–174). Mahwah, NJ: Lawrence Erlbaum.

Broderick, C. B. (1966). Socio-sexual development in a suburban community. *Journal of Sex Research, 2*, 1–24.

Camaioni, L., Castelli, M. C., Longobardi, E., & Volterra, V. (1991). A parent report instrument for early language assessment. *First Language, 11*, 345–359.

Ceci, S. J., Peters, D., & Plotkin, J. (1985). Human subjects review, personal values, and the regulation of social science research. *American Psychologist, 40*, 994–1002.

Craft, A. (1994). Issues in sex education for people with learning disabilities in the United Kingdom. *Sexual and Marital Therapy, 9*, 145–157.

Doherty-Sneddon, G., & McAuley, S. (2000). Influence of video-mediation on adult-child interviews: Implications for the use of the live link with child witnesses. *Applied Cognitive Psychology, 14*, 379–392.

Elias, J., & Gebhard, P. (1969). Sexuality and sexual learning in childhood. *Phi Delta Kappan, 50*, 401–405.

Finkelhor, D., & Berliner, L. (1995). Research on the treatment of sexually abused children: A review and recommendations. *Journal of the American Academy of Child and Adolescent Psychiatry, 34*, 1408–1423.

Fivush, R., Haden, C., & Adam, S. (1995). Structure and coherence of preschoolers' personal narratives over time: Implications for childhood amnesia. *Journal of Experimental Child Psychology, 60*, 32–56.

Fivush, R., & Schwarzmueller, A. (1998). Children remember childhood: Implications for childhood amnesia. *Applied Cognitive Psychology, 12*, 455–473.

Fortenberry, J. D., Costa, F. M., Jessor, R., & Donovan, J. E. (1997). Contraceptive behavior and adolescent lifestyles: A structural modeling approach. *Journal of Research on Adolescence, 7*, 307–329.

Fraley, M. C., Nelson, E. C., Wolf, A. W., & Lozoff, B. (1991). Early genital naming. *Developmental and Behavioral Pediatrics, 12*, 301–305.

Friedrich, W. N., Grambsch, P., Broughton, D., Kuiper, J., & Beilke, R. L. (1991). Normative sexual behavior in children. *Pediatrics, 88*, 456–464.

Gadpaille, W. J. (1975). *The cycles of sex.* New York: Charles Scribner's Sons.

Gagnon, J. H., & Simon, W. (1973). *Sexual conduct: The social sources of human sexuality.* London: Hutchinson.

Gilger, J. W. (1992). Using self-report and parental-report survey data to assess past and present academic achievement of adults and children. *Journal of Applied Developmental Psychology, 13*, 235–256.

Goldman, R., & Goldman, J. (1982). *Children's sexual thinking: A comparative study of children aged 5 to 15 years in Australia, North America, Britain, and Sweden.* London: Routledge and Kegan Paul.

Goldman, R., & Goldman, J. (1983). Children's perceptions of sex differences in babies and adolescents: A cross-national study. *Archives of Sexual Behavior, 12*, 277–294.

Gordon, B. N., Schroeder, C. S., & Abrams, M. (1990). Age and social-class differences in children's knowledge of sexuality. *Journal of Clinical Child Psychology, 19*, 33–43.

Gribble, J. N., Miller, H. G., Rogers, S. M., & Turner, C. F. (1999). Interview mode and measurement of sexual behaviors: Methodological issues. *Journal of Sex Research, 36*, 16–24.

Jaccard, J., Dittus, P. J., & Gordon, V. V. (1998). Parent-adolescent congruency in reports of adolescent sexual behavior and in communications about sexual behavior. *Child Development, 69,* 247–261.

Jackson, S. (1990). Demons and innocents: Western ideas on children's sexuality in historical perspective. In J. Money & H. Musaph (Series Eds.) & M. E. Perry (Vol. Ed.), *Handbook of sexology: Vol. 7. Childhood and adolescent sexology* (pp. 23–49). Amsterdam: Elsevier.

Jessor, R., & Jessor, S. L. (1977). *Problem behavior and psychological development: A longitudinal study of youth.* New York: Academic.

Kinsey, A. C., Pomeroy, W. B., & Martin, C. E. (1948). *Sexual behavior in the human male.* Philadelphia: W. B. Saunders.

Kinsey, A. C., Pomeroy, W. B., Martin, C. E., & Gebhard, P. H. (1953). *Sexual behavior in the human female.* Philadelphia: W. B. Saunders.

Lenderyou, G. (1994). Sex education: A school-based perspective. *Sexual and Marital Therapy, 9,* 127–144.

Meyer-Bahlburg, H. F. L., Dugan, T. M., & Ehrhardt, A. A. (1998). *Psychosexual Development Interview: Child version for sexual risk behavior, female (PDI-RISK-C-F).* Unpublished instrument, Columbia University, New York.

Nolan, K. (1992). Ethical issues: Assent, consent, and behavioral research with adolescents. *AACAP Child and Adolescent Research Notes, 2,* 7–10.

Offer, D., Kaiz, M., Howard, K. I., & Bennett, E. S. (2000). The altering of reported experiences. *Journal of the American Academy of Child and Adolescent Psychiatry, 39,* 735–742.

O'Sullivan, L. F., Jaramillo, B. M. S., Moreau, D., & Meyer-Bahlburg, H. F. L. (2000). Mother-daughter communication about sexuality in a clinical sample of Hispanic adolescent girls. *Hispanic Journal of Behavioral Sciences, 201,* 447–469.

O'Sullivan, L. F., Meyer-Bahlburg, H. F. L., & Wasserman, G. (2000). Reactions of inner-city boys and their mothers to research interviews about sex. *Journal of Psychology and Human Sexuality, 12*(1–2), 81–103.

O'Sullivan, L. F., Meyer-Bahlburg, H. F. L., & Watkins, B. X. (2000). Social cognitions associated with pubertal development in a sample of urban, low-income, African-American and Latina girls and mothers. *Journal of Adolescent Health, 27,* 227–235.

O'Sullivan, L. F., Meyer-Bahlburg, H. F. L., & Watkins, B. X. (2001). Mother-daughter communication about sex among urban African-American and Latino families. *Journal of Adolescent Research, 16,* 269–291.

Paikoff, R. L. (1995). Early heterosexual debut: Situations of sexual possibility during the transition to adolescence. *American Journal of Orthopsychiatry, 65,* 389–401.

Paikoff, R., Parfenoff, S. H., Williams, S. A., McCormick, A., Greenwood, G. L., & Holmbeck, G. N. (1997). Parenting, parent-child relationships, and sexual possibility situations among urban African American preadolescents: Preliminary findings and implications for HIV prevention. *Journal of Family Psychology, 11,* 11–22.

Pick, S., & Palos, P. A. (1995). Impact of the family on the sex lives of adolescents. *Adolescence, 30,* 667–675.

Rademakers, J., Laan, M., & Straver, C. J. (2000). Studying children's sexuality from the child's perspective. *Journal of Psychology and Human Sexuality, 12*(1–2), 49–60.

Rogers, A. S., Schwartz, D. F., Weissmann, G., & English, A. (1999). A case study in adolescent participation in clinical research: Eleven clinical sites, one common protocol and eleven IRBs. *IRB: A Review of Human Subjects Research, 21,* 6–12.

Ross, M. (1989). Relation of implicit theories to the construction of personal histories. *Psychological Review, 96,* 341–357.

Ross, M., & Newby-Clark, I. R. (1998). Construing the past and future. *Social Cognition, 16,* 133–150.

Rotheram-Borus, M. J., Meyer-Bahlburg, H. F. L., Koopman, C., Rosario, M., Exner, T. M., Henderson, R., et al. (1992a). Lifetime sexual behaviors among runaway males and females. *Journal of Sex Research, 29,* 15–29.

Rotheram-Borus, M. J., Meyer-Bahlburg, H. F. L., Rosario, M., Koopman, C., Haignere, C. S., Exner, T. M., et al. (1992b). Lifetime sexual behaviors among predominantly minority male runaways and gay/bisexual adolescents in New York City. *AIDS Education and Prevention* (Supplement, fall), 23–42.

Rubin, D. C., Wetzler, S. E., & Nebes, R. D. (1986). Autobiographical memory across the lifespan. In D. C. Rubin (Ed.), *Autobiographical memory* (pp. 202–221). Cambridge: Cambridge University Press.

Sandfort, T. G. M., & Cohen-Kettenis, P. T. (2000). Sexual behavior in Dutch and Belgian children as observed by their mothers. *Journal of Psychology and Human Sexuality, 12*(1–2), 105–115.

Sieber, J. E., & Baluyot, R. M. (1992). A survey of IRB concerns about social and behavioral research. *IRB: A Review of Human Subjects Research, 14,* 9–10.

Stanton, B., Li, X., Black, M., Ricardo, I., Galbraith, J., Kaljee, L., et al. (1994). Sexual practices and intentions among preadolescent and early adolescent low-income African-Americans. *Pediatrics, 93,* 966–973.

Thomson, R. (1994). Prevention, promotion, and adolescent sexuality: The politics of school sex education in England and Wales. *Sexual and Marital Therapy, 9,* 115–126.

Trian, F. (1997). Young children's memory: How good is it? How much do we know about it? *Child Psychology and Psychiatry Review, 2,* 150–158.

Udry, J. R. (1994). Integrating biological and sociological models of adolescent problem behaviors. In R. D. Ketterlinus & M. E. Lamb (Eds.), *Adolescent problem behaviors: Issues and research* (pp. 93–107). Hillsdale, NJ: Lawrence Erlbaum.

Visser, A. P., & van Bilsen, P. (1994). Effectiveness of sex education provided to adolescents. *Patient Education and Counseling, 23,* 147–160.

Wagenaar, W. A. (1988). People and places in my memory: A study on cue specificity and retrieval from autobiographical memory. In M. M. Gruneberg, P. E. Morris, & R. N. Sykes (Eds.), *Practical aspects of memory: Current research and issues: Vol. 1. Memory in everyday life* (pp. 257–261). Chichester: Wiley.

Wood, H., & Wood, D. (1983). Questioning the pre-school child. *Educational Review, 35,* 149–162.

Using the Parents as a Source of Information about the Child

With Special Emphasis on the Sex Problems Scale of the Child Behavior Checklist

HEINO F. L. MEYER-BAHLBURG AND
JENNIFER LYNNE STEEL

Modes of Assessing Childhood Sexual Behavior

If you were to conduct a study of the current sexual behavior of your (adult) peers, would you interview their parents? Presumably not. If you did, you would find that many, but not all, parents know whether their adult children are married, whether they have children of their own, and, if they are in jail, whether they are there for sexual offenses, but few know specifics about their adult children's sexual life. Likewise, if you were to conduct sex research on adolescents, you would want to ask the adolescents themselves rather than their parents because you know that adolescents are usually not interested in having their parents present when they engage in sexual activities, and most adolescents do not tell their parents in any detail, if at all, what kind of sexual practices they use with whom, etc.

But in sex research on children before puberty, parents often serve as informants. One reason is limited access. Unless the research evaluation takes place in a clinical setting to which the child has been referred because of a sexual concern, parents, school personnel, and other caretakers are quite protective of children and set high barriers to the enrollment of children in sex research. In addition, many children themselves find it difficult to talk about sex to adult interviewers (O'Sullivan, Meyer-Bahlburg, & Wasserman, 2000). Very young children, of course, do not even have the language and cognitive skills necessary for a language-based evaluation. Thus, much early work on childhood sexuality has relied on interviews with parents or with others who have opportunities to observe children in home situations, nursery schools, pediatric offices, and so forth (Berges, Neiderbach, Rubin, Sharpe, & Tesler, 1983; Conn & Kanner, 1940; Gundersen, Melås, & Skår, 1981; Kinsey, Pomeroy, & Martin, 1948; Kinsey, Pomeroy, Martin, & Gebhard, 1953; Levine, 1957; Newson & Newson, 1968; Newton & Newton, 1967; Rosenfeld et al., 1984; Schuhrke, Rank, Stadler, Pinz, & Hildner, 1998; Sears, Maccoby, & Levin, 1957). Most of these interviews were open-ended or semistructured and provided narrative or qualitative material, often on specific events, rather than easily quantifiable material. Psychometric and validation studies have usually not been performed, but we can assume that the typical problems of recall and bias affect parents' reports, augmented by sexuality-specific affects and values, and complicated by the likely differences in meaning children and adults associate with so-called sexual acts.

In spite of the limitations of reports by informants other than the child, we have learned a great deal about many aspects of childhood sexuality, such as erections in infant and preschool boys, the relationship of infant erections to breastfeeding, sexual self-exploration by infants, sexual curiosity in toddlers and preschoolers, masturbation, sexual games among preschoolers and elementary school children, etc. Such interview-based findings could sometimes be confirmed by direct observational studies, especially in nursery school and elementary school settings (e.g., Galenson, 1990; Galenson & Roiphe, 1974; Halverson, 1938; Thorne & Luria, 1986), although we are not aware of attempts to validate parental interview data directly. Relatively few studies have attempted to obtain information by interview with prepubertal children directly (for instance, Broderick, 1966; Elias & Gebhard, 1969; Ramsey, 1943), and some investigators found direct interviewing of children about sexual behavior so difficult that they resorted to quasi-projective techniques (Westney, Jenkins, & Benjamin, 1983). Only in the context of the current HIV epidemic and the apparent need for early intervention has research using direct sexuality-related interviews with children recently somewhat increased (e.g., Paikoff, 1995; Stanton et al., 1994). In clinical work with sexually abused children, interviews with the victims themselves are common (Gil & Johnson, 1993; Johnson, 1993), but they are mostly focused on the sex abuse events, and follow-up studies after intervention, for instance, tend to use parents as informants.

It is clear from the earlier studies that parents and other caretakers can provide very detailed descriptions of children's sexual behavior to the extent that the behavior occurs in the parents' presence, or that parents receive complaints about their child's sexual behavior from others. Nevertheless, only two standardized parent-administered screening instruments for childhood sexuality are available. One is the Child Sexual Behavior Inventory (CSBI) by Friedrich (1997). (A similar but much longer instrument, the Questionnaire for Child Sexual Behavior [QCSB], has been developed in the first author's unit, but has not yet been normed.) The other standardized one is the Sexual Problem Scale (SPS) of the Child Behavior Checklist (CBCL; Achenbach, 1991), for the age range of 4–11 years. A recently published child-administered Trauma Symptom Checklist for Children (TCC; Briere, 1996), for the age group 8–16 years, includes a Sexual Concerns scale, but the TCC is very limited in its scope and therefore not an appropriate replacement for the broadband screening questionnaires.

History of the SPS

When scanning PsycINFO and MEDLINE, we found that the SPS has been the most frequently reported standard assessment scale for childhood sexual behavior in the past two decades, although the SPS has not received much critical examination to support its use. As the SPS has undergone repeated modifications which make comparisons of results from different studies problematic, a brief review of its history will facilitate the understanding of its current status. Achenbach (1966, pp. 7–9) started his work with developing a general symptom checklist for the categorization of child psychiatric case histories. This symptom checklist was constructed from items that regularly appeared in published studies or were formulated on the basis of a review of 40 case histories from a child psychiatry unit. The item list included eight sexual items, which were conceptually sorted into four clusters: masturbation; sexual delinquency, incest, homosexuality; sexual perversions, exposing self; sexual preoccupation, precociousness (pp. 33–34). The checklist was used for the symptom coding (present/absent) of 300 case histories each of male and female child psychiatry inpatients and outpatients aged 4–15 years. Principal-factor analyses (followed by multiple rotations) of the data on males yielded 8 interpretable factors. They included one sexual problems factor with the following item loadings: masturbation .61; sexual preoccupation .50; sexual delinquency .45; sexual perversion .16; along with some nonsexual items (p. 12). No sexual problems factor emerged from the data on females; instead, the sexual items were scattered over various nonsexual factors.

Subsequently, the symptom checklist was modified and adapted for administration to parent informants by making the wording more colloquial and expanding the present/absent response alternatives to the current 0–1–2 scale (see below). New items were added on the basis of an updated literature search and consultations with clinicians working in settings where the new Child Behavior Checklist (CBCL) was to be used (Achenbach & Edelbrock, 1981, p. 7). The CBCL was administered to large samples stratified to approximate national demographic representativeness. Low-frequency items were excluded and principal-component analyses performed separately for several age/sex groupings. The resulting scales included a Sex Problems Scale (SPS) for girls aged 6–11 years (Achenbach & Edelbrock, 1979). The first comprehensive Manual for the CBCL was published by Achenbach and Edelbrock (1983). It now included one SPS each for boys 4–5, girls 4–5, and girls 6–11 years old. At that time, the scales were apparently based strictly on the results of the principal-components analyses (followed by varimax rotation) and included all items with factor loadings exceeding .30, regardless of whether the item content was sexual or not. Thus, the age-by-sex-specific versions of the SPS differed in content.

In their work on abused children, Friedrich, Urquiza, and Beilke (1986) suggested and used a CBCL-derived sexual problem scale limited to six items and applied to both genders equally. The scale was referred to by several names: both "Sexualization" and "Sexual Behavior Scale" by Friedrich, Urquiza, and Beilke (1986); "Sex Problems" by Friedrich, Beilke, and Urquiza (1987, 1988; Friedrich, 1993, p. 61, confirmed it as the six-item scale) and by Friedrich and Luecke (1988), and "Sexualization" by Einbender and Friedrich (1989; confirmed as the six-item scale by Friedrich, personal communication, February 24, 1998). Achenbach (1991) presented a factor-based scale of the same six items for 4–5- and 6–11-year-olds (boys and girls separately) in a major revision and restandardization of the CBCL designed to improve the CBCL scales by applying both statistical and conceptual criteria for item selection. Table 1 summarizes the modifications of the SPS items and scales from 1979 to 1991. Because most studies since 1991 involving the SPS have employed the six-item version, its further discussion here will be limited to that version.

Current Version of the SPS

In its current (1991) form, the CBCL is a broadband, parent-administered, behavior problem–focused questionnaire designed to obtain "a picture of the child's behavior as the parent sees it" (Achenbach, 1991, p. iii) and standardized on large samples. The first part of the CBCL assesses "social competence" and the second "behavioral/emotional problems," which includes several sexual items. For each item of the latter part, the parent is to mark whether the item is "very true or often true" of a child (response score: 2), "sometimes or somewhat true" (1), or "not true" (0); the time frame is "now or within the past six months." Eight syndrome scales were derived from principal component analyses of the problem items and orthogonal (varimax) rotation. The Sex Problem Scale (SPS) was identified as an additional scale by the same procedures among 4–5- and 6–11-year-old children, but not among adolescents.

The scores for the 1991 version of the SPS can range from 0 to 12. As is typical of symptom scales, the actual score distribution in community samples is highly skewed, and the majority of children have zero scores. Achenbach (1991) provided both raw score and T-transformed scores for the eight syndrome scales and the SPS. (Note that the T-scores do not represent straightforward linear transformations but involve some nonlinear transformations of the upper 2.4% of the raw scores [pp. 50–51].) In contrast to the other syndrome scales of the CBCL, Achenbach did not define a clinical range of SPS scores, presumably because of the relatively small difference in means between samples of clinically referred and nonreferred children (see below). According to Achenbach (p. 94), the SPS "should be

Table 1. *Factor Loadings of Items That Constitute the SPS in Different CBCL Editions*

	1983 CBCL			1991 CBCL
	Males 4–5	Females 4–5	Females 6–11	Males and Females 4–11
5. Behaves like opposite sex	.57	.47		≥.30
59. Plays with own sex parts in public[a]	.51	.33		≥.30
60. Plays with own sex parts too much[b]	.42	.44	.33	≥.30
73. Sexual problems (describe): _____[c]	.44	.50	.54	≥.30
96. Thinks about sex too much[d]		.63	.59	≥.30
110. Wishes to be of opposite sex	.60	.50		≥.30
31. Fears he/she might think or do something bad[e]				.37
39. Hangs around with others who get in trouble[f]		.31		
52. Feels too guilty			.34	
63. Prefers being with older kids[g]			.38	
93. Talks too much			.30	

Notes. Sources: For CBCL 1981, Achenbach & Edelbrock (1981), pp. 72–76; for CBCL 1983, Achenbach & Edelbrock (1983), pp. 3, 4, 199, 205, 207; for CBCL 1991, Achenbach (1991), pp. 11, 12, 37, 251. The factor loadings reported for females aged 6–11 in the 1983 CBCL are identical with those provided in Achenbach & Edelbrock (1979), p. 227. Factor loadings are based on varimax rotation after principal components extraction.

Earlier item wording:
[a]CBCL 1981: Plays with sex parts in public
[b]CBCL 1981: Plays with sex parts too much
[c]CBCL 1981: Sexual problems
[d]CBCL 1981: Sexual preoccupation
[e]CBCL 1981: Fears impulses
[f]CBCL 1983: Hangs around with children who get in trouble
[g]CBCL 1983: Prefers playing with older children; CBCL 1981: Prefers older children

viewed as providing supplementary data about a particular class of problems rather than as a strong indicator of need for professional help."

Item Content

The six items that now constitute the SPS for both boys and girls aged 4–11 years are listed in Table 1. They include four sex behavior items and two (cross-)gender items, i.e., conceptually two quite different domains. We expected that these two item sets would form separate factors if one were to conduct a factor analysis of the six items only. We used principal factor analyses of the six SPS items from community samples of 326 boys and 349 girls aged 6–10 years from an ethnically diverse school district in

New Jersey (Meyer-Bahlburg, Dolezal, & Sandberg, 2000) and from an inner-city sample of 126 boys aged 5–11 years who were at increased risk for the development of aggressive behavior (Meyer-Bahlburg, Dolezal, Wasserman, & Jaramillo, 1999); 112 of these boys were assessed a second time 15 months after baseline. (Principal axis factor analysis is a more appropriate procedure than principal-component analysis for variables with significant measurement error, especially when the number of variables is small; see Dunteman, 1989). As Table 2 shows, all analyses produced two (nonforced) factors. For the community sample of boys and girls combined (both unrotated and rotated solutions) as well as for the girls alone (unrotated solution only), the four sex items separated from the two gender items, but not for the three samples of boys. Thus, there was only partial support for the hypothesis that the two gender items and the four sex behavior items would segregate. We would expect a more consistent separation with high-variance samples including sexually abused and/or gender-identity-disturbed children, and this was shown by Friedrich (1989) in an unpublished dataset involving sexually abused children.

In our own data, the two subscales, sex and gender, correlated $r = .22$ ($p < .001$) in community boys, $r = .08$ ($p = .161$) in community girls, and $r = .36$ ($p < .001$) in boys at risk. The internal consistency coefficients for the four-item sex scale were not systematically different from those of the six-item SPS (see below), while the Cronbach alphas for the two-item gender scale ranged from .11 to .35, that is, were unsatisfactory (Meyer-Bahlburg, Steel, & Dolezal, 1997).

Of the SPS's four sex behavior items, two deal with masturbation and overlap considerably in content, while the other two are rather nonspecific. None of them explicitly include sexual behavior with a partner. Thus, the coverage of the sexual domain is very limited.

Two of the sex behavior items (#60 and #96) present "problem" statements rather than plain behavioral descriptions. That is, the parents are asked to endorse not whether or not a specific behavior occurs, but whether it is a problem ("too much"). Therefore, these items reflect, in part, the parents' evaluation of their children's behavior as problematic rather than just behavior observations, and their endorsement may vary with the parents' attitude to sexuality in general. As we know from routine clinical inquiry about the CBCL, parents vary considerably in the degree to which their endorsement of items #60 and #96, or of the others, reflects a "problem" perspective. It is for this reason that, despite the name of the SPS, we do not necessarily consider the behaviors captured by the individual items or their aggregation as "problems" or as "psychopathology."

Reliability

Internal consistency. Achenbach (1991, pp. 252, 254) reports for the SPS a Cronbach alpha of .56 for boys aged 4–11, and of .54 for girls aged 4–11

Table 2. *Rotated Principal Axis Factor Loadings of the SPS in Diverse Samples*

				Items			
			Sex			Gender	
Samples / Factors	Item #	59	60	73	96	5	110
Community boys and girls (*N* = 675)							
Factor 1		.64	.60	NA	.14	.13	.02
Factor 2		−.02	.15	NA	.11	.69	.26
Community boys (*N* = 326)							
Factor 1		.52	.82	NA	.16	.36	.04
Factor 2		.18	−.07	NA	−.01	.11	.62
Community girls (*N* = 349)							
Factor 1		.68	.54	NA	.15	.03	.01
Factor 2		−.07	.13	NA	.17	.64	.40
Boys at risk, baseline (*N* = 126)							
Factor 1		.83	.43	.03	.67	.04	.79
Factor 2		−.09	.20	.76	.10	.44	.00
Boys at risk, 15 months later (*N* = 112)							
Factor 1		.03	.67	.03	.84	.34	.79
Factor 2		.70	.41	.70	.42	−.08	−.06

years; the values are based on large demographically matched samples of clinically referred and nonreferred children combined (Achenbach, personal communication, August 9, 1999). Meyer-Bahlburg et al. (2000) determined for their community sample of boys aged 6–10 years a Cronbach alpha of .41 and for girls of .37, and Meyer-Bahlburg et al. (1999) found for a sample of boys at risk for the development of antisocial behavior a Cronbach alpha of .61 (and of .66 for the same sample 18 months later). The values are considerably lower than those for the other syndrome scales provided in the 1991 Manual for the CBCL, and also clearly lower than desirable for individual clinical assessment. The lowest alphas were found for community samples, presumably reflecting their particularly low frequencies of childhood sexual behaviors as compared to clinical samples (see Validity, below).

Test-retest reliability. Achenbach (1991, pp. 72–73) provided data on 24 boys and 29 girls, aged 4–11, whose parents were tested twice with a one-week interval; nonreferred children were used because it was thought that their scores would be less susceptible to regression toward the mean than those of referred children. The intraclass coefficient was .85 for boys and

.80 for girls. Clearly, retest reliability data on other samples would be desirable.

Stability. Long-term stability data are available from two sources. In a longitudinal project on low-birth-weight and normal-birth-weight children, Achenbach (1991, p. 79) obtained retest correlations of the SPS over one year of $r = .41$ from age 6 to 7 years ($p = .01$; $N = 76$ boys and girls) and $r = .20$ from age 7 to 8 (NS; $N = 65$ boys and girls), and over two years $r = .39$ from age 6 to 8 ($p = .01$; $N = 70$ boys and girls). Meyer-Bahlburg et al. (1999) followed 112 boys aged 6–12 years over approximately 15 months; the SPS at baseline correlated with the SPS at 15 months, $r = .22$ ($p = .02$). Thus, long-term stability of the SPS in middle childhood appears low—as one would expect, given the sporadic nature of childhood sexual behavior.

Interparent agreement. Achenbach (1991, p. 76) reports an interparent agreement on the basis of both clinically referred and nonreferred children as $r = .54$ for 4–11-year-old boys ($N = 182$) and $r = .50$ for 4–11-year-old girls ($N = 141$). These values are considerably lower than for most of the other syndrome scales. This may not only reflect the brevity of the SPS. On the basis of our clinical experience, we would expect that parents differ considerably in opportunities to observe sexual behaviors on the part of their children and in their characterization of such behaviors as problems.

Variations of SPS Scores with Demographic Variables

Gender. As Achenbach (1991) provides norms separately for males and females, no statistical test of a gender difference on the SPS is reported. However, SPS means are reported for girls and boys aged 4–11 in the CBCL Manual (Appendix B, pp. 252 and 254). The SPS mean for clinically referred boys ($N = 582$) is 0.5 ± 1.1 SD, for clinically referred girls ($N = 619$) 0.6 ± 1.2 SD, which is a nonsignificant difference on t-test. For nonreferred boys ($N = 582$), the mean is reported as 0.1 ± 0.5 SD, and for nonreferred girls ($N = 619$) as 0.2 ± 0.5 SD; this difference is significant ($p < .001$). In their community sample (which did not exclude clinically referred children), Meyer-Bahlburg et al. (2000) found SPS means of 0.2 that were identical for $N = 326$ boys and $N = 349$ girls. Thus, gender differences on the SPS seem to be inconsistent and, where significant, of small size.

Other. Analyzing for the effects of other demographic variables in his combined clinically referred and nonreferred norm samples, Achenbach (1991) found no effect for ethnicity or socioeconomic status, a minimal age effect (accounting for less than 1% of variance, with younger children having higher values) for boys only, and a small effect of referral status (accounting for 5% of variance, with referred children having higher values) for both boys and girls. In their community sample, Meyer-Bahlburg et al. (2000) did not find a significant association of the SPS with age or ethnicity for either gender; however, the SPS was minimally, but significantly, associated with parental education among boys ($r = -.13$, $p < .018$), but not girls.

Validity

Criterion validity. Achenbach (1991) did not provide any correlation of the SPS with another measure of child sexual behavior. Meyer-Bahlburg et al. (1999) reported on a sample of boys at increased risk for the development of antisocial behavior; at the time of the second assessment 15 months after baseline, when the boys were 6–12 years old, the SPS correlated $r = .42$ with Friedrich's Child Sexual Behavior Inventory, which indicates a moderate degree of criterion validity (Meyer-Bahlburg et al., 1997).

Discriminant validity. Given the fact that the SPS is positively correlated with the other syndrome scales of the CBCL (Achenbach, 1991; Meyer-Bahlburg et al., 1999), we would expect SPS scores to be higher in psychiatric samples than in community samples, and higher in community samples that include clinically referred cases than in community samples from which such cases have been excluded. Moreover, given the data on the increase of sexual behavior in many children with a history of sexual abuse, we would expect that samples of sexually abused children score higher than general psychiatric samples. To test these hypotheses, we conducted an extensive literature search of Medline 1966–2000 and PsycINFO 1967–2000, using the key words "Child Behavior Checklist" and "sexual abuse." A total of 2,512 abstracts were reviewed, and out of these, 189 articles were screened in which the abstract indicated that some type of standardized assessment of sexual behavior had been used. The criteria for inclusion in the current report were that (a) the study was published in English, French, German, or Spanish, (b) there was sufficient information on the sex composition and age of the samples, and (c) the report provided the numeric mean (raw score or T-score) of the SPS. Excluded were case studies and articles reporting on very few children as well as articles that did not employ the six-item version of the SPS. Data from the CBCL Manual (Achenbach, 1991) were added. All reports with sufficient information came from North American studies. Note that only the nonreferred norm samples of Achenbach (1991) are representative of the U.S. population. Unfortunately, the published reports vary too much in the reports of study details so that a formal meta-analytic approach could not be employed.

In some of the reports, CBCL data were presented as T-scores and in others as raw scores. Table 3 lists the available data on T-score means arranged by size within each sample category. Inspection of the table shows that there is little discrimination between community samples excluding

Table 3. *SPS Means (T-scores) of the 1991 CBCL for Diverse Populations*

Source	Sample description	Mean	SD	Sex	N	Age (yrs.)
	Community, excluding clinically referred children					
A	Nonreferred[a]	51.6	5.0	M	582	4–11
A	Nonreferred[a]	52.0	5.4	F	619	4–11
	Community, not excluding clinically referred children					
B	School, Toronto	50.8	3.1	F	52	8–13
C	School, New York Chinese	51.0	3.8	M	45	4–11
C	School, New York Chinese	51.6	5.3	F	59	4–11
	Medically defined					
D	Routine physical	50.7	3.4	M	107	6–17
E	Well-child clinic[b]	52.6	5.9	M,F	57	4–14
B	Turner's syndrome	52.4	5.9	F	103	7–13
	Psychiatrically defined					
D	ADHD[c]	52.7	7.7	M	93	6–17
E	Thumb-suckers	53.5	7.5	M,F	57	4–13
A	Referred[d]	54.9	8.8	M	582	4–11
A	Referred[d]	55.6	8.9	F	619	4–11
E	Psychiatric outpatients[b]	59.0	10.1	M,F	57	4–14
D	ADHD + social disability	64.3	13.9	M	26	6–17

Notes. A Achenbach, 1991; B Rovet & Ireland, 1994; C Chang, Morrissey, & Koplewicz, 1995; D Greene et al., 1996; E Friman, Larzelere, & Finney, 1994.
[a]Excluding those who had not received mental health services or special remedial school classes within the preceding 12 months (Achenbach, 1991, p. 20).
[b]Thumb-suckers excluded.
[c]Attention-deficit hyperactivity disorder.
[d]Referral for mental health services, including special education classes for behavioral/emotional problems.

clinically referred children, community samples including such children, and medically defined samples. However, psychiatric samples consistently have the highest means. There were no sex abuse samples reported in terms of SPS T-scores.

Table 4 lists the SPS means available in terms of raw scores, again arranged by size within sample categories. The lowest values are reported for community samples. Psychiatric samples are generally higher than community samples but overlap with medically defined samples. There is a major increase of the means in samples of sexually abused (clinically referred)

Table 4. *SPS Means (Raw Scores) of the 1991 CBCL for Diverse Populations*

Source	Sample description	Mean	SD	Sex	N	Age (yrs.)
	Community, excluding clinically referred children					
A	Nonreferred[a]	0.1	0.5	M	582	4–11
A	Nonreferred[a]	0.2	0.5	F	619	4–11
	Community, not excluding clinically referred children					
B	School controls, excluding SA[b]	0.13	0.40	F	46	6–14
C	School, day care controls excluding SA[b]	0.16	0.51	M,F	67	4–11
D	School, low-income	0.2	0.9	M	458	5–11
E	School	0.2	0.7	M	326	6–10
E	School	0.2	0.6	F	349	6–10
D	School, low-income	0.3	0.3	F	432	5–11
	Medically defined					
F	Short stature	0.1	0.3	M	83	4–11
G	Well-child clinic controls	0.15	0.56	M,F	78	3–12
F	Short stature	0.3	0.8	F	50	4–11
H	Well-child clinic controls excluding SA[b], PR[c]	0.8	1.1	M	32	4–8
	Psychiatrically defined					
I	At-risk[d]	0.4	1.0	M	126	5–11
A	Referred[e]	0.5	1.1	M	582	4–11
A	Referred[e]	0.6	1.2	F	619	4–11
G	Outpatients excluding SA[b] and severe developmental disabilities	0.7	1.6	M,F	64	3–12
H	Outpatient	0.8	1.1	M	32	4–8
	Sexually abused					
K	Sexual abuse, without PTSD	0.74	1.6	M,F	39	6–16
C	Sexual abuse, general	1.27	1.51	M,F	32	4–8
K	Sexual abuse, with PTSD	1.29	2.4	M,F	24	6–16
L	Sexual abuse, post-therapy	1.3	No SD	M	22	5–13
B	Sexual abuse	1.49	1.94	F	46	6–14
C	Sexual abuse, ritualistic	1.59	1.94	M,F	35	4–11
G	Sexual abuse	3.1	2.6	M,F	93	3–12
I	Sexual abuse	3.6	2.1	M	31	3–8

Continued on the next page

Table 4. *Continued*

Source	Sample description	Mean	SD	Sex	N	Age (yrs.)
	Sexually aggressive					
L	Sexually aggressive	5.9	No SD	M	9	4–11
L	Sexually aggressive	6.8	No SD	F	3	5–9

Notes. A Achenbach, 1991; B Einbender & Friedrich, 1989; C Kelley, 1989; D Raadal, Milgrom, Cauce, & Mancl, 1994; E Meyer-Bahlburg et al., 2000; F Sandberg, Brook, & Campos, 1994; G Friedrich, Beilke, & Urquiza, 1987; H Friedrich, Beilke, & Urquiza, 1988; I Meyer-Bahlburg et al., 1999; K Ruggiero & McLeer, 2000; L Friedrich & Luecke, 1988.
[a]Excluding those who had not received mental health services or special remedial school classes within the preceding 12 months (Achenbach, 1991, p. 20).
[b]SA Sexually abused.
[c]PR Psychiatrically referred.
[d]Brothers of adjudicated juveniles.
[e]Referral for mental health services, including special education classes for behavioral/emotional problems.

children, and the highest means are shown by two very small samples of "sexually aggressive" children. Thus, despite its brevity and the low frequency of its items in community samples, the SPS shows considerable discrimination at the group level.

Friedrich (1997, p. 5) compared the SPS of the CBCL to his 38-item Child Sexual Behavior Inventory (CSBI). As one would expect, the much longer CSBI outperformed the SPS in correctly classifying sexually abused and nonabused children both by ROC curve-analyses and by discriminant analysis.

Conclusions Regarding the Psychometric Quality of the SPS

The existing versions of the SPS differ in the number and content of the items included in the scale. Therefore, data obtained with different versions cannot be meaningfully compared.

Although the latest version of the SPS (Achenbach, 1991) constitutes a conceptual improvement, its general utility is limited because of its modest internal consistency and the lack of a criterion for clinical interpretation. Conceptually, the present version of the SPS is still heterogeneous in that it combines sex behavior items with gender items. The coverage is unsatisfactory; in particular, of the four sex behavior items none explicitly addresses sexual behavior with a partner. In spite of these difficulties, the SPS shows good discriminant validity at the group level. A raw score sample mean above 1.0 suggests that the sample represents sexually abused children. However, the published standard deviations imply that there is considerable overlap of samples of clinically referred children in general with children specifically identified as "sexually abused," and the scale's utility for the screening of individuals is unsatisfactory.

At the root of the unsatisfactory psychometric quality of the SPS lies the fact that the scale consists of items that are endorsed with low frequency in the standardization samples. Most children are scored zero, and therefore the item distributions are extremely skewed. As a consequence, for many of the reported samples, the scale-score distributions are also extremely skewed, the scale means lower than the variance (which implies gross violation of basic assumptions underlying most statistical procedures used in data analysis), and the internal consistencies and related indices of reliability poor. This situation is not unusual in the construction of symptom scales, but is usually overcome by using clinical samples for scale analysis. As Tables 3 and 4 show, however, general child psychiatric samples are only modestly (albeit significantly) increased in SPS means over nonclinical samples. It is conceivable that this is explained in part by the fact that children with sexual problems are often channeled into specific sex abuse programs and may thereby be underrepresented in general child psychiatric samples. The data on discriminant validity clearly imply that the use of samples of sexually abused children (and presumably of other samples of children identified as having sexual problems) should provide a more appropriate basis for scale development.

Recommendations for Improvement

Given the clinical need for a brief screening instrument concerning problematic sexual behavior, the inclusion of a sexual behavior scale in a comprehensive screening instrument such as the CBCL is highly desirable. We therefore suggest the following improvements: (1) The two gender items should be removed from the sexual behavior scale (The two gender items could be maintained as independent items; if they were to form an independent cross-gender scale, a few more gender items ought to be added for that purpose.); (2) The scale should be lengthened by the addition of a few sexual items, preferably including items that cover sexual activities with a partner; (3) Psychometric characteristics should be obtained on samples that include at least a significant percentage of sexually abused children. Such a sample would provide item distributions that are much more appropriate for factor analysis and other scaling procedures and yield a scale with better psychometric qualities; (4) To underline its function as a screening instrument, the validation of such a sexual behavior scale should include sensitivity/specificity analysis for the identification of children with clinically relevant sexual behavior problems; (5) Such a revised scale would also permit the definition of a clinical range.

Parental Reactions to Their Children's Sexual Behavior

How much do parents really know about the sexual behavior of their children? It is well known that parents and children differ in their reports during child psychiatric interviews and screening questionnaires. Parents tend to report externalizing (norm-violating) behavior by their children more than the children themselves do, whereas children report more internalizing symptoms about themselves than their parents report about their children. When one works clinically with children and parents on sexual issues, it becomes apparent that there are many parents and other caretakers of children in this society who are very uncomfortable with discussing sexual matters in general. This includes discussing the children's potential sexual behaviors and feelings with other adults, and even more so discussing sexual matters with the children themselves.

In their landmark study *Patterns of Child Rearing*, Sears, Maccoby, and Levin (1957) documented in great detail the enormous range of mothers' reactions—from almost complete permissiveness to disgust—to their children's sexual curiosity, masturbation, and sexual play. They described many different methods of control mothers used to inhibit the expression of sexual interest and behavior by their children, ranging from mild expressions of disapproval, prevention of any sexual stimulation, and distraction, to severe punishment. Some mothers also deliberately avoided teaching their children any labels for sexual body parts or any form of sexual behavior, and avoided opportunities for giving information about sexuality when children asked questions. Other studies have yielded similar results (e.g., Gagnon, 1965, 1985; Newson & Newson, 1968; see also Martinson, 1994; Roberts, Kline, & Gagnon, 1978; Rutter, 1980).

Now, almost two generations later, after a sexual revolution and in the presence of what to many looks like a constant barrage of sexual stimuli from the media, especially television, it may well be that the number of mothers with difficulties in this area is lower than it used to be. It is encouraging, for instance, that in our recent study of inner-city boys and their mothers (O'Sullivan et al., 2000), 92% of the mothers said they would be willing to participate again, and only a small minority had significant misgivings. In another recent pilot study, which was conducted by Alice Scharf-Matlick, 40 mother-child dyads from ethnically diverse inner-city neighborhoods participated in a study examining family influences on child sexual socialization. Participating women had to have a child between 6 and 12 years old. The interviews were conducted in the families' homes. One of the interviews, our Sexual Socialization Assessment Schedule (SESOAS; Meyer-Bahlburg & Scharf-Matlick, unpublished) included a section on mothers' perceived comfort in answering hypothetical questions from 7- or 12-year-old sons and daughters about differences between boys and girls' bodies, differences between men and women's bodies, pregnancy, menstruation, masturbation, erection, sexual intercourse, wet dreams, orgasm, and birth control. One example is "Imagine you have a 7-year-old daughter who is in first grade. How comfortable would you feel answering her questions about what pregnancy is?" Response options ranged from 1="Very uncomfortable" to 5="Very comfortable." The majority of mothers reported that they would be quite comfortable discussing various sexuality-related topics with their children. Yet there were dramatic differences in the mothers' comfort level as a function of the child's age (7 versus 12 years) and of sexual topic by child's gender. Mothers reported being much more comfortable when talking to daughters about "female" issues such as menstruation and to sons about "male" issues such as erections and wet dreams, and when talking about sexuality-related topics to 12-year-old sons and daughters rather than to 7-year-olds (Scharf-Matlick & Meyer-Bahlburg, 2001). These are mothers who volunteered to participate in a study that they knew would deal with child sexuality.

In our clinical work and in several sexuality-related studies we have conducted in the New York City area, we still encounter many parents who feel very uncomfortable in discussing sexual matters about and with their children. (In fact, some variation of a comfort scale such as ours or the one by Aquillo and Ely, 1985, might be a good tool to screen parents for the need for help in dealing with their children's sexuality.) Similarly, the continuing battles about sex education in schools also point to significant vociferous minorities among parents of schoolchildren who are concerned about what they consider premature exposure of children to sexual information or induction of undue sexual interest in their children by having sexuality openly discussed.

In our clinical experience, children are quite sensitive to parental expression of dislike of sexual talk or sexual activities. When they experience parental disapproval, some children will in fact be less likely to talk about or do sexual things, but others will simply limit their sexual talk and activities to situations where the parents or other adults are not present. These are the "sexual-possibility situations" which Paikoff (1995) has described as likely situations in which older children or young adolescents have an increased probability of transitioning to adolescent sexual activities. Likewise, the extant literature on childhood sexuality contains many examples of children trying to hide sexual talk and activities from their parents (for instance, Sears et al., 1957). Hiding sexual talk and sexual activities from adults is probably reflected in the decline of scores with age for certain parent-administered items on the CBCL or on the total scale of Friedrich's Child Sexual Behavior Inventory, and is also the likely basis for the psychoanalytic interpretation of middle childhood as a period of sexual latency, now a largely discredited concept (see Rutter, 1980).

Thus, when making sex unspeakable by not providing a vocabulary for sexual matters to their children or by denigrating all matters sexual as "nasty," parents not only block their communication with their children about sex but also contribute to the children's increasing secrecy about sexual activities. These developmental trends are probably also reflected in part in the increasing development of shame reactions and modesty in the child between the ages of 3 and 9 years (Ferguson & Stegge, 1995; Griffin, 1995; Rosenfeld et al., 1984; Schuhrke et al., 1998).

Conclusions

During early childhood, systematic direct observation or, if that is not feasible, interviews with parents and other informants—possibly enhanced by diaries—are the methods of choice. Interviews are especially useful in view of the sporadic or phasic nature of childhood sexuality. After the toddler age of their children, parents are progressively less likely to know about their children's sexual thinking and activities and therefore progressively less useful as informants. Therefore there is a compelling need to develop interviews and related methods for the direct assessment of children's sexuality.

Of the few parent-based screening instruments available, the Sex Problems Scale (SPS) of the Child Behavior Checklist (Achenbach, 1991) has been particularly frequently used. A critical examination of its psychometric quality shows a need for psychometric improvement, but also a considerable degree of validity on the group level. Although, in the United States, there has been a gradual increase in openness about human sexuality, there are still many parents who are uncomfortable in communicating with their children or others about sexual matters, which continues to pose a challenge for the development of disclosure-facilitating sexual assessment instruments.

Acknowledgments

This research was supported in part by Center Grant 2-P50-MH43520 from NIMH (Principal Investigator: Anke A. Ehrhardt, Ph.D.). Jennifer L. Steel, Ph.D., was supported by postdoctoral Training Grant 5-T32-MH19139 from NIMH (Zena Stein, M.D., Training Director). Ms. Patricia Connolly provided word processing assistance.

References

Achenbach, T. M. (1966). The classification of children's psychiatric symptoms: A factor-analytic study. *Psychological Monographs, 80*(615).

Achenbach, T. M. (1991). *Manual for the Child Behavior Checklist/4–18 and 1991 Profile*. Burlington: University of Vermont, Department of Psychiatry.

Achenbach, T. M., & Edelbrock, C. (1978). The classification of child psychopathology: A review and analysis of empirical efforts. *Psychological Bulletin, 85,* 1275–1301.

Achenbach, T. M, & Edelbrock, C. (1979). The Child Behavior Profile: II. Boys aged 12–16 and girls aged 6–11 and 12–16. *Journal of Consulting and Clinical Psychology, 47,* 223–233.

Achenbach, T. M., & Edelbrock, C. (1981). Behavioral problems and competencies reported by parents of normal and disturbed children aged four to sixteen. *Monographs of the Society for Research in Child Development, 46* (Serial No. 188).

Achenbach, T. M., & Edelbrock, C. (1983). *Manual for the Child Behavior Checklist and Revised Child Behavior Profile.* Burlington: University of Vermont, Department of Psychiatry.

Aquillo, M. L., & Ely, J. (1985). Parents and the sexuality of preschool children. *Pediatric Nursing, 11,* 41–46.

Berges, E. T., Neiderbach, S., Rubin, B., Sharpe, E. F., & Tesler, R. W. (1983). *Children and sex: The parents speak.* New York: Facts on File.

Briere, J. (1996). *Trauma symptom checklist for children: Professional manual.* Odessa, FL: Psychological Assessment Resources, Inc.

Broderick, C. B. (1966). Socio-sexual development in a suburban community. *Journal of Sex Research, 2,* 1–24.

Chang, L., Morrissey, R. F., & Koplewicz, H. S. (1995). Prevalence of psychiatric symptoms and their relation to adjustment among Chinese-American youth. *Journal of the American Academy of Child and Adolescent Psychiatry, 34,* 91–99.

Conn, J. H., & Kanner, L. (1940). Spontaneous erections in early childhood. *Journal of Pediatrics, 16,* 337–340.

Dunteman, G. H. (1989). *Principal components analysis.* Newbury Park: Sage.

Einbender, A. J., & Friedrich, W. N. (1989). Psychological functioning and behavior of sexually abused girls. *Journal of Consulting and Clinical Psychology, 57,* 155–157.

Elias, J., & Gebhard, P. (1969). Sexuality and sexual learning in childhood. *Phi Delta Kappan, 50,* 401–405.

Ferguson, T. J., & Stegge, H. (1995). Emotion states and traits in children: The case of shame and guilt. In J. P. Tangney & K. W. Fischer (Eds.), *Self-conscious emotions: The psychology of shame, guilt, embarrassment, and pride* (pp. 174–197). New York: Guilford.

Friedrich, W. N. (1989, June). *The Child Sexual Behavior Inventory: A comparison of normal and clinical populations.* Paper presented at the 15th annual meeting of the International Academy of Sex Research, Princeton, NJ.

Friedrich, W. N. (1993). Sexual victimization and sexual behavior in children: A review of recent literature. *Child Abuse & Neglect, 17,* 59–66.

Friedrich, W. N. (1997). *CSBI Child Sexual Behavior Inventory: Professional manual.* Rochester, MN: Mayo Clinic Foundation.

Friedrich, W. N., Beilke, R. L., & Urquiza, A. J. (1987). Children from sexually abusive families: A behavioral comparison. *Journal of Interpersonal Violence, 2,* 391–402.

Friedrich, W. N., Beilke, R. L., & Urquiza, A. J. (1988). Behavior problems in young sexually abused boys: A comparison study. *Journal of Interpersonal Violence, 3,* 21–28.

Friedrich, W. N., & Luecke, W. J. (1988). Young school-age sexually aggressive children. *Professional Psychology: Research and Practice, 19,* 155–164.

Friedrich, W. N., Urquiza, A. J., & Beilke, R. L. (1986). Behavior problems in sexually abused young children. *Journal of Pediatric Psychology, 11,* 47–57.

Friman, P. C., Larzelere, R., & Finney, J. W. (1994). Exploring the relationship between thumb-sucking and psychopathology. *Journal of Pediatric Psychology, 19,* 431–441.

Gagnon, J. H. (1965). Sexuality and sexual learning in the child. *Psychiatry, 28,* 212–228.

Gagnon, J. H. (1985). Attitudes and responses of parents to pre-adolescent masturbation. *Archives of Sexual Behavior, 14,* 451–466.

Galenson, E. (1990). Observation of early infantile sexual and erotic development. In J. Money and H. Musaph (Series Eds.) & M. E. Perry (Vol. Ed.), *Handbook of sexology: Vol. 7. Childhood and adolescent sexology* (pp. 169–178). Amsterdam: Elsevier.

Galenson, E., & Roiphe, H. (1974). The emergence of genital awareness during the second year of life. In R. C. Friedman, R. M. Richart, & R. L. Vande Wiele (Eds.), *Sex differences in behavior* (pp. 223–231). New York: John Wiley and Sons.

Gil, E., & Johnson, T. C. (1993). *Sexualized children: Assessment and treatment of sexualized children and children who molest.* Rockville, MD: Launch.

Greene, R. W., Biederman, J., Faraone, S. V., Ouellette, C. A., Penn, C., & Griffin, S. M. (1996). Toward a new psychometric definition of social disability in children with Attention-Deficit Hyperactivity Disorder. *Journal of the American Academy of Child and Adolescent Psychiatry, 35,* 571–578.

Griffin, S. (1995). A cognitive-developmental analysis of pride, shame, and embarrassment in middle childhood. In J. P. Tangney & K. W. Fischer (Eds.), *Self-conscious emotions: The psychology of shame, guilt, embarrassment, and pride* (pp. 219–236). New York: Guilford.

Gundersen, B. H., Melås, P. S., & Skår, J. E. (1981). Sexual behavior of preschool children: Teachers' observations. In L. L. Constantine & F. M. Martinson (Eds.), *Children and sex: New findings, new perspectives* (pp. 45–61). Boston: Little, Brown.

Halverson, H. M. (1938). Infant sucking and tensional behavior. *Journal of Genetic Psychology, 32,* 365–430.

Johnson, T. C. (1993). Assessment of sexual behavior problems in preschool-aged and latency-aged children. *Child and Adolescent Psychiatric Clinics of North America, 2*(3), 431–449.

Kelley, S. J. (1989). Stress responses of children to sexual abuse and ritualistic abuse in day care centers. *Journal of Interpersonal Violence, 4,* 502–513.

Kinsey, A. C., Pomeroy, W. B., & Martin, C. E. (1948). *Sexual behavior in the human male.* Philadelphia: W. B. Saunders.

Kinsey, A. C., Pomeroy, W. B., Martin, C. E., & Gebhard, P. H. (1953). *Sexual behavior in the human female.* Philadelphia: W. B. Saunders.

Levine, M. I. (1957). Pediatric observations on masturbation in children. *Psychoanalytic Study of the Child, 6,* 117–124.

Martinson, F. M. (1994). *The sexual life of children.* Westport, CT: Bergin and Garvey.

Meyer-Bahlburg, H. F. L., Dolezal, C., & Sandberg, D. (2000). The association of sexual behavior with externalizing behaviors in a community sample of pre-pubertal children. *Journal of Psychology and Human Sexuality, 12*(1–2), 61–79.

Meyer-Bahlburg, H. F. L., Dolezal, C., Wasserman, G. A., & Jaramillo, B. M. (1999). Prepubertal boys' sexual behavior and behavior problems. *AIDS Education and Prevention, 11*, 174–186.

Meyer-Bahlburg, H. F. L., & Scharf-Matlick, A. A. (unpublished manuscript). *The Sexual Socialization Assessment Schedule, parent version (SESOAS-P), 1999 Edition.* New York: HIV Center for Clinical and Behavioral Studies, NYS Psychiatric Institute.

Meyer-Bahlburg, H. F. L., Steel, J. L., & Dolezal, C. (1997, July). *The Child Behavior Checklist (CBCL) Sex Problems Scale as a measure of childhood sexual behavior.* Poster session presented at the 23rd annual meeting of the International Academy of Sex Research, Baton Rouge, LA.

Newson, J., & Newson, E. (1968). *Four years old in an urban community.* London: George Allen and Unwin.

Newton, N., & Newton, M. (1967). Psychologic aspects of lactation. *New England Journal of Medicine, 277*, 1179–1188.

O'Sullivan, L. F., Meyer-Bahlburg, H. F. L., & Wasserman, G. (2000). Reactions of inner-city boys and their mothers to research interviews about sex. *Journal of Psychology and Human Sexuality, 12*(1–2), 81–103.

Paikoff, R. L. (1995). Early heterosexual debut: Situations of sexual possibility during the transition to adolescence. *American Journal of Orthopsychiatry, 65*, 389–401.

Raadal, M., Milgrom, P., Cauce, A. M., & Mancl, L. (1994). Behavior problems in 5- to 11-year-old children from low-income families. *Journal of the American Academy of Child and Adolescent Psychiatry, 33*, 1017–1025.

Ramsey, G. V. (1943). The sexual development of boys. *American Journal of Psychology, 56*, 217–233.

Roberts, E. J., Kline, D., & Gagnon, J. (1978). *Family life and sexual learning: A study of the role of parents in the sexual learning of children.* Cambridge, MA: Population Education.

Rosenfeld, A., Siegel-Gorelick, B., Haavik, D., Duryea, M., Wenegrat, A., Martin, J., et al. (1984). Parental perceptions of children's modesty: A cross-sectional survey of ages two to ten years. *Psychiatry, 47*, 351–365.

Rovet, J., & Ireland, L. (1994). Behavioral phenotype in children with Turner Syndrome. *Journal of Pediatric Psychology, 19*, 779–790.

Ruggiero, K. J., & McLeer, S. V. (2000). PTSD Scale of the Child Behavior Checklist: Concurrent and discriminant validity with non-clinic-referred sexually abused children. *Journal of Traumatic Stress, 13*, 287–299.

Rutter, M. (1980). Psychosexual development. In M. Rutter (Ed.), *Scientific foundations of developmental psychiatry* (pp. 322–339). London: Heinemann.

Sandberg, D. E., Brook, A. E., & Campos, S. P. (1994). Short stature: A psychosocial burden requiring growth hormone therapy? *Pediatrics, 94*, 832–840.

Scharf-Matlick, A. A., & Meyer-Bahlburg, H. F. L. (2001, October). *Mothers' comfort level as a function of children's characteristics and discussion content when talking to children about sexuality.* Abstract of poster presented at the annual meeting of the Society for the Scientific Study of Sexuality, San Diego, CA, *Program and Abstracts* (p. 23).

Schuhrke, B., Rank, A., Stadler, A., Pinz, D., & Hildner, B. (1998). *Kindliche Körperscham und familiale Schamregeln*. Köln, Germany: Bundeszentrale für gesundheitliche Aufklärung.

Sears, R. R., Maccoby, E. E., & Levin, H. (1957). *Patterns of child rearing*. Evanston, IL: Row, Peterson.

Stanton, B., Li, X., Black, M., Ricardo, I., Galbraith, J., Kaljee, L., et al. (1994). Sexual practices and intentions among preadolescent and early adolescent low-income African Americans. *Pediatrics, 93,* 966–973.

Thorne, B., & Luria, Z. (1986). Sexuality and gender in children's daily worlds. *Social Problems, 33,* 176–190.

Westney, O. E., Jenkins, R. R., & Benjamin, C. A. (1983). Sociosexual development of preadolescents. In J. Brooks-Gunn & A. C. Petersen (Eds.), *Girls at puberty: Biological and psychosocial perspectives* (pp. 273–300). New York: Plenum.

Discussion Paper

KENNETH J. ZUCKER

My comments on the papers by O'Sullivan and by Meyer-Bahlburg and Steel will be offered, in part, from the perspective of a developmental approach. The developmental approach seeks to understand the factors that predict adaptation vs. maladaptation over time. Over the past 20 years, the developmentalist who studies normative development has often been one who also studies atypical development; hence, the fields of developmental psychology and developmental psychopathology have become strongly integrated. Adaptation and maladaptation, normal and abnormal, are mutually defining (Cicchetti, 1990; Sroufe & Rutter, 1984).

As noted by Sroufe (1990), development is organized around a set of critical developmental issues (e.g., attachment formation to caregivers, peer competence, etc.) and patterns of adaptation are defined with respect to these. But how can one know an issue is critical without examining the consequences of adaptational failure, that is, maladaptation and pathology, with respect to those issues? One cannot demarcate important deviations without first defining crucial developmental issues and normal patterns of adaptation with respect to those issues. But one cannot demonstrate the critical importance of any developmental issue without examining its consequences, or delimit the range of normal adaptive patterns without demarcating the pathological.

If we adopt the developmental approach to the study of sexuality, it is legitimate to ask the question, "What is sexual behavior development the development of?" From O'Sullivan's paper, we hear about two rather radical and opposing "worldviews" of childhood sexuality, likely ideological more than anything else, that have influenced our approach to the topic. The first view casts the child as an "asexual rookie," to be protected from the sexual disinhibitions of adulthood. This assumption has likely been one of the underlying factors that fueled interest in the topic of sexual abuse, or even child-to-child sexual interactions ("sex play"), namely, that premature exposure to sexual experiences (or too much exposure or too intense exposure) would abnormally accelerate a child's sexual development. The other view casts the child as a "sexual veteran," to be protected from the sexual inhibitions of adulthood. This assumption has likely been one of the underlying factors that have fueled interest in those variables that will promote, over time, a more sex-positive developmental outcome. Surely, both views, at least in their extreme, are incorrect and the developmental approach would argue for some kind of intermediate position, that is to say, childhood sexuality (whether we are talking about knowledge, attitudes, feelings, or subjectivity) has some kind of developmental form to it, with specific mature end-states to be reached.

O'Sullivan identified several institutional and methodological constraints in studying childhood sexuality. I want to make only a few remarks about the institutional matters, particularly with regard to IRBs. The examples provided by O'Sullivan illustrate the more general problem that sexology as a field has had to face, namely that it remains, at least in some quarters, an outlaw discipline (Bullough, 1994). Of course, much progress has been made in allaying institutional anxieties about studying sexuality, but there are, no doubt, many researchers in the field who have had to work hard at overcoming obstacles. Given the emotionally charged nature of sexuality research, perhaps this should surprise no one.

O'Sullivan notes that retrospective studies are hampered by the phenomenon of childhood amnesia (or forgetting), faulty recall (e.g., in the recovered memory debate, this problem is cast along the lines of "implantation of illusory memories"), and even retrospective distortion—this last problem adopting the view of memory as representing a dynamic process of reconstruction (again, in the recovered memory debate, on the distinction between "true" and "false" memories) (Conway, 1997; Pezdek & Banks, 1996; Williams & Banyard, 1999). All of these problems are legitimate. Indeed, in the fields of developmental psychology and psychopathology, the problems inherent to retrospective research have fueled several generations of prospective studies. The problem of retrospective research was actually commented upon by Freud (1920/1955), in his essay entitled "The psychogenesis of a case of homosexuality in a woman," where he wrote that

> So long as we trace . . . development from its final outcome backwards, the chain of events appears continuous, and we feel we have gained an insight which is completely satisfactory or even exhaustive. But if we proceed the reverse way, if we start from the premises . . . and try to follow these up to the final result, then we no longer get the impression of an inevitable sequence of events which could not have been otherwise determined. We notice at once that there might have been another result, and that we might have been just as well able to understand and explain the latter. The synthesis is thus not so satisfactory . . . in other words, from a knowledge of the premises we could not have foretold the nature of the result. (p. 167)

While accepting O'Sullivan's concerns about retrospective research and Freud's view that there may well be radical disjunctions in explaining long-term outcome depending on where one starts in the developmental sequence, I do not believe that retrospective strategies need to be abandoned entirely, nor do I believe that there are complete disjunctions between prospective and retrospective data sets in terms of developmental outcomes. For example, if we look at the relation between childhood sex-typed behavior and sexual orientation—a topic addressed at the 1998 Kinsey Conference on the Role of Theory in Sex Research (Bancroft, 2000) —we know that retrospective and prospective studies have provided reasonable evidence for convergence (Bailey & Zucker, 1995; Green, 1987). Moreover, we have some data suggesting that adult children and their mothers recall, with reasonable concordance, patterns of childhood sex-typed behavior (e.g., Bailey, Miller, & Willerman, 1993). Perhaps recalling patterns of childhood sex-typed behavior, which extend over a period of years, represents a type of semantic memory task, i.e., one that taps relatively permanent knowledge. Here let me flag one particular issue that is of great interest to developmentalists: the whole debate on continuity vs. discontinuity in development. Some developmentalists are strong adherents of the continuity perspective, including attention to "sleeper effects," i.e., evidence for coherence in development that might not be apparent unless one tracks children over long periods of time (see Sroufe, 1990). The other perspective, however, argues in favor of discontinuity, i.e., that coherence across development is not particularly strong (Lewis, 1997).

Another domain for which there are interesting recall data pertains to age of onset of signs of pubertal development in gay and straight men. Beginning with the Kinsey, Pomeroy, and Martin (1948) study, there are now about a baker's dozen of studies that all find, with one exception, that gay men recall an earlier pubertal onset than straight men (Bogaert & Blanchard, 1996). The most recent study, by Bogaert, Friesen, and Klentrou (2002) analyzed data from Laumann, Gagnon, Michael, and Michael's (1994) national probability sample. It would, of course, be desirable to replicate these findings from a prospective standpoint. Nonetheless, the fact that these studies measured pubertal onset in diverse ways—age of first masturbation, age of first orgasm, age of onset of sexual feelings, age of voice change, and so on—and yet found similar results lends some credence to their validity.

It is likely the case that research from a retrospective standpoint needs to take into account a whole host of variables that contribute, for example, to recall accuracy vs. distortion, and these factors need to be entertained in planning particular studies. It is likely, for example, that relatively objective vs. subjective markers (physical or behavioral) are extremely important in this regard. One final example of this will suffice: We have recently completed a study of birth weight in boys with gender identity disorder (GID) compared to clinical control boys and girls (Blanchard et al., 2001). Birth weight is sex-dimorphic. In our study, we found that boys with GID weighed less than clinical control boys, but not significantly more than clinical control girls. For the boys with GID, we had both maternal recall data on birth weight and hospital records. The correlation between the two data sources was .94. Recall may well be reconstructive in some instances, but not in others.

Meyer-Bahlburg and Steel's paper considers the use of the parent as an informant about child sexual behavior. They present the sobering fact that there are apparently only two standardized parent-screening instruments that pertain to childhood sexual behavior available in the literature: the Sexual Problems Scale (SPS) of the Child Behavior Checklist (Achenbach, 1991) and the Child Sexual Behavior Inventory (CSBI) developed by Friedrich and colleagues (Friedrich, Fisher, Broughton, Houston, & Shafran, 1998; Friedrich et al., 1992; Friedrich, Sandfort, Oostveen, & Cohen-Kettenis, 2000; see also Sandfort & Cohen-Kettenis, 2000). Given that parent-report questionnaires are so widely used in the developmental literature, it is indeed astonishing that there has been such a paucity of psychometric work in the area.

I will make only two specific comments about Meyer-Bahlburg and Steel's psychometric review. (1) First, they noted that the 15-month correlation for the SPS was only .22, which they interpreted as reflecting in part the "sporadic nature of childhood sexual behavior." Perhaps a more cautious interpretation is that the stability of very specific parent-reported childhood sexual behaviors is very low. Sampling a wider range of childhood sexual behaviors (say, e.g., early "crushes") might yield stronger stability estimates. (2) Second, Meyer-Bahlburg and Steel note that the CSBI shows reasonable evidence for discriminant validity, with sexually abused children having higher scores than clinical control children, who, in turn, have higher scores than nonclinical controls.

These data represent a clear advance in research on potential sexual behavior problems in children. Ten years ago, when I co-authored a narrative review of the child sexual abuse literature (Beitchman, Zucker, Hood, DaCosta, & Akman, 1991), I was frankly amazed at the paucity of well-designed empirical studies. At that time, we reviewed 42 articles that included a sample of sexually abused children. Of these, 43% did not employ a control group, 19% only employed nonclinical controls, 31% only employed clinical controls, and only 7% (3 of 42 studies) employed both clinical and normal controls. This state of affairs was moderately better than at the time of two previous reviews of the child sexual abuse literature: A review by Alter-Reid, Gibbs, Lachenmeyer, Sigal, & Massoth (1986) only contained 1 reference (out of 39) of sexually abused children that included a control group, and the widely cited review by Browne and Finkelhor (1986) contained only 1 reference (out of 49) that included a control group in which the results were published in a peer-reviewed journal.

At the time of the Beitchman et al. (1991) review, one of my doctoral students completed a dissertation in which sexually abused girls were compared to demographically matched clinical control girls and nonreferred or normal control girls (Maing, 1991). Maing found many nonspecific effects of clinical status, i.e., that both the sexually abused and clinical control girls had more general behavioral problems than did the nonreferred controls; however, she did find that the sexually abused girls under the age of 7 showed more sexualized behavior than the two comparison groups. Although it is beyond the scope of this commentary to discuss Maing's data in detail, I will mention that it made a nice contribution to describing the variability of sexual abuse experiences among the abused sample, which was to some degree correlated with the extent of sexualized behavior. Over the past 10 years, there have clearly been some good advances in the design and execution of studies in this particular domain.

Both O'Sullivan and Meyer-Bahlburg and Steel describe in their papers some broader approaches to obtaining information about childhood sexuality that go beyond the delimited focus influenced by the pressing clinical issues activated by the problem of childhood sexual abuse. It is likely that these approaches will contribute to a more comprehensive and developmental perspective in providing some type of phenomenological taxonomy pertaining to childhood sexual behavior, at least with regard to what might be construed in the broadest sense as normative phenomena within particular cultural groups. Consider, for example, the finding by Meyer-Bahlburg and Steel pertaining to maternal comfort level, which varied as a function of the sexual topic and the child's age and sex. These data reminded me of some data I found in two unpublished studies that I have conducted regarding the measurement of children's erotic preference (Zucker, 1989, 1990). As part of these studies, which included children ranging in age from 4 to 12, I collected information about children's exposure to peers and adults (including parents) in underclothing and in the nude. I found evidence for sex of child x sex of adult effects. In general, children had greater exposure to same-sex peers and same-sex adults in the nude and, to a lesser extent, in underwear, than to cross-sex peers and cross-sex adults. It is likely that these patterns speak to something important about implicit assumptions regarding sexual socialization.

Meyer-Bahlburg and Steel's data also have relevance to what I believe is a relatively understudied area with regard to childhood sexuality from the child's point of view, namely a good understanding of its emotional salience. Although we have some data on this (e.g., on the emergence of inhibitions about sexuality; e.g., Schuhrke, 1996, 2000), it seems that we can learn a great deal more about how and when children become sensitive to sexual stimuli. For example, if one used some type of reaction time experiment to words or pictures, what types of developmental trends would emerge regarding children's learning about the special significance of sexual cues?

Lastly, I would like to suggest several target groups for which we might learn more about the whole process of sexual socialization during childhood. First, I would endorse O'Sullivan's emphasis on the importance of the peer group. In our laissez-faire culture, it is likely that children learn a great deal about sexuality, accurate and inaccurate, within the peer group (see Thorne, 1993). Second, it might be quite useful to study transcripts of sex abuse investigations to code how children respond to sex matters in one particular environmental setting. Third, we should consider other special groups of children in which transmission of sexual information might be particularly unique: One group that comes to mind would be that of children whose parents are practicing "nudists"; the second group would be that of children who are treated by a particular subgroup of child psychoanalysts: the Kleinians. Many Kleinians interpret much of what children do in their play as sexual—it would be quite interesting to study transcriptions of audiotapes of these analytic sessions to gain an appreciation of how young children receive the comments of their therapist. Of these suggestions, I suspect that the last idea would be least viable, as it is likely that publication of the results would lead to the arrest and imprisonment of the therapist.

References

Achenbach, T. M. (1991). *Manual for the Child Behavior Checklist/4–18 and 1991 Profile*. Burlington: University of Vermont, Department of Psychiatry.

Alter-Reid, K., Gibbs, M. S., Lachenmeyer, J. R., Sigal, J., & Massoth, N. A. (1986). Sexual abuse of children: A review of the empirical findings. *Clinical Psychology Review, 6*, 249–266.

Bailey, J. M., Miller, J. S., & Willerman, L. (1993). Maternally rated childhood gender nonconformity in homosexuals and heterosexuals. *Archives of Sexual Behavior, 22*, 461–469.

Bailey, J. M., & Zucker, K. J. (1995). Childhood sex-typed behavior and sexual orientation: A conceptual analysis and quantitative review. *Developmental Psychology, 31*, 43–55.

Bancroft, J. (Ed.). (2000). *The role of theory in sex research*. Bloomington: Indiana University Press.

Beitchman, J. H., Zucker, K. J., Hood, J. E., DaCosta, G. A., & Akman, D. (1991). A review of the short-term effects of child sexual abuse. *Child Abuse & Neglect, 15*, 537–556.

Blanchard, R., Zucker, K. J., Cavacas, A., Allin, S., Bradley, S. J., & Schachter, D. C. (2001). *Fraternal birth order and birth weight in probably prehomosexual feminine boys*. Manuscript submitted for publication.

Bogaert, A. F., & Blanchard, R. (1996). Physical development and sexual orientation in men: Height, weight, and age of puberty differences. *Personality and Individual Differences, 21*, 77–84.

Bogaert, A. F., Friesen, C., & Klentrou, P. (2002). Age of puberty and sexual orientation in a national probability sample. *Archives of Sexual Behavior, 31,* 73–81.

Browne, A., & Finkelhor, D. (1986). Impact of child sexual abuse: A review of the research. *Psychological Bulletin, 99,* 66–77.

Bullough, V. L. (1994). *Science in the bedroom: A history of sex research.* New York: Basic.

Cicchetti, D. (1990). Perspectives on the interface between normal and atypical development. [Editorial]. *Development and Psychopathology, 2,* 329–333.

Conway, M. A. (Ed.). (1997). *Recovered memories and false memories.* Oxford, England: Oxford University Press.

Freud, S. (1955). The psychogenesis of a case of homosexuality in a woman. In J. Strachey (Ed. & Trans.), *The standard edition of the complete psychological works of Sigmund Freud* (Vol. 18, pp. 145–172). London: Hogarth. (Originally published 1920).

Friedrich, W. N., Fisher, J., Broughton, D., Houston, M., & Shafran, C. (1998). Normative sexual behavior in children: A contemporary sample. *Pediatrics, 101*(4), e9.

Friedrich, W. N., Grambsch, P., Damon, L., Hewitt, S. K., Koverola, C., Lang, R. A., et al. (1992). Child Sexual Behavior Inventory: Normative and clinical comparisons. *Psychological Assessment, 4,* 303–311.

Friedrich, W. N., Sandfort, T. G. M., Oostveen, J., & Cohen-Kettenis, P. T. (2000). Cultural differences in sexual behavior: 2–6-year-old Dutch and American children. *Journal of Psychology and Human Sexuality, 12*(1–2), 117–129.

Green, R. (1987). The "sissy boy syndrome" and the development of homosexuality. New Haven, CT: Yale University Press.

Kinsey, A. C., Pomeroy, W. B., & Martin, C. E. (1948). *Sexual behavior in the human male.* Philadelphia: W. B. Saunders.

Laumann, E. O., Gagnon, J. H., Michael, R. T., & Michaels, S. (1994). *The social organization of sexuality: Sexual practices in the United States.* Chicago: University of Chicago Press.

Lewis, M. (1997). *Altering fate: Why the past does not predict the future.* New York: Guilford.

Maing, D. M. (1991). *Patterns of psychopathology in sexually abused girls.* Unpublished doctoral dissertation, University of Windsor, Windsor, Ontario.

Pezdek, K., & Banks, W. P. (Eds.). (1996). *The recovered memory/false memory debate.* San Diego, CA: Academic.

Sandfort, T. G. M., & Cohen-Kettenis, P. T. (2000). Sexual behavior in Dutch and Belgian children as observed by their mothers. *Journal of Psychology and Human Sexuality, 12*(1–2), 105–115.

Schuhrke, B. (1996, June). *Shame of urination and defecation in 2- to 9-year-old children.* Poster session presented at the meeting of the International Academy of Sex Research, Rotterdam, the Netherlands.

Schuhrke, B. (2000). Young children's curiosity about other people's genitals. *Journal of Psychology and Human Sexuality, 12*(1–2), 27–48.

Sroufe, L. A. (1990). Considering normal and abnormal together: The essence of developmental psychopathology. *Development and Psychopathology, 2,* 335–347.

Sroufe, L. A., & Rutter, M. (1984). The domain of developmental psychopathology. *Child Development, 55,* 173–189.

Thorne, B. (1993). *Gender play: Girls and boys in school*. New Brunswick, NJ: Rutgers University Press.

Williams, L. M., & Banyard, V. L. (Eds.). (1999). *Trauma and memory*. Thousand Oaks, CA: Sage.

Zucker, K. J. (1989, June). Can "erotic preference" be measured in children? In K. J. Zucker (Chair), *Sexual behavior and eroticism in childhood*. Symposium conducted at the meeting of the International Academy of Sex Research, Princeton, NJ.

Zucker, K. J. (1990, August). *Can "erotic preference" be measured in children? II. Effects of increasing the salience of the putative erotic stimuli*. Poster session presented at the meeting of the International Academy of Sex Research, Sigtuna, Sweden.

General Discussion

Dennis Fortenberry: I want to comment on some issues related to the entry of children and adolescents into research projects on sexual behavior as part of a larger study. We're evaluating and asking parents to give us reasons that they consent to participation of their middle-adolescent daughters in a sexual behavior and sexual diseases research project. We're also asking those that decline consent, permission, to give reasons. For those that give permission, the most common reason is the kind of volunteer bias you might expect. They see the research as kind of an ally for them in terms of helping their daughters with their sexual behavior. For those that decline, the least common, although not absent, reason is the sexual content of the research. The most common reason for nonparticipation is the time. Now time might be said because it's a polite way of not talking about sex, but given the fact that our research lasts more than two years and we're in their house once a week for six months of each of those two years, that's probably correct. The second most common reason is not the sexual content, it's the research itself. I think what that suggests is, rather than be extraordinarily sensitive to the sexual content of our work, is that we have to be more proactive in promoting research as the public good and perhaps a social responsibility.

Lucia O'Sullivan: I would like to respond to that in part because the reaction to the study instrument that was included in our study with boys did ask the parents what benefits they saw this research as having and prompted them in terms of the greater good. Very few mothers recognized such benefit. They did not see how their interview or the interview with the boy, their son, could possibly benefit other women or families that they knew, and yet one part of the consent process was to explain that even though they might not benefit directly from this research beyond $30, we expect that these findings are going to be of use to a broader group. That was not understood or processed in some way, or at least not retrieved when we prompted for it at the end of the interview. There's some work to do on this aspect, I totally agree.

John Bancroft: To what extent is that socioculturally determined?

Lucia O'Sullivan: The families that we have been interviewing in our research program are from impoverished neighborhoods of New York City, a definite benefit no doubt being the financial reimbursement for their participation. I'm not sure how much social desirability factors come into play but these are all concerns, of course, as they would be with all researchers in this field.

Heino Meyer-Bahlburg: Our neighborhood is close to Harlem, and most of our African American participants would regard themselves as belonging to Harlem. Any research at Columbia University involving African Americans, especially studies that are focused predominantly on inner-city minorities, are under close political scrutiny. The larger study, onto which our study piggybacked, dealt with the development of aggressive behavior and provoked posters, marches, and political demonstrations. Also individual participants may be suspicious. For instance, one mother instructed her boy, before they came to our unit for their interviews, not to take any food or drink from us because it might be poisoned. She was amazed and relieved when a black interviewer greeted her at the door, to whom she then told these details. So the political climate for defining benefits of a study for an inner-city population around Columbia University can be difficult. That situation does not necessarily apply to other places.

Philip Jenkins: Two comments about that; there's an excellent book called *I Heard It through the Grapevine*, by Patricia A. Turner, which is about African American urban folklore. One of the case studies is on the elaborate folklore surrounding what urban university medical schools do to black people and specifically black children. In studying refusals to participate, I wonder if one factor might be media coverage, or media stereotypes over the last eight to ten years and the suggestion is, if you allow your children to be interviewed about sex then the interviewers are likely to evolve bogus charges of child sexual abuse.

Heino Meyer-Bahlburg: That is very difficult to research, and we don't have any pertinent data from this study. The particular study onto which we piggybacked involved the younger brothers of juvenile delinquents. Almost everybody who we approached for our substudy, which was conducted separately from the main study, participated. At baseline, we had almost 100% compliance. The drop off to Time 2, 15 months later, was very minor. This was a preselected sample in the sense that the families had already participated in the main study, which may explain why we had such a high participation rate. From other studies that I've done, my impression is that in some cases fears about sexual abuse reporting could play a role in refusal, but clear-cut supportive evidence is difficult to obtain.

Jay Paul: On the question of people's reaction to participating in research, there are a number of things that work against us and for which we have to take some responsibility. In the Urban Men's Health Study, if people were willing to go so far as to get screened, most were willing to participate. It wasn't a question of the topic matter that really threw people off in this case. Of course, this was a study of men who have sex with men so it's a particular subgroup, but it was a matter of getting people to participate in any kind of screening, any kind of research; that's the big stumbling block in telephone surveys. There are a number of things that work against us. Research is used by a lot of people who have less benign interests than we do as academicians: marketing research, research that's exploring behaviors relevant to the researcher's own economic ends. There is also the issue of making sure that results of studies get back to participants, get back to the communities that have provided the data. One of the difficulties, in that respect, is deciding what information to provide back to the community which isn't going in some way to bias further research. A lot of respondents who have been tracked for the Urban Men's Health Study were complaining at the six-month intervals that they had not yet heard of data coming out of the study in which they had participated initially. This is something that we really have to take seriously. We should be respectful of the time given by respondents in prior studies, making sure that they understand that important information has come out of their participation.

Ken Zucker: What do we know about the representativeness of samples in childhood sexuality studies compared to other childhood domains? Has anybody attempted to look at the feasibility of representative, stratified samples being willing to participate as compared to other domains of developmental research? Could any of the epidemiologists in the room comment about the comparability of participants in adult sexual studies compared to other types of studies?

Bill Friedrich: In the third sample that I collected with the Child Sexual Behavior Inventory, we did attempt to obtain a sample that was much more diverse economically and demographically. We did not deliberately stratify it but we sought out lower-income samples, less educated samples than you typically obtain in Olmsted County, Minnesota; the first study I did was 98.1% Caucasian and middle class to upper middle class. When we did get this much more diverse sample there was interestingly a much clearer relationship between education and income and the reporting of sexual behavior. So more educated parents reported more sexual behavior, parents who were more affluent reported more sexual behavior in their kids. That leads to another comment. Lucia mentioned the interviews that we did with parents when we were first developing the Child Sexual Behavior Inventory. These were parents of kids who came in because of concern that they were sexually abused and we would ask them about sexual behaviors. We did that in another study. I haven't published this data, but we found that more educated parents would volunteer behaviors as sexual; less educated parents had not thought of or categorized their child's behavior as sexual.

Janet Hyde: Sampling is everything if we're really trying to find out about normative sexual behavior in children. Bill Friedrich has a great idea in terms of interviewing people coming in for routine checkups, but I'd really like to hear more from those of you who are doing this research. It's clear to me that I can't go to the Madison schools and say I'd like to interview 2nd, 3rd, and 4th graders as I might with some other developmental study, that's just not going to work here. How can one go about recruiting samples of children that will end up being reasonably good samples of the general population?

Lucia O'Sullivan: With our focus group studies, we recruited [mothers] from community locations literally off the street, and that resulted in a total of 27 focus groups by the end of the study. Of course that means that you have a sampling bias of mothers who happen to be out on the streets of Harlem and Washington Heights at that time and who had daughters in that range in age from 6 to 17. Right now for our interview studies, we're recruiting from community agencies and school groups, in recreational centers and such, but all convenience samples with, of course, their built-in biases. However, we're hoping these samples are somewhat more representative than a clinic population that we might have used in the past.

Elsie Pinkston: Do you ever question whether it is normative sexual behavior that we should be looking for? Or should we rather be studying the circumstances that bring about different kinds of behavior? When you're working with children who have been designated as sexually aggressive, the criterion that ends up being used is "unexpected sexual behavior" and my question always is, if you've been through six foster homes and have been abused by one or two relatives, what is "expected behavior?" So in fact norms seem to get used to the detriment of children who actually are not from those norms.

Lucia O'Sullivan: I'm a social psychologist and I appreciate the broad strokes more than the finer detail in research and I think that it's a matter of what you consider most useful. I cannot understand what "aggressive" is without understanding what "nonaggressive" is. I'm not sure how much I agree with Ken Zucker that they are mutually defining; I don't necessarily think that's so. I think you do need to lay a foundation of research that captures what is typical. We always get into these issues of statistical deviance, and how you define normal and abnormal, but in my mind you answered the question yourself: How can you say what is unexpected sexual behavior unless you're very clear on what is expected?

Meredith Reynolds: Focus groups are a promising way of looking at norms of sexual behavior. Have you ever had a chance to compare the girls who are active participants with the girls who are more passively involved? In my limited experience with focus groups, it seems that if you're disagreeing with what's going on in the group you're more likely to be targeted by the focus group leader to elaborate on those differences. So I'm curious about the extent to which you're able to look at the norms that get established in the group, what the participants feel able to talk about, and to what extent they don't express disagreement because they don't want to be targeted. Is there any exit survey or debriefing approach that would help you get into that?

Lucia O'Sullivan: One problem with focus groups is that they do quickly develop consensus. So you get a norm in the sense of a broader average kind of response. What we did at the very beginning with the older groups was to have girls respond to a couple of items addressing their own views or beliefs at the start of the group before the group had established a consensus of what was normal or acceptable. (They were not asked to report on their own sexual behavior.) We followed up with individual interviews, which I really think is the only way you can capture the more personalized sexual behaviors. A group is not the place to get that information.

Meredith Reynolds: I'm not speaking so much of revealing one's personal experiences to the group, but rather one's opinions of what the group considers to be peer norms. If the group appears to be in consensus about what peers are doing and if you disagree with that, then it's difficult, especially in those age groups, to voice your disagreement. Doing so may be seen as revealing something of your own personal experiences and it may set you up for feeling really different or weird compared with the other group members.

Lucia O'Sullivan: We actually did have some luck with getting a range of perspectives and more with the older groups than with the younger. If there was one girl in the younger group who said, "OOHH, sex is gross and boys are disgusting," there it went, and all girls would chime in similarly. But, if you were able to encourage the girls to give the alternative view, "Well, you know some girls don't think that *all* sex is nasty or dirty," they're curious about what's going on and can express the range of perspectives. But the point of the focus groups was really to capture perceived norms and that is a different and perhaps a slightly distracting topic if we're really talking here about what actually happens, and so I think the interview data is much more valuable in that sense.

Ed Laumann: The various comments and presentations have been very psychologically premised. That is, there's an idea of some kind of developmental process that's rooted in the individual organism that somehow we would like to identify through asking about markers of their sexual activities and so on. To my mind, sexuality is fundamentally a social phenomenon and thinking about networks might be very helpful in raising the issues of normalization. For example, one could easily imagine childhood sex playgroups which, in a sense, recruit people through some discovery that they learn about these things through self-exploration. This is not something 3-year-olds are talking about, but at some point there is a recruiting process. Basically the strategy of the controlling society is to isolate people by not talking about these things. The theory is, if you don't talk about it, you don't produce the behavior.

Methodological Issues Involved in Adult Recall of Childhood Sexual Experiences

CYNTHIA A. GRAHAM

Empirical studies of the validity and reliability of adults' retrospective reports of childhood sexual experiences have largely been restricted to recall of child sexual abuse (CSA), reflecting the serious lack of research in the area of normative childhood sexual behavior. In the area of CSA, the issue of the validity of retrospective reports is certainly not a recent concern. However, triggered by the debate surrounding recovered memory, and the resultant questioning of the accuracy of adults' reports of CSA (e.g., Rich, 1990; Briere, 1990), the last decade has seen an increasing number of studies that have focused on the stability and accuracy of recall of CSA. The majority of these studies have addressed the question of how common it is for adults to fail to recall CSA experiences, and the correlates of such "forgetting," when it occurs.

In this paper I will review some of the recent research on adult recall of CSA and discuss some of the "gaps" that exist in this area as well as provide recommendations for future research. Recent studies that compared adolescent reports of sexual behavior with adult recall of adolescent behavior will also be briefly discussed. The question of whether adults can create "false" memories of CSA will not be addressed, nor will the issue of the reliability and credibility of children's reports of sexual abuse (for a recent review on this topic, see Bruck, Ceci, & Hembrooke, 1998).

Studies of Adult Recall of CSA

Studies of the prevalence of CSA based on adult recall vary widely (Goldman & Padayachi, 2000). Most researchers believe that prevalence rates reported based on adult retrospective reports are underestimates (Finkelhor, 1994; Williams, 1994), with failure to disclose related to the stigma and secrecy of CSA experiences. Although there is much disagreement about the rates of "false negatives" versus "false positives" in retrospective reports, few would disagree that there are significant problems with distortion and loss of information associated with retrospective recall (Widom & Morris, 1997).

There have now been a large number of studies which have asked the question, "How common is it for adults to fail to recall CSA?" Early studies primarily used clinical samples, mainly individuals in therapy, for self-reported CSA (e.g., Briere & Conte, 1993; Cameron, 1996; Herman & Schatzow, 1987), and in one study, women in outpatient treatment for substance abuse (Loftus, Polonsky, & Fullilove, 1994). More recent research has used nonclinical samples (Elliott, 1997; Epstein & Bottoms, 1998) and there have now also been a small number of prospective studies where individuals with previously documented histories of CSA have been followed up and interviewed about their recall of the abuse incident (Widom & Morris, 1997; Williams, 1994). Although the proportion of respondents who reported delayed recall varied widely across the above studies (range 19–59%, with higher percentages generally reported by clinical samples), all of these studies have found that a sizeable proportion of adults who recall CSA report prior periods during which they did not "remember" the abuse. The two prospective studies found substantial underreporting of sexual abuse among women: 38% in the Williams study and 32–60% (depending on the particular measure of sexual abuse) in the Widom and Morris sample. The findings from these studies have generated considerable controversy, mainly because of the issue of whether repression is the underlying mechanism for the delayed recall (Loftus et al., 1994). However, it is important to keep in mind that the phenomenon of delayed recall is not limited to CSA experiences. Elliott (1997) examined the issue of delayed recall of different types of traumatic events in a random sample of 724 adults and found that delayed recall occurred across a variety of traumas, although it was particularly high for traumatic events involving interpersonal victimization such as sexual abuse. Elliott also cited a large number of studies that documented partial or complete memory loss associated with trauma experiences. In another context, Widom and Morris discussed the fact that nonreporting by crime victims is well established and because of this researchers have conducted validity and reliability studies for victimization surveys for years. Given that survivors of CSA may be asked to recall events that occurred up to 30 years ago, these authors suggest that we should not be surprised if recall is often imperfect.

There has been some methodological criticism of the above studies (e.g., Pope & Hudson, 1995) and much discussion in the literature regarding the meaning of a failure to report CSA, particularly in relation to documented cases of abuse. Ornstein, Ceci, and Loftus (1998) argued that the lack of a report of a sexual abuse history may arise for any one of the following reasons: (a) there was no abuse to report; (b) abuse occurred but was not stored in memory; or (c) information about abuse was entered in memory, but it was forgotten over time. Another explanation for failure to report sexual abuse experiences has been that individuals may purposely prefer not to think about the events (rather than that the memories were unavailable) (Loftus, 1993).

Studies of the prevalence of delayed recall have also received criticism because of the wording of specific questions used to inquire about memory loss; as mentioned above, most of this debate has been about whether the prevalence of delayed recall can be taken as evidence for the prevalence of "repression" (Loftus et al., 1994). Typically, participants have been asked whether there was ever a time when they did not remember the abuse. Loftus and colleagues argued that questions such as these do not rule out the possibility that participants simply did not think about the abusive experience at some point during their lives. They gave the hypothetical example of a woman who thought, "I spent one nice summer in Europe where I didn't think about the abuse at all" (p. 81) and who might nonetheless be classified in the "forgot then regained memory category."

Factors That Affect Adults' Recall of CSA

A number of studies have explored factors that may play a role in adult recall of CSA. These include demographic characteristics such as race, gender, and age, and characteristics of the abuse (e.g., abuse severity, relationship to the perpetrator, threats or promises made by the perpetrator). Recall of abuse in childhood is also likely to be affected by current level of functioning, mood state, etc. (Cicchetti & Rizley, 1981), although there is little data available on this. Factors such as rehearsal (Harris & Liebert, 1991) and salience of the event (Brainerd & Ornstein, 1991) may also play a role, but these have not been systematically studied in relation to recall of CSA. Results on the relationship between abuse characteristics such as abuse severity and closeness to perpetrators have been inconsistent (Epstein & Bottoms, 1998). The two variables whose effects on rates of forgetting of CSA have received the most attention are gender and age of onset of abuse. A number of studies reported that younger age at the time of the abuse experience was associated with a greater likelihood of forgetting or delayed recall of the events (Briere & Conte, 1993; Cameron, 1996; Herman & Schatzow, 1987; Williams, 1994). Many different interpretations have been put forward for these findings, including cognitive developmental factors, infantile amnesia, etc. It is also worth noting that other studies have not found this association between age of onset of abuse and recall ability (Elliott & Briere, 1995; Melchert, 1996).

Of all the correlates of forgetting, the most consistent findings relate to the influence of gender on reporting of CSA. Women have been found to be more likely to temporarily "forget" their abusive experiences (Epstein & Bottoms, 1998). In one of the few studies that used a sample of adults who had documented histories of CSA, Widom and Morris (1997) reported a striking gender difference in the extent to which women and men recalled having experienced CSA (16% of men with documented histories of abuse reported their early experiences as "abuse" versus 64% of women). Widom and Morris speculated about possible explanations for these marked gender differences, for example, greater difficulty for men in disclosing abuse, differences in the meaning of these behaviors for men and women, etc.

Relationship between Aspects of Study Design and Recall of CSA

Despite recommendations that researchers explore the role of variables such as method of interview, different wording of abuse inquiry, and order of presentation of questions on the frequency and extent of reports of CSA (Briere, 1992; Widom & Morris, 1997), almost no research has been done in this area.

Question Wording and Number of Questions

Despite the concern about participants' correct interpretation of questions about delayed recall, discussed above (Loftus et al., 1994), very few researchers have systematically varied the questions used in studies or made any attempt to create less ambiguous questions. One exception to this was a recent study by Epstein and Bottoms (1998). To measure forgetting, participants were asked, "Was there ever a time when you could not remember this abuse experience?" but for a subsample, the question used differed slightly, ending with the additional " . . . *even if you tried to?*" Epstein and Bottoms found no differences between rates of forgetting in this subsample compared with the rest of their sample. In response to concerns about question ambiguity, one researcher reported the results of pretesting of the questions they used to assess delayed recall in their study (Elliott, 1997); 96% of the individuals apparently understood the questions to refer to a lack of access to memory (rather than normal forgetting or an active attempt to avoid the memory).

Although researchers have suggested that the number of questions asked of respondents in studies of CSA is likely to be of critical importance to prevalence rates (Briere, 1992; Goldman & Padayachi, 2000), systematic study of this possibility has been lacking. Goldman and Padayachi reviewed prevalence studies of CSA and found that studies using only one screening question reported fairly low rates in comparison with those that used more than one question. Studies that used behaviorally specific, detailed questions (termed "inverted funnel questions" by Wyatt & Peters, 1986) do report higher prevalence rates of CSA than those that used general screening questions. However, comparisons of information obtained using different types of questions in a single study of CSA have not been made (Martin, Anderson, Romans, Mullen, & O'Shea, 1993).

Mode of Data Collection

Goldman and Padayachi (2000) compared the prevalence rates of CSA for women across 17 studies that used three different modes of data collection: self-administered questionnaire (SAQ), face-to-face interview (FFI), and telephone interview. Not surprisingly, prevalence rates varied widely across studies (with a range of 7–62%); rates also varied within each category (e.g., rates of 8–34% for SAQs, and rates of 7–62% for FFI). The authors concluded, "there appears to be some relationship between the mode of data collection and the prevalence of child sexual abuse" (p. 312). However, given the wide variations in definitions of CSA used by researchers (Roosa, Reyes, Reinholtz, & Angelini, 1998), one might question whether comparisons of different data collection techniques across studies are meaningful. Goldman and Padayachi also suggested that of the three modes of data collection they surveyed, FFI appeared the most likely method to reduce the problems associated with retrospective recall and for this reason such interviews appear to have an advantage over SAQs or telephone interviews. In support of this, they argued that interviewers are able to establish rapport, convey a nonjudgmental approach, and generally encourage respondents to disclose their sexual abuse. While I agree with the authors that different modes of data collection may have considerable effects on the prevalence rates, the fact is that there is little or no research addressing the issue of which mode of data collection is most likely to produce more "accurate" reports of CSA. One of the few studies that provided a direct comparison between two methods of data collection (postal SAQ and FFI) suggested that interviews had no clear advantages over SAQs (Martin et al., 1993). In this two-stage retrospective survey, a postal questionnaire that included measures of general and mental health as well as questions on CSA was sent to a random sample of women; within one month, 492 women who completed the SAQ were interviewed. Although the results indicated some discrepancy between rates of CSA obtained from the SAQ and from the interview, a limitation of this study was that the SAQ questions were less precisely worded than the interview questions. However, this study did report one potentially very important difference between the two methods: A significant number of women (comprising 15% of those who reported CSA that involved a relative) reported CSA by a close family member in the postal questionnaire but not during the FFI; in comparison, incidents mentioned at the interview were more likely to involve a stranger.

Recent developments of computerized technologies have suggested that these new methods of data collection may lead to increased reporting of sensitive sexual behaviors, in comparison with interviewer-administered methods (Gribble, Miller, Rogers, & Turner, 1999). Increased reporting of behaviors with a particular mode of data collection is assumed to indicate more accurate responses (Minnis & Padian, 2001). Different modes of data collection have also been found to affect the likelihood of reporting sexual behaviors, even when no interviewer is involved. For example, in one study adolescent males reported significantly higher levels of a number of "stigmatized" sexual behaviors (including masturbation) in an audio computer-assisted self-interview (A-CASI) than on a paper-and-pencil SAQ (Turner et al., 1998). In a study of female adolescents, an automated telephone diary elicited increased reporting of risky sexual behaviors compared with a written calendar diary (Minnis & Padian, 2001). In a recent study of the prevalence of CSA among men who have sex with men, a computer-assisted telephone interviewing (CATI) procedure was compared with a telephone-automated computer-assisted self interview (T-CASI), which eliminates the need for a live interviewer (Paul, Catania, Pollack, & Stall, 2001). No differences by mode of interview were found for any self-reports of sexual abuse, suggesting that reports of the prevalence of CSA were unaffected by the presence of a live telephone interviewer.

Reliability of Abuse Reports

In part because there have been so few longitudinal studies that have followed into adolescence or adulthood children who were sexually abused (Widom & Morris, 1997), test-retest reliability data on CSA reports are almost nonexistent. One study examined the consistency of abuse reports (sexual, physical, and psychological abuse) in a sample of adults enrolled in a community-based, prospective cohort study (Friedrich, Talley, Panser, Fett, & Zinmeister, 1997). Participants completed questionnaires about their abuse experiences on two separate occasions, separated by an average of 20 months; 85.6% provided consistent reports of sexual abuse (kappa coefficient = .64, reflecting "good" agreement). Noncontact sexual abuse appeared to be less consistently reported, and overall women provided more consistent reports of sexual abuse than men. The authors concluded that adults' reports of sexual and physical abuse were relatively consistent, whereas reports of psychological abuse were less consistent across time. A limitation of this study was that the follow-up questionnaires differed from the initial questionnaire, both in the amount of detail requested about abuse experiences and, more importantly, in the wording of the screening questions; the initial questionnaire asked whether sexual acts had occurred "against your will," and the follow-up questionnaire asked about "important, unwanted" experiences.

In a study of a new interview measure of life events and post-traumatic stress for children and adolescents (aged 8–17), Costello, Angold, March, and Fairbank (1998) assessed the test-retest reliability of events reported on two occasions. At the first interview, ten of the children reported a history of sexual abuse; two weeks later, nine participants reported such a history (kappa coefficient = .81). The authors concluded, "it is particularly significant for research on sexual abuse that these children's retest reliability for sexual abuse was . . . excellent" (p. 1283); however, given the small sample and the very short recall period, these conclusions appear premature. A more recent study that assessed self-report consistency at different time points in adolescents found inconsistent rates of CSA over a seven-month time period (Fortenberry & Aalsma, 2003). Overall, 23% of their participants were "inconsistent reporters" of CSA (in that they either endorsed items of CSA at baseline but not at seven months, or did not endorse an item at baseline but did at seven months). Interestingly, there was an overall *decrease* in reporting of CSA from baseline to seven months. The authors suggested that this might have been due to the participants' being less willing to report CSA as having occurred as they become more comfortable with the research assistant (although it seems equally likely that this situation might have produced the opposite effect).

Adolescent versus Adult Recall of Sexual Experiences

There have been a small number of longitudinal studies that have compared adolescent reports of a variety of experiences (including, but not limited to, sexual experiences) and later adult recall of their adolescent experiences. Although not all of these included reports of CSA, the findings are interesting and relevant to the topic of this paper. In a study by Femina, Yeager, and Lewis (1990), 69 individuals interviewed during adolescence (mean age 15 years) were followed up and reinterviewed nine years later about negative childhood experiences (including sexual abuse). All of the adolescents had been incarcerated as adolescents and, as a result, had undergone extensive neuropsychiatric evaluation at the time of the first interview. Of the 69 respondents, 26 gave responses concerning CSA that were discrepant with information obtained when they were adolescents. Eighteen individuals failed to report physical and/or sexual abuse that was documented during the first interview, and eight participants reported abuse at the second interview that they had denied during the first interview. One interesting aspect of this study was that when the researchers confronted the participants with their discrepant reports, a variety of reasons for failing to report abusive experiences were provided, such as embarrassment, desire to forget the experience or to protect the perpetrator, etc.

A more recent study by Halpern, Udry, Suchindran, and Campbell (2000) compared self-report data on adolescent sexual experience collected from 59 males (mean age 13.2 years) with retrospective reports from these same individuals as young adults (mean age 21.5 years). Comparison of adolescent and adult reports showed that masturbation during adolescence (but not coitus and wet dreams) was more likely to be reported in young adulthood than during adolescence. In contrast, nonsexual "problem" behavior (e.g., vandalizing property, alcohol use) occurring during adolescence was more likely to be reported in adolescence than in early adulthood. The authors interpreted these findings as indicating that "adulthood is a condition that would reduce the reporting bias in sensitive behavior, and that higher rates of reporting may . . . therefore be interpreted as more accurate" (p. 330).

In another recent study, differences between adult memories of adolescence and what was actually reported during adolescence were examined;

73 14-year-old males were interviewed in 1962, and 67 of these individuals were reinterviewed at age 48 (Offer, Kaiz, Howard, & Bennett, 2000). The interviews covered a wide range of topics, including sexuality, dating, family relationships, and parental discipline; most of the responses were simple yes/no endorsements of statements made by the interviewer. Results indicated that accurate memory was generally no better than expected by chance. The authors' interpretation of these findings is interesting in that, unlike Halpern and colleagues, they clearly assume that the adolescent report was the more accurate one.

Recommendations for Future Research

Almost ten years ago, Briere (1992) suggested a number of ways in which retrospective research in the area of CSA might be improved. Unfortunately, although concern about the issue of accuracy of adult recollections of CSA has not lessened, there have been almost no studies conducted on the test-retest reliability of CSA reports, little systematic investigation of the effects of variables such as question wording, order of presentation of questions, and mode of data collection on recall, and almost no attempt to assess construct or discriminant validity of self-report measures. One good example of the latter type of study was done by Widom and Morris (1997), who examined the way four different self-report measures were related to other variables (such as diagnoses of alcohol use, depression, etc.) in a sample of individuals who had court-substantiated histories of CSA. This study also assessed the ability of retrospective self-report measures to predict individuals with documented CSA histories by calculating a "relative improvement over chance" index. On the basis of their findings, Widom and Morris questioned whether a single question would produce the same degree of accuracy as a series of questions and concluded, "we believe the focus of future research should not be on whether reports of childhood sexual abuse are valid or not but on the best way to ask questions to make answers more valid" (p. 44).

One other area in which there appear to be significant gaps in our understanding of memory relates to the question of how traumatic memories are different from "ordinary" memories. Although memory researchers have argued that memories for events that are traumatic may be harder to alter than neutral ones, reports of memory loss or partial forgetting are also well documented in the trauma literature (Ornstein, Ceci, & Loftus, 1998). Future research might investigate differences in adult recall of traumatic versus neutral memories (Elliott, 1997).

Finally, as this paper reflects, almost all of the data we have concerning the validity and reliability of retrospective recall of childhood sexual experiences relates to recall of CSA experiences. Future studies involving adult recall of normative childhood sexual behavior should aim to assess the validity and reliability of self-report measures.

References

Brainerd, C., & Ornstein, P. A. (1991). Children's memory for witnessed events: The developmental backdrop. In J. Doris (Ed.), *The suggestibility of children's recollections: Implications for eyewitness testimony* (pp. 10–20). Washington, DC: American Psychological Association.

Briere, J. (1990). Accuracy of adults' reports of abuse in childhood: Dr. Briere replies. [Invited letter]. *American Journal of Psychiatry, 147*(10), 1389–1390.

Briere, J. (1992). Methodological issues in the study of sexual abuse effects. *Journal of Consulting and Clinical Psychology, 60,* 196–203.

Briere, J., & Conte, J. (1993). Self-reported amnesia for abuse in adults molested as children. *Journal of Traumatic Stress, 6,* 21–31.

Bruck, M., Ceci, S., & Hembrooke, H. (1998). Reliability and credibility of young children's reports. From research to policy and practice. *American Psychologist, 53*(2), 136–151.

Cameron, C. (1996). Comparing amnesic and nonamnesic survivors of childhood sexual abuse: A longitudinal study. In K. Pezdek & W. P. Banks (Eds.), *The recovered memory/false memory debate* (pp. 41–68). San Diego: Academic.

Cicchetti, D., & Rizley, R. (1981). Developmental perspectives on the etiology, intergenerational transmission, and sequelae of child maltreatment. *Directions for Child Development, 11,* 31–55.

Costello, E. J., Angold, A., March, J., & Fairbank, J. (1998). Life events and posttraumatic stress: The development of a new measure for children and adolescents. *Psychological Medicine, 28,* 1275–1288.

Elliott, D. M. (1997). Traumatic events: Prevalence and delayed recall in the general population. *Journal of Consulting and Clinical Psychology, 65*(5), 811–820.

Elliott, D. M., & Briere, J. (1995). Posttraumatic stress associated with delayed recall of sexual abuse: A general population study. *Journal of Traumatic Stress, 8,* 629–639.

Epstein, M. A., & Bottoms, B. L. (1998). Memories of childhood sexual abuse: A survey of young adults. *Child Abuse & Neglect, 22,* 1217–1238.

Femina, D. D., Yeager, C. A., & Lewis, D. O. (1990). Child abuse: Adolescent records vs. adult recall. *Child Abuse & Neglect, 14,* 227–231.

Finkelhor, D. (1994). Current information on the scope and nature of child sexual abuse. *Future of children: Sexual abuse of children, 4*(2), 31–53.

Fortenberry, J. D., & Aalsma, M. C. (2003) *Abusive sexual experiences before age 12 and adolescent sexual behaviors.* In J. Bancroft (Ed.). *Sexual Development in Childhood* (pp. 359–369). Bloomington: Indiana University Press.

Friedrich, W. N., Talley, N.J., Panser, L., Fett, S., & Zinsmeister, A. R. (1997). Concordance of reports of childhood abuse by adults. *Child Maltreatment, 2,* 163–171.

Goldman, J. D. G., & Padayachi, U. K. (2000). Some methodological problems in estimating incidence and prevalence in child sexual abuse research. *Journal of Sex Research, 37,* 305–314.

Gribble, J. N., Miller, H. G., Rogers, S. M., & Turner, C. F. (1999). Interview mode and measurement of sexual behaviors: Methodological issues. *Journal of Sex Research, 36*, 16–24.

Halpern, C. J. T., Udry, J. R., Suchindran, C., & Campbell, B. (2000). Adolescent males' willingness to report masturbation. *Journal of Sex Research, 37*, 327–332.

Harris, J., & Liebert, R. (1991). *The child*. Englewood Cliffs, NJ: Prentice Hall.

Herman, J. L., & Schatzow, E. (1987). Recovery and verification of memories of childhood sexual trauma. *Psychoanalytic Psychology, 4*, 1–14.

Loftus, E. F. (1993). The reality of repressed memories. *American Psychologist, 48*, 518–537.

Loftus, E. F., Polonsky, S., & Fullilove, M. T. (1994). Memories of childhood sexual abuse: Remembering and repressing. *Psychology of Women Quarterly, 18*, 67–84.

Martin, J., Anderson, J., Romans, S., Mullen, P., & O'Shea, M. (1993). Asking about child sexual abuse: Methodological implications of a two-stage survey. *Child Abuse & Neglect, 17*, 383–392.

Melchert, T. P. (1996). Childhood memory and a history of different forms of abuse. *Professional Psychology: Research and Practice, 27*, 438–446.

Minnis, A. M., & Padian, N. S. (2001). Reliability of adolescents' self-reported sexual behavior: A comparison of two diary methodologies. *Journal of Adolescent Health, 28*, 394–403.

Offer, D., Kaiz, M., Howard, K. I., & Bennett, E. S. (2000). The altering of reported experiences. *Journal of the American Academy of Child and Adolescent Psychiatry, 39*, 735–742.

Ornstein, P. A., Ceci, S. J., & Loftus, E. F. (1998). Adult recollections of childhood abuse: Cognitive and developmental perspectives. *Psychology, Public Policy, and Law, 4*(4), 1025–1051.

Paul, J. P., Catania, J., Pollack, L., & Stall, R. (2001). Understanding childhood sexual abuse as a predictor of sexual risk-taking among men who have sex with men: The Urban Men's Health Study. *Child Abuse & Neglect, 25*, 557–584.

Pope, H. G., & Hudson, J. I. (1995). Can memories of childhood sexual abuse be repressed? *Psychological Medicine, 25*, 121–126.

Rich, C. L. (1990). Accuracy of adults' reports of abuse in childhood. [Letter]. *American Journal of Psychiatry, 147*(10), 1389.

Roosa, M. W., Reyes, L., Reinholtz, C., & Angelini, P. J. (1998). Measurement of women's child sexual abuse experiences: An empirical demonstration of the impact of choice of measure on estimates of incidence rates and of relationships with pathology. *Journal of Sex Research, 35*, 225–233.

Turner, C. F., Ku, L., Rogers, S. M., Lindberg, L. D., Pleck, J., & Sonenstein, F. L. (1998). Adolescent sexual behavior, drug use, and violence: Increased reporting with computer survey technology. *Science, 280*, 867–873.

Widom, C. S., & Morris, S. (1997). Accuracy of adult recollections of childhood victimization: Part 2. Childhood sexual abuse. *Psychological Assessment, 9*, 34–46.

Williams, L. M. (1994). Recall of childhood trauma: A prospective study of women's memories of child sexual abuse. *Journal of Consulting and Clinical Psychology, 62*, 1167–1176.

Wyatt, G. E., & Peters, S. D. (1986). Methodological considerations in research on the prevalence of child sexual abuse. *Child Abuse & Neglect, 10*, 241–251.

Using Computer-Assisted Self-Interview (CASI) for Recall of Childhood Sexual Experiences

MEREDITH A. REYNOLDS AND
DEBRA L. HERBENICK

A computer-assisted self-interview (CASI) was used as part of a 1998–99 study carried out at The Kinsey Institute that examined childhood sexual experiences and sexual development in adolescence and young adulthood through adult retrospective recall. Three hundred and three college students (154 women, 149 men) participated in the study as paid research subjects. The mean age of the men was 20.3 and the mean age of the women was 20.1. (For details of the results related to childhood sexual experiences with peers and later sexual development, see Reynolds, Herbenick, & Bancroft, 2003; for the results of masturbation experiences and sexual development, see Bancroft, Herbenick, & Reynolds, 2003.)

The use of CASI is an innovative alternative to in-person interviews and paper-based surveys. Subjects can be asked survey questions that are tailored to their experiences (CASI questions are responsive to subjects' answers), as would occur in an in-person interview, and yet anonymity can be preserved in data collection.

Subjects were required to come to The Kinsey Institute twice to complete the CASI sexuality survey. Subjects completed the survey individually at private computer stations where neither they nor their computers could be seen. An experimenter was available at all times to answer questions. The CASI survey was divided into four sections encompassing (a) childhood experiences, (b) high school experiences, (c) college experiences, and (d) current attitudes and beliefs. These sections were administered in two sittings, each lasting between one and one-and-a-half hours, that took place approximately four days apart. The childhood and high school sections were always completed together, as were the college and attitudes/beliefs sections. The order of completing these two pairs was randomly determined by code number.

Prior to beginning the CASI survey, each subject completed a series of practice screens with the experimenter in order to ensure that the subject understood how the CASI program worked (e.g., how to indicate numerical responses, how to indicate a response on a Likert scale, how to enter narrative data, etc.). The program was responsive to subjects' answers such that subjects received appropriate questions regarding their own experiences. For example, subjects who indicated that they had not masturbated in the previous 12 months were asked about the most important factors underlying their decision to abstain from this sexual activity during this time period. Subjects who had masturbated were asked about their frequency of masturbation, degree of sexual gratification via masturbation, and experience of guilt associated with their masturbation.

The content and sequence of each of the four sections is outlined below. The childhood, high school, and college sections were designed to together cover the subjects' entire lives. Childhood encompassed the subjects' lives from as far back as they could remember to the first day of high school. The high school section covered the subjects' lives from the first day of high school until the end of the summer following high school graduation, while the college section covered the subjects' lives from the September following high school graduation (regardless of whether they had started college at that time or had taken time off) to the day the subject completed the survey. Each section began with warm-up questions and items designed to trigger the recall of events during that period of time, prior to presenting items dealing specifically with sexual experiences. Subjects were also given paper and pencils and urged to begin by writing down what grades each of the time periods consisted of for them and the ages that they were in these grades. While most of the items of the CASI survey were written by the authors for this study, some preexisting questionnaires were converted into computer format and utilized as noted below.

Childhood

The childhood section began with questions regarding location of upbringing, school characteristics, significant life events (e.g., parental divorce/remarriage/death, moving, hospitalization, birth of siblings), involvement in organized children's groups/activities, family structure during elementary and middle school, enjoyment ratings of nonsexual play activities/games, and friendship and play patterns. Subjects also rated their parents separately on several items pertaining to parental affection/support, health, and discipline. Following these questions, the survey moved into the realm of sexuality, beginning with the "sexual environment" of the family, followed by autoerotic behaviors of the subject, sexual experiences with peers, and unwanted sexual experiences with adults, and ending with an assessment of sex role behaviors.

Childhood family sexual environment was assessed along multiple dimensions, including (a) parental nudity in the home, (b) shared bathing and sleeping arrangements, (c) presence of and access to pornographic materials, (d) the open display of physical affection and sexual behaviors between parents, and (e) parents' likely reaction to sexual behaviors and questions on the part of the subject as a child (regardless of whether these events actually occurred). Sexual curiosity and attraction were then assessed, as well as autoerotic/self-stimulation activities, childhood orgasm, and sexual fantasy.

Sexual play behavior with peers was assessed separately for three different periods of childhood demarcated by school transitions—pre-elementary, elementary, and middle school/junior high school. For each period subjects reported on all of the different kinds of sexual play behaviors they engaged in and provided specific details regarding the sexual experience they remembered best. These details included the sexual behaviors that occurred, the subject's level of participation, the number, gender, and relationship of the peer(s) involved, reasons for engaging in the experience, and whether or not an adult had found out. Subjects also indicated how typical this experience was in comparison to other experiences they had during the time period and provided an estimate of how many experiences they had overall. After completing each of the three sections on experiences during pre-elementary, elementary, and middle school/junior high, subjects were asked to evaluate their entire childhood sexual history as a whole.

In addition, subjects completed a brief series of questions regarding sexual experiences with an adult or child who was more than five years older than them, and that occurred prior to the subject age of 16. Experiences with and without actual touching were asked about separately. And, so as not to end this portion of the survey with potentially unwanted sexual experiences, subjects completed Mitchell and Zucker's (1991) Gender Identity Scale, a 24-item scale designed to assess sex role behavior and identification during childhood.

High School

Warm-up questions for this section included subjects' participation in high school organizations (e.g., sports teams, academic clubs), free-time activities, friendship patterns, perceptions of popularity among and similarity to their same- and opposite-sex peers, and parental affection/support, health, and discipline. The transition to sexuality questions began with sources of learning about sexual matters, sexual knowledge, formal sex education, use of sexually explicit materials, and autoerotic behaviors of the subject. Interpersonal sexual experiences were introduced by questions regarding parent-imposed dating rules, subjects' dating experiences, and subjects' interpersonal sexual behaviors (e.g., frequency, number of partners, enjoyment). Subjects were then asked a series of questions about a variety of sexual behaviors (kissing, light fondling, heavy fondling, oral sex, anal sex), about their first sexual intercourse experience after starting high school ("post-childhood"), and about their first post-childhood same-sex sexual experience involving genital contact.

College

Like the high school section, the college section began with questions regarding the subjects' schooling that were followed by the subjects' current relationship status, relationship history in the previous 12 months, sexual fantasy experience, masturbation experience in the previous 12 months, and use of sexual materials (pornography, sex toys, etc.) in the previous 12 months. An intensive history of college dating and sexual experiences (beginning the September following high school graduation) was obtained. A section was devoted to the subjects' experiences and relationship with their most important sexual partner or, if they had only had a one-night stand, the details of this experience. Subjects were also asked whether they had experienced a variety of sexual problems in the previous 12 months (pain during penile-vaginal intercourse, experiencing orgasm too soon, lack of pleasure in sexual activity, inability to orgasm, lack of interest, difficulty with vaginal lubrication, difficulty with erection) and whether they had been diagnosed with any sexually transmitted infections.

Attitudes/Beliefs

The attitudes/beliefs section consisted of the following surveys: (a) the Sociosexual Orientation Inventory (Simpson & Gangestad, 1991)—a 7-item survey assessing subjects' orientation (restricted/unrestricted) toward engaging in uncommitted sexual encounters; (b) the Sexual Self-Concept Inventory (Reynolds, 1997)—a 45-item measure with six subscales used to assess subjects' experience of themselves as sexual beings; (c) the Sexual Opinion Survey (Fisher, White, Byrne, & Kelley, 1988)—a 21-item measure assessing erotophobia/erotophilia; (d) the sexual morality and sexual motivation subscales of the Sexual Experiences Survey (Frenken & Vennix, 1981), assessing attitudes, norms, and values regarding premarital sex and the sexual socialization of children and sexual interactions with partners, respectively; and (e) the Kinsey Institute Sexual Inhibition/Sexual Excitation Scales (SIS/SES) (Janssen, Vorst, Finn, & Bancroft, 2002).

A version of the CASI program was available at the workshop at which this paper was delivered, for participants to explore.

References

Bancroft, J., Herbenick, D. L., & Reynolds, M. A. (2003). Masturbation as a marker of sexual development: Two studies 50 years apart. In J. Bancroft (Ed.), *Sexual development in childhood* (pp. 156–185). Bloomington: Indiana University Press.

Fisher, W. A., White, L. A., Byrne, D., & Kelley, K. (1988). Erotophobia-erotophilia as a dimension of personality. *Journal of Sex Research, 25,* 123–151.

Frenken, J., & Vennix, P. (1981). *Sexuality Experience Scales manual.* Lisse, the Netherlands: Swets and Zietlinger.

Janssen, E., Vorst, H., Finn, P., & Bancroft, J. (2002). The Sexual Inhibition (SIS) and Sexual Excitation (SES) Scales: I. Measuring sexual inhibition and excitation proneness in men. *Journal of Sex Research, 39,* 114–126.

Mitchell, J. N., & Zucker, K. J. (1991, August). *The Recalled Childhood Gender Identity Scale: Psychometric properties.* Poster session presented at the meeting of the International Academy of Sex Research, Barrie, Ontario.

Reynolds, M. A. (1997). *The development of sexuality: The impact of childhood sexual play on adult sexuality.* Unpublished doctoral dissertation, University of Michigan.

Reynolds, M. A., Herbenick, D. L., & Bancroft, J. (2003). The nature of childhood sexual experiences: Two studies 50 years apart. In J. Bancroft (Ed.), *Sexual development in childhood* (pp. 134–155). Bloomington: Indiana University Press.

Simpson, J. A., & Gangestad, S. W. (1991). Individual differences in sociosexuality: Evidence for convergent and discriminant validity. *Journal of Personality and Social Psychology, 60,* 870–873.

The Use of Meta-analysis in Understanding the Effects of Child Sexual Abuse

JANET SHIBLEY HYDE

The publication of Rind, Tromovitch, and Bauserman's 1998 meta-analysis of studies of the sequelae of child sexual abuse touched off a firestorm, raging from psychologists to members of Congress (Dodgen, 2000; Haugaard, 2000; Rind, Bauserman, & Tromovitch, 2000). In this article I will provide a brief overview of the technique of meta-analysis and methodological issues associated with it. Then I will evaluate the meta-analytic methods used in Rind and colleagues' 1998 meta-analysis.

Meta-analysis: An Overview

Meta-analysis is a statistical technique for synthesizing the results of numerous studies on a given scientific question. It is generally considered to be superior to traditional narrative (or qualitative) reviews, which often rely on the subjectivity of the reviewer and, even with an unbiased reviewer, can lead to false conclusions (Glass, McGaw, & Smith, 1981). Moreover, meta-analysis, more than traditional reviews, permits one to reach conclusions not only about whether effects exist, but also about how large they are.

A meta-analysis generally proceeds in four steps (for a very readable explication, see Hedges & Becker, 1986; for an advanced textbook, see Hedges & Olkin, 1985). In the first, the researcher locates all available studies on the question of interest. Essentially the researcher is sampling from a population of studies and ideally the researcher would like to locate every study in the population. Computerized databases such as PsycINFO are extremely helpful in this regard, although care must be taken in the choice of keywords.

In the second step, the researcher extracts statistical information from each study and, for each study, computes an effect size. Two different designs are possible, with corresponding statistics for effect size. One possible design is the two-group experiment or quasi-experiment. Examples would be whether psychotherapy is effective (therapy group versus waitlist control) or whether there are gender differences in mathematics performance. In such cases one computes the effect size d using the following formula:

$$d = \frac{M_E - M_C}{sd_w}$$

where M_E is the mean for the experimental group and M_C is the mean for the control group; sd_w is the pooled within-group standard deviation. In these two-group designs, d can also be computed from a t or F statistic. Notice that d can take on positive or negative values, depending on which group scores higher. d behaves much like z scores—that is, the distribution is centered on 0, and scores very far from 0 are unlikely. One of the virtues of d is that, unlike significance tests, it is unrelated to sample size.

The other possible design is a correlational study in which the outcome is a Pearson correlation, r, which itself can be used as an effect size in a meta-analysis. d and r are related according to the following formula:

$$d = 2r \: / \: (\text{sqrt } (1 - r^2)$$

An approximation is $d = 2r$.

In the third step, the meta-analyst uses statistical methods (e.g., Hedges & Olkin, 1985) to compute a weighted average effect size—whether d or r—over all studies. This overall effect size conveys whether there is an effect by whether the effect size is significant. It also conveys the magnitude of the effect. Cohen (1988) has suggested the following guidelines for interpreting the magnitude of effects: $d = .20$ is a small effect, .50 is a moderate effect, and .80 is a large effect.

In the fourth step, the meta-analyst tests whether the effect sizes collected across all studies are homogeneous, that is, close enough to each other so that one can assume that they were drawn from a single population. Invariably the effect sizes are not homogeneous. The researcher can then proceed to group studies into subcategories, identified a priori to test questions of interest in that research area. These analyses are called homogeneity analyses or moderator analyses. If the question is gender differences in mathematics performance, age might be important. Are gender differences small or nonexistent in elementary school and then large in adolescence? One can compute the average effect size for studies of elementary-aged children and for studies of adolescents and test whether the two effect sizes differ significantly.

Methodological Issues in Meta-analysis

Perhaps the most critical methodological issue in meta-analysis is described by the old dictum "Garbage in, garbage out." That is, if the studies reviewed in the meta-analysis are themselves of poor quality, riddled with methodological flaws, then the results of the meta-analysis will contain those same flaws. The problem, in such cases, is not with meta-analysis, but rather with the area of research being reviewed. Meta-analysis cannot make silk purses out of sows' ears. It is worth noting that this garbage-in, garbage-out problem is not unique to meta-analysis, but rather is common to many other statistical techniques, including factor analysis and structural equation modeling.

Meta-analysts do not need to passively accept garbage. When the topic being reviewed has been investigated in studies of varying quality, the meta-analyst may set a quality criterion and exclude studies that do not meet it. For example, if one were reviewing studies of the efficacy of a particular drug, one might accept only studies that used random assignment and double-blind methods. Alternatively, the meta-analyst can accept all studies or most studies, rate or categorize each on its methodological rigor, and then analyze effects separately for the best studies and for all studies. An example is my own work on gender and mathematics performance, in which sampling is a key issue. In that meta-analysis, we included samples of any sort, but then coded them as nationally representative, moderately selective (e.g., college samples), and highly selective (e.g., graduate students, Harvard students) (Hyde, Fennema, & Lamon, 1990). As it turned out, the magnitude of the gender difference varied considerably depending on the selectivity of the sampling.

A second methodological issue in meta-analysis is sampling of studies. Just as in primary research one samples participants from some population, in meta-analysis one samples research studies from some population of studies. The ideal is to identify all relevant studies. Care should be taken to locate unpublished studies that remained unpublished simply because they did not find significant effects. The meta-analyst must think carefully about defining the population of studies. In the study of gender differences in mathematics performance, for example, should studies of children with learning disabilities be excluded or included?

A third methodological issue concerns what to do with the vexing problem of studies that report only "significant, $p < .05$," and do not report the means and standard deviations or correlations that one needs to compute effect sizes. The first line of attack here should be to write to authors and request the exact numbers. I do this routinely and have experienced moderate success, with response rates around 20 to 25%. Nonetheless, there remain numerous studies for which an accurate effect size cannot be computed. What should the meta-analyst do? One solution would be to exclude those studies. The problem with that strategy is that it may systematically exclude more studies with nonsignificant effects and therefore small effect sizes, because it is precisely in those cases that authors are very likely to report nonsignificance only and provide no other statistics. An alternative strategy is to estimate effect sizes using the following rubric. Nonsignificant effects are converted to an effect size of 0. If significance is at the .05 level, one converts to the t or r that would yield that significance level and uses it to compute effect size. If significance is at the .01 level, corresponding *t* or *r* values are obtained, and so on. Clearly these estimates of effect size systematically underestimate the true effect size, but they are thought to be better than nothing. In my view, the ideal is to report all analyses twice, once using all effect sizes (exactly computed and estimated) and then using only exactly computed effect sizes.

A fourth methodological issue arises from conceptual confusion in the research area under study. For example, in research on self-esteem, some experts make a distinction between self-esteem (global self-worth) and self-concept (domain-specific self-worth, e.g., math self-concept), whereas other experts use the two terms interchangeably. If the question is whether there are gender differences in self-esteem defined as global self-worth, the meta-analyst will have to contend with the unwanted intrusion of studies of domain-specific self-concept that were labeled "self-esteem," and at the same time risk missing appropriate studies of self-esteem that were labeled "self-concept" (Kling, Hyde, Showers, & Buswell, 1999). In the case of child sexual abuse (CSA), imagine a case of an 8-year-old girl who engages in genital fondling with her 11-year-old brother. Is that child sexual abuse? If numerous studies include such incidents as CSA, should they be included in or excluded from the meta-analysis? Child sexual abuse is a research area that is plagued with such definitional problems and they will necessarily have an impact on any meta-analysis.

A fifth methodological issue is that meta-analysis cannot yield causal inferences if the studies contributing to the meta-analysis were not experimental.

A sixth issue concerns interpretation of the magnitude of the effect. As noted earlier, Cohen (1988) has offered guidelines that $d = .20$ is a small effect, .50 is moderate, and .80 is large. When r is the metric, he suggested that $r = .10$ is a small effect, .30 is moderate, and .50 is large (although an r of .50 is mathematically equivalent to a d of 1.15, i.e., a much larger effect). Rind and colleagues used r as their measure of effect size and the Cohen guidelines for interpreting r.

Analysis of the Rind, Tromovitch, and Bauserman (1998) Meta-analysis

Rind and colleagues located 59 studies, all based on college samples, that examined the association between child sexual abuse and psychological adjustment. The first thing to note is that one might investigate a variety of outcomes in adulthood, such as functioning in relationships, sexuality, or academic performance; this particular meta-analysis focused on only one outcome, adjustment.

The next point to note is that the review was limited to studies using college samples. This methodological feature has some advantages and disadvantages compared with other alternatives. It is a clear advance over reviews that focus on clinical or legal populations, which are biased toward those with more pathological outcomes. It also permits the assessment of a well-defined and comparable control group. The disadvantage is that these studies may miss precisely those who have experienced the most severe effects of child sexual abuse and who are so impaired that they are not capable of attending college. Other reviews that focus on clinical samples probably overestimate the negative impact of child sexual abuse. The Rind, Tromovitch, and Bauserman review probably underestimates the impact to some extent.

The question of the appropriate samples to include in the meta-analysis in turn relates to the question being addressed. If the question is, "In the population of persons with a history of CSA, does this experience cause intense psychological harm on a widespread basis for both genders?" (Rind et al., 1998, p. 22), then college samples may be appropriate because the question was stated in extreme form, and if any reasonable samples can be shown not to manifest severe harm, then the hypothesis is falsified. Alternatively, the question might have been stated more neutrally, for example, "Does CSA have negative psychological effects and, if so, how widespread and how large are they?" This question would demand that sampling include college samples, clinical samples, and samples of the general population.

Other criteria for inclusion in the meta-analysis were that the study had to include a control group that contained no students with CSA experiences, and that the CSA group had to be specific and not include other kinds of abuse.

A key issue is how the construct "child sexual abuse" was defined and what was included. Rind and colleagues defined it as "sexual interaction involving either physical contact or no contact (e.g., exhibitionism) between either a child or adolescent and someone significantly older, or between two peers who are children or adolescents when coercion is used" (1998, p. 23). The definition therefore excludes consensual contact between two adolescents, a decision that most researchers would probably agree with. At the same time, it includes a wide range of activities, from very mild (e.g., one incident of exposure from an exhibitionist) to severe (incest that is repeated over many years). If the preponderance of activities that occur and are reported in college samples are on the mild end of the continuum, the result may be small consequences for adjustment, thereby masking large effects on adjustment that result from severe cases. (See their Table 6, which addresses this issue to some extent.)

Rind and colleagues chose to examine one possible category of outcomes, adjustment. They might have chosen to focus on other outcomes, such as school performance or success in forming relationships (Davis & Petretic-Jackson, 2000).

Rind and colleagues located 59 relevant studies. That is an acceptable sample size for meta-analysis. Occasionally one sees attempts at meta-analysis with 10 or fewer studies, a practice that is simply unacceptable. The core idea in meta-analysis is to synthesize results over numerous studies. Furthermore, in meta-analysis one typically separates studies into subcategories and estimates effect sizes for different categories. It is preferable to have at least 10 studies per category, and five studies per category would be an absolute minimum. For the most part, Rind and colleagues maintained this minimum standard. A notable exception is their Table 6 (p. 35), in which the number of studies in a category is often two or three. The findings in that table are, in my judgment, worthless. One cannot estimate a population effect size based on two or three samples.

Rind and colleagues handled the problem of missing effect sizes by estimating them using the methods I outlined previously, and, for the most part, they reported double summary statistics, one with the estimated effect sizes included and one with only the accurately computed effect sizes.

Rind and his colleagues used r as the measure of effect size rather than d. On the one hand, this choice puzzles me because all studies involved a two-group design: CSA compared with no CSA. One might therefore have expected d to be reported. On the other hand, the use of r reminds the reader that the studies are correlational or quasi-experimental. Participants were scarcely randomly assigned to CSA and no CSA groups, and causal inferences simply are not warranted.

The crux of Rind and colleagues' results are found in Table 3 (p. 32) and the text associated with it (pp. 31 ff.). Overall, the relationship between CSA and psychological adjustment was $r = .09$, a small effect but nonetheless a significant one. They eliminated outlier effect sizes (a practice of some meta-analysts). One was an r of .36 in a study of incest cases and another was an r of .40 from a study with a large number of incest cases. The removal of outliers is debatable. In this meta-analysis, two studies of probably the most severely affected populations were removed, although, interestingly, the average r was still .09 even after removal of the outliers. The overall picture in Table 3 is that most of the psychological indicators were significantly associated with CSA, but the effects are all small, generally running around $r = .10$. When all studies are aggregated, then, the effects are small, although we should remember that the use of college students probably underestimates the magnitude of the effects in the general population.

Rind and colleagues then conducted a number of moderator analyses. I won't dwell on them, but rather will focus on their analyses concerning family environment. Their argument is that CSA is not the cause of adjustment problems, but rather that CSA is associated with a disturbed family environment and that the family environment, not CSA, is the source of the adjustment problems (Figure 1, top portion). CSA and family environ-

Rind's Model

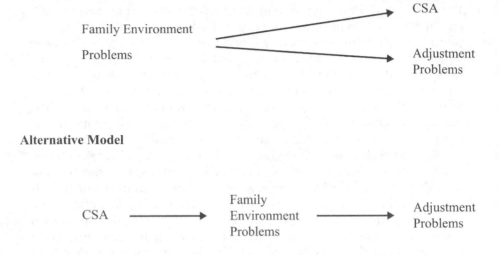

Alternative Model

Figure 1. Two alternative causal models for the relationship between child sexual abuse (CSA), family environment, and adjustment.

ment are essentially confounded, according to Rind. CSA was significantly correlated with family factors such as abuse, neglect, and lack of support (Table 10), and the effect sizes are of about the same magnitude as the CSA-adjustment relationships. The relationship between family environment and adjustment was actually somewhat stronger than between CSA and adjustment, and when family environment was controlled, the CSA-adjustment relationship became nonsignificant in many cases, leading the authors to conclude that the CSA-adjustment relationship was spurious. A notable alternative hypothesis is that family environment mediates or partially mediates the relationship between CSA and adjustment (Figure 1, bottom portion). That is, the CSA, at least if discovered in the family, may itself create the disordered family environment and it in turn is responsible or partially responsible for the negative effects on adjustment.

In summary, the Rind meta-analysis was generally well conducted. There is cause for concern that the CSA-adjustment relationship was under-estimated by restricting the sample to studies of college students, thereby perhaps eliminating those who suffered the most severe effects. Rind and colleagues' interpretation of the family environment effects could be challenged.

Other Meta-analyses of Studies
of the Sequelae of Child Sexual Abuse

It is worth noting that, prior to the Rind article, three other meta-analyses on the relationship between child sexual abuse and adjustment had been published (Jumper, 1995; Neumann, Houskamp, Pollock, & Briere, 1996; Rind & Tromovitch, 1997). One was by the same team and was published in the *Journal of Sex Research* in 1997 (Rind & Tromovitch, 1997) and touched off no controversy. More recently, Paolucci and colleagues published a meta-analysis in the *Journal of Psychology* in 2001 (Paolucci, Genuis, & Violato, 2001). And, of course, numerous narrative reviews on the question have been published (see Rind et al., 1998, for a complete list).

In 1997, Rind and Tromovitch published a meta-analysis on the effects of child sexual abuse, focusing on national samples such as the National Health and Social Life Survey (Laumann, Gagnon, Michael, & Michaels, 1994). They located seven such studies. The 1997 Rind meta-analysis has some strengths and some weaknesses compared with the 1998 one. The national samples clearly are superior to the college samples. However, these national studies, probably because CSA was not their focus, were less careful in defining CSA and often measured adjustment casually. For example, in the NHSLS, the crucial question asked whether the respondent had been sexually touched before puberty by someone who was past puberty. This definition excluded, for example, exposure to an exhibitionist and sexual abuse past puberty. Effect sizes were again small; for example, for the NHSLS, r was .07 for males and .05 for females. Methodologically it should be noted that reliability of measurement of the outcome variable affects effect sizes. The less reliable the measure, the smaller the effect sizes. In the NHSLS, adjustment was measured by a single item. Therefore, small effect sizes may be a result of unreliable measurement.

The meta-analysis by Paolucci and colleagues (2001) was disappointing. It did not cite the Rind meta-analysis published three years before and therefore any possibility of cumulating scientific evidence was missed. Paolucci looked at some of the same adjustment outcomes and added others as well, including PTSD, sexual promiscuity, and academic performance. Only 37 studies were located, fewer than Rind had. The samples were not restricted to college students. The authors used d as the measure of effect size and obtained weighted effect sizes of .40 for PTSD, .44 for depression, .44 for suicide, .29 for sexual promiscuity, and .19 for academic performance. These effect sizes are larger than the ones found by Rind and colleagues, and they—at least those for adjustment-related outcomes—are more in the moderate, rather than small, range. It seems likely that the overall effect sizes are larger in this meta-analysis than in the Rind analysis (1998) because this one included clinical samples.

Conclusion

Does child sexual abuse influence adjustment, according to the results of meta-analyses? According to the Rind et al. (1998) meta-analysis of college samples, there is a significant association between CSA and adjustment, but the effect is small. According to the Rind and Tromovitch (1997) meta-analysis using nationally representative samples, the answer is the same: There is a significant association but the effect is small.

Before we rush to the conclusion that CSA has no effect on adjustment, several caveats must be stated. First, the effect in the Rind et al. (1998) meta-analysis was significant. Second, the 1998 meta-analysis probably underestimated the magnitude of the effect because of the sample limitation to studies of college students, who are preselected to an unknown degree for good adjustment. Third, the 1997 Rind and Tromovitch meta-analysis probably underestimated the magnitude of the effect because of inadequate measurement of adjustment (e.g., in the NHSLS, only a single item measured adjustment).

Perhaps most importantly, the small effect may represent an average of large effects for some individuals and no effect for many others. Whether force was used, whether the individual consented, the duration of the abuse, and whether it was incestuous abuse are all likely sources of variation in outcomes. Rind et al.'s (1998, Table 6) attempt to analyze these moderators was inadequate because there were too few studies available that examined these effects.

For all these reasons, a conclusion that child sexual abuse has no effect on adjustment would be premature and probably inaccurate.

References

Cohen, J. (1988). *Statistical power analysis for the behavioral sciences* (2nd ed.). Hillsdale, NJ: Lawrence Erlbaum.

Davis, J. L., & Petretic-Jackson, P. A. (2000). The impact of child sexual abuse on adult interpersonal functioning: A review and synthesis of the empirical literature. *Aggression and Violent Behavior, 5,* 291–328.

Dodgen, D. (2000). Science, policy, and the protection of children. *American Psychologist, 55,* 1034–1035.

Glass, G. V., McGaw, B., & Smith, M. L. (1981). *Meta-analysis in social research.* Beverly Hills, CA: Sage.

Haugaard, J. J. (2000). The challenge of defining child sexual abuse. *American Psychologist, 55,* 1036–1039.

Hedges, L. V., & Becker, B. J. (1986). Statistical methods in the meta-analysis of research on gender differences. In J. S. Hyde & M. C. Linn (Eds.), *The psychology of gender: Advances through meta-analysis* (pp. 14–50). Baltimore: Johns Hopkins University Press.

Hedges, L. V., & Olkin, I. (1985). *Statistical methods for meta-analysis.* New York: Academic.

Hyde, J. S., Fennema, E., & Lamon, S. J. (1990). Gender differences in mathematics performance: A meta-analysis. *Psychological Bulletin, 107,* 139–155.

Jumper, S. (1995). A meta-analysis of the relationship of child sexual abuse to adult psychological adjustment. *Child Abuse & Neglect, 19,* 715–728.

Kling, K. C., Hyde, J. S., Showers, C. J., & Buswell, B. N. (1999). Gender differences in self-esteem: A meta-analysis. *Psychological Bulletin, 125,* 470–500.

Laumann, E. O., Gagnon, J. H., Michael, R. T. & Michaels, S. (1994). *The social organization of sexuality: Sexual practices in the United States.* Chicago: University of Chicago Press.

Neumann, D. A., Houskamp, B. M., Pollock, V. E., & Briere, J. (1996). The long-term sequelae of childhood sexual abuse in women: A meta-analytic review. *Child Maltreatment, 1,* 6–16.

Paolucci, E. O., Genuis, M. L., & Violato, C. (2001). A meta-analysis of the published research on the effects of child sexual abuse. *Journal of Psychology, 135,* 17–36.

Rind, B., Bauserman, R., & Tromovitch, P. (2000). Science versus orthodoxy: Anatomy of the congressional condemnation of a scientific article and reflections on remedies for future ideological attacks. *Applied and Preventive Psychology, 9,* 211–225.

Rind, B., & Tromovitch, P. (1997). A meta-analytic review of findings from national samples on psychological correlates of child sexual abuse. *Journal of Sex Research, 34,* 237–255.

Rind, B., Tromovitch, P., & Bauserman, R. (1998). A meta-analytic examination of assumed properties of child sexual abuse using college samples. *Psychological Bulletin, 124,* 22–53.

Discussion Paper

SUSAN F. NEWCOMER

Philip Jenkins, in his paper, described the interest in child sex abuse as a cyclical thing. But as several papers have noticed, we don't in the U.S. have much information about childhood sexuality except from studies of abused children and problems. Still, the studies of adult sexual behavior and teen sexual behavior all point to determinants appearing long before the time when respondents responded. So if we're going to ever get at "causation" in a world where we can't randomly assign individuals to the ways in which they deal with sex, it's important to have longitudinal data. Longitudinal data help deal with endogeneity bias, the economists' term for that which is *really* causing whatever it is you report.

I see two sorts of issues here: one is the quantity of data and one is the quality of the evidence. As Dr. Hyde observes, a meta-analysis needs a lot of evidence—developing a meta-analysis is a science in itself. One might say it's rather like doing secondary data analysis. One has little control over the quality of the material available for analysis. One winces with the wish that the investigator had only asked some other questions or wonders why a study so clearly flawed actually made it through peer review. So the challenge is to set your criteria for acceptance of a study for inclusion. It is, I should imagine, rather tempting to move outside the boundaries. I've been working on another report recently in which the issue of biological plausibility has been a sticking point in that, even if the data aren't there, "everybody knows that this really works in such and such a way" if it makes perfect sense that X is related to Y and there are a number of studies which suggest that relationship exists. As a counter to the "everybody knows . . . " we have to keep in mind that it made perfect sense many years ago that the world was flat, malaria was caused by bad air, leprosy was caused by impure thoughts or actions, and we won't mention the beliefs that some people in this world hold about the spread of HIV/AIDS.

When we think about data quality, the biomedical types sometimes sneer at the measures that social and behavior scientists use as being squishy and unverifiable. As an aside, that drives me to wonder if doctors believe what's in the medical histories their patients provide them. After all, that's self-report, too. I'm sure that some people lie and some people forget and some people get saved and are born again and some investigators may set up their studies in ways that support, reward, or encourage respondents to stretch the truth. Think about postintervention evaluation forms passed out by the intervention team—we all have tales about the born-again virgins, the admitted liars, and the people who age their age at first sex as they themselves age.

There is also the perplexing question concerning whether more of something is actually closer to the facts or the truth. If more men report same-sex behavior in a computer interview than to an interviewer, who's doing what to whom? If she says they have sex once a week and he says they have sex once in a blue moon, who's right? But CASI and audio CASI and T-CASI have other advantages as well as perhaps the issue of getting more of something reported. At least right now they do. Data are entered at the time of collection, skip patterns are set in from the start, which of course means people are skipped out of things where an interviewer might be able to do a little bit of probing and find out that, yes indeed, they had done it although they said they hadn't done it. It's also easier to translate into other languages, and people who are unfamiliar with computers can and do learn to use them. We're finding some studies with adolescents in Kenya who are doing just fine with CASI; the only thing is the cost of the computers and the batteries there. There are also even newer methods: Web based and voice mail–activated interviewing. One trembles at the fate of all of the NORC and RTI interviewers who are going to be unemployed perhaps at some point. I also just read briefly Nancy Padian's article in the most recent issue of the *Journal of Adolescent Health* on diaries, paper-pencil diaries versus telephone diaries. The data weren't that different but the kids liked the telephone diaries.

There's the issue in terms of methodology of biomarkers. A newly diagnosed case of gonorrhea is pretty convincing evidence of sexual intercourse since the last test. There are now sensitive tests that can pick up traces of infection from a much longer time ago and tests that can detect semen in vaginal tracts for a period of time. It is unlikely that such measures will ever be able to replace self-report, nor should they. Tagging biomarkers onto a social and behavioral study is often as convincing to the biomedical people as it is when doctors add one scale to their clinical studies. We don't believe that, they don't believe this, so we do have a long way to go to meet in the middle someplace.

And then we have the perpetual problems of retrospective recall—revisionist history at a personal level. If someone remembers something after a period of denying it, is it evidence of repression, or of what? I don't know. I'm a sociologist, not a psychologist. So then what is forgetting? What does it mean and what triggers the remembrance after the forgetting? There do seem to be gender differences. Are there other differences as well in who remembers what, when, and why? Now addressing sexual abuse is a multiple challenge.

The parent of a child who knows or suspects that the child is being abused is probably less likely to permit the child to be interviewed. Also, on discovering evidence of child abuse, in many states and jurisdictions, the interviewer is obliged to report it. What does that do to the whole family, let alone to your research project? Those are perpetual problems, which lead to mediocre question quality, such as "Has anybody ever done something to you that you didn't want done to you?" That's a sexual abuse question, I guess. Research on sexual abuse, while almost the only data we have in the U.S. on sexuality of the not-yet-teens, is not really very helpful about normal sexual development. We do need more information on that issue. It's a continuing challenge not to let the search for the perfect questions and the perfect data design drive away the merely excellent. However, it seems to me that research on sexual behavior is progressing; it's progressing slowly but we're doing a lot better than we used to be. Maybe the NIH study sections, which are extremely conservative, are slower to get the message than are the foundations, but nonetheless progress is being made.

General Discussion

Ken Zucker: What do people actually mean when they use the phrase "normal sexual development?" In that context, we have to think about distinctions between terms like "normal" and "normative." In other aspects of development, we can use them as some kind of framework; for example, we know what normative attachment development is in babies and young children. We know about signs of attachment as it emerges over time and we also know about qualitative differences in attachment formation. One domain where I think there would be some consensus is what Heino Meyer-Bahlburg often studies in his adolescent or young adult samples of people with intersex conditions—sexual milestones, which seem to have a Guttman-like sequence; first you do this, then you do that, then you do this. It's rare for there to be disjunctions (e.g., to have intercourse before you have a crush). We know in some groups that they have delays in sexual milestones but what do we actually think about sexual milestones in childhood, what's the sequence?

Deborah Tolman: I was very interested in the reasons that were offered to participants in the CASI for why they had masturbated. I looked over the reasons and I thought, "Hmmm, there might be a lot of other reasons why," and I noticed there wasn't an "other" section. I'm wondering if there's any way for you to offer participants a way to explain what their other reasons are. I was also very curious about how those reasons were derived in the first place.

Meredith Reynolds: There are a lot of questions like that where we had to come up with a list. We used questions from previous research to try to come up with a comprehensive list that people could use for motivations for doing things, reasons for doing things or not doing things, and we tried to always have the "other" category. If you select "other" as your answer for a question, the next screen you get is a box where you type in what "other" is. So we did get some of this more narrative data. For example, the screen where subjects indicate all the various sexual behaviors they had engaged in during childhood had an "other" option. Those who checked off "other" often wrote about games involving miming sexual behaviors or having their stuffed animals or Barbie dolls do sexual behaviors. So that is something that you can incorporate into a CASI format.

I'd like to respond to a comment by Susan Newcomer about the benefit of the interview, i.e., it's easier to go back and change things. You can incorporate that to some extent with the CASI. For example, there was a screen where subjects checked off all the behaviors on the list that they had experienced during high school. If they had not checked off that they had engaged in intercourse, they got a screen later down the road asking about why they had chosen not to have intercourse in high school. Included in the list of potential reasons was the option "I made a mistake, I did have intercourse during high school." If a subject checked that answer, the program would loop them back to the appropriate follow-up questions regarding their high school intercourse experiences, such as frequency, number of different partners, etc. So there is some flexibility, although it's never going to be as much as you have with a face-to-face interview.

Dennis Fortenberry: I want to compliment your use of the "don't want to," or no answer, alternative. Most research using CASI has not used that, and that surprises me, that they've been able to pass that through IRBs. But I wonder if you've analyzed the pattern of use of that alternative. In a CASI study that I'm doing in Indianapolis, there are some significant patterns or variations in the use of the "don't want to answer" alternative.

Meredith Reynolds: We've not looked at that so far as much as we should. One of the things I've noticed looking at that data is in some cases people appear to choose the "no answer" option perhaps accidentally, because they answered either an earlier or subsequent question that reveals the same information they were refusing to give. Oftentimes, unless it's a fill-in type question, the default answer selected for the questions when the subject first gets the screen is "no answer" and subjects have to actively unselect the "no answer" option. So, if there are, say, five questions on the screen and then there's the next button, they may answer only four questions, accidentally leaving one of the questions as "no answer" and click on "next" without realizing they skipped a question.

Lucia O'Sullivan: How well did it work and what were the mistakes, because I know it's so expensive to buy the platform, get the programming done, and implement it; did everyone do it well?

Meredith Reynolds: For the most part, but you have to understand that it's going to depend on the sample. We're using college students who are computer-savvy so you know it works well with that sample. People enjoyed it for the most part. People often haven't thought of those experiences before and it's kind of fun to remember. But that's college students and I think you have to be very careful in terms of generalizing to other samples. Susan Newcomer can speak more about use of CASI in Kenya.

Susan Newcomer: I haven't seen the data from it, I just know that the acceptability among the young people is very good and researchers aren't having qualms about using it.

Meredith Reynolds: As to the question of expense, the program we used is actually relatively inexpensive. It was $2000, but what we used cost only $1000. I originally did want to have an audio component because I was concerned about college students flying through screens and not really reading carefully, and then there were some points where I really wanted to have the audio component so that they were forced to hear the whole set of instructions. The second part of the computer software, which is Sensus Q&A from Sawtooth Technologies, is an audio and a video component and that was an extra thousand dollars, but we ended up not using it. So it was really only a $1,000 package that's quite flexible. It really worked out well for someone like me with minimal programming experience.

Janet Hyde: On this question of using computer-assisted data collection techniques with younger kids, I've been using computer data collection with third graders on nothing to do with sex and they love it. Contrary to the notion that they're not computer savvy, it's the neatest toy they've seen in a while and we've been doing it with a touch screen so they just have to touch the answer, they don't even have to use a mouse. It's just a big hit. I think they would much rather do that than interact with an interviewer.

Ed Laumann: I would like to join Dennis in adding a caution about trooping after CASI mechanisms. I think that these have been way oversold because there's not really been effective evaluation of some of the rapport-building aspects of personal interviews for these sorts of things. One in four Americans has a literacy competency of less than sixth grade, so the focus on being able to read the whole thing is something that has not been really thought about. Moreover, even if they have the option of hearing it, CASI turns out to be extremely slow and boring. We did this in China and our experience was that people just simply wouldn't bear sitting through this thing reading to them in this very slow fashion. They'd thus ask for assistance so you have this systematic selection for having assistance for the very group that you might have been most interested in. So I think the technical implementation of this technique leaves a lot to be desired, and I do not think it's a guarantee of quality or even willingness to disclose hypersensitive material. If you think about it properly and motivate people to share those sorts of things, I think you can finesse some of those issues.

Bill Friedrich: On considering the Rind paper (Rind & Tromovitch, 1997), David Finkelhor co-authored a paper with Boney-McCoy (Boney-McCoy & Finkelhor, 1995) looking at a large, well-collected sample and noted a clear relationship between a variety of types of victimization, including sexual abuse, and academic underachievement. So you do have a very significant selection bias when you're only looking at college students. The second issue is the simple choice of outcome measure. Looking at generic psychological adjustment in studies with children and adolescents, minimal effect sizes have been found for such psychological adjustment variables as depression, anxiety, aggression, self-concept, but more significant effect sizes have been identified for things that are more specific to sexual victimization, such as sexual behavior or symptoms consistent with post-traumatic stress disorder.

Janet Hyde: I just wanted to clarify one thing because I think I may have misled people. When I said that in the Rind meta-analysis they looked just at adjustment and not at a variety of other things they could have done like academic performance, they have a lot of indices of adjustment including anxiety, depression, eating disorders, and the usual suspects. One of those is sexual adjustment, so they did include various sexual adjustment scales and I think the effect size for this was .09, which is exactly what it was overall. So they did do some analysis of sexual adjustment and I didn't mean to mislead people into thinking that they hadn't.

Chris Browning: I have a question for Cynthia with respect to the issue of forgetting. We often think about either remembering or completely forgetting, but I'm wondering if you saw any reference to studies that had been done on partial patterns of forgetting. For me, one way of getting around the problem of cross-sectional versus prospective research designs is to examine patterns of item nonresponse within a sample survey so you might be able to at least get some insight into some of these hypotheses about what's driving forgetting. For instance, if it's repression you might expect more severe cases, e.g., incestuous relationships, to involve more partial forgetting, such as failure to recall whether specific behaviors occurred during the event.

Cynthia Graham: Yes, there were studies that reported "partial forgetting." There were also a number of studies that hypothesized that more severe abuse experiences would be more likely to be forgotten if repression was the mechanism. I came across one interesting community study, involving a nonclinical sample, by Epstein and Bottoms (1998), that looked at what triggered remembering or "delayed recall," and of the different triggers that people gave for remembering abusive experiences, media reports of abuse were most often mentioned; therapy was much less frequently mentioned. There's evidence from a number of studies that much of the forgetting of abusive experiences is "partial" forgetting rather than complete amnesia for the event.

David Finkelhor: I'd like to articulate a principle. I think that the methods that are appropriate for the study of any particular problem depend on the stage of development of scientific knowledge and the questions that are being asked about the issue. One has to take that into account in thinking about some of these methodological issues. It seems to me that for issues about which we have very little information, such as some sexual development issues, long-term retrospective recall information is probably a pretty good place to start. In an area like child sexual abuse, where I feel there's been a lot of both research and theoretical development, I think that the limitations of that methodology become more and more serious and more and more of a constraint. In fact, I'm very discouraged myself, personally, about the retrospective recall methodology, especially the long-term, and I'm not doing studies of that kind anymore. The kind of evidence that Cynthia reported on shows that there are really serious validity problems, some of which haven't yet even been tested. For example, the possibility of being associated with certain kinds of negative psychological or life conditions, so that people who have been more affected by the experience are more likely to have had a reason to be thinking about it or to be talking about it or disclosing it. Also issues related to historical trends—whether the meaning of having a history of sexual abuse changes over time as a result of the attention it has received and the existence of survivor movements and so on—that may have affected the nature of what people are willing to disclose or how they define what's happened to them. It seems to me to be critically important before we carry out a whole lot more retrospective recall studies, especially ones that are trying to test important theoretical ideas about development, that we really can establish that there is some validity to that approach for answering those kinds of questions. The dilemma, of course, is that if we don't have that methodology, do we have any other methodology? The finding that you cited (Halpern, Udry, Suchindran, & Campbell, 2000), of which I was unaware, that at least there are some studies that show that adults do a little bit better than adolescents, is also discouraging because it would be my inclination to try and get information about experiences as close to the time of occurrence as possible. In fact, the methodological literature from the criminology field, for example the crime victimization area, suggests very strongly that information that you gather after more than about a year is of very suspect validity and subject to enormous biases, not just about its occurrence but also about the details of the event. My inclination is to look for methodologies to get the recall information from youth close to the time of the occurrence or, next best, from young people who were recently out of childhood.

John Bancroft: There are varying sources of bias here. The study that Cynthia mentioned where the adolescents were underreporting masturbation compared with what they reported as young adults is relevant to attitudes and concerns about masturbation at different stages in one's lifecycle. There are certain points in life where you may feel more comfortable talking about something in your past than other times. Similarly it appeared from that data that the adolescents were more comfortable talking about more delinquent-type behaviors when they're adolescents than recalling them when they're adults. That makes sense as well. Somehow we need to take into account that there may be certain types of questions which we may expect a young adult to recall more accurately than an adolescent, and vice versa. So far that hasn't been addressed in any systematic way.

Cynthia Graham: Halpern et al. (2000) also looked at predictors of recall of masturbation in adolescents and one of the predictors that came out strongly was attitude towards masturbation. Those with more negative attitudes towards masturbation were less likely to report adolescent masturbation. But returning to David's point, I think there are ways of improving retrospective recall and I don't think studies using adult recall should be abandoned. However, the effects of varying question wording and order or presentation, mode of presentation, and mode of data collection, and so on need to be evaluated. Looking at the research on sexual behavior and HIV/AIDS, much more attention has been paid to methodological issues by researchers such as Joe Catania. This seems such a contrast to the area of child sexual abuse where there's been hardly any research of this kind.

David Finkelhor: There's another discouraging thing; the variability in the rates of sexual abuse are so great across studies and they seem to be explained by so many different things that actually pinpointing the things that explain that variability may take an enormously long time.

Deborah Tolman: I was curious about the Halpern article (Halpern et al., 2000), which I had not seen, so I looked at it. Perhaps this comes from my perspective as someone doing research on early adolescent sexuality, but I've noticed that the concern that's been voiced most frequently around the table has been about underreporting. My question tends to be about overreporting. How do we know that the adults were not retrospectively overreporting their adolescent masturbation when in adulthood they realized they should have been masturbating more as teenagers? I'm curious why you're all so confident that the adult reports are more "accurate," because I'm not.

John Bancroft: As it happens, adults are not terribly comfortable talking about masturbation either.

Bill Friedrich: I'm doing some research with a new adolescent sexual behavior inventory that took a lot of effort to get IRB approval. It's like an upper extension of the CSBI. One of the items is "I masturbate," and then they're allowed to rate frequency. The proportion of adolescents who acknowledge that they've masturbated at least once is somewhere around 8%. They just won't answer that question. They'd just rather answer questions like "I get used sexually by others," "I don't like my own body." It's something about masturbation. We've done some piloting with that item, masturbation, and it looks like serious underreporting.

Jany Rademakers: I have one question about this underreporting. Do they know the word "masturbation"? Is it such a common word that everyone in America knows what it is? I think especially for children and young adolescents it might be a behavior they engage in but not words they know of the concept. So do you explain in your inventory what kind of behavior you're referring to?

Bill Friedrich: Masturbation is defined in the preface.

Julia Heiman: What I'm interested in are the limits of each methodology and when they might be best used. We'll always need good ways to get retrospective data, especially if we're doing clinical studies, so we need to keep working on the methodology and which methodology to use, as all of these have limitations. Maybe we can point to some principles that might guide our thinking. One other point, does it ever make sense to ask people how sure they are of their answers? It wouldn't, of course, when you know that attitudes are biasing, but it might be worth asking in some cases. I also wanted to ask Janet Hyde about the Rind article. He argued at the end for a continuum of child sexual abuse as opposed to a dichotomous variable. Could you comment on that?

Janet Hyde: I agree personally with him on that point, because he defined child sexual abuse, as a lot of others do, as a very broad category ranging from exposure to exhibition on one occasion to repeated intercourse with a close family member. Clearly there's a range there and a number of studies have shown that you get more severe effects depending on where you are on that range. So as long as we lump all of those incidents together, we're not going to get very far in research looking at the effects. On the ambiguity of retrospective reports, I've just completed a study with Joanna Cantor, who is also at the University of Wisconsin in the Department of Communication and Arts, to look at the effects of sexual media on children. Because of the difficulty of getting into schools and otherwise recruiting children, we used retrospective reports by college students. We had them write open-ended responses in which they were asked to recall a time when viewing something sexual in the media had a big impact on them. We tell them we want them to write for 15 or 20 minutes, so they give us a page or two pages' worth of a narrative about this. It's quite fascinating. One of the nice things is that they are asked to tell exactly what the media was—were they watching a pretty woman in a movie theater, on video, or something like that—and that gives us an opportunity to assess the accuracy of the reports, because there's the Motion Picture Association of America directory that will tell you what movies were out which years and when they were in the theaters and so on. They are amazingly accurate in their recall. So if they said "I was watching the so-and-so movie in 1989," and you look it up in this directory, that's exactly when that movie was out. I think that's given them a very good tag to their experience at that time, whether they felt angry or upset or guilty for watching the movie and so on. Now this is a little off the topic of directly finding out about child sexual behavior because that wasn't directly the point of the study, but the point is the extent to which we can improve retrospective recall by giving concrete tags of this kind. This one is striking to me because they sure can remember what movie they saw in what year and what grade they were in and so on. Those incidents are rooted in their memories in a very fascinating way. I would like all of us to think more about how we can improve memory using techniques such as that.

Ken Zucker: I have a question about sampling with regard to the Rind meta-analysis. You mentioned his other meta-analysis on community samples. Has there been a third meta-analysis with regard to clinic samples by anybody?

Janet Hyde: There's a third meta-analysis but it's not clinical samples.

Ken Zucker: One of the things I'm thinking about is that each of these different groups can help with understanding mechanisms, so it might be legitimate to study people who are part of survivor movements in terms of what the mechanisms might be. One of the impressions I've had clinically is that people who become part of those subcultures develop a new identity which perpetuates the issue and reminds me of a less pernicious area in child psychopathology where it's been shown that kids with antisocial behavior who are in groups to learn social skills get worse because they learn how to do antisocial things from each other.

Suzanne Frayser: I'm addressing the issue that Ken raised of how to define normal sexual behavior and normal sexual development. I wanted to mention the importance of cross-cultural studies and interdisciplinary research. A lot of what we've been talking about here has been intracultural; to formulate an adequate definition of what is normal we have to look at the *human* population, not just the American population. For instance, if we consider the findings of evolutionary research, including cross-species and primate studies, what would we expect normal sexual behavior to be like among human beings? And though the cross-cultural research in traditional cultures is very spotty, nonetheless there are different standards for what is normal in other cultures. This gives us an idea of the range of variation of what is considered normal. Also, in the United States, we need more studies among different ethnic populations that have very different conceptualizations of what is normal. The thread that we've been following all morning is the importance of context and the importance of the types of questions that we ask. When I conduct interviews, I start out in a specific sequence, one that reminds me of Cynthia's point about warm-up questions. The context of the interview, as well as the sequence of questions asked, shapes so much of what the data will look like.

References

Boney-McCoy, S., & Finkelhor, D. (1995). Psychosocial sequelae of violent victimization in a national youth sample. *Journal of Consulting and Clinical Psychology, 63,* 726–736.

Epstein, M. A., & Bottoms, B. L. (1998). Memories of childhood sexual abuse: A survey of young adults. *Child Abuse & Neglect, 22*, 1217–1238.

Halpern, C. J. T., Udry, J. R., Suchindran, C., & Campbell, B. (2000). Adolescent males' willingness to report masturbation. *Journal of Sex Research, 37*, 327–332.

Rind, B., & Tromovitch, P. (1997). A meta-analytic review of findings from national samples on psychological correlates of child sexual abuse. *Journal of Sex Research, 34*, 237–255.

Part 3.

Some New Studies of Normal Sexual Development

Studies of Sexuality of Nonabused Children

WILLIAM N. FRIEDRICH

Introduction

This paper reviews a number of studies examining sexual behavior of nonabused children. In keeping with the principles of developmental psychopathology, normative sexual behavior is informed by research with non-normative samples, including psychiatric nonabused samples and sexually abused samples. In addition to establishing the ubiquity of sexual behavior from ages 2 through 12, sexuality in children is related to a number of individual and family factors. These include age, gender, various aspects of family sexuality, life stress, family violence, peer relationships, and number of hours per week in day care, as well as maternal attitudes toward sexuality. Related research on correlates of sexually aggressive behavior is also briefly discussed in this paper.

I would like to preface my comments on normative sexual behavior in children with a brief statement that my initial foray into research on sexual behavior in children was driven by my view of sexual behavior in children as a clinical issue. This is unlike the sexologists here, who research sexual behavior in children without any eye toward its being abnormal. However, after realizing in my first large normative study that sexual behavior in children is ubiquitous, I have begun to appreciate the normative aspects of sexuality in children. I also have come to realize that children's sexuality is, quite surprisingly, a relatively uncharted area.

For example, before analyzing the data in the first normative study with the Child Sexual Behavior Inventory (Friedrich, Grambsch, Broughton, Kuiper, & Beilke, 1991), I felt quite secure in my expectation that this measure would become a very powerful discriminating tool for sexually abused children. The problem of nondisclosing children who have been abused continues to be a huge issue in the clinical field. Researchers and clinicians are still searching for an assessment tool with maximal sensitivity and specificity. Imagine my surprise when the data informed me that with a very carefully screened sample, every sexual behavior item, no matter how unusual, was endorsed by a minimum of four to six parents ($N = 880$). On subsequent interview, these parents provided examples to support their reports of behaviors such as "put mouth on genitals of another child" and

Table 1. *Sexual Behavior Items from the CBCL* (Achenbach, 1991)

  5. Behaves like the opposite sex
 59. Touches sex parts in public
 60. Plays with sex parts too much
 73. Sexual problems (describe):
 96. Thinks about sex too much
110. Wishes to be of opposite sex

"inserts objects into vagina." The follow-up interviews with parents have been very illuminating, since they clarify the context of the behavior. This additional information clarifies and typically normalizes the sexual behavior.

This paper first reviews studies on sexual behavior in children using six items from the Child Behavior Checklist (CBCL; Achenbach, 1991), and then reviews the development of the Child Sexual Behavior Inventory. I will also include a review of subsequent research with the Child Sexual Behavior Inventory, including cross-cultural samples and correlations of sexual behavior with a variety of family variables. Factor analysis of the Child Sexual Behavior Inventory has led to interesting perspectives on the continuity and discontinuity of these factors across age groups. Finally, I would like to briefly synopsize related research on the correlates of sexually intrusive behavior.

Research with the Sex Items from the Child Behavior Checklist

My first research with sexually abused children was developed without an appreciation that sexual behavior was an important correlate of sexual abuse (Friedrich, Urquiza, & Beilke, 1986). Early research in the field had typically utilized nonstandardized instruments, and I was determined to use a measure that was objective and valid. Consequently, I used the Child Behavior Checklist for reasons other than the fact that it does contain six items which are related to sexual behavior in children (Achenbach, 1991). Behaviors sampled include "touches sex parts in public" and "thinks about sex too much." The six items are shown in Table 1.

Because these six items were present in the Child Behavior Checklist, I became aware that sexual behavior was a key feature with sexually abused children (Friedrich et al., 1986). Subsequent research demonstrated that sexual behavior measured by these six items discriminated sexually abused from nonabused children. For example, sexually abused boys exhibited more sexual behavior problems and less aggression than a comparable sample of boys receiving outpatient psychotherapy for externalizing disorders (Friedrich, Beilke, & Urquiza, 1988). Sexually abused children had more problems than a nonabused nonpatient comparison sample, but were not as disturbed on the Child Behavior Checklist as a similar sample of psychiatric outpatients; as a group, sexually abused children displayed significantly more sexual problems than either of the comparison samples (Friedrich, Beilke, & Urquiza, 1987). Additional research with the CBCL sex items with a large community sample of 6- to 10-year-old children has also demonstrated a relationship between sexual behavior and total behavior problems (Meyer-Bahlburg, Dolezal, & Sandberg, 2000). The relationship for externalizing behavior is the strongest in male children.

While these studies continued to show the sensitivity of the six-item scale, I was bothered by their lack of specificity and invitation to subjectivity. For example, what did the qualifier "too much" mean in items 60 and 96? In addition, an unpublished factor analysis of these six items suggested that items 5 and 110 loaded on one factor related to gender-role issues and was only minimally correlated with the remaining four items (Friedrich, 1997). Achenbach (1991) also found that these latter four items did make up a "syndrome" with younger children, but not with older children, and thus it was excluded as a core syndrome.

Development of the Child Sexual Behavior Inventory

As a way to address these concerns, I began to interview female caregivers of sexually abused children about sexual behavior exhibited by their children. The interview was typically in response to their comments on item 73 from the CBCL, "Sexual problems (describe)." Typical responses by caregivers of these children included such behaviors as exposing genitals, sexually intrusive behaviors with children and adults, and heightened sexual interest.

Some comments about the qualitative aspects of these interviews are in order. The typical parent had not thought of the behavior of these children as sexual. Consequently, when I asked them about "other sexual behaviors," my query typically drew a blank. After some thinking, they responded with a preface such as "I had never thought about it as sexual, but now that you mention it," and then an example, e.g., a child who would change into a bathing suit whenever a man visited the house.

Using the six items from the Child Behavior Checklist as a start and adding other behaviors reported by mothers, either on the CBCL or in direct interview, resulted in a 54-item measure of sexual behavior in children. I had several goals when developing this measure. First, I wanted the items to reflect overt behavior, and be as little influenced by subjectivity as possible. Secondly, while I wanted the same six-month timeline as used by the CBCL, the answer format of the CBCL added to its subjectivity, i.e., "not true," "somewhat or sometimes true," and "very true or often true." Consequently, the four-point answer format I developed emphasized the actual frequency of the item, e.g., "less than 1 time per month."

This first version of the Child Sexual Behavior Inventory was studied with 71 nonabused children from low-income families and 35 sexually abused children (Purcell, Beilke, & Friedrich, 1986). Significant between-groups differences were noted on most items. However, the response rate for many of the more unusual items was very low.

I then moved to my current position in the Department of Psychiatry and Psychology at the Mayo Clinic and was faced with a new institutional review board. The topic of sexual behavior was viewed as quite sensitive, and my proposal to obtain a large normative sample with the revised, 35-item Child Sexual Behavior Inventory required fairly constant shepherding through the IRB. I was required to keep an account of complaints received, and was asked to stop the study in response to any major protest. However, of the 1,231 subjects that were approached in the Community Pediatrics waiting room where they were recruited, only four mild complaints about the items were received.

The results from the first large sample of 880 2- to 12-year-old children from primarily middle-class and Caucasian families were published in 1991 (Friedrich et al., 1991). This sample had been screened for the absence of sexual abuse and children who had developmental disabilities or who had received mental-health counseling in the previous six months were excluded. In addition to the Child Sexual Behavior Inventory, the child's mother also completed the Child Behavior Checklist. Information on age, gender, marital, financial, and education status of the parents, family size, quality of peer relationships, hours per week spent in day care, life stress, and family sexuality was also obtained.

Ten of the 35 items were endorsed by more than 20% of the overall sample, and four of the items were endorsed by at least 50% of the sample. These included "scratches crotch," "if a boy, plays with girl toys; if a girl, plays with boy toys," "walks around in underwear," and "shy with strange men." Six of the 35 items were endorsed by fewer than 2% of the sample ("puts mouth on another child/adult's sex parts," "asks others to engage in sexual acts with him or her," "masturbates with objects," "inserts objects in vagina/anus," "imitates intercourse," and "makes sexual sounds"). Subsequent analysis with this normative sample found a significant and direct relationship between overall sexual behavior and family sexuality. Total sexual behavior was also significantly correlated with both internalizing and externalizing behavior from the Child Behavior Checklist.

Age differences in total sexual behavior were also noted, and the sample was divided into 2–6 years and 7–12 years old. More behaviors were reported in younger children, but some behaviors, e.g., sexual interest, were more common in the older age group. A factor analysis revealed one large factor, and this lack of variability was attributed to the low endorsement frequency of many of the items.

A series of follow-up interviews with some of the mothers who had reported unusual behaviors was again quite illuminating. For example, we heard several benign instances of sexual behavior that on face value would seem to be quite deviant. For example, the parent of a preschooler reported one instance of her daughter "inserting an object into vagina." The interview illuminated this as natural exploration with a small doll as a follow-up to a schoolmate's having told the little girl that she "had two holes down there." No actual penetration occurred, but the doll head was interlabial.

A subsequent study with this normative sample of 880 contrasted the CSBI with 276 children with a documented history of sexual abuse (Friedrich et al., 1992). Significant between-group differences were noted for 27 items and ROC curve analyses indicated that the longer CSBI was better than the six-item CBCL scale for both specificities and sensitivities. In addition, very adequate test-retest reliability was calculated as well as significant correlations between parent and teacher reports. Ratings by mothers and fathers were also highly correlated, although mothers tended to report more sexual behavior overall.

A second version of the CSBI was developed. The majority of the initial 35 items (27) were retained. The revised scale was tested with 141 nonabused children and 133 sexually abused children, and 35 of the 36 items differed between the abused and nonabused samples (Friedrich, 1993). Endorsement frequencies for this normative sample were similar to those of the 1991 sample across most of the items.

A 38-item CSBI was then developed. See Table 2 for a copy. The majority of the items (22) were retained in their original form. However, 12 items were rewritten to read more simply and clearly, three items were added, and one was dropped. In addition, the 1,114 2 to 12-year-old children in the sample were much more ethnically and socioeconomically diverse, due in large part to 280 children from public and private day care programs in Los Angeles County (Friedrich, Fisher, Broughton, Houston, & Shafran, 1998). Again, every item was endorsed by at least a few mothers, with the most unusual items typically reported for the younger children. Test-retest reliability was excellent and mother and father ratings were also significantly correlated.

Age and maternal education were significantly related to total score, but gender and family income were not. Younger children had significantly higher scores than older children and more highly educated mothers reported more sexual behavior. Total sexual behavior was significantly and positively related to family violence, hours per week in day care, life stress, and family sexuality. Both internalizing and externalizing behavior problems were also significantly related to total sexual behavior.

Research with three versions of the CSBI clearly indicated that sexual behavior was ubiquitous in preteen children. Consequently, I began to increasingly consider the normative aspects of children's sexuality. Toward this end, I identified developmentally related sexual behaviors. These were

Table 2. *Child Sexual Behavior Inventory* (Friedrich, 1997)

Appendix A

Please circle the number that tells how often your child has shown
the following behaviors *recently or in the last 6 months:*

	Never	Less than 1/month	1–3 times/month	At least 1/week
	0	1	2	3

1.   0 1 2 3   Dresses like the opposite sex
2.   0 1 2 3   Stands too close to people
3.   0 1 2 3   Talks about wanting to be the opposite sex
4.   0 1 2 3   Touches sex (private) parts when in public places
5.   0 1 2 3   Masturbates with hand
6.   0 1 2 3   Draws sex parts when drawing pictures of people
7.   0 1 2 3   Touches or tries to touch their mother's or other women's breasts
8.   0 1 2 3   Masturbates with toy or object (blanket, pillow, plastic toy)
9.   0 1 2 3   Touches another child's sex (private) parts
10.   0 1 2 3   Tries to have sexual intercourse with another child or adult
11.   0 1 2 3   Puts mouth on another child/adult's sex parts
12.   0 1 2 3   Touches sex (private) parts when at home
13.   0 1 2 3   Touches an adult's sex (private) parts
14.   0 1 2 3   Touches animals' sex parts
15.   0 1 2 3   Makes sexual sounds (sighs, moans, heavy breathing, etc.)
16.   0 1 2 3   Asks others to engage in sexual acts with him or her
17.   0 1 2 3   Rubs body against people or furniture
18.   0 1 2 3   Puts objects in vagina or rectum
19.   0 1 2 3   Tries to look at people when they are nude or undressing
20.   0 1 2 3   Pretends that dolls or stuffed animals are having sex
21.   0 1 2 3   Shows sex (private) parts to adults
22.   0 1 2 3   Tries to look at pictures of nude or partially dressed people
23.   0 1 2 3   Talks about sexual acts
24.   0 1 2 3   Kisses adults they do not know well
25.   0 1 2 3   Gets upset when adults are kissing or hugging
26.   0 1 2 3   Overly friendly with men they don't know well
27.   0 1 2 3   Kisses other children they do not know well
28.   0 1 2 3   Talks flirtatiously
29.   0 1 2 3   Tries to undress other children against their will (opening pants, shirt, etc.)
30.   0 1 2 3   Wants to watch TV or movies that show nudity or sex

Table 2. *Continued*

	Never 0	Less than 1/month 1	1–3 times/month 2	At least 1/week 3
31.	0 1 2 3	When kissing, tries to put their tongue in other person's mouth		
32.	0 1 2 3	Hugs adults they do not know well		
33.	0 1 2 3	Shows sex (private) parts to children		
34.	0 1 2 3	Tries to undress adults against their will (opening pants, shirt, etc.)		
35.	0 1 2 3	Is very interested in the opposite sex		
36.	0 1 2 3	Puts their mouth on mother's or other women's breasts		
37.	0 1 2 3	Knows more about sex than other children their age		
38.	0 1 2 3	Other sexual behaviors (please describe)		
		A. _____		
		B. _____		

behaviors that were endorsed by at least 20% of the mothers for a specific age-gender group. The items overlapped considerably across genders, and demonstrated a clear and understandable developmental transition, i.e., interest in the opposite sex appeared in the 10- to 12-year-old group. The items are listed in Table 3.

The inclusion of a sexually abused sample ($N = 620$) and an outpatient psychiatric sample ($N = 577$) allowed contrasts between these three groups. Further analyses illustrated the fact that sexual behavior was elevated, relative to the normative sample, in the outpatient psychiatric sample, although still significantly less than the sexually abused sample (Friedrich et al., 2001). It appeared that sexual behavior was directly related to both internalizing and externalizing behavior problems, and while it was a psychometrically distinct type of behavior, these correlations suggested that sexual behavior problems share some of the same etiologic elements as other behavior problems.

Cross-Cultural Research with the CSBI

Four published studies have used all or a portion of the CSBI to research sexual behavior in the children of their countries. The first study used a 25-item CSBI to contrast 500 American children with two samples of Dutch children, $N = 460$ and $N = 297$ (Friedrich, Sandfort, Oostveen, & Cohen-Kettenis, 2000). Considerable differences were noted between the three groups across a number of the behaviors rated, with a persisting ten-

Table 3. *Developmentally Related Sexual Behaviors*

Age Group	Item	Endorsement %
2–5 Boys	Stands too close to people	29.3
	Touches sex parts when in public places	26.5
	Touches or tries to touch their mother's or other women's breasts	42.4
	Touches sex parts at home	60.2
	Tries to look at people when they are nude or undressing	26.8
2–5 Girls	Stands too close to people	25.8
	Touches or tries to touch their mother's or other women's breasts	43.7
	Touches sex parts at home	43.8
	Tries to look at people when they are nude or undressing	26.9
6–9 Boys	Touches sex parts at home	39.8
	Tries to look at people when they are nude or undressing	20.2
6–9 Girls	Touches sex parts at home	20.7
	Tries to look at people when they are nude or undressing	20.5
10–12 Boys	Is very interested in the opposite sex	24.1
10–12 Girls	Is very interested in the opposite sex	28.7

dency for the parents of the children from the Netherlands to report higher rates of sexual behavior. This was true for very common behaviors as well. For example, "touches sex parts at home" was rated as having occurred at least once in the previous six months for 64.1% of 2- to 6-year-old U.S. boys. However, the percentages increased to 91.8 and 96.6 across the two Dutch samples of 2- to 6-year-old boys. Family sexuality was similarly related to sexual behavior in all three samples.

There were far fewer differences between American and 917 Dutch-speaking children from Belgium who were rated by their mothers on the first version of the CSBI (Schoentjes, Deboutte, & Friedrich, 1999). Significant age trends were noted for 34 of the 46 items studied, with 26 of the behaviors more common in the younger age group, e.g., "touches sex parts in public," and eight more common in the older groups, e.g., "shy about undressing." Age and maternal education were again related to total score on the CSBI in the same direction as in Friedrich et al. (1998). In addition, a number of features related to more relaxed maternal attitudes toward sexuality were associated with higher levels of sexual behavior.

The third study examined a sample of 185 3- to 6-year-old children from Sweden, screened for the absence of sexual abuse. They were studied with a 25-item scale derived from the CSBI (Larsson, Svedin, & Friedrich, 2000). The Swedish children were contrasted with 467 American children. Swedish children, particularly boys, exhibited more sexual behavior than American children. Intrusive and sexually explicit behaviors were unusual in both samples. Family sexuality was significantly correlated with total sexual behavior in both the U.S. sample ($r = .18$, $p < .05$) and the Swedish sample ($r = .16$, $p < .05$).

The last study focused on the overlap of parent and day care provider reports of sexual behavior in 185 3- to 6-year-old children in Swedish day cares (Larsson & Svedin, 2002). Extensive questionnaires were used and parents observed significantly more sexual behavior in their children at home than did teachers at the day care centers at all age groups. The authors concluded that day cares were more structured and monitored, thus inhibiting the expression of sexual behavior. This study helps us understand the influence of context on children's sexual behavior. Further cross-context research is clearly needed.

Factor Analytic Studies of the CSBI

There is reason to believe that sexual behavior in children becomes increasingly diverse with time and includes a broader range of heterogeneous behaviors. However, early attempts at factor analysis with the CSBI normative samples suggested a single factor (Friedrich et al., 1991). Presumably, this was due to the heterogeneity of the sample and the lack of variance for many of the items.

Schoentjes et al. (1999) used a principal component analysis with varimax rotation with the Dutch translation of the first version of the CSBI. They identified seven stable factors with their Belgian sample of 2- to 12-year-olds. These factors, along with a sample item, are as follows: shamelessness, e.g., "sits with crotch or underwear exposed"; sexual interest, e.g., "talks about sex acts"; boundary problems, e.g., "stands too close"; gender identity problems, e.g., "wants to be opposite sex"; sexualized play, e.g., "imitates the act of sexual intercourse"; sexual intrusiveness, e.g., "touches animal's sex parts"; and genital manipulation, e.g., "masturbates with hands." While these factors are quite interesting and clinically compelling, their validity and their correlation with various family and demographic variables were not calculated.

A subsequent factor analysis utilized the 1,114 normative, 577 outpatient psychiatric, and 620 sexually abused children making up the sample first reported in Friedrich et al. (2001). The sample was divided into three age groups that are more reflective of developmental changes, 2–5, 6–9, and 10–12 years old. A principal components analysis with promax rotation was completed with five factors identified across three different age groups, accounting for 45–55% of the variance in the data (Trane & Friedrich, in preparation [2002]). Four of the five factors were relatively similar across the three age groups. These four are self-stimulating behavior, sexual intrusiveness with children, inappropriate boundaries with adults, and sexual knowledge/interest. Sexualized play was a factor noted in the youngest age group, and sexual intrusiveness with adults was a factor noted with the two older age groups. The factors were significantly intercorrelated, suggesting the presence of a higher-order latent factor of sexualized behavior. Correlations of demographic variables with the factors varied across age group. For example, hours/week in day care was positively associated with self-stimulation and sexual knowledge/interest only in the 9–12 age group. Family sexuality was correlated .30 to .35 with sexual knowledge/interest at all age groups, and with sexual intrusiveness with children at the youngest age group, $r = .30$, but not with sexual intrusiveness in the oldest age group, $r = .07$. These results appear to indicate that future research on normative sexual behavior in children should not treat sexual behavior as a single entity, but rather examine underlying dimensions.

Family sexuality has typically been treated as a single factor in prior research with the CSBI, including the correlations reported above. However, the scale used to rate this domain includes items pertaining to co-sleeping, co-bathing, family nudity, the presence of pornography in the home, and witnessing parental intercourse. A factor analysis of these items suggests two factors, family nudity—e.g., co-bathing, nudity in the home, etc.—and overt family sexuality—witnessing intercourse, availability of pornography. Co-sleeping does not load on either factor, and its frequency drops off drastically after the age of 6 years. Co-sleeping is not associated with elevated sexual behavior or behavior problems as measured by the CBCL in children under 7 years of age, but is associated with total behavior problems in older children. This suggests that there are normative aspects of this co-sleeping that are developmentally related. The factor of overt family sexuality was significantly correlated with sexual behavior and total behavior problems at all age groups.

Related Research

Sexually intrusive behavior in children has taken center stage in educational and political circles. The criminalization of these children is increasingly commonplace. However, policy and treatment recommendations are being made with little research guidance. For example, what are the

Table 4. *Correlates of Sexually Intrusive Behavior*

Dependent Variable   **Sexually Intrusive Behavior**

Independent Variable	R2	Beta	r
1. PTSD	.09	.17	.33
2. Life Events	.14	.12	.27
3. Age	.15	−.16	−.10
4. External	.16	.12	.31
5. Family Sexuality	.17	.08	.18
6. Race	.18	.07	.06

$F = 45.2$ $(6, 1277)$ $p < .00001$

correlates of intrusive behavior? Do any of these correlates suggest that these are children with transient or more persisting problems?

Utilizing the three groups reported in Friedrich et al. (2001), I created a face valid subset of CSBI items labeled sexual intrusiveness. It consists of CSBI items 9, 10, 11, 13, 14, 16, 27, 29, 31, and 34. Initial analyses with stepwise multiple regression analyses are reported in Tables 4 and 5. As you can see from Table 4, sexual intrusiveness was related to the following variables: PTSD as defined by a subscale from the Child Behavior Checklist, life stress, age (inversely), externalizing behavior from the Child Behavior Checklist, family sexuality, and race (white). This latter variable has a simple correlation of .06, which is significant with this sample size, but is exceedingly small and difficult to interpret. Sexual abuse was not included in the analyses reported in Table 4.

The PTSD variable is a subscale derived from the CBCL via confirmatory factor analysis (Friedrich et al., in press). It includes items such as "fears certain animals, situations, or places," "nightmares," etc., and appears to be related to behavioral reactivity and hyperarousal.

When sexual abuse status was introduced as an independent variable, the independent variables were PTSD, life stress, age, sexual abuse status, externalizing behavior, and family sexuality. See Table 5. Only 18% of the variance could be accounted for with both of these equations, suggesting that we know very little about what accounts for this behavior. In fact, sexual abuse accounted for only 1% of the variance. The results from Tables 4 and 5 suggest that intrusive sexual behavior is related to children who are behaviorally reactive and aggressive, are younger than average, and have grown up in more stressful and sexualized family environments. While sexual abuse is related to sexually intrusive behavior, it is not the most important predictor of this type of behavior.

Of the variables listed in Table 4, the one most likely to be related to

Table 5. *Correlates of Sexually Intrusive Behavior*

Dependent Variable   **Sexually Intrusive Behavior (with Sexual Abuse Status Added to the Equation)**

Independent Variable	R2	Beta	r
1. PTSD	.09	.16	.33
2. Life Events	.14	.12	.27
3. Age	.15	−.16	−.10
4. Sexual Abuse Status	**.17**	**.11**	**.25**
5. External	.18	.12	.31
6. Family Sexuality	.18	.08	.18

$F = 47.4$ $(6, 1274)$ $p < .00001$

Table 6. *Correlates of Sexually Intrusive Behavior*

Dependent Variable   **Sexually Intrusive Behavior**

Independent Variable	R2	Beta	r
1. Witness parental sex	.06	.23	.27
2. Pornography in home	.07	.06	.08
3. Observe sex on TV/movie	.07	.06	.12
4. Bathing with parent	.07	.05	.04

$F = 48.9$ $(4, 2439)$ $p < .00001$

a pessimistic outcome is externalizing behavior from the CBCL. My contention is derived from research suggesting that childhood-onset conduct problems are more likely to persist over the course of the lifetime (Moffitt, 1993). However, externalizing behavior accounted for only 1–2% of the variance in the analyses listed in Tables 4 and 5.

When similar analyses were conducted using individual family sexuality behaviors, sexual intrusiveness was significantly related to witnessing parental intercourse, the presence of pornography in the home, witnessing sex on TV/movie, and showering or bathing with an adult. The first three of these items suggest a more overt family sexuality factor, and in fact the first variable, witnessing parental intercourse, has a correlation of .27. The size of the correlation with co-bathing is quite small, and an examination of Table 6 suggests that the magnitude of the relationships between sexually intrusive behavior and family sexuality is typically small.

Summary

In summary, sexual behavior in children can be validly studied with parent report. Research clearly indicates that children are sexual beings, and will exhibit a broad range of sexual behaviors in the absence of sexual abuse. The results can inform us of the developmental course of sexual behavior as well as familial correlates of this behavior. Research that identified a significant relationship between elevated sexual behavior and sexual abuse in children has overshadowed the fact that sexual behavior in children is typically nonpathologic, follows a developmental course, and can be quite varied. Sexually intrusive behavior in children is more typically seen in young, hyperaroused children who tend to act out rather than act in, and who live in families that have more relaxed sexual beliefs and practices. Children's sexuality continues to be a relatively uncharted terrain and further research is needed.

References

Achenbach, T. M. (1991). *Manual for the Child Behavior Checklist/4–18 and the 1991 profile*. Burlington: University of Vermont, Department of Psychiatry.

Friedrich, W. N. (1993). Sexual behavior in sexually abused children. *Violence Update, 3*(5), 1, 7–11.

Friedrich, W. N. (1997). *Child Sexual Behavior Inventory: Professional manual.* Odessa, FL: Psychological Assessment Resources.

Friedrich, W. N., Beilke, R. L., & Urquiza, A. J. (1987). Children from sexually abusive families: A behavioral comparison. *Journal of Interpersonal Violence, 2,* 391–402.

Friedrich, W. N., Beilke, R. L., & Urquiza, A. J. (1988). Behavior problems in young sexually abused boys: A comparison study. *Journal of Interpersonal Violence, 3,* 21–28.

Friedrich, W. N., Fisher, J., Broughton, D., Houston, M., & Shafran, C. R. (1998). Normative sexual behavior in children: A contemporary sample. *Pediatrics, 101*(4), e9.

Friedrich, W. N., Fisher, J., Dittner, C. A., Acton, R., Berliner, L., Butler, J., et al. (2001). Child Sexual Behavior Inventory: Normative, psychiatric, and sexual abuse comparisons. *Child Maltreatment, 6,* 37–49.

Friedrich, W. N., Grambsch, P., Broughton, D., Kuiper, J., & Beilke, R. L. (1991). Normative sexual behavior in children. *Pediatrics, 88,* 456–464.

Friedrich, W. N., Grambsch, P., Damon, L., Hewitt, S. K., Koverola, C., Lang, R. A., et al. (1992). Child Sexual Behavior Inventory: Normative and clinical comparisons. *Psychological Assessment, 4,* 303–311.

Friedrich, W. N., Sandfort, T. G. M., Oostveen, J., & Cohen-Kettenis, P. T. (2000).

Cultural differences in sexual behavior: 2–6-year-old Dutch and American children. *Journal of Psychology and Human Sexuality, 12*(1–2), 117–129.

Friedrich, W. N., Trane, S., Lengua, L., Fisher, J., & Davies, H. (in press). Development of PTSD and dissociation subscales for the Child Behavior Checklist. *Journal of Traumatic Stress Studies.*

Friedrich, W. N., Urquiza, A. J., & Beilke, R. L. (1986). Behavior problems in sexually abused young children. *Journal of Pediatric Psychology, 11*, 47–57.

Larsson, I., & Svedin, C. G. (2002). Teachers' and parents' reports on 3- to 6-year-old children's sexual behavior: A comparison. *Child Abuse & Neglect, 26*, 247–266.

Larsson, I., Svedin, C. G., & Friedrich, W. N. (2000). Differences and similarities in sexual behavior among preschoolers in Sweden and USA. *Nordic Journal of Psychiatry, 54*, 251–257.

Meyer-Bahlburg, H. F. L., Dolezal, C., & Sandberg, D. E. (2000). The association of sexual behavior with externalizing behaviors in a community sample of prepubertal children. *Journal of Psychology and Human Sexuality, 12*(1–2), 61–79.

Moffitt, T. E. (1993). Adolescent-limited and life-course-persistent antisocial behavior: A developmental taxonomy. *Psychological Review, 100*, 674–701.

Purcell, J., Beilke, R. L., & Friedrich, W. N. (1986, August). *The Child Sexual Behavior Inventory: Preliminary normative data.* Paper presented at the 94th annual convention of the American Psychological Association, Washington, DC.

Schoentjes, E., Deboutte, D., & Friedrich, W. (1999). Child Sexual Behavior Inventory: A Dutch-speaking normative sample. *Pediatrics, 104*, 885–893.

Trane, S. & Friedrich, W. N. (2002). *Dimensions of sexual behavior in children: A factor analytic study.* Manuscript in preparation.

Body Awareness and Physical Intimacy

An Exploratory Study

JANY RADEMAKERS, M. J. C. LAAN, AND
CORNELIS J. STRAVER

Introduction

To date, little scientific research has been carried out on the sexual development and the sexual behavior of children under the age of 12 (Constantine & Martinson, 1981; Sandfort, 1989; Sandfort & Rademakers, 2000; van der Zanden, 1992). The lack of theory, methodological knowledge, and empirical data in the area of normal child sexuality is regrettable for several reasons:

1. Criteria about what behavior is to be considered within the normal (age/gender/population-appropriate) range with respect to child sexuality and development are virtually absent. Early intervention with respect to a problematic or dysfunctional sexual development process, which might result in the prevention of adolescent or adult sexual dysfunction, is therefore extremely difficult.
2. Since child sexual abuse has become an important and major topic in policy, research, and counseling, negative aspects of child sexuality and possible harmful outcomes of sexual contact in childhood are emphasized, while neutral or even positive experiences and children's need for and interest in intimate physical contact are ignored. Moreover, much is still unknown about how children's sexual experiences are integrated into their sexual development process, what factors contribute to negative outcomes and what factors protect against them.
3. Since children are confronted with images of sexuality in the media and society at large, it is important to give them a frame of reference, a context to put these scattered and widely varying pieces of information into perspective. More research could inform the design and conduct of sex education programs for (young) children and provide guidance for parents and professionals working with children on how to deal with sexual issues. At present, research-based guidelines in the area of sex education for children hardly exist.

Most studies that do address childhood sexuality use observational or retrospective methods of research. Obviously, these methods have some serious limitations. One of them is that through observation or retrospection, it is impossible to gain insight into the meaning specific behaviors have for children at that moment and the emotions which are attached to them at the time.

But addressing children directly is very difficult as well. Young children don't have the verbal capacities to express themselves on more personal and complicated issues, and until age 7 or 8, boys and girls are not able to reflect on topics at a more abstract level. New instruments have to be developed, and questions about the validity and reliability of these instruments have to be faced.

For this reason, a small-size exploratory study on body awareness and experiences with physical intimacy from children's own perspectives was conducted. The aims of this study were

1. To gain more insight into the way children experience their own body, their experiences with and appreciation of (non-intimate and intimate) physical contact with peers and parents, and their experiences with one specific aspect of intimacy, e.g., being in love;
2. To generate more knowledge about methodological aspects of sex research with children. More specifically, the feasibility and usefulness of the research method used in this study were evaluated.

Study Design and Methods

In a qualitative study design, 15 girls and 16 boys were interviewed about body awareness and their experiences with physical intimacy. Because the children had to master verbal and reflexive skills to a certain degree and the developmental differences within the sample shouldn't be too large, the decision was made to select only children of 8 and 9 years of age. The children were contacted in the context of a routine school medical examination.

In a semistructured interview situation, a female interviewer talked with the children about romping (as a non-intimate form of physical contact), cuddling, and being in love. Furthermore, the children were invited to mark on drawings of a same-sex naked child's body which parts they considered pleasant and which parts they found exciting. The children were also asked to tell stories on the basis of four drawings which portrayed scenes such as playing doctor or having a bath with an adult, and they were asked about their own experiences in this respect. All parts of the research instrument were pretested in this age group. On average, the interviews took about 20 minutes. The data were analyzed qualitatively. After a preliminary coding of the material, categories were made per theme on the basis of the content of the answers. The number of children whose answers fitted in these categories was counted.

Data were also collected from the parents of the children. This part of the study was intended to determine whether parents know how their child experiences and appreciates intimate physical contact. During the period the child was interviewed, 30 parents (26 mothers and 4 fathers) filled out a structured questionnaire. (This study has also been described in Rademakers, Laan, & Straver, 2000.)

Results

Half of the children (eight girls, seven boys) described romping as pretend-fighting, something that involves the whole of the body and that was seen as positive. One-third (five girls, four boys) saw it as real fighting. They mentioned specific physically aggressive behavior, such as kicking, hitting, and biting. The other children (one girl, four boys) saw romping variously as pretend and real. Half of the children reported romping with their parents, while brothers and sisters, grandparents, and peers were also mentioned. Of the parents, almost all answered that they or their partner romped with the child.

Cuddling was described by almost all children (15 girls, 15 boys) in terms of hugging, kissing, and sitting on someone's lap. One boy didn't know what cuddling was and, after having heard an explanation by the interviewer, stated that he had never done it. Almost all of them regarded cuddling as something positive, either because of the bodily sensations or because of the feeling of safety it gives them. They expressed their feelings regarding cuddling as safe, nice, soft, cheerful, fun, kind, and comforting.

Many more children than parents said that children have a definite need for cuddling. Yet while all parents reported cuddling with their child, one in five children gave the impression this never happened. Half of the children (15) cuddled with both humans and cuddly toys, dolls, or stuffed animals. One-third (9) only cuddled with people. Generally, these people were close relatives such as brothers and sisters and grandparents; one child mentioned peers. Five children stated they only cuddled with toys, dolls, or stuffed animals, and never with people.

Questions about being in love were likely to elicit some tension, which was evident in nonverbal signs (giggling, sighing, voice changes). Being in love was sometimes described in terms of feelings (more often by girls) and sometimes concretely and factually (more often by boys). One boy was not able to give a definition of "being in love."

More than half of these 8- and 9-year-old children (18) said they were in love at the moment or had been in love before. One girl reported being in love with another girl; the others were in love with someone of the opposite sex. Most of the children who had experience with being in love also had fantasies about the person with whom they were in love. Parents were more inclined to believe that their children had been in love than the children's own reports suggested.

Most children (23) reported being in love to be a positive experience. They mentioned that it's good, fun, and nice, it's a tickling sensation, and it makes you feel proud. Three children thought it was negative—they didn't have any experience with it and they were not interested in it either. The other children had no opinion in this respect.

Though being in love is generally regarded as a positive experience, most children (22) wouldn't tell anyone when they're in love, because they feared (or had experienced) other children and adults teasing them.

The children were asked to mark on a drawing of a same-sex naked child's body (front and rear) which parts they considered to be pleasant and which they considered exciting, without further definition. While all children were able to indicate pleasant parts, fewer children (25) were able to mark exciting parts. Head and shoulders were indicated most in both categories, whereas arms and legs, belly and back, and chest were in the middle position. Genitals, bottom, and anus were least indicated, either as pleasant or as exciting. There was also no difference in the indications of boys and girls. A lot of the parents could not anticipate the answers of their son or daughter on this task: One-third (11) were unable to name pleasant body parts and half (14) could not name exciting parts.

Combining the answers of the children on several questions, the children appeared to fall into three categories. The largest of these (seven girls, nine boys) had a positive attitude toward intimate physical contact, but were relatively uninterested in the idea of being in love. Most of them didn't have any experience in this respect. Another group (six girls, five boys) displayed a positive attitude toward physical intimacy and were actively involved in the domain of love. They had been in love once or more and they appeared to be much more self-conscious about their own behavior, experiences, feelings, and motives. The smallest group (two girls, two boys) gave indications of wanting to avoid discussion of the topics at issue.

In general, parents reported more occurrences of physical contact between them and their child than the children did. This was described for romping and cuddling. A question about whether the parent and the child bathed or showered together produced highly conflicting answers: While almost two-thirds of the parents said they did, three-quarters of the children denied that it happened.

Feasibility and Usefulness of the Research Method

An important purpose of this research project was to test the research method with regard to its feasibility and usefulness with young children. Designing this study revealed once again just how little methodological knowledge there is in this area.

In this study it proved to be possible to obtain information directly from relatively young children on sensitive topics. However, questions with respect to the validity of the data have to be acknowledged. Children might interpret questions differently than adults, which may partly account for the discrepancies of the answers of children and their parents. Because of the sensitivity of the subject, children may have experienced feelings of reservation or shame in answering the questions. But validity problems and effects of social desirability are not specific for research with children —they are intrinsic to all social and sexological research.

The qualitative method used in this study seems quite appropriate, especially when the child's motives, thoughts, and feelings are the subject under study. But unlike interview material from studies with adults, the children's answers are brief, and the information they give is fragmented and has little depth. Therefore, the possibilities for content analysis are limited.

With respect to the phrasing of questions and the choice of topics discussed, it seems important to stay close to children's own level of experience. Since 8- and 9-year-old children enter the phase of concrete operational thinking, they can more easily answer questions which relate to concrete experiences than they can elaborate on more abstract questions. Some of these children, however, were already quite capable of reflecting on certain situations and the roles of themselves and others in those situations.

The combination of activities (being interviewed, drawing, talking about pictures) helped the children to concentrate. However, around 20 minutes really seemed the maximum time the children could stay focused in the interview.

References

Constantine, L., & Martinson, F. (1981). *Children and sex: New findings, new perspectives.* Boston: Little, Brown.

Rademakers, J., Laan, M., & Straver, C. (2000). Studying children's sexuality from the child's perspective. *Journal of Psychology and Human Sexuality, 12*(1–2), 49–60.

Sandfort, T. (1989). *Seksuele ervaringen van kinderen: Betekenis en effecten voor later.* Deventer, the Netherlands: Van Loghum Slaterus.

Sandfort, T., & Rademakers, J. (Eds.). (2000). *Childhood sexuality: Normal sexual behavior and development.* New York: Haworth.

van der Zanden, I. (1992). Sexueel gedrag van kinderen: Een literatuuroverzicht. *Tijdschrift voor ontwikkelingspsychologie, 19,* 133–153.

Discussion Paper

ANKE A. EHRHARDT

This conference has been coming for a long time. We have talked over the years about getting together to discuss children's sexuality and I'm very pleased that it has finally happened. And by children's sexuality I mean prepubertal children up to about age 12 rather than adolescents. I do think that it is very important that we stay on target in dealing with the issue of normal childhood sexuality. We could easily get lost in strictly methodological issues or in child abuse and not come at the end to a consensus on what we think is the normal expression of sexuality in childhood. It was good to start with these very good papers on methodology to warm us up. But now we have these two papers by Bill Friedrich and by Jany Rademakers which bring us right to the core of the issue. In other areas we have no problem dealing with normality. When you think of gender-related behavior, we certainly have no doubt about what is normal. We could be considering the range of normal behavior or alternatively what Bill Friedrich describes as behavior expression that doesn't have any consequences or implication for long-term development. Right now, and particularly in this country, we are looking at childhood sexuality without any standards. We have somehow lost sight of the ranges of normalcy.

Philip Jenkins reminded us that it is very good to go to the literature beyond the last 15 years. I was doing so recently, and went back to some summaries we wrote of normal childhood sexual behavior. Heino Meyer-Bahlburg had almost forgotten what he and I wrote 25 years ago. It's an old dusty reprint which I had him dig out where he summarized at that time the Kinsey data. There were two sources of Kinsey data, recall data from adolescents and actual reports by prepubertal children. In the discussion of that paper, I focused on what we actually know about gender differences in sexual behavior; are girls expressing their sexual behavior differently than boys? Of course we are very far from having those kinds of normative data. But in looking at those Kinsey tables we learnt that girls and boys clearly reported a high incidence of sociosexual behavior; about half of girls and more than half of boys talked about such behavior. There were significant numbers reporting same-sex behavior—33% girls, 48% boys. And there were descriptions in detail of some of the techniques of heterosexual play. Another piece for rereading is Michael Rutter's superb summary of normal psychosexual development published first in 1971 and then reedited in 1982. He goes back to the 1920s to review what kind of data there was, from different kinds of samples, about the expression of kids' sexuality. This was not restricted to coital behavior but the much broader range of sexual interest. Rutter, already in 1971, was challenging the whole notion of the latency period, the idea that children stop being interested in sexuality in middle childhood, between ages 5 and 10. He regarded this as a misconception of Freud and of psychoanalytic theory. He concluded from all the evidence that we have that there's an increasing interest into adolescence about each other's bodies, and about sexual expression of varying kinds. Over the last several years I have quoted that to residents, because the "latency period" concept had taken such hold in psychiatry. Everybody believed that as of 5 and 6 kids become asexual. The other very important point which Rutter makes is that sexual behavior is a learned behavior; we're not born as fully functioning sexual beings. I was thinking of Friedrich's point about the correlation to family sexuality. Rutter doesn't exactly make that point, but it occurred to me, since parents ask us about what is normative in this country much more than in northern Europe. There's really a profound insecurity for educators and for parents, about what is normal, what should parents do? Should we encourage parents to allow co-bathing or the occasional nudity? Where are children actually going to learn about physiology, about male and female bodies, etc.? Or are we seeing it as one of the criteria for abnormal sexual expression? It's really something for us to think about. Rutter, in the same article (and I have not found anybody else in a long time raising this in terms of adolescent sexuality) quotes Schofield's study of the '50s and '60s (Schofield, 1965) and states that it is very important to ask, when adolescents are not sexual, what happens to their sexuality in adulthood? The follow-up studies of Schofield show that in the '50s and '60s in England, those who didn't have any sexual experience as adolescents actually found it more difficult in their 30s to become sexual, to have sexual well-being and to be free from sexual problems. So to think about the angle we are taking here, when there is a tendency to see it all so much from the pathological and abuse angle, we should make sure that we are anchoring our approach correctly. Jany's last point is that it is maybe not as important to know the average level or normal ranges of expressions of behavior as it is to see it within the development context.

I wasn't surprised that in Jany's sample the kids were just as interested in having good feelings about their shoulders and about other parts of their bodies as about the genitals, or even more. Children explore their bodies and that is how we approach the incident or the anecdote about the young child kissing the genitals of the baby sister. That's what kids do before they become sexually much more directed in early adolescence.

So what do we know about normal sexual behavior? We do know that physiological responses in terms of erection and in terms of pleasure are there very early on in both boys and girls. Even that is not a given anymore; at Gil Herdt's conference in San Francisco two years ago, which John Bancroft and I attended, a biologist stood up and attacked Kinsey because, she said, "we all know that boys can't have erections before puberty." So any child who showed such responses was obviously an abused child. So we are really in a very strange no-man's-land here. The same, of course, is true for masturbation, and we have a long history, in this country and elsewhere, of how we regard masturbation. It's not that long ago that there were all kinds of medical interventions to prevent masturbation.

Clinically, I certainly get asked by parents, "What is normal?" Parents are at a loss about that. They sometimes give funny messages to kids; e.g., "you only do it in the bathroom" or "you do it in the dark" or "it's okay, but it is private and you shouldn't talk about it." I don't hear those messages so often, but parents are still very much at a loss how to deal with it. Bill Friedrich, you came from an "abuse perspective" and ended up— almost like a surprise journey—with lots of the behaviors that you anticipated were indications of abuse being endorsed by many parents. Jany Rademakers, you come from a different perspective, already thinking that childhood sexuality is something normal, and therefore you just looked at what was expressed. Both of you reached the conclusion, which I'm sure many here would endorse, that childhood sexuality by itself is not pathological, that there are developmental patterns and that there is great diversity. There is a range of expression of sexual behavior in childhood, as there is in adolescence and adulthood. The methodologies, I thought, were very interesting, both of them dealing with the parents and then also the more difficult issue of how to elicit data in that broad sexual sense from children. I found Jany's approach to be very developmentally anchored—to elicit from children by drawing, by activity, by asking about meaning, and by staying with the child. This is a very good approach for us to think about. The relationship between cuddling and sexuality makes a lot of sense developmentally. Obviously, cuddling is very important for most children, something which feels good and which they relate to pleasure. That is intuitively understandable. Why kids get embarrassed and feel ashamed when they begin to talk about falling in love is an interesting question. Whether that is a message that this is something which is forbidden—that may not be the only explanation. An alternative explanation is that it's just something private; that when falling in love, being infatuated and preoccupied with another person becomes something you don't want to share with anybody and that already starts in childhood. I have also seen in children the kind of infatuation patterns that are very similar to later in the life course. So falling in love is an interesting phenomenon.

So what do we need to know? Developmental mapping of childhood sexual behavior by gender and by different background factors and by cultural norms; to have a repertoire of good methodologies to approach children's sexual expression, both child-centered and parent-sampled, and maybe teacher-sampled or other informant–sampled, would be very important. Since behavior is so diverse and we know so little, we should be cautious in attributing pathology to sexual expression in children before we know more. I would suggest that if we get a good consensus document from this conference, it should go beyond consensus. We should perhaps end up, on the basis of the consensus, highlighting some research priorities.

References

Rutter, M. (1971). Normal psychosexual development. *Journal of Psychological Psychiatry, 11,* 259–283.

Rutter, M. (1982). Psychosexual development. In M. Rutter (Ed.), *Scientific foundations of developmental psychiatry* (pp. 322–338). London: Heinemann.

Schofield, M. (1965). *The sexual behaviour of young people.* London: Longman.

General Discussion

Jany Rademakers: When you were talking about the uncertainty of the parents in the United States, we see some of that uncertainty as well in the Netherlands, but not so widespread. Because parents in the U.S. are very much aware of the topic and of the concern about sexual abuse, they might more quickly label certain behaviors of their child as sexual. Therefore the free exploring space which children normally have would be restricted because parents are looking over their shoulder much more at what they are doing than in the Netherlands. In the Netherlands they are more laid back, they don't get so excited over such things. But that contradicts the cross-cultural findings of Bill Friedrich and Theo Sandfort and Peggy Cohen-Kettenis, who found that the Dutch parents reported more sexual behavior in their children. So an alternative explanation is that American parents are more afraid of it and they just turn away and don't look, so it doesn't happen.

David Finkelhor: The issue of what is "normal sexual behavior" among children most frequently comes up when a parent approaches a professional or a doctor, and in the same way that they would ask the question, "My child has a rash, is that something to be worried about?" It is actually a question not so much about normal behavior as it is about pathological behavior, and it seems to me that there are two classes of behavior that we ought to be clearly distinguishing. One is behavior that is clearly part of a normal range but that may be an indicator of some kind of problem; behaviors that are statistically much more or relatively more frequent among problem groups. The other is behavior that almost always indicates some kind of abnormality. What are the criteria that we should use for distinguishing between these two categories of behavior? For example, are there things like engaging in penetrative sexual activities with another child prior to age 6 which we can say are always indicative of a problem? I don't think we know that.

Anke Ehrhardt: Children do engage in exploratory play behavior and it is not necessarily indicative of a problem.

David Finkelhor: So you're saying there's nothing that we can put in that most extreme category, but there may be some things that we can put in the risk category. What would they be?

Anke Ehrhardt: I can give you one example about which I am periodically consulted: so-called excessive masturbation. You might think that doesn't exist but it does exist. I saw a child years ago in Buffalo, a little girl who was masturbating everywhere, in the waiting room, waiting for me, anywhere, in a kind of compulsive way. Parents in the U.S. typically see that as something sinful, terrible, an indication of serious behavior pathology. I saw ten families like that over time, always with little girls. I advised the parents (who were often foster parents) not to be punitive, but to use a very simple behavioral approach; whenever your child does this just take her on your lap and hold her and cuddle her. For the most part, if they followed the recommendations, the masturbation disappeared. If we had more systematic studies of sexual behavior problems like that where rather than being punitive parents and other adults would do something that is more developmentally appropriate, it might help us to understand what abnormal behavior like that may mean.

David Finkelhor: One of the things that is interesting about the example you give is that it suggests that one of the criteria that we use for deciding what is abnormal or risky childhood sexual behavior is not necessarily evidence that it's associated with pathology but that it is disturbing to other people.

Anke Ehrhardt: And it may be disturbing to the child also.

David Finkelhor: If the professional working with the child says that that kind of behavior is going to be disturbing to other kids or disturbing to other adults who work with the kids, and that's going to end up with that child having some stigma as a result, then they might decide that that is a problem. I don't know if that's an appropriate criterion for applying the term "abnormal." It might be entirely appropriate even though it may not be indicative of any pathological process in the child.

John Bancroft: This is an issue of boundaries that you've raised and the question of whether behavior is appropriately done in front of other people and when it's appropriate to be done privately. This is something that children have to learn about and they learn very quickly that this is taboo behavior. I wanted to ask Bill whether his parent questionnaire actually gave him evidence of behaviors which children have learned to keep secret because they learn the taboos. We see other problems, developmental or learning problems with young people who show inappropriate behavior in their teens because they have a problem learning appropriate behavior. So there's a question of whether you would expect this child at this developmental stage, and in this context, to have learned appropriate ways of dealing with their sexuality, and whether it is appropriate seems to be one of the yardsticks that we're looking for.

Julia Heiman: I wonder if there could be a label developed for something called "sexual manners," the sort of etiquette adopted by current cultures, that changes over time, about what one expects to be done in public versus in private. We have all sorts of behaviors that are both social and personal and which in some ways are also pleasant. You can have the capacity for pleasure in both sexual and eating behaviors, some you do in private and some you do in public. Maybe there need to be more categories than just normal and abnormal.

Ken Zucker: Just amplifying that from a developmental perspective: If you believe that parents actually socialize their children and what parents or others do matters, which is debatable, sexual socialization is how I would describe what you're referring to as sexual manners. It is interesting that almost no children masturbate in public and almost no adults masturbate in public. How does that come about? In some respects sexuality is probably one of the most private behavioral acts that people engage in and the precursors obviously start with these kinds of limits in childhood. The problem in our culture is that sexual socialization is so undefined; there are no clear guidelines as to what to do. In ritualized cultures, such as Papua New Guinea, it seems that it's very clear what to do. But in our society there are just so many views on how to socialize sexuality, which is why we're so hesitant to make prescriptions.

Elsie Pinkston: One of the things that strikes me is how very difficult it is to stay on the topic of normal sexual behavior. It immediately goes to pathology, and if that happens in this group then you certainly have to think about what happens in the broader culture. One of the problems is normally we think of parents as socializing their children, but now, as we have different kinds of caregivers, there are other people who are the agents for socializing children and we only hear about it when someone objects to the way that's being done, often the parent. But since such a large proportion of the children who are being labeled as pathological are in the care of public agencies, one of the things that we might ask ourselves is how important is access to privacy? We have a whole population of children who are deprived of privacy. After you've been through seven or eight foster homes, you really haven't had much privacy. You've had many people express an opinion about your behavior, and many opportunities to learn a variety of behaviors that you might not have learned in a single family. So I hope we will take Anke Ehrhardt's advice and continue to look for normal sexuality with a very broad brush. If you've got holes and you have fingers you're going to explore them. So once a child has received a pathological label then there are a lot of people who believe that that behavioral problem cannot be cured because it's a disease rather than a temporary social malfunction. So I hope that we can emphasize the caution that should be exercised by the outside world in making pathological interpretations of the data that are provided about such children.

Meredith Reynolds: I want to comment about Jany Rademakers's observation. It is reasonable to consider these children being in different phases of development; you had the earliest development group showing a positive attitude, and the next group showing a positive attitude and active exploration, and so on. But I am often struck by individual differences in sexuality at the adult level and I just want to raise the possibility that individual differences in sexuality might be evident in all phases of the life-cycle. So you may have very different types of children, with different developmental patterns, who will vary in how they respond to environmental input.

Jany Rademakers: It's true that you have a very large individual variability in adulthood and in adolescence as well. But adolescents usually don't start with having sexual intercourse; they start with body explorations on another level. So there is some kind of hierarchy of behaviors or development. What we try to do is acknowledge the diversity but nevertheless look for a kind of development model which should fit across the diversity.

Anke Ehrhardt: Elsie Pinkston commented that we only really hear about it when somebody asks, is there a problem. I don't think we should be going down that road. There are other reasons to know about normal sexual development in children. It's not just when it becomes a problem, when the pediatrician gets asked or when the counselor gets asked. It's a much broader issue with day care providers, teachers wanting to know what are the correct responses, what is normal, what are the boundaries? "Normal" has, as I mentioned before, to be seen from different levels, not what is the most frequent but what are the kinds of behaviors which are expressed by children without raising concern or without raising the issue of pathology. It's important to map the whole spectrum.

Janet Hyde: Bill, with your descriptions of sexually intrusive behaviors and maybe also sexually intrusive children, are these maybe ADHD kids who are just really active and they're doing too much of everything including sex? If that is the case, then it is not a specifically sexual issue and because of the kinds of children they are, they also lack inhibitory control and so they haven't learned how to inhibit the way other kids their age have.

Bill Friedrich: That's a really good point. When I was trying to figure out what the PTSD meant, I first thought it might be like a summary variable for sexual abuse but it didn't turn out to be that way. This conference has been good because it has gotten me away from clinical practice and I was thinking after I had presented that the next thing I'm going to do when I get back home is pull out the ADHD items from the CBCL and assess the degree to which they are related. When I was trying to explain what the PTSD meant, it wasn't necessarily so much PTSD as lack of restraint, things of that sort, which would be consistent with impulsive, in-attentive kids.

The Nature of Childhood Sexual Experiences

Two Studies 50 Years Apart

MEREDITH A. REYNOLDS, DEBRA L.
HERBENICK, AND JOHN BANCROFT

Introduction

Over the past 15 years, we have seen escalating concern about childhood sexual abuse, an increase in its reporting, an increasing tendency to see any sexual expression in children as evidence that sexual abuse has already occurred, and a growing campaign to teach children to avoid anything which could be construed as sexual. In the process, there is active and widespread denial that "normal" childhood sexual expression exists. In recent years, research into childhood sexuality has been largely confined to delineating the negative sequelae of sexual abuse, with few studies focused on normative childhood sexuality and basic, healthy sexual development. Without a more complete picture of normal childhood sexual behaviors and development, not only will parents and teachers be at a disadvantage when dealing with "normal" children, interpretation of the abuse literature will be hazardous. If this imbalance is to be redressed, it will be necessary to study childhood sexuality in its own right.

Both direct studies of children and those utilizing parent reports of children's behavior are reviewed elsewhere in this volume (Friedrich, 2003; Meyer-Bahlburg & Steel, 2003; O'Sullivan, 2003; Rademakers, Laan, & Straver, 2003). Most studies have relied on retrospective recall by adults of their own childhood. Green (1985) reported the frequency of these experiences while Leitenberg, Greenwald, and Tarran (1989) assessed features of the most "advanced" episode and Finkelhor (1980) focused on experiences with siblings. Haugaard and Tilly (1988) studied the characteristics of sexual play experiences and concluded that subjects' reactions to those events were driven by features of the experience, such as coercion, the relationship between participants, and the gender of those involved, rather than the type of sexual behavior itself. Lamb and Coakley (1993) and Kilpatrick (1992) studied the childhood experiences of women. In some studies, childhood experiences have not been distinguished from those of adolescence (Bauserman & Davis, 1996; Kilpatrick, 1992; Leitenberg et al., 1989), making it difficult to determine experiences specific to childhood.

Estimates of the prevalence of childhood sexual experiences with peers (CSEP) range from 39% to 85%, depending on several factors: how "childhood" is defined (e.g., prior to age 6, prior to age 13, inclusive of adolescence), the method of assessment (parental reports vs. adult retrospective recall), and the type of memory elicited by researchers (e.g., a "sexual game," "most meaningful" experience). Few studies have also considered the development of psychological aspects of sexuality, such as onset of sexual fantasy and first experience of sexual attraction.

Despite differences in methodology, it is notable that study results generally support the idea that non–sexually abused children engage in a range of overt sexual behaviors while very young which become increasingly covert as the child ages (perhaps around age 4 or 5) and becomes aware of cultural norms and taboos. Also, advanced sexual behaviors such as oral-genital contact and anal or vaginal insertion of objects/fingers— while uncommon—do constitute a part of some non–sexually abused children's sexual experiences.

That sexual play often occurs in secret makes these experiences particularly challenging to study. Parent reports and naturalistic observations will be atypical. Longitudinal prospective studies of children are not only difficult to execute but also raise concerns regarding potential effects on children's sexual development and behavior. Once children are old enough to be aware of the associated taboos, they may be reluctant to report them even to sensitive researchers (see O'Sullivan, 2003). Although the use of retrospective accounts by adults of their own childhood presents a number of potential problems, including recall, reporting and volunteer biases, and the impact of current attitudes about childhood sexuality, it is at present the most reasonable method for studying childhood sexual experiences, particularly those that occur during the developmental phase when secrecy prevails, and their relation to adult sexuality.

In both study A and study B, reported in this paper, we used young adults (aged 18–22), so that the length of time from childhood was relatively short, yet they were old enough to be able to report childhood experiences without undue embarrassment. In addition, this allowed us to relate childhood sexual experiences to sexual development during adolescence and early adulthood.

Study A: 1998–99

This study focused on recall by adults exploring in detail specific sexually relevant events that occurred in different periods of childhood, including the individual's subjective experience of these events. All questions pertaining to childhood experiences with peers and autoerotic experiences during childhood were asked prior to inquiring about childhood sexual experiences with adults. Subjects were presented with an extensive series of warm-up questions about childhood experiences in general to get them into the mindset of that time period prior to asking about any experiences that might be construed as sexual in nature.

Method and Sample

Study A was carried out at The Kinsey Institute with data collected during 1998–99. Undergraduate students of Indiana University were sampled in a two-stage process in order to assess the extent and nature of participation bias.

Stage 1 involved random selection of 1,869 students, aged 18–22, from the registrar's list (838 females and 1,031 males), who were mailed a set of questionnaires purporting to assess demographic and personality characteristics of college students. Nine hundred fifty-three students (496 females and 457 males) returned completed questionnaires, for a response rate of 51% (59% for females and 44% for males). A "permission to be contacted for future research" form was returned by 684 (352 females and 332 males); 553 of these who were still available were invited to participate in Stage 2. The final sample for Study A consisted of 154 females and 149 males. The response rate was 55% (55% for females and 54% for males). Details of the Stage 1 survey and participation bias in Stage 2 are to be reported elsewhere. However, there were no major differences with respect to personality and demographic characteristics between the non-participants and participants in Stage 2.

All information was obtained by means of computer-assisted self-interview (CASI). Details of the CASI interviews are given in Reynolds and Herbenick (2003), together with a list of the items covered. For items related to puberty, age at puberty was taken as age at menarche for females, and age at first ejaculation for males.

Results

CHILDHOOD SEXUAL EXPERIENCES WITH PEERS

Childhood sexual experiences with peers (CSEP) were asked about separately for each of the following time periods: pre-elementary school, elementary school, and junior high (prior to starting high school). Table A1 shows the percentage of males and females reporting CSEP, by type of behavior reported. Overall, 87.2% of males and 84.4% of females reported having sexual experiences with peers prior to starting high school. More males than females reported having engaged in some kind of experience for all three time periods, although these differences were not significant. However, during the junior high period, more males reported CSEP that involved direct genital contact (43.6% vs. 27.3%, $\chi^2 = 8.9$, $p < .01$). Experiences with peers involving the most advanced behaviors were extremely rare in the pre-elementary period, but increased in prevalence over time.

Table A1. *Proportion of Subjects Who Reported Engaging in Childhood Sexual Experiences with Peers (CSEP) by Sex, Time Period, and Type of Behavior Reported*

	Time Period							
	Pre-elementary		Elementary		Jr. High		Total	
	F	M	F	M	F	M	F	M
	%	%	%	%	%	%	%	%
No genital contact	14.9	23.5	53.2	61.1	53.2	60.4	79.9	83.9
Genital contact	5.2	12.8*	29.2	32.9	27.3	43.6**	47.4	57.7
Insertion/ oral-genital/ intercourse	1.3	4.0	12.3	10.1	17.5	24.2	26.0	32.2
Any CSEP	15.6	24.2	58.4	63.8	57.1	63.1	84.4	87.2

N=154 for females, N=149 for males
* = $p<.05$, ** = $p<.001$ for sex difference comparison within same time period χ^2

Prior to high school, 9% of females and 16% of males had engaged in oral-genital contact; 3% of females and 4% of males had engaged in anal insertion (with object or finger); 18% of females and 22% of males reported vaginal insertion (with object or finger); and 2% of females and 5% of males reported penile-vaginal intercourse. Not surprisingly, subjects reported having more CSEP in the later time periods.

Although overall the majority did not have more than five experiences, 20% reported engaging in CSEP 11–50 times. There was no sex difference in the overall number of CSEP that subjects engaged in prior to starting high school. When asked to compare their own experiences to those of the "average child," 13% stated they thought they probably had more CSEP than other children, while 48% said they had less and 39% thought they had a comparable number of experiences.

Because of the small sample size, it is difficult to look at the continuity of CSEP across the three time periods. However, the data suggest that there is continuity in these experiences for some subjects. For males, 69% of those who reported pre-elementary CSEP also reported experiences in elementary school. Among those who first engaged in these behaviors during the elementary school period, 70% reported having CSEP during junior high school. Results were similar for females.

Details of the most memorable CSEP that subjects reported for each time period are presented in Table A2. The majority of these experiences were dyadic, involving a friend of the opposite sex. Experiences with several peers were more likely to occur in junior high, while experiences with same-sex peers were more likely to occur during elementary school.

Table A2. *Characteristics of "Most Memorable" CSEP, by Time Period and by Gender*

	Pre-elementary		Elementary		Jr. High	
	F N = 24	M N = 36	F N = 90	M N = 95	F N = 88	M N = 94
Number of peers involved						
1	77%	79%	73%	65%	80%	77%
2	18%	15%	14%	24%	4%	9%
3	5%	3%	6%	7%	5%	7%
≥ 4	0	3%	7%	4%	11%	7%
Relation to peers						
Relatives (siblings/cousins)	26%	11%	23%	18%	14%	11%
Friends	78%	69%	82%	90%	92%	89%
Acquaintances	—	19%	5%	5%	8%	10%
Strangers	—	3%	—	—	—	—
Sex of peer(s)						
Same-sex only	26%	14%	38%	20%	10%	14%
Opposite-sex only	65%	78%	43%	64%	80%	69%
Mixed	9%	8%	19%	16%	10%	17%
Initiator of event						
Subject	—	20%	11%	20%	—	23%
Peer	56%	37%	49%	40%	53%	34%
Just happened	44%	43%	39%	40%	47%	43%
Subject participation						
Completely voluntary	58%	61%	58%	68%	67%	69%
Acquiescing	29%	33%	27%	24%	20%	22%
Pressured	13%	6%	14%	8%	9%	7%
Coerced	—	—	1%	—	4%	2%
Reasons for participating						
Curiosity	67%	61%	63%	73%	49%	66%
Thrill of the "forbidden"	21%	36%	41%	60%	36%	60%
Physical/sexual pleasure	8%	19%	19%	24%	48%	68%
To feel "grown-up"	17%	17%	18%	17%	41%	37%
To be accepted by peers	4%	6%	20%	13%	33%	30%
Didn't want to do it	13%	3%	8%	2%	5%	3%

Table A2. *Continued*

	Pre-elementary		Elementary		Jr. High	
	F	M	F	M	F	M
	N = 24	N = 36	N = 90	N = 95	N = 88	N = 94
Adult discovered CSEP	21%	31%	23%	25%	21%	10%
	(N=5)	(N=11)	(N=21)	(N=23)	(N=18)	(N=9)
Adult reaction(s)						
Ignored it	40% (2)	9% (1)	5%	22%	—	33%
Told never to do it again	40% (2)	45% (5)	38%	57%	17%	22%
Criticism/threats	—	18% (2)	14%	39%	6%	11%
Physical punishment	—	—	—	17%	—	11%
Laughed/thought it funny	20% (1)	27% (3)	33%	22%	22%	33%
Told to do only in private	—	—	5%	9%	17%	22%
Subject's experience						
("moderate" or "a lot")						
Happiness	33%	50%	41%	53%	62%	71%
Curiosity	64%	77%	60%	83%	57%	75%
Sexual pleasure	8%	9%	20%	30%	34%	57%
Excitement	38%	53%	46%	66%	66%	75%
Embarrassment	38%	12%	30%	18%	21%	16%
Shame/guilt	25%	27%	50%	14%	15%	20%
Fear/anxiety	21%	32%	37%	42%	35%	28%
Overall						
Very negative (1)	8%	11%	9%	—	7%	4%
(2)	8%	—	15%	13%	7%	6%
Mixed (3)	46%	54%	43%	40%	33%	29%
(4)	25%	23%	22%	28%	30%	31%
Very positive (5)	13%	12%	12%	19%	23%	30%

There were no sex differences in number of peers involved, sex of peer(s), or relation of peer(s), with the exception that during the pre–elementary school period, males were the only subjects to report having experiences with acquaintances (rather than friends or relatives; 19% vs. 0%, $\chi^2 = 5.3$, $p < .03$). A sex difference did emerge in the elementary school period with respect to the sex of the peer(s) involved, with more females than males stating it was same-sex only (38% vs. 20%) and more males stating it was opposite-sex only (64% vs. 43%).

Interestingly, subjects generally did not report themselves as having

Table A3. *Positive and Negative Aspects of all CSEP Ever Engaged in, by Gender*

	F $N = 132$	M $N = 126$
Positive aspects of CSEP overall:	%	%
Satisfied curiosity about sexual matters	73.5	87.3**
Physical/sexual pleasure	40.2	52.4*
Thrill/adventure of doing something forbidden	28.8	54.8***
They were part of the positive experiences subjects had with their peers, generally speaking	34.8	43.7
Felt grown-up/mature	32.6	29.4
Helped prepare subjects for post-childhood sexual experiences	30.3	39.7
Helped subjects learn how their body worked	31.8	42.9
Increased subjects' status/reputation among peers	9.1	22.2**
Negative aspects of CSEP overall:	%	%
Fearful of getting caught	49.2	46.8
Feelings of guilt	45.5	37.3
Confusion: wasn't sure if they were right or wrong	32.6	31.7
Ashamed about things subjects did or who subjects did them with	35.6	27.0
Feeling bad, immoral	23.5	20.6
Learning about sexual matters too early	7.6	9.5
Being teased/taunted for doing them by other kids	6.8	3.2
Being punished/criticized or getting into trouble	3.8	6.3

† Trend $p < .1$ * Significant, $p < .05$ ** Significant, $p < .01$ *** Significant, $p < .001$ (χ^2)

initiated the event, and roughly equal proportions stated that peers had initiated or that the event had "just happened" in all three time periods; no females admitted to initiating CSEP for the pre-elementary and junior high periods. Few subjects felt pressured into the activity, and almost no one indicated that they had been coerced. Both the thrill or adventure of doing something "forbidden" and curiosity were commonly cited reasons for having engaged in CSEP during all three time periods. Physical or sexual pleasure, being accepted by peers, and feeling "grown-up" were increasingly important reasons for engaging in CSEP as subjects grew older.

Subjects' overall ratings of all of their CSEP prior to high school were assessed for both positive and negative aspects (Table A3). These questions were asked at the end of the childhood section and were different from those asked for each specific time period. What subjects identified as the positive aspects overall paralleled the reasons they gave for engaging in their most memorable experiences. Satisfying curiosity about sexual matters was a positive aspect of CSEP for most subjects, although more so for males than females. More males than females also reported physical or sexual pleasure, the thrill or adventure of the "forbidden," and an increase in status or reputation with their peers as positive aspects of their experiences. More than a third of the subjects indicated that their CSEP were simply a part of the overall positive relations they had with their peers. No sex differences emerged for negative aspects of CSEP. Fear of getting caught was the most frequently endorsed negative aspect, followed by feeling guilty, for both males and females. Few subjects reported getting into trouble or being punished, suggesting that getting caught was not common. Few subjects said that they learned things about sexual matters as a result of CSEP that they felt they were too young to know about.

Having engaged in CSEP was not related to having masturbated in childhood. However, among those who had both experiences, frequency of CSEP was significantly correlated with frequency of masturbation ($R^2 = .34$, $p < .01$). (See Bancroft, Herbenick, & Reynolds, 2003, for a more detailed analysis of masturbation data.)

SEXUAL ATTRACTION, AROUSAL, AND FANTASY

As was to be expected, age at first sexual attraction was correlated with age at onset of sexual fantasies and age at first sexual arousal for both males and females. Onset of these experiences in relation to age at puberty is shown in Table A4.

Relations between onset of attraction, arousal, and fantasy and the onset, frequency, and range of CSEP were investigated. There were trends for females who had experienced pre-elementary CSEP to report sexual arousal earlier. Boys with pre-elementary CSEP reported earlier sexual attraction and fantasy.

In addition, having engaged in a broader range of sexual behaviors during CSEP was associated with earlier onset of arousal ($r = -.20$, $p < .05$), attraction ($r = -.21$, $p < .05$), and sexual fantasy ($r = -.17$, $p < .05$) for the females. For male participants, this association was only found with age at first sexual fantasy ($r = -.24$, $p < .01$).

ACCESS TO PORNOGRAPHY

While 43% of males and 30% of females reported the presence of pornography in the home, 80% of males and 49% of females reported having access to such materials outside of home during childhood (e.g., at a friend's house). Males reported more access to pornography during childhood than females both in and outside the home (in the home, 83% vs. 55%, $\chi^2 = 27.8$, $p < .001$; outside the home, 67% vs. 33%, $\chi^2 = 7.0$, $p < .01$), and reported viewing pornography significantly more often than females during both the elementary ($t = -4.2$, $p < .001$) and junior high ($t = -7.5$, $p < .001$) periods. Among those who viewed pornography, significantly

Table A4. *Sex Differences in First Intrapsychic Sexual Experiences in Relation to Puberty Onset*

		Prepubertal	Postpubertal
Sexual arousal			
	Male	70%	30%
	Female	63%	37%
Mean age			
	Male	8.8	12.0
	Female	9.2	13.6
Sexual attraction			
	Male	67%[a]	33%[a]
	Female	38%[b]	62%[b]
Mean age			
	Male	11.0	12.1[a]
	Female	10.2	13.7[b]
Sexual fantasy			
	Male	55%[a]	45%[a]
	Female	29%[b]	71%[b]
Mean age			
	Male	10.8	12.6[a]
	Female	10.5	14.4[b]

a significantly different from *b* for sex difference comparisons ($p < .05$) (χ^2)

more males reported having been caught by an adult doing it (24% vs. 8%, $\chi^2 = 11.8$, $p = .001$).

Males and females with access to pornography in or out of home during "childhood" (pre–high school years) were not more likely to report CSEP in the pre-elementary years, but were more likely to report CSEP in the elementary school period (females: 67% vs. 48%, $\chi^2 = 5.8$, $p < .02$; males: 68% vs. 44%, $\chi^2 = 5.1$, $p < .03$). This difference was also found for the middle school period among females only, 67% vs. 45%, $\chi^2 = 7.6$, $p < .01$.

SEXUAL EXPERIENCES WITH ADULTS OR PERSONS
AT LEAST FIVE YEARS OLDER

Fourteen percent of females and 22% of males reported at least one sexual experience that involved touching which occurred prior to beginning high school with an adult or person at least five years older. Only 4% indicated having had more than five such experiences. Details of these experiences and the reactions to them are given in Table A5. No significant

Table A5. *Characteristics of Subjects' Sexual Experiences with an Adult or Someone at Least 5 Years Older, That Involved Touching, and Occurred Prior to Beginning High School*

	Females	Males
Total # of such experiences		
None	86%	78%
1–5	11%	16%
6–10	2%	2%
11–50	1%	3%
50+	—	1%
Relationship between subject and all adults with whom these experiences occurred (N = 21 for females, N = 32 for males)		
Relatives	10%	16%
Friends	33%	47%
Acquaintances	48%	44%
Strangers	14%	3%
Sex of adult perpetrator		
Same-sex only	6%	24%
Opposite-sex only	94%	73%
Both same- and opposite-sex	—	3%
Subjects' participation in the experiences		
Largely voluntary	28%	31%
Acquiescing	16%	35%
Pressured	28%	17%
Coerced	28%	17%
How subject felt about experiences at the time		
Very negative (1)	44%	28%
(2)	6%	10%
Mixed (3)	27%	35%
(4)	17%	17%
Very positive (5)	6%	10%
If anyone found out about experiences before subject turned 18		
Yes	25% (N = 5)	20% (N = 6)
No	75% (N = 15)	80% (N = 24)

relationship was found between having reported CSEP in pre-elementary and elementary school years and reporting a "touching" sexual experience with an older person (females: 16% of those with CSEP vs. 11% without CSEP; males: 20% vs. 27%).

Nine percent of females and 15% of males reported at least one non-touching sexual experience prior to beginning high school that involved an adult or a person at least five years older. The large majority of these reported one to five such experiences (7% females, 14% males). The remaining participants reported six to ten experiences; no one reported more than that. There was no significant relationship between such nontouching experiences with an adult or older person and having engaged in "early" CSEP (pre-elementary or elementary period; females: 8% of those with early CSEP vs. 9% without early CSEP; males: 15% for both groups).

CSEP AND THEIR RELATION TO ADOLESCENT SEXUAL DEVELOPMENT

Subjects who engaged in CSEP in either the pre-elementary or elementary time periods were categorized as having reported "early CSEP," and this grouping was used to examine relationships with adolescent sexuality variables. Sixty-four percent ($N = 98$) of females and 72% ($N = 107$) of males were categorized as having early CSEP, and relationships between this history and adolescent sexuality variables are shown in Table A6.

For the females, those with early CSEP were more likely to report having had sexual intercourse by the time of the survey (84% vs. 63%, $\chi^2 = 8.8$, $p < .01$). However, for those who had experienced sexual intercourse, there were no significant differences for age at first intercourse. Females with early CSEP were also more likely than the rest of the females to have had a same-sex sexual experience during either high school or college years (23% vs. 3%, $\chi^2 = 6.5$, $p < .02$).

For the males, those with early CSEP were not more likely to have had sexual intercourse, but those who had reported a younger age at first intercourse (16.7 vs. 18.0 years, $F = 9.7$, $p < .01$). No relationship was found between early CSEP and high school or college period experiences with a same-sex partner (15% with early CSEP and 17% without early CSEP reported such experiences).

Study B: The Original Kinsey Sample

In order to explore the extent to which childhood sexual play and other childhood sexual experiences may have changed over the past 50 years, a sample of university students from Kinsey's original interview study was selected and their interview data used. Inevitably, the number of items relating to childhood sexuality which can be directly compared to Study A are limited, but some broad comparisons are possible.

In this paper, we consider childhood sexual experiences with peers and older persons, and how they relate to adolescent sexual activity. Mas-

Table A6. *Relationship of "Early" CSEP (i.e., CSEP Occurring in Either the Pre-elementary or Elementary School Periods) to Later Sexual Development Variables*

	Females		Males	
	Early CSEP[a]	Later or no CSEP[b]	Early CSEP[c]	Later or no CSEP[d]
Sexual intercourse, ever‡	84%**	63%	80%	69%
First sexual intercourse, age	17.0	17.1	16.7**	18.0
Number of lifetime sexual partners	3.9†	2.3	3.4	2.6
Total number of sexual partners in college years (experiences involving genital contact)	6.3**	3.7	6.2	4.8
Age at first crush	8.7	8.8	8.3**	9.9
Age at first kiss	13.3	13.8	12.5**	13.9
Age at first date	14.6	14.3	14.1†	14.8
Age at first boyfriend/girlfriend	13.1	13.3	12.0*	13.3
Age at first orgasm	15.6	15.6	13.0	13.6
Frequency of high school masturbation[e]	3.4*	2.6	5.3	5.0
Frequency of viewing pornography in high school period[e]	3.2	3.0	4.9*	4.4
Total # of different sexual behaviors subject engaged in during high school (possible range of 0 to 8)	4.6†	4.0	4.7**	3.4
# of advanced sexual behaviors subject engaged in during high school (e.g., oral, anal, penile-vaginal behaviors), possible range 0–5	2.0†	1.6	2.0**	1.3
Age at first light fondling during high school	15.1	15.0	15.1	15.5
Age at first heavy fondling during high school	15.7	15.6	15.5	15.8
Frequency of condom use during sexual intercourse (high school)[f]	4.8	5.0	4.4	5.5

‡ χ^2; remainder ANOVA
† Trend, $p < .10$
* Significant, $p < .05$ (a from b, or c from d)
** Significant, $p < .01$ (a from b, or c from d)
e scale of 1 to 6 where 1 = never, 2 = < 5 times, 3 = 6–10 times, 4 = 11–20 times, 5 = 21–50 times, 6 = > 50 times
f scale of 1 to 5 where 1 = never, 2 = rarely, 3 = some of the time, 4 = most of the time, 5 = every time

turbation history is reported in a separate paper (Bancroft, Herbenick, & Reynolds, 2003).

Method and Sample

In order to create a sample comparable to that of Study A, all subjects from the Kinsey interviews who were enrolled in college and between the ages of 18 and 22 at the time of the interview were selected. This starting sample consisted of 3,683 participants (1,913 women, 1,770 men). Whereas subjects in Study A all came from one university, those in Study B were from a number of universities.

Because of our emphasis on sexual experience in relation to the timing of puberty, it was first necessary to use the same definition of puberty as in Study A (i.e., age at first ejaculation for men and age at menarche for women). Thus we recoded the age at puberty used by Kinsey (Kinsey, Pomeroy, & Martin, 1948; Kinsey, Pomeroy, Martin, & Gebhard, 1953). The recoded age at puberty, using our definition, and the original age at puberty were equal for 95% of women and 80% of men. (See Bancroft, Herbenick, & Reynolds, 2003, for further details of this recoding.)

In the Kinsey interview, many questions were asked in reference to the original age at puberty. If the recoded age was older than the original age, what was meant to be prepubertal in the interview would still be considered prepubertal in the secondary analysis, so these subjects remained in the sample. However, subjects whose recoded age at puberty was less than the original age were excluded, as what was considered prepubertal during the original interview might not meet the current definition. Approximately 1% of women ($N = 18$) and .5% of men ($N = 8$) were excluded on this basis.

Three women were excluded from analyses because they had never menstruated, due to pathology, and thus we could not establish pre- or postpubertal time periods. Two additional women were excluded from analyses because they could not remember their age at menarche. One man was excluded from analyses as he had never ejaculated, and three men were excluded because of missing data. After these exclusions, the final sample consisted of 3,648 participants (1,890 women and 1,758 men).

Measures

Participants were interviewed in person by Alfred Kinsey and his colleagues using the method described in *Sexual Behavior in the Human Male* (Kinsey et al., 1948). Data reported in this paper include ethnicity, socioeconomic status, pubertal development, number and sex of siblings, child nudity in the home, childhood sexual experiences with same- and opposite-sex peers, masturbation, sexual encounters with adults, and postpubertal and premarital sexual experiences.

Results

The sample consisted of 1,890 women (52%) and 1,758 men (48%). Men were significantly older than women at the time of the interview (20.3 vs. 19.6 years, $t = 16.0$, $p < .001$). Ninety-six percent of women and 99% of men were Caucasian; 3% of women and 1% of men were African American.

The majority of subjects reported a family socioeconomic status at subject ages of 14–17 years old of middle (46% women, 54% men), upper middle (37% women, 24% men), or lower middle class (9% of women and 11% of men).

NUDITY IN THE HOME

Subjects were asked to report how frequently there was nudity in the home while they were growing up. There was no significant difference between men and women in this respect. Of the valid data, 75% of participants (76% women, 73% men) indicated that there was "never" nudity, 5% (4% women, 6% men) said "seldom," 3% (3% women, 4% men) said "often," and 17% (17% women and men) said that nudity was "usual" in their home growing up.

CHILDHOOD SEXUAL EXPERIENCES WITH PEERS

Table B1 displays information by subjects' most advanced CSEP behavior types, for females and males. For the purpose of comparison with Study A, the age ranges were compiled to create likely time periods of pre–elementary school, elementary school, and junior high years. It is important to note that as questions were only asked about prepuberty, and the year before puberty was not included, some subjects are lost in the elementary grade, and more from the junior high period, because they had reached the year before puberty or later. Also, subjects were not asked about all behaviors, but the most advanced for each year until the year before puberty. These numbers will be underestimates of CSEP in comparison to Study A because they all involve genitals to some extent—note that kissing is not listed here.

Men were more likely than women to report CSEP in general (68% men, 42% women, $\chi^2 = 247.4$. $p < .001$), with opposite-sex peers (48% men vs. 25% women, $\chi^2 = 194.8$, $p < .001$) and with same-sex peers (51% men vs. 30% women, $\chi^2 = 159.8$, $p < .001$).

SEXUAL EXPERIENCES WITH ADULTS OR PERSONS FIVE OR MORE YEARS OLDER

There is a great deal of missing data for this variable. For women, 27% have missing data, whereas for 97% of the men it is missing. Two hundred seventy-three women and 46 men reported prepubertal sexual experiences with adults, including (nongenital and genital) touching as well as

Table B1. *Most Advanced Behaviors Experienced as Part of CSEP in Each Time Period*

	Pre-elementary (ages 4–5)		Elementary (ages 6–11)		Jr. High (ages 12–14)		TOTAL*	
	F	M	F	M	F	M	F	M
No genital contact ("showing only")	5% (N = 93)	4% (n = 72)	14% (N = 264)	14% (N = 253)	1% (N = 25)	5% (N = 87)	18% (N = 337)	17% (N = 303)
Genital contact ("touching only")	4% (N = 80)	4% (N = 78)	14% (N = 271)	20% (N = 351)	2% (N = 34)	11% (N = 184)	17% (N = 321)	24% (N = 429)
Insertion/oral-genital/intercourse	2% (N = 29)	5% (N = 84)	7% (N = 132)	23% (N = 395)	1% (N = 21)	8% (N = 146)	8% (N = 142)	26% (N = 460)
Any type of CSEP N =							42% 800	68% 1192

*Total is the total number of subjects whose most advanced behavior in CSEP (ages 4–14) is of each type.

nontouching (exposing genitals) experiences. As the 46 men amount to 87% of the sample for whom there was data, it must be assumed that for much of the missing data, either the question was not asked or a negative response was given and not recorded. This limited data, particularly for the males, cannot be considered representative of the sample as a whole. Women were only asked about experiences with older men; men were asked about older men and women.

Two hundred fifty-eight women and 35 men reported prepubertal sexual experiences (nontouching and/or touching) with at least one adult male (or male at least five years older). The mean age for first prepubertal sexual experience with an adult male was 9.0 years for women (SD = 2.2, range = 4–13) and 9.9 years for men (SD = 2.5, range = 4–15).

Table B2 displays information about subjects' experiences with the first adult male, together with age of male (when known), nature of relationship, type of contact, and subjects' emotional response to the experience. Most subjects indicated that the adult was either a stranger or an acquaintance and that the experience with this particular adult male did not involve touching and occurred only once.

The age at which these experiences occurred was compared with the age at first CSEP. One hundred sixty-eight women and 34 men were included in the analysis. There were no significant differences in the ages for women (8.6 years for first CSEP vs. 8.9 years for first prepubertal sexual experience with an adult). However, men reported a significantly earlier age for their first CSEP (8.4 years vs. 9.9 years, t = 2.7, p < .02). This comparison was also carried out for experiences with older people that only involved touching. Seventy-four women and 25 men were included in the analysis. This produced essentially similar results.

Twelve men reported prepubertal sexual experiences with older women, and their mean age was 12.5 years for the first occasion (range = 4–13). In seven cases, coitus or attempted coitus was involved.

RELATIONSHIP OF CSEP TO OTHER CHILDHOOD EXPERIENCES

More subjects reporting childhood nudity in the home reported CSEP (with either same- or opposite-sex peers; 60% vs. 53% of those without childhood nudity in the home; χ^2 = 10.97, p < .01).

Females who reported CSEP were more likely to have had brothers (62%) than those who did not report CSEP (57%; χ^2 = 4.8, p < .03), though no such difference emerged for males.

RELATIONSHIP BETWEEN CSEP AND POSTPUBERTAL SEXUAL EXPERIENCES

Females with CSEP were significantly more likely to report postpubertal masturbation (45% vs. 26%, χ^2 = 77.8, p < .001). This difference was not apparent for the males.

Both females and males who had experienced CSEP were also more

Table B2. *Childhood Experiences with an Older Male (Differences in Ns Indicate Missing Data for Some Variables)*

	Women	Men
Mean age of first adult male for women (N = 131) and men (N = 24)	32.8 years	29.9 years
Relationship to first adult male for women (N = 169) and men (N = 16)		
Stranger	76.3% (N = 129)	50.0% (N = 8)
Acquaintance	9.5% (N = 16)	37.5% (N = 6)
Friend	7.7% (N = 13)	6.3% (N = 1)
Relative (sibling)	1.2% (N = 2)	6.3% (N = 1)
Relative (uncle, etc.)	3.6% (N = 6)	0
Relative (parent or grandparent)	1.8% (N = 3)	0
Subject's response to experience with first adult male for women (N = 173) and men (N = 18)		
Negative (fear, horror, upset)	79.2% (N = 137)	44.4% (N = 8)
Neutral or indifferent	13.9% (N = 24)	22.2% (N = 4)
Slight positive (curiosity/interest/ amusement/surprise)	5.8% (N = 10)	0
Positive	0	5.6% (N = 1)
Negative and arousal	0	5.6% (N = 1)
Slight positive and arousal	.6% (N = 1)	5.6% (N = 1)
Positive and arousal	.6% (N = 1)	0
Orgasm	0	16.7% (N = 3)
Type of experience with first adult male for women (N = 256) and men (N = 33)		
Approach	8.2% (N = 21)	18.2% (N = 6)
Exhibition of genitals	49.2% (N = 126)	3.0% (N = 1)
Nongenital touching	16.4% (N = 42)	21.2% (N = 7)
Genital touching	17.6% (N = 45)	33.3% (N = 11)
Mouth-genital contact	0.8% (N = 2)	12.1% (N = 4)
Coitus or attempted coitus/anal insertion	5.1% (N = 13)	9.1% (N = 3)
Assault with any of above	2.7% (N = 7)	3.0% (N = 1)

likely to have had a postpubertal same-sex experience (females: 7% vs. 3%, X^2 = 12.0, p < .01; males: 35% vs. 16%, X^2 = 67.1, p < .01).

Both females and males who reported CSEP were more likely to have engaged in (a) postpubertal petting (females: 96% vs. 93%, χ^2 = 10.1, p < .01; males: 97% vs. 95%, χ^2 = 5.6, p < .02); (b) either petting or coitus during high school years (females: 74% vs. 65%, χ^2 = 16.4, p < .001; males: 86% vs. 75%, χ^2 = 28.4, p < .001); and (c) petting or coitus after high school (females: 94% vs. 90%, χ^2 = 9.4, p < .01; males: 96% vs. 93%, χ^2 = 5.9, p < .02). Although these differences are significant, it is noteworthy that the large majority in both groups had engaged in these behaviors. However, more strikingly, both males and females who reported CSEP were more likely to have experienced orgasm during postpubertal petting (females: 38% vs. 29%, χ^2 = 16.9, p < .001; males: 59% vs. 49%, χ^2 = 13.9, p < .001).

More females with CSEP (21%) had engaged in premarital sexual intercourse than those without CSEP (16%; χ^2 = 6.3, p < .02). However, females with and without CSEP who had experienced sexual intercourse did not differ in their age when this first occurred. Males with CSEP were also more likely to have engaged in premarital sexual intercourse (51% with CSEP vs. 35% without CSEP, χ^2 = 39.3, p < .001), and also reported an average age at first intercourse that was significantly younger than coitally experienced men without CSEP (17.4 vs. 17.9 years, F[1,918] = 9.2, p < .01), though the effect size was low (adj. R2 = .009).

Having had CSEP had no bearing on whether or not the females engaged in coitus with a fiancé or someone who subsequently became their spouse, though males with CSEP tended to be more likely to do so (47% vs. 35%, χ^2 = 3.9, p = .05).

In addition, participants with and without CSEP were compared for the frequency of specific petting behaviors (see Table B3). Although a number of these show significant differences, all in the same direction, with the CSEP group reporting higher frequencies, the effect sizes are small.

Discussion

Although differences in the ways questions were asked limit the amount of direct comparison that is possible, there are nevertheless some interesting similarities and differences between these two data sets. The likelihood of having engaged in CSEP was somewhat underestimated in Study B, as it was the most advanced behavior for each age that was recorded. However, taking the overall percentages who had engaged at some stage prior to high school, we find a somewhat higher percentage for males in Study A (87.2% vs. 68%) and a more substantial difference in females (A, 84.4% vs. B, 42%). This gender difference apparent in Study B but not Study A is evident in a number of areas, reflecting a more wide-

Table B3. *Frequency of Engaging in Specific Premarital Petting Behaviors by Gender and CSEP (0 = never, 1 = rare, 2 = little, 3 = some, 4 = much)*

Premarital Petting Behaviors	Females		Males	
	No CSEP	CSEP	No CSEP	CSEP
Hugging	3.7**	3.8	3.8**	3.9
Kissing	3.7**	3.8	3.7**	3.9
Tongue kissing	2.6**	2.9	2.7**	3.1
Male hand on nude female breast	2.3**	2.6	2.9**	3.2
Male mouth on nude female breast	1.2**	1.5	1.2**	1.7
Male hand on nude female genitals	1.3**	1.6	1.8**	2.4
Female hand on nude male genitals	0.9**	1.2	1.2**	1.7
Male mouth on nude female genitals	0.2	0.3	0.1	0.2
Female mouth on nude male genitals	0.2†	0.3	0.2*	0.3

ANOVA: † Trend, $p < .10$ * Significant, $p < .05$ ** Significant, $p < .01$

spread reduction in gender differences in sexual behavior over the past 50 years. Thus, we see this with experience of sexual intercourse; although at both time periods involvement in CSEP appears to increase the likelihood of coital experience by the time of entering college, the proportions of both genders with coital experience have increased, particularly for the females, where for both those with and without CSEP the increase has been fourfold.

The relationship between CSEP and same-sex sexual experience post-puberty is also of interest. For females in Study B, 7% of those with CSEP reported postpubertal same-sex sexual experience, compared to 3% with no CSEP. However, in Study A we find the comparable figures to be 23% and 3%. Thus not only has CSEP been associated with more same-sex behavior postpuberty, but this effect has substantially increased among females. In males, the picture is somewhat different; in Study B, 35% with CSEP reported same-sex postpubertal behavior compared with 16% without CSEP. In Study A, however, the figures are 15% CSEP and 17% no CSEP. This would appear to indicate an increase in adolescent same-sex behavior in females, and a decrease in males, over the past 50 years. This reduction in males has been commented on in other studies (e.g., Schmidt, Klusmann, Zeitzschel, & Lange, 1994), and as Gagnon and Simon (1973) pointed out, a substantial proportion of Kinsey's 37% of men

with same-sex orgasmic experience since puberty were boys in early adolescence (Bancroft, 1998).

For sexual experience with adults, Study B is of limited value, particularly for the males, and in Study A we made the mistake of not establishing
at what age these experiences occurred other than before age 16. The impression from the female data is that Study A females were less likely to
have encountered male exhibitionists than those in Study B. The most confident conclusion from both data sets is that such experience with adults
does not relate to whether the child had sexual experiences with peers.
Although it is clear that some sexually abused children do become more
sexually interactive with their peers, our data would suggest that for the
majority of sexual abuse experiences there is no such effect. This "sexualization," when it occurs, may relate to the severity and duration of the
abuse.

Overall, we find evidence from both studies that childhood sexual experience with peers is associated with earlier and more extensive sexual
experience in adolescence, although in several respects the effects are subtle.
The crucial question is whether this is a causal relationship, i.e., because of
childhood sexual experiences children become more sexually aware, or
whether both aspects of development are manifestations of an innately
greater sexual awareness or responsiveness in some children than in others.
An intermediate interactive explanatory position may have more credibility,
in which children with a greater innate awareness of sexual pleasure are
more likely to initiate sexual games, but any child participating in such
games, providing they are not aversive experiences, may find an increased
awareness of sexual interest and pleasure as a consequence. The extent to
which such games result in increased sexual awareness may depend on the
child's innate propensity for sexual pleasure, which probably varies substantially across children.

The association between exposure to pornography and CSEP during
elementary school years is also of interest. It is again not clear whether
children who engage in CSEP are more likely to be aware of or recognize
the significance of pornography when they come across it. But it is also
possible that encountering such material induces curiosity which leads
to CSEP.

In the accompanying paper on masturbation (Bancroft, Herbenick, &
Reynolds, 2003), we stressed the gender contrast in age of onset of masturbation, with females showing a much wider distribution both pre- and
postpubertally. Whereas we do not see this pattern with CSEP, we do find
a wider range of age of onset of sexual arousal, attraction, and fantasy
among the females in Study A. It is also noteworthy that the females with
early CSEP are more likely to masturbate postpubertally, a relationship
which is not evident in the males, presumably because the large majority
of boys masturbate postpubertally anyway.

This paper has focused on childhood sexual play. Such play is likely to have functions in cognitive and emotional development similar to those of other types of play. The full theoretical consideration of the role of play in development will be covered in a separate paper.

References

Bancroft, J. (1998). Alfred Kinsey's work 50 years later. Introduction. In A. C. Kinsey, W. B. Pomeroy, C. E. Martin, & P. H. Gebhard, *Sexual Behavior in the Human Female* (pp. a–r). Bloomington: Indiana University Press.

Bancroft, J., Herbenick, D. L., & Reynolds, M. A. (2003). Masturbation as a marker of sexual development: Two studies 50 years apart. In J. Bancroft (Ed.), *Sexual development in childhood* (pp. 156–185). Bloomington: Indiana University Press.

Bauserman, R., & Davis, C. (1996). Perceptions of early sexual experiences and adult sexual adjustment. *Journal of Psychology and Human Sexuality, 8*(3), 37–59.

Finkelhor, D. (1980). Sex among siblings: A survey on prevalence, variety, and effects. *Archives of Sexual Behavior, 9,* 171–194.

Friedrich, W. N. (2003). Studies of sexuality of nonabused children. In J. Bancroft (Ed.), *Sexual development in childhood* (pp. 107–120). Bloomington: Indiana University Press.

Gagnon, J. H., & Simon, W. (1973). *Sexual conduct: The social sources of human sexuality.* Chicago: Aldine.

Green, V. (1985). Experiential factors in childhood and adolescent sexual behavior: Family interactions and previous sexual experiences. *Journal of Sex Research, 21,* 157–182.

Haugaard, J. J., & Tilly, C. (1988). Characteristics predicting children's responses to sexual encounters with other children. *Child Abuse & Neglect, 12,* 209–218.

Kilpatrick, A. (1992). *Long-range effects of child and adolescent sexual experiences: Myths, mores, menaces.* Hillsdale, NJ: Lawrence Erlbaum.

Kinsey, A. C., Pomeroy, W. B., & Martin, C. E. (1948). *Sexual behavior in the human male.* Philadelphia: W. B. Saunders.

Kinsey, A. C., Pomeroy, W. B., Martin, C. E., & Gebhard, P. H. (1953). *Sexual behavior in the human female.* Philadelphia: W. B. Saunders.

Lamb, S., & Coakley, M. (1993). "Normal" childhood sexual play and games: Differentiating play from abuse. *Child Abuse & Neglect, 17,* 515–526.

Leitenberg, H., Greenwald, E., & Tarran, M. (1989). The relation between sexual activity among children during preadolescence and/or early adolescence and sexual behavior and sexual adjustment in young adulthood. *Archives of Sexual Behavior, 18,* 299–313.

Meyer-Bahlburg, H. F. L., & Steel, J. L. (2003). Using the parents as a source of information about the child, with special emphasis on the sex problems scale of the Child Behavior Checklist. In J. Bancroft (Ed.), *Sexual development in childhood* (pp. 34–53). Bloomington: Indiana University Press.

O'Sullivan, L. F. (2003). Methodological issues associated with studies of child sexual behavior. In J. Bancroft (Ed.), *Sexual development in childhood* (pp. 23–33). Bloomington: Indiana University Press.

Rademakers, J., Laan, M., & Straver, C. J. (2003). Body awareness and physical intimacy: An exploratory study. In J. Bancroft (Ed.), *Sexual development in childhood* (pp. 121–125). Bloomington: Indiana University Press.

Reynolds, M. A., & Herbenick, D. L. (2003). Using computer-assisted self-interview (CASI) for recall of childhood sexual experiences. In J. Bancroft (Ed.), *Sexual development in childhood* (pp. 77–81). Bloomington: Indiana University Press.

Schmidt, G., Klusmann, D., Zeitzschel, U., & Lange, C. (1994). Changes in adolescents' sexuality between 1970 and 1990 in West Germany. *Archives of Sexual Behavior, 23,* 489–513.

Masturbation as a Marker of Sexual Development

Two Studies 50 Years Apart

JOHN BANCROFT, DEBRA L. HERBENICK,
AND MEREDITH A. REYNOLDS

Introduction

Although childhood sexual play experiences are common, possibly more so in recent years, prepubertal children appear to vary in their level of awareness of and interest in sexual issues.

In this paper we explore masturbation and the age of onset of masturbation, particularly prepubertal masturbation, as potentially valuable markers of early sexual development. Although child masturbation can be the result of sexual interaction with other children or adults, it often isn't, and from the perspective of understanding sexual development, it has the advantage of being a solitary behavior relatively independent of social context and peer group influences. And whereas the likelihood of masturbation during adulthood is often influenced by the availability of sexual partners, masturbation during childhood is not. As such, it may be a more direct indicator of a child's sexual interest and awareness. Why do some children and adolescents masturbate and others do not? How do those who do and don't masturbate compare in other aspects of sexual development? Is early onset of masturbation an indication of greater sexual awareness or responsiveness? How does age of onset of masturbation relate to sexual adjustment during early adulthood?

In children under the age of 5, some degree of genital self-stimulation may be apparent to parents, though typically after the age of 5 such behavior becomes less apparent (Friedrich, Grambsch, Broughton, Kuiper, & Beilke, 1991). This may be because it stops, or more probably because the child learns that it is something that should be done in private and conceals it from the parents. It is presumably at this stage of cognitive development that children start to learn the "sexual significance," or at least the "taboo" nature, of such behaviors, resulting in their greater secrecy. We understand very little about this process of sexual labeling in childhood, but it can obviously be affected by reactions of parents to their child's self-stimulation as well as by sexual interaction with adults or older children and the reaction of parents and others to such sexual exploitation. We should not be

156

surprised if children who have learnt the "sexual taboos" are reluctant to talk about their sexual experiences to researchers. Halpern, Udry, Suchindran, and Campbell (2000) recently demonstrated the reluctance of young teenagers to report masturbation, by finding that the same individuals, interviewed later as young adults, recalled substantially higher incidence of masturbation than was reported at the time. It is also possible that whereas today young adults find it less embarrassing to admit to masturbation than teenagers, 50 years ago young adults may also have underreported masturbation for the same reason. While we are therefore largely dependent on recall of childhood memories by older subjects to explore more normal aspects of children's masturbatory behavior, we should keep in mind the possibility of underreporting in our earlier sample.

Arafat and Cotton (1974), in a study of 230 male and 205 female college students, reported that 13% of the males and 12% of the females had started to masturbate between the ages of 5 and 8, and 37% of the males and 19.5% of the females between the ages of 9 and 12. Leitenberg, Detzer, and Srebnik (1993) found that in a sample of 280 college students, 30% of the men and 23% of the women reported having masturbated prior to age 13.

In this paper we also focus on the childhood memories of college students. Two studies are involved: Study A is a recent study of students at a Midwestern university carried out between fall 1998 and summer 1999, and Study B involves an age-matched sample of college students interviewed in the original Kinsey study. We thus have two samples collected approximately 50 years apart. This will allow us to look for changing patterns over that time period.

We focus on masturbation and orgasm associated with masturbation as relatively "pure" markers of individual sexuality, and our principal objectives are to explore the age of onset of masturbation, and masturbatory orgasm, in relation to the age at puberty, in males and females. Having identified those with prepubertal onset of masturbation and those with pubertal or postpubertal onset, we then explore early experiences which might account for these different developmental patterns and also consider whether the age of onset of masturbation has implications for later sexual development in adolescence and early adulthood.

Study A

Subjects

Subjects were recruited as part of a larger study on the relationship between childhood sexual experience and later sexual adjustment (for full details see Reynolds, Herbenick, & Bancroft, 2003). One hundred fifty-four women and 149 men, a representative sample of non–first semester students between the ages of 18 and 22, participated in a computer-assisted self-interview (CASI) study on sexuality. (For full details of the CASI procedure, see Reynolds & Herbenick, 2003.)

The mean age of the men was 20.3 years; of the women, 20.1 years. Ninety-three percent of women and 67% of men were Caucasian; the remainder were from various racial groups.

Five percent of the males described themselves as homosexual; 4% of females and 3% of males reported a bisexual orientation; 3% of females and 2% of males were uncertain; and the remainder self-identified as heterosexual.

AGE AT PUBERTY

Puberty, for the purpose of this study, was defined as the age at first ejaculation for the males and menarche for the females. As age at puberty is a key variable in this analysis, we excluded those subjects whose pubertal ages, as defined, were younger than 10 or older than 16 years, on the grounds that outside this age range spermarche and menarche are relatively abnormal and potentially problematic. Three women and 10 men were excluded on this basis, and there were two women and five men with missing data for age at puberty. This leaves a total of 149 women and 134 men for analyses.

Methods

The computerized interview was in two parts. One part dealt with childhood and adolescence, the other with the present time. The order of these two parts was balanced across subjects.

1. Definition of masturbation and age at first masturbation
For the purpose of this study, we defined masturbation as self-stimulation to the point of arousal, but not necessarily to orgasm or climax. It was also emphasized that questions about masturbation related to solitary masturbation rather than masturbation involving another person. Following the definition, subjects were asked at what age they first masturbated.

2. Frequency of masturbation and related experiences
Subjects were asked to estimate the frequency of masturbation in each of the following time periods: elementary school, middle or junior high school, and high school. Were they caught masturbating by an adult? What was the adult's reaction? What were their reasons for masturbating?

3. Experience of prepubertal orgasm
Orgasm was not specifically defined for participants; rather, it was assumed that their present knowledge of orgasm would be sufficient to report on whether orgasm had occurred in the past.
Subjects were asked, as best as they could recall, to report the fre-

quency with which they reached orgasm or climax during masturbation as a child (i.e., prior to starting high school), and to indicate whether they had reached orgasm prepubertally (i.e., yes, no, or "I think so"). Those who reported "yes" or "I think so" were asked at what age they first experienced orgasm. On this basis we can estimate the proportion who experienced first orgasm prepubertally.

4. Family influences

We determined whether subjects lived with both parents or one while growing up (and if one parent, which one); the number of siblings; whether subjects had same-sex siblings within five years of their age; whether subjects had opposite-sex siblings within five years of their age; whether subjects had same-sex siblings at all; and whether subjects had opposite-sex siblings at all. We also asked about the extent of maternal and paternal support of the subjects prior to high school; maternal and paternal verbal and physical abuse of the subjects prior to high school; maternal and paternal health when subjects were children; parents' open display of affection for each other; subjects' closeness to their mothers and their fathers; and whether subjects had shared a bed with same-sex or opposite-sex children while growing up. We investigated family bathing practices, parental comfort discussing sexual matters, and family sexual environment (a composite of several variables such as bathing practices, comfort talking about sex, etc.).

5. Peer group influences (nonsexual)

We asked about the number of other children subjects played with at least a couple of times a week during elementary and junior high school years, and the proportion of friends that were same and opposite sex.

6. Childhood and adolescent sexual experiences

Participants were asked a wide variety of questions pertaining to sexual experiences occurring during different time periods as delineated by school (i.e., pre-elementary, elementary, junior high school, and high school). These included sexual play and experiences with peers; the timing of the first date, first crush, first feelings of sexual attraction, first sexual arousal, and first explicit sexual fantasies; how much access to pornography they had in and away from the home; and interest in and frequency of looking at pornography and at nonpornographic sexual material (e.g., underwear advertisements).

7. Childhood sexual experiences with adults

Subjects were asked about sexual experiences (separately for "touching" and "nontouching" experiences) with adults or individuals more than five years older than them that occurred prior to age 16. Full details about these experiences and how the subject reacted to them are given in Reynolds, Herbenick, and Bancroft (2003).

8. Current sexuality

We assessed subjects' current sexuality by asking about their level of current sexual satisfaction; their lifetime number of sexual partners; the number of people they had dated since high school graduation; how frequently they had masturbated in the previous 12 months; how consistently they had experienced orgasm during masturbation during the previous 12 months; and how frequently they had felt guilty after masturbating. We asked about the frequency with which they discuss personal sexuality or other sex topics with others; how frequently they had had oral sex in the past year; the number of partners with whom oral sex was given or received; their enjoyment of giving and receiving oral sex; and the consistency with which they have experienced orgasm during oral sex during their college years. Regarding sexual intercourse, we investigated the number of people with whom they have had sexual intercourse (i.e., penile/vaginal), and their frequency of sexual intercourse, during their college years; their enjoyment of sexual intercourse during their college years; and whether orgasm was experienced during sexual intercourse. We also asked about the frequency of genital contact not involving sexual intercourse, and the number of different people involved, during their college years; their enjoyment of non-intercourse sexual activity during their college years; how frequently they had experienced sexual problems during the previous 12 months (pain, lack of pleasure in sex, inability to experience orgasm, lack of sexual interest, erectile or vaginal lubrication difficulties); how frequently they had experienced premature ejaculation in the previous 12 months; and the number of times they had been verbally or physically pressured into sexual activity. We also queried subjects' current level of sexual satisfaction.

Statistical Analysis

For both Studies A and B, comparisons of prepubertal and postpubertal masturbators on other variables have involved analysis of variance or t-tests for continuous or ordinally rated variables and χ^2 analysis for categorical variables.

Results

AGE AT PUBERTY

Women's mean age at puberty (i.e., menarche) was 12.6 years (median = 12.0, SD = 1.6, range = 6–18). Mean ages for other pubertal markers were: first bra, 11.2 years (median = 11.0, SD = 1.4, range 6–16); development of pubic hair, 11.4 years (median = 11.0, SD = 1.4, range = 6–14).

Men's mean age at puberty (i.e., first ejaculation) was 12.5 years (median = 13.0, SD = 1.7, range = 7–19). For other pubertal markers, their mean ages were: voice change, 12.6 years (median = 13.0, SD = 1.4, range

= 8–16); development of pubic hair, 11.5 years (median = 12.0, SD = 1.7, range = 5–15).

MASTURBATION HISTORY

There was missing data for 5% of women and less than 1% of men. Of those with valid data, 17% of women and <2% of men had never masturbated, 40% of women and 38% of men had masturbated prepubertally, and 43% of women and 61% of men had first masturbated postpubertally.

For establishing whether masturbation had started prepubertally, eight women and one man had incomplete data. Of the valid data, 40% (N = 57) of women and 38% (N = 50) of men had masturbated prepubertally. For these subjects, the mean age for onset of prepubertal masturbation was earlier for women than for men (8.3 vs. 10.1 years, t = −3.3, p < .01). This method of calculation may underrepresent the extent of prepubertal onset of masturbation, since subjects with first masturbation and puberty occurring in the same year (7% of women, or 8, and 37% of men, or 49) were categorized as pubertal or postpubertal onset, when some of them may have masturbated before first ejaculation or menarche.

For all those subjects who had masturbated by the time of the study, age at first masturbation is shown in Figure A1 and age at first masturbation in relation to age at puberty is shown in Figure A2.

Women whose first masturbation occurred prepubertally had a significantly later age at puberty than women whose first masturbation occurred postpubertally (12.8 years vs. 12.3 years, F(1,115) = 5.3, p < .03). There was a similar trend for men (12.8 years vs. 12.4 years, F(1,129) = 3.8, p = .055).

Subjects were not specifically asked how frequently they masturbated prior to puberty. Therefore, this information was derived from information on how frequently they masturbated during elementary school years, since elementary school years (typically ages 6–12) were prepubertal years for most subjects. The mean age for puberty was greater than the mean age for beginning middle/junior high school. On average, women with prepubertal masturbation were 11.6 years old at starting middle school but 12.8 at reaching puberty; men with prepubertal masturbation were 11.7 at starting middle school and also 12.8, on average, at reaching puberty. Frequencies of masturbation for women and men during elementary school years are shown in Table A1. There was no gender difference in this respect.

The pre- and postpubertal onset masturbation groups were compared for (a) their stated reasons for masturbating prior to high school, (b) ever having been caught masturbating prior to high school, and (c) adult reaction if caught.

The groups did not differ, for either men or women, for the following stated reasons for masturbating: curiosity about self (women: 72% pre,

Females

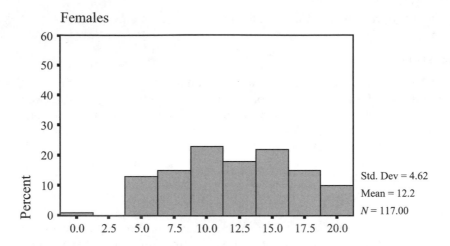

Age in years

STUDY A: Data were included only for subjects who reported masturbation. 17% of females had not yet masturbated at the time of the survey.

Males

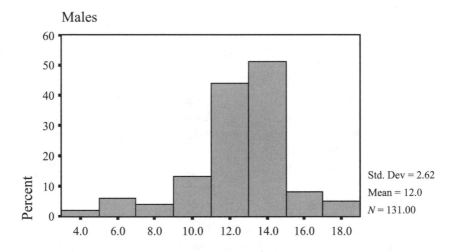

Age in years

STUDY A: Data were included only for subjects who reported masturbation. Less than 2% of males had not yet masturbated at the time of the survey.

Figure A1.   Age at First Masturbation: Study A

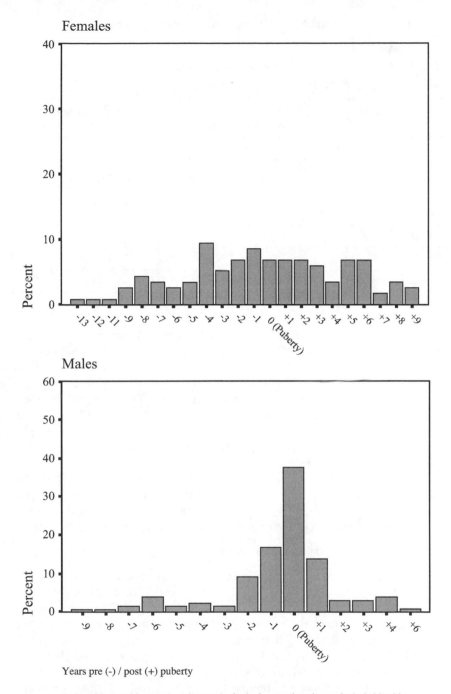

Years pre (-) / post (+) puberty

Only subjects with complete data and who had masturbated were included in this figure. 16% of women and 2% of men had not masturbated and 5% of women and 1% of men had incomplete or missing data.

Figure A2. Onset of Masturbation in Relation to Age at Puberty: Study A

Table A1. *Frequency of Masturbation during Elementary School Years for Women and Men Reporting Prepubertal Masturbation*

Frequency	Women (of those who masturbated prepubertally)	Men (of those who masturbated prepubertally)
	$N = 57$	$N = 50$
Never	14%	32%
Less than 5 times	26%	22%
6–10 times	16%	12%
11–20 times	12%	10%
21–50 times	12%	10%
50+ times	19%	14%

82% post; men: 70% pre, 72% post); to self-soothe when upset, frightened, or angry (women: 14% pre, 4% post, men: 8% pre, 9% post); to help fall asleep (women: 21% pre, 7% post; men: 16% pre, 17% post). The male groups did not differ in masturbating for physical pleasure or excitement (84% pre and 92% post) or to entertain self when bored or lonely (40% pre and 32% post), whereas the female groups did differ on these two variables: physical pleasure or excitement: (68% pre, 41% post; $\chi^2 = 5.83$, $p < .02$;) or to entertain self when bored or lonely (33% pre, 11% post; $\chi^2 = 4.68$, $p < .04$).

Twenty-three percent of women and 12% of men with prepubertal onset of masturbation were discovered masturbating by an adult, compared to only one woman (4%) and three men (5%) who began masturbating postpubertally. Details of adults' reactions are shown in Table A2.

EXPERIENCE OF ORGASM BEFORE PUBERTY

Eighteen women (12%) and 18 men (13.5%) reported ages at first orgasm that were younger than their age at puberty. For women, the mean age at first prepubertal orgasm was 8.5 (median = 9.0; $SD = 2.6$; range = 4–13 years). For men, the mean age at first prepubertal orgasm was 9.6 years (median = 10.5; $SD = 3.1$; range = 5–13).

All of the 18 women and 16 of the 18 men indicated that their first prepubertal orgasm occurred as the result of a solitary experience. For one man, the first experience of prepubertal orgasm involved same-sex peers; for another man it involved an older person.

A further six women and four men answered "I think so" to the question about orgasm and gave ages at first orgasm earlier than puberty. When they were combined with the previous group, the mean age for first or-

Table A2. *Pre–high school Masturbation and Adult Reaction*

Masturbation Onset Groups	Prepubertal Onset		Postpubertal Onset	
	Women	Men	Women	Men
Ever caught by an adult masturbating prior to high school	N	N	N	N
Caught	13	6	1	3
Not caught	44	44	26	62
Adult reaction (s)				
Ignored it	6	3	0	2
Criticized or threatened subject	3	1	1	0
Laughed/thought it was funny	2	0	0	0
Physically punished subject	1	0	0	0
Told subject it was okay but only in private	3	2	0	2
Told subject to never do it again	4	1	1	0

gasm and source of first orgasm remained very similar; one of these additional women indicated that her first orgasm occurred with a same-sex peer.

ASSOCIATION BETWEEN MASTURBATION HISTORY AND OTHER VARIABLES

Comparison of masturbators with nonmasturbators

Although only 17% of women had not masturbated by the time of the interview, they were compared with the remainder of the women on other variables because of the striking differences between masturbators and nonmasturbators in Study B. There were too few nonmasturbating men, in either study, to make this comparison worthwhile.

These two groups were compared on more than 150 variables, and they differed on 31 variables at the 5% or 1% significance level. These differences were consistent, showing the masturbators to have had more CSEP during elementary school (particularly involving looking at or displaying genitals), more physical/sexual pleasure during these experiences, and, during college years, more interest in unconventional sexual fantasies (e.g., use of vibrator, sex with another woman, watching others in sexual activity), with more sexual partners, more oral sex, and greater enjoyment of oral sex. They also reported being more perceptive of when someone was interested in them sexually.

Comparison of prepubertal and postpubertal onset groups

1. Family influences

Males. The only variable tending to discriminate between the groups indicated that prepubertal masturbators were less likely to share a bedroom with other boys (31% prepubertal, 47% postpubertal; χ^2 = 2.9, p = 0.09).

Females. Women with opposite-sex siblings were more likely to report postpubertal onset of masturbation (59% of women with opposite-sex siblings, 40% without, had a postpubertal onset of masturbation; χ^2 = 3.7, p = .054). This trend did not appear for the men.

Women who reported prepubertal onset of masturbation tended to be less close to their fathers (p = .085).

2. Peer group influences (nonsexual)

Males. The mean number of childhood (elementary school and middle school) friends for the prepubertal group was 9.9 (*SD* = 4.9; range 3–24); for the postpubertal group, 11.6 (*SD* = 4.6; range 4–23). This difference approached significance: t = −1.9, p = .059. In particular, men in the prepubertal group reported playing with fewer friends during middle school years than did men in the postpubertal group (9.9 vs. 11.6 friends, t = 1.7, p = .097). This difference was not found during elementary school years. The female groups did not differ in this respect for either time period.

Females. Significantly more women in the prepubertal masturbation group reported having memories of childhood sexual experiences with peers during elementary school years than did those in the postpubertal group (77% vs. 52%, χ^2 = 8.3, p < .01).

3. Childhood and adolescent sexual experiences

Of the variables listed under this heading, those showing a difference between prepubertal and postpubertal onset masturbators are shown in Table A3. For the males, only two variables discriminated: Prepubertal masturbators were more likely to have engaged in "heavy fondling" and oral sex during high school years. For females, there are many more discriminators. Prepubertal masturbators were younger at first crush, first sexual arousal, first sexual attraction, first experience of explicit sexual fantasies, and light and heavy fondling, and were more likely to have viewed both pornographic and nonpornographic but sexual materials during their elementary school years; all of which showed earlier experiences in the prepubertal masturbators.

4. Same-sex sexual experiences during high school

Ten percent of males and 6% of females reported having had at least one same-sex partner during their high school years. No relationship was found with age of onset of masturbation.

Table A3. *Significant Differences between Pre- and Postpubertal Onset of Masturbation on Measures Related to Childhood and Adolescent Sexual Experiences for Women and Men*

	Women	
	Prepubertal group	Postpubertal group
Age at first crush	8.2 years*	9.2 years
Age at first sexual arousal	10.0*	11.8
Age at first sexual attraction	12.2†	13.1
Age began having explicit sexual fantasies	12.4*	14.1
Grade when peers began light fondling	7.0*	7.6
Grade when peers began heavy fondling	8.0*	8.6
Frequency of viewing pornographic materials during elementary school years (scale of 1 to 6 where 1 = never, 6 = 50 + times)	1.8* (< 5 times)	1.5
Frequency of viewing nonpornographic but sexual materials during elementary school years	2.9* (6–10 times)	2.4 (< 5 times)
Frequency of viewing nonpornographic but sexual materials during junior high school years	3.8† (11–20 times)	3.3 (6–10 times)

	Men	
	Prepubertal group	Postpubertal group
Engaged in heavy fondling during high school years	88%*	70%
Performed oral sex during high school years	64%*	43%

*Statistically significant difference, $p < .05$
† $p < .10$

5. Sexual experiences before the age of 16 with adults (or someone at least five years older)

Experiences involving touching. There were no differences between prepubertal and postpubertal masturbators in the occurrence of such experiences for either males or females. For the women, 14% ($N = 8$) of prepubertal and 14% ($N = 8$) of postpubertal masturbators reported such experiences. For the men, 19% ($N = 9$) of prepubertal and 25% ($N = 20$) of postpubertal masturbators reported these experiences.

Experiences not involving touching. There were again no differences between the two groups for nontouching sexual experience. (For women, 5% of prepubertal vs. 9% of postpubertal masturbators reported such experiences; for men, 15% of prepubertal vs. 16% of postpubertal masturbators did so.)

6. Current sexuality

Variables relating to the sexual experience of college years which discriminated between pre- and postpubertal onset masturbators are shown in Table A4. Here again we find a striking gender difference. For males, the postpubertal onset masturbators show a trend toward more frequent masturbation, more frequent sexual fantasies, more enjoyment of giving and receiving oral sex, greater likelihood of orgasm during oral sex and during vaginal intercourse, and greater likelihood of premature ejaculation than the prepubertal group. For females, on the other hand, we find the prepubertal group tending to report a higher level of current sexual satisfaction, a higher frequency of masturbation, a lower frequency of orgasm during oral sex, and a significantly higher likelihood of buying or renting X-rated videos. Also of interest, females with prepubertal masturbation were less likely to report having had any STDs (2% vs. 13%, $\chi^2 = 5.0$, $p < .03$).

Study B

Subjects

For the purpose of comparison with Study A, an initial sample was chosen from the original Kinsey interviews of subjects between the ages of 18 and 22 who were enrolled in college at the time of the interview.

AGE AT PUBERTY

Kinsey and his colleagues had calculated puberty using a variety of variables, including voice change, growth spurt, and development of pubic hair, as well as first ejaculation for men and menarche for women. For the purpose of comparison with the sample in Study A, age at puberty was recoded to match that in Study A (i.e., age at first ejaculation or menarche), and the sample further restricted to those who reached puberty, so

Table A4. *Significant Differences Related to Subjects' Current Sexuality Based on Onset of Masturbation*

	Women	
	Prepubertal group mean	Postpubertal group mean
Frequency of masturbation in previous 12 months (0 = not at all, 9 = once a day)	4.8† (*t* = 1.8, *p* = .082)	4.1
Current level of sexual satisfaction (1 = very dissatisfied, 5 = very satisfied)	3.8† (*t* = 1.9, *p* = .057)	3.4
Frequency with which subject reached orgasm as a result of receiving oral sex during college years (1 = never, 5 = every time)	2.8 † (*t* = 1.8, *p* = .069)	3.2
Number of times subject engaged in non-intercourse sexual activity with genital contact in previous month	5.3† (*t* = 1.7, *p* – .096)	2.9
Subject bought or rented an X-rated video or movie in the last 12 months to enhance sexual enjoyment	37%* (χ^2 = 5.9, *p* < .02)	17%

	Men	
	Prepubertal group mean	Postpubertal group mean
Frequency of masturbation in previous 12 months (0 = not at all, 9 = once a day)	6.6† (*t* = 1.9, *p* = .06)	7.0
Frequency of sexual fantasy (1 = < once a month, 5 = several times a day)	3.9* (*t* = 3.2, *p* < .01)	4.4
Subject's enjoyment of performing oral sex (1 = never, 5 = every time)	3.4* (*t* = 2.5, *p* < .02)	3.9
Subject's enjoyment of receiving oral sex (1 = never, 5 = every time)	4.1* (*t* = 2.2, *p* < .03)	4.5

Continued on the next page

Table A4. *Continued*

	Men	
	Prepubertal group mean	Postpubertal group mean
Frequency with which subject reached orgasm as a result of receiving oral sex during college years (1 = never, 5 = every time)	3.3† ($t = 1.7$, $p = .10$)	3.7
Frequency with which subject's partner reached orgasm while subject performed oral sex during college years	2.0† ($t = 1.7$, $p = .093$)	2.2
Frequency with which subject had orgasm via penile-vaginal sex (1 = never, 5 = every time)	4.0† ($t = 1.95$, $p = .054$)	4.4
Frequency of experiencing orgasm too soon in previous 12 months (1 = never, 2 = a few times, 3 = several times, 4 = many times)	1.9* ($t = 2.0$, $p < .05$)	2.2

* Statistically significant difference, $p < .05$
† $p < .10$

defined, between the ages of 10 and 16. From this narrowed pool, it was found that the "new" age at puberty and the original age at puberty were equal for 95% of women and 82% of men (correlations between new and old ages were .97 for women and .89 for men).

Because many of the original Kinsey interview questions were asked in relation to puberty (e.g., whether prepubertal masturbation occurred, ages at various prepubertal sexual experiences, etc.), we further excluded from the sample those whose "new" age at puberty was less than their original age at puberty (1% of women and 0.5% of men). The decision was made to keep the 4% of women and nearly 18% of men whose "new" puberty ages were greater than their original puberty ages. Thus, although we might have lost some examples of prepubertal behavior with this re-coding, we can be certain that all behavior reported as prepubertal met both Kinsey's and our definition of prepubertal.

As a result of these various exclusions, the final subject pool for Study B consisted of 3,597 subjects (1,875 women and 1,722 men). The mean age for women at the time of the interview was 19.6 years (median = 19.0,

$SD = 1.2$, range $= 18-22$), and for men, 20.3 (median $= 20.0$, $SD = 1.3$, range $= 18-22$), a difference which was significant ($t = 15.7$, $p < .001$).

Methods

All of this data was obtained by face-to-face interview.

1. Definition of masturbation
   Masturbation was not specifically defined. However, if a subject seemed not to know what masturbation was, the interviewers would give a brief description using the vernacular of the time (e.g., "some call it 'rubbing off'") until they were certain that the subjects understood the term. Questions about postpubertal masturbation were often more specific, however, as the techniques were elicited.

2. Age at first masturbation
   Subjects were asked to report their age at first masturbation. If the age was prepubertal, it was recorded and whether or not orgasm occurred was ascertained.

3. Occurrence of prepubertal orgasm
   While data on prepubertal female orgasm were included in the marginal tabulations of the 1938–63 interviews, these data, unlike the same data for males, were never entered into a computer database. The original interview sheets were reexamined and one of the authors (DH) was trained in the coding by Paul Gebhard and through the use of existing codebooks. This information was available for all of the college women who reached puberty between the ages of 10 and 16 (inclusive), and includes reports of subjects' age at first orgasm from a variety of sources (e.g., masturbation, petting, same-sex experience, coitus, dreams, etc.).

4. Family and other early influences
   Subjects were asked to report on the following: their relationship with each parent at ages 14–17; the interparental relationship when subjects were aged 14–17; their age if or when their genetic parents separated or divorced; the number of sisters and brothers; the frequency of childhood nudity in the home; their health as a child; their main source of sex education; and the contribution of each parent to their sexual knowledge.

5. Peer group influences
   Subjects were asked the numbers of their male and female playmates at ages 10–11, and the numbers of their male and female friends and companions at ages 16–17.

6. Childhood and adolescent sexual experiences
   Subjects were asked about their same- and opposite-sex childhood sexual experiences with peers; most advanced sexual play technique during

each year of preadolescence (age 4 through the year prior to puberty); petting techniques (hugging, kissing, tongue kissing, oral and manual breast contact, and oral and manual genital contact); age at first intercourse; and enjoyment of first intercourse.

7. Childhood sexual experiences with adults

Subjects were asked their age at their first sexual experience with an adult (or person five years older when subject was a child), and the frequency of their prepubertal sexual experiences with an adult male. This data was incomplete for no clear reason (missing in 27% of women and 97% of men; see Reynolds, Herbenick, & Bancroft, 2003, for more details). Men, but not women, were asked about prepubertal sexual experiences with an adult female.

8. Current sexuality

Subjects were asked about their number of petting or coital partners after high school; their precoital petting experiences; whether they had ever experienced orgasm in coitus; and their enjoyment of first coitus.

Results

AGE AT PUBERTY

Mean age at puberty was, for women (i.e., menarche), 12.3 years, and for men (i.e., first ejaculation) 13.1 years.

MASTURBATION HISTORY

Data on masturbation was missing from 187 women (10%) and 39 men (2%). Of the 1,688 remaining women, 61.4% had never masturbated at the time of the interview; 13.2% reported prepubertal onset and 25.4% pubertal or postpubertal onset of masturbation. Of the 1,683 men, 5% had never masturbated at the time of the interview, whereas 26.9% reported prepubertal and 68.1% pubertal or postpubertal onset of masturbation. Among those reporting prepubertal onset of masturbation, the women reported a significantly younger age of onset than the men—8.38 years vs. 9.99 years, $t = 7.8$, $p < 0.001$.

Distribution of the age of onset of masturbation for males and females, and age of onset in relation to age at puberty, are shown in Figures B1 and B2.

EXPERIENCE OF ORGASM DURING PREPUBERTAL MASTURBATION

Eighty-four percent ($N = 100$) of the 119 women who reported a prepubertal orgasm indicated that masturbation was the source of their first orgasm. Other sources included same-sex experience (6%), petting experience (3%), and dreams (2%); 3% of women couldn't remember. Animals, psychological means (i.e., fantasy), and music or other means were re-

Females

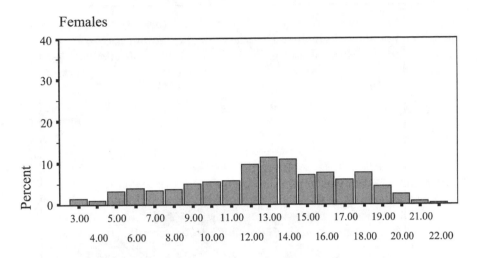

Age in years

STUDY B: Data were included only for subjects who reported masturbation.
56% of females had not yet masturbated at the time of the interview.

Males

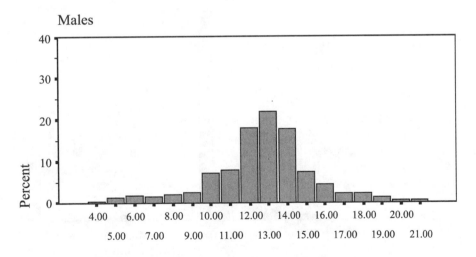

Age in years

STUDY B: Data were included only for subjects who reported masturbation.
5% of males had not yet masturbated at the time of the interview.

Figure B1.   Age at First Masturbation: Study B

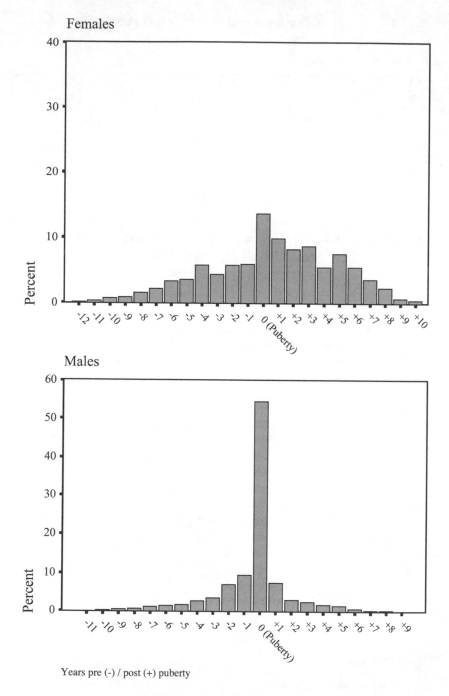

Females

Males

Years pre (-) / post (+) puberty

Only subjects with complete data and who had masturbated were included in this figure.
55% of women and 5% of men had not masturbated and 10% of women and 2% of men
had incomplete or missing data.

Figure B2.   Onset of Masturbation in Relation to Age at Puberty: Study B ported by one woman in each case. Women's average age at first prepubertal orgasm (regardless of source) was 9.2 years (median = 10.0; SD = 2.5; range = 3–14).

Of the men, only 9% (N = 162) of the total sample had valid data for this question. Of these males, 75% (N = 122) reported masturbation as the source and 11% reported a same-sex sexual experience as the source. The remaining subjects indicated the following sources: 7% spontaneous; 4% dreams; <3% in coitus; <1% in petting.

One hundred and six women and 124 men gave their age when orgasm first occurred as a result of prepubertal masturbation. This was significantly earlier for women than for men (9.2 vs. 10.4 years, t = 3.9, p < .001).

ASSOCIATION BETWEEN MASTURBATION HISTORY AND OTHER VARIABLES

Comparison of masturbators with nonmasturbators
In view of the small number of men who had never masturbated, this comparison is restricted to the women, the majority of whom had never masturbated. These two groups were compared on all 55 potentially relevant variables, with 26 showing differences at the 1% or 0.1% level of significance, all in a consistent direction. Most of these significant differences are given in Table B1.

The family variables that discriminated the masturbators were the greater likelihood of child nudity in the home and somewhat worse relationships with both parents between the ages of 14 and 17. The masturbators were more likely to have reported childhood sexual play experiences with peers, and reported significantly more "advanced" play behaviors during elementary school years. Masturbators also reported more prepubertal sexual experiences with adults. Masturbators reported more sexual experiences postpuberty in a number of ways, consistent with their being more sexually arousable and prepared to engage in more advanced sexual activities with their partners.

Comparison of prepubertal and postpubertal onset groups

1. Family and other early influences
Males. Only one variable, childhood nudity in the home, discriminated between pre- and postpubertal onset masturbators: 33% of the prepubertal and 25.5% of the postpubertal group (χ^2 = 8.1, p < 0.01).
Females. Two variables discriminated: the relationship subjects reported between their parents (at subject age 14–17) and subjects' health as a child. On a four-point scale (bad, poor, fair, good), women in the postpubertal onset group reported an interparental relationship that was slightly but significantly better than that reported by women in the prepubertal group (3.5 vs. 3.3, F = 5.2, p < .03). Subjects reported their health as a child on a five-point scale (1 = bad, 5 = good), and women in the postpubertal onset

Table B1. *Comparison of Women Who Had Ever and Those Who Had Never Masturbated*

Reported masturbating	**Never**	**Ever**	Significance
Family Environment			
Relationship with father at ages 14–17*	3.5	3.3	$t = 3.4, p = .001$
Relationship with mother at ages 14–17*	3.6	3.4	$t = 3.8, p < .001$
Childhood nudity in the home	20%	30%	$\chi^2 = 20.4, p < .001$
Childhood sexual experiences			
CSEP with opposite-sex peer	19%	36%	$\chi^2 = 62.8, p < .001$
CSEP with same-sex peer	26%	40%	$\chi^2 = 35.0, p < .001$
Prepubertal experience with an adult male	11%	18%	$\chi^2 = 12.7, p < .001$
Postpubertal sexual experiences			
Ever same-sex contact	3%	9%	$\chi^2 = 33.1, p < .001$
Ever orgasm in petting	26%	45%	$\chi^2 = 63.1, p < .001$
Apposition of nude genitalia without penetration (0 = never, 4 = often)	0.6	1.2	$t = 7.5, p < .001$
Oral sex experiences			
Male to female (receiving)†	0.2	0.4	$t = 3.9, p < .001$
Female to male (performing)†	0.2	0.3	$t = 3.8, p < .001$
Ever orgasm from receiving	1%	3%	$\chi^2 = 8.1, p < .01$
Sexual intercourse			
Ever premarital intercourse	13%	27%	$\chi^2 = 49.0, p < .001$
Enjoyment of first sexual intercourse (0 = none, 3 = much)	1.0	0.9	$\chi^2 = 0.2$, n.s.
Ever regret premarital sexual intercourse	21%	31%	$\chi^2 = 3.8, p = .053$
Ever had orgasm during sexual intercourse	70%	68%	$\chi^2 = 0.2$, n.s.
Current Sexuality			
Current arousal in response to opposite sex (1 = none, 4 = much)	2.1	2.5	$t = 8.3, p < .001$
Vaginal lubrication (0 = none, 4 = much)	1.9	2.5	$t = 8.9, p < .001$

* 1 = bad, 4 = good
† 0 = never, 4 = much

group reported slightly but significantly higher scores of good health as a child (4.7 vs. 4.4, $F = 15.1$, $p < .001$).

2. Peer group influences

None of these discriminated between the two groups for either males or females.

3. Childhood (prepubertal) sexual experiences

To look at differences in types of childhood sexual experiences with peers (CSEP) between the prepubertal and postpubertal groups, it was first ascertained what each subject's most advanced behavior was for time periods comparable to those used in Study A (i.e., for pre-elementary, ages 4 and 5; for elementary years, ages 6–12; for middle school/junior high, ages 13 and 14).

Males. Sixty-two percent of the prepubertal group engaged in prepubertal sex play with girls, compared with 44% of the postpubertal group ($\chi^2 = 44.0$, $p < 0.001$). Seventy-six percent of the prepubertal group engaged in prepubertal sex play with other boys, compared with 43% of the postpubertal group ($\chi^2 = 142.9$, $p < .001$).

There were also significant group differences for each of the three time periods (see Table B2), such that men in the prepubertal masturbation group more often reported "advanced" behaviors (i.e., oral-genital contact, coitus or attempted coitus, insertion in vagina or urethra, or anal contact) than did men in the postpubertal group.

Females. There was a trend for same-sex CSEP, with 44% of the prepubertal and 37% of the postpubertal group having engaged in sex play with other girls ($\chi^2 = 2.8$, $p = .095$). The difference for sex play with boys was not significant (40% in pre group, 34% in post group).

The two groups did not differ in their most advanced CSEP for either pre-elementary or junior high school years, though there was a significant difference for elementary school years, such that girls in the prepubertal group engaged in more advanced behaviors than girls in the postpubertal group (see Table B2).

4. Postpubertal sexual experiences

Males. Men in the prepubertal group started postpubertal petting earlier (14.9 vs. 15.3 years, $F = 14.9$, $p < .001$) and reported significantly more petting and coital partners through high school than did men in the postpubertal group (median, 5.0 vs. 4.0, $F = 5.2$, $p < .03$).

Subjects were asked to report the frequency with which they engaged in various sexual behaviors as part of premarital petting, and this frequency was coded using a five-point scale where 0 = never and 4 = much. Males in the two groups differed on several of these behaviors (see Table B3). They did not differ in reported age at first postpubertal orgasm during petting (17.4 years for both the pre- and postpubertal groups), or age at

Table B2. *The Most Advanced CSEP for the Prepubertal and Postpubertal Onset Groups*

	Women		Men	
	Prepubertal	Postpubertal	Prepubertal	Postpubertal
Pre-elementary			*	
Showing	40%	38%	22%	36%
Touching	40%	48%	29%	34%
"Advanced" †	20%	14%	49%	30%
Elementary	*		*	
Showing	22%	34%	14%	31%
Touching	47%	45%	34%	36%
"Advanced"	31%	21%	52%	33%
Jr. high school			*	
Showing	15%	30%	12%	27%
Touching	55%	35%	47%	41%
"Advanced"	30%	35%	41%	32%

* Significant, $p < .05$
† "Advanced" is oral-genital contact, coitus or attempted coitus, insertion in vagina or urethra, or anal contact.

first postpubertal sexual intercourse (17.3 for the prepubertal and 17.5 years for the postpubertal group). There was a trend for men in the prepubertal group to report greater enjoyment during first sexual intercourse than men in the postpubertal group (1.83 vs. 1.66 on a scale where 0 = did not enjoy and 3 = enjoyed very much; $p = .092$).

Females. The two groups did not differ in the age at which they first engaged in postpubertal petting or in the number of petting and coital partners they reported through high school (3.7 prepubertal group, 3.8 postpubertal group), or in the frequencies of different types of petting they had experienced (see Table B3), or in the reported age at first postpubertal orgasm during petting (17.9 years for both the pre- and postpubertal groups), or the age at first postpubertal intercourse (18.5 years prepubertal, 18.4 years postpubertal), or enjoyment reported during first intercourse (prepubertal 0.92, postpubertal 0.96).

Table B3. *Frequency of Engaging in Premarital Petting (0 = "never," 4 = "often")*

	Women		Men	
	Prepubertal	Postpubertal	Prepubertal	Postpubertal
Hugging	3.8	3.8	3.9	3.8
Kissing	3.8	3.8	3.9	3.8
Tongue kissing	3.2	3.0	3.1	3.0
Manual breast contact	3.0	2.9	3.2	3.1
Oral breast contact	1.8	1.8	1.8*	1.4
Manual genital contact on man by woman	1.3	1.5	1.8*	1.5
Manual genital contact on woman by man	1.9	2.0	2.5*	2.2
Oral-genital contact on woman by man	0.30	0.38	0.2	0.2
Oral-genital contact on man by woman	0.35	0.32	0.3	0.2
Apposition of genitalia without penetration	1.1	1.2	1.3*	1.1
Orgasm in postpubertal petting	1.2	1.4	1.4	1.4

*Significant, $p < .05$

5. Childhood sexual experiences with adults

We have incomplete data here, particularly for the men, the large majority of whom were apparently not asked about such experiences. Two hundred seventy-three women and 46 men reported such experiences, including both "touching" and "nontouching." These experiences were not more likely to occur in either of the masturbation onset groups. For women, 20% in the prepubertal group and 16% in the postpubertal group reported an experience with an adult or older male ($\chi^2 = 1.7$, $p = .196$). Ages at which these experiences occurred did not differ between the masturbation onset groups. (For further details of these experiences, see Reynolds, Herbenick, & Bancroft, 2003.)

Those in the prepubertal onset group with experiences involving older males or females were looked at to compare their age at first masturbation with their age at first prepubertal experience with an adult. These did not differ significantly in either direction. Women in this narrowed pool had an average age of 8.5 for first masturbation and 8.7 for first experience with an adult (male), whereas men had an average age of 9.8 years for both masturbation and for first experience with an adult (male or female).

6. Postpubertal same-sex experience
   Males. Thirty-nine percent of the prepubertal and 27% of the postpubertal masturbation group reported same-sex sexual contact (with or without orgasm) since onset of puberty ($\chi^2 = 22.8$, $p < 0.001$), with age at first such contact being earlier in the prepubertal group (13.9 years vs. 14.3 years, $F = 5.4$, $p < .03$).
   Females. Twelve percent of the prepubertal and 8% of the postpubertal group reported postpubertal same-sex contact, with or without orgasm (trend: $\chi^2 = 2.8$, $p = .096$), but the age at which this first occurred did not differ significantly between groups (14.6 years for the prepubertal group, 15.2 years for postpubertal).

7. Current and college sexual experience
   For details of premarital experiences, see Table B3.
   Males. Fifty-two percent of the prepubertal group and 46% of the postpubertal group had experienced premarital sexual intercourse ($\chi^2 = 4.1$, $p < 0.05$). The two groups did not differ in the number of post–high school petting and coital partners reported (15.9 pre, 15.7 post).
   There are no significant group differences for men in regard to degree of feeling sexually aroused by the opposite sex (none, little, some, much) and too few to analyze in regard to feelings of arousal for the same sex.
   Females. Fifty-seven percent of the prepubertal and 43% of the postpubertal group reported sexual intercourse with a fiancé or subsequent spouse prior to marriage (trend: $\chi^2 = 3.1$, $p = 0.08$). The two groups did not significantly differ in the number of reported post–high school petting and coital partners (each group reported an average of 6.4).
   There were no significant group differences for women in regard to degree of feeling sexually aroused by the opposite sex (none, little, some, much) and too few to analyze in regard to feelings of arousal for the same sex.

Comparison of Studies A and B

Apart from the substantially different sample sizes in the two studies, there are many differences in the information available to analyze which limit the amount of direct comparison possible.

For the two samples as a whole, the age at puberty was significantly younger for the males in Study A than in Study B (mean age 12.5 years in Study A, 13.1 years in Study B, $t = 2.76$, $p < 0.01$), and younger for the females in Study B than Study A (12.6 years in Study A, 12.3 years in Study B, $t = 5.25$, $p < 0.001$). These mean ages were unchanged by adding in those subjects excluded because they did not reach puberty between ages 10 and 16.

Masturbation in Females

There was a dramatic decrease in the proportion of women who had never masturbated, from 61.4 % in Study B to 16% in Study A, and also a substantial increase in the proportion who reported prepubertal masturbation (13.2% in Study B, 40% in Study A). There were substantial differences between the masturbators and nonmasturbators in Study B, suggestive of the masturbators' being more sexually aware and responsive. These differences were less substantial and more subtle in Study A, although, given the different questions asked in the two studies and the lower power in Study A, the comparisons between masturbators and nonmasturbators were broadly similar.

When we consider factors which might be related to early onset of masturbation within the limits of comparison that the data allow, we find some interesting changes over the 50 years. Whereas the early onset subjects in Study B tended to show more childhood sexual experience with peers, and of a more advanced type, they did not differ much from the postpubertal onset group when it came to high school and college years. In Study A, we find the prepubertal onset group reporting earlier sexual interest, arousal, and fantasy, and earlier experiences with "heavy fondling." They also tended to report more sexual activity, including masturbation, and greater satisfaction with their sexual lives during college years than the postpubertal onset women.

There was little change between Studies B and A in same-sex sexual experience or its relationship to age of onset of masturbation.

Masturbation in Males

The proportion of men who had never masturbated at the time of interview was slightly lower in Study A (1.5%) than Study B (5%). Also, in Study A a higher percentage reported prepubertal onset of masturbation (40.4%, Study A; 26.9%, Study B). We find in Study B that the prepubertal onset group experienced more petting and had more petting partners during high school, and were more likely to have engaged in premarital intercourse. In Study A, the situation is similar for high school experiences, but by college years we find the postpubertal onset group tending to report more masturbation, more orgasm during oral sex, more enjoyment from oral sex, and a greater likelihood of ejaculating quickly.

Although the information was collected somewhat differently in the two studies, there appears to be substantially more same-sex behavior among the males in Study B than in the later study. In addition, in Study B, males in the prepubertal onset group were significantly more likely to engage in same-sex behavior as adolescents; this was not the case in Study A.

Comparison of Males and Females

Although we see the predictable gender difference in the proportion of college students who masturbate, we do not find a gender difference in Study A in the proportion of men and women who masturbated before puberty, or in their frequency of prepubertal masturbation.

Also striking is the significantly earlier mean age of onset of prepubertal masturbation for females, the differences in age between females and males being almost identical in the two studies. The distributions of age of onset in relation to age at puberty are also strikingly similar for the two studies (see Figures A2 and B2).

In Study B, we find both female and male prepubertal masturbators showing evidence of more sexual awareness and responsiveness. In Study A, this relationship is even more marked for the females, but the picture changes for the males; the prepubertal onset group seem to be in some way "desensitized" sexually later during adolescence.

Discussion

These two studies show two striking and contrasting findings. On the one hand, we see a substantial increase over 50 years in the proportion of women who report masturbation, and who start to masturbate prior to puberty, to the extent that there is no gender difference in either the occurrence or frequency of prepubertal masturbation in the later study. On the other hand, we find a gender difference in the age of onset of masturbation and its relationship to puberty which is very similar in these two samples 50 years apart.

Leitenberg et al. (1993) commented that if the predictable gender differences in the likelihood and frequency of masturbation were due to different "social scripts" for men and women, then the changing attitudes toward women's sexuality as well as toward masturbation should have resulted in a decline in this gender difference. Because they found gender differences to persist in relation to masturbation, in spite of major reductions in other gender differences in relation to sex, they wondered if biological factors might be responsible. Our findings suggest the impact of both sociocultural and biological influences. The increased likelihood of women reporting masturbation probably results from a reduction in the taboo around masturbation, making it easier to admit to masturbation as well as increasing the likelihood of its happening, both prepubertally and postpubertally. In addition, the substantial differences between women 50 years ago who reported and didn't report masturbating in other aspects of their sexuality suggest a level of societal constraint on women's sexual expression at that time which has substantially lessened.

In the males, by contrast, the robust pattern that emerges from our two studies, and which is largely consistent with the rest of the literature, is of a more predictable, peri-pubertal pattern of masturbatory onset, suggesting that the hormonal, physical, and psychosocial changes at puberty play an important organizing and activating role, which hasn't changed over the 50 years and which results in the large majority of males' starting to masturbate either shortly before or shortly after puberty onset. Our use of first ejaculation as the indicator of puberty onset may accentuate this pattern, but using other indicators of puberty onset, as our own data show, would make little difference to this pattern.

The much more variable pattern of masturbatory onset in females, with its relative lack of association with puberty, implies that it is less hormonally organized, or alternatively that hormones are more relevant to some females than others. The early prepubertal starters may be manifesting a relatively high and innate level of sexual awareness and responsiveness which, according to our limited data, does not appear to be determined by environmental factors, and hence may have a genetic basis. This early onset may be activated by hormonal changes at adrenarche, which typically occurs around eight years of age. The middle-range onset masturbators may, like the males, be showing more responsiveness to peri-pubertal hormonal change, while the late-onset masturbators or non-masturbators may be expressing a generally lower level of sexual responsiveness.

What our data also show for females is a suggestion of a link between early-onset masturbation and more positive sexual experiences in adolescence and early adulthood, although by college years social factors will be increasing the likelihood of sexual involvement in the majority of women, so that by then the relevance of this early onset is relatively subtle. The late-onset group, who we have postulated may be less sexually responsive, may not differ in their ability to establish rewarding and enjoyable sexual (and reproductive) relationships, but it is possible that they may end up attaching less importance to orgasm and genital response and more to other, more socially validated aspects of the sexual experience. That is a researchable question. (For a more comprehensive comparison of hormonal influences in male and female sexuality, see Bancroft, in press.) It would be of interest to use such markers as early masturbation onset as possible predictors of later patterns of sexuality in women, including the impact of the menstrual cycle, pregnancy and lactation, and the menopause—but that will best be done with longitudinal studies, as with older subjects retrospective recall of childhood masturbation experience will be more fallible. We can begin to see how biological and sociocultural factors might interact in the sexuality of women. If we postulate that women vary in their propensity for sexual responsiveness on genetic or at least biological grounds, as suggested above, then what we may have seen over this 50-year period is a reduction of the social constraints which previously were inhibiting some of the early starters and many of the late starters. As a result we are seeing the basic biologically determined variability of female sexual responsiveness given freer expression.

In the male we find the impact of puberty on the organization of emerging sexuality, at least through masturbation, markedly apparent at both time periods. There may have been some more subtle changes. We suggested above some form of "desensitization" of the early masturbators. Perhaps the early masturbation experience had dulled sexual responsiveness over the years, or perhaps the early masturbators had well-established patterns of penile stimulation which were less easily incorporated into their sexual interactions with a partner. The hint, in Study A, that the early-onset masturbators are more isolated from their peer group warrants further inquiry. It is otherwise difficult to see how changing social influences could account for this difference.

We found no support, in either study, for the idea that early masturbation is a manifestation of the "sexualizing" of children that results from sexual abuse, although the finding that women who didn't masturbate at all were less likely to report such abuse experiences during childhood, in Study B, raises the possibility that the child's level of sexual awareness might influence her likelihood of being sexually exploited by an older person. We found no evidence of this in the later study. We also found a greater likelihood of childhood sexual experience with peers in women who had masturbated, although this association was less striking and more subtle in the later study. Whether the CSEP increased the likelihood of masturbation or vice versa, we cannot clearly answer.

We found that, in Kinsey's time, the early-onset masturbating male was more likely to engage in same-sex behavior postpuberty; this no longer appears to be the case. The more general decline in same-sex sexual activity among teenage boys is discussed more fully in the accompanying paper (Reynolds, Herbenick, & Bancroft, 2003).

One unexpected finding, which was restricted to the females, was an association between prepubertal masturbation and exposure to pornography as a child. This deserves closer examination. At present it is not clear whether the pornography awakened sexual interest or whether the greater innate interest in sex may have increased awareness of pornography, or recall of it.

Other studies of college students (Arafat & Cotton, 1974; Leitenberg et al., 1993) show some variability but are consistent with this general picture. The proportion of females who had ever masturbated is higher in the Arafat and Cotton study (61%) than in the later Leitenberg et al. study (45%), both falling between our findings in Studies A and B.

In these other studies, precise age of puberty has not been reported. However, Arafat and Cotton (1974) report the proportions of males and females starting masturbation at different ages pre- and postpubertally. Their distributions are very similar to ours, with a much flatter pattern in the females than the males.

In conclusion, the results reported here suggest that masturbation is an important marker of sexual development, which is particularly valuable in exploring the inherent variability of sexual responsiveness and interest in women.

References

Arafat, I. S., & Cotton, W. L. (1974). Masturbation practice of males and females. *Journal of Sex Research, 10,* 293–307.

Bancroft, J. (in press). Androgens and sexual function in men and women. In C. Bagatell & W. J. Bremner (Eds.), *Androgens in health and disease.* Totowa, NJ: Humana.

Friedrich, W., Grambsch, P., Broughton, D., Kuiper, J., & Beilke, R. (1991). Normative sexual behavior in children. *Pediatrics, 88,* 456–464.

Halpern, C. J. T., Udry, J. R., Suchindran, C., & Campbell, B. (2000). Adolescent males' willingness to report masturbation. *Journal of Sex Research, 37,* 327–332.

Leitenberg, H., Detzer, M. J., & Srebnik, D. (1993). Gender differences in masturbation and the relation of masturbation experience in preadolescence and/or early adolescence to sexual behavior and sexual adjustment in young adulthood. *Archives of Sexual Behavior, 22,* 87–98.

Reynolds, M., & Herbenick, D. (2003). Using computer-assisted self-interview (CASI) for recall of childhood sexual experiences. In J. Bancroft (Ed.), *Sexual development in childhood* (pp. 77–81). Bloomington: Indiana University Press.

Reynolds, M., Herbenick, D., & Bancroft, J. (2003). The nature of childhood sexual experiences: Two studies 50 years apart. In J. Bancroft (Ed.), *Sexual development in childhood* (pp. 134–155). Bloomington: Indiana University Press.

Discussion Paper

JOHN D. DELAMATER

I appreciate being invited to participate in the workshop, and also the opportunity to comment on these two papers: "Masturbation as a marker of sexual development: Two studies 50 years apart," by Bancroft, Herbenick, and Reynolds, and "The nature of childhood sexual experiences: Two studies 50 years apart," by Reynolds, Herbenick, and Bancroft. The two papers present results from the same two datasets. I am not going to say much about the methodology of the Kinsey study (Study B). I do have comments about the methodology of the recent study. Then I would like to highlight some of the findings reported in the two studies and point in some directions that I think these results take us.

Methodological Issues

We have been talking about the need to learn about normal sexual development or to identify what normative sexual development is. To do this, we need data from representative samples; a number of people this morning cited problems with data coming from very highly selected samples, so that we are not sure what they represent. Study A was obviously an important attempt to get data from a representative sample of students. Recruitment proceeded in two stages. The first stage involved the questionnaire that was mailed to a random sample of students on campus. There was a 51% response rate to that questionnaire, which is about typical, I suppose, for a mailed questionnaire. But it is unfortunate, because they started with a random sample, and half of the people did not return the questionnaire. An even smaller percentage returned the form giving permission to contact them again. Only 684 out of 1,800 returned a "permission to be contacted" form. Of this group, 553 were invited to participate in Stage 2, by completing a computer-assisted self-interview (CASI). It was completed by only 55%, so in fact the response rate from the original base is 16% of the original sample. The authors do report in one paper that there was no difference in Stage 2 between people who did and did not complete the CASI. I would be even more interested in a comparison of people who completed the CASI in Stage 2 and all of the people who completed the questionnaire in Stage 1 because the latter is a larger group that approaches being representative. Having done such studies myself, I can certainly appreciate the difficulties of working even with a population that is this close at hand.

Bancroft, Herbenick, and Reynolds

John Bancroft and his co-authors propose masturbation as an important marker of sexual development. We discussed this morning the need for a model of normal sexual development, and the identification of markers or milestones in that process. I think they are right; I think masturbation is probably a very important marker. They suggest that masturbation "has the advantage of being a solitary behavior relatively independent of social context and peer group influences." Thus, it may be a relatively "pure" marker of individual sexuality. As a sociologist, I have to suggest that there may be some very important social influences even on solitary masturbation. I certainly remember in my male peer groups a lot of discussion about masturbation. People have suggested that men in particular, at least in my generation, often learned about masturbation from other young men, either in conversation or actually in childhood sex play (Rook & Hammen, 1977). People have said that women of my generation typically did not have that experience; I don't know whether that is true. People also say that young women today talk about sex in a way that they did not 30 years ago. It may be that there is actually more peer group social interaction around sexuality and masturbation now than there was in the past, whereas I suspect the amount of that kind of activity for men has more or less remained the same. I think we need to take into account the possibility of peer group influence on the onset of masturbation and possibly on the frequency of masturbation. I remember my friends reporting some number of instances of masturbation per day or week; like all self-report, we have to be skeptical of that, especially when we were standing on the street corner smoking cigarettes, but I suspect it had a motivating influence on some of the other young men who were listening to the conversation.

The analysis that is reported in Study A systematically compares young people who started masturbating before puberty with those who started after puberty. I thought it was very interesting that females in the pre-pubertal group are more likely to report memories of childhood sexual experience with peers during elementary school, compared to females who first masturbate postpuberty (77% vs. 52%). This suggests peer influence. It is especially important to notice that whether people started before or after puberty is not related to the likelihood of having a same-sex partner during high school for males or females, nor to likelihood of a sexual experience with an adult before age 16. So there is no evidence that the patterns we observe in masturbation might relate to other atypical experiences, particularly abuse, which we discussed at length this morning. So in that sense masturbation may be a very important marker of normal sexual development.

I also noted the dramatic decrease in the proportion of women who had never masturbated, from 61% of the women interviewed by Kinsey (1938–56) to 16% in Study A (1998–99). This is a huge change in behavior. There is also a dramatic increase in prepubertal masturbation among women, from 13% in the Kinsey data to 40% in the more recent study. The authors suggest that these changes are due to the lessening of constraints on female sexuality between the 1940s and the end of the century, and a reduction in the taboo in our society against masturbation. I would add to that the possibility that there is increased peer interaction for young women around sexuality and around masturbation, which may have contributed to the increase, as, possibly, has access to information in sex education programs in schools. Sex education is certainly more common now than it was then. There is a lot of variability in sex education courses, but I am sure some of them do provide good information about sexuality. Finally, we have the mass media. There are certainly much more open portrayals of a variety of sexual activities in the mass media today. I think most young people must be influenced by that, to some extent.

Reynolds, Herbenick, and Bancroft

The paper by Reynolds, Herbenick, and Bancroft reports a variety of data regarding childhood (and adolescent) sexual experience with peers (CSEP). The first significant finding is, as we saw from the bar graphs in their presentation, the vast majority of young men and women reported sexual experience with peers prior to high school (87% of the males and 84% of the females). The second finding is that the most advanced behavior during the pre-elementary years was relatively non-intimate, and there is a gradual increase in the prevalence of the more intimate forms of sexual behavior—oral/genital and anal and vaginal insertion—as the person moves into adolescence. The third finding is that a majority of respondents recalled five or fewer episodes in childhood. The fourth finding that I thought was particularly interesting was that the most memorable experience for the majority of these young people was dyadic and it involved a person of the opposite gender; I think this is consistent with socialization and other patterns in our society.

These four findings are consistent with a model of developmental progression. Such a progression occurs pretty commonly across our society. I think the progression goes from kissing to light petting/breast fondling, heavy petting/genital fondling, to intercourse and possibly to oral/genital contact.

One of the really interesting things about this progression is that it takes time in the life of an individual. In Table 1, I have put some data from a couple of the tables in Meredith's [Reynolds and colleagues'] paper, specifically the ages at which young people reported their first kiss, their first experience of light fondling, their first experience of heavy fondling, and their first experience of intercourse. What you see, first for men, is that the first kiss occurs between the ages of 12½ and 14, light fondling 15 to 15½, heavy fondling a bit later in their 15th years, and the age of first intercourse 16.7 to 18, for the men that completed the study. You see for the women the same kind of pattern; it starts a bit later with the first kiss being at age 13.3 to 13.8, but then the other ages are comparable: 15.1, 15.7 and 17.1. So the progression takes three to four years in the development of a particular individual.

I published a book in 1979 (DeLamater & MacCorquodale) that has the exact same data from a large sample of students at the University of Wisconsin who we interviewed in face-to-face interviews in 1973. Here (see Table 1) you have the ages at which our student sample reported their first participation in the same four behaviors. First, you see the same pattern; it takes time for the progression to occur. More importantly, you see that the process is happening earlier now (in the Reynolds, Herbenick, & Bancroft data) than it did 25 or 26 years ago; this is consistent with the social changes that John Bancroft mentioned earlier. Notice also that this progression is what we observe as a particular relationship develops, from least to most intimate behavior. Also, it is what we observe when we study the sexual scripts of young people in our society (Jemail & Geer, 1977); this is the order in which they tell us these behaviors occur within their dating relationships. So I think there is a very clear pattern here that resonates to a number of aspects of sexual expression in our contemporary society.

Concluding Remarks

There is evidence in both studies, the analysis of the data collected by Kinsey and the analysis of data from contemporary college students, that childhood sexual experience with peers is associated with earlier and more extensive sexual experience in adolescence. As John Bancroft says in his paper, the crucial question is whether this is a causal relationship. That is, do young people become more sexually aware and active in adolescence because of childhood sexual experience, or do incidence and frequency of both childhood and adolescent sexual activity reflect an innately greater interest in or awareness of sexuality in some children compared to others? There is a third possibility, and that is that both of these could reflect something else. The something else that occurred to me as I read the papers and listened to the discussion this morning is family influence. It could be that children growing up in families that are more openly sexual in the ways that are measured in the studies we discussed, have more open discussion regarding sexuality, more nudity, where children have the opportunity to

Table 1. *Comparison of Ages of First Experience of Sexual Intimacy*

	Reynolds, Herbenick, & Bancroft (1) (1998–99)		DeLamater & MacCorquodale (2) (1973)	
Behavior	*Male*	*Female*	*Male*	*Female*
First kiss	12.5 to 13.9	13.3 to 13.8	14.2	14.8
Light petting/ breast fondling(3)	15.1 to 15.5	15.1	15.8	16.6
Heavy petting/ genital fondling	15.5 to 15.8	15.7	16.6 to 16.8	17.2 to 17.4
Intercourse	16.7 to 18	17.1	17.5	17.9

1. See Reynolds, Herbenick, & Bancroft, Table A6.
2. See DeLamater & MacCorquodale, 1979, Table 4.1, p. 59.
3. "Petting" used by Reynolds, Herbenick, & Bancroft, "Fondling" by DeLamater & MacCorquodale.

observe adults engaging in sexual behavior—such a family environment may create greater awareness which leads to both more childhood exploration with peers and more sexual activity in adolescence. I was particularly interested in Bill Friedrich's data showing a positive correlation between his measure of family sexuality and reports by the mothers of their children's behavior. Another possible third factor was suggested by Ed Laumann this morning, that we pay attention to patterns of recruitment. It is possible that those young people who engage in childhood sex play were recruited into it by someone. This may reflect something about the social environments that kids grow up in. There may be some social environments where that kind of recruitment is much more likely to happen, thereby producing a person who has earlier childhood sexual experience.

I think, in summary, that these two studies provide the foundation for a model of normal sexual development. They identify some of the markers. We have some interesting data on the timing of the occurrences of those markers, at least in populations of college students. I think the interpretation of these patterns could be the subject of a great deal of lively debate.

References

Bancroft, J., Herbenick, D. L., & Reynolds, M. A. (2003). Masturbation as a marker of sexual development: Two studies 50 years apart. In J. Bancroft (Ed.), *Sexual development in childhood* (pp. 156–185). Bloomington: Indiana University Press.

DeLamater, J., & MacCorquodale, P. (1979). *Premarital sexuality: Attitudes, relationships, behavior.* Madison: University of Wisconsin Press.

Jemail, J. A., & Geer, J. (1977). Sexual scripts. In R. Gemme & C. C. Wheeler (Eds.), *Progress in sexology* (pp. 513–522). New York: Plenum.

Reynolds, M. A., Herbenick, D. L., & Bancroft, J. (2003). The nature of childhood sexual experiences: Two studies 50 years apart. In J. Bancroft (Ed.), *Sexual development in childhood* (pp. 134–155). Bloomington: Indiana University Press.

Rook, K. S., & Hammen, C. L. (1977). A cognitive perspective on the experience of sexual arousal. *Journal of Social Issues, 33*(2), 7–29.

Discussion Paper

DEBORAH L. TOLMAN

I am a senior research scientist at the Center for Research on Women at Wellesley College, where I founded and direct the Gender and Sexuality Project, an umbrella for a number of different studies on gender and sexuality in adolescent development. I have primarily done my research with girls. I began including boys in the last five years, when I had the brilliant insight that things are not going to be changed much for girls until we figure out what's going on with boys. So I have read these papers through the lens of my prospective perspective, rendering one of the key questions in these papers, that of recall, especially interesting and thought-provoking for me.

There are some really complicated issues running through these papers that had a great deal to bear on our larger project here of developing a consensus statement. First, I want to say that as someone who does work on adolescent sexuality, it is such a treat to think about and read about and discuss data about sexuality that is potentially positive and not traumatic and not bad and not focused on risk. I want to acknowledge how these papers jettisoned out of the reigning discourse about the sexuality of people under the age of 20. I commend the authors for engaging in what constitutes an unspeakable and risky activity, not because these behaviors are inherently problematic, but because to study them in the current (and past) hostile environment is.

I want to invite us to consider some of the meta-level issues embedded in these papers that I think are crucial for our overall agenda. What these papers offer is an important foray, the start of a foray, into our understanding about childhood sexuality, which is what I would argue our mission at the very least involves and which, interestingly and perhaps ironically, we have not in fact talked much about today. So far, prior to these papers, only Jany Rademakers addressed childhood sexuality directly (see Rademakers, Laan, & Straver, 2003). While I wish to consider how these papers move our understanding of childhood sexuality forward, I will organize my remarks around my observation that these papers contain several cautionary tales.

My initial reaction to the papers was to be overwhelmed by the sheer volume of data reported. I found this cornucopia of information quite difficult to hold in my head, in fact, and I wondered why that was so. Setting aside personal, idiosyncratic explanations (exhaustion, overwork, mothering two small children), I recalled an anecdote told to me by Carol Gilligan, with whom I studied. She recounted the difficulty that she had had in keeping Kohlberg's system for coding levels of moral development in her head. She always had to go back to the coding book; she couldn't remember it, because the framework did not make sense to her. Without a compelling theoretical framework within which to hold these categories, they simply kept slipping out of her mind. I realized that in the case of these papers, I was having a comparable processing problem. It wasn't so much that I had an alternative framework that intruded upon my reading of the papers, but that I felt the absence of an explicit theoretical framework keenly, and so I felt at sea about how to make sense of these analyses.

As a wonderful statistics professor of mine once wisely remarked, data don't speak, people do. I was missing crucial guiding information, and I found myself wanting to know some really basic things; please take my queries as what they are intended, a genuine need to know. What exactly were the research questions? What did these authors hypothesize? What did they predict they would find—and we'll get to the "and why" part in a second. I think that these hypotheses actually appear in the conclusions of these papers, cloaked as findings in a way, and signify a sort of missing or at least subterranean discourse throughout the papers. My analysis of these papers suggests that we must know, from the outset, how the authors conceptualize sexuality in order to understand and evaluate how this conception informs their hypotheses and the questions that they are pursuing in secondary analyses of these large and very compelling data sets.

Let me be so bold as to unearth, retrospectively and retroactively, what I think some of their research questions may have been. Is there an innate dimension to sexuality that may inform sexual behavior in childhood and beyond? Is there an interaction between internal factors (e.g., hormonal, personality) and external or contextual (e.g., demographic, family) factors and how childhood sexuality emerges, as well as for how early sexuality relates to later sexual experiences? Does masturbation or childhood sexual experience with peers (CSEP) relate to—and, at the true heart of things, don't they, and we all, really want to know if such behavior *causes*—coital experiences among adolescents or early adults? Are there gender differences in these associations, and how did these associations change over time? Does early masturbation or CSEP relate to earlier or perhaps better sexual experiences in adolescence and early adulthood, and if so, how?

I truly do not mean to be condescending in this exercise, but what I do want to do is call attention to how vital it is to articulate these questions up front, because they do and they should drive the design of our studies. Such an exercise forces us to come clean about what our theories and thus our endeavors are (Fine & Gordon, 1989), rather than offering them as after-the-fact explanations, which makes me a bit uncomfortable. In this instance, my discomfort springs in part from not being convinced that these data supported some of the explanatory claims being offered in the conclusions of these papers. Yet I did find what were dressed up as conclusions to be compelling and important theories. I am certainly not the first to notice that how we conceptualize sexuality and sexual development and sexual processes will organize what questions we do and do not ask, how we interpret our data, and, ultimately, what knowledge is and also is not generated about the development of human sexuality (Foucault, 1980; Tiefer, 1995). Let me offer an example that ties these two papers together.

In what I think constitutes an answer to the question "How are prepubertal masturbation and childhood sexual experiences with peers related to later sexuality for girls?" the authors report that there were no differences in later female sexuality found to be associated with prepubertal CSEP, but there was one found with prepubertal masturbation, that is, prepubertal masturbation was associated with what the authors called a more positive later sexuality. Let me offer a completely different way of thinking about these findings than the potential role of hormones or "innate sexuality" offered as explanatory in the paper—and representing one conception of sexuality. The interpretation I offer is grounded in a feminist social constructionist view (Tiefer, 1995; Tolman & Higgins, 1996) mixed up with a feminist perspective on female development (Brown & Gilligan, 1992; Debold, 1991; Gilligan, Rogers, & Tolman, 1991). That is, female adolescents learn to objectify themselves as a "normative" part of their development (Bartky, 1990; de Beauvoir, 1961; Fredrickson & Roberts, 1997; McKinley & Hyde, 1996). This process has been referred to as self-objectification. In my own work, I have articulated and measured how girls internalize and construct femininity as a process of dissociation from their own bodies, or disembodiment (Tolman & Porche, 2000). Recent research on preadolescent girls provides evidence of young girls' embodiment, which is found to diminish significantly as they go through puberty (Brown, 1999; Debold, Tolman, & Brown, 1996; Gilligan, 1991). It has also been theorized that developing girls, whose bodies are changing into women's bodies, are being constructed as objects of desire by others. Such objectification processes, incited and accompanied by the onslaught of patriarchal norms, may restrict female sexual desire, agency, and subjectivity (Fine, 1988; Tolman, 2002; Tolman & Debold, 1993).

Given this theoretical framework, here is another interpretation of this particular finding. Perhaps girls who masturbate prepubertally have developed a sense of themselves as sexual agents, have solidified their own embodiment, and thereby have developed a form of resistance to or protection from such pressures, and thus enjoy more positive sexuality as they develop. Prepubertal CSEP was reported by girls to be initiated by others or as having "just happened." No girls reported initiation, so that these behaviors would not enhance sexual subjectivity or agency, and thus we would expect to find no association with more positive sexual experiences later in their development—as was found. The right interpretation—who knows? Plausible? You bet. My point is that how we can conceptualize sexuality will be key in the knowledge about sexuality that we produce. With 20/20 hindsight as a college student, it was evident to me that Kinsey's construction of sexuality in terms of whether or not it was marital, along with his focus on orgasm as a privileged form of pleasure, produced certain forms of knowledge while glossing over others. We have the advantage of the work of Ken Gergen (1985), Amedeo Giorgi (1970), and Ken Plummer (1995), to name a few, who have provided theories to help us be aware of, and make explicit and careful choices about, how we are constructing sexuality and thus producing knowledge about it. These papers seem to be organized by a chicken or egg approach to childhood sexuality. I understand where it's coming from, but I urge us to have a critical perspective on it, because I think it might get us into an endless feedback loop that we may not be able to resolve with the types of research designs to which we have access at this point in history. And so, on to another, related question: Why is causality the most important question? Why this high and perhaps unachievable bar? It invites a perhaps unproductive focus on whether or not or to what extent sexuality is innate. In fact, it may even be construed as a kind of defensive question and, after listening to our discussion all day, I think that the centrifugal force of defensiveness is very evident. Perhaps in service of this pursuit, the authors of the second paper assert that masturbation is a "pure" indicator of sexuality or relatively uncomplicated, and I'm going to echo John DeLamater here: I'm not convinced that this is an assertion that is even supported by these data or by what the authors asserted regarding how early children learn that masturbation is in some fashion taboo. And such a construction of masturbation doesn't square with their concluding argument about the impact of both sociocultural and biological influences. This canon should be cleaned up by coming clean about the conceptions, theories, and hypotheses with which we are working.

Since I'm standing in the proverbial bully pulpit, I'm going to ask some other questions about sexuality research that a focus on childhood sexuality can generate. Why do we tend to privilege onset of behavior, and what does "onset" mean: engaging in the behavior once (which I refer to as being "sexually activated") or regularly, and don't such variations matter in how we make sense of these findings? And frequency of behavior, that is, questions about prevalence—what else might we want or need to know about sexuality in general and childhood sexuality in particular? Such questions lead us into the land of experience and meaning into which Jany Rademakers has convincingly invited us, and call for different designs, questions, and analysis. In the first of the two papers there was movement in that direction that I thought was absolutely fascinating. I refer in particular to the data on the characteristics of most memorable CSEP by time and gender and the positive and negative aspects of all CSEP ever engaged in by gender. Weren't you dying to know the stories of these participants' most memorable CSEP? I commend you for asking "most memorable"; that's a great strategy. I, for one, wanted a lot more information, which I, tending toward a phenomenological perspective on sexuality, believe we can garner through eliciting and listening to participants' stories (Mishler, 1986; Tolman, 2002). This method can operationalize a different and, the reported data would suggest, most necessary next set of research questions: How do early and/or late adolescents describe their most memorable CSEP and, while we're at it, early masturbation? How do they make sense of this experience and in what ways might they feel there is a connection between their childhood sexual experience, their adolescent sexual experiences, and their current sexuality? Okay, these are not easy questions to ask, and they pull for conscious processes. But why should we approach our research participants with suspicion rather than an openness to connection with them, working within a more relational model of research? One could argue that Kinsey spearheaded this perspective in some ways (though not in others!). This approach has been very fruitful with adolescents, who are not accustomed to being listened to; rather, they find it an unusual and meaningful departure from being talked at regarding their sexuality.

Let me shift to a related issue with a story that a female colleague of mine told about an experience she had when she was junior faculty. She was at a full faculty meeting with her colleagues, most of whom were male, when a sexual harassment suit that was being brought against a fellow (male) colleague was being discussed. The discussion essentially constituted denigration of the young women bringing the suit, the kinds of nasty things that one would imagine. My friend, because she was junior and female, felt she couldn't speak up and say what she thought might have occurred or why the students might be justified in their actions or how it was possible that they should be believed. As she tells this story, she got up, and she left the room, and she went to the women's room—and she masturbated. Her reason for masturbating had nothing to do with sexuality or sexual feelings; it had to do with regaining a sense of control. The point of the story is that we cannot assume that there is a sexual meaning associated with all sexual behavior; perhaps this is especially true with childhood sexual behavior. Masturbation may have nothing whatsoever to do with sexuality, and I think this conversation has already started here today. As I read these papers I kept wondering, what did masturbation mean or signify to these participants? The definition of self-stimulation to arousal made me more rather than less curious. Consider Charlene Muehlenhard and colleagues' recent discovery through narrative data that the participants in her studies had a totally different idea about what token resistance to sex, her area of expertise, meant than had the researchers, despite refined definitions. These newly discovered differences in the very conception of the construct under study had serious consequences for the interpretations they had been making all along of their quantitative data (Muehlenhard & Rodgers, 1998). Might there be experiences that adolescents, and I suppose I'm thinking in particular of girls but why not boys too, may have had that they would not label in this way but that would fit into one or a broader conception of childhood sexuality?

A video called *The Match That Started My Fire* is a case in point. It's about young women's descriptions of experiences of the joy of sexual pleasure in childhood. It sounds like these women were interviewed on the phone. It's not a study, so I don't know what the questions were or who these women were, but I think it still has something to tell us. Let me briefly recap the story in this video. A woman is remembering being in gym class and climbing a rope. She says that her feet were very sensitive, and so she liked climbing. She relays how the rope really felt good between her legs, and that she really liked that, and so she climbed a little bit higher. Before reaching the top, she slid down the rope, and she really liked that, and so she started climbing up again, and it really felt good, and so she slid down again—and she never made it to the top. That is her story. Now would that have been reported as masturbation in study A? I don't know, but such an experience may be elicited if we ask participants to tell us stories about remembered early sexual experiences, especially pleasurable ones. I think there may be an important difference between recall of traumatic experiences and recall of pleasurable or what we're trying to describe as normative experiences. Perhaps one of the reasons for the structure of these papers, which is, I suppose, at least in part what I'm commenting on, is the very real concern with the credibility of data that we can collect about childhood sexuality, which we've been talking about ad infinitum all morning and will probably not stop talking about, because it is indeed a serious problem for sexuality research. And I appreciated the detail with which the authors of both papers outlined the limitations of the use of retrospective accounts. They argue that such is the best that we can do—but is it indeed good enough? What else can we do to enhance the credibility or validity of our data?

I think narrative data can contribute to this challenge. While any individual story shifts, changes, and emerges over time (Plummer, 1995), such narratives convey information about remembered experience. At the same time, they provide a compelling context within which we can make sense of and have more confidence in other forms of information reported about childhood sexuality. Narrative data can enable us to learn what masturbation meant to participants, at least in retrospect, and its perceived impact on current sexuality. It can convince others that typical nonsexual childhood behaviors can be associated with sexuality that is not tainted or harmful. While narrative data offer different kinds of challenges, such as how to make a good interpretation or even how to think about "reliability" and "validity," there are methodologies available for enhancing those processes. As in all other forms of research, the clarity of the underlying conceptions, hypotheses, and research questions will enhance the credibility of such data and outline their limitations. Narrative data also offer the advantage of identifying aspects of sexual experience that we researchers may not have thought to ask about.

Being here at The Kinsey Institute, I feel obliged to comment on the use of Kinsey's data in these papers, because I was puzzled at first by it. I studied history and literature in college. I wrote my junior paper comparing scenes of seduction and rape in Victorian pornography to those in *Tess of the d'Urbervilles* by Thomas Hardy, and my senior honors paper on sexual awakening in George Eliot's *Middlemarch* (and no, it is not a non sequitur). So I am honestly very intrigued by historical material. But my sense was that the use of these historical data was in the service of answering questions about the potential innateness of sexuality such that, if continuities were found, it would suggest the presence of such an innate quality to sexuality. This approach disregards what we know about the changes in beliefs and norms over the past 50 years, which were mentioned by the authors and by John DeLamater, and, from my perspective, in well-recognized social constructions of sexuality via available discourses. While I honestly love these analyses and find them fascinating, I'm not sure how much they do for the larger project of understanding contemporary childhood sexuality, and I think that this approach should be discussed, especially given limited resources. In this larger project of coming to a consensus in which we are engaged as a group, we need to incorporate our conceptions of sexuality into our statement about how and why the study of childhood sexuality should be pursued. I think we have to name our favorite theories and hypotheses and research questions and tussle over them in order to design the very best studies possible, because, as we all know, we have to be impeccable. And I urge us to consider the different forms of data that can and should be collected and analyzed in an organized, coordinated fashion to bolster all of our findings and claims.

References

Bartky, S. L. (1990). *Femininity and domination: Studies in the phenomenology of oppression*. New York: Routledge.

Brown, L. M. (1999). *Raising their voices: The politics of girls' anger*. Cambridge, MA: Harvard University Press.

Brown, L. M., & Gilligan, C. (1992). *Meeting at the crossroads: Women's psychology and girls' development*. Cambridge, MA: Harvard University Press.

de Beauvoir, S. (1961). *The second sex*. New York: Bantam.

Debold, E. (1991). The body at play. In C. Gilligan, A. G. Rogers, & D. L. Tolman (Eds.), *Women, girls, and psychotherapy: Reframing resistance* (pp. 169–184). Binghamton, NY: Haworth.

Debold, E., Tolman, D., & Brown, L. M. (1996). Embodying knowledge, knowing desire: Authority and split subjectivities in girls' epistemological development. In N. R. Goldberger, J. M. Tarule, B. M. Clinchy, & M. F. Belenky (Eds.), *Knowledge, difference, and power* (pp. 85–125). New York: Basic.

Fine, M. (1988). Sexuality, schooling, and adolescent females: The missing discourse of desire. *Harvard Educational Review, 58*(1), 29–53.

Fine, M., & Gordon, S. (1989). Feminist transformations of/despite psychology. In M. C. M. Gentry (Ed.), *Gender and thought: Psychological perspectives* (pp. 146–174). New York: Springer-Verlag.

Foucault, M. (1980). *The history of sexuality: Vol. 1. An introduction* (R. Hurley, Trans.). New York: Vintage.

Fredrickson, B. L., & Roberts, T. A. (1997). Objectification theory: Toward understanding women's lived experiences and mental health risks. *Psychology of Women Quarterly, 21,* 173–206.

Gergen, K. J. (1985). The social constructionist movement in modern psychology. *American Psychologist, 40,* 266–275.

Gilligan, C. (1991). Joining the resistance: Psychology, politics, girls, and women. *Michigan Quarterly Review, 29,* 501–536.

Gilligan, C., Rogers, A. G., & Tolman, D. L. (Eds.). (1991). *Women, girls, and psychotherapy: Reframing resistance.* New York: Harrington Park.

Giorgi, A. (1970). *Psychology as a human science: A phenomenologically based approach.* New York: Harper and Row.

McKinley, N. M., & Hyde, J. S. (1996). The Objectified Body Consciousness Scale: Development and validation. *Psychology of Women Quarterly, 20,* 181–215.

Mishler, E. G. (1986). The analysis of interview-narratives. In T. R. Sarbin (Ed.), *Narrative psychology: The storied nature of conduct* (pp. 233–255). New York: Praeger.

Muehlenhard, C. L., & Rodgers, C. S. (1998). Token resistance to sex: New perspectives on an old stereotype. *Psychology of Women Quarterly, 22,* 443–463.

Plummer, K. (1995). *Telling sexual stories.* London: Routledge.

Rademakers, J., Laan, M., & Straver, C. J. (2003). Body awareness and physical intimacy: An exploratory study. In J. Bancroft (Ed.), *Sexual development in childhood* (pp. 121–125). Bloomington: Indiana University Press.

Tiefer, L. (1995). *Sex is not a natural act and other essays.* Boulder, CO: Westview.

Tolman, D. L. (2002). *Dilemma of desire: Teenage girls and sexuality.* Cambridge, MA: Harvard University Press.

Tolman, D. L., & Debold, E. (1993). Conflicts of body and image: Female adolescents, desire, and the no-body body. In P. Fallon, M. Katzman, & S. Wooley (Eds.), *Feminist perspectives on eating disorders* (pp. 301–317). New York: Guilford.

Tolman, D. L., & Higgins, T. (1996). How being a good girl can be bad for girls. In N. B. Maglin & D. Perry (Eds.), *Good girls/bad girls: Women, sex, violence, and power in the 1990s* (pp. 205–225). New Brunswick, NJ: Rutgers University Press.

Tolman, D. L., & Porche, M. V. (2000). The Adolescent Femininity Ideology Scale: Development and validation of a new measure for girls. *Psychology of Women Quarterly, 24,* 365–376.

General Discussion

Meredith Reynolds: I first want to talk about the use of narrative accounts because that actually was my first step. My dissertation was based largely on narrative data and I agree with you about the value of that for getting at the meanings of sexuality. My training is in clinical psychology at the University of Michigan, which is psychoanalytically oriented. I also have the benefit of learning methodologies using narrative recall and I worked with Marty Mayman there, who developed a good technique for studying early memories. We used his early memory questionnaire, a modified version of the Early Memory Test (Karliner, Westrich, Shedler, & Mayman, 1996), as a basis for getting narratives about sexual experience. We got up to three narratives from subjects, including their most memorable and second most memorable experiences, and if they were caught in the experience they were asked to write about that as well. It was a free open response followed by six probe questions. That is absolutely fascinating data. It's a wide spectrum of people's accounts and it's something that we didn't pursue in this study because we wanted to get a larger sample and you can only do the narrative approach with small samples. But the stories that are told and the emotional intensity that came out in some of those narratives was compelling and guided the development of the CASI questions.

John Bancroft: There's a lot of data in these two papers here, as you rightly point out, and this is the first time we've actually presented it. As far as John's comments were concerned, I think the word "pure" was improper and I shouldn't have used it. The point I was trying to make is that relative to other types of sexual expression, masturbation is perhaps the simplest marker of a person's sexual interest. Of course there are major social influences on masturbation too. I'm interested, for example, in whether there might have been more peer group influences on masturbation 50 years ago among boys than there are now because of greater awareness of masturbation and more stigmatization. The same thing applies to same-sex behavior. This is very striking. Kinsey reported that 37% of men had experienced orgasm with someone of the same sex since puberty. As John Gagnon and Bill Simon pointed out in a later paper, the large majority of that 37% involved sexual activity during the early teens. Günter

Schmidt has shown that in Germany in a series of studies of the students, there has been a steady decline in the amount of same-sex behavior amongst young people. I'm wondering whether the same thing might have happened in relation to circle jerk–type phenomena and the way that boys now learn about masturbation. I was intrigued by our finding that the early-onset masturbating boys tended to be a bit more isolated from their peer groups than the late-onset masturbating, which doesn't quite fit with the peer group determination model.

David Finkelhor: I have two methodology issues which occurred to me. One concerns the difference between the distribution of male and female masturbation onset. You defined puberty for males as first orgasm and you define puberty for females as menarche; now because masturbation was very likely involved with the act that signals the onset of puberty, the association of that first memory of their masturbation would be very likely enhanced or facilitated by the fact that they had an orgasm at the time and that would be the one that they'd most likely remember, it seems to me. So that produces an artifactual clustering for the boys around the time of first orgasm as the time that they would remember themselves first masturbating, whereas because it wasn't associated in the same way for girls, you might have had less of that clustering. I don't think that explains the whole thing, but it could explain some of it.

The other thing that occurred to me is the possibility that the social groups that are coming to be undergraduates at Indiana University have changed quite a bit since the 1940s and in particular, for example, I wonder how many African Americans there were here in the 1940s. I believe it's true, for example, that African American girls probably engage in more early sexual behavior and maybe more masturbatory activity. Could there be something about the changing social composition of the student bodies in these two historical times that would at least explain some of those differences?

John Bancroft: There are probably more African Americans now but there's still not very many, so I don't think a change in either composition could account for much. As for other types of sociocultural changes, one would assume that they would be reflecting the sexual changes that are going on in those 50 years anyway. So I don't see that as being necessarily a confound; it seems to be part of the process of social change. It is true that we're focusing on college students and it is true that in Kinsey's time there were quite substantial differences in the likelihood of masturbating between the lower and upper socioeconomic strata. You probably wouldn't find that degree of effect of socioeconomic status in the current sample. Your first point was about using ejaculation as the marker of puberty. When we took Kinsey's definition of puberty, which in some respects is a more conventional definition using a variety of puberty changes, and we changed it to make age of first ejaculation the indicator, the age remained the same for 80% with a correlation between the ages of .87. It was even closer for the females. But you're right, we've thought about this a lot, the confounding effect of using ejaculation as a marker to divide pre- and post-puberty given that is part of or likely to be part of masturbation. I agree with you that it probably amplifies that point to some extent. What you're suggesting is that boys may be more likely to remember masturbating when they ejaculate and therefore they are having a different pattern of recall than the girls; that is conceivable. You could say that maybe ejaculation is an organizing factor in boys' masturbation histories. But it doesn't explain why the girls seem to start predictably earlier than boys. So the only other explanation to explain that gender difference that I've heard is the one that you've just offered, that the boys recall their first masturbation more around the time that they first ejaculated whereas the girls' memories are not going to be organized that way. That is an interesting possibility.

Janet Hyde: Was the Kinsey sample of Indiana University students based on his 100% sampling of sororities and fraternities, because I know he used that sampling technique here? That raises the question, how much of the Kinsey sample was from those 100% sorority and fraternity sub-samples, and how would that compare to your sampling with the current Indiana University students? I do think young women who are in sororities are a little different from young women who aren't in sororities.

John Bancroft: The book says he did a 100% sampling in sororities and fraternities; however, they obtained two such samples from sororities and nine from fraternities, so the majority were partial samples.

Janet Hyde: I would argue that women in sororities are hyper-feminine and therefore perhaps less expressive of solitary sexuality.

John Bancroft: Well, certainly today's "frat boys" are hyper-masculine, no question about that, and some of the other research that we're doing at the moment into sexual risk-taking is making us quite concerned about the patterns of behavior in fraternity boys.

Debra Herbenick: I want to clarify that the Kinsey college sample was not all Indiana University students. It involved enrollment in colleges in other places in the country.

David Finkelhor: I wonder what your distribution would look like if you compared masturbation to orgasm for both the male and the female group?

John Bancroft: We reported in the paper on the number who recalled experiencing orgasms before puberty and it was a substantial minority who did that.

Dennis Fortenberry: I want to react to John DeLamater's commentary about the developmental hierarchy of sexual behaviors. My problem with it is that I think it fits the sample that he was referring to—college students. But it does not resonate well with other populations and I think that that's an important issue. It may be the same for masturbation as a marker of sexual development. I can't attach this to a substantial number of life stories that I know from young people, most of whom are inner city and African American, but a few now are Latino or even lower-middle-class European Americans. I think we ought to be careful in making generalizations in the absence of sufficient data.

John Bancroft: You're absolutely right, we should be very cautious about extrapolating beyond college students. The people you study are teenagers who are much less likely to end up in college. And if you go back to Kinsey's original studies, he found major differences in the males between different socioeconomic groups. But my impression is that most surveys since have found these socioeconomic differences to be less marked. But obviously they've not disappeared.

Dennis Fortenberry: I believe that there really are no data to allow us to extend even masturbatory behaviors to other ethnic and socioeconomic groups.

John Bancroft: You're dealing with young teenagers who get STDs.

Dennis Fortenberry: Not entirely; we're dealing with teenagers in clinics, many of whom have STDs but many of whom are not there just for that, they're there to get their eyes examined or their "sport physical" carried out. Our experience is not entirely with the teenagers who are infected.

John Bancroft: What exactly in the masturbation data is causing you concern?

Dennis Fortenberry: The idea that it's a substantial marker of the development of sexual behavior, because I see a significant number of particularly young men who actually describe, as best I can tell, at a fairly early age—somewhere between 9 and 11—an initial sexual experience that is coitus. They don't describe antecedent masturbatory activity, they don't describe a lot of kissing, they don't describe a lot of oral sex, they describe no oral/genital contact and no hand fondling or "petting," however you want to describe it.

Jay Paul: The close relationship of masturbation onset for the males in both studies could be a process of defining what is masturbation for the males. What is masturbation may change once puberty hits and you ejaculate. So I think that an important issue is what's defined as masturbation with these males, what do they perceive of as masturbation versus perhaps playing with their penis. I think it also suggests that part of what we're grappling with in terms of normal sexual development is this whole process, not just of biological and physical development and the sense of bodily awareness, but the whole process of differentiating sexual pleasure from other pleasures, sexual interest from other appetites.

Heino Meyer-Bahlburg: First, I want to agree with Dennis that in our inner-city samples we find substantial minorities of African American and

Latino children who start sex very early, before puberty or around the time of early puberty (Rotheram-Borus, Meyer-Bahlburg, Koopman, et al., 1992; Rotheram-Borus, Meyer-Bahlburg, Rosario, et al., 1992).

John DeLamater has described in 1968 the effects of the sex of the interviewer, which was particularly important in its effects on young women (DeLamater, 1974). Male interviewers with young women were less successful at getting disclosure than any other interview/subject pairings that were compared. Kinsey's interviewers were all male. As far as I remember he did not have female interviewers, and so I would think that talking about something as unspeakable at that time as masturbation was probably more difficult for women responding to male interviewers than for males. Thus, some of the sex differences that were found by Kinsey's team may have to do with the sex of the interviewer.

Your interpretation of the difference between women and men in onset of masturbation, and its relation to possible early pubertal events such as adrenarche, reminds me of our retrospective study on idiopathic precocious puberty in girls (Meyer-Bahlburg et al., 1985). Sociosexual and romantic behavior were only slightly advanced, whereas masturbation was advanced by 5½ years in those who masturbated. There is no good explanation other than it is somehow linked to the early onset of puberty.

Finally, I want to make a brief comment on Meredith's talk. I appreciate very much that you delineated the influence of sexual socialization factors in the family. We did something similar using a very different approach in our boys' study, which has not yet been published. In that study, we were interested in the relationship of childhood sexual behavior before puberty to such variables as conduct disorder or externalizing behaviors. Basically, we wanted to extend the problem behavior theory (Jessor & Jessor, 1977; Ketterlinus & Lamb, 1994) from adolescence to childhood. Using existing data from the main study, onto which we piggybacked, we could show that family factors predicting externalizing, aggressive, and delinquent behaviors also predicted sex behavior.

This is as expected, since the correlations between those two classes of behavior have already been demonstrated for adolescents. When we added on family sexual socialization, using variables very similar to the ones you employed, then the predictive value almost doubled (Meyer-Bahlburg, Wasserman, Dolezal, & Bueno, 1996). Thus, family sexual socialization variables seem to differentiate children who show externalizing behaviors without sexual behaviors from those who show both.

Anke Ehrhardt: Your masturbation findings in girls are very interesting. While everything became earlier over time in terms of sexual behavior and girls became more like boys in terms of coitus, masturbation always stayed with a huge gender difference. So it's actually the first time that I have seen some data where there is a bigger change in masturbation in the females, however representative or unrepresentative your sample may be.

That the girls who masturbated early also had more sexual enjoyment later is a very interesting finding and fits well into the whole sex therapy movement in women's sexuality. Teaching women to masturbate who have difficulty in becoming orgasmic is quite common as part of therapy. So it makes perfect sense to me that those young women who report earlier masturbation also had more sexual enjoyment.

References

DeLamater, J. D. (1974). Methodological issues in the study of premarital sexuality. *Sociological Methods and Research, 3,* 30–61.

Jessor, R., & Jessor, S. L. (1977). *Problem behavior and psychosocial development: A longitudinal study of youth.* New York: Academic.

Karliner, R., Westrich, E. K., Shedler, J., & Mayman, M. (1996). Bridging the gap between psychodynamic and scientific psychology: The Adelphi Early Memory Index. In J. M. Masling & R. F. Bornstein (Eds.), *Psychoanalytic perspectives on developmental psychology: Vol. 6. Empirical studies of psychoanalytic theories* (pp. 43–67). Washington, DC: American Psychological Association.

Ketterlinus, R. D., & Lamb, M. E. (Eds.). (1994). *Adolescent problem behaviors: Issues and research.* Hillsdale, NJ: Lawrence Erlbaum.

Meyer-Bahlburg, H. F. L., Ehrhardt, A. A., Bell, J. J., Cohen, S. F., Healey, J. M., Feldman, J. F., et al. (1985). Idiopathic precocious puberty in girls: Psychosexual development. *Journal of Youth and Adolescence, 14,* 339–353.

Meyer-Bahlburg, H. F. L., Wasserman, G., Dolezal, C. L., & Bueno, Y. (1996, November). Predictors of sexual behavior in boys aged 7–12 years [Abstract]. Society for the Scientific Study of Sexuality, 39th Annual Meeting, Houston, TX, *Program and Abstracts,* p. 22.

Rotheram-Borus, M. J., Meyer-Bahlburg, H. F. L., Koopman, C., Rosario, M., Exner, T. M., Henderson, R., et al. (1992). Lifetime sexual behaviors among runaway males and females. *Journal of Sex Research, 29,* 15–29.

Rotheram-Borus, M. J., Meyer-Bahlburg, H. F. L., Rosario, M., Koopman, C., Haignere, C. S., Exner, T. M., et al. (1992). Lifetime sexual behaviors among predominantly minority male runaways and gay/bisexual adolescents in New York City. *AIDS Education and Prevention* (Supplement, fall), 23–42.

Antecedents of Sexual Activity at Ages 16 and 17 in a Community Sample Followed from Age 5

JOHN E. BATES, DOUGLAS B. ALEXANDER,
SARAH E. OBERLANDER, KENNETH A. DODGE,
AND GREGORY S. PETTIT

Sexual activity versus restraint is an important dimension of individual difference in high school–age individuals. Differences in sexual activity reflect not only biological maturation, but also social roles that youths have adopted. Powerful social forces seek to constrain expression of sexuality, and similarly powerful forces seek to promote sexuality. Teens are urged to emphasize nonsexual endeavors, such as advanced schooling, and sex is often negatively sanctioned and portrayed, with some reason, as fraught with social and physical risks. We have recently seen billboards, showing attractive teens, with the words "Sex can wait. I'm worth it." We have also heard this slogan on a popular music radio station in a message that features teens talking about the dangers of sex, such as sexually transmitted diseases with "disgusting names," and about their alternative activities. At the same time, the potential rewards of sex are portrayed even more vividly. Media aimed at teens are heavily saturated with sexual images and ideas. On the one hand, we want our young people to forego sex during a prolonged adolescence for the sake of achieving advanced education and the wisdom to handle the dangers of sex in a mature way. On the other hand, we want our young people to develop "healthy" attitudes and sexual abilities so that they can enjoy sex and successfully create and rear the next generation of children. And young people themselves actively seek and respond to sexual concepts. Because teens are making the transition from restraint to activity in an atmosphere of conflicting social values, their sexual behavior choices are regarded as intensely meaningful.

This chapter considers the antecedents of sexual behavior choices in middle adolescence, ages 16–17, in a sample studied since early childhood. We are particularly interested here in antecedents of variations in the number of sexual partners. On the one hand, number of partners could reflect level of adventuresomeness and sexual maturity; on the other, it could reflect some degree of disconnection from the mainstream society. Moreover, it could reflect subcultural values differing according to social class or ethnicity. Most research on individual differences in sexual behavior in teens has used cross-sectional designs. Longitudinal studies are critical for describing the developmental process. And, in fact, several longitudinal studies have appeared. However, many questions remain, some of which the current study can address.

Previous Literature

This chapter is not intended as a thorough review of the previous literature, even of the relatively small part of it that reports on longitudinal research. Reflecting an occupational hazard of longitudinal research, we are too new to this topic to presume an authoritative review; it seems like only last month that we were scrambling to understand the parenting, peer relations, and other literatures relevant to making sense of the children's development in the preschool era, last week the elementary era, and yesterday the middle school era. We have recently presented data on the role of father absence and involvement in sexual development (Ellis, Dodge, Pettit, & Bates, 1999; Ellis et al., 2003), but we are still neophytes in this area. Fortunately, there have recently been some authoritative reviews. One, by Kotchick, Shaffer, Forehand, and Miller (2001), focuses on risky sexual behavior, such as unprotected sex and multiple partners. Kotchick and colleagues also consider findings on teen pregnancy, viewing it as a possible outcome of risky behavior. Another review, by Miller, Benson, and Galbraith (2001), focuses on teen pregnancy, but also reviews findings on differences in sexual activity in general and risky behavior in particular. Although these two reviews yield largely converging pictures of variables associated with teens' sexual activity, we were surprised to note that they review largely nonoverlapping sets of studies. Our own search for articles published on the topic in the past two years, using PsycINFO and nonsystematic browsing of the journals, suggests that the Kotchick et al. (2001) and Miller et al. (2001) reviews converge with the issues and major findings of the most recent papers, even though, again, there are a number of studies not represented in either of the two reviews. This suggests to us that research on teens' sexual risk behavior is a vigorous and diverse field, but that there are some fundamental concepts and facts spanning the field.

Clustering of Externalizing Problem Behaviors

The most fundamental observation spanning the wide field of adolescent sexuality is, as Jessor and his colleagues (e.g., Costa, Jessor, Donovan, & Fortenberry, 1995) have noted for many years, that sexual activity in adolescence often occurs in a cluster of rebellious, externalizing, "problem" behaviors, such as negative interactions with teachers, parents, and peers, poor schoolwork, and delinquent behavior of all kinds. Delinquency is associated with higher numbers of sexual partners for both boys and girls, as well as pregnancy for girls (Kotchick et al., 2001). The externalizing behaviors of substance use and delinquency in 9th grade were found to precede adolescent pregnancy status by 12th grade in European American boys and girls (Scaramella, Conger, Simons, & Witbeck, 1998), and sociometric ratings of aggressiveness in elementary school predicted child-bearing by age 14 in a sample of African American girls (Miller-Johnson et al., 1999). A wide variety of "unconventional" behaviors and attitudes predicted how early first sexual intercourse occurred in white and Hispanic youths (Costa et al., 1995). Moreover, there is some evidence that rates of tobacco use and risky sexual activity grow in step with one another in individuals followed over 18 months (Duncan, Strycker, & Duncan, 1999).

Academic deficiencies are often found to be associated with externalizing behavior problems (e.g., Coie & Dodge, 1998), and are also found to be associated with adolescent sexual behavior. However, interestingly, academic ability and achievement variables might be associated with sexual risks independently of the externalizing behavior variables. The longitudinal path model of Scaramella et al. (1998), describing rural youths in Iowa, showed that academic deficiencies predicted girls' becoming pregnant or boys' causing pregnancy independent of the externalizing problem pathway. This was confirmed by the findings of Fergusson and Woodward (2000) in a sample of girls followed in New Zealand. In the same sample, Woodward and Fergusson (1999) showed that conduct problems at age 8 predicted later teen pregnancy. However, this relation was mediated by sexual intercourse by age 16 and multiple sexual partners and smoking (all of which were associated with having a deviant peer group and school problems). Similarly, Fagot, Pears, Capaldi, Crosby, & Leve (1998) found that in addition to low family income, low academic achievement in 6th grade and arrests and drug use in 12th grade were the best predictors of teens' fathering children.

Origins of Externalizing Behavior Traits

The currently dominant models of how adjustment differences develop are complex system models, in which multiple influences are expressed over time in both additive and multiplicative fashion (Collins, Maccoby, Steinberg, Heatherington, & Bornstein, 2000; Wachs, 2000). The most heavily emphasized developmental origin of externalizing behavior is poor parenting, with ineffective and harsh discipline and lack of warm, dependably supportive involvement (e.g., Patterson, Reid, & Dishion, 1992). Consistent with the wide array of findings and the theoretical models (e.g., Rothbaum & Weisz, 1994), our prior findings suggest that externalizing behavior problems typically emerge in the preschool era, in association with harsh parenting and physical abuse (Dodge, Bates, & Pettit, 1990; Dodge, Pettit, & Bates, 1994) and the absence of positive parenting (Bates & Bayles, 1988; Bates, Bayles, Bennett, Ridge, & Brown, 1991; Bates, Maslin, & Frankel, 1985; Pettit & Bates, 1989; Pettit, Bates, & Dodge, 1997).

Another important predictor, in theory, is child temperamental traits (Bates, 1989; Rothbart & Bates, 1998). Whether through genetic inheritance or through other processes (e.g., intrauterine environment), individual children bring distinctive motivational and self-regulatory qualities into their social relationships. Our longitudinal studies have found that externalizing problems are predicted by temperamental traits of negative emotionality and resistance to control (Bates & Bayles, 1988; Bates et al., 1991; Bates et al., 1985), and this has been largely confirmed by other studies (Rothbart & Bates, 1998). In addition, we have found, in two studies, that observed maternal control can moderate the prediction from unmanageable or resistant temperament to externalizing behavior problems in middle childhood (Bates et al., 1998). Children with resistant temperament and highly controlling mothers showed a weaker linkage from early temperament to later externalizing behavior than resistant children with mothers observed to be low in control. Conversely, children with nonresistant temperament and highly controlling mothers had a greater chance of being high in externalizing behavior than nonresistant children with low control mothers. This was true of both teacher- and mother-rated externalizing behavior outcomes. We can interpret this as showing, in part, that active maternal management limited the later expression of early-appearing externalizing tendencies.

Besides problematic parenting and challenging temperament, children with externalizing behavior problems often have a history of problems in getting along with peers, especially at school (Coie & Dodge, 1998). Such children arrive at school with coercive tendencies, poorly equipped for the flexible adoption of cooperative and compliant roles that are often called for in the classroom and on the playground (Patterson et al., 1992). In our own prior results, we have found that individual trajectories of children who are sociometrically rejected by their peers in kindergarten diverge from those of the majority of children. Rejected children show increases in externalizing behavior problems over the years of elementary and middle school, even controlling for their initial levels of externalizing behavior (Dodge et al., 2003; Keiley, Bates, Dodge, & Pettit, 2000). This may partly be due to the rejected child's finding similarly antisocial peers, especially by early adolescence, which might, in conjunction with ineffectual parental supervision, lead to increased opportunities for externalizing behaviors. Patterson (1993) found in a longitudinal study that boys who became more antisocial in the transition from middle childhood to early adolescence showed increases in unsupervised time out wandering the streets.

Demographic Variables Associated with Externalizing and Sexual Behavior

Family background and gender of the child are possible demographic correlates of the cluster of externalizing behavior problems, as well as sexual activity differences.

Lower socioeconomic status (SES), which includes low education and occupational status, is often found associated with both behavior problems and low academic achievement (Coie & Dodge, 1998). However, SES is not in itself meaningful as a psychological or developmental variable, so researchers have studied the processes that might explain how SES comes to predict adjustment or achievement. For example, Olson, Bates, and Bayles (1984) showed that observed qualities of mothers' stimulation of their infants and toddlers accounted for the association between family SES at birth and children's cognitive-verbal development by age 24 months. Similarly, Dodge et al. (1994) showed that harsh parental discipline practices accounted for the association between family SES and child behavior problems at ages 5–8.

In accounting for risky sexual behavior differences, SES is included often as a control variable, that is, showing that a given variable, such as parental supervision quality, is predictive even controlling for differences in social class. However, it is not as often examined as a factor in its own right, according to Kotchick et al. (2001), and so its relation to sexual risk is not clear. However, Miller et al. (2001) cite a number of studies that show that lower SES is associated with earlier and more sexual activity, as well as some studies that show that this association is via permissive attitudes and low levels of supervision.

Another family background variable that could influence sexual development is ethnicity. Studies have typically indicated similar predictors of sexual activity and risk behaviors in African American and European American children, such as parental monitoring and early aggressiveness (Kotchick et al., 2001; Miller et al., 2001). Studies often report that African American youths have relatively high levels or rates of increase of externalizing behavior problems (e.g., Keiley et al., 2000), as well as sexual activity and pregnancy (Kotchick et al., 2001), but the role of SES in this is uncertain, and studies have seldom compared African American and European American teens in the same study (Miller et al., 2001). One major study that did compare models of antecedents of sexual behavior, the Costa et al. (1995) study of sexual debut in early adolescence, did not find that its predictive models worked as well in an African American sample as in white and Hispanic samples. In considering the effects of ethnicity it is important to control for SES. It is difficult to be sure that effects of African American ethnicity, in particular, are independent of economic status.

Yet another family background predictor of both externalizing behavior problems (Coie & Dodge, 1998) and sexual activity in teens has been parental divorce and single-parent family status (Kotchick et al., 2001). A complication in interpreting this factor is that it overlaps with many parenting factors and SES.

Finally, gender is a demographic factor that could make a difference. It certainly makes a difference in externalizing behavior problems: On the average, boys show higher levels of externalizing behavior than girls, especially in the school setting (e.g., Keiley et al., 2000). However, the difference is not so clear-cut when it comes to sexual behavior in adolescence. Kotchick et al. (2001) commented that few studies have compared male and female teens on sexual risk behaviors, but among the few relevant findings are that boys tended to have more sexual partners and that girls were less likely to use condoms. This paucity of salient findings, in conjunction with the Scaramella et al. (1998) report that the correlates of being involved in a teen pregnancy were similar for girls and boys and the Costa et al. (1995) report that the unconventional behavior and sociodemographic antecedents of age of first sexual intercourse were not different for girls and boys, raises the possibility that there may not be important differences in the developmental antecedents of sexual activity in girls and boys. However, given the many differences in development, it would be worthwhile to continue searching for gender effects in sexual development. Maccoby (1991) has argued that there should be important differences in the origins of male and female sexual behavior characteristics.

Other Predictors

A number of other variables have been considered in the origins of both externalizing behavior problems and teen sexual activity. The ones mentioned so far in this chapter have been the ones that seem theoretically the most critical and general. Some others were set aside for later consideration because we saw them as reflecting more basic processes of parental control and warmth and child externalizing adjustment style (e.g., the variable of "psychological control," which involves perceptions of verbal hostility and shaming; Miller et al., 2001; Pettit, Laird, Bates, Dodge, & Criss, 2001), or yielding unclear findings regarding sexual behavior in previous literature (e.g., the role of neighborhood factors). Others, for example, parent-teen communication about sexual matters and values (Miller et al., 2001), were omitted not only because they had unclear implications for our research, but because we did not measure them in our longitudinal study. And yet another, father involvement, has been omitted because it is the special focus of another paper (Ellis et al., 2003).

However, one additional predictor that we did consider important enough to measure in early adolescence was pubertal development. Previous research has suggested that early puberty plays an important role in the cluster of problem behaviors, including early sexual activity, various forms of delinquency and psychological adjustment problems, and academic declines (Magnusson, 1988; Simmons & Blyth, 1987), especially in girls who are subjected to the attentions of older boys (Caspi, Lynam, Moffitt, & Silva, 1993). Kotchick et al. (2001) report that early pubertal development is associated with early initiation of sexual relations, but whether early physical development has a role in sexual risk behaviors is not established. The present chapter asks whether early puberty might play a role in the middle adolescence era of development.

Further Questions

The literature we have reviewed leaves open a number of questions. First, of course, is the extent to which previously replicated findings will replicate yet again. Will early externalizing behavior tendencies predict sexual activity in advance? Will academic performance predict sexual activity independent of externalizing behavior? Will parental monitoring in early adolescence predict sexual risk-taking? Such answers would constitute more of a solidification of a phenomenon than a new discovery, but most in the social sciences would agree that the risks from underreplication of findings are greater than the costs of overreplication. Our risk of over-replication is particularly low in that very few longitudinal studies have been done on the question of sexual activity, especially ones that have followed teens from as early in development as our study and with measures representing as many domains of children's development.

There have been calls recently for theoretically informed integrations of the various domains of antecedents of sexual activity, including biological and self-system factors in the child/teenager, family background and process factors, and extrafamilial factors, such as peer relations (Kotchick et al., 2001). Some useful path models have been constructed, most notably the one by Scaramella et al. (1998). However, while we have evaluated path models in past research, we felt that the current state of knowledge in this area would be better advanced by a more general exploration, using models that are less concerned with evaluating theories of development of sexual activity than with advancing the empirical basis for a theoretical model. Our special focus in this chapter is origins of differences in the number of sexual partners at ages 16 and 17. We will also, however, consider in passing the question of whether the teen had been involved in creating pregnancies at these ages. These are the only measures of sexual activity that we have at this time.

In previous work, we have established a large body of findings about the developing adjustments of the participants in our study from age 5 to early adolescence. These findings have both replicated and extended the previous literature on factors in the development of adjustment. Now we can see whether our sample might confirm and augment previous findings on sexual behavior differences. One goal of the study was to simply see if relevant antecedent factors are predictive of later sexual behavior in our own study. This will be addressed in simple correlations and analyses of variance. Another goal stemmed from an apparent need for further consideration of how the various predictor variables, many of which have at least moderate overlap with one another, might *combine* to predict later sexual behavior. This will be addressed in multiple regressions. The Costa et al.

(1995) study is a notable prior example of the use of multivariate models. And finally, the prior literature we have seen is extremely sketchy on the question of how antecedent variables might *moderate* one another. Our question was, "Do teens' gender and ethnicity in some way interact with other predictor variables in forecasting sexual activity, or will we learn that the processes are substantially the same?" We will address this issue by considering multiplicative terms in multiple regression equations and patterns of correlation difference. Costa et al. (1995) found that their prediction equations forecasted transition into sexual activity in their white and Hispanic teens, but not African American teens, except for the subsample living in intact families. They also found that interactions between gender and unconventionality were not significant, meaning that unconventionality predicted loss of virginity for both boys and girls in the same way. However, this does not establish whether the same would be true for a somewhat different outcome—the number of sexual partners.

The Child Development Project

The Child Development Project (CDP) was designed to identify processes in children's adjustment, especially to describe the origins of conduct problems or externalizing behavior. From the outset (Dodge et al., 1990), we have been concerned with how a wide range of environmental and child characteristics explain variations in social development. Following the developmental psychopathology model (Sroufe & Rutter, 1984), we have been interested in not only problems, but also competencies and normal developmental processes, and in learning things that might ultimately contribute to the prevention of disorders and maximization of growth.

Sample

We recruited a sample of 585 children and their parents as the children were about to begin kindergarten. We did this at three sites, Bloomington, IN, Knoxville, TN, and Nashville, TN, and in two cohorts, starting in 1987 and 1988. We made special efforts to get representation from lower-SES families and to avoid the strong middle-upper-SES bias that characterizes many community samples. In fact, 26% of the sample was in the lowest two classes according to the Hollingshead (Hollingshead, 1979) classification, based on parent occupation and education. The mean Hollingshead four-factor SES score for the sample was 39.4, and the range was 8 to 66. Further demographics were as follows: boys 52%, girls 48%; European American plus a few Asian and other ethnic groups 83%, African American 17%. The median birth date of the first cohort was April 3, 1982, and that of the second cohort was March 14, 1983.

Of the original 585, 485 provided information about sexual activity at age 16 or 17 (or both). We compared the participating 83% with the 17%

not participating at this point. There were no significant differences according to gender or ethnicity. The nonparticipants were on average lower in SES (35.5) than the participants (39.9) and higher in teacher-reported externalizing behavior problems in kindergarten (9.74 versus 6.00); they did not differ significantly on mother-reported externalizing problems at age 5 or in family stress up to that age. The tendency of nonparticipants to have shown higher externalizing behavior scores at school and to be from lower-SES families seems likely to bias the findings, if at all, against finding effects from early conduct problems and social class. However, ranges on the variables are still comparable for participants and nonparticipants.

Procedures

At age 5, we conducted detailed interviews with the parents, in which we learned about family background, including a variety of stressors, but especially whether the parents had divorced, parental discipline practices, and the child's developmental history, including a retrospective account of the child's temperament. The temperament questionnaire had been shown to yield information that converged with information collected in infancy (Bates, Pettit, Dodge, & Ridge, 1998). In the kindergarten, 1st, 2nd, and 3rd grades we collected reports about the child's behavioral adjustment from mothers using the Child Behavior Checklist (CBCL; Achenbach, 1991a) and teachers on the Achenbach Teacher's Report Form (TRF; Achenbach, 1991b), and from peers using sociometric measures (Dodge et al., 2003) in the child's classroom. In each of these years, and beyond, up to year 13 or child age 17, we also sought parent reports (almost always from mothers) about family stresses over the past year and about the child's behavioral adjustment on the CBCL, and we got teacher reports up to year 9 or age 13.

Assessments were done by questionnaires mailed to the home or school or administered over the phone in some years, and in other years were part of a more detailed interview conducted at the home or, in the case of sociometrics, at the school. In year 9 (child age 13), we asked about the parent-child relationship, particularly about monitoring versus permissiveness. At year 8 (age 12), the youths themselves started rating their own adjustment on the Youth Self-Report (YSR; Achenbach, 1991c), and did so each year (except in year 9) up to year 13 (age 17). In addition, we also used the Adolescent Behavior Questionnaire, which we constructed to measure a wide variety of risky behaviors in years 12 and 13 (ages 16 and 17). Two of the 39 items on this questionnaire asked about sexual behavior, as will be detailed below. At year 8 (during the school year; average age of child = 12.98), we administered a questionnaire on pubertal development (Carskadon & Acebo, 1993). Finally, from school records we collected information about the child's academic performance from year 2 to 12. We also administered a standard short form of the WISC in year 9.

To produce a more reliable estimate and to maximize the sample represented in each analysis, we averaged across several years on indexes that we collected in multiple years. Most participants contributed data in the majority of years in each epoch. Epochs were the following: Epoch 1: years 1–6 (ages 5–10); Epoch 2: years 7–9 (ages 11–13); and Epoch 3: years 10–13 (ages 14–17), which correspond to middle childhood, early adolescence, and middle adolescence, respectively. (Some Epoch 1 variables involve development prior to age 5, measured retrospectively at age 5.) For the major analyses to be reported, we focused on predictions from Epochs 1 and 2, although we also computed relations between Epoch 3 measures and the sexual activity variables. The N for the different analyses varies, because not every teen, family, or teacher contributed data every year. However, as indicated above, the basic bias is for higher rates of nonparticipation in the lower-SES families and children with higher behavior problems, as is typical in longitudinal studies. So missing data are unlikely to bias toward spurious findings, and the sample sizes and ranges are still large enough that there are fair chances to observe statistically significant effects, which means that contrasting findings of nonrelations might have some meaning, as well.

Sexual Activity: Basic Findings

We considered first the intercorrelation of the two sexual activity items in years 12 and 13 (at ages 16 and 17). For all items in the questionnaire, teens were asked to describe activities in the last 12 months. The first item asks, "With how many different persons have you had sexual relations?" The second item asks, "How many times have you been pregnant (or gotten someone else pregnant)?" Within a given year, when a teen's reported number of sexual partners was higher, so was their frequency of impregnating or becoming impregnated ($r = .47$ and $.42$, for years 12 and 13, respectively, both $p < .001$; all probability values for correlations are two-tailed). Across years, number of sexual partners correlated $.64$ ($p < .001$), and number of pregnancies correlated $.45$ ($p < .001$). Interestingly, the number of sexual partners in year 12 predicted pregnancies in year 13 ($r = .50$, $p < .001$), but year 12 pregnancies had little to do with year 13 sexual partners ($r = .08$, $p = .111$). Perhaps this latter finding reflects the actual births that occurred to some of our more sexually adventurous participants, which may have reduced their opportunity or inclination for variety in partners. Noticing a considerable range in the reports of number of sexual partners, and coming from a historical era and social class that led us to question the veracity of the higher numbers, we selected the cases where the number of different sexual partners in year 12 was 5 or more ($N = 25$) and computed the same set of intercorrelations. In fact, the matrix was virtually identical to that for the whole sample, showing that the validity coefficients were the same. The same was true for the larger sub-sample who were moderately active, with two or more partners. In short, as in prior literature, numbers of sexual partners and likelihood of pregnancy are correlated both within and across years, suggesting that despite the psychometric limitations of single items, these items have some validity and that a composite of items would be meaningful. We chose to focus on number of sexual partners, and so created a composite of these two items, averaging across years 12 and 13. Sixty-five percent of the teens with scores on this composite contributed this item in both of the years.

The mean number of sexual partners increased from 0.88 to 1.30 from year 12 to 13 (paired t (378) = −3.53, p = .000). On the averaged year 12–13 index, 52.6% (254 of 483 answering this question) of the sample reported no sexual partners across the two years. This is similar to previous findings in the literature (Kotchick et al., 2001), in which a slight majority of high school–age adolescents describe themselves as abstaining from sexual intercourse. Of the sexually active 47.4%, 128 or 56% reported an average of between 1 and 1.5 partners per year; 55 or 24% reported between 2 and 3 partners per year; and 46 or 20% reported more than 3 partners per year. For some analyses, we created groups corresponding to these segments of the sample, in hopes of seeing some non-linear patterns of antecedents, e.g., for the externalizing behavior problems to be associated with only the most extremely active group. However, in general, the patterns were regular and linear, with the mean level of a given antecedent variable changing in parallel with the group's level of sexual activity. Therefore, we ultimately chose to focus upon simple, correlation analyses. The important point here is that the majority of the teens told us that they were not engaging in sexual intercourse by age 17, and that of those who were sexually active, the majority had fewer than two different partners per year.

Distributions for the male and female adolescents' numbers of sexual partners were quite similar. This was slightly surprising, based on the literature cited above. There was no mean difference; the correlation between gender and number of sexual partners was −.03 (n.s.). There was an ethnicity effect (r = .16, p < .001), which shows that African American teens reported more partners. However, the meaning of this, given the important overlap between ethnicity and SES, is not clear. As will be seen later, ethnicity has less predictive value when considered in the context of other descriptors.

Antecedents of Sexual Activity

Are there antecedents of sexual activity, operationally defined as the number of sexual partners? Our findings suggest that there are, indeed, many such antecedents, and many of these conform to the general themes of prior findings we reviewed. We examined the antecedents in sections according to the developmental era. First, we describe the measures for each developmental epoch.

Description of Predictor Measures

As Epoch 1 variables we considered predictors that reflect early and middle childhood characteristics of the child's family background, as well as temperament and social and academic adjustment. For all the parent and teacher Achenbach reports, we computed scores for the second-order factors of *internalizing* (composed of 32 items for mothers and 36 for teachers), which includes first-order factors of anxious/depressed, social withdrawal, and somatic complaints, and *externalizing* (composed of 33 items for mothers and 34 for teachers), whose first-order factors are aggressive (including disruption and noncompliance items) and delinquent. Internalizing and externalizing behaviors are conceptually distinct, but it is important to note that they are empirically correlated (e.g., Achenbach, 1991a). This suggests that each scale also reflects adjustment in a general sense. Peer sociometric rejection was based on the numbers of like-most and like-least nominations from classmates (up to three from each peer in each category) standardized within class. *Rejected status* was coded if the child's like-most nominations minus the number of like-least nominations was one standard deviation or more below the mean of the class, and their like-most score was less than the average and their like-least score was greater than the average. *Popular status* was coded for the reverse set of scores: like-most minus like-least one standard deviation or more above average, and like-most score average or above and like-least score below the mean. We then created indexes by averaging popular or rejected status across the years, with scores ranging from 0.00 to 1.00. We measured *harsh parental discipline* in early childhood in our initial interview with mothers based on reviewer ratings growing out of extensive discussions about parental discipline from ages 1 to 4 and from ages 4 to 5, with inter-rater agreement $r = .73$ (further details in Deater-Deckard, Lansford, Dodge, Pettit, & Bates (in press); Weiss, Dodge, Bates, & Pettit, 1992). High scores reflect parent report of frequent use of corporal punishment. From this same interview we took a measure of whether the child had experienced the parents' *divorce prior to age 5* (coded as 0 or 1). Mothers rated their children's *early temperamental difficultness* (8 items on negative emotionality), *unadaptability* (4 items on distress in response to novelty), and, of greatest interest to us here, *resistance to control* (3 items, e.g., doesn't stop when told "no"). Temperamental resistance was of interest because of its consistently differential links to externalizing behavior (Bates, 1989; Bates, Pettit, Dodge, & Ridge, 1998). Preliminary analyses showed negligible relations between the other two temperament scales and later sexual behavior, so we omitted them from further analysis. Academic performance measures were derived from

school records. We computed *grade point average* across the years of the epoch, and also the numbers of *absences*. We included WISC IQ in this epoch,
which consisted of an estimated IQ based on the scaled scores on the Vocabulary and Block Design scales (Sattler, 1982). We did so even though
we had actually administered the test at age 13, because it is theoretically
a characteristic that would be present in the first epoch. All other Epoch 1
measures were collected between ages 5 and 10, using data from parents,
peers, teachers, and school records.

In Epoch 2, ages 11 to 13, we considered similar adjustment variables,
including parent, teacher, school record, and now the Achenbach Youth
Self-Report Internalizing (32-item) and Externalizing (30-item) scales.
We also computed a measure of youth description of *association with antisocial peers*, using ten items of peers' frequency of behaviors such as drinks,
smokes, or gets into trouble at school, adapted from Dishion, Patterson,
Stoolmiller, and Skinner, 1991. This was completed by youths in regard to
two best friends, rated separately, in the year 7 (age 11) interview, and in
regard to kids in their group, rated as a group, in the year 8 (ages 12–13)
interview. Ratings from the two years were standardized and averaged together (alpha = .49). In addition, we included measures from the age 13
interviews with parents and teens concerning the parent-teen relationship.
First, on the basis of factor analysis of scales of parent-reported monitoring,
teen-reported monitoring, parent-reported psychological control (Barber,
1996), teen-reported psychological control (see Pettit et al., 2001, for details), teen-reported parental permissiveness, parent-reported involvement
with the teen, and parent-reported involvement with the teen's school,
we created unweighted composites representing five factors: teen-report
permissiveness, teen-report parental monitoring, parent-report positive
involvement and monitoring, and parent-report school involvement. In
preliminary analyses, we correlated the composite scales with the sexual
activity variable, and found that the three teen-report composites did correlate, but the two parent-report composites did not.[1] We omitted the
parent-reported factors for the present analyses. We retained two teen-
report measures, *permissiveness* (4 items, rated for each parent separately,
on a scale from 1 = not like him/her to 3 = a lot like him/her, including
items such as "lets me go out any evening I want," alpha reliability = .68)
and *monitoring* (5 items, completed for each parent on a scale from 1 =
don't know to 3 = know a lot, e.g., "My parent (mother/father) really
knows about what I do with my free time," alpha = .65). We found that
permissiveness and monitoring were correlated to only a modest degree
($r = -.14$, $p = .004$), which is perhaps surprising, given their conceptual
relationship. On the basis of the ages 12–13 self-reports, we computed, using the Carskadon and Acebo (1993) procedure, the *pubertal development
scale*, which indexes the degree of progress toward puberty.

In Epoch 3, ages 14 to 17, the adjustment variables were similar, except that we used parent, youth, and school record data, but not teacher reports. The association with deviant peers score was based on the youths' descriptions of their groups (as in year 8) in years 10, 11, and 12 (alpha = .81). It is somewhat of a misnomer to describe the Epoch 3 variables as antecedents, since half the years' assessments were approximately concurrent to the measurement of the sexual behavior variables. Descriptions of a few additional variables will be given subsequently, as findings regarding the variables are discussed.

Bivariate Correlations between Antecedents and Sexual Activity Outcomes

Here we will focus only on the first column of Table 1, which lists the correlations between number of sexual partners and the predictor variables in the sample as a whole. The correlations within subsamples are present in other columns of the table for the sake of later analysis of interaction effects. The overall pattern in the full sample is that the Epoch 1 predictions are numerous, but of a slightly smaller magnitude than the Epoch 2 predictions. Perhaps not surprisingly, the Epoch 3 correlations are larger yet. In other words, to a modest or moderate degree, it is possible to predict sexual activity at ages 16–17 from early and middle childhood. From the early to middle childhood epochs, lower socioeconomic status, experience of parental divorce prior to age 5, harsh maternal discipline practices (spanking, etc.), temperamental resistance to control, and mother- and teacher-reported externalizing behavior all predicted the reported higher number of sexual partners, as did peer rejection, low GPA, low IQ, and absences from school. Internalizing behavior did not predict later sexual activity. The strongest predictor was teacher-reported externalizing behavior: When children had been seen by teachers as disruptive, aggressive, or noncompliant in grades K–5, they were more likely later to report more sexual partners. Individually, none of the correlations was large, but it is striking that there were so many significant links to such a specific outcome measured so many years later, involving different sources of information, and all pertaining to difficulties with authority, social relations, and academic achievement.

Epoch 2 variables predicted in the same fashion as the Epoch 1 variables. Teens' externalizing behavior in early adolescence, whether reported by the mother, the teacher, or the teen, accounted for variance in numbers of sexual partners at ages 16–17. Youths reporting more association with deviant peers were also a bit more likely to report higher numbers of sexual partners later. One difference from the previous epoch's predictors was that early adolescent internalizing behavior (anxious, depressed, socially withdrawn), as reported by mothers and teachers, was significantly predictive of sexual behavior, as it was not in Epoch 1. At this point, the reports from mothers and teachers of internalizing behavior could reflect youths'

Table 1. *Correlations between Number of Sexual Partners at Ages 16–17 and Developmental Antecedents*

Predictor	Correlations (*p*) with Average Number of Sexual Partners				
Variable	Full Sample	Boys	Girls	Euro-/Other	Afro-Ethnicity
A. *Epoch 1 variables*					
1. Family/child					
a. SES	−.20***	−.31***	−.09	−.15**	−.10
b. Divorce 1–5	.10*	.12	.08	.08	.18
c. Harsh discipline	.11*	.13*	.09	.07	.08
d. Resistant temperament	.10*	.09	.12	.09~	.15
e. Mother-rated internalizing	.06	.04	.07	.06	.08
f. Mother-rated externalizing	.18***	.23***	.13*	.16***	.25*
2. School					
a. Teacher-rated internalizing	.06	.04	.08	.07	−.03
b. Teacher-rated externalizing	.30***	.26***	.39***	.31***	.18
c. Peer-rejected	.19***	.08	.31***	.21***	.07
d. Peer-popular	−.07	−.01	−.11~	−.10*	.16
e. GPA	−.17***	−.19**	−.14*	−.19**	.09
f. School absences	.13**	.11	.14*	.09	.09
g. IQ	−.12**	−.18**	−.08	−.11*	.09
B. *Epoch 2 variables*					
1. Family/child					
a. Mother-rated internalizing	.12**	.14*	.12	.09~	.30*
b. Mother-rated externalizing	.25***	.30***	.21**	.22***	.34**
c. Youth-rated internalizing	.04	−.02	.10	.05	−.01
d. Youth-rated externalizing	.32***	.27***	.26***	.24***	.31*
e. Permissiveness	.08	.29***	−.10	−.03	.30*

Table 1. *Continued*

Predictor	Correlations (*p*) with Average Number of Sexual Partners				
Variable	Full Sample	Boys	Girls	Euro-/ Other	Afro- Ethnicity
f. Monitoring	−.26***	−.33***	−.21**	−.23***	−.39***
g. Pubertal development	.09~	.20*	.05	.11*	.05
h. Deviant peers	.13**	.17*	.09	.12*	.04
2. School					
a. Teacher-rated internalizing	.20***	.07	.33***	.21***	.13
b. Teacher-rated externalizing	.32^***	.34***	.31***	.28***	.29*
c. GPA	−.28***	−.31***	−.31***	−.23***	−.27*
d. School absences	.11*	.24***	.03	.01	.23~
C. *Epoch 3 variables*					
1. Family/child					
a. Mother-rated internalizing	.19***	.10	.27***	.20***	.20
b. Mother-rated externalizing	.36***	.28***	.43***	.35***	.31**
c. Youth-rated internalizing	.19***	.13*	.26***	.20***	.25*
d. Youth-rated externalizing	.38***	.38***	.37***	.35***	.52***
e. Deviant peers	.38***	.42***	.35***	.38***	.43***
2. School					
a. GPA	−.33***	−.36***	−.33***	−.32***	−.26*
b. School absences	.23***	.37***	.13~	.19***	.21~

Notes. *N*s for full sample 394–482, depending on variable (median = 451); *N*s for boys 197–246 (median = 223); *N*s for girls 197–236 (median = 224); *N*s for European American plus Other 337–406 (median = 383); *N*s for African American 57–76 (median = 68).
Significance: *p* less than or equal to: ~ .10   *.05   **.01   ***.001

willingness to display negative affect and withdrawal from the home or school settings as well as distressed affect resulting from conflicts with parents and teachers. As in Epoch 1, school absences and low grades predicted number of sexual partners, but the prediction from GPA was slightly stronger from the later epoch than from the earlier epoch. Of the teen-parent relationship measures collected at age 14, teens' report of parental permissiveness was not consistently correlated with sexual partners, but their report of parental monitoring was: The more monitoring the teen reported, the less sexual activity was shown at ages 16–17. Not reported in the table was a similarly modest to moderate significant correlation between sexual activity and teen-reported parental psychological control, as well as nonsignificant relations between sexual behavior outcomes and the two parent-reported factor composites, reflecting their monitoring of and positive involvement with the teen. Also of interest because of prior findings about externalizing behavior in general and teen sexual activity, and reported in the table, is the finding that level of pubertal development was associated, weakly but in the expected direction, with the sexual behavior outcome: Teens who were physically more mature at the average age of nearly 13 tended, to a borderline degree, to report greater numbers of sex partners at ages 16–17.

Findings from later adolescence, Epoch 3, were closely parallel to those for the preceding two developmental eras, with consistent predictions from both mother- and teen-rated internalizing and externalizing problems in the teen to higher numbers of adolescent sexual partners. The main difference between the Epoch 3 and the Epoch 1 or 2 findings is that the Epoch 3 correlations were on the average slightly stronger than those of the first two epochs. To the extent that future analyses support the increasing degree of relationship between internalizing adjustment as the time draws closer to the sexual activity measure, this may reflect increasing evidence that sexually active teens are showing more emotional distress, along with more association with peers engaging in socially disapproved activities like stealing, fighting, and consuming alcohol and other drugs. If the relationship between externalizing-type behaviors and sexual activity is actually growing with proximity in age, this could be due to two opposite processes. On the one hand, it could be a function of newly emerging instances of acting-out behavior in teens who as younger children had been average or only a little higher than average on externalizing behavior, so their earlier behavior would not have contributed to the prediction of later sexual activity. Such youths are referred to by Patterson, DeBaryshe, and Ramsey (1989) as late starters. If this is, in fact, what has happened, an interesting question would be whether it is specifically the power of sex that centrally motivates increased levels of defiance and decreased levels of academic performance, or whether sexual activity is just an incidental perquisite of the amplified rebelliousness. On the other hand, however, the pattern of stronger correlation between adolescent adjustment and sexual activity could be due to teens who had been hard to manage in middle childhood, but who became better behaved, and perhaps more academically oriented, in adolescence, and who were not sexually active. Resolution of these issues will come only with future research.

Another type of possible antecedent of sexual activity is personality. To an extent, our measures of internalizing versus externalizing behavior problems reflect personality in the form of a stable adjustment style. However, do personality measures that are more independent of psychopathology, namely the Big Five dimensions, predict sexual behavior? At year 8 (ages 12–13), the CDP teens filled out a 25-item Big Five personality questionnaire adapted by Richard Lanthier from his longer questionnaire (Lanthier, 1993). We found that the only one of these variables to correlate with sexual activity was neuroticism ($r = -.13$, $p = .006$). To a modest extent, teens describing themselves as fearful, worrying, and nervous were less likely to be sexually active later. Extraversion, agreeableness, conscientiousness, and openness to experience were not significantly correlated with later sexual behavior. Some part of the noncorrelation could be due to youths of the age of nearly 13 providing less reliable or valid descriptions of their personalities than they would at later ages. However, it is also possible that teens' sexual activity is not related to these dimensions. It is interesting, however, that neuroticism was a better predictor of later sexual restraint than was the conceptually related youth self-report of internalizing behavior problems, despite a correlation of .42 ($p = <.001$) between neuroticism and self-reported internalizing across ages 11–13. It is also interesting that it predicted in the opposite direction of the mother- and teacher-reported teen internalizing prediction of sexual behavior: the more self-described neuroticism, the *less* sexual activity, but the more internalizing behavior, the *more* sexual activity. This provides an interesting phenomenon for future exploration of the psychological distinctions between the neuroticism and the internalizing adjustment variables.

Glancing now at the correlations for the subsamples of boys and girls and those of European American (and a few others, mostly Asian American) ethnicity versus African American ethnicity, our major impression is of similarity in the relations between the predictors and the sexual behavior outcome. There are several differences, most of which we will address in the context of multiple regression analyses, using the gender and ethnicity variables as moderators of relevant predictors. However, the dominant pattern of similar correlations across subgroups solidifies the meaningfulness of the correlations computed in the full sample. Of course, a correlation of modest size that is significant in the full sample is less likely to be statistically significant in a subsample.

Comparisons of Sexual Activity Groups

In supplemental analyses, predictors were also examined as dependent variables in one-way ANOVAs with the four levels of sexual activity (no sexual partners across the two years, an average of 1.5 or fewer sexual partners, an average of between 2 and 3 partners, and 3.5 or more partners) as the independent variable. We looked for patterns in which predictors were relevant only for some levels of the sexual activity variable. For example, did the behavior problem antecedents only account for differences between the nonactive and the extremely active teens? Might moderately active teens be essentially similar to, or even superior to, the nonactive teens in signs of positive adjustment, such as grades and peer popularity? The overall pattern, however, was one of linear relationship: The nonactive teens had the lowest levels of most of the negative adjustment variables, the somewhat active teens had higher levels of negative adjustment, and the most highly active teens had the highest levels, even if differences between adjacent groups were not always significant. And the reverse was true for the positive adjustment variables. The only exception to this was in the case of peer rejection: The mean proportion of years the child achieved the peer sociometric status of "rejected" was very similar for the three lowest sexual activity groups, and they were all significantly different from the most highly active group. So, for this one variable, teens with just a few different sexual partners were essentially the same as the teens who had no sexual partners—all were quite unlikely to have been rejected by peers in elementary school (averages of .08, .09, .07)—whereas the most active teens had more than twice the likelihood of having been rejected (.21). In short, except for one somewhat interesting exception, the overall pattern of relations between predictors and the levels of sexual activity was a linear one. The more well adjusted the child and the more advantageous the family background, the less sexual activity reported in middle adolescence.

We also searched in another way for exceptions to the emerging trend of our data. We asked whether there could be subgroups of sexually active teens with well-adjusted prior backgrounds, including good grades, success with peers, good relations with parents and teachers, etc. We had not seen descriptions of such kinds of teens in past literature, but we reasoned that they might exist, for example, the stereotype (or is it a myth?) of a popular, successful high school boy with an active sex life. Cluster analysis is an approach that groups individuals according to their similarity of profile across a set of variables. It allows for nonlinear profiles, for example, one kind of teen could be high on sexual partners and low on adjustment measures, whereas another could be high on both sexual partners and adjustment measures. We conducted an exploratory series of cluster analyses, but did not find the kinds of groups we were looking for. This does not mean that they do not exist, but the variables we used did not produce configurations that transcended the linear relations previously described. We can think of a few other variables to key the clusters on, such as sports success, but these were not available for analysis, and given the discouraging trend of our analyses in this vein so far, we set aside the question of well-adapted groups of sexually active teens for the time being.

Multiple Regression Models of Antecedents of Sexual Activity

Therefore, we turned finally to the question of how the various predictors of sexual activity in middle adolescence would combine in linear regression equations—that is, to see how a given variable predicted when other variables were statistically controlled. We also wished to see how gender and ethnicity might affect the nature of the predictions in some instances. We decided to focus on the more distant antecedents, from Epochs 1 and 2, and to exclude those from Epoch 3. The Epoch 3 predictors would, of course, account for the largest portions of variance in the sexual behavior index, but we were more interested in the development of sexual activity than the concurrent correlates of it. Because of statistical power limitations, even with a moderately large sample such as ours, we decided to conduct separate regression analyses for the two epochs, rather than combining their predictors into one regression equation. For the same reason, we excluded a few variables that had nonsignificant bivariate correlations with the sexual behavior outcome and a larger number that were shown in preliminary regression analyses to have nondiscriminating relations with the outcome because of overlap with other predictors (e.g., harsh discipline was not predictive in the context of SES, externalizing behavior, etc.). This enabled us to consider interaction terms involving gender and ethnicity. The interaction terms, selected on the basis of hints of possible interactions in the correlation matrix shown in Table 1, consisted of the dichotomous gender or ethnicity variable multiplied by a standardized version of the continuous predictor variable (mean approximating zero, standard deviation approximating 1). In the first step of a two-step hierarchical model, we entered the main effects terms for gender, ethnicity, and the continuous predictor variables. In the second step, we entered the set of interaction terms. For both the Epoch 1 and the Epoch 2 equations, the set of interaction terms provided a significant contribution. For Epoch 1, the R^2 increase due to adding the interaction terms was .05, with $F(4,462) = 6.82$, $p < .001$; and for Epoch 2 it was .08, with $F(4,347) = 9.35$, $p < .001$. We will present standardized regression coefficients for only the final step of the models. The results of the models are summarized in Tables 2 and 3.

Predictors from Developmental Epoch 1

As shown in Table 2, a moderate amount of the variance in number of sexual partners was predicted by background and adjustment characteristics from early and middle childhood. Statistically significant predictors

Table 2. *Multiple Regression Results for Epoch 1 Predictors of Number of Sexual Partners*

Multiple correlation: .40

$F(10,462) = 8.81, p < .001.$

Predictor Variable	Beta	Significance
Gender	.07	.120
African American ethnicity	.06	.185
SES	−.20	.003
Mother-rated externalizing 1	.14	.041
Teacher-rated externalizing 1	.13	.046
Peer rejection	−.08	.193
SES x gender	.16	.012
Mother ext. x gender	−.15	.029
Teacher ext. x gender	.19	.008
Peer reject x gender	.16	.015

included SES, mother and teacher reports of child externalizing behavior, and the interaction between gender and SES, as well as three adjustment variables. Lower levels of family SES predicted higher levels of sexual activity, even controlling for gender and ethnicity. However, neither gender nor ethnicity had significant main effects. SES was significantly more predictive of later sexual activity for boys than girls, as can be seen by comparing the relevant correlations for boys and girls in Table 1. (The correlations in Table 1 were computed with all cases available for a given pair of variables [i.e., using pairwise deletion]; however, the correlations on the sample corresponding to those included in the multiple regression analysis [i.e., using listwise deletion] were virtually identical to those in Table 1.)

Mother-reported externalizing was significantly more predictive of later sexual activity for boys than for girls. In contrast, teacher-reported externalizing was more predictive for girls than for boys. Since both mother and teacher reports of externalizing were directly predictive of later sexual behavior, for both boys and girls, the interaction effects show difference in the degree of prediction, not in whether externalizing tendencies were predictive. We remind ourselves to be restrained in interpreting interaction effects found in only one sample, even in as large a sample as the present one. However, the school versus home distinction here illustrates a conclusion that we have drawn previously (e.g., see Keiley et al., 2000), that problem behaviors rated at school signify different things than those rated at home, despite moderate convergence between mothers' and teachers' ratings. Mothers tended to see higher levels of externalizing behavior in middle childhood, and saw it decline over the years, whereas teachers tended to see lower levels of externalizing, and saw it remain relatively constant, except for some children, including those experiencing peer rejection and those of African American descent, who showed increases (Keiley et al., 2000). Perhaps the externalizing tendencies of girls at home were less meaningful for later sexual behavior because they were more reflective of particular mother-daughter relationships than they were for boys, or because they were not so strongly reflective of a general personality. In school, on the other hand, there may also have been differences in the ways in which girls and boys came to be rated as showing externalizing problems. Both boys and girls can be disruptive and uncooperative with the teacher, and both can get into conflicts with peers. However, relative to girls, perhaps young boys' externalizing tendencies reflected reactions to the constraints of the classroom (sit still, pay attention), in part, and to this extent had less to do with tendencies to pursue risks and rewards in the sexual arena. And perhaps girls' externalizing tendencies at school were less reflective of difficulties in paying attention, and relatively more reflective of social relationship difficulties that transcended difficulties with the task demands of school, and perhaps these social difficulties forecasted later sexual risk-taking.[2] This interpretation will require further data, but for the moment, it converges with the final interaction effect in the Epoch 1 model, described next.

Peer rejection was considerably more predictive of later sexual behavior for girls than for boys. The main effect for peer rejection was not significant in the regression model, and among the boys the bivariate correlation between peer rejection and later sexual behavior did not reach significance. However, among girls the correlation was highly significant. Recall that the correlation between peer rejection and later sexual behavior is largely accounted for by the tendency of the most extremely sexually active group of teens, those in the top 20% of sexually active teens, to have been rejected more than all of the other teens. Again, this may mean that for girls, being rejected by peers signifies an enduring problem in adhering to the norms of girls' social relationships. Perhaps girls who are aggressive or disruptive are in violation of such strong norms for their gender that they are strongly disposed to risk-taking, or are so consistently ostracized by their girl peers that they are likely to find peer support only in adolescence with similarly risk-taking boys. Other interpretations are possible, but we will continue on with this interpretation later, when we talk about an interaction effect found in the Epoch 2 model.

We also asked whether the model in Table 2 would be augmented by additional variables, and thus, added variables to the equation one at a time, to see whether they made an incremental contribution. We considered grade point average in the first epoch, harsh maternal discipline in early childhood, IQ, and the stress of divorce in early childhood. None of these added significantly, despite having significant bivariate correlations with the sexual activity outcome variable. We also considered the predictive power of six CBCL items relevant to sexual problems. On the basis of principal components analysis, we sorted the six items into composites describing excessive masturbation, cross-gender wishes, and thinking about sex too much plus an idiosyncratically specified sexual problem item, and added them across ages 5–7 (because of marked drop-off in frequency of endorsement of these items across middle childhood). Only the latter had a relation to the outcome: Children described by their mothers as thinking about sex too much and having some form of sexual problem reported higher numbers of sexual partners. This held true even after control for all of the other predictor variables in the Epoch 1 multiple regression, with a beta of .09 ($p = .035$). We are currently exploring the meaning of the measure. It might index consequences of early sexual abuse, or it could reflect a wide variety of different factors.

Predictors from Developmental Epoch 2

In addition to the Epoch 2 predictors, the Epoch 2 model also included the basic background variables: gender, SES, ethnicity, and SES x gender. As can be seen in Table 3, neither gender nor ethnicity approached significance as a predictor of sexual behavior in this context. SES did approach significance, in the same direction as in the Epoch 1 model, with higher-SES teens likely to have fewer sexual partners. (The SES variable accounted for less variance in the context of the Epoch 2 predictors than it did in the context of the Epoch 1 predictors, but not significantly less.) And the same SES x gender moderator effect described for Epoch 1 was still significant in the context of the Epoch 2 variables. Lower SES was more predictive of sexual activity for boys than for girls. However, there were not direct effects of mother- and teacher-reported externalizing behavior in Epoch 2, despite substantial bivariate correlations (as seen in Table 1). This may be due to the youths' report of their own externalizing behavior accounting better for the same portion of variance in later sexual behavior than mother and teacher reports accounted for (youth-report externalizing correlated .35 with both mother- and teacher-report externalizing, $p < .001$ for both).

Youths' report of parental permissiveness did not have a direct effect. However, their report of parental monitoring did: Teens who perceived their parents as high in supervision of them in early adolescence tended to have fewer sexual partners later. This may be more due to the teens' own characteristics in relationship with the parents than the parents' efforts at monitoring, especially given that the parents' report of monitoring plus involvement at the same point in development did not have a substantial correlation with later teen sexual behavior. As pointed out by Kerr and Stattin

Table 3. *Multiple Regression Results for Epoch 2 Predictors of Number of Sexual Partners*

Multiple correlation: .52

$F(14,347) = 9.17, p < .001.$

Predictor Variable	Beta	Significance
Gender	−.02	.719
African American ethnicity	.03	.642
SES	−.13	.087
Mother-rated externalizing 2	.06	.311
Teacher-rated internalizing 2	−.06	.373
Teacher-rated externalizing 2	.10	.140
Youth-rated externalizing 2	.12	.019
Permissiveness	.09	.196
Monitoring	−.14	.004
Pubertal development	−.10	.062
SES x gender	.14	.038
Teacher int. x gender	.25	.000
Permissiveness x gender	−.22	.002
Permissiveness x ethnicity	.17	.004

(2000), the dominant interpretation of the deviance-inhibiting effect of parental monitoring might be incorrect. Rather, their findings argue that what the parents know about their teens' activities might depend in large part upon what the teens are willing to let them know. (For a more detailed exploration of the developmental processes in parental monitoring and the development of externalizing behavior in CDP adolescents, see Laird, Pettit, Bates, & Dodge, 2001.) The rate of pubertal development had only a borderline-significant direct effect.

The relation between teacher-reported internalizing behavior in Epoch 2 and later sexual behavior was moderated by gender, as shown in Table 3. Internalizing behavior was significantly predictive for girls, but not for boys, as seen in the relevant correlations of Table 1. Apparently, the anxiety, depression, and social withdrawal shown by boys in early adolescence at school has little to do with later sexual behavior, but internalizing symptoms shown by girls forecast higher numbers of sexual partners. Based on the moderately high correlation between internalizing and externalizing symptoms, we can speculate that the present finding may have something to do with the consequences of externalizing behavior and peer rejection in elementary school, discussed in the previous section. It seems possible, based on Patterson's (1982) coercion theory, that as children mature enough to recognize the stable deficits in their lives, some who are chronically coercive ultimately display depression as a result of the social and academic failures they experience. It may also be possible, however, that for some children, depression shown to teachers may reflect their negative adaptation to school rather than a more general affective disturbance. For some girls, either kind of process might ultimately produce an increased likelihood of multiple sexual partners. Aggressive, uncooperative tendencies might lead to peer rejection and academic failures in middle childhood, with depression as a consequence in early adolescence, and in later adolescence to either multiple, non-exclusive, perhaps shallow sexual relationships or a succession of exclusive but short relationships.

Teen-reported parental permissiveness also predicted sexual behavior as moderated by gender. Boys who described parents as permissive in early adolescence were more likely to report multiple sexual partners. Among girls, however, parental permissiveness did not make a significant difference, and in fact, if there was a relation, it ran in the opposite direction. We have a difficult time even speculating on what developmental processes account for this gender x permissiveness interaction effect. Perhaps it has to do with the different norms held by girls and boys for risky behavior of all kinds. Perhaps sense of freedom of movement is not especially salient in girls' actual sexual practices, while boys' image of the latitude they have may be more relevant to their freedom to engage in sexual relations. However, why this should be so is not clear. Since the finding is apparently unique in the literature, and since there are not converging interactions within our own data, we will avoid further speculation for now.

One additional interaction effect in predicting sexual behavior was found: permissiveness x ethnicity. For African American youths, perceptions of parental permissiveness were associated with increased numbers of sexual partners, but for European American youths, permissiveness had essentially nothing to do with later sexual activity. This effect, and our basic inability to provide an interpretation, are the same as for the permissiveness x gender effect described in the preceding paragraph.

Finally, as we did in the Epoch 1 model, we tested a few additional predictors in the Epoch 2 model; each had shown a significant bivariate correlation with sexual activity. We tested the effects of grade point average in early adolescence; it did not make a significant contribution in the context of the other variables in the model. We also considered a measure of teens' association with deviant peers, defined by the teens' descriptions of their friends' frequencies of externalizing or petty delinquent behaviors at ages 11 and 12–13. It failed to make a significant contribution in the context of other, more centrally placed indexes of child adjustment.

In summary, a moderate portion of the variance in numbers of sexual partners reported by teens at ages 16–17 was accounted for by variables from early adolescence, as well as by the same family background measures and the SES x gender interaction that predicted in the Epoch 1 model. Unlike the middle childhood model, where girls' teacher-rated externalizing and peer rejection were more strongly predictive of later sexual behavior than boys' externalizing was, in the early adolescence model, the girls' teacher-rated internalizing behavior predicted the later sexual behavior more than boys' internalizing behavior did. We interpret this as consistent with Patterson's model (Patterson et al., 1992) of developmental consequences of acting-out behavior problems.

Conclusions

This longitudinal study has shown that a wide variety of social background and adjustment measures from early childhood to adolescence forecast, to a moderate degree, self-reported numbers of sexual partners at ages 16–17. This provides an addition to the relatively small number of prospective studies of sexual behavior. It confirms previous studies, with both cross-sectional and longitudinal designs, in showing that the central predictor of sexual activity in adolescence is externalizing behavior tendencies, as well as environmental circumstances that are likely to support or reflect such tendencies. Since only a few previous studies have been designed to show whether conduct problems are truly an antecedent of sexual activity, it is useful that the present study confirms that they are. It is also useful that the present study shows that such behaviors are predictive from as early as kindergarten age, and that measures from multiple sources of information converge on the same picture.

How shall we frame the association between early externalizing tendencies and later sexual activity? Prior interpretations have typically been that it reflects a version of psychopathology, or at least a form of social deviance. Indeed, it does seem quite possible that the main findings of this and other studies reflect a developmental process in which sexual restraint is the result of better adaptations throughout childhood, and higher levels of sexual activity reflect poorer adaptations. It certainly seems to be the case for those who are in the group with the highest numbers of sexual partners. However, we think it might also be helpful to remain aware of the possibility that future research will show that some patterns of sexual activity in middle adolescence are associated with normal development, and perhaps even advantages in later adulthood, especially in cases where the sexual risk-taking has not resulted in a crippling disease or premature parenthood. We do not know if prior studies have searched for possible subgroups of sexually active teens who were not showing adjustment difficulties in earlier development; but if so, we have not yet encountered such studies, and our preliminary efforts in this direction were not successful in identifying such successful or nonproblem paths. However, at the same time, we must emphasize that the problems shown by the children of this study were at the level one would expect to find in a community sample. Relatively few of them showed externalizing problems that would be interpreted by Achenbach (1991a, 1991b) as of potential clinical significance, meaning, above a T-score of 60 (15% and 14% on the mother and teacher reports, respectively, in Epoch 1, and 18% and 19%, on mother and teacher reports in Epoch 2). Although we well recognize the major social harm done by aggressive and impulsive people, it is possible that the externalizing tendencies shown by some of the children in the sample, despite associations with lower SES, lower grades, etc., were reflective of social qualities that could be valuable in society, indicating levels of independence, adventurousness, and aggressiveness that could actually prove useful in some possible futures. Perhaps society maintains in its children externalizing behavior levels that are sometimes annoying or nonoptimal in the dominant settings of current society, especially schools, but which express qualities that might be richly reinforced in other contexts. This may resemble the fact that our genome carries along genes that are dysfunctional or nonfunctional in some environments, but which become adaptive in other environments (Ridley, 2000). Belsky, Steinberg, and Draper (1991) have argued, for example, that it is possible to view early sexual activity and the externalizing behaviors that precede and accompany it as adaptive in a socially stressful ecology.

For the most part, prior studies have not addressed interaction effects in forecasting sexual behavior differences. We have done so by considering the ways in which predictions may be moderated by gender and ethnicity. In most instances, relations between predictors and the sexual behavior outcome variable were similar for male and female and for European American and African American teens. However, in several intriguing instances, mostly involving gender, there were differences.

The most interesting departure from the prior literature is the set of findings that suggest that developmental antecedents of sexual activity for girls may be different than those for boys. Externalizing behavior as rated by mothers was more predictive for their sons than their daughters. On the other hand, adjustment as rated by teachers was more predictive for girls than for boys, with teacher-rated externalizing behavior and peer rejection both showing this effect in elementary school, and teacher-rated internalizing behavior showing it in early adolescence. We speculated, tentatively, that these interaction effects might imply a process in which aggressive girls are consistently socially rejected by their girl peers and ultimately are vulnerable to emotional distress in adolescence and to relatively shallow or short-lived relationships with boys. How did the present study find effects of gender interactions with prior adjustment when previous studies did not? Perhaps our outcome measure, number of sexual partners at ages 16–17, is sufficiently different from those of the studies that showed no such effects—pregnancy in late adolescence (Scaramella et al., 1998) and sexual debut in early adolescence (Costa et al., 1995). Nevertheless, there have been so few attempts to find interaction effects previously that our finding of them cannot be viewed as highly anomalous. Additional findings of interaction effects, for example, those involving gender-moderating relations between family socioeconomic status and sexual activity, are of possible interest, but there is not a coherent enough pattern in the present data to justify further interpretation until they are replicated.

Another finding of previous studies that we thought we might repeat, but did not, was the independent association between school achievement and sexual behavior outcomes. The previous findings (Fergusson & Woodward, 2000; Scaramella et al., 1998), however, focused on pregnancy or childbearing outcomes rather than number of sexual partners. So our finding of no incremental prediction for grade point average measures should be seen not as a true nonreplication, but rather as a supplemental finding.

In conclusion, the study has clearly confirmed the externalizing behavior aspects of teen sexual activity in middle adolescence, and it has raised some interesting questions about possible gender differences in the developmental bases of sexual activity differences. There are a number of ways in which the answers here might be improved, such as use of a wider array of predictor measures, including indexes of positive adjustment that are independent of negative adjustment measures, for example, perhaps, creativity. In addition, as theories of sexual development are refined, it would be helpful to use structural equations which control for unreliability of measurement of the outcome and antecedent variables, as well as growth curve models to more precisely model the relations between specific trajectories and the outcomes. For the present, however, these findings both confirm previous trends in the development of differences in sexual behavior in adolescence and raise interesting new questions.

Acknowledgments

This work was supported by National Institute of Mental Health grants MH28018 and MH42498 and National Institute of Child Health and Human Development grant HD30572. We also thank the families participating in this study, Bruce Ellis for his comments, and Richard Viken for his statistical consultation.

Notes

Editor's comment: This paper was to have been presented at the workshop, but due to unforeseen circumstances, this was not possible. For this reason, there is no discussion of this paper.

1. The composite used for our preliminary analyses differed in important respects

from the one used by Ellis et al. (2003). The most important difference is that it used only year 9 data, whereas Ellis et al. use year 7 data as well. Ellis et al. find a significant difference between a group reporting early sexual activity and a group not reporting it on parentally reported monitoring. In subsequent analyses, we will consider the sources of the difference in findings.

2. Supplemental analyses provide a bit of support for the suppositions about the different meanings of externalizing behaviors for boys and girls. A teen-report index of parent-child relationship quality was more correlated with female teens' externalizing behavior as rated by mothers, and more correlated with male teens' externalizing behavior as rated by teachers; and male teens' self-reported personality was somewhat more strongly correlated with externalizing behavior than was female teens' personality.

Teen-rated psychological control (10 items, e.g., "Blames me for other family members' problems," "Brings up my past mistakes when he/she criticizes me," rated for each parent; Barber, 1996; Pettit et al. 2001) related slightly to teacher-rated externalizing behavior of boys in Epoch 1 ($r = .13$, $p = .06$) and Epoch 2 ($r = .15$, $p = .03$). This same index was essentially uncorrelated with mother-reported externalizing of boys in Epochs 1–3 ($r = .02, .03, .02$, respectively, all n.s.). However, psychological control ratings showed the opposite pattern for girls, with nonsignificant relations between the index of parent-teen relationship quality and teacher-reported externalizing behavior ($r = .06$, .08, n.s., for Epochs 1 and 2, respectively), but more substantial ones with mother-reported externalizing behavior ($r = .16$, $p = .02$; .26, $p < .001$; .22, $p = .001$; for the three epochs, respectively).

A brief, youth-oriented Big Five personality questionnaire (Lanthier, 1993), administered to the teens at year 8 (ages 12–13), produced a complementary pattern. For both boys and girls, extraversion correlated significantly ($r = .14$–.22) with both teacher and mother reports of externalizing behavior. However, agreeableness, conscientiousness, and neuroticism showed stronger relations for boys than for girls. Boys' agreeableness correlated −.15 ($p = .03$) with teacher reports of externalizing in Epoch 1, −.10 ($p = .13$) in Epoch 2. It correlated −.12 ($p = .09$) with mother reports in Epoch 1, −.16 ($p = .02$) in Epoch 2, and −.18 ($p = .01$) in Epoch 3. Corresponding correlations (and ps) for girls were .04 (.57), −.01 (.87), −.11 (.11), −.06 (.36), and −.02 (.77). Boys' neuroticism had negative relations with teacher ratings of externalizing behavior, to at least a trend degree, in Epochs 1 ($r = −.12$, $p = .07$) and 2 ($r = −.17$, $p = .01$).

References

Achenbach, T. M. (1991a). *Manual for the Child Behavior Checklist/4–18 and 1991 profile.* Burlington: University of Vermont, Department of Psychiatry.

Achenbach, T. M. (1991b). *Manual for the Teacher's Report Form and 1991 profile.* Burlington: University of Vermont, Department of Psychiatry.

Achenbach, T. M. (1991c). *Manual for the Youth Self-Report and 1991 profile.* Burlington: University of Vermont, Department of Psychiatry.

Barber, B. K. (1996). Parental psychological control: Revisiting a neglected construct. *Child Development, 67,* 3296–3319.

Bates, J. E. (1989). Applications of temperament concepts. In G. A. Kohnstamm, J. E. Bates, & M. K. Rothbart (Eds.), *Temperament in childhood* (pp. 321–355). Chichester, England: Wiley.

Bates, J. E., & Bayles, K. (1988). Attachment and the development of behavior problems. In J. B. T. Nezworski (Ed.), *Clinical implications of attachment* (pp. 253–299). Hillsdale, NJ: Lawrence Erlbaum.

Bates, J. E., Bayles, K., Bennett, D. S., Ridge, B. & Brown, M. M. (1991). Origins of externalizing behavior problems at eight years of age. In D. P. K. Rubin (Ed.), *Development and treatment of childhood aggression* (pp. 93–120). Hillsdale, NJ: Lawrence Erlbaum.

Bates, J. E., Maslin, C. A., & Frankel, K. A. (1985). Attachment security, mother-child interaction, and temperament as predictors of behavior problem ratings at age three years. *Monographs of the Society for Research in Child Development,* special issue, *Growing points in attachment theory and research,* I. Bretherton & E. Waters (Eds.), Serial No. 209.

Bates, J. E., Pettit, G. S., Dodge, K. A., & Ridge, B. (1998). The interaction of temperamental resistance to control and restrictive parenting in the development of externalizing behavior. *Developmental Psychology, 34,* 982–995.

Belsky, J., Steinberg, L., & Draper, P. (1991). Childhood experience, interpersonal development, and reproductive strategy: An evolutionary theory of socialization. *Child Development, 62,* 647–670.

Carskadon, M. A., & Acebo, C. (1993). A self-administered rating scale for pubertal development. *Journal of Adolescent Health, 14,* 190–195.

Caspi, A., Lynam, D., Moffitt, T. E., & Silva, P. A. (1993). Unraveling girls' delinquency: Biological, dispositional, and contextual contributions to adolescent misbehavior. *Developmental Psychology, 29*(1), 19–30.

Coie, J. D., & Dodge, K. A. (1998). Aggression and antisocial behavior. In W. Damon (Ed. in Chief) & N. Eisenberg (Vol. Ed.), *Handbook of child psychology: Vol. 3. Social, emotional, and personality development* (5th ed., pp. 779–862). New York: John Wiley.

Collins, W. A., Maccoby, E. E., Steinberg, L., Hetherington, E. M., & Bornstein, M. (2000). Contemporary research on parenting: The case for nature and nurture. *American Psychologist, 55,* 218–232.

Costa, F. M., Jessor, R., Donovan, J. E., & Fortenberry, J. D. (1995). Early initiation of sexual intercourse: The influence of psychosocial unconventionality. *Journal of Research on Adolescence, 5,* 93–121.

Deater-Deckard, K., Lansford, J. E., Dodge, K. A., Pettit, G. S., & Bates, J. E. (in press). Adolescents' attitudes about corporal punishment: The role of sociocultural context and experiences involving physical punishment and abuse. *Journal of Family Psychology.*

Dishion, T. J., Patterson, G. R., Stoolmiller, M., & Skinner, M. L. (1991). Family, school, and behavioral antecedents to early adolescent involvement with antisocial peers. *Developmental Psychology, 27,* 172–180.

Dodge, K. A., Bates, J. E., & Pettit, G. S. (1990). Mechanisms in the cycle of violence. *Science, 250,* 1678–1683.

Dodge, K. A., Lansford, J. E., Burks, V. S., Bates, J. E., Pettit, G. S., Fontaine, R., et al. (2003). Peer rejection and social information processing factors in the development of aggressive behavior problems in children. *Child Development, 74,* 374–393.

Dodge, K. A., Pettit, G. S., & Bates, J. E. (1994). Socialization mediators of the relation between socioeconomic status and child conduct problems. *Child Development, 65,* 649–665.

Duncan, S. C., Strycker, L. A., & Duncan, T. E. (1999). Exploring associations in developmental trends of adolescent substance use and risky sexual behavior in a high-risk population. *Journal of Behavioral Medicine, 22,* 21–34.

Ellis, B. J., Dodge, K. A., Pettit, G. S., & Bates, J. E. (1999). Quality of early family relationships and individual differences in the timing of pubertal maturation in girls: A longitudinal test of an evolutionary model. *Journal of Personality and Social Psychology, 77,* 387–401.

Ellis, B. J., McFadyen-Ketchum, S., Bates, J. E., Dodge, K. A., Fergusson, D. M., Horwood, L. J., et al. (2003). Does early father absence place daughters at special risk for early sexual activity and teenage pregnancy? *Child Development.*

Fagot, B. I., Pears, K. C., Capaldi, D. M., Crosby, L., & Leve, C. S. (1998). Becoming an adolescent father: Precursors and parenting. *Developmental Psychology, 34,* 1209–1219.

Fergusson, D. M., & Woodward, L. J. (2000). Teenage pregnancy and female educational underachievement: A prospective study of a New Zealand birth cohort. *Journal of Marriage and the Family, 62,* 147–161.

Hollingshead, A. A. (1979). Four-factor Index of Social Status. Unpublished manuscript, Yale University, New Haven, CT.

Keiley, M. K., Bates, J. E., Dodge, K. A., & Pettit, G. A. (2000). A cross-domain growth analysis: Externalizing and internalizing behaviors during 8 years of childhood. *Journal of Abnormal Child Psychology, 28,* 161–179.

Kerr, M., & Stattin, H. (2000). What parents know, how they know it, and several forms of adolescent adjustment: Further support for a reinterpretation of monitoring. *Developmental Psychology, 36,* 366–380.

Kotchick, B. A., Shaffer, A., Forehand, R., & Miller, K. S. (2001). Adolescent sexual risk behavior: A multi-system perspective. *Clinical Psychology Review, 21,* 493–519.

Laird, R. D., Pettit, G. S., Bates, J. E., & Dodge, K. A. (2001). *Parents' monitoring-relevant knowledge and adolescents' delinquent behavior: Evidence of correlated developmental changes and reciprocal influences.* Unpublished manuscript, University of Rhode Island.

Lanthier, R. P. (1993). *The Big Five dimensions of personality in middle childhood and adolescence.* Unpublished doctoral dissertation, University of Denver.

Maccoby, E. E. (1991). Different reproductive strategies in males and females. *Child Development, 62,* 676–681.

Magnusson, D. (1988). *Individual development from an interactional perspective: A longitudinal study.* Hillsdale, NJ: Lawrence Erlbaum.

Miller, B.C., Benson, B., & Galbraith, K. A. (2001). Family relationships and adolescent pregnancy risk: A research synthesis. *Developmental Review, 21,* 1–38.

Miller-Johnson, S., Winn, D.-M., Coie, J., Maumary-Gremaud, A., Hyman, C., Terry, R., et al. (1999). Motherhood during the teen years: A developmental perspective on risk factors for childbearing. *Development and Psychopathology, 11,* 85–100.

Olson, S. L., Bates, J. E., & Bayles, K. (1984). Mother-infant interaction and the development of individual differences in children's cognitive competence. *Developmental Psychology, 20,* 166–179.

Patterson, G. R. (1982). Coercive family process. Eugene, OR: Castalia.

Patterson, G. R. (1993). Orderly change in a stable world: The antisocial trait as chimera. *Journal of Consulting and Clinical Psychology, 61,* 911–919.

Patterson, G. R., DeBaryshe, B. D., & Ramsey, E. (1989). A developmental perspective on antisocial behavior. *American Psychologist, 44,* 329–335.

Patterson, G. R., Reid, J. B., & Dishion, T. (1992). *Antisocial boys.* Eugene, OR: Castalia.

Pettit, G. S., & Bates, J. E. (1989). Family interaction patterns and children's behavior problems from infancy to age 4 years. *Developmental Psychology, 25,* 413–420.

Pettit, G. S., Bates, J. E., & Dodge, K. A. (1997). Supportive parenting, ecological context, and children's adjustment: A seven-year longitudinal study. *Child Development, 68,* 908–923.

Pettit, G. S., Laird, R. D., Bates, J. E., Dodge, K. A., & Criss, M. M. (2001). Antecedents and behavior-problem outcomes of parental monitoring and psychological control in early adolescence. *Child Development, 72,* 583–598.

Ridley, M. (2000). *Genome.* New York: Harper-Collins.

Rothbart, M. K., & Bates, J. E. (1998). Temperament. In W. Damon (Ed. in Chief) & N. Eisenberg (Vol. Ed.), *Handbook of child psychology: Vol. 3. Social, emotional, and personality development* (5th ed., pp. 105–176). New York: John Wiley.

Rothbaum, F., & Weisz, J. R. (1994). Parental caregiving and child externalizing behavior: A meta-analysis. *Psychological Bulletin, 116,* 55–74.

Sattler, J. M. (1982). *Assessment of children's intelligence and special abilities.* Boston: Allyn and Bacon.

Scaramella, L. V., Conger, R. D., Simons, R. L., & Witbeck, L. B. (1998). Predicting risk for pregnancy by late adolescence: A social contextual perspective. *Developmental Psychology, 34,* 1233–1245.

Simmons, R. G., & Blyth, D. A. (1987). *Moving into adolescence: The impact of pubertal change and school context.* New York: Aldine de Gruyter.

Sroufe, L. A., & Rutter, M. (1984). The domain of developmental psychopathology. *Child Development, 55,* 17–29.

Wachs, T. D. (2000). *Necessary but not sufficient: The respective roles of single and multiple influences on individual development.* Washington, DC: American Psychological Association.

Weiss, B., Dodge, K. A., Bates, J. E., & Pettit, G. S. (1992). Some consequences of early harsh discipline: Child aggression and a maladaptive social information processing style. *Child Development, 63,* 1321–1335.

Woodward, L. J., & Fergusson, D. M. (1999). Early conduct problems and later risk of teenage pregnancy in girls. *Development and Psychopathology, 11,* 127–141.

Part 4.

Cross-Cultural Aspects

Normative Sexual Behavior of African American Children

Preliminary Findings

JEFFRY W. THIGPEN, ELSIE M. PINKSTON,
AND JAY H. MAYEFSKY

The Sexually Aggressive Children and Youth (SACY) program of the Illinois Department of Children and Family Services was created in 1994 to provide clinical treatment to wards who exhibit sexual behavior. The creation of this specialized program was an outgrowth of the Legal Assistance Foundation of Chicago's realization that the state of Illinois provided few resources to state wards who sexually abused other children. The goals of the SACY program are to identify children who exhibit sexual behavior, provide clinical services to address their sexual behavior, and monitor children designated "sexually aggressive."

A complaint made to Cook County's Office of the Inspector General (OIG) of the Illinois Department of Children and Family Services by a foster parent, who questioned the removal of her foster child by reason of the foster child's alleged display of sexual behavior in a previous foster home, launched a series of investigations into the practices of the SACY program. These investigations, based on reviews of random samples of SACY cases, revealed several disquieting practices (OIG, 2000). First, the SACY program designates and labels children sexually aggressive without consideration of the frequency and severity of the displayed sexual behavior, the child's psychosocial and developmental history, or the specific circumstances surrounding the sexual behavior. Further, most designations were made by telephone without interviewing the children or, in many cases, the foster parents. Second, the SACY program espouses an adult model of sexual aggression that assumes incurability and emphasizes the potential for reoffense. To reduce the probability of reoffense, all adults acting in a supervisory role with a SACY-designated child are informed of the designation. Further, the child's name is placed and maintained on a permanent statewide database. Third, and perhaps the most important, the SACY program determines whether a child's sexual behavior is problematic or aggressive according to *usual and expected* age-appropriate sexual behavior. This practice is particularly alarming and ironic given that little is known about normative sexual behavior of children, especially African American children. These practices, in tandem, have detrimental and long-lasting effects on children designated sexually aggressive. In many cases, the sexually aggressive label resulted in siblings being separated, children being alienated from their peers, and more beneficial placement alternatives, such as adoption, being denied.

Of critical importance is the possibility that some of the children designated sexually aggressive were inappropriately labeled, and consequently will be subjected to the harmful effects of the label. This possibility approaches certainty because the majority of children designated sexually aggressive are African American,[1] and what constitutes usual and expected age-appropriate sexual behavior for these children is unknown. Researchers have noted that participants involved in child sexual behavior studies are typically white and from higher socioeconomic backgrounds (Gordon & Schroeder, 1995). Thus the findings from these studies may not represent the full range or frequency of sexual behavior exhibited by children from different ethnic and social class families.

To begin filling this important empirical gap, this study investigates the range and frequency of sexual behavior in a sample of African American children without histories of sexual abuse. As physicians and mental health practitioners report that parents often inquire into the normalcy of their children's sexual behavior (Johnson, 1991), the knowledge gained from this study will assist practitioners in determining when a child's sexual behavior is within an acceptable range and when it is cause for concern. Similarly, the knowledge gained from this study will facilitate the development of empirically informed child welfare programs and policies.

Sexual Behavior in Children: A Cursory Review of the Literature

Although sexuality and sexual functioning are widely accepted as fundamental and important aspects of human life, few empirical studies are available regarding the sexual behavior of children. This paucity of empirical research is no doubt connected to prevailing societal beliefs that children are asexual in thought and behavior. It is plausible to associate this "age of innocence" belief to religious and cultural ideologies about sex that suggest that children are overtly uninterested in sex until puberty. Regardless of the sources of this belief, restrictive cultural attitudes about sex in general, and more specifically about children and sex, impede a comprehensive understanding of the sexual behavior of children. Two recent lines of scientific inquiry purporting to understand the nature, extent, and effects of child sexual abuse, and a related literature that examines children as a category of sexual aggressors who prey upon other children, illuminate the poor state of knowledge regarding the normative sexual behavior of children. Although empirical studies investigating normal sexual behavior of children have recently surfaced (Friedrich, Grambsch, Broughton, Houston, & Shafran, 1998; Friedrich, Grambsch,

Broughton, Kuiper, & Beilke, 1991; Okami, Olmstead, & Abramson, 1997), the findings are preliminary, and our knowledge and understanding is still growing.

Notwithstanding the dearth of empirical studies that have investigated the sexual behavior of children cross-culturally, psychosexual development and the capacity for sexual response are believed to be present at or before birth (Goldman & Goldman, 1982; Martinson, 1981). For example, male babies have penile erections and female babies are capable of vaginal lubrication (Martinson, 1981). Similarly, Rutter (1971) reported a variety of sexualized behaviors seen in young children, including orgasmic-like responses in boys as young as five months, and thigh rubbing by female preschoolers; exhibitionism and voyeurism with other children and adults by male and female nursery school children; sexual exploration games in boys and girls by the age of 4 years; and asking questions about sex by both boys and girls by the age of 5 years.

Psychosexual development and sexual behavior continue throughout childhood. Routh and Schroeder (1981) identify masturbation and sexual play as the most common sexual behaviors in children. Friedrich et al. (1991) found that children between the ages of 2 and 12 display a wide variety of sexual behavior at high frequencies (e.g., being interested in the opposite sex, kissing nonfamily adults and children, touching breasts, touching their genitals, undressing in front of others, etc.). The study also found that younger children more frequently display sexual behavior than older children do. Martinson (1991) distinguishes masturbation from genital play. Masturbation is described as a volitional act that requires rhythmic and repeated manipulation of the genitals resulting in pleasurable sensations. In contrast, genital play is viewed as bodily exploration that involves fingering, simple pleasurable handling of the genitals, and random exploration. Martinson contends that infants are not capable of the small-muscle control that masturbation requires, and are not innately motivated to this degree of self-stimulation. However, masturbation in male infants as young as five to seven months, and in female infants from four months, has been suggested (Kinsey, Pomeroy, & Martin, 1948).

Sexual play is a common sexual phenomenon among children, and is viewed as a nonpathological peer sexual interaction (Okami et al., 1997) motivated by a child's curiosity about his/her own body as well as the bodies of others (Gordon & Schroeder, 1995). Lamb and Coakley (1993) reported that 85% of their sample of college women recalled engaging in sexual games during childhood, at an average age of 7.5 years. The study further reported that 86% of childhood sexual play occurred between male and female friends, and over 40% of the sexual play activities involved fantasy play or other activities in which the children experimented with sexual stimulation (including sexual intercourse), rape, prostitution, strip shows, playing "doctor," and exposing their genitals. In a longitudinal study investigating the long-term correlates of early childhood peer sexual experiences, Okami et al. (1997) found that almost half of the sample had engaged in sex play before age 6.

Cultural and Family Context

The psychosexual development and sexual behavior of children are influenced by cultural norms and expectations, familial interactions and values, and interpersonal experience (Friedrich et al., 1991; Martinson, 1981). Goldman and Goldman (1982), in discussing the universality of sexuality, point to the existence of sexual taboos in every society, and highlight Western society's unwillingness to recognize children as sexual beings. Societies have been classified into three general categories with respect to their sexual attitudes, beliefs, and practices: restrictive, semirestrictive, and permissive (Ford & Beach, 1951). Western societies fall within the restrictive category, purposely impeding or limiting the acquisition of sexual knowledge and sexual experiences during childhood (Goldman & Goldman, 1982). What is permissible for children to know, explore, and practice varies considerably between the categories of this sexual typology (Goldman & Goldman, 1982). For example, Larsson, Svedin, and Friedrich (2000) found that children in Sweden, a sexually permissive society, more frequently exhibit sexual behavior than American children. Culture is of considerable import as a mediating factor in shaping the psychosexual development and sexual behavior of children.

The psychosexual development and sexual behavior of children are strongly influenced by the sexual culture of the family in which the child is reared. Finkelhor (1978) conceptualizes family sexuality as having three dimensions: attitude toward sexuality (family culture); the actual eroticization of family relationships; and the family's respect for personal boundaries. Further, families are characterized as either sex-positive or sex-negative. This characterization is described as follows:

> In sex-positive families, children receive accurate information about sex, are given positive attitudes about their bodies and are shown physical affection. In sex-negative families, sex and discussions about sex are loaded with anxiety and taboos. In highly sexualized families, members use one another as objects to their sexual role-playing. Each member tries to test out his or her powers of attraction and adequacy on the others. (p. 47)

In families where personal boundaries exist, personal privacy is respected and the sex roles of adults and children are clearly differentiated. Conversely, in families where poor boundaries exist, child sexuality is not clearly distinguished from adult sexuality.

Methodology

To investigate the range and frequency of sexual behavior in African American children, project research assistants recruited primary caregivers of African American children 2 to 12 years of age from the waiting area of a well-child clinic in Cook County that provides non-emergent, routine pediatric care to low-income African American children. The primary caregivers were approached, provided with general information regarding the nature of the study, and asked about their interest in participating. Very few primary caregivers declined receiving further information about the study or exploring their eligibility for participation. In instances where primary caregivers refused further information about the study or their participation, reasons such as "I'm too tired" or "I don't have time" were offered. All project research assistants were African American graduate social work students.

Given the study's focus on the sexual behavior of African American children without a known history of sexual abuse, and without chronic mental, physical, or developmental disabilities, children with these histories were excluded from the sample. Also excluded were primary caregiver–child pairs residing outside of the county or who had not resided in the same household for the past six months, and pairs in which the primary caregiver was younger than 18, had received mental health counseling in the past six months, or also cared for a child younger than 2 or older than 12. To ensure that each primary caregiver was eligible for participation in the study, project research assistants conducted an eligibility screen with each primary caregiver before beginning the informed consent process and completing the survey. Additionally, eligibility was again ascertained and ensured via exclusionary questions on the actual survey. No discrepancies between eligibility information obtained during the eligibility screen and eligibility information obtained during the interview process were found. Having children below 2 years of age was the single most common reason primary caregivers were excluded from the study. A second and less frequent reason was the presence of a developmental disability.

Subsequent to determining eligibility for participation in the study and obtaining consent, primary caregivers were asked to respond to 116 questions posed by project research assistants regarding the behavior of the child being seen in the clinic. Responses to the 116 questions were recorded on the survey form by the interviewing research assistant. Primary caregivers with more than one child were allowed to report on the behavior of up to two children, provided the child–primary caregiver pair met all eligibility criteria, both children were patients of the well-child clinic, and both were present at the time of the interview. Arrangements were made to conduct all of the interviews privately or at least semiprivately; however, some primary caregivers chose to be interviewed in the waiting area of the clinic. To help defray the cost of transportation, each participant was given $10.

Measures

The third version of the Child Sexual Behavior Inventory (CSBI; Friedrich et al., 1991) was used to measure the range and frequency of specific dimensions of sexual behavior, including self-stimulation, personal boundaries, gender-role behavior, exhibitionism, sexual anxiety, sexual interest, sexual knowledge, voyeuristic behavior, and sexual intrusiveness. The 42-item CSBI captures the frequency of sexual behaviors displayed over the past six months. It is scored as 0, 1, 2, or 3 to reflect levels of observed frequency (i.e., 0 = never; 1 = less than once per month; 2 = one to three times per month; and 3 = at least once per week). The reliability of the scale has ranged from alpha coefficients of .72 (Friedrich et al., 1998) to .82 (Friedrich et al., 1991).

Various sociodemographic data were collected, including the age and sex of the child, family size, and the marital, financial, and educational status of the primary caregiver. Data regarding the peer relationships of the child, day care characteristics, life events, TV-watching practices, family nudity, opportunities the child has had to witness intercourse, family attitude(s) and belief(s) about the normalcy of sexual feelings and curiosity in childhood, and family and child church attendance were also collected.

Preliminary Findings[2]

At the time of writing, there were 56 children in the sample.

Eighty-nine percent of the primary caregivers of the children in the sample reported being the biological mother of the child, 7% grandmother, 2% adoptive mother, and 2% other relative. The majority (60%) of the primary caregivers identified themselves as single, 21% reported being married, and 19% were separated, divorced, or widowed. Nearly all of the primary caregivers reported having at least a high school diploma or the equivalent. Reports of family size most frequently specified two children and a median annual household income of less than $15,000.

Fifty-seven percent of the children in the sample were 6 years of age or younger; 43% were 7 years of age or older. Fifty-five percent of the children were male, and 45% female. None of the children were reported as having a developmental disability or a history of sexual abuse, and nearly all school-age children (98%) were reported as being in regular educational classrooms.

Range of Sexual Behavior

Table 1 presents each item of the CSBI, and provides the percentage of overall endorsement in the sample. The percentage of endorsement by age and gender is also presented in Table 1. Eighteen items received no endorsement in this sample. These unendorsed items primarily fall within the personal boundaries and sexual intrusiveness dimensions of sexual behavior.

Overall, 24 of the 42 sexual behavior items making up the CSBI were endorsed conservatively by primary caregivers in the sample. A broader range of items was endorsed for children 2–6 years of age. Twenty of the items were endorsed for the younger age category (2–6 years of age) compared to 13 items for the older age category (7–12 years of age). Gender differences in the total number of endorsed items are also noted both within and between the two age categories. Overall, more items were endorsed for boys (20) than girls (18). However, within the younger age category, more sexual behavior items were endorsed for girls. Conversely, more items were endorsed for boys in the older category.

The dimensions of sexual behavior highly endorsed in this sample include self-stimulation, sexuality anxiety, sexual interest, and personal boundaries. Higher percentages of endorsement for self-stimulation and sexuality anxiety behaviors were reported for younger children. Two items were consistently endorsed at higher percentages for boys and girls in both age categories. "Interested in the opposite sex" was endorsed at higher percentages, but consistently lower for girls. The percentage of endorsement increased with age for boys, and declined for girls. "Stands too close" was also endorsed at consistently high percentages within and between the categories; however, the percentage of endorsement was highest for 7- to 12-year-old girls.

Frequency of Sexual Behavior

The frequencies with which sexual behavior items of the CSBI were endorsed are shown by age and gender categories in Tables 2–5. In a review of these frequencies, several patterns emerge. First, most of the endorsed behaviors were reported as occurring less than once per month for all groups. Second, endorsed behavior items were more frequently displayed (i.e., reported as occurring at least once per week) by children in the younger age category. Third, boys more frequently displayed behavior items that were endorsed at higher frequencies in both age categories. Fourth, the reported frequencies of endorsed items declined as age increased. No sexual behavior items endorsed for 7- to 12-year-old girls were reported as occurring more than 1–3 times per month.

Discussion

The above preliminary findings suggest that this sample of African American children displays a range of sexual behaviors at differential frequencies that vary in accordance with the age and gender of the child. The sexual behavior items were endorsed conservatively by the primary caregivers; however, the range of endorsed items covers all dimensions of the CSBI, except behaviors that were related to sexual intrusiveness (e.g., trying to undress children and adults against their will, or forcing children to engage in sexual acts). Analysis of data from future subjects is needed to confirm the patterns of relationships that have emerged in this study, and

Table 1. *Endorsement of Sexual Behavior Items (Percentage of Endorsement), N=56*

Item (Abbreviated)	Overall Sample	Boys 2–6	Girls 2–6	Boys 7–12	Girls 7–12
1. Dresses like the opposite sex	5.4	10.0	0.0	0.0	7.7
2. Stands too close to people	27.0	25.0	25.0	27.3	30.8
3. Wants to be the opposite sex	0.0	0.0	0.0	0.0	0.0
4. Touches private parts in public	5.4	15.0	0.0	0.0	0.0
5. Masturbates with hand	1.8	0.0	8.3	0.0	0.0
6. Draws sex parts when drawing pictures of people	1.8	0.0	0.0	9.1	0.0
7. Touches women's breasts	18.0	25.0	33.3	0.0	7.7
8. Masturbates with toy/object	2.0	0.0	8.3	0.0	0.0
9. Touches another child's sex parts	2.0	5.0	0.0	0.0	0.0
10. Tries to have sexual intercourse with children/adults	0.0	0.0	0.0	0.0	0.0
11. Puts mouth on another child's sex parts	0.0	0.0	0.0	0.0	0.0
12. Touches private parts when at home	12.5	20.0	16.7	9.1	0.0
13. Touches adults' sex parts	3.6	5.0	8.3	0.0	0.0
14. Touches animal sex parts	0.0	0.0	0.0	0.0	0.0
15. Makes sexual sounds	0.0	0.0	0.0	0.0	0.0
16. Asks others to engage in sexual acts	0.0	0.0	0.0	0.0	0.0
17. Rubs body against people/furniture	0.0	0.0	0.0	0.0	0.0
18. Puts objects in vagina/rectum	0.0	0.0	0.0	0.0	0.0
19. Tries to look when people are nude/undressing	10.7	5.0	25.0	9.1	7.7
20. Pretends that dolls/stuffed animals are having sex	10.7	0.0	25.0	18.2	7.7
21. Shows sex parts to adults	0.0	0.0	0.0	0.0	0.0
22. Tries to look at pictures of nude/partially dressed people	7.2	0.0	8.3	18.2	7.7
23. Talks about sexual acts	1.8	0.0	0.0	9.1	0.0
24. Kisses adults they do not know well	0.0	0.0	0.0	0.0	0.0
25. Gets upset when adults are kissing/hugging	14.3	15.0	24.9	9.1	7.7

Table 1. *Continued*

Item (Abbreviated)	Overall Sample	Boys 2–6	Girls 2–6	Boys 7–12	Girls 7–12
26. Overly friendly with men they don't know well	3.6	5.0	8.3	0.0	0.0
27. Kisses other children they do not know well	1.8	0.0	8.3	0.0	0.0
28. Tries to undress other children against their will	0.0	0.0	0.0	0.0	0.0
29. Talks flirtatiously	0.0	0.0	0.0	0.0	0.0
30. Wants to watch TV/movies that show nudity/sex	5.4	0.0	0.0	18.2	7.7
31. Tries to put tongue in other person's mouth when kissing	1.8	0.0	8.3	0.0	0.0
32. Hugs adults they don't know well	7.2	5.0	25.0	0.0	0.0
33. Shows sex parts to other children	1.8	5.0	0.0	0.0	0.0
34. Tries to undress adults against their will	0.0	0.0	0.0	0.0	0.0
35. Interested in the opposite sex	35.6	35.0	25.0	63.7	23.1
36. Puts mouth on mother's/women's breasts	5.4	5.0	16.6	0.0	0.0
37. Knows more about sex than other children their age	1.8	0.0	0.0	9.1	0.0
38. Touches other children's sex parts after being told not to	0.0	0.0	0.0	0.0	0.0
39. Plans how to sexually touch other children	0.0	0.0	0.0	0.0	0.0
40. Forces other children to do sexual acts	0.0	0.0	0.0	0.0	0.0
41. Puts finger/object in other children's vaginas/rectums	0.0	0.0	0.0	0.0	0.0
42. Other sexual behavior	0.0	0.0	0.0	0.0	0.0

Table 2. *Endorsement Frequencies of Sexual Behavior Items for Boys 2–6, N=20*

Item (Abbreviated)	< Once per month	1–3 times per month	Once per week	Percentage of endorsement
1. Touches another child's sex parts	1	0	0	5.0%
2. Touches adults' sex parts	1	0	0	5.0%
3. Hugs adults they don't know well	1	0	0	5.0%
4. Shows sex parts to other children	1	0	0	5.0%
5. Puts mouth on mother's/women's breasts	1	0	0	5.0%
6. Dresses like the opposite sex	2	0	0	10.0%
7. Tries to look when people are nude/ undressing	0	1	0	5.0%
8. Overly friendly with men	0	1	0	5.0%
9. Touches private parts in public	2	1	0	30.0%
10. Gets upset when adults are kissing/ hugging	1	2	0	30.0%
11. Touches private parts when at home	0	1	3	40.0%
12. Stands too close	2	2	1	50.0%
13. Touches women's breasts	2	2	1	50.0%
14. Interested in the opposite sex	1	1	3	50.0%

to identify other sociodemographic and sociocultural factors that are correlated with sexual behavior. Given that children in Cook County were designated "sexually aggressive" following one display of alleged sexual behavior not of a sexually intrusive or aggressive nature in 70% of the randomly selected cases (OIG, 2000), these preliminary findings offer some support for the earlier claim that some of the children designated "sexually aggressive" in Cook County were inappropriately labeled.

Although these preliminary findings provide evidence that African American children without histories of sexual abuse display a range of sexual behavior at varying frequencies, the primary caregivers' reports are conservative in comparison to findings presented in earlier studies using the CSBI with children of other ethnic backgrounds (e.g., Friedrich et al., 1991, 1998). One plausible explanation for this difference is that restrictive sexual beliefs and attitudes, culturally or religiously based, may affect a

Table 3. *Endorsement Frequencies of Sexual Behavior Items for Girls 2–6, N=12*

Item (Abbreviated)	< Once per month	1–3 times per month	Once per week	Percentage of endorsement
1. Masturbates with hand	1	0	0	8.3
2. Masturbates with toy/object	1	0	0	8.3
3. Tries to look when people are nude/ undressing	1	0	0	8.3
4. Pretends that dolls/stuffed animals are having sex	1	0	0	8.3
5. Tries to look at pictures of nude/partially dressed people	1	0	0	8.3
6. Tries to put tongue in other person's mouth when kissing	1	0	0	8.3
7. Touches adults' sex parts	0	1	0	8.3
8. Overly friendly with men they don't know well	0	1	0	8.3
9. Kisses other children they don't know well	0	1	0	8.3
10. Puts mouth on mother's/women's breasts	1	0	1	16.7
11. Interested in the opposite sex	1	0	1	16.7
12. Touches private parts when at home	0	0	2	16.7
13 Hugs adults they don't know well	1	2	0	24.9
14. Gets upset when adults are kissing/hugging	1	1	1	24.9
15. Stands too close	1	0	2	24.9
16. Touches women's breasts	1	0	3	33.0

caregiver's interpretation of a child's behavior or a child's display of sexual behavior. This possibility has extreme relevance for this sample, as 55% of the primary caregivers in the sample reported attending church two or more times per month; less than 20% reported no church attendance. Additionally, 80% of the primary caregivers reported that their child had never shown sexual behavior, 64% reported having never seen their child touch his/her genitals, and 32% reported that sexual feelings and curiosity in children are abnormal. A better understanding of the effects of culture

Table 4. *Endorsement Frequencies of Sexual Behavior Items for Boys 7–12, N=11*

Item (Abbreviated)	< Once per month	1–3 times per month	Once per week	Percentage of endorsement
1. Draws sex parts when drawing pictures of people	1	0	0	9.1
2. Pretends that dolls/stuffed animals are having sex	1	0	0	9.1
3. Talks about sex acts	1	0	0	9.1
4. Gets upset when adults are kissing/hugging	1	0	0	9.1
5. Touches private parts when at home	0	1	0	9.1
6. Tries to look when people are nude/undressing	0	1	0	9.1
7. Knows more about sex than other children their age	0	1	0	9.1
8. Tries to look at pictures of nude/partially dressed people	0	2	0	18.2
9. Wants to watch TV/movies that show nudity/sex	1	1	0	18.2
10. Stands too close	1	1	1	27.3
11. Interested in the opposite sex	2	3	0	45.5

and religious participation on parental and caregiver reports of the sexual behavior of children is needed. In addition, research exploring the attitudes and beliefs of African American parents regarding sexuality and sexual behavior in children should be conducted, because parental interpretation of and reaction to sexual behavior of children will affect the extent to which children are comfortable in exploring and expressing their sexuality, which has consequences for both adolescent and adult sexuality.

Limitations of the Research

As previously mentioned, the findings presented in this paper are preliminary; data collection and analysis are ongoing. In addition to the preliminary nature of the findings, several limitations exist. First, the meth-

Table 5. *Endorsement Frequencies of Sexual Behavior Items for Girls 7–12, N=13*

Item (Abbreviated)	< Once per month	1–3 times per month	Once per week	Percentage of endorsement
1. Tries to look when people are nude/ undressing	1	0	0	7.7
2. Pretends that dolls/stuffed animals are having sex	1	0	0	7.7
3. Tries to look at pictures of nude/partially dressed people	1	0	0	7.7
4. Wants to watch TV/movies that show nudity/sex	1	0	0	7.7
5. Interested in the opposite sex	1	0	0	7.7
6. Dresses like the opposite sex	0	1	0	7.7
7. Touches women's breasts	0	1	0	7.7
8. Gets upset when adults are kissing/hugging	0	1	0	7.7
9. Stands too close	2	2	0	30.8

odology of this study was designed to exclude children with histories of sexual abuse; however, it is possible that children with this history are represented in the sample due to the history being unknown or not reported. Second, given that these findings are derived from parental and caregiver reports of the sexual behavior of children, the accuracy of the data is questionable given that parents and caregivers may either underreport observances of sexual behavior, in line with prevailing attitudes and beliefs about childhood sexual behavior, or may be unaware of the sexual behavior of their children, given that behavior can occur unbeknownst to the parent. Finally, the external validity of the findings is limited to the sample population, and consequently does not reflect normative ranges and frequencies of the sexual behavior of all African American children.

Notes

1. This is not due to an oversampling of African American children, but is related to the overrepresentation of African American children in foster care in Cook County.

2. It should be noted that the findings presented herein are preliminary, and based on descriptive analysis of the data. Data collection and further analyses are ongoing.

References

Finkelhor, D. (1978). Psychological, cultural and family factors in incest and family sexual abuse. *Journal of Marriage and Family Counseling, 4*, 41–49.

Ford, C. S., & Beach, F. A. (1951). *Patterns of sexual behavior.* New York: Harper.

Friedrich, W. N., Fisher, J., Broughton, D., Houston, M., & Shafran, C. (1998). Normative sexual behavior in children: A contemporary sample. *Pediatrics, 101*(4), e9.

Friedrich, W. N., Grambsch, P., Broughton, D., Kuiper, J., & Beilke, R. (1991). Normative sexual behavior in children. *Pediatrics, 88*, 456–464.

Goldman, R., & Goldman, J. (1982). *Children's sexual thinking: A comparative study of children aged 5 to 15 years in Australia, North America, Britain, and Sweden.* New York: Academic.

Gordon, B., & Schroeder, C. (1995). *Sexuality: A developmental approach to problems.* New York: Plenum.

Johnson, T. (1991). Understanding the sexual behavior of young children. *SIECUS Report, 5*, 8–15.

Kinsey, A. C., Pomeroy, W. B., & Martin, C. E. (1948). *Sexual behavior in the human male.* Philadelphia: W. B. Saunders.

Lamb, S., & Coakley, M. (1993). "Normal" childhood sexual play and games: Differentiating play from abuse. *Child Abuse & Neglect, 17*, 515–526.

Larsson, I., Svedin, C. G., & Friedrich, W. N. (2000). Differences and similarities in sexual behaviour among pre-schoolers in Sweden and USA. *Nordic Journal of Psychiatry, 54*, 251–257.

Martinson, F. (1981). Eroticism in infancy and childhood. In L. Constantine & F. Martinson (Eds.), *Children and sex: New findings, new perspectives* (pp. 23–35). Boston: Little, Brown.

Martinson, F. (1991). Normal sexual development in infancy and early childhood. In G. D. Ryan & S. L. Lane (Eds.), *Juvenile sexual offending: Causes, consequences, and correction* (pp. 57–82). Lexington, MA: Lexington.

Office of the Inspector General, Illinois Department of Children and Family Services. (2000). *An investigation of current practices in Cook County with state wards (eight to twenty) who are designated as sexually aggressive.* Chicago: Author.

Okami, P., Olmstead, R., & Abramson, P. (1997). Sexual experiences in early childhood: 18-year longitudinal data from the UCLA Family Lifestyles Project. *Journal of Sex Research, 34*, 339–347.

Routh, D., & Schroeder, C. (1981). Masturbation and other sexual behaviors. In S. Gabel (Ed.), *Behavior problems of childhood* (pp. 387–392). New York: Grune and Stratton.

Rutter, M. (1971). Normal psychosexual development. *Journal of Psychological Psychiatry, 11*, 259–283.

Cultural Dimensions of Childhood Sexuality in the United States

SUZANNE G. FRAYSER

Child sexual abuse has emerged as an issue that expresses a well-placed concern for the welfare and healthy development of children. Child sexual abuse has also become an issue that triggers moral outrage, fuels a victim-perpetrator paradigm for judging sexual cases, and provides justification for attacks on researchers whose research topics do not conform to politically correct formulations about the meaning of abuse or children's sexual behavior. The deep emotions that the issue arouses are often difficult to articulate, and suggestions that outcomes other than long-term harm can result from childhood sexual experience are likely to be met with disbelief, horror, or hostility. To feel or think otherwise rocks our sense of comfort in our cultural home, because we then have to question the assumptions that we take for granted as natural, stable, and valid to structure our lives.

The issue is broader than child sexual abuse. It is a challenge to think about the meaning of the concepts of childhood, sexuality, and abuse in the United States. How have our cultural beliefs about childhood and sexuality channeled what we perceive as normal, what we define as a problem, and what we ignore or deny? What are the consequences of these patterns for scientific investigations of, developmental theories about, and therapeutic approaches to childhood sexual experience?

This paper will approach identification of the cultural contours of thinking about childhood sexuality in the United States by looking from the outside in. It builds on a previous article in which I used an anthropological approach to define normal childhood sexuality (Frayser, 1994). I want to highlight some of the findings of that overview of evolutionary and cross-cultural research to indicate what we know about childhood sexuality as a human and culture-bound experience. I'll then discuss the cultural pattern that I think guides our thinking about childhood sexual experience in the United States. I'll conclude with the implications of continuing that pattern.

Evolutionary and Cross-Species Research

Evolutionary and cross-species research provides the broadest basis for exploring what is normal about childhood sexuality (Daly & Wilson, 1978;

255

Fisher, 1992; Symons, 1979). While humans share many biological and social features of their sexuality with other sexually reproducing animals (e.g., courtship), mammals (e.g., viviparity, breastfeeding, parenting), and primates (e.g., longer gestation period, longer period of infant and juvenile dependence, investment in fewer offspring, attachment, the importance of social life as a context for learning [including sexual play and learning how to love], nonreproductive sexual interactions, more reliance on touch and vision), they depart from their nonhuman relatives in distinctive ways. Humans accentuate all of the previously mentioned biological and social features of sexually reproducing animals, mammals, and primates, but the pattern of their adaptations defines what is human about human sexuality; these features frame what we can expect as normal sexual behavior during childhood.

Longer Dependency Period

Human infants are born at an earlier stage of neurological development than other primates and mammals. The brain grows from 25% to 70% of its adult size in the first two years after birth, and brain growth is not complete until puberty, when the child is physiologically capable of reproduction (White & Brown, 1973). Therefore, human children require more parenting and attachment to caretakers to survive (Bowlby, 1969). Childhood is extended.

More Reliance on Learning in a Social Context

Because most of brain growth occurs after birth, human development includes more learning from the environment, particularly the social context. Initially, sensory communication through sight, sound, smell, and touch provides the basis for having needs met. Breastfeeding provides a model for the infant's first intimate social relationship, blending touch, giving and receiving, and pleasure (Raphael, 1976). Play provides a way for children to explore their environment and try different kinds of behavior in a safe context. And interaction with adults and other children allows them to learn how to love. As Harlow demonstrated in his famous experiments with rhesus monkeys, even nonhuman primates have to learn how to attach, love, and have sex (Harlow, 1973).

Disjunction between Reproductive and Nonreproductive Sex and the Importance of Learning Behavioral Cues

Upright posture with bipedal locomotion and the "loss" of estrus has resulted in more reliance on behavioral cues of sexual receptivity and proceptivity and less on physiological changes (e.g., fluctuation in hormones) and anatomical signals (e.g., sex skin). It also means that much sexual activity does not coincide with peak fertility and lead to reproduction, as it does during the breeding season of many mammals. Consequently, much of human sexual behavior is nonreproductive.

Anterior sex organs favored face-to-face intercourse (and partner recognition). A highly innervated clitoris in females and the absence of a penis bone in males added more significance to physical stimulation (e.g., touching, visual appeal) and interaction to foster arousal. Therefore, social learning needs to include learning about sexual interactions, stimulation, and responses.

Cultural and Cognitive Maps for Sexual Interaction

Humans significantly departed from the rest of the animal kingdom when they specialized in culture to adapt to different ecological niches. They codified social learning into patterns of meaning, synthesized in symbolic form, and passed their cultural concepts down from one generation to the next as significant conceptual tools for survival. Shared ideas and beliefs intervened between a stimulus and response so that context and conceptualization became the filters for interpreting meaning and played a significant role in channeling behavior. Therefore, the interpretation of behavior became a significant guide to action. Language developed as a symbolic medium for communicating concepts. Cultural adaptation meant that there would be wide variation in the meaning and patterns of sexual behavior. This network of cultural assumptions would then influence individual cognitions about sexual behavior and interpretation of personal experiences. The physical body became a powerful symbol itself, as an intermediary between sociocultural messages and individual experience. Douglas (1966) analyzed ways in which the body becomes a metaphor for the society and symbolically communicates cultural messages to the individual.

The Pattern of Human Childhood Sexuality

The foregoing features lead to the conclusion that "it would be surprising if children did not have an interest in or express sexual behavior, particularly because humans rely on learning to such a great extent and engage in so much nonreproductive sexual behavior" (Frayser, 1994, p. 180). We would expect that a human baseline for social learning would include how to follow social rules, interact with others in a group, and interpret behavior through cultural beliefs, so that the child learns how to love (attach) and be sexual. Sexual responses during breastfeeding, sexual play as practice for how to interact sexually, and learning about appropriate partners and responses would be logical consequences of the human evolutionary heritage.

Variations on Evolutionary Themes: The Cross-Cultural Evidence

Cross-cultural research demonstrates the variety of beliefs, sexual expressions, and social responses to childhood sexual behavior that the evolution of human sexuality would predict. Also, it shows that there are some constant themes that underlie this variety, particularly during infancy and early childhood.

Close Physical Contact between Mother and Infant

Breastfeeding is one of the first social contexts within which the infant can experience intimacy. The infant needs to suck the mother's nipple to stimulate the release of oxytocin, which then triggers the letting-down of the milk. Mother and infant learn how to give to and receive from each other in a highly tactile and sensuous way. Infant boys may have erections while feeding and mothers may experience sexual arousal, thus contributing to the pleasure and satisfaction of both mother and infant (Martinson, 1994). Breastfeeding generally lasts two to three years in traditional societies (Barry & Paxson, 1971), and postpartum sex taboos of less than a year (many of these for one to five months) reinforce this initial close interaction of mothers with infants (Frayser, 1985, p. 318).

Sleeping arrangements also facilitate close physical contact between mother and child in traditional societies. Mothers often sleep with their infants, with or without the father, who may sleep elsewhere. Barry and Paxson (1971) found that none of the 126 societies they analyzed separated the sleeping area of infants from that of their caretakers. Mothers will frequently hold and carry the infant beyond routine care, particularly during the first nine months (Barry & Paxson).

Infants and small children may receive nurturance from a variety of caretakers, most of whom are women. Barry and Paxson's data show that caretakers in most of the 120 societies nurture infants and small children with gentleness and affection. This gentle, affectionate caretaking usually continues through the first four or five years, after which caretakers in some societies may treat their children more harshly (Barry & Paxson). In her cross-cultural study of child abuse and neglect, Korbin (1981) cautions against jumping to conclusions that behaviors mean abuse or neglect without considering their context: the value of children, beliefs about categories of children, beliefs about the age capabilities and developmental stages of children, and integration of childrearing into kin and community networks.

The Incest Taboo Begins: Setting the Stage
for Social Control of Sexual Expression

The incest taboo is one of the most widespread elements of the cultural map that guides sexual behavior worldwide. It stands out in its importance as one of the first cultural concepts about socially approved sexual interaction that applies to the infant and child and its lifelong application from infancy through adulthood and old age also marks its significance. It is a prohibition on sexual relations between kin of a specified category; it is *not* a reproductive prohibition, even though the prohibition on sex has reproductive consequences.

The incest taboo varies from society to society in the kin to whom it applies. The *core taboo* prohibits sexual relations between parents and children and between siblings in the nuclear family. Most societies have this taboo, but may regard some pairings as more serious than others. The greatest variation occurs in the definition of the *extended taboo,* an extension of the sexual prohibition to relatives beyond the nuclear family. Cross-cultural research (Cohen, 1964; Frayser, 1985) demonstrates that the pattern of extension correlates with the type of kinship system in the society. Patrilineal systems extend their prohibition patrilaterally or to the lineage; matrilineal systems, matrilaterally or to the lineage; and bilateral systems, to kin related to ego on both paternal and maternal sides. This suggests that the taboo defines a cultural boundary that organizes the behavior of socializers so that children can learn their sexual scripts and establish their gender identity in a stable, systematically structured context. Such a social setting can allow for sexual play and the exploration of gender roles; it does not exclude all sexual behavior between relatives or between adults and children.

Punishments for incest indicate the significance of incestuous relationships in other societies. They vary from one extreme to the other: either very mild (e.g., temporary disapproval, a verbal reprimand, ostracism) or very severe (e.g., death, mutilation, sterility, expulsion from the community) (Frayser, 1985, p. 105). In addition, many societies do not perceive the negative consequences of incest as confined to the participants themselves; someone else (e.g., children of offenders) or the entire social group will suffer (e.g., through a plague or other calamity) for their transgression (p. 106).

Variations in Childhood Sexual Activity

Ford and Beach (1951) found that adults in only a few of the traditional societies in their sample "attempt to deny young children any form of sexual expression" (p. 180). After reviewing the cross-species and cross-cultural evidence about sexual behavior before puberty, they concluded that "tendencies toward sexual behavior before maturity and even before puberty are genetically determined in many primates, including human beings. The degree to which such tendencies find overt expression is in part a function of the rules of the society in which the individual grows up, but some expression is very likely to occur under any circumstances" (p. 198). Studies of children's sexual behavior in contemporary Western societies also confirm that children engage in a wide variety of sexual behaviors and that parents differ in those behaviors that they find acceptable (Friedrich, Grambsch, Broughton, Kuiper, & Beilke, 1991; Friedrich, Grambsch, Damon, et al., 1992; Martinson, 1994).

Social rules and cultural concepts of what is acceptable are important qualifiers for understanding childhood sexual expression. A wide range of sexual activities occur in childhood. Although there is little systematic, documented cross-cultural evidence about adult attention given to the sexual behavior of infants and small children, the research we have indicates that restrictions on sexual expression are likely to increase according to age and gender. However, cultural prescriptions may be at odds with children's interest in sexual activity. Societies may impose mild restrictions on heterosexual play, masturbation, and other erotic activities during early childhood and apply stronger restrictions in later childhood, particularly for girls (Barry, Josephson, Lauer, & Marshall, 1976). However, there is wide variation in parents' and adults' attitudes toward children's expressing sexual interest or engaging in sexual behavior. Parents may encourage children's sexual activities, and games with other children may include sexual interaction. Homosexual as well as heterosexual behavior in childhood is accepted as a normal part of childhood in many societies (Herdt, 1990). Children may have opportunities to observe adults engaging in sexual relations, and they may talk with adults about sex. Sometimes children may engage in sexual relations with adults, more often in ritual contexts (Feierman, 1990). However, most societies disapprove of child-adult sexual relations involving prepubescent children.

Cross-cultural research in traditional as well as contemporary societies confirms this diversity in attitudes about children's sexuality. Goldman and Goldman's research (1982) on children's sexual thinking in the United States, England, Australia, and Sweden demonstrated that there is no latency period in thinking about sex, as Freud hypothesized. Each of these societies differs in the permission they give children to think about sex, with the United States being the most restrictive and Sweden the least.

In sum, responses to childhood sexuality vary according to cultural context. Social organization may channel the types of cultural responses to similar behavioral expressions of sexuality. Therefore, we would expect that the "objective realities" of childhood sexual expression could be and often are at odds with the social responses to and cultural conceptualizations of such expression. Philip Jenkins noted this phenomenon in his analysis of moral panics about child sexual abuse (2003). Consequently, we need to consider variations in children's sexual expression not only across cultures but also within them. Cultural interpretations of biological changes illustrate this point.

Biological Changes and Cultural Interpretations

The physiological changes of puberty (e.g., greater testosterone and sperm production in males, maturing ova and menstruation in females), as well as the appearance of secondary sexual characteristics (e.g., body hair in both males and females, budding breasts in females), take on major social significance as indicators of the transition from nonreproductive to potentially reproductive capabilities (Schlegel & Barry, 1991). This means that the sexual activities of postpubescent children could result in producing a new member of the society. Consequently, the group has a more significant stake in how and with whom sexual activities occur. Many traditional societies educate their children about the meaning of puberty. Often this training begins before puberty, as preparation for changes in emotions and anatomy that will occur later. Initiation ceremonies, particularly those for boys, provide lessons about the meaning of adulthood, gender, and sexual interaction and their concomitant responsibilities. They are social and cultural tools for effecting a psychological transition to socially acceptable adult sexuality. They may imprint the depth of the change with physical ordeals and permanent changes in the body (e.g., circumcision, clitoridectomy, tattooing, scarification). After initiation, boys and girls become men and women whose having sex, marrying, and/or having children is socially accepted. Many traditional societies do not interpose a period of adolescence between childhood and adulthood; their lives proceed directly from the stage of childhood to that of adulthood (Schlegel & Barry, 1991).

In traditional societies, age at first marriage usually was under 17 for girls (most married between 12 and 15) and over 18 for boys (most married between 18 and 21) (Frayser, 1985, p. 208). In addition, premarital sex was permitted more often than restricted, and often restrictions on marriage were related to kin involvement and property transmission (p. 215). This means that sexual expression often occurred in a socially acceptable context after puberty and before marriage. Therefore, the disjunction between physical sexual development and social approval of expressing sexuality was not so great. Sexual learning and practice were part of normal social life in many societies. However, there were probably as many societies in which such learning and practice was restricted, particularly for girls.

The Relevance of Cultural Maps for Sexual Behavior

If we assume that the conceptualization of childhood sexuality and rules about children's sexual behavior are preparation for participating in adult sexual roles, then cultural maps of adult sexuality may inform us about why we see such variability in how societies deal with childhood sexuality.

In *Varieties of Sexual Experience*, I identified two major models of adult sexuality (Frayser, 1985, p. 334). Using variables that indicated the degree to which sexual activity was confined to a reproductive context (e.g., premarital and extramarital restrictions, difficulty of divorce and remarriage, sanctions for barrenness, involvement of kin in marriage), I found that patterns of sexual restriction, particularly of women's sexuality, were significantly related to defining sex in terms of reproduction; sexually permissive patterns were significantly related to social practices that allowed sexual expression outside of a reproductive context. Since the evolutionary evidence demonstrates that reproductive and nonreproductive sexuality do not typically coincide in humans, these patterns demonstrate the role of culture in channeling sexual behavior so that it does or does not coincide with reproduction. Therefore, reproductive cultural maps would more likely restrict the sexual behavior of children or view it negatively, while nonreproductive ones would allow more expression and permit a more positive view of childhood sexuality. Ford and Beach (1951) noted, "most . . . societies that discourage infantile and childhood sex play also attempt to control premarital experimentation in sexual matters on the part of adolescents or young adults" (p. 185).

I found that these restrictive patterns occur significantly more often in societies with patrilocal residence (usually associated with patrilineality but also with some bilateral kinship systems). I concluded that the restrictions served to confine female sexuality in a reproductive context to provide more assurance of paternity, which was the foundation of many social institutions (e.g., marriage, economics, and politics) in these societies (Frayser, 1985, pp. 323–359). It is interesting to note how some of these cultures constructed female sexuality; they extolled motherhood, a reproductive interpretation of female sexuality, but devalued nonreproductive aspects of womanhood (p. 340).

Laumann, Gagnon, Michael, and Michaels (1994) point out the variety of these models of sexual orientation in contemporary U.S. culture; they label the reproductive model the "procreational" normative orientation, and the nonreproductive model "relational" and "recreational." The normative orientations toward sexuality vary according to their assumptions about the primary purpose of sexuality: Procreational models stress the significance of reproduction; relational models center on the significance of sexual activity as a component of a loving, intimate relationship; and recreational models focus on sexual activity as pleasure.

Defining the Cultural Map of Childhood Sexuality in the United States

How, then, does this spectrum of variety in sexual behavior and restrictions during childhood and adulthood help us to understand the cultural contours of thinking about childhood sexuality in the United States? The roots of our cultural map lie in the construction of sexuality at the end of the 19th century. I would characterize that map as a reproductive model of sexuality that structured ideas about love, sex, marriage, and children in a very precise way. The question becomes whether and how the cultural concepts of the 19th century have changed in meaning in tandem with the social changes that have occurred over the last century.

A Reproductive Model and Childhood Innocence

Historical research shows that the conceptualization of childhood sexuality is historically specific. Jackson (1993) argues that the concept of childhood sexuality is relatively recent in the West; it was only in the 16th and 17th centuries that children came to be regarded as a special group of people, and even later, in the 19th century, that sex was defined as a distinctive part of life. He emphasizes the social and cultural impact of three centuries of economic transition to a market economy. In the past, households and the workplace were located in the same community. Households were composed of relatives, servants, and boarders in a structure that afforded little privacy. Consequently, children could observe some aspects of adult sexual interaction as well as hear and participate in bawdy verbal exchanges. Childhood was a social status, and children were integrated into work and community life.

By the 19th century the shift from an agrarian to a capitalist economy had changed family and community organization. The household and the workplace were separated, thus detaching family and personal relationships from economic production (Cancian, 1987, pp. 15–21). Nuclear families resided in households of their own, and they enjoyed more privacy from the world of work and less public scrutiny and supervision of their behavior. Therefore, children were separated from work and community. Childhood was viewed as a developmental phase during which children should be educated in preparation for later roles. Sex became an important way to distinguish between childhood and adulthood; children were innocent (i.e., not sexually aware or experienced) and immature while adults were sexually experienced and mature.

This concept of childhood innocence fitted into a reproductive model of adult sexuality, because it reinforced the belief that sexual thoughts and behavior should not occur outside of a reproductive context. The acceptable pattern for sexual expression was to fall in love, marry, have sex with the goal of having children, and achieve the roles of mother and father, which would take precedence over those of husband and wife. As Cancian (1987) notes, "Motherhood was the key to being a real woman" (p. 20), much as being a mother is extolled in other sexually restrictive societies.

Love, Sentiment, and Social Control

A new division of labor separated the genders into different, specialized arenas. In the domestic sphere, women dealt with the emotional life of the family; in the world of economic production, men acted in ways calculated to enhance individual achievement. Shorter points out that mothers were expected to be sentimentally attached to their children (1977); as moral guardians of the family, women were to protect their children. Love, whether interpreted as the essential bond between parents and children or the major criterion for selecting a spouse, became the new basis for defining relationships; it became feminized. This cultural shift in the meaning of love and gender meant a shift from social control over partner choice and sexual activity. Because choices based on feelings of love were unique to each individual, love released individuals from some of the external community standards that had previously guided their behavior. Thus, individual development and feelings became more central in the interpretation of sexuality. As sentiment and love centered themselves in a woman's domain, nonreproductive sex was cast out of the domestic realm; sex became masculinized (Cancian, 1987, pp. 15–29).

A Natural Order

A new worldview was also taking shape at the end of the 19th century. Darwin's *Origin of Species* (1859) shook Christianity's assumptions of a great chain of being and God's special creation of humans from their throne of prominence and offered in their place a natural order of being, where humans were subject to the same principles of biological adaptation as other animals. This worldview paved the way for the flowering of the social and behavioral sciences, the task of which was to discover and articulate natural laws to explain human behavior. Scientists supplanted priests and ministers as the new experts in interpreting the meaning of human behavior. Krafft-Ebing's *Psychopathia Sexualis* (1906) redefined sexual deviance as psychopathology, removing it from a religious context of sin and moral condemnation. Health and normalcy became the new standards for understanding sexual behavior.

Part of this natural order entailed an examination of the coherence of the biological, social, cultural, and psychological aspects of sexuality. Just as the cultural map bundled love, sex, marriage, and children into a well-structured package, so too did it interpret biological, social, cultural, and psychological dimensions of sexuality as necessarily concordant with physical attributes. The anatomy of the person defined his or her role, identity, orientation, and interpretation of sexual behavior. Discordance between these dimensions led to definitions of aberrance or abnormality that the new experts tried to align with their conceptions of normalcy. For example, females who did not conform to their gender roles were labeled "insane" and sent to asylums for domestication and reeducation into socially acceptable behavior (Showalter, 1985). Treatment of unrestrained sexuality could include clitoridectomies or leeches applied to the cervix and labia to draw out the socially disruptive feelings and behavior (p. 75). Likewise, the assumption of childhood sexual innocence alerted parents, particularly mothers, that they should suppress and punish the sexual behaviors of their children.

Another consequence of Darwin's theory was the idea of social evolution and progress, a theory quite in keeping with the industrialization, urbanization, and exploration of the day. It provided a framework for explaining differences between people in different societies and ethnic groups and put a positive spin on the economic changes taking place in the United States. It also reinforced beliefs in individual achievement as a way to effect progress.

Ambivalence about and Denial of Sexual Desires

These cultural shifts highlighted beliefs consonant with the new economic order: childhood innocence, love and sentiment, reproduction, individuality, and development. But, as Tafoya (1990) said so well in his plenary speech to the Society for the Scientific Study of Sexuality, "A system of knowledge is also a system of ignorance." This is the cultural dilemma that emphasis on a reproductive model posed for the early adherents of these beliefs. Where did sex and desire fit into this model? Many of the cultural solutions to this 19th-century dilemma persist today. Because people see what they believe and have difficulty seeing what they cannot accept, emphasis on some beliefs entails ignoring or denying other ways of perceiving behavior.

Darwin's theory was at odds with the increasing tendency to distinguish children as special and sexually innocent, because he posited that all animals have sexual desires, including men, women, and children of the human species. It challenged the prevailing view that humans were different from other animals. Members of late-19th- and early-20th-century society developed a series of cultural solutions for dealing with unacceptable thoughts about childhood sexuality.

Postulation of Stages of Development. The first solution to Darwin's challenge was to define different stages of social and individual development to explain why Western society stood firm as the pinnacle of civilization and why children were asexual. Social evolutionists (e.g., Bachofen, Briffault) distanced themselves from animals with theories of social evolution; some groups had evolved from their "primitive" state into "civilized" societies. Promiscuity, multiple partners (whether in marriage or not), and nonreproductive sexual behavior occupied the basement level of social development. Civilization entailed adherence to cultural values of fidelity, monogamy, reproductive sex, and sexual restraint.

Suppression of Sexual Language or Interest. Second, members of society tried to ignore nonreproductive sex by publicly suppressing any suggestion of sexual language or sexual interest. Without an acceptable language for discussing sex, cultural transmission of ideas about it became difficult. And, without legitimate behavioral outlets for sexual expression, the sexual underworld of prostitution, pornography, and sexually transmitted diseases flourished. Women who participated in these industries were "fallen women" and men, "immoral." As Foucault (1978) points out, sex became a powerful force in people's lives and became a basis for interpretation of and social control over their behavior. Sexuality became conspicuous by its absence from conventional discourse.

Labeling of Nonreproductive Sexual Behavior as Bad. Third, they labeled nonreproductive sexual behavior as bad. Masturbation, oral sex, and sexual desire or activity separated from an intent to reproduce could lead to illness or insanity. Consequently, they took preventive measures to restrain these activities and feelings: spiked penis rings to counter nocturnal erections, clitoridectomies and ovariectomies to remove sources of sexual desire, and predictions of weakness from loss of sperm with frequent sex.

Although diminished in their prominence, religious traditions fueled negativity about nonreproductive sex. The filtering of the Hebraic philosophy, which affirmed the unity of the spirit and flesh in sexual unions, through the dualistic mind/body ideology of the early Greco-Roman Christian church resulted in the deprecation of the body and the elevation of the spirit (Lawrence, 1989). Consequently, the absence of sexual knowledge or experience in children put them in a more spiritually positive light.

View of Childhood Sexual Behavior as Pathology. Finally, they reinforced the idea of childhood innocence in developmental theories by labeling childhood sexual behavior as, at best, immature, but at worst, abnormal. Freud's theory of normal sexual development (1962) at least acknowledged that children had sexual desires. However, the task of developing maturity was to control and displace those immature desires in socially acceptable ways; to do otherwise was to risk psychological abnormality. Thus, clitoral stimulation as a route to sexual satisfaction was labeled "immature" and vaginal intercourse, "mature." Note that the "mature" route was a potentially reproductive behavior. Although some early research on the sexual life of children (e.g., Moll, 1924) suggested that no harm resulted from children's sexual behavior or knowledge, these results fell on deaf ears. Since the early 20th century, few of the major developmental theories have included sexual issues as an integral part of their formulations.

The Contemporary Cultural Map of Childhood Sexuality and Its Consequences

On the face of it, our current cultural map would appear to be quite different from that of the 19th century. We seem to have shifted away from a reproductive to a nonreproductive model of adult sexuality. However, the shift has not been linear or homogeneous. Rather, there are now a variety of coexisting models for sexuality that include reproductive and nonreproductive maps.

Although the cultural concepts of love, sex, marriage, and children have stayed with us, their meaning has changed in relation to different social trends and contexts. When happiness rather than having children became a dominant requirement for marriage (Hareven, 1982), the conceptual ground for a reproductive model shifted. Although this was not explicit, happiness implied that relationships rest on the satisfaction of feelings rather than producing children. Although not new, this emphasis on sentiment opened the door for a variety of sexual arrangements, whether marital or not, and whether heterosexual or not. Love, sex, marriage, and children could go their separate ways, combining in whatever form made individuals the happiest. Self-development and independence for both men and women grew in importance. Research in the social and behavioral sciences enriched knowledge of the biological, social, cultural, and psychological bases of sexual behavior. With this expansion of knowledge also came an expansion of the definition of sex—from sex to sexuality, embracing biological, social, cultural, and psychological dimensions. In addition, the reproductive or procreational model of sexuality expanded and multiplied, so that reproductive and nonreproductive (e.g., relational and recreational) models coexist in different segments of the population. These shifts have affected the approach to childhood sexuality.

An examination of the concept of incest as it existed in the 19th century shows that it expressed the reproductive model of the time: a taboo on sexual intercourse between mother and son, father and daughter, or brother and sister. The consequences of inbreeding were the rationale for the taboo. Sex meant heterosexual intercourse. The reason for the taboo was to prevent the mating of inappropriate reproductive partners.

An expanded view of sexuality has meant an expanded interpretation of what is sexual; sexual activity is not synonymous with intercourse. Words, looks, touches, pictures, and movements can all be construed in sexual ways. And, as the definitions of what is sexual have expanded, so too have the interpretations of what is abusive.

Acceleration of the consumer economy since the beginning of the 20th century has increased emphasis on what people *want* rather than what they *need* (Birkin, 1988). Ambivalence about sexuality has fueled the power of messages in advertising and encouraged people to believe that they can get what they desire by buying products or services. The disappointment resulting from trying to satisfy emotional needs with products and services only adds to the frustration that people feel in not knowing where to turn (Jhally, 1995). Globalization, changes in the demographic composition of the country (e.g., more Hispanics and Asians), and the electronic revolution (e.g., reliance on telecommunications and computers for quick information) have blurred or weakened the structural boundaries that have traditionally provided guidance for behavior and decision making. And children as well as adults may be exposed to experiences (e.g., infection with HIV, rape, pornography in cyberspace) that they did not seek but that require some meaningful interpretation. The overwhelming number of choices that individuals can exercise and the range of experiences to which they are exposed may have led to a sense of powerlessness and victimization, a feeling that no one is taking care of them.

Part of the problem we face is that social life has changed faster than some of the cultural concepts that have given coherence to behavior. An adequate cultural framework has not evolved to structure increased emphasis on the individual, independence, choice, and desire. We are in what Turner (1969) would term a marginal cultural period, betwixt and between a former cultural model and a new one, the contours of which have yet to coalesce. Suspension in such an uncertain state elicits a variety of responses, from feelings of fear and danger to excitement about creating new social forms and cultural interpretations.

Reliance on the cultural concepts and language of the past provides some structure until a new, more satisfactory map is codified. This is in line with the principle that a system of knowledge is also a system of ignorance. The support provided by socially accepted knowledge excludes other possibilities, and its structure provides a sense of psychological security. This may be what has happened in thinking about childhood sexuality.

Expansions of Fear Rather Than Knowledge. As the definition of sexuality has expanded, acknowledgment of normal sexual behavior in children has not; rather, fear of abuse of innocent children has expanded. The language is instructive. There is less talk about incest and more about child sexual abuse. Unlike extended incest taboos in other cultures, the prohibition of sex with children radiates beyond specified kin to see sexual danger in a wide range of behavioral expressions and social interactions.

The perception of danger associated with childhood sexual activity has extended to the interpretation of sexual activity during adolescence. In *Dangerous Passage* (1991), Nathanson argues that sexually active and reproductively uncontrolled adolescent women pose a threat to cultural beliefs that uphold the social order. Allowing premarital sex threatens a system based on a reproductive model. Focusing on individual "failures" rather than the culture and its social institutions diverts attention from the real issue: the inadequacy of the society to deal with "deviance" from its model. Consequently, limiting access to birth control becomes a tool of social control for those who want to retain sex as a part of marriage, that is, maintain a reproductive model of sexuality. As long as teenage women continue to violate social prescriptions, they will be dangerous to the society. It becomes society's duty to protect youth against such deviations.

Likewise, Jenkins (2003) points out that protective measures are assertions of control. By definition, a child is denied the "full rights of choice appropriate for an adult" (p. 6). He hypothesizes that such concepts may become popular as a way to reassert control that has been forfeited, perhaps due to major social changes.

Extension of Innocence. Another form of denial of the normalcy of sexual expression during childhood has been extension of the innocence of childhood to adolescence, thus sidestepping the issue of sexuality altogether. Research that compared Danish and U.S. socialization practices concluded that "in the United States parents treat their adolescents as children longer than in Denmark. . . . We would suggest that children in the United States are subject to a delayed socialization" (Kandel & Lesser, 1972, p. 89). These practices reflect beliefs and emotions about sexuality. Bresee sums up the differences: "For American teens, sex is generally considered a private and often prohibited activity, whereas many Danish teens and their parents consider it "natural and acceptable . . . In the Danes' view, . . . restrictions demonstrated unwarranted lack of trust and fear of teenage sexual activity" (Bresee, 1986, pp. 13–14).

Accentuation of Fear and Danger. Even though there is definite research to substantiate normal childhood sexual behavior in this society (e.g., Friedrich et al., 1991, 1992; Martinson, 1994), most sex education materials and programs stress the dangers of nonreproductive sex (e.g., illness, disease, and unacceptable pregnancies) and continue to instill fear about sexual activity, as they have for the past century (Campbell, 1986). The very real consequences of infection with HIV have fueled the emphasis on the dangers of sexual contact since the early 1980s.

Despite the efforts of groups such as Planned Parenthood and SIECUS, a reproductive model of sexuality prevails in sex education, informing children about reproductive anatomy and physiology without including information about sexual response, pleasure, and intimacy. As Krivacska points out (1990), we have been educating our children in the worst aspects of the sexual experience.

Suppression of Acceptable Language of Sex. The psychological denial of the pleasures of sexual activity that such education engenders may add to the confusion that children already have about sex. Early on, children learn that it is unacceptable to talk about sex, and they notice that the only language available for talking about it is the austere vocabulary of the medical profession or the demeaning terms of slang. Fisher (1989) discusses the consequences of children's feeling sexual pleasure (e.g., from genital exploration or masturbation) but experiencing the cultural denial of their own experiences (e.g., punishment by parents for sexual interest, no discussion of sexuality, dolls with no genitalia). Money warns of the paraphilias that can result from lack or punishment of juvenile sex play (Money, 1986).

The absence of an adequate language for and permission to talk about sexuality also removes one of the main bases for teaching new generations the lessons of satisfactory sexual behavior. Therefore, the young have to rely on their own perceptions and behavior with each other to construct a meaningful interpretation of their experiences. In the absence of informed dialogue about sexuality with their parents, teachers, or doctors, they rely on distorted depictions of sexuality (e.g., the Internet, pornography, MTV) to construct their view of sexuality. As Goldman and Goldman (1982) point out, children have an interest in sexuality that persists from early childhood. Avoiding the issue will not eradicate the interest. Unlike many traditional societies, the United States does not seize the opportunity to interpret sexuality in a socially productive way—rather, it avoids the issue.

Behavioral Consequences of Sexual Innocence. Children's lack of accurate information about normal sexual behavior may account for other serious behavioral consequences: The United States has one of the highest rates of teen pregnancy in the industrialized world, higher incidence of STDs, high teen suicide rates stemming from gender orientation issues, and a high incidence of sexual assault. In the earlier part of the 20th century, Moll (1924) concluded that sexual knowledge was necessary for children to interpret behavior and protect themselves. He foresaw more harm from lack of knowledge than knowledge. In a recent M.A. thesis, Glabach (1998) coins the term "asexual abuse" to sum up the consequences of suppressing sexual interest, play, knowledge, and behavior.

Despite the plethora of findings about different dimensions of personhood that deconstruct the idea of concordance between biological, social, cultural, and psychological aspects of sexuality, adherence to the idea of concordance between these dimensions persists. Consequently, abnormality still means that behavior and thoughts are out of synch with anatomy.

Therapeutic Interventions without a Baseline. Therapeutic interventions may also suffer from lack of knowledge about normal childhood sexuality. Without a baseline of normalcy, it is difficult to assess abnormality. With research and theory biased toward abuse, it is difficult to see other interpretations and outcomes of the presenting problem. Without adequate language to talk about sex, it is difficult to develop a meaningful dialogue. And, without a cultural context supportive of honest dialogues about sexual behavior, the discussion of sexual issues may be bypassed or be introduced for the first time with iatrogenic, harmful effects. As Money concludes, "Without a well-researched science of developmental sexology, today's methods of intervention . . . barely surpass trial and error" (1990, p. 19).

Restrictions on Scientific Research on Childhood Sexuality. Culturally defined fear as well as resistance to altering the idea of sexual innocence in childhood has limited scientific investigations of children's sexuality. Few socially approved funding sources legitimize scientific studies of normal childhood sexuality, because they assume that children, by definition, are asexual. What is there to study except abnormality and perversion?

As Kuhn (1962) so compellingly argued in *The Structure of Scientific Revolutions,* scientific paradigms are slow to change and will shift only when both the evidence and the scientific community support a new theory. Since scientists are members of the culture at large, they are subject to some of the same unspoken assumptions about sexuality as members of the broader culture (Fausto-Sterling, 1985). Moral panic about child sexual abuse in the culture at large affects the construction of scientific theory about the consequences of childhood sexual expression (Jenkins, 2003). And the line between scientific discourse and political agendas may become blurred (Okami, 1990).

Nevertheless, scientists have status in their role as experts who explain "natural" patterns of behavior. The evolutionary and cross-cultural evidence confirms that children are sexual beings. Past and present research within the United States substantiates the existence of normal sexual behavior among children. Will our cumulative knowledge as scientists modify the prevailing paradigm of sexual innocence? Will we assume the role of cultural authorities to provide perspective on and coherence to the variety of sexual models and experiences to which children and adults are currently subject?

References

Barry, H., & Paxson, L. M. (1971). Infancy and early childhood: Cross-cultural codes 2. *Ethnology, 10,* 466–508.

Barry, H., Josephson, L., Lauer, E., & Marshall, C. (1976). Traits inculcated in childhood: Cross-cultural codes 5. *Ethnology, 15,* 83–114.

Birkin, L. (1988). *Consuming desire: Sexual science and the emergence of a culture of abundance, 1871–1914.* Ithaca, NY: Cornell University Press.

Bowlby, J. (1969). *Attachment and loss: Vol. 1. Attachment.* New York: Basic.

Bresee, D. (1986). Exchange program teenagers compare life in Denmark and the U.S.A. *Occasional Papers in Intercultural Learning, 10,* June 1985. Cambridge, MA: AFS International/Intercultural Programs, Inc.

Campbell, P. J. (1986). *Sex guides: Books and films about sexuality for young adults.* New York: Garland.

Cancian, F. M. (1987). *Love in America: Gender and self-development.* Cambridge, England: Cambridge University Press.

Cohen, Y. A. (1964). *The transition from childhood to adolescence: Cross-cultural studies of initiation ceremonies, legal systems, and incest taboos.* Chicago: Aldine.

Daly, M., & Wilson, M. (1978). *Sex, evolution, and behavior: Adaptations for reproduction.* North Scituate, MA: Duxbury.

Darwin, C. (1959). *On the origin of species by means of natural selection, or the preservation of favoured races in the struggle for life.* London: Watts.

Douglas, M. (1966). *Purity and danger: An analysis of concepts of pollution and taboo.* New York: Praeger.

Fausto-Sterling, A. (1985). *Myths of gender: Biological theories about women and men.* New York: Basic.

Feierman, J. (Ed.). (1990). *Pedophilia: Biosocial dimensions.* New York: Springer-Verlag.

Fisher, H. (1992). *Anatomy of love: The natural history of monogamy, adultery, and divorce.* New York: Norton.

Fisher, S. (1989). *Sexual images of the self: The psychology of erotic sensations and illusions.* Hillside, NJ: Lawrence Erlbaum.

Ford, C. S., & Beach, F. A. (1951). *Patterns of sexual behavior.* New York: Harper.

Foucault, M. (1978). *The history of sexuality: Vol. 1. An introduction* (R. Hurley, Trans.). New York: Pantheon.

Frayser, S. G. (1985). *Varieties of sexual experience: An anthropological approach to human sexuality.* New Haven, CT: HRAF.

Frayser, S. G. (1994). Defining normal childhood sexuality: An anthropological approach. *Annual Review of Sex Research, 5,* 173–217.

Freud, S. (1962). *Three essays on the theory of sexuality* (J. Strachey, Ed. & Trans.). New York: Basic.

Friedrich, W. N., Grambsch, P., Broughton, D., Kuiper, J., & Beilke, R. L. (1991). Normative sexual behavior in children. *Pediatrics, 88,* 456–464.

Friedrich, W. N., Grambsch, P., Damon, L., Hewitt, S. K., Koverola, C., Lang, R. A., et al. (1992). Child Sexual Behavior Inventory: Normative and clinical comparisons. *Psychological Assessment, 4,* 303–311.

Glabach, D. (1998). *Child sex play: Its historic role in natural development and the psychological impact of its deprivation.* Unpublished master's thesis, Vermont College, Norwich University.

Goldman, R., & Goldman, J. (1982). *Children's sexual thinking: A comparative study of children aged 5 to 15 years in Australia, North America, Britain, and Sweden.* London: Routledge and Kegan Paul.

Hareven, T. (1982). American families in transition: Historical perspectives on change. In R. Walsh (Ed.), *Normal family processes* (pp. 446–465). New York: Guilford.

Harlow, H. F. (1973). *Learning to love.* New York: Ballantine.

Herdt, G. (1990). Cross-cultural issues in the development of bisexuality and homosexuality. In J. Money and H. Musaph (Series Eds.) & M. E. Perry (Vol. Ed.), *Handbook of sexology: Vol. 7. Childhood and adolescent sexology* (pp. 52–63). Amsterdam: Elsevier.

Jackson, S. (1993). Childhood and sexuality in historical perspective. In A. Yates (Ed.), *Child and adolescent psychiatric clinics of North America: Vol. 2. Sexual and gender disorders* (No. 3, pp. 355–368). Philadelphia: W. B. Saunders.

Jenkins, P. (2003). Watching the research pendulum. In J. Bancroft (Ed.), *Sexual development in childhood* (pp. 3–20). Bloomington: Indiana University Press.

Jhally, S. (1995). Image-based culture: Advertising and popular culture. In G. Dines & J. M. Humez (Eds.), *Gender, race, and class in media: A text-reader* (pp. 77–87). Thousand Oaks, CA: Sage.

Kandel, D., & Lesser, G. (1972). *Youth in two worlds.* San Francisco: Jossey-Bass.

Korbin, J. (1981). *Child sexual abuse and neglect: Cross-cultural perspectives.* Berkeley: University of California Press.

Krafft-Ebing, R. von. (1906). *Psychopathia sexualis* (F. J. Rebman, Trans., 12th ed.). New York: Rebman.

Krivacska, J. J. (1990). *Designing child sexual abuse prevention programs: Current approaches and a proposal for the prevention, reduction, and identification of sexual misuse.* Springfield, IL: C. C. Thomas.

Kuhn, T. S. (1962). *The structure of scientific revolutions.* Chicago: University of Chicago Press.

Laumann, E. O., Gagnon, J. H., Michael, R. T., & Michaels, S. (1994). *The social organization of sexuality: Sexual practices in the United States.* Chicago: University of Chicago Press.

Lawrence, R. L., Jr. (1989). *The poisoning of Eros: Sexual values in conflict.* New York: Augustine Moore.

Martinson, F. M. (1994). *The sexual life of children.* Westport, CT: Bergin and Garvey.

Moll, A. (1924). *The sexual life of the child* (E. Paul, Trans.). New York: Macmillan.

Money, J. (1986). *Lovemaps.* New York: Irvington.

Money, J. (1990). Historical and current concepts of pediatric and ephebiatric sexology. In M. E. Perry (Ed.), *Handbook of sexology, Vol. 7: Childhood and Adolescent Sexuality* (pp. 3–21). Amsterdam: Elsevier.

Nathanson, C. A. (1991). *Dangerous passage: The social control of sexuality in women's adolescence.* Philadelphia: Temple University Press.

Okami, P. (1990). Sociopolitical biases in the contemporary scientific literature on adult human sexual behavior with children and adolescents. In J. R. R. Feierman (Ed.), *Pedophilia: Biosocial dimensions* (pp. 91–121). New York: Springer-Verlag.

Raphael, D. (1976). *The tender gift: Breastfeeding.* New York: Schocken.

Schlegel, A., & Barry, H., III, (1991). *Adolescence: An anthropological inquiry.* New York: Free.

Shorter, E. (1977). *The making of the modern family.* London: Fontana.

Showalter, E. (1985). *The female malady: Women, madness, and English culture, 1830–1980.* New York: Pantheon.

Symons, D. (1979). *The evolution of human sexuality.* New York: Oxford University Press.

Tafoya, T. (1990, November). *A new way of seeing.* Plenary speech presented at the annual meeting of the Society for the Scientific Study of Sexuality, Minneapolis, MN.

Turner, V. (1969). *The ritual process: Structure and anti-structure.* Chicago: Aldine.

White, E., & Brown, D. M. (1973). *The first men.* New York: Time-Life.

Discussion Paper

GILBERT HERDT

Both of the papers that I've been assigned to discuss certainly deserve serious scrutiny, because each deals with vital topics that are important and in some way or another had been neglected in the intellectual community, particularly with regard to the African American sample, which is just so under-studied. Both of these papers share a philosophical commitment to the norm and to norm-based studies as well as to an idea of the normal as a way of understanding human experience. Both share a methodological conundrum in valuing the meaning of the norm within a group while comparing this meaning to other groups. Issues of cultural relativism are informative for understanding both "proximate" and "ultimate" accounts of child development and sexual culture in both these cases. In both cases, there is an assumption of cultural adaptation and this, it seems to me, is problematic. Specifically, we need to problematize the relationship between Culture, with a big C, sexuality, and adaptation better than in the past, if we're to rediscover childhood sexuality and how and why sexual coercion occurs in the context of cultural adaptation.

In composing my commentary, three images came to mind that I wanted to share with you briefly. The first is John Money's wise statement, in 1967, that childhood sexuality is the last taboo in the frontier of sex research. This is certainly still true today. The second is Bob Stoller's remark to me in 1982 that until we could systematically study children's sexual behavior we'd never know how right or wrong Freud was in his assertion that sexuality begins in infancy. The third image comes from the studies that Martha McClintock and I have conducted since 1996 (Herdt & McClintock, 2000; McClintock & Herdt, 1996), which try to establish the importance of the development of sexual attraction by age 10 in males and females, heterosexual and homosexual, using the best data that exists from studies in the United States. When I present these findings around the country, parents typically are troubled by them. Although college students and teens are fascinated by the idea that their sexuality reaches a memorable phase by age 9½ or 10, their parents are perplexed, and even academic, middle-class parents can become anxious and troubled by the thought that the children living with them at home right now are sexual beings.

Hypothesis: American middle-class people remain wedded to an ideology of childhood sexual innocence, just as Suzanne was strongly asserting. But this seems surprising to me and the surprise should be registered in view of the fact that we've had two sexual revolutions in the 20th century, the Pill, the epidemic, television sex, the end of the Cold War with globalization, and now the Internet. Something does not compute. I would like to come back to this point later.

My comments about Jeffry Thigpen's paper are primarily methodological, but this is a critical research topic and we should be very grateful to Jeffry and his colleagues for making the painstaking effort and also probably having had many hassles with the IRB at the University of Chicago to gather data at Cook County Hospital on young African Americans' sexual behavior. As I suggested above, I am perplexed by the problem of identifying a normative model of African American children's sexuality, which is precisely Jeffry's problem. How do we establish what is normal in the absence of study? How do we establish what is normal in the presence of so much chaos? Clearly this needs to be done in order to overcome racist conceptions of the past, stereotypes that exist in the present, as well as inappropriate comparisons to white middle-class or European children. But exactly how do we do this?

The Cook County Hospital sample so carefully weeds out problems of sexual trauma in the population, substance abuse, mental dysfunction, and so on that only a very, very small percentage of the total population could possibly remain at the end of the day. I could not figure out the frequency of those selected compared to those not selected in this population. Nor could I figure out the total number of the sample from the text, understanding that this is, of course, a study in progress. What does emerge is the highly culturally conservative church-attending nature of the women caretakers in this sample, as Jeffry has pointed out. Granted, the significance of the church in the African American community must be understood as a vital part of its adaptation. This may represent a typical tendency of African American communities, but also is a perplexing problem for us in establishing what is the norm. Is this normative with respect to African American communities in the United States? How do we define cultural norms in such an oppressed population? Eighty percent of these people, mostly women, say their children up to age 12 show no interest in sexuality. Now I ask you, is this an observation or a culturally self-fulfilling prophecy?

An analysis of the gender differences between boys and girls in the sample would be telling, and age differences, especially for older boys as they get closer to gonadal puberty, would be very important to know, as they may conflict with the express desires or aims of their caretakers. I was surprised at the protocol asking about sexual interactions across genders but not asking about same-gender sexual interest. Why is this? Clearly we could not make the methodological mistake of so many adolescent studies in the '60s and '70s that assumed the entire population is heterosexual. That introduces a sample bias.

Methodologically I think the study needs a component, difficult to construct but certainly doable, in which the women caretakers, about 90% of whom are biological mothers, are asked to reflect upon their own comfort level regarding their sexuality. This would help to both establish a central tendency in this particular population and secondly provide a lens to interpret mothers' observations of their kids, particularly as they get older and approach an age of independence when they would depart from the caretakers' norms. If sexual shame and sexual silence, as I suspect, are part of the background of this sexual culture, perhaps those reflective questions will begin to reveal the difficulties of establishing a norm.

This study neglects, it seems to me, the qualitative and ethnographic studies of the past, particularly coming from sociology, which would inform a norm in the real world beyond Cook County Hospital: classics such as *Tally's Corner*, Lee Rainwater's work from the '60s, Michelle Fine's work on African American girls in New York in the 1980s (Fine, 1988), Elijah Anderson's more recent work (Anderson & Anderson, 1996), and others. But back to the norm: Why question the norm? What is it going to be used for? Why do we want to know what the norm is? What policies will be constructed from it? Can we really base a norm on an extraordinarily selected subsample from a hospital? Perhaps before we focus on the norm we ought to determine some contrast across populations, both clinical and in more naturalistic settings, and then be sure that we do not set the stage to restigmatize those people within the African American community who do not live up to the norm of a policy implemented by thoughtless bureaucrats in the state.

Now moving on to Suzanne's paper, this is a notable integrated attempt to synthesize evolutionary reproductive development and anthropological perspectives, building upon her work over a very long time. I share with Suzanne her commitment to cross-cultural study and the need to problematize sexuality in cultural context. The language which she invokes, "traditional" versus "nontraditional," it seems to me is very problematic today. Indeed the text reads in many respects as if the world that it represented, which is before 1985 to 1990 in the research literature which she primarily cites, more or less came to a stop at that point. Decolonization, the end of the Cold War, and structural violence, which are very much on the agenda of anthropology today, are largely ignored in this paper. Let's briefly outline the two models of cross-cultural study which are invoked. First the human relations area file factoids, which represent dubious frequencies of dubious samples of cultures, aggregated 50 or 60 years ago when sexuality had a very different set of meanings in the West, and yet it still remains the most important comparative data set we have, albeit very, very flawed.

Second, of course, the good old-fashioned anecdotal veto approach made famous by Margaret Mead: "Not in my culture, it isn't." This approach emphasizes the specificity of meanings and social practices in local context. The trouble is, with a few exceptions most anthropologists neglected sexuality, or, as Carol Vance has often said, treated it as subservient to the core of reproduction, even going so far as to equate marriage with the totality of sexuality for adults in some societies. Of course children were typically ignored in this approach to sexuality and so, of course, was same-gender sexual contact. That brings me to what I feel was left out of Suzanne's paper that needs to be put back in. First of all, no mention of AIDS or HIV or sexually transmitted diseases in the paper, when for instance, in the United States, we know the creation of sexuality education programs beginning in 2nd and 3rd grade clearly is an extraordinary change in the last 15 years. Second, it never mentions new reproductive technologies that impact sexuality in many places, even in non-Western worlds. Third, it doesn't mention the Internet or children's access to it; whether children from Pakistan or adolescents from rural Montana get on the Net and find available to them information and experiences never before obtainable throughout the world. These omissions surely underscore the extent to which sexuality has rapidly changed since 1985, subject to forces of globalization, the epidemic, and the Net, in many places but not of course all. Certainly it has not touched all places in the world.

Today, anthropologists such as Paul Farmer (1999) challenge us to understand the impact of structural violence, that is to say racism, poverty, homophobia, as major variables that impact on sexuality and the lives of children in many lands. Among these impacts is the increasing presence of sexual tourism, sexual migration, and child prostitution, which are not mentioned in this paper. Again, the problem is, what is the norm? There is no attention in the text to a definition of what is normal or abnormal, the concept nearly always used in public policy to regulate, which has been suspect in anthropology since at least the days of Ruth Benedict, writing in 1932 (Benedict, 1934). Also, what is a child? How do we mark off the category of this very, very important variable? What constitutes a child? Is it purely a matter of age? Clearly Suzanne says no, it is more than that. It is a social status. She is right; it is also about power and relationships. Here I worry about discontinuities between childhood and adult sexuality, which are an important source of intergenerational difference and conflict. Suzanne Frayser's study, like Jeffry's on African Americans, perhaps accepts too globally the notion that culture equals adaptation, or if something is cultural it will promote child development. Culture in such a relativist epistemology is too large and vague, too far removed from the shame, silence, stigma, and oppression of real people in real-life communities.

American parents are very, very uncomfortable in general in dealing with sexual behavior in their children, especially girls. Americans remain worried about cross-gender tendencies in their children, especially boys. They worry about sexual abuse and coercion and this is for good reason, I suspect. However, all of this worry is obviously not just about sexuality; it registers many other things in their social world. It is certainly overdetermined by power relationships, gender role changes, and alterations in the family. Think for instance of the report this week, coming out of the census, that only 25% of American families conform to nuclear family status now, which obviously changes greatly the meaning of who the caretakers are in early development. These points do not simply reflect sexual anxiety.

I would point to two hypotheses for understanding the overall meaning of culture in this setting. The first, which I share with Suzanne, is the American ideological commitment to 19th-century models of reproductive sexuality and family structure. For multiple reasons still unclear, this ideology remains intact even as the family structure has drastically changed in the last 35 years. Second, the American worldview, which knows not the past, is committed to the future; specifically ideal future horizons in insecure and uncertain times. Childhood sexual innocence is the last cultural icon on which Americans still agree. Their consensus is surprising in view of television sex and the sexualization of the child in the media and advertising. But their commitment to this ideal is not difficult to understand. Their children are their link via their bodies, flesh and bones, DNA, and even their mental world to this future legacy. Americans give up so much to attain their material dreams, and these are expressed in and through their children. Even gays and lesbians are no different, and that's why many of them decide to have children.

But here is a problem for policymakers, as a way to end my comments. Sexuality study ultimately is always about control and regulation; how will society establish its norms? In contrast to the previous discussant, juvenile delinquency, it seems to me, is a poor field for comparison and, with all due respect to David Finkelhor, I think juvenile delinquency has a very different trajectory. It aims toward the law and its bureaucracies, which are ultimate legal arbitrators of what is black and white. Sexuality is not this; it is fuzzy, it has fuzzy boundaries. It represents different sexual cultures in a multicultural society such as ours. Surely there is enormous variation in antecedence, social approval, and desired outcomes, as Jeffry's project, I think, is attempting to establish. Policy should not just be for control.

We should strive to establish a range of acceptable and approved behaviors, not just a target norm but a range of norms, which provide a context for thinking about differences across communities as a goal of policy. We need to build a consensus model. But this is a democracy, not an authoritarian society, in which we should be much more sensitive to cultural differences, to interpersonal contexts, and to family values, because these differences are ultimately what make each one of us individuals.

References

Anderson, A., & Anderson, E. (1996). The code of the streets. In L. C. Mahdi, N. G. Christopher, & M. Meade (Eds.), *Crossroads: The quest for contemporary rites of passage* (pp. 91–98). Chicago: Open Court.

Benedict, R. (1934). *Patterns of culture.* New York: Houghton Mifflin.

Farmer, P. (1999). *Infections and inequalities: The modern plagues.* Berkeley: University of California Press.

Fine, M. (1988). Sexuality, schooling, and adolescent females: The missing discourse of desire. *Harvard Educational Review, 58*(1), 29–53.

Herdt, G., & McClintock, M. (2000). The magical age of 10. *Archives of Sexual Behavior, 29,* 587–606.

McClintock, M., & Herdt, G. (1996). Rethinking puberty: The development of sexual attraction. *Current Directions in Psychological Science, 5,* 178–183.

General Discussion

Jeffry Thigpen: Dr. Herdt's critique of the study is duly noted, and I think his critique echoes a lot of what has already been said here during the workshop, particularly related to ideologies of normality. However, in the context of this particular study I think that it is important to begin to have a better understanding or a better picture of what normal sexual behavior looks like, particularly given that the absence of information has consequences, negative consequences, for the children that are being labeled as sexually aggressive. One point that you raised that we've considered a lot since starting this study is the need to collect more ethnographic information from the mothers, particularly about their own sexuality and also how they are actually interpreting sexual behavior.

Elsie Pinkston: The people who make decisions about these children in the welfare system come from the same social class or same religious background as these mothers, so at least I expected these to be conservative, but I didn't expect them to be this conservative, and so to me that was a very good piece of information to see in this data. What it tells us about young children's sexual behavior—who knows? But also the fact that the children are on the streets at an earlier age with their peer group probably means that their mothers aren't lying, they simply don't witness a lot of sexual behavior. Secondly, I would like to defend the IRB at the University of Chicago, which put us through in an expeditious manner. However, Cook County was a little bit more political and more protective of its research subjects.

Suzanne Frayser: First, I want to clarify a couple of points. Gil inferred that a lot of the data I was referring to were taken from the precoded information in the Human Relations Area Files, but it was not. Many of the cross-cultural findings that I cited were based on data from the Standard Cross-cultural Sample, a database specifically developed by Murdock and White (1969) at the Cross-cultural Cumulative Coding Center at the University of Pittsburgh to test hypotheses using a representative sample of the world's cultures. The bulk of the cross-cultural findings to which I referred are based on over 10 years of my own research with complete primary and secondary sources that describe the cultures in the Standard Cross-cultural Sample; I operationalized variables relating to sex and reproduction in an effort to transcend culture-bound concepts. I share Gil's concern about reliance on HRAF alone for generalizing about worldwide cultural patterns. The precoded materials in HRAF are adequate for quick research, e.g., for testing hypotheses when time is not available to read complete sources. The issue of generalizability prompted Murdock to reframe many of the societies and cross-cultural sources of HRAF into the 186 pinpointed groups that make up the Standard Cross-cultural Sample.

The point of my paper was to identify cultural patterns in the U.S. that help us to understand the paucity of research and dialogue about normal childhood sexuality. The cross-cultural generalizations from previous research helped me to establish a range of behaviors and beliefs within which to position the current conceptualization of childhood sexuality in the U.S. Cross-cultural research in more contemporary societies demonstrates the cultural differences between the U.S. and other industrialized cultures. For example, the comparison between Danish and American socialization practices revealed that the Danes thought that U.S. parents treat their adolescents as children longer, extending the period of childhood innocence; parental restrictions demonstrate a fear of teen sexual activities and a lack of trust in teens making their own decisions. That finding fits with Jany's comments about the Netherlands, where young people are given more responsibility for making their own sexual decisions. Complementing the findings of the SCCS with research from contemporary cultures would certainly enrich the conclusions that we draw from these data.

I appreciate Gil's suggestion that we need to consider the impact of the Internet and globalization on cultural authority about sexuality. Incorporation of findings in these areas could expand our understanding of the consequences of lack of structure or boundaries that I referred to in the later part of my paper. It dovetails with my concern about the absence of an adequate language or socialization process for adults to transmit knowledge about sexuality to children. Without competent adult guidance about the meaning of sexuality, children, like many adults in the culture, must draw their own conclusions about sexual images and behavior imposed on them through the media.

I believe that cultural patterns strongly influence behavior and psychological adjustment. My paper demonstrates that there is a disjunction between the sexual behavior that children express and the cultural interpretation of that behavior. I think we agree that some traditional, reproductive concepts about sexuality from 19th-century ideology persist in dialogue about childhood sexuality. So the question is: Why does this cultural pattern persist? The distinction between what is social and behavioral and what is cultural is important to keep in mind when addressing this question. We know that behavior can change a lot more quickly than ideology does; right now we're "out of synch." For example, Gil said that only 25% of families in the U.S. are nuclear families (mother, father, and their children); yet a lot of family policy and school/educational programs still assume that we have this kind of a family. I'm talking about the same kind of process as it relates to children's sexuality; traditional meanings are very slow to change, despite changes in social behavior. I don't think we're a sexually free society by any means. Even though there are a lot of sexual images on the Internet, on MTV, and in print advertising, they do not mean that we have had a real sexual revolution in the culture. Rather, I think that advertisers and the media play on the ambivalence and lack of direction that people feel about their sexuality. I conduct research for advertising agencies and marketing firms, and one of the psychological factors that they key in on is the fact that people are insecure about their sexuality. Just because there's more sexual behavior doesn't necessarily mean that the culture has changed or that participants in sexual behaviors feel better about what they're doing or themselves.

The cultural trend toward more individuality means that more individuals have to create structure in their own lives, organizing and making sense of the differing social contexts in which they participate—a difficult and stressful task. This may explain greater participation in more conservative political groups and religions; they provide both ideology and organization to readily structure the world. Dialogue that confirms a structured world has become popular. For example, Dr. Laura Schlessinger's radio program is one of the most popular programs on the air. Her model of sexuality is quite traditional; she says that sex should only occur in marriage and that parents' major responsibilities center on the well-being of their children. The dialogue on the program reinforces a traditional sexual ideology and maligns more liberal interpretations of sexuality. The popular emphasis on victimology expresses this sense of individual powerlessness and need for social direction and structure. The focus given to child sexual abuse and abnormal sexual development to the neglect of considerations of identifying the parameters of normal childhood sexual development is probably part of this search for meaning and individual power. Censure of children's sexual activities may serve to uphold a reproductive model of sexuality in the face of other nonreproductive interpretations of sexuality. We cannot assume that there's just one model for childhood sexuality in the U.S.

Dennis Fortenberry: I want to pick up on the issue mentioned by Gil, and that's the influence of HIV and STDs on the way childhood sexuality will be constructed over the next decade or two. The reason that I think it may be important is because of the survival into adolescence and young adulthood now of a significant number of congenitally infected children. In many adolescent HIV programs around the country, a third of the clients are congenitally infected who survived into adolescence and are beginning to have sex in a variety of ways. The actual number of those adolescents is very small, but we all know that it doesn't take an epidemiologically large proportion of kids to set an agenda that is going to be very contentious, especially around issues like HIV. As we begin to think about childhood sexuality with that in the discussion, it changes the context a great deal.

Gil Herdt: Following up on Suzanne's point about cultural regulation of sexuality. Most of us would agree that culture or society regulates to some extent. But what's to me so interesting, and this again is why I would highlight the changes since 1985 and roughly the coincidence with the AIDS epidemic, is how cultural authority has been undermined with regard to sexual instruction. I think that compared to what happened 15–20 years ago, even the sexual revolution, there is no longer the same relationship between the process of cultural socialization of sexuality and the outcome with regard to child development. What the epidemic has done and the Internet globalization with regard to mass migration, it has created more flux, dislocated and, to a certain extent, dislodged the traditional or received authority of who had the knowledge to instruct about sexuality; whether the parents, the church, a community organization; whether there was a ritual initiation, a ring of leaders, or a ceremonial system. Throughout much of the third world today, there is increasingly a disruption of those cultural authorities and that has two components. It's the knowledge that you have access to information on the Internet. I didn't have that opportunity when I was a child and you ask yourself, what difference would it make in the process of growing up? Secondly, the outcome for expression: Where can they go to have sexual experiences with partners known or unknown? That also has loosened up. There is more of a disconnect between the traditionally selected or targeted appropriate partners for sexual relations and the known circle of people with whom you could have sex, which has expanded. So the challenge of cultural authority at a variety of levels, medical authority, community leaders, religious authority, and so on, creates a new situation for all kinds of possibilities for sexual outcomes that are diverse from those of the parents or the preceding generation.

Suzanne Frayser: That brings to mind an enduring 19th-century concept about sexuality—the idea that sexual knowledge is a demarcation between adult and child; a child, by definition, was sexually innocent. This boundary may be disappearing with globalization and the Internet. How, then, are we going to define a child? Fear of losing the idea of childhood innocence might be one of the reasons that people are so tenacious in resisting ideas of normal childhood sexuality and so ardent in eradicating child sexual abuse. At the same time, children are exposed to a plethora of sexual images in the media and the Internet; and, they may be facing the consequences of infection with HIV or sexual abuse. They are acquiring sexual knowledge through their experiences, often without the benefit of adult guidance in its meaning.

I'm wondering who or what groups retain cultural authority for sex education in the U.S.? What are the cultural contours of sex education in this country? Language is a significant symbolic way of transmitting information and cultural concepts, but children rarely have an appropriate language for talking about sex, unless it's slang. So, how are these ideas transmitted? The lack of a language points to another way to perpetuate childhood sexual innocence. Consequently, each generation of children has to discover information about sexuality anew. There isn't the acceptable cultural continuity that we see in other aspects of culture, except transmission of the idea that it's dangerous. Patricia Campbell conducted a review of sex education books for juveniles over the last 100 years and found that fear and danger persist as dominant themes (Campbell, 1986). Even our college textbooks on human sexuality contain many chapters related to the fear and danger of sex, e.g., violence, pornography, unwanted pregnancies, sexually transmitted diseases. In contrast, the media promulgate ideas of sexual excitement. What cultural authorities will intervene to provide accurate, balanced views of sexuality?

Anke Ehrhardt: It is obviously very important that we take diversity in our society into consideration, while at the same time we are really in a time of change. Ed was saying that one of the factors for the trajectory is whether kids come from intact families. Well, if intact families are now less than 25% in this country, then we obviously cannot have that as a norm anymore.

Jany Rademakers: It's a lot easier to get funding for studies of problems than nonproblems. But we should not forget that studying childhood sexuality is a perfectly valid scientific aim in itself. Understanding normal sexual development is important as a basis for developing sex education programs and for developing support for parents and teachers who don't know what to do with the children they have or they work with. Not specifically with the aim of preventing problems, but to give children and adolescents the help and support they need for growing into happy, healthy sexual adults when we look at the kind of studies which are being funded. Children now are much more exposed to sexual messages in the media and through the Internet than they were 20 years ago. It's very important that parents and teachers and professionals are aware that children need a context in which to interpret these messages. Now, especially in the United States, they get very conflicting messages from their educators and from the media. We see that when we study adolescent sexuality and causes of teenage pregnancy. The mixed messages make it very difficult to behave in a consistent manner or make it more difficult to find your own way.

Janet Hyde: A question for Suzanne. You reminded us that there have been numerous societies where the average age of marriage for girls was something like 12 or 13. What's the age of menarche in those societies?

Suzanne Frayser: I don't know.

Janet Hyde: Do you have a guess?

Suzanne Frayser: No. That was one of the gaps in the data. Most of the sources I used noted that menarche was one of the indicators of puberty; budding breasts were another. Usually they did not note the chronological age. Nevertheless, an advantage of cross-cultural research is finding out what the gaps are; there are a lot of them in the area of sexuality, particularly children's sexuality.

Janet Hyde: Okay. Yesterday, we were attaching a lot of significance to puberty at 12½ years of age and I just want to mention a comment I heard at the Society for Research in Child Development meeting a couple of weeks ago. It was a talk by Ron Dahl, who is a very noted adolescence researcher. He made a point that if we take it as known that in Western countries 100–150 years ago biological puberty for girls was occurring at 17–18 years of age and now has declined to 12.5 in the United States, new fMRI evidence indicates that the prefrontal cortex, which has a lot to do with our capacity for rational decision making, planning ahead, etc., does not mature until about 18 years of age and that age has not dropped over the last 100–150 years. So his argument was that 100–150 years ago, and I also suspect in these contemporary cultures where there's early marriage, because there's less nutrition puberty occurs around 18 and you have a nice pairing of reproductive capacity, menarche, and maturation of the prefrontal cortex all occurring around age 18. What we have in the United States now is a disjuncture, with capacity for reproduction and capacity for menstruation and ovulation occurring much earlier than maturation of the prefrontal cortex. I think that's very provocative for our discussions because we've been attaching so much significance to puberty occurring at 12.5 years of age, which may be historically and cross-culturally unusual.

Anke Ehrhardt: Why cross-culturally unusual?

Janet Hyde: I'm not talking about other Western European nations but other nations where they don't have as prolific nutrition as we do.

Cynthia Graham: A short question for Suzanne: You mentioned that in some societies longer periods of breastfeeding and co-sleeping with mother especially were very common. Have you found any relationship in your studies or other research between attitudes toward childhood sexuality and prevalence of prolonged breastfeeding (e.g., four years or more) and co-sleeping with parents? It seems that in North American society, especially, there are still very negative attitudes toward long periods of breastfeeding and also toward co-sleeping.

Suzanne Frayser: I did not test that hypothesis with my data, but it would be interesting to do so. The women in most of the groups in my sample did not bottle-feed their infants. Therefore, close physical contact between mother and infant during sleep and breastfeeding might have adaptive advantages for infant survival, regardless of attitudes about sexuality. One study found that infants in traditional societies always slept with their mothers, regardless of whether the fathers slept with them. The longest period of breastfeeding that I know of was six years; since the postpartum sex taboos lasted as long as the breastfeeding, lengthy breastfeeding created difficulties for the marriages, because the men did not want to wait that long to resume sexual relations. The common practices in the U.S. of putting infants in separate rooms and then separating children into separate rooms become symbolic of the individuality that the culture stresses.

Anke Ehrhardt: On the issue of what is family sexuality and what is appropriate nudity or co-bathing, it is in many ways more important whether the child experiences it as forbidden or as appropriate and not as intrusive but as natural. It's probably more important to get that kind of data rather than just whether co-bathing occurred or not. There are lots of families that do that and it is totally fine and there are others where suddenly it is disconnected for the child or experienced as being intrusive. So probably the context may be much more important than the behavior. But we don't have in this country good research on this issue.

Bill Friedrich: I did collect information on co-sleeping with parents. It was one of eight items in a family sexuality index. Another item pertained to co-bathing. Co-sleeping didn't load on either of the two factors derived from these eight items. The first factor included the co-bathing item and items about family nudity. The second factor included items measuring exposure to adult sexual activity, including pornography. Occasional co-sleeping in my sample of over 2,800 kids was relatively common (at least 8–10%) at every age group from 2 to 12. It certainly decreased with the age of the child, but it's actually quite common and apparently not correlated with the other domains of family sexual behavior that I measured.

I am reminded of Gil's comment about norms being used to regulate. Jany has suggested that information about normative behavior is actually quite useful because it can help us with sex education. The theory that I had when I first started researching sexual behavior was that sexual behavior was a learned social behavior, and that a sexually abusive experience would accelerate the learning curve. I also expected that the interaction between the abuse and the child's characteristics would find that some children would exhibit more sexual behavior than would others.

While the data on sexually abused children bears out this hypothesis, I firmly believe that the utility of the normative information about the sexual behavior of children is related to the finding that some sexual behaviors are ubiquitous. If sexual behaviors were very unusual, then the information could be used to regulate. But since that is not the case, the normative data can provide information to service providers. For example, it can help day care providers of preschoolers be less punitive about genital self-touching in the children in their care.

John Bancroft: I'm very pleased that Jeffry and Elsie are doing their study. It's coming from a particular socially driven situation which obviously limits it, but we've also got Dennis working with a lot of African American teenagers in Indianapolis and Lucia and Heino in New York. So insofar as we're striving to understand normal or unproblematic and appropriate childhood sexual development, the comparison of the African American community with the other communities in this country could be particularly important. We know that there are some substantial differences. We know that African American boys in particular start intercourse a lot earlier than white boys do, and in our recent survey, which is not yet published, on women in the United States, we found some differences between black and white women across the age range which suggested to me that African American women are actually more in touch with their own sexuality. They're more comfortable about their own sexual pleasure. They're more assertive in their relationships with their male partners, and I'm intrigued to know whether that comes from the developmental process. There's a paradox here. In the secondary analysis, Ed, that was reported in your second book, where you looked at cultural issues, there was this discrepancy between the attitudes of the African Americans and their behaviors. Here we have the African American caregivers expressing very conservative attitudes about sexuality in children and yet somehow black kids are growing up with a seemingly more positive feel about sexuality than white kids have. Why is that the case?

Janet Hyde: One of the things I think we need to be careful about is not to treat Americans as homogeneous, and at the same time we have to be careful not to treat African Americans as homogeneous. There are huge social class variations. Some of the discrepancies we've been hearing in the conversation today are not about one person having the right findings and the other being wrong, but people dealing with different aspects of that continuum. We shouldn't forget that there are middle-class blacks and some of what we have been characterizing as patterns of black/white difference are in fact social class differences more than anything else.

Gil Herdt: Janet's point that the African American community is not homogeneous is precisely what I was driving at in saying that we don't want to set up a norm which is based on a sample of a population which has had a terribly oppressive history in a whole variety of ways. There is really no agreement yet on how we think about the central tendencies in different African American communities. Clearly social class will be very important to this, also probably gender differences, perhaps even more than in white middle-class communities. So if you create a norm which is based upon a white middle-class sample or an African American middle-class sample, which would be a minority demographically of the entire population of the United States, and you use that as a policy framework and then compare all others to that, obviously you're creating the classic situation for a deficit or a deprivation model. So rather than seeking a single target norm, create a range of possible behavior that falls within what a group of leaders and experts would consider appropriate, rather than a single norm, because then that allows flexibility with regard to context, social class, the history of the particular family. I'm trying to defend against the danger that a single norm would be held as a model for everybody and that in a heterogeneous population there are going to be children who won't live up to it and then they're going to be stigmatized.

John Bancroft: I'm reacting to what you said, Gil, and to some extent to what Janet said about African Americans. Obviously you're both right that they're a heterogeneous group socially. But if I understood you correctly you were implying that if we focused on them as a group and in any way looked for norms there, we would be dealing with a deficit situation. Janet was implying the differences are socioeconomically determined. We should keep our minds open to the idea that even people who may be socioeconomically deprived may have grown up in a more sex-positive culture and environment than the puritanical people from Europe that have descended on this continent.

Anke Ehrhardt: I don't think we have that evidence. I was thinking that, having done a number of studies with my colleagues on African American women in the lower class or working class, it's a lack of information which most of those women have about sexuality and about their body which is impressive, together with the wish to learn more. So it's not that they have great or a better repertoire of knowledge.

John Bancroft: I'm not talking about a better repertoire of knowledge. I have been looking at the literature on African Americans and there's not a lot, unfortunately. But this picture of the African American women having grown up in a very different sociopolitical environment in terms of their relationship to men is important in its impact on the way that they've developed. We should consider the possibility that there may be some positive aspects to that.

Anke Ehrhardt: No question. I just think that right now the data which we have is not as strongly supportive of a uniform difference, that's my point. There are quite a few other voices and other studies, which have come out in the whole HIV arena, which wouldn't support that.

Ed Laumann: Implicit in some of Gil's and Suzanne's comments is the issue about cultural change and the loss of authority. Maybe I'm being a bit pessimistic but I would argue that the compositional changes in the population of the United States are moving rather strongly in a more conservative direction on sexual matters because of immigration. Koreans, Asians, and Hispanics are quite conservative populations that have been added to the contemporary mix. African Americans are actually also a very conservative group culturally (Laumann & Michael, 2001). They're much more so among women than among men. It seems to me that, thinking about where cultural changes are to be expected, I would not really expect the newly arriving people, as they become more politically represented, to want to move anything in a more "sexually positive way," which is the implication of some of the preceding comments.

The cultural character of the United States, Western Europe, or much of Asia is relatively conservative on these matters. Blaming it all on 19th-century Victorianism is really to arrest us in our understanding of why contemporary groups are the way they are and why they believe as they do.

References

Campbell, P. J. (1986). *Sex guides: Books and films about sexuality for young adults*. New York: Garland.

Laumann, E. O., & Michael, R. T. (Eds.). (2001). *Sex, love, and health in America: Private choices and public policies*. Chicago: University of Chicago Press.

Murdock, G. P., & White, D. R. (1969). The standard cross-cultural sample. *Ethnology, 8*, 329–369.

Part 5.

Retrospective Studies of Effects of Child Sexual Abuse on Adolescent Sexuality

Sexual Contact between Children and Adults

A Life Course Perspective with Special Reference to Men

EDWARD O. LAUMANN, CHRISTOPHER R. BROWNING, ARNOUT VAN DE RIJT, AND MARIANA GATZEVA

Introduction

Christopher Browning and I have been collaborating on the analysis of adult-child sexual contacts reported by respondents in the National Health and Social Life Survey (NHSLS) conducted in 1992 (cf. Laumann, Gagnon, Michael, & Michaels, 1994/2000, chap. 9; Browning & Laumann, 1997, 2003). Today we have divided our task into two parts. In the first part, I will present a basic description of the prevalence of adult-child sexual contacts among men in the NHSLS—a part of the population that was not included in our original article (1997) because of space constraints. In addition, I will also report comparable data collected in the Chicago Health and Social Life Survey (CHSLS) in 1995 and 1997 that will permit us to assess the replicability of our original results in a large urban sample and to go into somewhat greater depth because of the inclusion of some additional questions in the CHSLS. In the second part, Browning will expound in greater detail the theoretical perspective we have been developing to account for these findings and those reported in the literature.

In 1994, Ross Cheit, a professor of public policy at Brown University, publicly revealed that a boys' choir director in San Francisco had sexually abused him during the 1960s. The case received a great deal of publicity because of Cheit's willingness to come forward as a victim of abuse and, perhaps more important, because of his claim that the memory of abuse had surfaced only recently at the age of 36. In the context of increasing popular and academic interest in the possibility that memories of sexual abuse can be repressed, Cheit's story was particularly compelling. Yet the case was also interesting because of a less visible but undeniable fact: Cheit was an award-winning, successful, articulate professional and widely acknowledged as such. Moreover, he was happily married and, by all accounts, mentally healthy. The image of the victim of sexual abuse as emotionally unstable and permanently afflicted by the trauma of abuse was clearly at odds with the picture that Cheit presented (Freyd, 1996).

How did Cheit manage to endure the experience of sexual abuse with such apparent success? What sets cases like his apart from those that lead to substantial problems in adulthood? When sexual abuse began receiving more academic attention in the 1970s, researchers were primarily interested in establishing the nature of its effect on subsequent well-being. This largely descriptive research focused on both the severity of negative effects in adulthood and their breadth. Analyses of clinically based samples have revealed strong and consistent associations between experiences of early sexual contact with an adult and a host of adverse outcomes. A secondary and often ignored finding of this descriptive research, however, was the clearly nondeterministic relation between adult-child sex and poor adult adjustment. Individuals who reported early sexual experiences did not inevitably suffer long-term negative effects: Some exhibited no discernible effect at all.

This finding has called attention to a critical question: Why do some children who experience sexual abuse suffer a host of negative consequences while others do not? In the absence of measures to prevent the occurrence of child sexual abuse, it is critical for parents, therapists, and policy makers to understand the mechanisms by which such experiences lead to poor adjustment in adolescence and adulthood. Without knowledge, intervention efforts may be misguided and ineffective.

Data and Measures

Conducted in 1992, the National Health and Social Life Survey (NHSLS) is currently the only national probability sample to combine information on childhood sexual experiences with detailed accounts of the respondent's subsequent sexual history and current sexual practices. The richness of the NHSLS thus offers a unique opportunity to contextualize early sexual experiences within a life history. Indeed, the tendency of previous studies to ignore experiences occurring in the aftermath of adult-child sex may derive from the limited quality of the available data.

The NHSLS is a nationally representative probability sample of 1,511 men and 1,921 women between the ages of 18 and 59 living in households throughout the United States. That subpopulation covers about 97% of the population in this age group—roughly 150 million Americans. It excludes people living in group quarters (barracks, college dormitories, and prisons) as well as those who do not know English well enough to be interviewed. The sample includes an oversampling of African Americans (*N* = 458) and Hispanics (*N* = 267). The survey was conducted by the National Opinion Research Center (NORC) at the University of Chicago between February and September 1992. The sample's response rate was over 79%, at the higher end of such rates obtained in national surveys in recent years. Checks against other high-quality samples (e.g., the Census Bureau's Current Population Survey) suggest that the NHSLS succeeded in obtaining a truly representative sample of the population. Each respondent was surveyed in person by experienced interviewers from NORC. Interviews averaged 90 minutes in duration, and both direct questioning by the interviewer and self-administered questionnaires, filled out by the respondent at various points during the interview and given to the interviewer in a sealed envelope (to ensure the confidentiality of the respondent's answers), were employed. (Extensive discussion of the sampling design and evaluation of sample and data quality can be found in chapter 2 and appendices A and B in Laumann et al., 1994/2000.)

The Chicago Health and Social Life Survey (CHSLS), conducted in 1995, with a brief field operation in 1997 to complete the field operations interrupted in 1995 due to lack of funds and to add another sample neighborhood to the study, closely replicated the main features of the research design and interview schedule used in the NHSLS, with some new questions added to enhance and clarify several issues asked about in the original study. The CHSLS consists of five sample survey data sets and a textbase of fieldnotes from open-ended key informant interviews. The survey data were collected closely following the procedures employed in the NHSLS. The samples are representative of five geographical areas: Cook County as a whole (the city of Chicago and the inner ring of suburban communities) ($N = 890$), and four community areas within the city of Chicago: (a) a predominantly Mexican neighborhood ($N = 349$), (b) a Puerto Rican and mixed Hispanic neighborhood ($N = 210$), (c) a neighborhood dominated by affluent, white, young singles with a concentration of gay men ($N = 358$), and (d) an African American neighborhood ($N = 307$). Response rates ranged from 60% to 78% across samples. (A more comprehensive discussion of the research design is available in Laumann, Ellingson, Mahay, Paik, & Youm, 2003.)

In addition, 160 interviews were conducted with community leaders and service providers in the health, religious, social service, and legal institutional domains.

The retrospective nature of the NHSLS and the CHSLS data on early sexual experiences, however, renders them vulnerable to three primary error-generating mechanisms: memory repression ("motivated" forgetting), memory failure ("conventional" forgetting), and refusal (or misrepresentation). The psychoanalytic concept of repression posits a psychodynamic process by which the memory of highly emotionally charged or traumatic events is transferred from the conscious to the unconscious mind. In this view, traumatic childhood sexual experiences are not forgotten in the conventional sense; rather, while memory of the trauma is not available to the conscious mind, it is expressed in hysterical symptoms (Freud, 1896/

1955; Freyd, 1996). Bias due to memory repression would result in under-reporting of those experiences that were most traumatic—and possible underestimation of the long-term negative effect of childhood sexual experiences.

Memory loss may also be a function of conventional processes of forgetting. The details of early childhood events can be difficult to remember, especially for older respondents, some of whom are recounting an event that took place 40 to 50 years ago. Memories of early sexual experiences may also be subject to revision over time, as the meaning of the event changes within an evolving personal biography. Finally, a respondent may not disclose the event (or part of the event) in an interview because of the perceived social stigma that may accompany such a revelation.

Ultimately, we cannot know the extent to which particular sources of measurement error affect estimates of the prevalence or effects of early sexual experiences taken from the NHSLS data. However, an analysis of *partial* patterns of nonresponse in the NHSLS data (i.e., the tendency not to report components of an early sexual experience) does not provide evidence that events typically thought to be more traumatic (incestuous, repeated, penetrative, etc.) are associated with "partial amnesia" (Browning, 1997).

Evidence that nonresponse may be a significant source of error, however, does exist. Some researchers have gathered evidence designed to measure the tendency not to report early sexual experiences. Williams (1994) identified a sample of women who had documented histories of sexual abuse during childhood by reviewing hospital records of all sexual abuse victims examined between April 1973 and June 1975. Williams contacted a total of 129 women some 17 years later (when the women were between the ages of 18 and 31) in order to estimate the reported rate of abusive childhood sexual experiences in adulthood. When asked about childhood sexual experiences, 38% of the sample of adult women did not report the "index" (or documented) abuse experience.

The implications of measurement error in data on early sexual experiences differ, however, depending on the question addressed. Estimations of the prevalence of early sexual contacts, for instance, will be biased downward if significant proportions of individuals do not recall or report such experiences. On the other hand, parameter estimates describing the long-term *effects* of early sexual experiences will be biased only if those respondents who disclose early sexual experiences are systematically different from those who had early sexual experiences but do not report them. That is, an analysis of long-term effects may be immune to bias generated by reporting failure. An interesting finding from Williams's study relevant to this issue is the degree of similarity between women who did and women who did not report the index sexual abuse. No statistically significant differences were found between the two groups with respect to the proportions reporting other sexual assaults (in addition to the index abuse), the experience of abortion, prostitution, or having a sexually transmitted disease (one summary variable indicating any of the three outcomes), alcohol or drug problems, or having a close friend or family member who was killed. Moreover, the two groups were remarkably similar with respect to characteristics of the event, including the use of physical force, the occurrence of penetrative sexual activity, and genital trauma. The two groups, then, did not vary on a variety of important measures of subsequent behavior and well-being and differed only marginally with respect to characteristics of the event. Although Williams's findings call into question the accuracy of prevalence estimates drawn from self-reported data, they do not offer evidence that an analysis of long-term effects will be subject to significant error. Unfortunately, similar investigations of retrospective reporting of early sexual contacts among men have not been undertaken.

Acknowledging the potential for measurement error, the NHSLS and the CHSLS took a number of steps to promote accuracy and candor in respondents' reports of their early sexual experiences. First, questions regarding early sexual experiences were not asked until well into the interview. Inquiries into childhood, adolescent, and forced sexual experiences were placed in section 8 of a 10-section questionnaire. At this stage of the interview, respondents had already discussed intimate details of their sex lives, reducing the marginal social cost of further revelations. Second, while memory problems are difficult to surmount, the surveys avoided unduly taxing or ambiguous questions concerning details of the event. Evidence also exists that respondents were generally willing to discuss sensitive issues relating to sexuality. Nearly 80% of the NHSLS sample responded to the survey—a high response rate even for surveys not oriented toward sensitive behavior.[1] Despite the retrospective nature of the reports and the inevitably lower-bound estimates derived from them, the accuracy of the data gathered in the NHSLS, particularly for an analysis of early sexual experience effects, should be considered exceptionally high.

Construction of Early Sexual Contact Variables

The NHSLS and the CHSLS asked respondents (face-to-face) whether they had been touched sexually before puberty or the age of 12 or 13. If a positive response was given, the respondent was asked a number of questions about the experience, including the age of the respondent and the partner, when the sexual contact began and ended, what happened sexually (specific acts), the frequency of contact, the relationship of the respondent to the partner, and whether the respondent experienced sexual contact with anyone else during childhood. If more than one person touched the respondent, comparable summary information was requested regarding those experiences.[2] Adult-child sexual contact was defined as any genital fondling or oral, vaginal, or anal sex before age 14 with a partner who was at least four years older than the respondent and no younger than age 14. By this definition, 12% of women and 6% of men in the NHSLS reported experiencing sexual contact with an adult during childhood. The comparable rates for the CHSLS are 10% for women and 7% for men.

Childhood sexual experiences were also partitioned on the base of the severity of the event. Early sexual experiences were assigned a severity score based on the number of the following characteristics reported: (a) the type of sexual contact that occurred: oral, vaginal, or anal sex versus only fondling of the genitals; (b) whether the partner was a father/stepfather (for women) or relative/stepfather (for men); (c) the number of times sexual contact occurred: many times versus a few times or only once; (d) the number of individuals with whom contact occurred: two or more versus one; and (e) the age of the respondent when the sexual contact began: 9 or younger versus 10 to 13.[3]

We also constructed a variable indicating whether the respondent reported experiencing childhood sexual contact with a peer but not with an adult. Respondents were coded as having experienced *peer* or *mild asymmetrical* contact if they reported being touched sexually only by another child under age 14.[4] These events were distinguished exclusively by the age of the parties involved, not by any other aspect of the sexual contact. By this definition, 4% of men and 1% of women in the NHSLS reported a sexual experience with another peer during childhood. The comparable rates of child-peer sexual contact in the CHSLS are 7% for men and 2% percent for women. While, at first glance, this proportion appears low, it should be emphasized that the wording of the filter questions, "Did anyone touch you sexually?" (Laumann et al., 1994/2000, p. 650) was intended to capture events in which a partner or partners engaged in overtly sexual behavior with the respondent during childhood. It is reasonable to expect that a relatively small number of respondents would have experienced explicitly sexual contact initiated by another child age 13 or under. Moreover, respondents who reported sexual contacts with peers *and* adults were not included in the proportions (4% of women and 9% of men reported any peer sexual contact). Unfortunately, because of the low number of women who reported only peer sexual contacts, analysis of this experience independent from that of adult-child sexual contact was not feasible for this group. Consequently, only peer sexual contacts reported by men were analyzed. Finally variables measuring the occurrence of oral sex during the early event (occurrence vs. nonoccurrence) and the gender of the sex partner (at least one male partner vs. no male partners during childhood) were constructed.

Dependent Measures

Sexual Behavior Measures

A set of items measuring patterns of sexual activity in the aftermath of early sex was constructed to test the hypothesis of a bipolar versus a unidirectional behavioral response to early sexual experiences. Three category outcome variables were constructed, measuring age at first intercourse (19 or over/never, 16–18, or younger than 16), number of sex partners in the last year (zero, one, or two or more), number of sex partners in the last five years (zero or one, two or three, or four or more), and number of sex partners since age 18 (women: zero to two, three to six, or seven or more; men: zero to two, three to eight, or nine or more).[5] Measures of the tendency to engage in oral sex (both passive and active) with a primary partner in the last year (never, sometimes/rarely, always/usually) were also constructed.

Well-Being

A second set of outcomes attempts to assess the respondent's well-being both generally and with respect to current intimate relationships. The overall measure of well-being was based on an item inquiring into the general level of happiness the respondent experienced in the last year. The item asks the respondent, "Generally, how happy have you been with your personal life during the past 12 months? Have you been . . . Extremely happy, . . . Very happy most of the time, . . . Generally satisfied, pleased, . . . Sometimes fairly unhappy, or . . . Unhappy most of the time?" (Laumann et al., 1994/2000, p. 659). The well-being measure collapses the two categories at the low end of the happiness scale owing to the small number of cases. The measure of relationship satisfaction was constructed on the basis of responses to a question asking how emotionally satisfied the respondent felt with his or her current or "primary" partner in the last year. The respondent was asked, "How emotionally satisfying did you find your relationship with (PARTNER) to be, extremely satisfying, very satisfying, moderately satisfying, slightly satisfying, or not at all satisfying?" (Laumann et al., 1994/2000, p. 627). Again, the two low-satisfaction categories were collapsed. For both outcomes, higher categories represent lesser well-being.

Sexual Dysfunction

The NHSLS asked a number of questions designed to tap the respondent's level of dysfunction along both physical and emotional dimensions of sexual adjustment (for an extended analysis of these data, see Laumann, Paik, & Rosen, 1999, 2001). A latent class analysis (LCA) of a subset of these items identified typical categories of sexual dysfunction.[6] The content of the latent class solutions is consistent with clinical descriptions of typical constellations of symptoms and their associated features, if not precisely correspondent with specific sexual disorders.

For men, the best-fitting latent class solution produced three classes— one characterized by little or no sexual dysfunction, a second characterized by a high probability of anxiety interfering with sexual activity, and a third, a highly dysfunctional class (including problems achieving erection, adverse emotional responses to sexuality, and diminished pleasure). The fact that two independent surveys such as the NHSLS and the CHSLS find similar latent class solutions testifies to their robustness.

Independent Measures

Covariates included in the analyses were designed to capture background factors that are potentially associated with the occurrence of early sexual contacts as well as sexually active careers and subsequent well-being. These include race (black or Hispanic vs. white), cohort (1933–42, 1943–52, 1953–62, or 1963–74/78[7]), mother's education (finished high school, some high school, or less than high school), mother's work status when the respondent was age 14 (working or not working), family structure at age 14 (intact or non-intact), the respondent's number of siblings, and the type of place in which the respondent was living at age 14 (rural, small town, medium-sized city or suburb, or large city).

Intervening Measures

For men, four categories of measures were tested for the extent to which they mediate the long-term effect of childhood sexual experiences: (a) two measures of adolescent deviance: an item indicating whether the respondent had ever spent at least one night in jail[8] and a dichotomous item measuring whether the respondent left home before age 18; (b) two variables measuring the stability and consequences of the respondent's sexual trajectory: a dichotomous item measuring whether the respondent reported sex with a stranger to be very or somewhat appealing versus not or not at all appealing[9] (for the NHSLS only) and a measure of the experience of STD-related symptoms in the last 12 months (including painful or difficult urination, painful intercourse, lesions or sores in the genital area, or intense chronic itching of the genital area);[10] (c) marital status (whether the respondent was currently married); and (d) physical health status (whether the respondent self-reported fair or poor health in the last 12 months).

Finally, a measure of the exclusivity of sexual preference with regard to the sex of the respondent's sex partners was constructed. The base category for the variable is exclusive opposite-sex attraction. Categories 2 and 3 represent sexual attraction toward both sexes and exclusive same-gender sexual attraction, respectively. This variable was constructed out of two items: one measuring the respondent's reported attraction to only women, mostly women, both women and men, mostly men, or only men, and another asking the respondent whether he found having sex with someone of the same gender very appealing, somewhat appealing, not appealing, or not at all appealing. The advantage of the latter construction of the response categories was that it allowed the respondent to mark a negative category but to indicate some distance from the extreme negative category. This is where we might expect men who are experiencing some conflict about their sexual preferences to fall. Thus, those men who reported attraction to the opposite sex as well as any attraction to members of the same sex or who marked any category of appeal for same-gender sexual activity other than the extreme category (not at all) were coded as having non-exclusive sexual preference with regard to gender of partner.

Tables 1A and 1B provide univariate descriptive statistics for variables in the analysis and bivariate associations between childhood sexual experiences and subsequent outcomes, respectively, for both the NHSLS and the CHSLS. These tables support the findings of previous research, that adverse outcomes in adulthood are more likely given an adult-child sexual experience but are by no means inevitable. (While we focus in this paper on men's experiences [reported in Table 1B], we have provided information for the women in Table 1A to facilitate comparison.)

Perhaps the most striking pattern revealed in Table 1B is the consistently comparable elevations in tendency to experience both heightened sexual behavior and adverse adult outcomes among men who report sexual contact with a peer during childhood but not with an adult and those who reported adult-child sex. In the NHSLS, while roughly 11% of those men who reported no childhood sexual interaction reported low levels of happiness, 22% of those who reported adult-child sex and 16% of those who experienced peer sexual contact did so. The comparable rates for the CHSLS are 11%, 18%, and 11%, respectively. Similarly, in the NHSLS, 18% of men who reported no childhood sexual interaction said that they were moderately or less satisfied with the current relationship, while 33% and 35% of those who reported adult-child and peer sexual contact, respectively, reported lower emotional satisfaction with their primary partner in the last year. The comparable rates for the CHSLS are 29%, 29%, and 35%, respectively. Finally, in the NHSLS, one in 10 of those who reported no early sexual contact reported anxiety interfering with sexual activity, and the same proportion reported high dysfunction in the last year. Seventeen percent of those who experienced both peer and adult-child sexual contact reported sexually related anxiety in the last year, and comparable proportions reported high dysfunction. Although in the CHSLS the

Table 1A. *Definitions, Percentages, and Bivariate Associations with Childhood Sexual Experience for Sexual Behavior Outcomes, Intervening Variables, and Adult Well-Being in the Analysis (Women)*

Variables	NHSLS				CHSLS				
	All	No CS[a]	Ad-ch[b]	N	All	No CS[a]	Peer[c]	Ad-ch[b]	N
Sexual behavior outcomes									
Age at first intercourse				1,716					1,156
19 or older	38%	40%	25%		45%	48%	31%	29%	
16–18	48%	48%	53%		37%	36%	42%	40%	
Under 16	14%	13%	29%		18%	16%	27%	31%	
Number of partners since age 18				1,647					1,208
0 to 2	51%	54%	36%		64%	66%	59%	50%	
3 to 8	31%	31%	31%		25%	25%	19%	26%	
9 or more	18%	15%	33%		12%	10%	22%	24%	
Number of partners in last 5 years				1,664					-
0 to 1	68%	69%	63%		-	-	-	-	
2 to 3	20%	20%	18%		-	-	-	-	
4 or more	12%	11%	19%		-	-	-	-	
Number of partners in the last year				1,743					1,219
0	14%	14%	11%		16%	16%	22%	16%	
1	75%	76%	72%		69%	71%	63%	55%	
2 or more	12%	10%	17%		13%	12%	11%	28%	
Passive oral sex with partner in last year				1,464					1,002
Frequently	15%	14%	16%		17%	15%	21%	28%	
Occasionally	52%	51%	58%		46%	45%	58%	53%	
Never	33%	35%	26%		37%	39%	21%	20%	

				N					N
Active oral sex with partner in last year				1,463					
Frequently	12%	11%	15%		21%	20%	16%	32%	
Occasionally	52%	51%	58%		47%	47%	68%	48%	
Never	35%	37%	27%		31%	33%	16%	20%	
Intervening variables									
Childbirth before age 18	24%	21%	28%	1,744	17%	16%	26%	23%	1,217
Number of sex partners since age 18				1,647					1,208
0 or 1	35%	37%	24%		40%	43%	30%	24%	
2 to 10	56%	56%	54%		51%	51%	48%	57%	
11 to 20	6%	5%	15%		5%	4%	15%	9%	
21 or more	3%	2%	8%		4%	3%	7%	10%	
STD in lifetime	18%	16%	30%	1,693	22%	19%	52%	39%	1,208
Coerced sexual experience				1,725					1,218
Never forced after childhood	85%	88%	66%		87%	91%	70%	62%	
Forced once after childhood	11%	9%	22%		8%	6%	19%	22%	
Forced more than once after childhood	4%	3%	13%		4%	3%	11%	17%	
Adult well-being									
Latent sexual dysfunction classes				1,599					1,160
Low dysfunction	69%	71%	56%		63%	66%	39%	41%	
Sexual desire dysfunction	18%	17%	21%		23%	23%	38%	24%	
Sexual response dysfunction	7%	6%	10%		7%	6%	12%	23%	
High dysfunction	7%	5%	15%		7%	5%	11%	12%	

Continued on the next page

Table 1A. *Continued*

Variables	NHSLS				CHSLS				
	All	No CS[a]	Ad-ch[b]	N	All	No CS[a]	Peer[c]	Ad-ch[b]	N
Overall well-being				1,741					1,216
Extremely happy	16%	17%	14%		12%	12%	7%	6%	
Very happy	41%	43%	33%		37%	39%	26%	29%	
Generally satisfied	29%	28%	35%		37%	36%	37%	39%	
Unhappy	14%	13%	19%		14%	13%	30%	26%	
Emotional satisfaction in relationship				1,482					1,172
Extremely satisfied	39%	39%	34%		36%	36%	39%	27%	
Very satisfied	38%	39%	30%		35%	35%	15%	34%	
Moderately satisfied	17%	15%	24%		21%	21%	23%	19%	
Slightly / not satisfied	7%	7%	11%		9%	7%	23%	21%	

a No childhood sexual experience
b adult-child sexual experience
c sexual experience with peers.

Table 1B. Definitions, Percentages, and Bivariate Associations with Childhood Sexual Experience for Sexual Behavior Outcomes, Intervening Variables, and Adult Well-Being in the Analysis (Men)

Variables	NHSLS					CHSLS				
	All	No CS[a]	Peer[c]	Ad-ch[b]	N	All	No CS[a]	Peer[c]	Ad-ch[b]	N
Sexual behavior outcomes										
Age at first intercourse					1,349					827
19 or older	32%	33%	22%	32%		38%	39%	27%	27%	
16–18	45%	46%	44%	34%		34%	35%	32%	30%	
Under 16	23%	22%	34%	34%		28%	26%	42%	43%	
Number of partners since age 18					1,339					872
0 to 2	32%	35%	11%	18%		40%	43%	23%	22%	
3 to 8	31%	32%	21%	26%		23%	25%	15%	19%	
9 or more	37%	33%	68%	56%		37%	33%	63%	59%	
Number of partners in last 5 years					1,329					—
0 to 1	53%	56%	29%	41%		—	—	—	—	
2 to 3	21%	22%	23%	22%		—	—	—	—	
4 or more	26%	23%	48%	38%		—	—	—	—	
Number of partners in the last year					1,406					887
0	10%	98%	10%	16%		10%	11%	5%	5%	
1	67%	70%	50%	46%		57%	59%	49%	45%	
2 or more	23%	20%	40%	38%		32%	29%	46%	48%	

Continued on the next page

Table 1B. *Continued*

Variables	NHSLS					CHSLS				
	All	No CS[a]	Peer[c]	Ad-ch[b]	N	All	No CS[a]	Peer[c]	Ad-ch[b]	N
Passive oral sex with partner in last year					1,230					703
Frequently	19%	18%	23%	28%		25%	24%	39%	32%	
Occasionally	51%	51%	51%	49%		49%	50%	47%	34%	
Never	30%	32%	26%	22%		26%	26%	14%	34%	
Active oral sex with partner in last year					1,228					703
Frequently	21%	19%	33%	27%		26%	24%	43%	34%	
Occasionally	50%	49%	51%	52%		48%	50%	43%	32%	
Never	30%	31%	16%	21%		26%	27%	14%	34%	
Intervening variables										
Left home before age 18	20%	18%	32%	32%	1,408	29%	28%	24%	42%	887
Spent at least one night in jail	23%	21%	36%	37%	1,407	16%	13%	27%	31%	
Fair or poor health last year	10%	9%	20%	11%	1,408	13%	13%	8%	16%	
Currently married	52%	54%	28%	41%	1,394	41%	43%	22%	39%	
STD symptoms in the last year	9%	8%	27%	17%	1,386	2%	1%	10%	2%	
Find anonymous sex appealing	31%	29%	54%	39%	1,402	—	—	—	—	—

Exclusivity of sexual preference					1,399					839
Attracted only to women	88%	90%	82%	70%		88%	91%	71%	73%	
Attracted to both genders	10%	9%	12%	23%		5%	4%	11%	11%	
Attracted only to men	2%	2%	6%	7%		7%	6%	17%	16%	
Adult well-being										
Latent sexual dysfunction classes					1,341					
Low dysfunction	78%	80%	65%	64%		79%	80%	73%	70%	
Anxiety interfered with sex	11%	10%	17%	17%		10%	9%	8%	11%	
High dysfunction	12%	10%	17%	19%		12%	11%	19%	18%	
Overall well-being					1,407					885
Extremely happy	18%	19%	12%	12%		13%	13%	13%	13%	
Very happy	41%	43%	24%	28%		39%	40%	32%	32%	
Generally satisfied	29%	28%	48%	38%		36%	36%	44%	37%	
Unhappy	12%	11%	16%	22%		12%	11%	11%	18%	
Emotional satisfaction in relationship					1,245					840
Extremely satisfied	41%	43%	33%	33%		35%	34%	33%	42%	
Very satisfied	38%	39%	33%	34%		36%	36%	33%	29%	
Moderately satisfied	16%	14%	30%	25%		21%	21%	25%	14%	
Slightly / not satisfied	5%	4%	5%	8%		9%	8%	10%	15%	

a No childhood sexual experience
b adult-child sexual experience
c sexual experience with peers.

rates for men reporting anxiety interfering with sexual activity are similar for men who report childhood sexual experience and men who don't report such experience, respondents who reported childhood sexual contact have elevated rates of reporting high dysfunction (roughly 19% of the men reporting both adult-child and peer contact and 11% of men reporting no such contact). We examine multivariate patterns of association between childhood sexual experiences and subsequent outcomes in the analyses to follow.

Analyses and Results

In order to adjudicate between the psychogenic hypothesis that adult-child sexual contact has a polarizing effect on sexual behavior outcomes (hypothesis 1A) and the life course expectation of a unidirectional positive effect of both peer and adult-child sexual experiences on subsequent sexual behavior (hypothesis 1B), we examined the effect of early sex on four trichotomous outcome variables measuring the extent of sexual activity during specific phases of the respondent's life course and two measures of the frequency of oral sex in the last year. We predicted the latter two outcomes using a measure of whether the respondent reported the occurrence of oral sex during childhood, a childhood sexual event without oral sex, or no childhood sexual interaction.

Multinomial logit analyses were performed decomposing the coefficients measuring the effect of childhood sexual experiences into linear and quadratic components. The linear component measures the extent to which peer or adult-child sexual contact increases the odds of falling in the higher categories (representing more sexually active or precocious behavior) of each outcome when compared with adults who report no childhood sexual contact. The quadratic effect measures the extent to which these experiences increase the odds of falling into each of the two extreme categories (compared to the middle category).[11] Table 2 presents the results of likelihood ratio χ^2 comparisons of models fitting only the linear effect of childhood sexual experiences with models including only background characteristics (col. 1 and col. 3 for the NHSLS and the CHSLS respectively), and of models fitting both the linear and the quadratic effects of childhood sexual contacts with models fitting only the linear effects (col. 2 and col. 4 for the NHSLS and CHSLS respectively). The life course perspective predicts significant improvements in fit with the inclusion of linear effects alone (but not quadratic effects), while significant improvements in model fit with the inclusion of quadratic terms conform to the expectations of the psychogenic perspective.

For men, including the linear effects of both peer and adult-child sexual contact resulted in significant improvements in fit for models of number of sex partners since age 18, in the last five years, and in the last year. For the

Table 2. *Likelihood Ratio χ^2 Comparison for Multinomial Logit Models of Sexual Behavior Outcomes*

| | Likelihood Ratio χ^2 Comparison[a] | | | |
| | NHSLS | | CHSLS | |
Construction of Child Sex Parameter and Behavior Outcome	χ^2: Model 2 vs. Model 1	χ^2: Model 3 vs. Model 2	χ^2: Model 2 vs. Model 1	χ^2: Model 3 vs. Model 2
Women				
Adult-child vs. no child sex				
Age at first intercourse (<16, 16–18, 19+/never)	25.10 **	.00	13.93 **	.01
Number of partners since age 18 (0–2, 3–8, 9+)	49.79 **	3.08	15.17 **	1.78
Number of partners in last 5 years (0–1, 2–4, 5+)	12.35 **	2.45	—	—
Number of partners last year (0, 1, 2+)	15.23 **	3.45	27.84 **	3.82
Childhood oral sex, childhood sex without oral sex, no child sex				
Active oral sex last year (frequently, occasionally, never)	11.01 **	1.77	7.97 **	1.32
Passive oral sex last year (frequently, occasionally, never)	3.63	2.30	16.16 **	2.18
Men				
Adult-child vs. no child sex, peer vs. no child sex				
Age at first intercourse (<16, 16–18, 19+/never)	3.49	2.66	11.10 **	.69
Number of partners since age 18 (0–2, 3–8, 9+)	38.57 **	.60	28.39 **	3.70
Number of partners in last 5 years (0–1, 2–4, 5+)	17.80 **	.05	—	—
Number of partners last year (0, 1, 2+)	6.15 *	7.29 *	12.26 **	3.36

Continued on the next page

Table 2. Continued

	Likelihood Ratio χ^2 Comparison[a]					
	NHSLS			CHSLS		
Construction of Child Sex Parameter and Behavior Outcome	χ^2: Model 2 vs. Model 1	χ^2: Model 3 vs. Model 2		χ^2: Model 2 vs. Model 1	χ^2: Model 3 vs. Model 2	
Childhood oral sex, childhood sex without oral sex, no child sex						
Active oral sex last year (frequently, occasionally, never)	9.07 *	2.48		13.57 **	2.51	
Passive oral sex last year (frequently, occasionally, never)	10.83 **	.89		11.70 **	2.27	

Note. Model 1: Sexual behavior outcome regressed on background factors only (see below). Model 2: Sexual behavior outcome regressed on background factors and linear effects of childhood sexual experience. Model 3: Sexual behavior outcome regressed on background factors and both linear and quadratic effects of childhood sexual experience.

a Likelihood ratio χ^2 comparisons tests are conducted on 1 degree of freedom for women and 2 degrees of freedom for men (since effects of both peer and adult-child sex are included in models 2 and 3). The models control for race (white, black, Hispanic), cohort (1933–42, 1943–52, 1953–62, 1963–74/78), mother's education (less than high school, high school, more than high school), mother's work status (working for pay when respondent was 14 or not) (for the NHSLS only), family structure at age 14 (intact vs. nonintact), the type of place respondent lived in at age 14 (rural, small town, medium-sized city/suburb, or large city), and respondent's number of siblings (for the NHSLS only).

* $p < .05$ (two-tailed test)
** $p < .01$ (two-tailed test)

CHSLS, including these linear effects improved the fit of the model predicting men's age at first intercourse, but it did not for the NHSLS. Also, including the linear effects of childhood sexual experiences with and without the occurrence of oral sex improved the fit of models of both measures of frequency of oral sex in the last year for both surveys. For the NHSLS, the linear effects of peer sexual contacts were positive and significant for all four sex partner outcomes, while adult-child sex was positively and significantly associated with number of partners since age 18 and in the last five years. The occurrence of childhood sexual contacts without and with oral sex was significantly and positively associated with the occurrence of both passive and active oral sex in the last year. For the CHSLS, the linear effects of both peer and adult-child sexual contact were positive and significant for all three sexual outcomes in adulthood, while only childhood sexual contact with active and passive oral sex was associated with more frequent oral sex in the last year.

In contrast to the expectations of the psychogenic perspective, for both surveys, fitting the quadratic term did not result in significant improvements in fit for models of age at first intercourse, number of sex partners since age 18, number of sex partners in the last five years, or frequency of passive or active oral sex in the last year, for men. Only for the NHSLS, in the case of number of sex partners in the last year, did the quadratic term result in a significant change in likelihood ratio χ^2. Yet an analysis of coefficients for adult-child and peer sexual contacts indicated that both have significant quadratic effects on number of sex partners in the last year. This finding suggests that polarized sexual activity in the last year may be more a function of an unstable sexual career than of opposing strategies to cope with lingering emotional disturbance. Over the life course, sexual careers marked by less relationship stability and a tendency to avoid marriage may lead to both an increasingly intermittent pattern of sexual partnering and higher probabilities of having multiple partners simultaneously. Measured over a relatively short time span, then, these men are more likely to appear sexually inactive *or* highly sexually active. In conformity with the expectations of the life course perspective, linear effects of early sexual experience were strong and positive, resulting in consistent improvements in goodness of fit across outcomes.

We next considered hypothesis 2—the extent to which individuals specialize in sexual behaviors and relationship characteristics specific to the early sexual contact. Table 3 reports the results of analyses examining this tendency through modeling the effect of the reported occurrence of oral and same-gender sex during early sexual contact on their occurrence in adulthood.[12] In order to isolate the effect of the specific characteristic itself on subsequent orientations most effectively, we compared early sexual experiences where the event occurred both to other cases of early sexual contact and to those reporting no early sex (the omitted category). For

Table 3. *Adult Oral Sex Activity and Appeal of Same-Gender Sex by Childhood Occurrence and Background Characteristics (Logistic Regression Models: Log-Odds Ratios) (Men)*

Characteristics of Sexual Contact (vs. No Child Sexual Contact)	NHSLS			CHSLS		
	Frequent Occurrence of Active Oral Sex (Last Year)	Frequent Occurrence of Passive Oral Sex (Last Year)	Appeal of Same-Gender Sex	Frequent Occurrence of Active Oral Sex (Last Year)	Frequent Occurrence of Passive Oral Sex (Last Year)	Appeal of Same-Gender Sex
Oral Sex:						
Did not occur	.242	.357	...	.440	.215	...
	(.202)	(.201)		(.275)	(.309)	
Occurred	1.365 **	.349	...	1.729 ***	1.082 **	...
	(.366)	(.419)		(.486)	(.365)	
Same-gender sex:						
Did not occur	...	...	−.570	...	...	−.738
			(.296)			(.743)
Occurred	...	...	1.267 **	...	...	3.004 ***
			(.255)			(.359)
Total N	1,304	1,306	1,496	699	699	870

Note. Numbers in parentheses are standard errors. The models control for race (white, black, Hispanic), cohort (1933–42, 1943–52, 1953–62, 1963–74/78), mother's education (less than high school, high school, more than high school), family structure at age 14 (intact vs. non-intact), the type of place respondent lived in at age 14 (rural, small town, medium-sized town/suburb, or large city), mother's work status (working for pay when respondent was 14 or not) (for the NHSLS only), and respondent's number of siblings (for the NHSLS only).

**p < .01 (two-tailed test)

***p < .001 (two-tailed test)

men, the magnitude of the effect of events in which the behavior did occur is considerably larger than the effect of events in which it did not for the frequent occurrence of oral sex in the last year and the appeal of same-gender sex. (These results are replicated for women too.)

Because of the paucity of measures of both deviance and paternal and other informal attachments during youth, the effect of early sexual experience on the manifestation of diversity in deviant behavior could not be considered as effectively with the NHSLS and the CHSLS. The life course perspective suggests that the generalization of deviant behavior in adolescence is an indirect effect of the attenuation of critical social bonds in the aftermath of early sex, not an expression of the emotional disturbance or strain induced by traumatic childhood sexual contact. Although the specific mechanism linking early sex with measures of deviance could not be tested using the NHSLS and the CHSLS, models predicting ever having spent a night in jail and leaving home early (analyses not presented), for men, indicate that both adult-child and peer sexual contact are associated with these events (at comparable magnitudes and levels of significance). This finding warrants examination of the potential mediating effect of deviance on long-term well-being.

In contrast to the life course focus on the events that may mediate the effects of early sex, the psychogenic perspective points to the severity of the childhood sexual experience as the key variable accounting for differences in adult well-being. To examine this dose-response hypothesis (3A), a cumulative measure of event severity (the number of severe characteristics reported by the respondent, ranging from zero to five) was included in a multinomial logit model predicting sexual dysfunction latent class membership and two ordered logit models predicting the four-category well-being and relationship-satisfaction measures (see Table 4). For both sexes, the cumulative severity measure was not a significant predictor of sexual dysfunction in the multinomial logit model, nor was it in either of the ordered logit models predicting levels of well-being and emotional satisfaction with the primary partner. (Note that the results reported in Table 4 are based on relatively small sample sizes.) The results of these analyses are not consistent with the psychogenic hypothesis that severity of early sexual experience accounts for variation in adult well-being.[13]

Finally, Table 5 reports the results of multinomial logit and ordered logit models measuring the effects of both peer and adult-child sexual contact as well as the intervening variables described above on the three measures of adult adjustment. For each outcome considered, an initial model is fit examining the effect of childhood sexual experience, controlling for background factors (col. 1 under each outcome heading). For the NHSLS, men's adult-child sex is associated with all the adult adjustment variables, while for the CHSLS, it is not associated with any of these variables. Moreover, consistent with the life course perspective, for the NHSLS, peer sexual

Table 4. *Adult Outcomes by Severity of Childhood Sexual Experiences and Background Characteristics (Logistic Regression Models) (Men)*

	NHSLS				CHSLS				
	Sexual Dysfunction		Well-Being		Sexual Dysfunction			Well-Being	
Independent Variables	Anxiety Interfered with Sex	High Sexual Dysfunction	Low Overall Well-Being	Low Satisfaction with Partner	Anxiety Interfered with Sex	High Sexual Dysfunction	More than 1 Dysfunction Reported	Low Overall Well-Being	Low Satisfaction with Partner
Number of severe characteristics	.381	.006	.142	.038	-.206	.179	.282	.117	.009
	(.235)	(.200)	(.127)	(.139)	(.295)	(.244)	(.248)	(.161)	(-.165)
Total N	...	165	173	149	...	...	124	126	121

Note. Coefficients are log-odds ratios. Numbers in parentheses are standard errors. The models control for race (white, black, Hispanic), cohort (1933–42, 1943–52, 1953–62, 1963–74/78), mother's education (less than high school, high school, more than high school, family structure at age 14 (intact vs. non-intact), and the type of place respondent lived in at age 14 (rural, small town, medium-sized town/suburb, or large city).

contacts were associated with both adult overall well-being and high sexual dysfunction, although the coefficients predicting emotional satisfaction and anxiety during sexual activity did not reach conventional levels of significance. These results also run counter to the psychogenic assumption that those who experience sexual contacts with age peers will not manifest similar adult outcomes. However, for the CHSLS no significant differences in adult well-being or sexual adjustment between men with and without peer sexual experiences were found.

Analyses examining the life course explanation of variation in the long-term effects of childhood sexual experience are presented in columns 2 and 3 of Tables 5 and 6. Models under columns 2 and 3 add in intervening variables in order to examine their mediating effect on the outcome considered. For men, model 2 adds in measures of leaving home early and delinquency, and model 3 adds marital and health status as well as sexual trajectory measures (experience of STD-related symptoms, the appeal of anonymous sex, and exclusivity of sexual preference).

For the NHSLS men, coefficients describing the association between both peer and adult-child sexual contact and low overall well-being in adulthood are significant in model 1. For those who experienced adult-child sex, the odds of reporting low overall well-being are (exp {0.841} =) 2.3 times* higher than the odds for those who experienced no childhood sexual contact. Similarly, the odds for those who report peer sexual contacts are (exp {0.6509} =) 1.9 times higher than the odds for those who report no childhood sexual contacts. The introduction of measures of deviance (specifically, jail time, which is associated with low overall well-being in adulthood) in model 2 results in modest reductions in the size of the coefficients for childhood sexual experiences. However, marital and health status, STD symptoms, and the appeal of anonymous sex are all associated with adult overall well-being and result in a dramatic drop in the magnitude and significance of the coefficient for peer sexual contacts and a further and more marked reduction (by comparison to model 2) in that of the adult-child coefficient (although it remains significant at the .05 level). Controlling for subsequent trajectories, the odds of reporting low overall well-being for men who report adult-child sex are 1.7 times higher than the odds for those who did not report a childhood sexual experience. The coefficient for peer sexual contacts is negligible and nonsignificant in model 3. Although no parallel coefficients in the CHSLS are statistically significant, they all decrease and their standard deviations increase as sexual trajectory variables are added.

The mediating effect of subsequent trajectories can also be seen in the analyses of the association between childhood sexual experience and low

*(exp {0.841} =) 2.3 times — this means that the exponential 0.841 equals 2.3, the odds.

Table 5. *Adult Well-Being by Childhood Sexual Experience, Intervening Sexual Trajectory, and Background Characteristics (Ordered Logit Models: Log-Odds Ratios) (Men)*

Independent Variables	NHSLS: Well-Being Last Year						CHSLS: Well-Being Last Year					
	Low Overall Well-Being			Low Satisfaction with Partner			Low Overall Well-Being			Low Satisfaction with Partner		
	(1)	(2)	(3)	(1)	(2)	(3)	(1)	(2)	(3)	(1)	(2)	(3)
Childhood sexual experience:												
Adult-child	.841 **	.755 **	.557 *	.623 **	.543 *	.425	.333	.253	.190	−.060	−.121	−.210
	(.212)	(.214)	(.220)	(.238)	(.241)	(.247)	(.254)	(.256)	(.260)	(.263)	(.267)	(.273)
Peer	.650 *	.543 *	.015	.542	.457	.040	.206	.147	.034	.077	.052	−.128
	(.259)	(.261)	(.270)	(.284)	(.287)	(.294)	(.246)	(.248)	(.256)	(.250)	(.249)	(.254)
Generalized deviance:												
Spent a night in jail	...	.488 **	.334 *	...	.479 **	.329 *	...	.454	.246	...	.279	.181
		(.125)	(.127)		(.131)	(.134)		(.182)	(.187)		(.184)	(.190)
Left home at 17 or younger	...	.222	.223	...	.160	.149	...	.124	.171	...	.036	.054
		(.133)	(.134)		(.141)	(.142)		(.142)	(.144)		(.141)	(.143)
Marital/health status and sexual trajectory:												
Currently married	...	...	−.869 **	...	...	−.983 **	...	...	−.549 ***	...	...	−.698 ***
			(.117)			(.128)			(.144)			(.145)
Poor health	...	...	.786 **	...	...	.208	...	...	1.136 ***	...	...	.458 *[1]
			(.183)			(.207)			(.210)			(.204)
STD symptomatology	...	...	.499 **	...	...	.054	...	...	.334	...	...	.876
			(.183)			(.203)			(.463)			(.503)

	Col 1	Col 2	Col 3	Col 4	Col 5	Col 6	Col 7	Col 8	Col 9	Col 10	Col 11	Col 12
Anonymous sex appealing	...	...	.425 **	...	...	.596 **	...	...	...	...	...	...
			(.114)			(.121)						
Sexual preference exclusivity:												
Attracted to both genders	...	...	.167	...	...	.304	...	...	.279	...	...	.292
			(.169)			(.186)			(.264)			(.266)
Attracted only to men	...	...	.643	...	...	-.187	...	...	.541	...	...	.321
			(.337)			(.418)			(.305)			(.310)
Threshold parameter estimates:												
$\_1$	-1.732	-1.615	-2.099	.312	.457	-.235	-2.244	-2.156	-2.339	-.622	-.571	-.963
$\_2$	.203	.339	-.038	2.044	2.205	1.627	-.246	-.148	-.261	.907	.961	.621
$\_3$	1.963	2.119	1.860	3.797	3.969	3.455	1.752	1.864	1.849	2.387	2.445	2.152
Log-likelihood	-1,678.3	-1,668.6	-1,612.6	-1,366.4	-1,358.6	-1,310.3	-1,077.1	-1,073.4	-1,045.6	-1,047.2	-1,046.0	-1,025.5
df	17	19	25	17	19	25	13	15	20	13	15	20
N	1,330	1,330	1,330	1,188	1,188	1,188	869	869	869	826	826	826

Note. Numbers in parentheses are standard errors. The models control for race (white, black, Hispanic), cohort (1933–42, 1943–52, 1953–62, 1963–74/78), mother's education (less than high school, high school, more than high school), family structure at age 14 (intact vs. non-intact), the type of place respondent lived in at age 14 (rural, small town, medium-sized town/suburb, or large city), mother's work status (working for pay when respondent was 14 or not) (for the NHSLS only), and respondent's number of siblings (for the NHSLS only).

*p < .05 (two-tailed test)   **p < .01 (two-tailed test)   *** p < .001 (two-tailed test)

1. In the CHSLS the number of degrees of freedom is different due to the absence of some control variables.

Table 6. *Adult Sexual Adjustment by Childhood Sexual Experience, Intervening Sexual Trajectory, and Background Characteristics (Multinomial Logit Models: Log-Odds Ratios) (Men)*

Independent Variables	NHSLS Dysfunction Classes						CHSLS Dysfunction Classes					
	Anxiety			High			Anxiety			High		
	(1)	(2)	(3)	(1)	(2)	(3)	(1)	(2)	(3)	(1)	(2)	(3)
Childhood sexual experience:												
Adult-child	.673 *	.616	.464	.688 *	.505	.435	−.186	.142	.090	.631	.610	.447
	(.335)	(.339)	(.347)	(.328)	(.339)	(.341)	(.442)	(.450)	(.464)	(.368)	(.371)	(.382)
Peer	.719	.630	.592	.892 *	.316	.288	−.256	−.430	−.462	.601	.612	.501
	(.415)	(.428)	(.170)	(.401)	(.421)	(.421)	(.505)	(.525)	(.530)	(.356)	(.366)	(.374)
Marital/health status and sexual trajectory:												
Currently married	...	−.132	−.078	...	−.414 *	−.390	...	−1.228 ***	−1.200 ***	...	.047	.171
		(.206)	(.209)		(.208)	(.209)		(.302)	(.308)		(.245)	(.254)
Poor health	...	.185	.173	...	1.160 **	1.159 **	...	.772 *	.816 *	...	.867 **	1.001 **
		(.342)	(.341)		(.257)	(.257)		(.351)	(.354)		(.323)	(.327)
STD symptomatology	...	.578 *	.543	...	.782 **	.777 **	...	−.090	−.187	...	.170	−.220
		(.291)	(.293)		(.280)	(.281)		(.832)	(.849)		(.689)	(.710)
Anonymous sex appealing	...	−.156	−.152	...	.693 **	.692 **	...	...	...	...	...	...
		(.214)	(.215)		(.196)	(.197)						

	(1)	(2)	(3)	(4)	(5)	(6)
Sexual preference exclusivity						
Attracted to both genders	.719 **	...	.576 *	...	.936	1.627 ***
	(.263)		(.284)		(.516)	(.411)
Attracted to men only	.887	...	.241	...	-.227	.295
	(.509)		(.671)		(.480)	(.432)
Log-likelihood	-829.6	-815.0	-799.9	-533.6	-518.7	-510.7
df	30	38	42	26	32	36
N	1,284	1,284	1,284	829	829	829

Note. Numbers in parentheses are standard errors. The models control for race (white, black, Hispanic), cohort (1933–42, 1943–52, 1953–62, 1963–74/78), mother's education (less than high school, high school, more than high school), family structure at age 14 (intact vs. non-intact), the type of place respondent lived in at age 14 (rural, small town, medium-sized town/suburb, or large city), mother's work status (working for pay when respondent was 14 or not) (for the NHSLS only), and respondent's number of siblings (for the NHSLS only).

*p < .05 (two-tailed test)   **p < .01 (two-tailed test)   ***p < .C01 (two-tailed test)

*1 In the CHSLS the number of degrees of freedom is different due to the absence of some control variables.

emotional satisfaction with the respondent's primary partner in the last year. In model 1, the odds of reporting low emotional satisfaction or worse are 1.86 times higher for those who report adult-child sexual experience than those for respondents reporting no childhood sexual contact. Again, the experience of jail time results in a modest reduction in the size of the coefficient for adult-child sex, but, with the introduction of marital status and the appeal of anonymous sex in model 3, subsequent trajectory controls result in a 40% reduction in the magnitude of the coefficient (vs. model 1) and render it nonsignificant (at the .05 level). For the CHSLS, no significant effects of adult-child or peer sexual experience are found, but all coefficients decrease and their standard deviations increase as sexual trajectory variables are added. The importance of marital status and the appeal of short-term sexual partnering as mechanisms linking early sexual contact with adult relationship satisfaction conform to the expectations of the life course perspective. Early sexual experience may result in the assimilation of models or scripts of sexual interaction that do not facilitate the development of stable intimate relationships. The durability of relationships may be of central importance to men. Evidence suggests that the benefits of stable relationships may not be apparent in the short term but are a cumulative and increasing function of the amount of time men spend in these relationships (cf. Waite & Joyner, 2001). Although it is not clear from the model whether the effect of marriage is state-dependent or the result of heterogeneity in the tendency to marry, these results, nevertheless, point to the potential importance of sexual and marital trajectories in mediating the effects of childhood sexual experiences on adult well-being.

Further evidence suggesting the importance of intervening trajectories was provided in the analysis of the association between childhood sexual experience and sexual dysfunction. Table 6 reports the results of multinomial logit models assessing the association between peer and adult-child sexual contact and membership in the two sexual dysfunction latent classes (compared with the low dysfunction class). Model 2 adds measures of marital and health status, STD symptoms, and the appeal of anonymous sex,[14] while model 3 adds sexual preference exclusivity. In model 1, for the NHSLS, adult-child sexual contact was associated with anxiety during sexual activity at the conventional level of significance (96% increase in odds over those reporting no childhood sexual contact), while both adult-child and peer sexual contacts were associated with high sexual dysfunction (99% and 144% increases in odds, respectively). For the CHSLS, all effects of adult-child and peer sexual contact on men's sexual dysfunction are insignificant.

With regard to the experience of anxiety during sexual activity, the introduction of marital status, physical health, and sexual trajectory variables modestly reduced the magnitude and the significance ($p > .05$) of the coefficient for adult-child sex. The significant effect of STD symptoms suggests that indications of a sexually transmitted disease may contribute to anxiety about the ability to perform sexually, the potential for passing the STD to a partner, or the partner's reaction to external symptoms, among other potential sources of anxiety. The CHSLS did not find such an effect of the presence of STD symptoms on sexual dysfunction. Model 3 introduces sexual preference exclusivity, which, for the NHSLS, results in a further 30% reduction in the magnitude of the coefficient. Although the effect of exclusive same-sex orientation is relatively large in magnitude, it does not achieve the conventional level of significance. Interestingly, the effect of reported attraction to both sexes is both highly significant and relatively large in magnitude (a 100% increase in the odds of anxiety interfering with sexual activity over respondents who reported no childhood sexual contact). Accompanying changes in the size of the adult-child sex coefficient suggest that this category of early sexual experience (which is more likely to involve an older male) may reinforce same-gender sexual activity and subsequently produce conflict over sexual preference in some individuals, with lasting implications for sexual adjustment.

The models yield different results on the CHSLS data. First of all, childhood sexual experience with a peer or an adult does not have an effect on sexual anxiety in any of the three models, nor do these coefficients reveal a pattern close to that of the NHSLS. Second, a large effect of marital status on sexual anxiety is found for the CHSLS but not for the NHSLS. Third, no effect of STD symptomatology is present in the models for the CHSLS, while it is present in the models for the NHSLS. And fourth, in contrast to the NHSLS models, no significant effect on bisexual preferences is found for the CHSLS models.

Finally, the significant associations between both peer and adult-child sexual contacts and high sexual dysfunction, found in the analysis of the NHSLS, were reduced (substantially in the case of peer contacts) and rendered nonsignificant ($p > .05$) in model 2. Similarly, the (nonsignificant) effect of the CHSLS in model 1 decreases and its standard deviation increases with the inclusion of sexual trajectory variables in models 2 and 3. For the NHSLS, all of the intervening variables included in model 2—marital and health status,[15] STD symptoms, and the appeal of anonymous sex—were associated with high dysfunction. For the CHSLS, health status is associated with high dysfunction, while for marital status and STD symptomatology no significant effects are present. The reduction in the magnitude and significance of the adult-child and peer sexual contact coefficients indicates that active sexual trajectories and their consequences may lead to higher rates of both physical problems during sexual activity (poor overall health and STD symptoms may increase the likelihood of erection difficulties or diminished pleasure) and emotional problems and anxiety associated with sexual activity. Although it is possible that sexual dysfunction precipitates a less-stable sexual trajectory, participation in heightened levels of sexual activity begins at relatively early stages of the life course for men who experience early sexual contact, indicating that patterns of interaction are established prior to, and may contribute to, the onset of adult sexual adjustment problems.

Model 3 adds the measure of sexual preference exclusivity. For both surveys, only attraction to both sexes had a significant effect on the likelihood of high sexual dysfunction. For the NHSLS, the coefficient for adult-child sex was only modestly reduced, but the pattern of significance for this item and the consistent sensitivity of the adult-child contact effect to its inclusion are suggestive of a potentially important mediating mechanism. Indeed, the extent to which the relatively limited number of intervening trajectory variables account for the association between childhood sexual experience and both adult well-being measures and sexual dysfunction suggests that the life course hypothesis that the long-term effects of childhood sex are largely indirect merits further exploration.

Discussion

The preeminent position of trauma-based conceptions of the long-term effects of early sexual experience has remained largely unchallenged. Although the notion of trauma is multivocal in the psychogenic literature, it anchors the vast majority of research attempting to account for the associations between childhood sex and subsequent well-being. Yet the key theoretical claims and expectations uniting psychogenic theories of the long-term effect of childhood sex received little support in analyses of a large, nationally representative sample of U.S. adults and of a large representative sample of the Chicago metropolitan area.

- The prediction that adult-child sex leads to a withdrawal from sexual activity received no support.
- The effect of adult-child sex on measures of sexual behavior over longer periods of the life course (last five years and since age 18) indicates that these experiences heighten levels of sexual activity for men but do not result in sexual withdrawal.
- The evidence suggests that childhood sexual contact tends to result in reinforcement of sexual activity generally as well as acts and relationship characteristics specific to the early sexual event. This conclusion is supported with respect to the heightened interest in oral sex if this occurred in the early event as well as the association between same-gender sexual activity during childhood and its subsequent appeal.[16]
- Contrary to the expectations of the psychogenic perspective, the level of event severity is not associated with long-term outcomes.
- Peer contacts were associated—at magnitudes and significance levels comparable to adult-child sexual contacts—with overall well-being

and sexual adjustment during adulthood. In short, age of the partner is not associated with sexual adjustment during adulthood.

- Respondents who reported adult-child sexual contact were significantly more likely also to report a peer sexual contact,[17] suggesting that early sexual practice may diffuse through networks of children tied to those who have experienced sexual contact with an adult. Moreover, of those men who reported a peer contact, half in the NHSLS and 35% in the CHSLS reported more than one such experience during childhood. The diffusion of sexual practices through peer networks may promote a social context in which continuity in sexual behavior patterns is maintained and reinforced.

- The effect of adult-child sex on adult sexual adjustment appears to be mediated by a range of intervening events in the life course.

- In sum, childhood sexual experience should be understood as embedded in dynamically unfolding lives. Research efforts that seek to track the consequences of early sexual events through behavioral pathways may prove more fruitful than the continued and restrictive focus on the severity and nature of event-specific trauma.

Notes

This paper draws heavily from those sections in Browning and Laumann (2003) pertaining to the male NHSLS respondents. Results, based on an analysis of the data from the CHSLS, have also been incorporated into the relevant tables, with an extended discussion of their implications for replication and extension of the empirical findings originally reported. We wish to express our appreciation for funding from the NICHD (RO1-HD28356) that supported the date collection and analysis of the CHSLS.

1. The more modest completion rates attained in the CHSLS have more to do with the abrupt termination of field operations because of funding shortfalls than any apparent reluctance on the part of the respondents to participate in the survey once they were successfully contacted to arrange an appointment for the interview. A number of active interviews in process were lost when field operations were stopped, so that interviewers were unable to do their regular follow-up procedures to bring a tentatively scheduled interview to fruition. These "lost" interviews had to be counted as not completed for purposes of calculating the completion rates. (See p. 295 for a full discussion of this situation.)

2. In cases where the respondent was touched by more than one person, however, the summary method of data collection rendered any clear connection between reported descriptions of the aggregated experiences and characteristics of the persons who touched the respondent impossible. In these cases, then, the occurrence of isolated characteristics (say, the experience of oral sex) during the respondent's childhood could be confirmed, but this information could not be linked with a specific partner. This data constraint clearly limits our knowledge of the experiences of respondents with multiple sexual contacts during childhood. For the vast majority of the cases involved, however, the construction of the variable employed ensures that relatively advanced sexual con-

tact occurred with at least one substantially older individual. In some cases, the respondent reported sexual contact both with an adolescent or adult (at least 14 years of age) and with another child (13 years old or younger). Since the percentage of cases involving older partners that did *not* involve at least fondling of the genitals was nominal, we included these cases despite ambiguity regarding the content of the sexual interactions. Because a small number of respondents reported that they reached puberty at ages well into adolescence (15, 16, 17), some sexual experiences that began after the respondent had reached age 13 were reported. These cases were excluded.

3. Determination of the cut point for age was based on previous research by Russell (1986), who identified age 9 as the critical point before which the probability of long-term effects was elevated. Freud suggested that sexual trauma before, but not after, age 9 would generate later hysterical symptomatology (Freud 1896/1955).

4. In the CHSLS there are several cases in which the toucher was older than 14 but the age difference was less than four years, e.g., a respondent reporting being sexually touched at the age of 12 by a 15-year-old. Due to considerations about the sample size, we included those cases in the analysis in the category of peer contact.

5. Cut points for the numbers of partners in each category were determined by selecting the number of partners roughly corresponding to the 33rd and 66th percentiles of the distribution, except in cases where the distribution was heavily skewed (e.g., partners in the last year and the last five years). A number of alternative specifications of the outcome variables were tested; the results did not alter the conclusions of the analysis.

6. LCA is the categorical data analogue of factor analysis (which is used for continuous variables). It provides a method of identifying a set of mutually exclusive latent classes that account for the association among a set of categorical variables. LCA arrives at a solution of T latent classes, such that the observed variables, controlling for the latent variable, are independent (i.e., LCA maximizes local independence among a set of observed categorical variables; cf. McCutcheon, 1987).

7. In the CHSLS, this cohort was extended by four years since the survey was conducted later than the NHSLS and therefore includes people from younger cohorts. Thus, the youngest CHSLS cohort becomes 1963–78.

8. This, of course, measures the occurrence of delinquent events that resulted in official intervention.

9. Since men, in general, are more likely to report multiple partners across the life course, the number of sex partners may not effectively identify those men most at risk of engaging in sexual behavior with adverse consequences. The subjective appeal of anonymous sex is highly correlated with high levels of sexual activity but may also, and more parsimoniously, capture a tendency to engage in a higher-risk, less stable pattern of sexual partnering for men.

10. Symptom measures more accurately describe the current effect of sexually transmitted infection and do not require the respondent to have been diagnosed by a doctor or have knowledge of the effects associated with a given infection (as do specific STD measures). Men, in general, have less direct contact with medical professionals regarding reproductive health issues and may be less likely to have knowledge regarding, or be willing to admit having, a sexually transmitted disease.

11. In this case, because there are only three outcomes, the model with both linear and quadratic effects is equivalent to the unconstrained multinomial logit model.

12. Because same-gender sexual behavior was so rare in the male population, we used a measure of the subjective appeal of this activity.

13. Each of the severe characteristics was considered individually in models predicting adult outcomes as well. The coefficients for more and less severe events for each

characteristic were roughly equivalent in the majority of cases. Indeed, the number of models in which the coefficient for less severe cases achieved significance while the coefficient for more severe cases did not exceeded the number in which the reverse result was obtained.

14. Since no obvious theoretical justification for including measures of deviance to predict these outcomes was apparent, these items were dropped from the analysis of adult sexual dysfunction.

15. In order to ensure that the results of the analysis were not driven by the health status item (which conceivably could be measuring sexual dysfunction as well), the health item was removed from the analysis. Removing the health item results in no change in the magnitude or the significance of the adult-child sexual contact coefficient in model 3.

16. The finding regarding same-sex activity, however, should be interpreted with considerable caution. The suggestion of a causal link between early same-gender sex and its later appeal should not be understood as a general theory of homosexual behavior. Nor should it be taken as evidence that every such experience will have a causal effect. Indeed, in some cases, the causal process may be reversed. To the extent that same-gender sexual preference is biologically based or established at a developmentally early stage, some same-gender childhood sexual experiences may occur as a result of a selection process. Nevertheless, patterns of sexual activity in the aftermath of early sex support the life course hypothesis that childhood sexual contact models and reinforces sexual activity in general and patterns of interaction specific to the childhood event.

17. Of men who reported adult-child sexual contact, 16% reported a peer sexual contact as well, compared with 4% of men who did not report an adult-child sexual contact. The comparable numbers in the CHSLS were 31% and 8%, respectively, and for CHSLS women, 14% and 2%, respectively. Comparable proportions for NHSLS women were 6% and 1%, respectively. Respondents who report adult-child sexual contacts are undoubtedly also more willing to acknowledge the occurrence of a peer sexual contact—nevertheless, the strength of the association between the two events warrants further attention.

References

Browning, C. R. (1997). *Trauma or transition.* Unpublished doctoral dissertation, University of Chicago.

Browning, C. R., & Laumann, E. O. (1997). Sexual contact between children and adults: A life course perspective. *American Sociological Review, 62,* 540–560.

Browning, C. R., & Laumann, E. O. (2003). The social context of adaptation to childhood sexual maltreatment: A life course perspective. In J. Bancroft (Ed.), *Sexual Development in Childhood* (pp. 383–403). Bloomington: Indiana University Press.

Freud, S. (1955). The aetiology of hysteria. In J. Strachey (Ed. & Trans.), *The standard edition of the complete psychological works of Sigmund Freud* (Vol. 3, pp. 146–158). London: Hogarth. (Originally published 1896.)

Freyd, J. (1996). *Betrayal trauma.* Cambridge, MA: Harvard University Press.

Laumann, E. O., Ellingson, S., Mahay, J., Paik, A., & Youm, Y. (2003). *Sex in the city: The structure of sexual markets and sexual relationships in an urban setting.* Chicago: University of Chicago Press.

Laumann, E. O., Gagnon, J. H., Michael, R. T., & Michaels, S. (2000). *The social organization of sexuality: Sexual practices in the United States.* Chicago: University of Chicago Press. (Originally published 1994).

Laumann, E. O., Paik, A., & Rosen, R. (1999). Sexual dysfunction in the United States: Prevalence and predictors. *Journal of the American Medical Association, 281,* 537–544.

Laumann, E. O., Paik, A., & Rosen, R. (2001). Sexual dysfunctions in the United States: Prevalence and predictors. In E. O. Laumann & R. T. Michael (Eds.), *Sex, love, and health in America: Private choices and public policies* (pp. 352–376). Chicago: University of Chicago Press.

McCutcheon, A. L. (1987). *Latent class analysis.* Newbury Park, CA: Sage.

Russell, D. E. H. (1986). *The secret trauma: Incest in the lives of girls and women.* New York: Basic.

Waite, L. J., & Joyner, K. (2001). Emotional and physical satisfaction with sex in married, cohabiting, and dating sexual unions: Do men and women differ? In E. O. Laumann & R. T. Michael (Eds.), *Sex, love, and health in America: Private choices and public policies* (pp. 239–269). Chicago: University of Chicago Press.

Williams, L. M. (1994). Recall of childhood trauma: A prospective study of women's memories of child sexual abuse. *Journal of Consulting and Clinical Psychology, 62,* 1167–1176.

Childhood/Adolescent Sexual Coercion among Men Who Have Sex with Men

Understanding Patterns of Sexual Behavior and Sexual Risk

JAY P. PAUL, JOSEPH A. CATANIA, AND
LANCE M. POLLACK

Our previous research has confirmed that the prevalence of childhood sexual coercion among men who have sex with men is far higher than among the general male population (Jinich et al., 1998; Paul, Catania, Pollack, & Stall, 2001). Given the linkages between this and numerous long-term health-related consequences, it is important to improve our understanding of this phenomenon. Multiple studies have shown a strong relationship between a history of what is generally referred to as "childhood sexual abuse" (CSA) and high-risk sexual behavior in adulthood for both females (e.g., Choi, Binson, Adelson, & Catania, 1998; Johnsen & Harlow, 1996; Parillo, Freeman, Collier, & Young, 2001; Whitmire, Harlow, Quina, & Morokoff, 1999; Zierler et al., 1991) and males (e.g., Bartholow et al., 1994; Carballo-Diéguez & Dolezal, 1995; Doll et al., 1992; Jinich et al., 1998; Lenderking et al., 1997; Paul et al., 2001). The broader linkages between childhood sexual experience and adult sexual behavior are far from clear, however, and reflect differences in methodologies, including disparate sources of study samples, divergent definitions of childhood sexual abuse, and variations in sexual outcome variables of interest to different researchers. They also reflect the difficulties inherent in attempting to identify developmental sequelae between a variable set of childhood experiences whose impact may be mediated or moderated by other situational/environmental factors (e.g., family functioning, subsequent help-seeking) and which yield such diverse symptom profiles among the affected children (Beitchman, Zucker, Hood, DaCosta, & Akman, 1991; Kendall-Tackett, Williams, & Finkelhor, 1993) and adults followed at diverse intervals subsequent to the victimization (Beitchman et al., 1992; Lipovsky & Kilpatrick, 1992; Rind, Tromovitch, & Bauserman, 1998; Romans, Martin, Anderson, O'Shea, & Mullen, 1995). Furthermore, the individual is not a passive recipient of these experiences; how these victimization experiences are cognitively processed may result in considerably different outcomes. Although Kendall-Tackett et al. (1993) acknowledge that no specific pattern of symptoms was found in a majority of the samples of abused children from the 45 studies they reviewed, they did find higher rates of PTSD and sexualized behavior among "sexually abused" children than nonabused children. Furthermore, the strongest effect sizes found were for acting-out behaviors, such as sexualized behaviors and aggression. Among adults, a variety of long-term sequelae in the area of sexuality (e.g., sexual dysfunction/dissatisfaction) have been reported, but these have primarily been with female samples (Beitchman et al., 1992; Mullen, Martin, Anderson, Romans, & Herbison, 1994).

This paper focuses on how early sexual coercion differentiates some of the patterns of sexual behavior among men who have sex with men (MSM), to better understand these findings of elevated sexual risk. It is important to gain a greater insight into the ways in which these developmental traumas may influence current sexual risk behavior, as research findings suggest that such variables can help to explain a substantial amount of variance in HIV risk behavior (Stiffman, Dore, Cunningham, & Earls, 1995).

Gender and Childhood Sexual Abuse

Males remain an under-studied population with respect to the two principal types of studies of childhood sexual abuse: those drawing upon clinical samples of victimized children, and those relying upon retrospective reporting of victimization to determine long-term effects of such experiences. Inconsistencies in research findings suggest that a great deal is yet to be clarified with respect to how gender differentially influences CSA experiences and their aftermath for victims. Finkelhor (1994) noted, "The clinical literature observes that boys are more likely than girls to act out in aggressive and antisocial ways as a result of abuse. Boys are also seen as having more concerns about gender role and sexual orientation because both victimization in general and homosexual victimization in particular are so stigmatizing to males. Although these observations may be accurate, outcome studies have actually had difficulty demonstrating consistent differences in symptomatology between abused boys and girls or men and women" (p. 47).

Gender may influence the specific characteristics identified as influencing the severity of impact of these victimization experiences (e.g., the presence of penetration, the closeness of the relationship between perpetrator and victim, the duration and frequency of an ongoing victimization relationship, the degree of threat/force involved, the age of the child victim; see Friedrich, Beilke, & Urquiza, 1988; Kendall-Tackett et al., 1993), and these effects also vary with respect to family environment and functioning (Pierce & Pierce, 1985). Gender may also be tied to the ways in which children understand the meanings/implications of these relationships, their patterns of coping with the distressful nature of these experiences (e.g., "externalizing" versus "internalizing" behaviors), and the specific ways in which these experiences impact adult interpersonal and sexual functioning (Homes & Slap, 1998).

We have recently proposed a social learning model of the CSA/sexual risk behavior relationship specific to MSM (Paul et al., 2001). This model integrates prior research findings on the overlap between specific long-term sequelae of CSA and observed correlates of HIV risk behavior (albeit primarily based upon research with heterosexual adult women; e.g., Fergusson & Horwood, 1998; Fergusson, Horwood, & Lynskey, 1996; Miller, 1999; Whitmire et al., 1999), with other empirical findings and theoretical formulations (Browne & Finkelhor, 1986; Catania & Paul, 1999; Hoier et al., 1992). In the proposed model, relationships are hypothesized between CSA and emotional, cognitive, and interpersonal outcomes that impact directly or indirectly upon two key components of HIV sexual risk-taking models (Catania, Kegeles, & Coates, 1990; Fisher & Fisher, 1992): the appraisal of potential risk, and the capacity to enact behaviors necessary to reduce risk. The proposed mediators of this CSA/risk behavior process include motivational factors (e.g., social motives, including need for social acceptance; sexual feelings; sexual impulse control; dysphoric states), coping strategies (in particular, escape/ avoidance coping), maladaptive risk appraisal processes, poor interpersonal regulatory abilities, and learned sexual scripts (involving dominant and submissive roles). This mediational model proposes a variety of pathways whereby key behavioral, cognitive, and emotional patterns are related to sexual risk, and incorporates a number of theoretical considerations with respect to CSA. Consistent with Hoier and her colleagues (1992), we focus on those more severe CSA experiences that are painful on many levels (e.g., physiological, psychological, emotional), in which fight-or-flight responses are aroused under conditions that deter physical escape or effective avoidance, and in which the victim may have been punished for attempts to change or evade the situation. The adaptations that the individual makes to these experiences can later be problematic in adult social and sexual adjustment. The severity and nature of these long-term outcomes of CSA-related trauma may vary tremendously, presumably reflecting the severity and characteristics of the CSA experience (Johnson, Pike, & Chard, 2001). The model that we have proposed does not exclude the potential for a concurrent effect consistent with the life course perspective articulated by Browning and Laumann (2003).

Preexisting CSA/sexual risk models based upon samples of women may be less meaningful when applied to men, due to the potential impact of gender-specific patterns and roles (e.g., compliance vs. resistance, passivity vs. activity, internalized vs. externalized patterns of distress). Reports suggest some differential responses to CSA by gender. CSA has been related to higher levels of eroticism, lower levels of sexual anxiety, and more sexualized behaviors among male victims of CSA than among female victims (Feiring, Taska, & Lewis, 1999; Watkins & Bentovim, 1992). A repeatedly reproduced finding is that males who have been sexually abused are more apt than their female counterparts to exhibit aggressive, hostile behavior (Watkins & Bentovim, 1992), and to victimize others—which may be a consequence of coping with the trauma by identifying with the aggressor (Becker, Cunningham-Rathner, & Kaplan, 1987; Burgess, Hazlewood, Rokous, Hartman, & Burgess, 1988; Carmen, Rieker, & Mills, 1984; Groth, 1979; Stevenson & Gajarsky, 1991) or related to patterns of coping with stress (Marshall, Serran, & Cortoni, 2000). In a chart review of 449 cases involving CSA, McClellan and colleagues (1996) found "sexually inappropriate behaviors" were similarly elevated for both males and females, but found gender differences in the patterns of sexual behavior: Females showed somewhat higher rates of hypersexual behaviors, while males showed markedly higher rates of victimizing behaviors. Gender differences have also been found with respect to the influence of CSA on sexual attitudes, experiences, satisfaction, and frequency (Meston, Heiman, & Trapnell, 1999). With some exceptions (e.g., Laumann, Paik, & Rosen, 1999), there does not seem to be a clear association between CSA and adult sexual dysfunction in males, although findings supporting such a link appear to be more robust for women (Kinzl, Mangweth, Traweger, & Biebl, 1996; Sarwer, Crawford, & Durlak, 1997).

This paper examines several questions, using some data from the Urban Men's Health Study (UMHS). First, we evaluate our overall strategy of operationalizing childhood sexual victimization, by comparing responses of respondents for our initial items on feeling forced or frightened into sex. Second, we describe differences in patterns of CSA experiences reported by age of onset in this sample of MSM. Finally, we attempt to explore two key aspects of this model for MSM who have been sexually victimized: (a) the manner in which CSA experiences may shape a victim's subsequent sexuality and sexual relationships, and (b) the ways in which the distressing nature of CSA and the relative powerlessness of the child in this situation can result in an overreliance on particular escape/avoidance strategies (possibly due to an overgeneralized learned response, e.g., "learned helplessness," see Abramson, Seligman, & Teasdale, 1978; Seligman, 1971). We are constrained by the limitations of our data to focus on substance use (in general, and in association with sexual activity) as a general marker for dissociative and other escape/avoidance strategies.

How do we anticipate that CSA experiences will influence sexual behavior? CSA is unique among other traumatic experiences in that it can directly shape patterns of sexual behavior and relationships. The distortions this may introduce are one of the key aspects of "traumatic sexualization" in CSA models (Browne & Finkelhor, 1986). Much of prior research has tended to focus on signs of "hypersexuality," including more sexualized behavior, a greater frequency of sexual encounters, and a greater number of sexual partners. Some have described the higher number of sexual partners among those with CSA histories than among the non-victimized as a sign of "compulsive" behavior (Dimock, 1988; Krug, 1989; for MSM, see Jinich et al., 1998). While "promiscuity" is a value-laden term whose subjective meaning is not always clear, studies of adult CSA survivors have described sexual promiscuity in clinical terms as a compulsive behavior motivated by anxiety and other disturbing emotions, which is reinforced by outcomes such as orgasm-related tension reduction (e.g., see Timms & Connors, 1992). This may be related to a greater emphasis on the sexual as a defining element of self, to a broader sense of the self as an object for others' gratification (with sexual behavior conceptualized as a "commodity" to get attention or meet nonsexual interpersonal needs), or to the reinforcement provided by childhood sexual experiences for the function of sexual behavior as a mechanism of relief/soothing. Elevated numbers of sexual partnerships among those with CSA experiences may also be a consequence of other CSA-related outcomes that may inhibit the development of long-term relationships (e.g., impaired interpersonal trust and attachment capacities). This is one arena where there are clear parallels between the description of the "sexual trajectory" in the life course model suggested by Browning and Laumann (2003) and traumagenic models. CSA is likely to disrupt the normative developmental process in which an individual synthesizes a coherent self-schema out of many disparate aspects of self and sexuality, learning how to "integrate personal desires into interpersonal contexts" (Bukowski, 1992, p. 278). This may be an especially critical concern for MSM, who must navigate the process of coming to terms with a stigmatized sexuality and identity—and must do so with less cultural and immediate social support than is available to most heterosexual men and women.

A CSA history may not only influence the frequency of sexual behavior, but may shape the adoption of specific sexual behaviors and sexual relationship dynamics. Males with a CSA history may directly learn from the sexually aggressive behavior and limited impulse control modeled by their predators, and subsequently display similar patterns of emotional response, sexual objectification, and predatory behavior in their adult sexual relationships. Research suggests that male CSA survivors are more likely to sexually victimize others (Becker et al., 1987; Burgess et al., 1988; Carmen et al., 1984; Groth, 1979; Stevenson & Gajarsky, 1991). Some view this as a means of reasserting control in situations that re-evoke feelings of helplessness generated by early CSA experiences, but a more parsimonious explanation may simply be that we are dealing with learned associations between power and eroticism. This association of the erotic with power may also influence the types of sexual behaviors in which these men engage (beyond simply those that are viewed as "high risk"). The UMHS dataset does permit some examination of the likelihood that power disparities in sexual relationships will be eroticized. In contrast to those men who might be said to imitate the behavior of their victimizers, the behavior and sexual relationships of other males with CSA histories may be shaped by a history of rewards for compliance in the face of aggression, reinforcing more passive, submissive responses. Both long-term patterns, of aggression or passivity in sexual encounters, may result in the establishment of rigid, invariant sexual scripts that promote sexual risk-taking.

As suggested by the above, CSA histories may be linked to problematic sexual partner selection in adulthood. Adult CSA survivors may be attracted to partners with "high-risk" psychological characteristics that are familiar to the victim and satisfy certain needs that arise from the CSA-perpetrator relationship. Those whose CSA experiences provide a template for later sexual and intimate relationships (with similarly skewed power dynamics) may attract (and be attracted to) men who are less empathic and more focused on self-gratification, which in extreme situations may extend to physical brutality, including forced sex (i.e., adult sexual "revictimization"; see, for example, Muehlenhard, Highby, Lee, Bryan, & Dodrill, 1998).

As noted earlier, overreliance upon escape/avoidance coping strategies —as a product of CSA experiences—may influence sexual behaviors, particularly risk-taking. While they are relatively primitive coping strategies, the ongoing practice of dissociative processes and substance use may be a consequence of their learned utility in managing the emotional distress of CSA experiences (Chu & Dill, 1990; Miller, 1999), as well as CSA-related long-term negative outcomes (e.g., anxiety, depression, impaired interpersonal functioning). Dissociation, or compartmentalizing aspects of one's conscious experience, allows one to achieve psychological or emotional distance from an experience that may not be possible to avoid physically. There are at least two key reasons why this is potentially dangerous. First, dissociative mechanisms have also been suggested as mediating between physical victimization in childhood and the potential for victimizing others (Narang & Contreras, 2000), and it is possible that this process also facilitates enacting the role of victimizer in adult sexual encounters. Second, this coping style reduces attention to danger cues, thereby impairing accurate risk appraisal and inhibiting self-regulatory processes needed for negotiating and enacting safer sexual practices. Substance use has been noted both as an outcome of CSA (Miller, 1999; Molnar, Buka, & Kessler, 2001; Stein, Golding, Siegel, Burnam, & Sorenson, 1988), and as a correlate of sexual risk-taking (e.g., Beltran, Ostrow, & Joseph, 1993; Ekstrand & Coates, 1990; Kelly et al., 1991; McKirnan, Ostrow, & Hope, 1996; Stall, Coates, & Hoff, 1988). As a behavioral escape/avoidance coping strategy, substance use may lead to high-risk sex by undermining interpersonal regulatory abilities that prevent unsafe sex, by reducing perceptions of risk or concerns about safety, or by facilitating sensation-seeking.

Our empirical exploration of these issues is constrained by the original purpose of the study, which was a broad-based general health assessment of MSM, rather than research specifically developed to allow an in-depth examination of the impact of childhood sexual victimization. Thus, our analyses utilize proxy variables that suggest but do not fully test these proposed relationships. In the current paper, we examine several substance use variables, including alcohol/drug use during sex, sexual partnerships (including "one-night stands"), and recent abusive relationships. These variables are believed to reflect underlying factors that mediate the link between CSA and sexual risk-taking in our hypotheses. There is evidence of the importance of disentangling the effects of CSA from the effects of aspects of the family environment (Beitchman et al., 1991; Boney-McCoy & Finkelhor, 1996; Fergusson & Horwood, 1998; Schaaf & McCanne, 1998), but given the sexual focus of our current analyses and the findings of independent effects of CSA and other adverse familial experiences in our previous analyses (Paul et al., 2001), we do not include these variables in this paper.

Methods

Sample

The data reported here come from the Urban Men's Health Study, a household probability-based sample of men who have sex with men (MSM)[1] in four United States cities (San Francisco, Los Angeles, New York, and Chicago). As it is less threatening for men to be asked about their behavior in the remote past than to be asked about current behaviors (Catania et al., 1990), a broad behavioral inclusion criterion (in terms of age when sex occurred with another man) was used to increase response rates. Disproportionate sampling (Kalton, 1993; heavier sampling of telephone exchanges of high MSM-density areas than those of lower MSM-density areas) and adaptive sampling techniques (Blair, 1999; release of sample is influenced by prior screening interview data identifying exchanges most likely to yield MSM-eligible households) were used to construct a random digit–dial (RDD) sample in each city. The strategies employed were congruent with guidelines previously suggested for generating representative samples of hard-to-reach populations for HIV studies (Fowler, 1989). All data presented in this paper are weighted to reflect probability of selection, adjusted for noncoverage and nonresponse, as well as to maintain proportionality between cities according to each city's estimated total MSM population.

Procedures

After presurvey community awareness efforts (publicity and public meetings), computer-assisted telephone interviewing (CATI) was used to successively determine (a) if households were within selected ZIP codes,

(b) if a male 18 or older resided there, and (c) if one such male was an MSM (using an adult male household resident to determine this last piece of information). A total of 2,881 interviews with MSM were completed, either in English or Spanish (yielding a 78% participation rate of "eligible" households, N = 3,700) between November 1996 and February 1998.

Measures

This study utilized standardized measures, items developed to fit specific study topics, and measures revised to suit the population or needs of the survey. Field-testing of measures followed established procedures, combining qualitative and quantitative methods of evaluating problematic items for respondents or interviewers (Cannell, Oksenberg, Kalton, Bischoping, & Fowler, 1989). Although this survey instrument was not developed solely to examine issues related to childhood sexual abuse, its breadth permitted the identification of indicators of many possibly pertinent long-term sequelae of such abuse (e.g., self-destructive behavior, problematic substance use, disturbed/distorted relationship patterns).

Dependent Variables

Early Sexual Abuse. CSA rates reported across various studies are strongly influenced by operational definitions of CSA (Finkelhor, 1994; Fromuth & Burkhart, 1987; Haugaard & Emery, 1989; Roosa, Reyes, Reinholtz, & Angelini, 1998; Watkins & Bentovim, 1992). There are a number of factors that differentiate such operationalizations. First, CSA definitions vary with respect to whether one is talking about adolescent as well as childhood sexual abuse (with upper age ranges varying from 12 to 18). Second, operationalizations differ with respect to how coercion is assessed: either directly (e.g., general self-report or more specific descriptions of the actions the perpetrator took to pressure the respondent into sex), or by inferred power inequities within a sexual dyad (e.g., based upon age differences or status/role differences, such as between a parental figure and a child). Third, these definitions may include a varying range of sexual activities (some of which may not involve any contact between the "assailant" and the "victim"). Fourth, CSA may be measured as a dichotomous or categorical variable based upon degree. In addition, concern has been raised about the accuracy of adult retrospective accounts of such reports of victimization (Widom & Morris, 1997).

As it appears that the cognitive appraisal of the sexual experience (as abusive/coercive or not) among males can have a significant effect on the impact of that event (Fondacaro, Holt, & Powell, 1999), we felt it was best to utilize an operationalization of CSA that explicitly asked respondents to judge whether such sexual experiences were coercive. Self-presentation bias may make it more difficult for males to disclose victimization, and in some circumstances, it may be difficult to pinpoint the manner of coercion.

However, our prior work[2] suggested that this would be preferable in this population to basing the definition of CSA on more conventional age differentials. Noncoercive sexual experiences with older males may conceivably be experienced as positive by some youth, given the sense of isolation typical in early gay identity development and socialization, and the fact that sex provides a means of bonding with other MSM. Thus, our inquiries focused on self-reported coercive sexual episodes ("Thinking back from your childhood to the present, have you ever been forced or frightened by someone into doing something sexually that you did not want to do?"). Respondents who answered in the negative were queried again ("Sometimes people's views about their experiences change over time. Did you ever have an experience when you felt at the time that you were forced or frightened into doing something sexually that you did not want to do?"). Given the sensitivity of the material, it was thought that this might capture some respondents whose first response would be to avoid any self-disclosure on this topic. We discuss the effect of using this series of questions in the Results.

Respondents who responded affirmatively were asked for the number of sexual coercion experiences, the number of perpetrators, and detailed information about experiences with the first and last (if multiple) coercive partner(s). Information gathered on a respondent's first or only coercive relationship included the respondent's and perpetrator's ages at the time of the initial victimization, whether this abuse was a single or repeated event, the period of time over which the abuse occurred, the perpetrator's relationship to the respondent, the type of coercion used (e.g., physical force or weapons, threats of physical force, or other kinds of pressure), the sexual activities involved (particularly whether penetrative sexual acts occurred), and the subjective level of distress about this experience (both at the time and in retrospect). For the purpose of initial comparisons, subjects were categorized as "never coerced," "sexually coerced before age 7," "sexually coerced between the ages of 7 and 12," or "sexually coerced between ages 13 and 17." Those who were sexually coerced only after age 17 (such coercion is hereafter referred to as "adult sexual victimization") were excluded from comparisons of the never-coerced and those coerced in childhood/adolescence. These age categories are based upon the groupings used in the review by Kendall-Tackett et al. (1993), which noted differences in symptoms for different age groups of sexually victimized children.

Independent Variables

Demographic Variables. Variables included race/ethnicity (multiethnic respondents were assigned to the lowest-prevalence category they reported), age (grouped by decade), formal educational attainment, employment status (working full-time, working part-time, or not working—e.g., disabled, unemployed, retired), household income (categorized by $20,000 increments), self-defined sexual orientation (gay/homosexual, heterosexual, bisexual, or other—e.g., "don't use labels," "inactive") and self-reported HIV status. Standardized assessment procedures came from both general population surveys and prior work with this population.

Number and Type of Male Sexual Partners. Respondents were asked how many male sexual partners they had had in the previous 12 months and how many of these men they had sex with only once (colloquially, "one-night stands"). The distribution of both these variables was extremely skewed, leading to their transformation into categorical variables. Number of male sexual partners was categorized as one of five values (0, 1, 2–3, 4–10, 11 or more). Number of one-night stands was dichotomized as none vs. one or more, as almost half of the respondents reported no one-night stands.

Sexual Behaviors. Global items asked about numbers of partners with whom respondents had engaged in a variety of sexual activities (performing/ receiving oral sex with a man, receptive/insertive anal intercourse, anal/ oral sex, fisting, use of sex toys/dildos with a man, bondage/discipline or S/M sexual activities). These were treated as dichotomous variables (respondents were categorized as having or not having engaged in each activity). In addition, the variety of a respondent's repertoire was measured by adding up the number of behaviors reported (categorized as none, 1–3 behaviors, 4–5 behaviors, 6–8 behaviors). This measure follows Kippax and her colleagues' reports (1998) that HIV seroconversion could be predicted by what they described as "cultures of sexual adventurism"—a set of practices linked with particular forms of gay community participation— which were associated with drug use, more esoteric sexual practices, and use of varied sexual venues.

Sexual Risk-Taking. Sexual behavior in the prior 12 months was measured primarily in two ways. "Global" items asked about the number of partners with whom respondents engaged in various sexual activities (e.g., receptive anal intercourse to ejaculation without a condom, receptive anal intercourse with a condom). "Partner-specific" items asked about sexual acts occurring with each of up to four of their last sexual partners in the given time window. These led to the creation of two dichotomized operationalizations of sexual risk. Using the global measures, if respondents either (a) reported any unprotected anal sexual behavior (e.g., unprotected insertive or receptive anal intercourse, either to ejaculation or with withdrawal) and did not have a primary partner, or (b) reported any specific unprotected anal sex activity with more than one partner, they were considered to have engaged in "non–primary partner sexual risk." The partner-by-partner assessment permitted a second measure of sexual risk-taking, based upon the HIV seroconcordance/discordance of sexual dyads as well as sexual behavior. "Serodiscordant sexual risk" was defined differently, based upon the respondent's HIV serostatus. If HIV-positive, it involved reporting unprotected insertive anal intercourse with an HIV-negative or serostatus-unknown male partner. If HIV-negative, it meant engaging in unprotected receptive anal intercourse with an HIV-positive or serostatus-unknown male partner. These two operationalizations of sexual risk behavior each have their own advantages and disadvantages. The first, based on global measures of sexual risk without adjusting for the seroconcordance or serodiscordance of the partners, may yield a higher rate of false positives. The second, while sensitive to HIV serostatus, is confined to behavior with no more than the most recent four male partners, and may yield a higher rate of false negatives.

Substance Use. Respondents were asked about frequency of use of alcohol, and typical quantity of alcohol used on each such occasion. "Heavy/frequent alcohol users" were those who reported at least five alcoholic beverages per drinking occasion, occurring at least on a weekly basis, after Cahalan (1970). Drinking problems were dichotomized between those who reported less than three and those who reported at least three of six drinking problems, derived from Cahalan (1970) (fear of dependence on alcohol, needing to have a few drinks to change a mood, loss of control once drinking starts, drinking to relieve a hangover, conflicts with a lover or close friend due to drinking, loss of a job due to drinking). Use of 11 categories of drugs (e.g., marijuana, psychedelics, cocaine, amphetamines) was summarized by total number of drugs reported and rate of use of the most frequently reported drug. Measures were derived of proportion of anal intercourse "under the influence," based upon two items in the partner-by-partner assessment of sexual behavior (frequency of anal sex under the influence of alcohol, and under the influence of other drugs, within the prior 12 months). Response categories were assigned numerical values (never = 0, sometimes = .25, about half the time = .50, almost all the time = .75, every time = 1); these values were then multiplied by the frequency of anal intercourse with a given partner, yielding a measure of the frequency of anal sex under the influence with that partner. These values for all assessed male non–primary partners (up to four) were summed, and divided by the frequency of anal intercourse summed across these male partners. The majority of respondents reported no anal sex under the influence with a secondary partner (alcohol: 76%; drugs: 83%), due, in large part, to these respondents' reporting either no secondary partners or no anal intercourse with secondary partners. Approximately 10% of men reported 40% or more of their anal sexual encounters with nonprimary male partners being "under the influence" of alcohol and approximately 10% were under the influence of drugs 40% of the time or more. These two proportions (for anal sex under the influence of alcohol and for anal sex under the influence of drugs) were dichotomized into "infrequent" (less than 40%) and "frequent" (40% or more).

Depression. Depressive symptoms were assessed with the Center for

Epidemiologic Studies–Depression (CES-D) scale (Radloff, 1977). This measure was dichotomized in analyses, using the conventional cut-off score of 16 or above as indicative of being "depressed."

Abusive Relationships. Twelve items asked about having been the recipient of "unwanted physical or emotional violence" in an intimate relationship over the prior five years (e.g., being hit "with fists or an open hand," "verbally threatened," "pushed or shoved"). For the purposes of this analysis, a dichotomous variable was defined that identified whether or not a respondent reported two or more of these experiences. This was treated as a marker for potential disturbances in intimate relationships. In addition, one item from this series, which specifically focused on being forced by a boyfriend to have sex, was used as a measure of recent adult sexual revictimization.

Data Analyses

To answer the first question of the analysis, we examined those who reported having been sexually victimized in childhood or adolescence, comparing those who responded with an affirmative to the first question in this series (as to whether they had ever been forced or frightened into doing something sexually that they did not want to do) with those who initially responded negatively, but when asked again, responded affirmatively. This was examined against both demographic variables and a variety of variables detailing the CSA experiences of the respondent. As these were all categorical variables, we utilized the χ^2 statistic in these univariate analyses. To explore how sexual victimization experiences differ by age of onset (using the three age categories), we again used the χ^2 statistic. Univariate analyses examining sexual behaviors and potential mediating behaviors to sexual risk (e.g., substance use) also utilized the χ^2 statistic. All data were weighted to deal with the likelihood of noncoverage and nonresponse.

Results

Approximately 19% of the total number of men reporting sexual coercion at any point in their lifetime answered in the negative when initially queried; when focusing solely on those who reported their first experiences before age 18, that number drops to approximately 10%. Answering affirmatively on the second rather than the first query was not associated with any demographic variables, but it was associated with particulars of respondents' initial childhood/adolescent victimization experience. As might be expected (see Table 1), those whose coercive experiences were in adolescence, who reported being less distressed by the incidents, who were coerced only once or for a brief period of time, whose victimizer was not a family member, or who did not feel threatened with immediate bodily harm were more likely to answer affirmatively only on the repeated question. However, over 19% of the men who initially answered "no" and then answered "yes" reported that their compliance was gained through the use of either physical force or weapons (an additional 7.7% reported threats of violence), over 45% reported being coerced by more than one individual, approximately one-third had been coerced by their victimizer more than once, and over 44% reported being moderately or extremely upset at the time of the coercive experience, suggesting that such additional queries are important to gain a reliable estimate of the prevalence of coerced sex. Disclosure patterns are correlated with current sense of distress over the incident(s): Over 60% who only responded to the repeat question (versus one-quarter of those who gave affirmative response the first time) reported their experiences with their initial assailant as currently being "not at all upsetting."

The prevalence of any childhood/adolescent sexual abuse was estimated to be 20.6% (95% confidence interval [CI] = 18.8%, 22.5%). In this sample, 4.1% reported an initial occurrence of CSA prior to age 7, 8.9% reported an initial occurrence between ages 7 and 12, and 7.6% reported an initial occurrence between ages 13 and 17. Another 14.7% (95% CI = 13.1%, 16.6%) reported adult sexual victimization (age 18 or older), and 64.7% (95% CI = 62.4%, 66.9%) reported no sexual coercion experiences.

Over half of the victimized men reported being sexually victimized by more than one person. Perpetrators were typically male, and although not likely to be family members (17.7% were in the victim's immediate family; 31.9% were at least members of the victim's extended family), they were unlikely to be strangers to their victims. More than half the respondents reported multiple victimization experiences, and those experiences involved more than one occasion. Over 27% reported an initial CSA relationship that extended for one year or more. Initial coercive experiences involved a high degree of physical threat (over two-fifths involved the use of weapons or physical force), as well as a high proportion of penetrative sex (with almost half involving attempted or actual anal intercourse). Respondents reported overwhelmingly that the initial CSA experience was "moderately" or "extremely" upsetting at the time, and approximately half reported these events to still be extremely or moderately upsetting.

Men who reported CSA were different with respect to several demographic characteristics from men who were never sexually victimized. Those reporting CSA (when compared to the never-coerced) were less likely to be white (73% vs. 82%) or Asian/Pacific Islander (1% vs. 4%), and more likely to have lower levels of formal education (38% vs. 26% with less than a college degree) and lower levels of household income (48% vs. 35% with an annual household income of $40,000 or less). They were

Table 1. *Initial vs. Belated Acknowledgment of CSA: Differences in Victimization*

	p	Acknowledged When 1st Asked %	Acknowledged Only in Follow-up %
Age at time of initial sexual victimization	.001		
0–6 years old		21.1	13.2
7–12 years old		44.8	26.4
13–17 years old		34.2	60.4
Number of times forced/frightened into sex	.0015		
Once		28.5	51.9
Twice		23.1	25.0
3–5 times		25.8	15.4
6 or more times		22.7	7.7
Maximum force used by initial perpetrator(s)	.00001		
Weapons or physical force		45.7	19.2
Threats of harm		9.2	7.7
Other pressure exerted		28.4	26.9
Type of pressure not clear		16.7	46.2
Duration of victimization by initial perpetrator(s)	.0003		
Once		43.5	67.9
Less than 1 year		27.0	26.4
1 year or more		29.5	5.7
Number of assailants	.05		
1		45.2	54.7
2		27.2	34.0
3 or more		27.6	11.3
Age difference between assailant and victim	n.s.		
5 years or less		20.0	31.4
6–15 years		34.1	29.4
16–25 years		26.3	29.4
26 or more years		19.6	9.8

Table 1. *Continued*

	p	Acknowledged When 1st Asked %	Acknowledged Only in Follow-up %
Initial assailant's relationship to respondent	.014		
Family member		33.9	14.8
Nonfamily, known to respondent		41.9	50.0
Stranger		24.2	35.2
Level of distress at time of initial victimization	.002		
Not at all upset/mildly upset		31.7	55.6
Moderately upset		27.7	24.1
Extremely upset		40.6	20.4
Current level of distress about initial victimization	.00001		
Not at all upset		25.8	60.4
Mildly upset		23.6	18.9
Moderately upset		19.8	17.0
Extremely upset		30.8	3.8

also more likely to be younger (23% vs. 20% were less than 30 years old), unemployed (24% vs. 18%), and HIV-positive (24% vs. 14%), and to not self-identify as gay (79% vs. 85%).

Table 2 shows the differences in CSA experiences by age of initial occurrence—thereby illustrating the problems involved in attempting to evaluate the effect of any single characteristic of a CSA history independent of the effects of other CSA variables. As can be seen, very early (up to age 6) CSA experiences were primarily perpetrated by family members, and were likely to be repeated, likely to be of longer duration, likely to involve greater force, unlikely to involve anal intercourse, and likely to be upsetting at the time of interview of the respondent. Experiences beginning in adolescence (age 13–17) were likely to involve a stranger, likely to involve less clear-cut types of coercion, likely to involve anal sex, unlikely to go beyond a single episode, unlikely to be followed by any further victimization experiences, and unlikely to be upsetting at the time of the interview.

Given that this data comes from a survey that was set up to examine a broad array of health issues other than sexual victimization, it was nec-

Table 2. *Characteristics of Sexual Victimization Differing by Age of Onset*

	p	Age 0–6 %	Age 7–12 %	Age 13–17 %
Initial assailant's relationship to respondent	.00001			
Family		51.4	39.8	12.1
Nonfamily, known to respondent		40.4	38.1	49.7
Stranger		8.3	22.1	38.2
Number of assailants	n.s.			
1		55.0	43.3	44.7
2		20.2	27.9	32.3
3 or more		24.8	28.8	23.1
Number of times forced/frightened into sex	.00001			
Once		30.1	24.2	38.4
Twice		11.7	25.1	27.3
3–5 times		29.1	23.4	24.2
6 or more times		29.1	27.3	10.1
Duration of victimization by initial perpetrator(s)	.00001			
1 incident only		29.1	38.8	62.8
Less than 1 year		28.2	23.7	30.2
1 year or more		42.7	37.5	7.0
Maximum force used by initial perpetrator(s)	.05			
Weapons or physical force		48.5	45.0	37.9
Threats of harm		8.7	12.1	5.6
Other pressure exerted		24.3	24.7	34.8
Type of sexual activity in initial victimization	.02			
None specified		2.9	5.7	1.5
Touching/fondling only		23.8	21.1	13.5
Penetrative acts (oral/anal/vaginal)		73.3	73.2	85.0

Table 2. *Continued*

	p	Age 0–6 %	Age 7–12 %	Age 13–17 %
Anal sexual activity in initial victimization	.00001			
None		63.3	62.6	40.5
Attempted anal intercourse		18.3	16.8	16.6
Anal intercourse		18.3	20.6	42.9
Level of distress at time of initial victimization	n.s.			
Not at all upset/mildly upset		39.0	34.9	30.7
Moderately upset		25.0	25.4	30.7
Extremely upset		36.0	39.7	38.7
Current level of distress over initial victimization	.0002			
Not at all upset		18.9	31.2	32.5
Mildly upset		23.6	19.2	27.4
Moderately upset		17.0	17.5	23.4
Extremely upset		40.6	32.1	16.8

essary to derive a measure of CSA severity from a limited set of variables (age at first CSA experience, number of experiences, number of coercive partners, length of the first coercive relationship, manner of coercion or pressure used, identity of coercive partner, and type of sexual acts involved in the initial coercive experience). We examined these potential markers of severity and their interaction effects with respect to a variety of measured adult social and psychological outcome variables that would be anticipated to vary according to level of sexual traumatization (including sexual risk behavior, one-night stands, boyfriend/partner abuse, heavy/frequent alcohol use, multiple drug use, frequent drug use, frequency of sex under the influence of alcohol or illicit drugs, any reported sexual problems, depression, and adult sexual revictimization). Number of CSA occasions (relative to other severity indices) was consistently the most powerful correlate in 9 of 13 CSA-relevant adult outcome regression models examining each of these outcome variables (considering indicator main effects and interactions). Duration of CSA was significant in five models, but was essentially redundant with number of coercion episodes ($r = .66$). Based upon this initial exploration of the data, further analyses used a trichoto-

Table 3. *Potential Mediators of Risk by CSA Severity*

	p	Never Coerced (N = 1753) %	Coerced 1–5 times (N = 440) %	Coerced 6 times (N = 119) %
Any boyfriend abuse in past 5 years?	.00001	31.4	55.5	64.7
Boyfriend coerced/forced sex in past 5 years?	.00001	1.0	9.5	24.4
Maximum frequency of drug use in past 6 months	.00001			
No drugs used		50.7	41.7	38.3
At least one used monthly or less		22.0	20.4	14.2
At least one used less than weekly		11.4	15.6	10.0
At least one used 1+ times a week		16.0	22.1	37.5
Number of drugs used in past 6 months	.00001			
None		50.2	41.6	39.0
1–2		34.4	35.0	28.0
3 or more (maximum: 11)		15.4	23.3	33.1
Alcohol-related problems	.001			
None		36.3	25.1	33.3
1–2		49.1	53.0	51.7
3 or more (maximum: 6)		14.6	21.9	14.9
Heavy/frequent alcohol use[a]	.05	6.5	10.3	8.4
Frequent anal sex under influence of alcohol[b]	.001	8.6	15.6	14.9
Frequent anal sex under influence of drugs[c]	.00001	6.5	12.4	18.4
Depressed (CES-D score 16 or higher)	.00001	24.3	41.6	39.8

[a] Heavy/frequent alcohol use = drinking 5 or more drinks at a time, at least once a week
[b] Frequent anal sex under influence of alcohol = at least 40% of time with secondary partners only
[c] Frequent anal sex under influence of drugs = at least 40% of time with secondary partners only

mous measure of the number of abuse experiences (never, 1–5 times, 6 or more times) as an index of CSA severity. Table 3 shows the effects of this index of CSA severity on a variety of proposed mediators of sexual risk-taking.

Table 4 shows some of the differences found in patterns of sexual activity based upon our operationalization of severity of CSA history. Consistent effects were found, not only in terms of some of the variables presumed to be related to sexual risk, but in terms of broader patterns of sexual behavior. CSA severity was positively correlated with numbers of male sexual partners in the previous year and with the range or repertoire of respondents' sexual activities. This relationship to sexual repertoire is also demonstrated by the statistically significant positive relationships between CSA severity and prevalence of anal-oral sex ("rimming"), fisting, use of sex toys/dildos, and bondage and discipline or S/M activities. We do not see as strong a relationship between CSA severity and receptive anal sex as we find with respect to insertive anal sex. Similarly, when looking at unprotected anal sex, insertive anal intercourse and not receptive anal intercourse with a nonprimary partner was found to be significantly correlated with CSA severity. Both measures of sexual risk-taking— non–primary partner sexual risk and serodiscordant sexual risk—had a strong positive dose relationship to CSA severity. It is not surprising, given these findings, that prevalence of HIV seropositivity was also positively correlated with CSA severity.

Table 5 examines the univariate relationships between potential mediators of the CSA/adult sexual risk-taking relationship and our most rigorous operationalization of risk (serodiscordant partner risk). With respect to sexual variables, number of male sexual partners, engaging in one-night stands, variety of the respondent's sexual repertoire, engaging in anal-oral sex, fisting, and bondage and discipline or S/M activities were positively related to risk-taking. Frequent/heavy alcohol use and number of alcohol-related problems were not linked to sexual risk, although frequency of anal sex under the influence of alcohol was positively associated with risk. All indicators of drug use (frequency of use, number of drugs used, and frequency of anal sex under the influence of drugs) were positively associated with sexual risk. Being in an abusive relationship in the previous five years and having been coerced into sex by a boyfriend were positively associated with serodiscordant partner risk. Depression was not associated with risk-taking.

Discussion

The high prevalence level of childhood sexual abuse (CSA) found among MSM is striking in contrast to prevalences reported for the general male population or adult male heterosexuals (Finkelhor, 1994; Molnar

Table 4. *Sexual Behavior Repertoire and CSA Severity*

	p	Never Coerced (N = 1753) %	Coerced 1–5 times (N = 440) %	Coerced 6+ times (N = 119) %
Number of male sex partners in past year	.00001			
None		13.7	10.7	9.2
1		28.6	24.4	14.3
2–3		16.3	16.9	14.3
4–10		22.7	23.5	21.0
11 or more		18.7	24.6	41.2
Variety of sexual repertoire (past year)	.00001			
No behaviors reported		15.6	11.1	10.2
1–3 behaviors		28.4	23.4	17.8
4–5 behaviors		39.3	38.0	40.7
6–8 behaviors		16.6	27.5	31.4
Sexual activities in the past year*				
Performed oral sex on a male	n.s.	78.3	81.5	83.2
Received oral sex from a male	.05	80.1	84.8	86.4
Receptive anal intercourse	.02	48.1	55.8	53.8
Insertive anal intercourse	.0004	57.7	66.1	73.7
Anal-oral sex (performed/received)	.002	48.8	54.1	63.9
Fisting (performed/received)	.00001	6.0	10.0	16.8

Use of sex toys/dildos with a male	.00001	22.7	30.0	39.0
Bondage/discipline or S/M activities	.00001	13.4	25.2	35.6
Sexual risk variables				
Non–primary partner sexual risk[a]	.00001	11.9	17.0	31.9
Serodiscordant sexual risk[b]	.00001	2.3	4.9	12.6
Unprotected receptive AI (nonprimary)	n.s.	10.3	12.7	14.6
Unprotected insertive AI (nonprimary)	.00001	15.0	21.0	38.5
HIV-positive serostatus	.00001	14.2	21.4	32.5

* Percentages do not sum to 100% because multiple affirmative responses are possible.
[a] Non–primary partner sexual risk = respondent had unprotected insertive or receptive anal intercourse (AI) with a man who was not his primary partner in the past year.
[b] Serodiscordant sexual risk = HIV-positive respondent had unprotected insertive anal intercourse with HIV-negative/sero-unknown partner, or HIV-negative respondent had unprotected receptive anal intercourse with HIV-positive/sero-unknown partner, in past year.

Table 5. *Potential Mediators of CSA/Serodiscordant Partner Risk Relationship*

	p	Serodiscordant Partner Risk	
		No (N = 2652) %	Yes (N = 92) %
Number of male sex partners in past year	.00001		
None		13.7	0
1		27.6	2.2
2–3		17.3	13.0
4–10		22.0	35.9
11 or more		19.4	48.9
One-night stands in past year	.00001	49.8	92.4
Variety of sexual repertoire with male partners	.00001		
No behaviors		15.3	0
1–3 behaviors		26.7	5.4
4–5 behaviors		39.5	48.9
6–8 behaviors		18.6	45.7
Engaged in anal-oral sex in past year?	.00001	49.6	82.6
Performed/received fisting with male in past year?	.00001	6.6	26.1
Bondage/discipline or S/M with male in past year?	.00001	15.8	37.0
Heavy/frequent alcohol use[a]	n.s.	7.8	12.4
Alcohol-related problems	n.s.		
None		34.7	23.5
1–2		49.6	54.4
3 or more (maximum: 6)		15.8	22.1
Maximum frequency of drug use in past 6 months	.001		
No drugs used		48.4	30.3
At least one used monthly or less		21.3	19.1
At least one used less than weekly		12.3	16.9
At least one used 1+ times a week		18.1	33.7

Table 5. *Continued*

| | *p* | Serodiscordant Partner Risk | |
		No (N = 2652) %	Yes (N = 92) %
Number of drugs used in past 6 months	.00001		
None		48.0	30.3
1–2		34.4	29.2
3 or more (maximum: 11)		17.6	40.4
Frequent anal sex under influence of alcohol[b]	.00001	9.9	31.0
Frequent anal sex under influence of drugs[c]	.00001	7.7	26.2
Any boyfriend abuse in past 5 years?	.00001	38.0	61.5
Boyfriend coerced/forced sex in past 5 years?	.00001	4.7	16.5
Depressed (CES-D score 16 or higher)	n.s.	29.3	37.1

[a] Heavy/frequent alcohol use = drinking 5 or more drinks at a time, at least once a week
[b] Frequent anal sex under influence of alcohol = at least 40% of time with secondary partners only
[c] Frequent anal sex under influence of drugs = at least 40% of time with secondary partners only

et al., 2001). Furthermore, the CSA experiences of these men were characterized by high levels of physical force, penetrative sex, and distress; a substantial subgroup also reported multiple assailants and/or coercion over an extended period of time. These characteristics suggest that a large proportion of MSM have encountered potentially traumatizing early sexually coercive experiences. Our initial univariate analyses of affirmative responses to the first versus the follow-up query about coercive sexual experiences suggest that we are dealing with at least two distinct phenomena affecting response patterns. This initial negative response followed by an affirmative response may be indicative of greater ambiguity with respect to whether respondents view themselves as having been coerced into sex. This may involve situations where the manner of coercion or force was less clear-cut, where it was a single event rather than an ongoing experience, or where the respondent did not see it as upsetting. Respondents appear to be more likely to respond to these questions according to their affective response to the events at the time of the interview (rather than the time of the event). Respondents who have managed to achieve some distancing or closure to the event may therefore be less likely to currently report these interactions as unwanted sex. It appears that the additional probe helped to focus them on their subjective experience of the events at the time. On the other hand, we are also dealing with a subset of men for whom the initial negative response may be construed as a reluctance to acknowledge the event in this interview context, despite the distress that may be associated with it (both historically and currently). As our measure of CSA requires a subjective assessment of coercion and/or pressure, it may appear to be less clear-cut than other measures that operationalize such coercion by focusing on the age differential between the participants in a childhood or adolescent sexual encounter. Yet those subjectivities are critical in understanding how this experience is constructed and processed by the child, and directly influence the observed outcomes of such events (Fondacaro et al., 1999).

Age is a key factor in determining the cognitive structures that the child has to make sense of an experience of sexual victimization. Over 60% of men reporting CSA histories report initial experiences beginning prior to age 13. Taking a developmental perspective requires an understanding of not only how the individual contextualizes his experience, but other factors that may be influenced by age. Despite the variability of experiences reported by respondents, modal characteristics of the initial coercive experiences appear to change with age. As the child becomes older, his social world broadens, and his independence from parental supervision grows, he is more likely to be victimized by nonfamilial and unfamiliar persons. The younger a respondent was at initiation of sexual coercion, the more likely it was that this experience involved longer relationships with the assailant and/or was the first of multiple coercive sexual relationships. Although adolescence (ages 13–17) signals a shift to less overt methods of coercion, it also signals a shift to a greater likelihood of penetrative acts being involved in these episodes, especially anal intercourse. While there are no differences in initial emotional distress responses to being coerced into sex by age of first event, there is a clear difference in the current emotional response to these memories, with earlier-onset events being far more distressing. These findings highlight some of the difficulties in utilizing any single characteristic of sexual coercion as a good marker of severity, although our subsequent analyses use the number of abuse experiences as the strongest of such markers, based upon our exploratory analyses. Table 3 shows that there is a clear correspondence between the indicator variable utilized for CSA severity and the effects found for selected potential mediators of adult sexual risk-taking.

An important focus of this paper was on the ways in which early coercive sexual experiences may shape patterns of adult sexual activity. As can be seen from Table 4, our data confirm the relationship found in prior research between CSA and "hypersexuality" in terms of higher numbers of sexual partners. This is likely due to the greater number of transient partners or one-night stands among these male sexual partners. It may be that higher numbers of sexual partners provide more varied sexual encounters, and thus account for the greater range in sexual repertoire for those who have had early coercive sexual experiences. However, this more extensive sexual repertoire may be linked to many other factors in a CSA history, including the undue emphasis that these experiences may place upon sex in one's sense of self, and the direct and indirect rewards that may be accrued by a breadth of range of sexual proficiency. The sexual behaviors that seem to be most strongly linked to CSA severity include both behaviors that focus on penetration (e.g., fisting, use of sex toys/dildos) and those that focus on sexual behavior as a power exchange (bondage/discipline or S/M activities). Sexual acts involving dominance and submission (a broader term that is frequently used within the sexual community that engages in bondage and discipline or S/M acts) typically involve sexual scripts with clearly defined power roles, frequently in conjunction with a variety of fetishized objects (e.g., uniforms, restraints, leather). Further research will be necessary to clarify the specificity of the linkage between adult sexual proclivities and aspects of sexually coercive events; these experiences may shape only a generalized sexual script associating sex and power. While other research has found associations between physical and emotional abuse histories and sexual fantasies, it has not previously found links between sexual abuse and sexual behaviors (Meston et al., 1999). More work is necessary in this area, as well as to extend what is currently a fairly limited research literature on those who participate in bondage and discipline activities.

It is intriguing that the higher prevalence of sexual risk-taking among those who had been sexually coerced in childhood or adolescence appears to be linked to a higher prevalence of unprotected insertive anal intercourse as opposed to unprotected receptive anal intercourse. This suggests a very different dynamic than what has been associated with higher sexual risk among women with a CSA history, and appears to corroborate our notions of the importance of developing gender-specific models of risk. While our current data cannot provide any definitive answers, this finding is at least consistent with the notion that some MSM with sexual abuse histories may come to identify with their aggressor and model the lack of concern for the well-being of their sexual partners shown by their childhood victimizers. We are in the process of further research to test models of sexual risk-taking among those who have CSA histories, and hope to clarify this and other points.

Our last table's findings on the mediators of sexual risk-taking for

MSM with CSA histories illustrate that sexual risk is embedded in a context of high numbers of sexual partnerships, many of which are casual one-night stands, with a higher propensity for these relationships to be ones in which the respondents are victimized physically, psychologically, or sexually. These findings are similar to those found in the broader population of MSM, yet are important because these are factors that we have found to be influenced by a history of early sexual victimization. Sexual risk is also embedded in a pattern of more diverse sexual practices, akin to what Kippax and colleagues (1998) described as a "culture of sexual adventurism." More in-depth research is necessary to draw a clearer understanding of how these sexual practices are linked, although one could suggest several hypotheses. They may be linked only insofar as such "esoteric sexual practices" may be associated with the use of drugs or other mind-altering substances in conjunction with sexual activity, thereby promoting dissociative states, poor judgment or assessment of risk, and inability to regulate what occurs in a sexual encounter. Because one of the traumatic outcomes of childhood sexual victimization is likely to be an increased reliance on dissociation and other escape/avoidance coping strategies, this may make it easier to engage in either sexual risk behavior or these other, less prevalent sexual activities. Such esoteric sexual practices may also be associated with a self-concept as a "sexual outlaw" who is not bound by any rules or conventions; this self-concept may then be incompatible with enacting sexual risk reduction strategies. These sexual practices may also be associated with participation in specific sexual networks in which the norm is to engage in unprotected anal intercourse, as a highly controversial sexual subculture devoted to "bare-backing" has arisen in the gay male community.

Finally, as noted in our findings, substance use is an important factor in shaping the sexual patterns of sexually abused MSM. Substance use has been noted as a coping strategy for dealing with distress associated with such a history. It may also (as noted by Browning & Laumann, 2003) be elevated as a result of early sexualization having led to membership in a deviant or "delinquent" peer group, in which sexual activity, alcohol or drug use, and flouting of rules are the norms. Such men are more likely to have sex under the influence of alcohol or drugs, and those for whom a high proportion of sexual activity is in an altered state are more likely to engage in sexual risk behavior. Sexual risk is also powerfully associated with both variety and frequency of drug use. This may be tied to frequency of sex under the influence, it may be linked to how and where one finds sexual partners, or it may be a proxy measure for a broader set of escape/avoidance strategies which are disruptive to any health-protective actions.

The data from which we are drawing these inferences have their limitations. We are using retrospective accounts in our measures, which may be influenced by many factors, although retrospective reports of both CSA (e.g., Whitmire et al., 1999) and sexual risk (Coates et al., 1988; Saltzman, Stoddard, McCusker, Moon, & Mayer, 1987) have been found to have good reliability and validity. Both the cross-sectional nature of the study and the limitations of univariate analyses mean that we cannot truly disentangle complex relationships between the multiple variables that we are proposing as mediators of sexual risk, our measures of childhood sexual victimization, and our measures of sexual risk behavior. Key variables that might be related to the aftermath of childhood sexual victimization or might mediate sexual risk-taking were not measured. Interpretations of our findings can only be viewed as suggestive, rather than definitive. Our operationalization of CSA may have missed some portion of those who did not see those coercive experiences as having been the result of "force" or being "frightened." Despite this disadvantage, we hope that our operationalization hints at or acknowledges the complexities of both normal and abnormal patterns of childhood sexual development. When we cannot rely on strict age-differentials to define "childhood sexual abuse," we must make some sense of the very personal, subjective constructions of these experiences by the child. This will require a more fine-tuned understanding of the course of healthy sexual development in conjunction with physical maturation and psychological development.

Acknowledgments

Primary support for this study was provided by NIMH/NIA Grant No. MH54320 (PI—Joseph Catania). Supplemental support came from NIMH Grant No. MH42459 (The Center for AIDS Prevention Studies, PI—Thomas Coates).

The random digit–dial (RDD) sample was constructed by the Survey Research Center (SRC) of the University of Maryland, in collaboration with Dr. Graham Kelton at Westat and University of California investigators.

This study would not have been possible without the selfless cooperation of the men who served as project informants and participants in the hope that the knowledge gained would be of benefit to other gay/bisexual men.

Notes

1. "Men who have sex with men" (MSM) were operationally defined by either having had sex with a male since age 14 or self-identification as gay or bisexual.

2. Forty-four percent of gay/bisexual males who had sexual experiences with part-

ners at least 10 years their senior when between the ages of 13 and 15 reported that no coercion was involved (Jinich et al., 1998).

References

Abramson, L., Seligman, M., & Teasdale, J. (1978). Learned helplessness in humans: Critique and reformulation. *Journal of Abnormal Psychology, 87,* 49–74.

Bartholow, B., Doll, L., Joy, D., Douglas, J., Bolan, G., Harrison, J., et al. (1994). Emotional, behavioral, and HIV risks associated with sexual abuse among adult homosexual and bisexual men. *Child Abuse & Neglect, 18,* 747–761.

Becker, J., Cunningham-Rathner, J., & Kaplan, M. (1987). Adolescent sexual offenders: Demographics, criminal and sexual histories, and recommendations for reducing future offenses. *Journal of Interpersonal Violence, 1,* 431–445.

Beitchman, J. H., Zucker, K. J., Hood, J. E., DaCosta, G. A., & Akman, D. (1991). A review of the short-term effects of child sexual abuse. *Child Abuse & Neglect, 15,* 537–556.

Beitchman, J. H., Zucker, K. J., Hood, J. E., DaCosta, G. A., Akman, D., & Cassavia, E. (1992). A review of the long-term effects of child sexual abuse. *Child Abuse & Neglect, 16,* 101–118.

Beltran, E., Ostrow, D., & Joseph, J. (1993). Predictors of sexual behavior change among men requesting their HIV-1 antibody status: The Chicago Macs/Ccs cohort of homosexual/bisexual men, 1985–1986. *AIDS Education and Prevention, 5*(3), 185–195.

Blair, J. (1999). A probability sample of gay urban males: The use of two-phase adaptive sampling. *Journal of Sex Research, 36,* 39–44.

Boney-McCoy, S., & Finkelhor, D. (1996). Is youth victimization related to trauma symptoms and depression after controlling for prior symptoms and family relationships? A longitudinal, prospective study. *Journal of Consulting and Clinical Psychology, 64,* 1406–1416.

Browne, A., & Finkelhor, D. (1986). Impact of child sexual abuse: A review of the literature. *Psychological Bulletin, 99,* 66–77.

Browning, C. R., & Laumann, E. O. (2003). The social context of adaptation to childhood sexual maltreatment: A life course perspective. In J. Bancroft (Ed.), *Sexual development in childhood* (pp. 383–403). Bloomington: Indiana University Press.

Bukowski, W. M. (1992). Sexual abuse and maladjustment considered from the perspective of normal developmental processes. In W. O'Donohue & J. H. Geer (Eds.), *The sexual abuse of children: Vol. 2. Clinical issues* (pp. 100–142). Hillsdale, NJ: Lawrence Erlbaum.

Burgess, A., Hazelwood, R., Rokous, F., Hartman, C., & Burgess, A. (1988). Serial rapists and their victims: Reenactment and repetition. *Annals of the New York Academy of Science, 528,* 277–295.

Cahalan, D. (1970). *Problem drinkers: A national survey.* San Francisco: Jossey-Bass.

Cannell, C., Oksenberg, L., Kalton, G., Bischoping, K., & Fowler, F. (1989). *New techniques for pretesting survey questions* (NCHSR# HS 05616). Ann Arbor, MI: Survey Research Center, University of Michigan.

Carballo-Diéguez, A., & Dolezal, C. (1995). Association between history of childhood sexual abuse and adult HIV-risk sexual behavior in Puerto Rican men who have sex with men. *Child Abuse & Neglect, 19,* 595–605.

Carmen, E., Rieker, P., & Mills, T. (1984). Victims of violence and psychiatric illness. *American Journal of Psychiatry, 141,* 378–383.

Catania, J., Kegeles, S., & Coates, T. (1990). Towards an understanding of risk behavior: An AIDS risk-reduction model (ARRM). *Health Education Quarterly, 17,* 53–72.

Catania, J., & Paul, J. (1999, November). *Sexual development and mental health among men who have sex with men.* Paper presented at the NIH workshop "New Approaches to Research on Sexual Orientation, Mental Health, and Substance Use," Washington, DC.

Choi, K.-H., Binson, D., Adelson, M., & Catania, J. (1998). Sexual harassment, sexual coercion, and HIV risk among U.S. adults 18–49 years. *AIDS and Behavior, 2,* 33–40.

Chu, J., & Dill, D. (1990). Dissociative symptoms in relation to childhood physical and sexual abuse. *American Journal of Psychiatry, 147,* 887–892.

Coates, T., Calavara, L., Soskolne, C., Read, S., Fanning, M., Shepherd, F., et al. (1988). Validity of sexual histories in a prospective study of male sexual contacts of men with AIDS or an AIDS-related condition. *American Journal of Epidemiology, 128,* 719–728.

Dimock, P. (1988). Adult males sexually abused as children: Characteristics and implications for treatment. *Journal of Interpersonal Violence, 3,* 203–221.

Doll, L., Joy, D., Bartholow, B., Harrison, J., Bolan, G., Douglas, J., et al. (1992). Self-reported childhood and adolescent sexual abuse among adult homosexual and bisexual men. *Child Abuse & Neglect, 16,* 855–864.

Ekstrand, M., & Coates, T. (1990). Maintenance of safer sexual behaviors and predictors of risky sex: The San Francisco Men's Health Study. *American Journal of Public Health, 80,* 973–977.

Feiring, C., Taska, L., & Lewis, M. (1999). Age and gender differences in children's and adolescents' adaptation to sexual abuse. *Child Abuse & Neglect, 23,* 115–128.

Fergusson, D., & Horwood, L. J. (1998). Exposure to interparental violence in childhood and psychosocial adjustment in young adulthood. *Child Abuse & Neglect, 22,* 339–357.

Fergusson, D., Horwood, L. J., & Lynskey, M. (1996). Childhood sexual abuse and psychiatric disorder in young adulthood: II. Psychiatric outcomes of childhood sexual abuse. *Journal of the American Academy of Child and Adolescent Psychiatry, 34,* 1365–1374.

Finkelhor, D. (1994). Current information on the scope and nature of child sexual abuse. *Future of Children: Sexual Abuse of Children, 4*(2), 31–53.

Fisher, J., & Fisher, W. (1992). Changing AIDS-risk behavior. *Psychological Bulletin, 111,* 455–474.

Fondacaro, K. M., Holt, J. C., & Powell, T. A. (1999). Psychological impact of childhood sexual abuse on male inmates: The importance of perception. *Child Abuse & Neglect, 23,* 361–369.

Fowler, F. J., Jr. (Ed.). (1989). *Health survey research methods: Conference proceedings.* Washington, DC: National Center for Health Services Research and Health Care Technology Assessment, Public Health Service, HHS.

Friedrich, W. N., Beilke, R. L., & Urquiza, A. J. (1988). Behavior problems in young sexually abused boys: A comparison study. *Journal of Interpersonal Violence, 3,* 21–28.

Fromuth, M., & Burkhart, B. (1987). Childhood sexual victimization among college men: Definitional and methodological issues. *Violence and Victims, 2,* 241–253.

Groth, A. (1979). Sexual trauma in the life histories of rapists and child molesters. *Victimology, 4,* 10–16.

Haugaard, J., & Emery, R. (1989). Methodological issues in child sexual abuse research. *Child Abuse & Neglect, 13,* 89–100.

Hoier, T. S., Shawchuck, C. R., Pallotta, G. M., Freeman, T., Inderbitzen-Pisaruk, H., MacMillan, V. M., et al. (1992). The impact of sexual abuse: A cognitive-behavioral model. In W. O'Donohue & J. H. Geer (Eds.), *The sexual abuse of children: Vol. 2. Clinical issues* (pp. 100–142). Hillsdale, NJ: Lawrence Erlbaum.

Holmes, W. C., & Slap, G. B. (1998). Sexual abuse of boys: Definition, prevalence, correlates, sequelae, and management. *Journal of the American Medical Association, 280,* 1855–1862.

Jinich, S., Paul, J., Stall, R., Acree, M., Kegeles, S., Hoff, C., et al. (1998). Childhood sexual abuse and HIV risk-taking behavior among gay and bisexual men. *AIDS and Behavior, 2,* 41–51.

Johnsen, L. W., & Harlow, L. L. (1996). Childhood sexual abuse linked with adult substance use, victimization, and AIDS-risk. *AIDS Education and Prevention, 8,* 44–57.

Johnson, D. M., Pike, J. L., & Chard, K. M. (2001). Factors predicting PTSD, depression, and dissociative severity in female treatment-seeking childhood sexual abuse survivors. *Child Abuse & Neglect, 25,* 179–198.

Kalton, G. (1993). Sampling considerations in research on HIV risk and illness. In D. G. Ostrow & R. C. Kessler (Eds.), *Methodological issues in AIDS behavioral research* (pp. 53–74). New York: Plenum.

Kelly, J., Kalichman, S., Kauth, M., Kilgore, H., Hood, H., Campos, P., et al. (1991). Situational factors associated with AIDS risk behavior lapses and coping strategies used by gay men who successfully avoid lapses. *American Journal of Public Health, 81,* 1335–1338.

Kendall-Tackett, K. A., Williams, L. M., & Finkelhor, D. (1993). Impact of sexual abuse on children: A review and synthesis of recent empirical studies. *Psychological Bulletin, 113,* 164–180.

Kinzl, J. F., Mangweth, B., Traweger, C., & Biebl, W. (1996). Sexual dysfunction in males: Significance of adverse childhood experiences. *Child Abuse & Neglect, 20,* 759–766.

Kippax, S., Campbell, D., Van de Ven, P., Crawford, J., Prestage, G., Knox, S., et al. (1998). Cultures of sexual adventurism as markers of HIV seroconversion: A case control study in a cohort of Sydney gay men. *AIDS Care, 10,* 677–688.

Krug, R. (1989). Adult male report of childhood sexual abuse by mothers: Case descriptions, motivations, and long-term consequences. *Child Abuse & Neglect, 13,* 111–119.

Laumann, E. O., Paik, A., & Rosen, R. C. (1999). Sexual dysfunction in the United States: Prevalence and predictors. *Journal of the American Medical Association, 281,* 537–544.

Lenderking, W., Wold, C., Mayer, K., Goldstein, R., Losina, E., & Seage, G. (1997).

Childhood sexual abuse among homosexual men: Prevalence and association with unsafe sex. *Journal of General Internal Medicine, 12,* 250–253.

Lipovsky, J. A., & Kilpatrick, D. G. (1992). The child sexual abuse victim as an adult. In W. O'Donohue & J. H. Geer (Eds.), *The sexual abuse of children: Vol. 2. Clinical issues* (pp. 430–476). Hillsdale, NJ: Lawrence Erlbaum.

Marshall, W. L., Serran, G. A., & Cortoni, F. A. (2000). Childhood attachments, sexual abuse, and their relationship to adult coping in child molesters. *Sexual Abuse: A Journal of Research and Treatment, 12,* 17–26.

McClellan, J., McCurry, C., Ronnei, M., Adams, J., Eisner, A., & Storck, M. (1996). Age of onset of sexual abuse: Relationship to sexually inappropriate behaviors. *Journal of the American Academy of Child and Adolescent Psychiatry, 34,* 1375–1383.

McKirnan, D., Ostrow, D., & Hope, B. (1996). Sex, drugs, and escape: A psychological model of HIV-risk sexual behaviors. *AIDS Care, 8,* 655–669.

Meston, C. M., Heiman, J. R., & Trapnell, P. D. (1999). The relation between early abuse and adult sexuality. *Journal of Sex Research, 36,* 385–395.

Miller, M. (1999). A model to explain the relationship between sexual abuse and HIV risk among women. *AIDS Care, 11,* 3–20.

Molnar, B. E., Buka, S. L., & Kessler, R. C. (2001). Child sexual abuse and subsequent psychopathology: Results from the National Comorbidity Survey. *American Journal of Public Health, 91,* 753–760.

Muehlenhard, C., Highby, B., Lee, R., Bryan, T., & Dodrill, W. (1998). The sexual revictimization of women and men sexually abused as children: A review of the literature. In R. Rosen, C. Davis, & H. Ruppel, Jr. (Eds.), *Annual Review of Sex Research, 9,* 177–223. Mt. Vernon, IA: Society for the Scientific Study of Sexuality.

Mullen, P. E., Martin, J. L., Anderson, J. C., Romans, S. E., & Herbison, G. P. (1994). The effect of child sexual abuse on social, interpersonal, and sexual function in adult life. *British Journal of Psychiatry, 165,* 35–47.

Narang, D. S., & Contreras, J. M. (2000). Dissociation as a mediator between child abuse history and adult abuse potential. *Child Abuse & Neglect, 24,* 653–665.

Parillo, K. M., Freeman, R. C., Collier, K., & Young, P. (2001). Association between early sexual abuse and adult HIV-risky sexual behaviors among community-recruited women. *Child Abuse & Neglect, 25,* 335–346.

Paul, J. P., Catania, J., Pollack, L., & Stall, R. (2001). Understanding childhood sexual abuse as a predictor of sexual risk-taking among men who have sex with men: The Urban Men's Health Study. *Child Abuse & Neglect, 25,* 557–584.

Pierce, R., & Pierce, L. H. (1985). The sexually abused child: A comparison of male and female victims. *Child Abuse & Neglect, 9,* 191–199.

Radloff, L. (1977). The CES-D Scale: A self-report depression scale for research in the general population. *Applied Psychological Measurement, 1,* 385–401.

Rind, B., Tromovitch, P., & Bauserman, R. (1998). A meta-analytic examination of assumed properties of child sexual abuse using college samples. *Psychological Bulletin, 124,* 22–53.

Romans, S., Martin, J., Anderson, J., O'Shea, M., & Mullen, P. (1995). Factors that mediate between child sexual abuse and adult psychological outcome. *Psychological Medicine, 25,* 127–142.

Roosa, M. W., Reyes, L., Reinholtz, C., & Angelini, P. J. (1998). Measurement of women's child sexual abuse experiences: An empirical demonstration of the impact of choice of measure on estimates of incidence rates and of relationships with pathology. *Journal of Sex Research, 35*, 225–233.

Saltzman, S., Stoddard, A., McCusker, J., Moon, M., & Mayer, K. (1987). Reliability of self-reported sexual behavior risk factors for HIV infection in homosexual men. *Public Health Reports, 102*, 692–697.

Sarwer, D. B., Crawford, I., & Durlak, J. A. (1997). The relationship between childhood sexual abuse and adult male dysfunction. *Child Abuse & Neglect, 21*, 649–655.

Schaaf, K. K., & McCanne, T. R. (1998). Relationship of childhood sexual, physical, and combined sexual and physical abuse to adult victimization and post-traumatic stress disorder. *Child Abuse & Neglect, 22*, 1119–1133.

Seligman, M. (1971). Phobias and preparedness. *Behavior Therapy, 2*, 307–321.

Stall, R., Coates, T., & Hoff, C. (1988). Behavioral risk reduction for HIV infection among gay and bisexual men: A review of results from the United States. *American Psychologist, 43*, 878–885.

Stein, J., Golding, J., Siegel, J., Burnam, M., & Sorenson, S. (1988). Long-term psychological sequelae of child sexual abuse: The Los Angeles Epidemiological Catchment Area Study. In G. E. Wyatt & G. J. Powell (Eds.), *Lasting effects of child sexual abuse* (pp. 135–154). Newbury Park, CA: Sage.

Stevenson, M., & Gajarsky, W. (1991). Unwanted childhood sexual experiences related to later revictimization and male perpetration. *Journal of Psychology and Human Sexuality, 4*(4), 57–70.

Stiffman, A. R., Dore, P., Cunningham, R. M., & Earls, F. (1995). Person and environment in HIV risk behavior change between adolescence and young adulthood. *Health Education Quarterly, 22*, 211–226.

Timms, R., & Connors, P. (1992). Adult promiscuity following childhood sexual abuse: An introduction. *Psychotherapy Patient, 8*(1–2), 19–27.

Watkins, B., & Bentovim, A. (1992). The sexual abuse of male children and adolescents: A review of current research. *Journal of Child Psychology and Psychiatry, and Allied Disciplines, 33*, 197–248.

Whitmire, L., Harlow, L., Quina, K., & Morokoff, P. (1999). *Childhood trauma and HIV: Women at risk*. Philadelphia: Brunner/Mazel.

Widom, C. S., & Morris, S. (1997). Accuracy of adult recollections of childhood victimization: Part 2. Childhood sexual abuse. *Psychological Assessment, 9*, 34–46.

Zierler, S., Feingold, L., Laufer, D., Velentgas, P., Kantrowitz-Gordon, I., & Mayer, K. (1991). Adult survivors of childhood sexual abuse and subsequent risk of HIV infection. *American Journal of Public Health, 81*, 572–575.

Abusive Sexual Experiences before Age 12 and Adolescent Sexual Behaviors

J. DENNIS FORTENBERRY AND
MATTHEW C. AALSMA

Introduction

A substantial body of research links early, unwanted sexual experiences with risky sexual behaviors during adolescence. These behaviors are risky because of potential sequelae such as sexually transmitted diseases (STD) or unwanted pregnancy. In order to expand understanding of this relationship, we've added four innovations to the study of childhood sexual abuse (CSA): distinction of childhood from adolescent unwanted sexual experiences; multi-item measurement of unwanted experiences; use of cross-time validated measures of unwanted sexual experiences; and use of behavioral outcome measures obtained separately from measures of unwanted sexual experience.

The distinction of childhood from adolescent unwanted sexual experiences is difficult to address in research projects. With increasing age, adolescents may have consensual sexual experiences with older partners. These experiences are generally not considered abusive, although large age differences between sexual partners are related to increased risk for unintended pregnancy and ineffective contraceptive behaviors (Darroch, Landry, & Oslak, 1999). Because of this, distinctions between CSA and consensual sexual experiences need to be made. Research in the area of CSA has addressed this difficulty in several ways. Some CSA research literature uses age to distinguish CSA from consensual adolescent experiences. Finkelhor (1979), for instance, defined sexual experiences with relatives and nonconsensual sexual contacts before the age of 12 as being sexually abusive. Similar age criteria have been adopted by other researchers assessing CSA (Russell, 1983; Wyatt, 1985). Thus, 12 years of age appears to be an appropriate age at which to distinguish between CSA and consensual sexual experiences. However, additional clarification of the distinct roles of CSA and unwanted adolescent sexual experiences is needed.

In general, surveys of adolescent behavior rely upon single-item self-report measures. This measurement approach is limited since sensitive or stigmatized experiences may be substantially misclassified. Given this possibility, some researchers have assessed the reliability of self-reports of behaviors such as timing of initial sexual experiences and lifetime sexual intercourse. The consistency of adolescent self-report of initial sexual experience timing, for example, appears poor (Alexander, Somerfield, Ensminger, Johnson, & Kim, 1993; Capaldi, 1996). In light of this fact, we must consider that self-report of other sensitive experiences, such as CSA, may also be inconsistently reported in adolescent populations. Hence, a goal of this study is to use cross-time validated measures of unwanted sexual experiences to assess the consistency of CSA reporting with adolescents.

The relationship between CSA and emotional, behavioral, and adjustment problems has previously been demonstrated (see Kendall-Tackett, Williams, & Finkelhor, 1997; Luster & Small, 1997). However, the specific mechanisms leading to these outcomes are not clearly understood. One reason for this lack of clarity is likely methodological in nature, given that CSA measurement varies greatly across studies (Briere, 1992; Goldman & Padayachi, 2000; Roosa, Reyes, Reinholtz, & Angelini, 1998). For example, in many self-report questionnaire studies, CSA is measured by a single item (Bensley, Van Eenwyk, Spieker, & Schoder, 1999; Luster & Small, 1997; Thompson, Potter, Sanderson, & Maibach, 1997), which eliminates the possibility of assessing internal reliability. Other studies use more extensive measurement methods, such as clinical interviews or medical/ psychosocial evaluations (Brown, Kessel, Lourie, Ford, & Lipsitt, 1997; Meyer, Muenzenmaier, Cancienne, & Struening, 1996). Using an interview to assess CSA can allow information concerning the duration and nature of the abuse to be gained. However, interviews are time-intensive and their reliability as research tools is poorly evaluated. In sum, studies using brief, multi-item scales to assess CSA are noticeably absent in the research literature.

No methodological research concerning the stability of CSA reporting has been conducted even though researchers have called for data to be collected at more than one time point to assess for developmental differences in symptomatology (Kendall-Tackett et al., 1997). Only one recent study (Costello, Angold, March, & Fairbank, 1998) measured the reliability of CSA reporting across two time points. In this study, 10 participants indicated they had been sexually abused. Two weeks later, 9 participants reported that they had been sexually abused, resulting in a kappa of .81. This study is limited by the small number of subjects who identified a CSA history and the short recall period. Given that this was the only article found in which the reporting of CSA over time was even assessed, the call for methodologically rigorous CSA research (Briere, 1992; Kendall-Tackett et al., 1997) is unanswered.

Self-report consistency at different time points is one measure by which to assess validity (i.e., correct classification as non-CSA or CSA). This method has proved effective in past studies of adolescent self-report consistency (Capaldi, 1996; Alexander et al., 1993). Utilizing two time points is expected to create three distinct groups of CSA reporting: consistent nonreporters (deny CSA at both time points), inconsistent reporters (endorse CSA at one point and deny it at the other), and consistent reporters (endorse CSA at both time points). If the two-time-point approach reduces misclassification (i.e., improves validity), we expect the following: Consistent nonreporters have a lower proportion of persons with a true experience of abuse; inconsistent reporters include persons with true positive and false positive reports; and the consistent CSA-reporting group will contain a larger proportion of true positive reports and a smaller proportion of false positive reports.

If the preceding premise is true, we would then expect problem behaviors associated with CSA to be differentially distributed across the three groups. Specifically, we expect lower levels of problem behaviors among consistent nonreporters, intermediate levels among inconsistent reporters, and higher levels among consistent reporters of CSA. The demonstration of differential problem behavior involvement will provide another measure of validity. Additionally, endorsement of two or more CSA items should be related to an increased likelihood of consistent reporting. Hence, the prediction of consistent and inconsistent CSA reporting will be explored via the number of CSA items endorsed.

A final innovation included in this analysis is the use of separate measurement of CSA reports and reports of some sexual behaviors. Our rationale for this distinction rests on the assumption of the substantial stigma and shame associated with sexual abuse and with adolescent sexual activity. This multimethod approach may allow distinction of common method variance associated with simultaneous measurement. Earlier research shows that diary reports of sexual behavior may be more accurate than retrospective self-reports, especially for subjects with high coital frequencies (Fortenberry, Cecil, Zimet, & Orr, 1997).

Methods

This study is part of a larger project evaluating factors associated with repeated bacterial and protozoan sexually transmitted infections (STI). Subjects were ages 14–25, attending a metropolitan STD clinic or one of three community adolescent health clinics. Subjects were eligible for entry if they were treated for *N. gonorrhoeae, C. trachomatis, T. vaginalis,* or nongonococcal urethritis (NGU), or were sexual contacts of these infections. Appropriate single-dose treatment was provided to each subject, along with condoms and counseling on the need to advise sex partners to be tested and treated. Each subject provided written informed consent, but the requirement for parental consent was waived. The institutional review board of Indiana University/Purdue University at Indianapolis approved the study.

Data were collected at two time points using a self-administered questionnaire. A baseline questionnaire was obtained at enrollment. Self-reports of sexual abuse and sexual coercion were obtained as well as details regarding sexual behavior, substance use, violence, and depression. The baseline questionnaire required 20–25 minutes for completion.

Following completion of study procedures at enrollment, participants were provided with pocket-sized calendars appropriate for the interval until the next follow-up visit. Participants were asked to indicate each day on which coitus occurred, the partner's first name or initials, whether a condom was used, and whether alcohol or marijuana was used within four hours of coitus. Subjects were taught a simple code to protect confidentiality.

Diaries were collected at return visits at one, three, five and seven months after the enrollment visit. At the seven-month visit, all items included on the enrollment questionnaire were repeated.

Measures

The sexual behavior outcome variables are aggregated from the daily diary records. *Coital frequency* was expressed as the average number of coital events per week. *Condom use* was computed as the number of condom-protected coital events divided by the total number of coital events. *Alcohol use* was computed as the proportion of alcohol-associated coital events divided by the total number of coital events. *Marijuana use* was computed as the total number of coital events associated with marijuana use divided by the total number of coital events.

The main independent variables, collected at enrollment and seven-month follow-up through self-report questionnaires, were history of sexual abuse and history of sexual coercion. These conceptual categories of unwanted sexual experiences were distinguished by events occurring before age 12 (sexual abuse) and from age 12 (sexual coercion). Age 12 was chosen because focus groups with adolescents identified this as an age at which a young person could differentiate wanted from unwanted sexual events, and this age captured the average age of initial voluntary sexual experiences of this sample. *History of sexual abuse* was assessed by four items contained in both the enrollment ($a = .85$) and seven-months questionnaire. Participants were asked to respond in terms of events occurring before age 12. Specific items are in Table 1. These items were chosen to reflect an overall general belief that sexual abuse had occurred. Additional items reflect use of force or coercion in the context of the participant's unwillingness to engage in sexual activities. Types of sexual behaviors were not

Table 1. *Sexual Abuse Items, by Gender (Ns with % of total N in parentheses)*

	Females		Males	
	Enroll *N* = 166	7-Month *N* = 166	Enroll *N* = 33	7-Month *N* = 33
I believe I have been sexually abused by someone.	42 (25.3)	33 (19.9)	5 (15.2)	3 (9.1)
Someone tried to touch me in a sexual way against my will.	57 (34.3)	39 (23.6)	5 (15.2)	1 (3.0)
Someone tried to make me touch them in a sexual way against my will.	36 (21.8)	24 (14.6)	5 (15.2)	2 (6.1)
Someone threatened to tell lies about me or hurt me unless I did something sexual with them.	21 (12.7)	11 (6.7)	3 (9.1)	0 (0)

specified in order to avoid the complexity of inquiry about a range of inappropriate behaviors. Issues such as the identity or relationship of the abuser and the age of onset and duration of abuse were deliberately omitted. *History of sexual coercion* (four items, a = .69) was framed in terms of unwanted sexual events occurring after age 12. "Unwanted" was defined as any kind of sex that the subject did not agree to, even if with someone known to them.

Predictor variables, also collected at baseline and seven-month follow-up via self-report questionnaires, include *age at initial coitus, number of lifetime sex partners, cigarette use, alcohol use, depression, marijuana use, violence, family support,* and *prior STD history. Alcohol use* was assessed by three items (scale range 3–18, a = .84) addressing quantity and frequency of alcohol use in the previous two months, as well as the number of episodes of five or more drinks in a single setting. *Depression* was assessed by four items (scale range 4–12, a = .85) addressing the frequency in the past six months of feelings of hopelessness, depression, and pessimism about the future. *Marijuana use* was assessed by two items (scale range 2–8, a = .84) addressing recent and lifetime frequency of marijuana use. *Violence* was assessed by four items (scale range 4–16, a = .63) addressing recent episodes of intimidation, aggression, and physical fighting. *Family support* (three items, scale range 3–12, a = .85) addressed the degree to which parents and other family members were available and helpful for emotional and medical problems. *Prior STD history* summed individual items about history of gonorrhea, chlamydia, trichomonas, and NGU (scale range 0–3 for females; 0–4 for males).

Statistical Analyses

The statistical analysis was carried out in sequential steps. First, baseline predictor variables were tested for differences between sexes using the student's t-test. The resulting diary data results are described, given the novelty of this data analysis approach. Second, the stability of CSA reporting over time was evaluated by calculating Pearson product-moment correlations between baseline and seven-month CSA scale scores. A second way to assess the stability of CSA reporting was to calculate the number of subjects who endorsed at least one item at one time point. We then determined the proportion of these individuals that endorsed at least one item at both time points (Consistent Reporters) and the proportion that endorsed at least one item at only one time point (Inconsistent Reporters).

The third analysis entailed distinguishing Consistent Reporters from Inconsistent Reporters in terms of demographic information, recent coercive sexual experiences, depression, substance abuse, sexual behaviors, parental support, and the diary data (coital frequency, condom use, alcohol use, marijuana use). One-way analysis of variance (ANOVA) was subsequently used for the aforementioned analyses.

Fourth, a t-test analysis was conducted on the individuals who endorsed at least one item from the CSA scale. For the purpose of this analysis, individuals who reported CSA at both time points (Consistent Reporters) were compared to Inconsistent Reporters of CSA on their CSA scale scores.

Results

A total of 199 subjects provided baseline, diary, and seven-month follow-up data. The average age of female participants ($N = 166$) was 16.7 years, and of male participants 18.3 years ($N = 33$). The average age of first sexual intercourse for females was 13.8 years compared to 13.2 years for males ($p < .01$ by t-test). The average number of lifetime sex partners at enrollment was 8.4 for females and 20.5 for males ($p < .01$ by t-test).

The median number of days from an initial to a final diary entry was 185 days (range: 24 days to 264 days). An entry for coitus was missing for 1,877 (6.3%) days. The diaries thus represented 30,956 days, with coitus on 3,914 (12.6%) days. The median number of coital events was seven, but 26 (13.1%) subjects recorded no coital events and 24 (12%) recorded 50 or more events. Condoms were used for 1,518 (38.8%) of coital events. Average proportion of condom-protected events was 56%. Alcohol preceded 144 (3.6%) coital events, with marijuana associated with 335 (8.6%) coital events.

The proportions of female and male participants reporting abusive sexual experiences are shown in Table 1. For each item, a larger proportion of females than males reported an abusive experience. Overall, 68/166 (41%) females and 7/33 (21.2%) males responded affirmatively to at least one item regarding sexually abusive experiences. Females were somewhat more likely to respond affirmatively to two or more items (60/199; 30.1%) compared to males (6/33; 18.2%). However, equal proportions of females and males (6.1% for each sex) responded affirmatively to all four items (data not shown).

The stability of CSA reporting over time was assessed via a Pearson product correlation of baseline and seven-month CSA reporting. The resulting correlation was significant ($r = .60$, $p < .001$) but not as strong as expected given that CSA prior to age 12 was being assessed. As an additional measure of stability, a Pearson product correlation was also conducted with baseline and seven-month CSA scores only among subjects who endorsed a history of CSA at some time point (85 participants). The resulting Pearson product correlation was again significant ($r = .27$, $p < .01$) and significantly lower. Hence, substantial variability in the number of CSA items endorsed was evident.

Table 2 reports CSA reporting over time. The majority of adolescents (113 participants; 57%) were Consistent Nonreporters of CSA across both time points. Forty participants (20%) were Consistent Reporters of CSA, indicating they endorsed at least one CSA scale item at both time points. Forty-five respondents (23%) were Inconsistent Reporters of CSA, in that either they endorsed at least one CSA item at baseline, but not at seven months (35 participants; 18%), or they did not endorse an item at baseline, but did at seven months (10 participants; 5%). These three groups (Consistent Nonreporters, Inconsistent Reporters, and Consistent Reporters) were then compared on relevant demographic, behavioral, and mental health variables from enrollment and diary data using one-way ANOVA with posthoc Scheffe contrasts.

Significant univariate effects were found for the coercive sexual experiences scale ($F = 28.03$, $p < .001$) as well as depression ($F = 3.71$, $p < .05$). The lifetime number of sexual partners variable evidenced outliers (0 to 100 partners), so the variable was standardized for the analyses. Subsequently, the lifetime number of sexual partners was significant ($F = 3.54$, $p < .05$). Table 3 contains significant means and standard deviations for the CSA groups. No significant differences were found between the consistency groups in terms of age at initial coitus, cigarette use, alcohol use, marijuana use, violence, family support, and prior STD history. Similarly, no

Table 2. CSA *Reporting over Baseline and Seven Months*

	7-month CSA scale endorsement	
	No	Yes
Baseline CSA scale endorsement		
No	113 (57%)	10 (5%)
Yes	35 (18%)	40 (20%)

Table 3. *Means and Standard Deviations by CSA Reporting Group**

Variable	Non-CSA reporters	Inconsistent CSA reporters	Consistent CSA reporters
Sexual coercion	4.8 (1.2)[a]	5.5 (1.6)[a]	6.9 (2.2)[a]
Depression scale	9.4 (3.6)[a]	10.5 (3.5)	11.1 (3.6)[a]
Lifetime sex partners	8.6 (12.0)[a]	9.2 (9.4)	15.6 (20.9)[a]

* Matching [a] superscripts indicate significance at the $p < .01$ level.

significant differences among consistency groups were found for coital frequency, condom use, and alcohol or marijuana use associated with sex.[1]

In order to assess the ability of the CSA scale to predict stable reporting, the Consistent Reporters of CSA (40 participants) were compared to Inconsistent Reporters (45 participants) in terms of their overall score on the CSA scale at baseline. The group differences were statistically significant (t [82] = 3.33, $p < .01$) with Consistent Reporters evidencing higher scale scores (mean = 2.69, SD = .99) than Inconsistent Reporters (mean = 1.56, SD = 1.25).

Discussion

Considerable instability of CSA reporting was evident over a seven-month time period. This instability was predominantly a function of inconsistent reports of abuse. Reports of no abuse were generally quite stable, in that 92% of those reporting no abuse at baseline continued to report no abuse at the seven-month follow-up. The pattern of instability was similar across all four items of the CSA scale.

Among subjects initially reporting CSA, fewer reported CSA at the seven-month survey. Reasons for this decline are unclear. Because data were initially collected in a clinical setting, the subject's level of stress may have been higher at baseline measurement, given the enrollment requirement of an STD diagnosis. This may have resulted in interpretations of past events that were reassessed by the seven-month report.

Significant differences existed between Consistent, Inconsistent and Nonreporters of CSA. Consistent CSA reporters endorsed the highest rates of sexual coercion experiences, depression, and lifetime number of sexual partners. CSA nonreporters were lowest on these measures, with Inconsistent reporters between. These data support the assumption that the Consistent CSA group contains a larger proportion of "true" experiences of abuse. The Inconsistent CSA group contains a proportion of individuals who subsequently reinterpret their experience. We suspect these inconsistent reports are largely "false positive" initial reports. Otherwise, the Inconsistent CSA group should show levels of problem behavior similar to that of Consistent CSA reporters. Since cross-sectional studies obtain only a single CSA assessment, our data suggest such studies overreport the prevalence of CSA. Such misclassification may represent a substantial bias in the existing research on the long-term effects of CSA.

In conclusion, our data support the importance of greater attention to the reliable and valid measurement of CSA. The continued absence of such research represents a substantial threat to research seeking to identify those at risk and reduce adverse outcomes among victims of CSA.

Acknowledgments

Sponsored in part by the National Institute of Allergy and Infectious Diseases (U19 AI31494) and the Maternal Child Health Bureau (MCJ 18965). The authors thank Patricia Brooks and Cathy Roberts for data collection.

Note

1. Although the CSA and coercive sexual experience scales use clearly different questions and the age range for each is distinct (prior to age 12 for CSA, age 12 and after for coercive sexual experiences), we wanted to make sure the CSA and coercive sexual experiences were distinct in this sample. Therefore, we created groupings of subjects based on consistency of coercive sexual experience reporting over the two time periods (Consistent Nonreporters, Inconsistent Reporters, Consistent Reporters). We then created a cross-tabulation table comparing the CSA groups to the coercive sexual experience groups. In general, the CSA groups were spread evenly across the coercive sexual experience groups. Hence, subjects endorsing CSA experiences are not necessarily endorsing consistent, high rates of coercive sexual experiences. This provides additional evidence that the participants in this study are able to differentiate between CSA prior to age 12 and coercive sexual experiences from age 12. Additionally, the importance of utilizing diary data variables was made evident by examining the coercive sexual expe-

riences groupings. Consistent reporters, for example, evidenced higher rates of alcohol ($p < .01$) and marijuana use ($p < .05$) in conjunction with coitus. Hence, the importance of a variety of measurement modalities for sensitive sexual behaviors was evident.

References

Alexander, C. S., Somerfield, M. R., Ensminger, M. E., Johnson, K. E., & Kim, Y. J. (1993). Consistency of adolescents' self-report of sexual behavior in a longitudinal study. *Journal of Youth and Adolescence, 22,* 455–471.

Bensley, L. S., Van Eenwyk, J., Spieker, S. J., & Schoder, J. (1999). Self-reported abuse history and adolescent problem behaviors. I. Antisocial and suicidal behaviors. *Journal of Adolescent Health, 24,* 163–172.

Briere, J. (1992). Methodological issues in the study of sexual abuse effects. *Journal of Consulting and Clinical Psychology, 60,* 196–203.

Brown, L. K., Kessel, S. M., Lourie, K. J., Ford, H. H., & Lipsitt, L. P. (1997). Influence of sexual abuse on HIV-related attitudes and behaviors in adolescent psychiatric inpatients. *Journal of the American Academy of Child and Adolescent Psychiatry, 36,* 316–322.

Capaldi, D. M. (1996). The reliability of retrospective report for timing first sexual intercourse in adolescent males. *Journal of Adolescent Research, 11,* 375–387.

Costello, E. J., Angold, A., March, J., & Fairbank, J. (1998). Life events and posttraumatic stress: The development of a new measure for children and adolescents. *Psychological Medicine, 28,* 1275–1288.

Darroch, J. E., Landry, D. J., & Oslak, S. (1999). Age differences between sexual partners in the United States. *Family Planning Perspectives, 31,* 160–167.

Finkelhor, D. (1979). *Sexually victimized children.* New York: Free.

Fortenberry, J. D., Cecil, H., Zimet, G. D., & Orr, D. P. (1997). Concordance between self-report questionnaires and coital diaries for sexual behaviors of adolescent women with sexually transmitted diseases. In J. Bancroft (Ed.), *Researching sexual behavior* (pp. 237–249). Bloomington: Indiana University Press.

Goldman, J. D. G., & Padayachi, U. K. (2000). Some methodological problems in estimating incidence and prevalence in child sexual abuse research. *Journal of Sex Research, 37,* 305–314.

Kendall-Tackett, K. A., Williams, L. M., & Finkelhor, D. (1997). Impact of sexual abuse on children: A review and synthesis of recent empirical studies. *Psychological Bulletin, 113,* 164–180.

Luster, T., & Small, S. A. (1997) Sexual abuse history and number of sex partners among female adolescents. *Family Planning Perspectives, 29,* 204–211.

Meyer, I. H., Muenzenmaier, K., Cancienne, J., & Struening, E. (1996). Reliability and validity of sexual and physical abuse histories among women with serious mental illness. *Child Abuse & Neglect, 20,* 213–219.

Roosa, M. W., Reyes, L., Reinholtz, C., & Angelini, P. J. (1998). Measurement of women's child sexual abuse experiences: An empirical demonstration of the impact of choice of measure on estimates of incidence rates and of relationships with pathology. *Journal of Sex Research, 35,* 225–233.

Russell, D. E. H. (1983). The incidence and prevalence of interfamilial and extra-familial sexual abuse of female children. *Child Abuse & Neglect, 7,* 133–146.

Thompson, N. J., Potter, J. S., Sanderson, C. A., & Maibach, E. W. (1997). The relationship of sexual abuse and HIV risk behaviors among heterosexual adult female STD patients. *Child Abuse & Neglect, 21,* 149–156.

Wyatt, G. E. (1985). The sexual abuse of Afro-American and white American women in childhood. *Child Abuse & Neglect, 9,* 507–519.

Discussion Paper

DAVID FINKELHOR

The two papers, one by Paul and colleagues and one by Laumann and Browning and colleagues, provide some important theoretical and empirical contrasts. One of the places they differ most clearly is in their theoretical orientation. Laumann and Browning, in what I think is an important contribution, point to the tendency of much previous theory, including that used by Paul and by myself in some of my work (e.g., Finkelhor & Browne, 1985) to see the long-term impact of SA as mediated by changed internal states and internal representations and their expressed behavioral patterns, which are then stable over time. For example, they point to my idea that the association of sexual abuse with subsequent employment problems could be explained by reduced self-efficacy as a result of being overpowered or coerced in sexual abuse experience. By contrast, they argue that sexual abuse may have many intermediary consequences, including delinquency, early home leaving, more sexual partners: cascades of accentuating effects that may be more responsible for later employment problems than any internal state. They introduce a number of these relevant environmental accentuaters to the discussion. They argue, in effect, that some of the internal consequences get frozen into environments, opportunities, external structures and constraints, so that even if the internal states dissipate or change, new enforcers of deviance and disadvantage remain. Thus, for example, as sexual abuse affects friendship choice or relationship with parents, these become the deviance-promoting and -maintaining structures.

I welcome this theoretical insight, but I do not see the changed states and life course cascades as mutually exclusive or alternative accounts. I see these as complementary accounts. Effects can be continuous through internal states and representations in some cases with some people, and they can also be mediated by environment and life course factors in others. It is notable that Laumann and Browning themselves relied on some internal state notions, at least in an original version of their paper, when they theorized about how sexual abuse may establish in some people a "same-gender sexual script," and thus can create some basis for subsequent homosexual or bisexual sexual activity. Nonetheless, I do think they are correct to say that the current theorizing has not noticed enough of the life course cascades that can occur—partly a result of the fact that there have been few longitudinal research designs.

In building on the complementarity of the lifestyle and changed internal representations views, I would argue that the developmental interaction between internal effects and environmental constraints and opportunities is potentially very complex.

There may be many more models than a simple internal representation model and a simple life course trajectory model. For example, it could be that the internal representation model actually has a variety of developmental subtypes. Here are two:

1. The internal representation is created by the abuse and expresses itself in later behaviors, e.g., sexual interests or responses are evoked and continue to be evoked under similar circumstances later.
2. The internal representation is created but then changes, although it still retains a deviant character throughout the developmental process, thus a sense of stigma that leads to social withdrawal in grade school and then to a negative sexual self-image at adolescence. In other words, one would not see a continuous trauma-induced trait, but the change would be due to developmental processes, not to environmental repercussions.

Then when we talk about environmental accentuaters or deviance maintainers, we probably can differentiate among subtypes here again:

1. Life course trajectories that simply have their effect through the external constraints they impose, for example, once you drop out of school, then various options are blocked for you.
2. Life course trajectories that act by creating or reinforcing internal states. Getting sexually assaulted again may create new and different traumas that may act on outcomes primarily through internal states again.

Another difference in the two papers—that reflects an ongoing unresolved issue in the field—has to do with how the relevant childhood events are conceptualized and operationalized. Laumann and Browning talk about and operationalize the childhood events primarily as sexual experiences (using questions about sexual touch and age difference). Paul, by contrast, uses a conceptualization that emphasizes much more the trauma element, "being forced or frightened to do something sexual." This will certainly have consequences for the outcomes that are found, with sexual experiences naturally more associated with sexual outcomes, and trauma experiences more associated with trauma outcomes.

Another issue raised by the juxtaposition of the two papers has to do with the contrast between general population surveys and targeted populations, and their implications for hypothesis testing. Laumann and

Browning have a national sample, whereas Paul has a highly targeted one intended to identify a marginal community, even though it uses probability sampling. If you look at the literature in many fields—the ones I know best include child maltreatment, family violence, sexual assault—you generally note a discrepancy of findings between studies from true community samples and those with more targeted populations. For example, the dynamics of spousal violence look very different among community samples than among samples from women's shelters. A possible conclusion from these discrepancies is that most of these phenomena are not simply continua of increasing seriousness from minor to severe, but perhaps better thought of as distinct phenomena. In spousal violence, the distinction has been made between "common couple violence" and "terroristic" assault (Johnson, 1995). With these problems in general, one might say there is a large "garden-variety" form of the problem and a smaller subset of a "clinical" extreme that characterizes a lot of the clinical case material, from which much of the theory is derived, but which isn't fully represented in general population surveys, either because it is relatively rare or perhaps because people in this category do not participate or are not candid in surveys. In a more targeted sample such as Paul's, findings more consistent with clinical impressions about the problem of sexual abuse may be easier to confirm.

Future research can benefit from the melding of the strengths of both of these approaches—tracking impact through both changes in internal representations and life course cascades, looking at the issue of both childhood sexual experiences and childhood sexual traumatic experiences, and testing hypotheses with both community samples and more targeted samples with potentially more of the most serious clinical cases. This should result in better theory and better research in this whole field.

References

Finkelhor, D., & Browne, A. (1985). The traumatic impact of child sexual abuse: A conceptualization. *American Journal of Orthopsychiatry, 55*, 530–541.

Johnson, M. P. (1995). Patriarchal terrorism and common couple violence: Two forms of violence against women. *Journal of Marriage and the Family, 57*, 283–295.

General Discussion

Heino Meyer-Bahlburg: The life course perspective really appeals to me. Yet one issue that is missing from the presentation and also from David Finkelhor's comments is the question of antecedents. Do we assume that child sexual abuse is randomly distributed across the population or does it not happen more frequently in some settings than others? From the longitudinal delinquency research, which was brought up by David, it is very clear that there are important intrafamily antecedents that set the trajectories. Individual events add to that, but they happen in a setting which is preloaded with disadvantageous factors. I think one has to extend backwards the life course perspective that you described today by getting data on factors that precede the sexual abuse itself. The second aspect I am missing throughout the discussion of child sexual abuse, in this country especially, are the effects that government or other agencies have that manage child sexual abuse. I am often appalled at the way child sex abuse is handled in this country; how the children and families are victimized by government policies and regulatory agencies, in comparison to what typically happens in Western Europe. In my clinical work, I have seen marked exacerbation of the effects of child sexual abuse by what happens as a consequence of agency interventions. I think that has to be taken into consideration, and yet typical research studies do not make these effects part of the evaluation. A third issue: Do investigators who conduct these large-scale studies have any data (in terms of "trauma" from sexual abuse) on those people who don't participate? Are traumatized people more likely to avoid participation because they know this topic is going to be touched upon? My final question is: Would you expect the same degree of long-term aftereffects as described for the total sample if you broke it down into the ones who were clearly abused or had child-adult contact before puberty compared to those whose experiences took place during or after puberty, since you had a relatively high cut-off around age 14 or 15?

Ed Laumann: We do have some relevant information that we haven't presented here. In general, we looked at what we called six master status attributes, which were marital status, age, religious background, racial background, ethnic background, and socioeconomic status. We did not see any clear patterns in the relationships between our social demography variables and the likelihood of reporting child sexual abuse so we haven't pursued that very much. What we do find, and report in our third volume (Laumann & Michael, 2001) in the chapter on the age at first intercourse, is a major change over time in the importance of class background and religious background on the deferral of sexual initiation. For respondents who came of sexual age before 1970, there are really strong deferral effects of having Catholic backgrounds or having a mother with a middle-class background. After 1970 these effects disappear and there's a huge convergence so that everybody looks very similar to one another. On the other hand, there is personal biography, which includes age of menarche, and intact family at respondent's age 14, which means that both the biological parents are present. If a stepfather is present at the age of 14, it makes it somewhat more likely that childhood sexual events will happen. So broken family and age of adult-child sexuality as an event have strong effects on transition issues of that kind. I defer to Elsie Pinkston and Jeff Thigpen on the scary adverse impact of the government on those they're trying to protect. With regard to selective refusals, in our data we have a 78% or 79% completion rate. The people who did not agree to participate in the survey, though they were told up front that they were going to be discussing sexual issues, looked pretty much like everybody else. We didn't say much about the extent to which we would be discussing the respondent's detailed sexual history. The most sensitive question in the survey, with the highest refusal to answer, was family income. We had a 12% refusal rate on that question. None of the items regarding sexual behavior got more than 2% refusal. So I think people have no particular problems talking about these things. Now we purposely avoided mentioning abuse or labeling the childhood experience as abusive. We merely said, did you ever have a sexual experience before you became pubertal, and we'd gone through some discussion of what that meant at the time. Only after they described all of these events did we ask whether any were experienced as negative. My memory is that only about half of these events were reported as emotionally negative; it was more common for women to label them negatively. Men were much less likely to label these experiences as negative although these experiences did exert the same effects of eroticizing the men's behavior. The other thing we thought might make a difference was if they were known to have occurred by other people at the time; did they tell anybody, or what people knew about it even though they didn't tell. About half of these events were known by parents or other people and our theory is that that would enhance the likelihood of negative outcomes; that the labeling process, with everybody's throwing up their hands and getting excited about it, would suggest that this was a very adverse event. There was, however, no effect of the public awareness of the event on the likelihood of an adverse outcome, as I recall.

Elsie Pinkston: We have drawn a random sample, and of the kids who were abused in our sample who were later labeled as having abused others, which in fact they didn't really, only 17% of the people who abused them were ever prosecuted or brought to court, etc. We don't know what those figures mean but they are certainly rather startling. We've been looking at kids who are considered sexually aggressive and basically this information is phoned in. No one goes out and interviews the children or the people involved. Very often it comes from a call to the hotline and they describe what the situation is to the gatekeepers and they put these children on a list. This list is referred to privately as "sexually aggressive children and youth" and you don't get off that list for at least two years and we actually never saw anybody come off the list. Part of our job was actually to eliminate that list. This is basically a social intervention project, but the slippery slope between being called a victim and being called a perpetrator or a "perp" just made you cry. We stopped at every meeting and just swore a little bit because it was so extreme and so irrational. That leads me into an issue—I was wondering why you don't focus more on the kids who have the experience but who are survivors and go ahead and do well because people take these markers, and they just have to have the marker, they don't have to have the behavior. The marker itself will be enough to get them put into a category that may cause them to be unable to return home because they have a sister or brother; not engage in contact sports, not go to summer camp, have all their teachers be told that they are perpetrators, etc. So it would be good if there was a countervailing process to help us look at the people who are not traumatized. In some areas, trauma theory has been discounted. So if they don't look at the survivors then the attribution that it is trauma that causes something is problematic.

Anke Ehrhardt: And they get on the list before they actually have done anything, just because they were victimized?

Elsie Pinkston: They get on the list because they do something; they may pee against the building, they may put their hands on someone's diaper, they may do anything that, if you were not in this system, would be something your family would handle. We looked at children from 2 through 6. We had 2½-year-olds on the list—and understand that the people put them on the list to help them. You must understand there's so little known about how to treat this, that people make horrendous errors with very good intentions.

John Bancroft: An interpretation of your results would seem to be that sexual contact with peers during childhood is almost as traumatic as sexual contact with adults in terms of its impact on the subsequent life course, although you had very few who acknowledged sexual contact with peers. I think this raises an important methodological point. You comment in your paper on how low that number was and that was because the question very much focused on the sexuality of the peer contact. I would suggest that the sequence of questions that you had in your interview, which started off with "had you ever been sexually touched as a child" and then started to inquire about who did it, very much got the respondent to focus on what would be regarded as abusive sexual experiences during childhood; then first of all were they done by adults and so on. So nonabusive sexual experiences with other children, which most studies which have looked at them have found to be widespread, probably would not be commented on in your survey. In our data, not all of the child sexual play experiences involve genital contact but quite a lot do, and we have no evidence that those experiences are in any way harmful. So I'm concerned that an interpretation of your data about peer sexual relationships might be very negative when in fact that data is the result of a methodological problem. Another issue, which applies I think to Jay Paul's study as well, is the emphasis which is being placed on the long-term consequences. Basically you made a bold statement that you found no evidence that child sexual abuse resulted in any withdrawal from sex, or avoidance of sex. I have certainly seen quite a few people in my clinical career who have withdrawn from sex as a result of child sexual abuse and I'm wondering what happens to them in the surveys. Is there a tendency for people whose behavior has been somewhat sexualized by their childhood experience and have much more developed and often risky sexual careers subsequently, to be more likely to report or recall sexual abuse experiences than people who have withdrawn or become sexually avoidant? Is that another methodological issue that we have to consider?

Ed Laumann: Regarding the second question concerning selection biases and participation, it's very difficult to know. It's not that there were no observed low levels of sexual activity in the population; there are lots of relatively sexually inactive people in the sample. About half the population of men and women were mutually monogamous with sex less than once a week. So there's certainly the potential for people reporting relatively inactive sex lives or for particularly women to report that they don't have sex partners for substantial periods of time, and they do exist in our sample. You'd have to come up with a rather complicated theory about why those people are less likely to admit to this sort of event early on in their childhood, when they're describing essentially a socially undesirable state of affairs in their current life. The other point you're making about child sexual experiences; I agree with you that we used a priming variable which led people to think of things more sexual than many childhood experiences might be considered to be. Having touched another little boy's "pee pee" when you were five, or something like that, may not have been picked up because the context of the interview at that point was focused more on sexual acts. So I think we definitely are underestimating the amount of child-child sex that's going on, and that we're taking from a subset of those people. In general, I might say that precocity or earliness of exposure to sexually interesting things does not necessarily mean an adverse outcome.

People become sexually interested, they start early, they tend to have more sexual concerns over time, they do things such as have partner turnover and other things that put them at risk, but I'm not labeling early sexual experiences and precocity in that regard as necessarily bad events. In a sense we're trying to argue that most people go through these sexual initiatory experiences relatively robustly and recover from whatever spins there may be. So the paper is certainly not intended in any way to describe these events as fundamentally negative. It helps to know that there are a lot of people who have had these experiences and that most of them come out of them in a fairly healthy, satisfactory way. The usual accounts in the literature are of these dramatic horror stories of clinically bad outcomes that have happened. But people need to be told that these things have happened to lots of people and most people survive them. So I think the survival story is the story that I want to emphasize, not the adverse outcome story, which I think has dominated the psychogenic literature.

I want to underscore David's remark about couple violence. Johnson's paper (1995) has an excellent review of the treatment of domestic violence and he argues that one often confounds two different populations: the more clinically out-of-control violent group versus the more common garden-variety physical fights that occur in domestic partnerships. Our data, for example, in Chicago described physical fights occurring in 15–35% of couples' relationships in the last year, so it's a very common pattern. But it's not an out-of-control pattern that is described by some people who are true wife batterers, and these have tended to get confounded in the literature. This is, again, a situation in which advocacy groups and others need to begin making difficult, careful distinctions in what's really going on.

Jany Rademakers: We should be very conscious about what terms we use. When I look at the program, we're in the session about effects of child sexual abuse. But half of these people we've heard about didn't have abusive experiences—they had adult-child sexual experiences. Therefore you cannot say anything about survival because in my opinion you don't survive a sexual contact, you survive abuse. Okay, sometimes you survive the sexual contact, but it's not appropriate terminology. When we talk about child sexuality and sexual experiences we should be very distinct about not generalizing everything into abuse.

Gil Herdt: Welcome to the United States. It seems to me that there were three dimensions that were marked off in these papers. One has to do with the frequency of contact; the second has to do with severity or intensity. I prefer intensity as a dimension which gets at the vertical meaning and of course both of these terms, in some sense, have an objective-subjective dimension. But the third dimension, and here I would put on my anthropology hat, is the degree of social approval of the event that has occurred. To make it absolutely explicit, what Jany is suggesting, and I think also the implications of Heino's question about antecedents, is to say, is this approved in the family or in the community? What is the degree to which it is known? This gets to the question of duplicity, of family agreement, secrecy, the extent to which people know that this is occurring and they approve of it. This may set up a problem in the extent to which we can consider there is continuity or discontinuity in the person's development, the extent to which it creates both a social and an intrapsychic conflict the person has to deal with. Whose standards are they following? This is why the juvenile delinquency example really is a very poor one. The example with regard to juvenile delinquency is the law. There is no agreed consensual uniform community standard, that's why Ed's example of the 36-year-old professor is a startling one. Why would this come forward now? So I would just want to venture to guess, in answer to what John and others have raised, which I think is very legitimate, who's not being included in the population-based samples? My hypothesis would be, it is the people who have experienced this degree of conflict between what they thought was socially approved or complicitly agreed upon when they were young and what the social community standard is as they grow up. That is to say, they genuinely are unclear about what this means. Obviously this can be construed in many, many ways and we're talking about an enormous degree of variation in people's subjective experiences. But the absolute standard has to be what is true in the mind of the victim.

Ken Zucker: The first sentence of Jay Paul's paper, "Our previous research has confirmed that the prevalence of child sexual abuse among men who have sex with men is far higher than among the general male population," will require the rewriting of every psychology, sociology, and psychiatry textbook about the relationship between homosexuality and sexual abuse, if it's correct. But it was difficult to present your data in such a short time and I just wanted to point out a couple of things that I found quite confusing about the data that have been talked about. First of all, you're talking about victimization experiences, yet if I look at your Tables 1 and 2, a substantial percentage of your participants are saying that at the time the event occurred or at the initial victimization, they didn't experience distress. How does one square the respondent saying there was no distress with calling it victimization? This gets at the point that Jany Rademakers just mentioned and I'm confused by it. Also when you asked them about their current level of distress, you also have lots of people saying that it's not at all upsetting. My question in terms of your study in general, in terms of looking at its relation to risky sexual behavior, is, if you only include people who were victimized under the age of 12, because I think after the age of 12 it gets much more ambiguous in terms of what's going on, and only those people who reported distress, what does that do to your data? Does it strengthen the predictions? Weaken them?

Jay Paul: I think that it's difficult to operationalize victimization solely on the basis of the emotional impact that the person can describe at the time or currently. Typically victimization is talking about some sort of acknowledged power differential between the people involved. We started off asking people about things happening against their will that they didn't want, so asking about the emotional distress is one piece of it, but it's not the only piece, it's not the golden rule in defining what is or what is not victimization. In terms of what we call childhood sexual abuse, childhood sexual coercion, childhood victimization, however you want to refer to it, I don't know that it's necessarily clear at what age we should draw that line.

Lucia O'Sullivan: I think the terminology that we use in our studies, the extent to which we define what child sexual abuse is, understanding what a victim is, is problematic. "Nonconsensual" is not synonymous with "unwanted." Obviously "unwanted" is not synonymous with "unwilling" and there are many reasons why people engage in unwanted sexual activity other than being forced or coerced. We need to be really careful, in any study we do, to delve into that much more carefully and to make sure that our understanding of what is sexually coercive or abusive is the same as the participants'. There are a number of very interesting studies coming out that have deconstructed these terms that we use so easily.

References

Johnson, M. P. (1995). Patriarchal terrorism and common couple violence: Two forms of violence against women. *Journal of Marriage and the Family, 57,* 283–294.

Laumann, E. O., & Michael, R. T. (Eds.). (2001). *Sex, love, and health in America: Private choices and public policies.* Chicago: University of Chicago Press.

Part 6.

Theoretical Models for Mediating Mechanisms

The Social Context of Adaptation to Childhood Sexual Maltreatment

A Life Course Perspective

CHRISTOPHER R. BROWNING AND
EDWARD O. LAUMANN

The recent increase in academic attention to child sexual abuse has both broadened concern with this phenomenon and deepened our understanding of its nature and consequences. Yet, despite the ever-increasing salience of child abuse, academic inquiry has remained largely confined to psychology and social work. Sociologists have remained only peripherally involved in the project of theorizing the dynamics and impact of child abuse. In what follows, we argue that sociological theory—particularly life course and contextual models of development—can aid in addressing some of the central research questions that continue to dominate the field. Toward this end, we describe a sociologically informed model of the long-term effects of child sexual abuse that addresses one of the most pressing questions confronting researchers and practitioners concerned with child abuse: Among those who experience sexual abuse, why do some suffer a host of long-term negative effects in adolescence and adulthood while others do not?

We offer a sociologically based life course model of the effects of child sexual abuse as an alternative to the currently dominant psychogenic perspective on early sexual experiences. The life course perspective emphasizes the role of adaptation to childhood sexual abuse and the cumulative consequences of behavioral trajectories in the aftermath of early sexual experiences (Browning, 2003; Browning & Laumann, 1997). In contrast, the psychogenic perspective conceptualizes childhood sexual experience as a variably traumatic event producing lingering emotional disturbance. In this view, adverse effects in adolescence and adulthood are seen as a result of the contemporary manifestation of durable negative affect induced by childhood sexual abuse. While we describe these models as competing in the discussion to follow, this strategy is, in part, heuristic. The psychogenic and life course perspectives need not be mutually exclusive. In fact, the most fruitful theoretical strategy may involve the integration of insights from the psychogenic and life course perspectives.

Theoretical Perspectives

Researchers only recently have returned to the project of developing theories to explain why childhood sexual experiences lead to long-term effects. The most notable early effort in this regard was outlined in Freud's 1896 essay "The Aetiology of Hysteria," wherein he attributed hysterical symptomatology among a subset of his patients to early sexual trauma (Freud, 1896/1955). In the context of this theory—now known as the "seduction hypothesis" (Gay, 1989)—Freud used the term "trauma" with reference to painful or overwhelming stressors that produce an intense emotional response. The quantity of affect produced by the traumatic event cannot be managed by the conscious mind and is repressed. This unresolved affect, however, remains in the unconscious and may periodically be manifest in hysterical symptoms. Freud's advocacy of the seduction hypothesis, however, provoked vociferous criticism among his colleagues in the medical community, and he subsequently abandoned the theory (Masson, 1984).

After Freud's retraction, there followed an extended hiatus in research on the effects of childhood sexual experiences that lasted until the topic was "rediscovered" in the 1960s. The research agenda that emerged during this period focused on understanding the impact of childhood sexual contacts (almost exclusively with adults) on several dimensions of subsequent well-being. Studies of the effects of adult-child sex on children observed a host of short-term consequences including affective disturbance (Deblinger, McLeer, Atkins, Ralph, & Foa, 1989; Gomes-Schwartz, Horowitz, & Cardarelli, 1990; McLeer, Deblinger, Henry, & Orvaschel, 1992), effects on sexual interests and behavior (Beitchman, Zuckee, Hood, DaCosta, & Akman, 1991; Beitchman et al., 1992; Browne & Finkelhor, 1986; Deblinger et al., 1989; Friedrich, 1988; Urquiza & Capra, 1990), and nonsexual problem behavior (Deblinger et al., 1989; Widom, 1989). Studies of the long-term effects of adult-child sex documented a comparable range of adverse outcomes, including diminished well-being on a variety of mental health assessment scales, relationship problems (Deblinger et al., 1989; Finkelhor, 1990; Finkelhor, Hotaling, Lewis, & Smith, 1990), and sexual dysfunction (Urquiza & Capra, 1990). The proliferation of these largely descriptive studies, however, and the persistent finding that not all those who experienced childhood sexual contact suffered long-term adverse outcomes called attention to the relative dearth of theoretical work in this area. In response, some researchers began redirecting their attention to developing explanations for the link between adult-child sex and long-term effects.

The dominant theoretical framework to emerge can be described as a "psychogenic" perspective on the long-term effects of childhood sexual experiences. This perspective encompasses a number of different approaches, including the Post-traumatic Stress Disorder framework (PTSD) (American Psychiatric Association [APA], 1994; Briggs & Joyce, 1997; Deblinger et al., 1989; McLeer, Deblinger, Atkins, Foa, & Ralph, 1988), Lenore Terr's typological trauma theory (Terr, 1991), the cognitive-behavioral model (Hoier et al., 1992), and elements of David Finkelhor's traumagenic dynamics model (Finkelhor, 1988). These theories share a core vision of childhood sexual experiences with adults as variably traumatic events that produce a lingering emotional disturbance that may affect well-being across long stretches of the life course.

We offer an alternative model to explain the long-term effects of childhood sexual experiences that integrates social learning theory (Akers, 1973; Bandura & Walters, 1963; Elliott, Huizinga, & Ageton, 1985), social control theory (Hirschi, 1969; Sampson & Laub, 1993), and concepts taken from the sociology of the life course (Caspi, 1987; Elder, 1985). In this view, both adult-child sex and explicitly sexual contacts with peers are understood as early transitions to sociosexual activity. Aspects of this transition induce vulnerability to subsequent experiences that have independent effects on adult well-being. From this perspective, the effects of childhood sexual contacts are largely indirect. That is, risky behavior patterns established in the aftermath of early sex and their unfolding impact over time account for the association between childhood sexual experience and adult mental, sexual, and interpersonal well-being (three of the most commonly affected areas of adult adjustment).

The Psychogenic Perspective

As noted above, the psychogenic perspective encompasses a number of distinct theories. We argue, however, that these theories share four fundamental assumptions about the long-term negative effects of childhood sexual experiences: (a) that "trauma"—although conceived in a variety of ways in the psychogenic literature (see "Conceptions of Trauma," below)—is the central concept to be used in characterizing the effects of these experiences; (b) that childhood sexual experiences fall on a continuum of severity that describes the level of stress induced and predicts the extent to which the child will suffer long-term negative consequences (the "dose-response" hypothesis [Rutter, 1988]); (c) that continuity in the emotional disturbance induced by childhood sexual trauma is principally responsible for adult symptomatology; and (d) that the behavioral response to childhood sexual contact is bidirectional—with some withdrawing from sexual activity (including behaviors associated with the original sexual event) and others engaging in heightened levels of sexual activity.

The psychogenic theories that hold these assumptions can be classified by their conceptions of the nature of sexual trauma. Traumatic scenarios can be organized into three broad categories:[1] (a) the presentation of negative stimuli (e.g., painful or overwhelming experiences of sexual intrusion); (b) the removal of positively valued stimuli (e.g., betrayal by a parent in the case of incest); and (c) blocked escape from negative stimuli (e.g., thwarted efforts to avoid repeated sexually abusive episodes). Below, we consider the content of psychogenic theories in more detail, focusing specifically on demonstrating the centrality of the four assumptions.

CONCEPTIONS OF TRAUMA

By far the most popular conception of the effects of adult-child sexual contact envisions the experience as the presentation of noxious stimuli to a child. In this view, sexual abuse is seen as a painful or overwhelming event that produces adverse emotional responses. This perspective is represented both by Freud's early seduction theory and by the more recent widespread application of the PTSD framework to the case of sexual abuse (Eth & Pynoos, 1985; Horowitz, 1976; Janoff-Bulman, 1985). Rooted in a psychoanalytic conception of trauma, the PTSD model suggests that the experience of stress during adult-child sex generates powerful psychic energy (memories and affect associated with the event) that, if unresolved, leads to adverse mental health outcomes (Gelinas, 1983). Thus negative outcomes in adulthood are "symptoms" of a lingering psychic disorder, the etiology of which is traced directly to the original adult-child sexual experience.

By implication, the PTSD framework suggests that the degree of traumatic stress experienced during the original sexual contact is the factor that best accounts for variation in the long-term adverse effects of adult-child sex. More severe events will induce more subsequent emotional disturbance and an increased likelihood of exhibiting PTSD symptomatology. Advocates of the PTSD perspective have operationalized the level of trauma experienced by examining characteristics of the event, such as the frequency and type (e.g., penetrative versus nonpenetrative) of sexual contact that occurred (Briggs & Joyce, 1997) and whether force was involved (Urquiza & Capra, 1990).[2]

In this view, the emotional disturbance induced by childhood sexual trauma may linger over long stretches of the life course and is largely responsible for the varied manifestation of adolescent and adult symptomatology. Green (1993), for instance, argues that symptoms such as chronic anxiety and depression "might be carried over directly from childhood," while other symptoms that are "apparently new, i.e., anxiety attacks, delayed PTSD and hysterical symptoms, may represent the breakthrough of long-repressed traumatic memories triggered by adult sexual experiences" (p. 894). Gelinas (1983) takes a similar tack, arguing that the long-term negative impact of incest, including nightmares, behavioral reenactments, dissociation, depression, and impulsivity, can be attributed to "chronic traumatic neurosis" (similar to the notion of delayed PTSD). In both models, the continuity of emotional disturbance may be heterotypic—meaning, it may be manifest in developmentally specific ways. This diversity of expression, however, has its roots in a single source—the traumatic childhood sexual experience.

Most psychogenic models of the effects of sexual abuse, however, do not explicitly state the hypothesis of continuity in emotional disturbance.

Rather, they imply that the impact of abuse is largely direct by consistently employing a "coping model" to account for specific outcomes. By stating that any given behavior in the short or long term is an effort to cope with the pain of abuse (e.g., substance use, delinquency, multiple or unstable sexual partnering, and so on), trauma models link behavioral outcomes directly with lingering affective disturbance. Hoier and colleagues (1992), for instance, argue that victims of sexual abuse may accelerate entry into sexual activity with intimate partners due to a desire to "get it over with." This strategy, like sexual withdrawal, is a method of coping with the residual pain and anxiety associated with sexual activity due to childhood trauma.

Felitti and colleagues' (1998) analysis of the association between child (including sexual) abuse and adult health problems illustrates the "default explanation" status of the coping model. They suggest that "high levels of exposure to adverse childhood experiences would expectedly produce anxiety, anger, and depression in children. To the degree that behaviors such as smoking, alcohol or drug use are found to be effective as coping devices, they would tend to be used chronically" (p. 253). Sexual activity is also cited as potentially providing "pharmacological or psychological benefit" as "a coping device in the face of the stress of abuse" (p. 253). The coping model, then, accounts for a wide range of responses in the aftermath of childhood abuse and can be enlisted to account for affective and behavioral problems well into adulthood.

While coping strategies may take myriad forms, the PTSD framework offers a specific hypothesis concerning the likely response to sexual stimuli resulting from the trauma of adult-child sex. On the one hand, PTSD typically involves the adoption of "avoidance strategies" designed to structure all reminders of the traumatic incident out of daily experience (APA, 1994). An alternative response, however, involves confronting stimuli associated with the traumatic experience in order to achieve mastery over the event (Horowitz, 1976). The PTSD perspective, then, suggests a polarized response pattern, with adverse reactions to sexual trauma taking the form of withdrawal from sexual activity (and the specific sexual acts associated with the sexual trauma) or compulsive sexual behavior (Green, 1992, 1993).

Some or all of the four assumptions embedded in the PTSD model—the centrality of trauma, the dose-response hypothesis, the continuity and predictive centrality of emotional disturbance, and the bidirectional behavioral orientation—are reproduced in other "noxious stimuli" models of the long-term effects of adult-child sex (Hoier et al., 1992) as well as in models that posit alternative trauma-generating scenarios. For instance, the notion of trauma as the removal of positive stimuli finds expression in perspectives that emphasize "betrayal" as the consequential component of adult-child sex (Freyd, 1996). From this point of view, the trauma of abuse results from the child's recognition that a valued caretaker is exploiting the child's trust. The key event characteristic predicting subsequent adjustment is the relationship of the child to the perpetrator. Betrayal by adults to whom the child is more attached (dose) is hypothesized to lead to more severe long-term effects (response).

Trauma stemming from the failure to escape negative stimuli has been emphasized by Terr (1991), who suggests that chronic exposure to a stressful event creates a sense of anticipation and recognition on the part of the child that he or she has little control over the occurrence of the stressor. The hypothesized consequences of this type of trauma include denial, psychic numbing, dissociation, and rage.

Finkelhor (1988) has offered a challenge to models of the long-term effects of adult-child sexual contact that focus exclusively on overwhelming or painful trauma. First, he questions the theoretical "fit" of PTSD to the case of adult-child sexual interaction. More often applied to survivors of war combat, natural disasters, and other life-threatening experiences, the PTSD framework may not address adequately cases of adult-child sexual interaction that involve more subtle manipulation over time rather than abrupt and forceful violation (Armstrong, 1978; Finkelhor, 1988). Second, Finkelhor notes the failure of those employing the PTSD perspective to articulate a more precise theory of the link between adult-child sexual contact and subsequent outcomes. The problem, he contends, lies in the construction of adult-child sexual contact as a discrete episode. Focusing on the trauma of the "event" obscures the cognitive impact of the unfolding process of an adult-child sexual relationship. This leads to a third problem with the PTSD perspective—its failure to integrate more than a fairly restricted range of "symptoms" within its conceptual purview. The presumption that the experience of adult-child sexual contact nearly universally induces high levels of stress in children leads scholars to focus on subsequent disturbances of affect to the exclusion of other potentially significant outcomes.

In an attempt to correct some of the inadequacies of the PTSD framework, Finkelhor has developed an alternative model of long-term effects that attempts to identify qualitatively distinct psychological dynamics that may operate during adult-child sexual relationships. In his Traumagenic Dynamics model, the effect of adult-child sexual contact is due to the presence or absence of four key dynamics—powerlessness, betrayal, traumatic sexualization, and stigmatization—each of which accounts, individually, for a particular class of long-term outcomes. The dynamic of powerlessness refers, first, to abuse situations in which the child experiences the threat of injury, and second, to those in which "a child's will, wishes, and sense of efficacy are repeatedly overruled and frustrated" (Finkelhor, 1988, p. 71). The first component of the powerlessness dynamic is equivalent to the traditional noxious stimuli trauma and is employed to account for those adult-child sexual relationships that are likely to produce PTSD-like symptoms. The second component is similar to Terr's "repeated exposure" trauma. Finkelhor attributes long-term outcomes similar to those discussed by Terr to the powerlessness dynamic, including phobias and dissociation, but adds more concrete behavioral manifestations of the dynamic such as running away from home, delinquency, employment problems, truancy, aggressive behavior, and becoming an abuser. The experience of anxiety and fear, the lowered sense of efficacy, the perception of oneself as a victim, and, potentially, identification with the aggressor all contribute to emotional and cognitive vulnerability to the long-term outcomes described.

A second dynamic, betrayal, refers to the process by which the child's trust in the adult involved comes into conflict with the discovery that the adult's actions are or were abusive and exploitative. The child's implicit expectation that his or her well-being is considered important by the adult is violated and undermined by the recognition that the child's interests have been disregarded. Finkelhor suggests that the experience of betrayal produces long-term feelings of depression, mistrust (typically of men), extreme dependency, anger, and hostility. As an example of the removal of positive stimuli, the betrayal dynamic more explicitly spells out the potential impact of "betrayal trauma" on adult well-being beyond the exclusive focus on repression offered in Freyd's model (Freyd, 1996).

Third, traumatic sexualization refers to the inappropriate sexual socialization of a child. Sexual contact with an adult may (a) condition the child to use sexuality inappropriately or manipulatively in interaction with others; (b) mislead the child cognitively so that incorrect or inappropriate beliefs about sexuality develop; (c) lead the child to fetishize certain acts or body parts; or (d) associate sexual activities with negative experiences, resulting in aversive and dysfunctional responses to sexuality (Finkelhor, 1988). The psychological impact of this dynamic includes preoccupation with sexual issues, potential confusion about sexual identity and sexual norms, confusion of sex with love, and aversion to sex intimacy. Traumatic sexualization involves cognitive distortions and sex-related learning that may result in precocious, aggressive, and promiscuous sexual behavior. Aversive conditioning, however, may result from adult-child sex leading to sexual dysfunctions (difficulty with arousal or orgasm) and avoidant or phobic reactions to sexual behavior. Finkelhor thus reproduces the hypothesis of a bipolar behavioral response to adult-child sex. He does not, however, adhere to the psychoanalytic/PTSD explanation for heightened levels of sexual activity (the "mastery" hypothesis). Rather, he suggests that adult-child sexual experiences involve inappropriate modeling of sexual interaction.

Finally, Finkelhor's fourth dynamic, stigmatization, refers to the range of processes that communicate negative messages to the child about the sexual contact. These messages can be expressed in a variety of ways. Perpetrators may communicate to the child that the relationship is illicit, and the child is to blame for its occurrence. Parental and institutional responses may, overtly or subtly, reinforce this construction of the sexual relationship, communicating to the child that he or she is responsible for the abuse or, at least, was a willing participant. In response, the child develops feelings of shame, guilt, and diminished self-esteem.

Finkelhor's model of the long-term effects of adult-child sexual contact, then, integrates all three of the trauma-producing scenarios described above. Negative affect may result from adult-child sex due to the emotionally shocking or overwhelming nature of early sexual experiences, repeated failure to escape the sexual contact, or recognition of the betrayal it often implies. Yet Finkelhor also considers the consequences of inappropriate sexual socialization for children who have experienced sexual abuse. First, Finkelhor emphasizes the importance of cognitive distortions in producing maladaptive orientations and behavior. Traumatic sexualization may result in aversive affective reactions to sexually related stimuli as well as distorted cognitive models of appropriate sexual behavior. Incorporating the cognitive impact of adult-child sex focuses attention on how the model provided by an early sexual relationship influences the child's future behavior. Second, Finkelhor's focus on the psychosocial dynamics embedded in adult-child sex highlights the contribution of contextual factors to its long-term impact. For instance, a child may feel stigmatized by the response of parents or agencies to the disclosure of adult-child sex. Disclosure, however, may occur long after the actual sexual contact has ceased. It is this observation that sets the Traumagenic Dynamics perspective apart from most other perspectives on adult-child sexual contact. The recognition that negative outcomes in adulthood may arise from processes and dynamics within which the adult-child contact is embedded—both prior and subsequent to the actual sexual contact—is an important advance over the medicalized conceptualization of long-term effects implicit in the psychogenic approach.

Nevertheless, the notion of trauma, though multivocal, remains an essential element of Finkelhor's model. A wide range of adult-child sex outcomes are seen to be products of emotional disturbances flowing from characteristics of the sexual relationship that measure its severity. For instance, in an oft-cited article reviewing the literature on adult-child sexual contact effects, Finkelhor devotes considerable attention to the developing focus on differential outcomes by type of abuse—including the duration of the sexual contact, the relationship of the child to the perpetrator, and the extensiveness of the sexual activities that occurred (Browne & Finkelhor, 1986). Thus he considers the severity of the sexual contact (as measured by the event characteristics noted above) to be a key determinant of variation in the experience of long-term effects. Subsequent experiences, such as behavior patterns developed during adolescence and young adulthood that may be related to early childhood sexual activity, are given less emphasis. Moreover, as in other psychogenically based models, Finkelhor hypothesizes a tendency either to avoid sexual stimuli or to experience heightened sexual interest and activity (reproducing the hypothesis of a polarized pattern of behavioral responses to adult-child sex [Finkelhor, 1988]).

By failing to locate early sexual experiences within an unfolding and extended life trajectory, Finkelhor is constrained to explain the wide-ranging consequences of adult-child sex as direct effects of one or another traumagenic dynamic—often resulting in awkward causal linkages. For instance, he links the posited effect of adult-child sex on later employment problems directly to feelings of inefficacy and lack of control traumatically instilled through the dynamic of powerlessness. A more plausible explanation of this outcome links adult-child sexual experiences with a range of subsequent adolescent outcomes such as increased numbers of sexual partners, delinquency, and leaving home before age 18, all of which (directly or indirectly) may be associated with reduced educational and employment prospects. The other major models considered earlier—the PTSD framework and the cognitive behavioral theory—focus attention almost exclusively on the sexual contact relationship itself. Implicit in these perspectives is the notion that much if not all of the explanation for long-term effects can be found in aspects of the sexual contact. If researchers can accurately measure the severity of the sexual contact and the degree of stress experienced by the child, predictive capacity will be maximized. Subsequent negative experiences should be seen as manifestations of trauma flowing from the original event.

In short, the Traumagenic Dynamics framework, the PTSD model, the cognitive behavioral theory, and other models rooted in the psychogenic perspective posit heterogeneity in the degree of trauma induced by the experience of adult-child sex and explain long-term effects as a result of contemporary continuity in the emotional disturbance stemming from it. The life course approach, considered in more detail below, explains the wide-ranging effects of childhood sexual experiences by exploring their impact on subsequent life trajectories rather than forcing an artificial linkage between an induced psychic condition and multiple, diverse, and temporally distant outcomes.

A Life Course Perspective on the Effects of Childhood Sexual Experiences

In contrast to the psychogenic perspective, the life course approach suggests that early sexual experiences must be contextualized in an unfolding life history in order to understand their impact across time. A critical concept is the notion of a "sexual trajectory," consisting of the transition to sociosexual interaction and intercourse, for instance, and patterns of entry into and exit from subsequent sexual partnerships. Below, we incorporate this concept into a theory of the link between early sexual experiences and subsequent outcomes based on a dynamic integration of social control and social learning theory.

Rooted in the criminological tradition, the social control perspective suggests that delinquency is a result of attenuated ties to conventional persons and institutions (Hirschi, 1969; Kornhauser, 1978). Social control is achieved through effective socialization (development of the internal capacity to regulate action [Gottfredson & Hirschi, 1990]) and the establishment of strong social bonds that enforce conformity to mainstream norms (Sampson & Laub, 1993). In the absence of adequate controls, individuals are "free" to pursue short-term gratification, resulting in a pattern of generalized deviance (Hirschi & Gottfredson, 1994).

In contrast to control theory, the learning perspective suggests that delinquency is the result of imitation and reinforcement of such behaviors through associations with delinquent individuals. In turn, the nature and extent of these associations will best predict delinquent outcomes (Akers, 1973; Bandura, 1973; Elliott et al., 1985). Sources of reinforcement include the social rewards of participating in peer group–supported delinquent activities as well as the intrinsic rewards of specific criminal behaviors (Wood, Gove, Wilson, & Cochran, 1997).

In essence, the life course perspective suggests that the long-term effects of early sexual experiences stem from two key processes: (a) reinforcement of particular sexual behaviors and "scripts"[3] for sexual interaction; and (b) inadequate sexual socialization or failure to develop effective internal control over sexual impulses. These processes are linked to central concepts of social learning (reinforcement) and control (internal control) perspectives, respectively. In the context of the life course, early reinforcement of sexual activity without adequate sexual socialization creates vulnerabilities to subsequent events that may have independent effects on adult well-being. These events may, for instance, contribute to attenuation in social bonds (or external controls). Examining the ramifications of these processes across the life course highlights the importance of structural sources of continuity (interactional and cumulative) that contribute to adverse outcomes in adulthood.

CHILDHOOD SEXUAL EXPERIENCES IN THE SHORT TERM

Early sexual experiences offer the child an introduction to the experience of sexual pleasure. This process of eroticization—meaning, the process by which specific acts are linked cognitively to sexual arousal[4]—should be seen as a relative novelty in the sensory history of a child (Gagnon & Simon, 1973). Through instilling specifically sexual impulses, then, early sexual interactions produce state-dependent effects on the child's level of sexual interest. Early sexual activity is likely to be reinforced not only by the incipient pleasure experienced but also by the nonsexual rewards for which it is exchanged (Finkelhor, 1988). As Finkelhor has noted, these may include love, affection, and approval, in addition to more concrete rewards. Indeed, for a child who has not experienced eroticization, social (and potentially material) reinforcements are a critically important component of the process by which early sexual interactions are initiated and maintained.

Having few if any alternative sources of knowledge regarding sexuality, children who participate in early sexual relationships assimilate a model or script of sexual interaction on which future relationships are based (Gagnon & Simon, 1973; Wyatt, Newcomb, & Riederle, 1993). Elements of this model may include (a) concrete sexual behaviors and sequences of acts constituting sexual interaction, and (b) aspects of the sexual relationship. Reinforcement of specific behaviors and characteristics of the sexual dyad will result in heightened interest in and preoccupation with these event-specific sexual practices.

Early sexual activity, however, generates sexual impulses and interests without also providing the capacity to manage or regulate them. Since these activities tend to occur before a child has been introduced to the normative definitions of appropriate courtship and sexual behavior and little knowledge of them is imparted during the interaction itself, the necessary internalized constraints on sexual behavior are not developed. While eroticization is a normal component of sexual development typically occurring during adolescence, this process is usually accompanied by information on socially defined parameters of appropriate sexual expression. The early timing of eroticization and the transmission of inappropriate sexual scripts, combined with poorly developed sexual impulse controls, lead to developmentally inappropriate sexual interests and behavior. Indeed, the most consistently documented short-term effect of sexual abuse is heightened or maladjusted sexual behavior (Beitchman et al., 1991; Knutson, 1995; Urquiza & Capra, 1990). Accordingly, the life course perspective emphasizes this discrepancy between sexual impulses and self-regulatory capacities—a process we refer to as "sexualization"[5]—as a critical link between early childhood sexual experiences and long-term adverse outcomes.

An important implication of this emphasis is that sexual contacts between adults and children may be no more likely to produce sexualized behavior than explicitly sexual contacts with adolescents or even peers. Sexual contacts with peers or slightly older children may also serve to eroticize a child, resulting in similar tendencies toward sexualized behavior. However, peer sexual contacts may involve different reinforcement contingencies, particularly with respect to characteristics of the partner. Peer sexual contacts are significantly less likely to involve a partner of the same gender for men, a distinction that may have important consequences for long-term outcomes.

The sexualization of the child induces vulnerability to subsequent experiences that are independent predictors of long-term adverse outcomes. Below, we demonstrate how the process of sexualization produces behavioral orientations that have implications for life trajectories.

CONTINUITY IN THE EFFECTS OF EARLY SEXUAL EXPERIENCES

As noted, childhood sexual experiences involve eroticization without the development of adequate self-regulatory capacities as well as potential reinforcement of specific behaviors and scripts for sexual interaction. Accordingly, we should observe an increase in the overall level of sexual activity and interest among individuals who experience early sexual activity, including early adolescent intercourse and increased numbers of sexual partners. As noted earlier, we should also observe heightened interest in or tendencies to engage in behaviors or relationship characteristics that were specific to the childhood sexual contact. First, early childhood sexual experiences will involve particular types of sexual contact and sequences of sexual activities. Sexual acts may include genital fondling and oral, vaginal, or anal sex (depending on the gender of the partner). To the extent that these activities are reinforced by early sexual contact, they will tend to remain significant components of an individual's sexual behavior repertoire —potentially over long spans of the life course.

Second, characteristics of the sexual dyad may also be reinforced. For instance, in some instances (mainly involving male children), sexual contact may occur with a partner of the same gender. Indeed, a relatively large percentage of childhood sexual experiences involving boys and adult partners are same-gender contacts (54%). Reinforced same-gender sexuality will increase the likelihood of subsequent same-gender sexual interest and behavior. Consistent with the predictions of the social learning perspective, then, individuals may specialize in particular types of sexual relationships reinforced at an early age.

Continuity in behaviors and interests learned through early sexual interaction will result not only from individual-level factors (e.g., their incorporation into fantasy [Gagnon & Simon, 1973]) but also from structural sources. The level of sexual awareness and, in some cases, "pseudo-maturity" of children who have experienced adult-child sexual contact may signal sexual availability. Mausert-Mooney, Trickett, and Putnam (1995) found that girls who had experienced sexual contact with an older male were perceived to be older, more personally attractive, and more flirtatious. Boys may provide comparable cues by engaging in assertive sexual behavior (Friedrich & Luecke, 1988). Moreover, boys who are perceived to be inclined toward same-gender sexual activity may be categorized as homosexual and, hence, unavailable for heterosexual relationships. Interactional continuity, then, will occur through responses of others that support a sexually active orientation or cement existing models of sexual interaction.

The establishment and maintenance of same-gender sexual scripts may be an important source of long-term effects for men who experience early sexual contact. Since a majority of adult-child sexual experiences occur with males (compared with a minority of peer sexual contacts), a possible effect of this experience may be sexual preference conflicts stemming from erotic impulses toward both genders. Long-term sexual adjustment problems may result from efforts to reconcile both same- and opposite-sex desire in a culture that emphasizes strict bipolar categories of sexual orientation—particularly for men (Bem, 1996). In this sense, learned same-gender sexual interest can be understood as a precursor to strain induced by conflict between an individual-level desire and social barriers to its fulfillment. Any same-gender interest (whether exclusive or non-exclusive) will likely encounter social resistance at some point during the life course. However, lasting emotional problems stemming from same-gender desire may be most likely for individuals who fall between the polarized categories of homo- and heterosexual. According to the expectations of this hypothesis, the problematic category—for men who experienced adult-child sex—would be reported attraction to both sexes, not one exclusively. By definition, this hypothesis exempts exclusively opposite-sex orientations as well as exclusively same-sex attraction from long-term sexual preference conflict.

Patterns of sexual activity established in the aftermath of childhood sexual experiences may have a cumulative impact on long-term well-being for both men and women. Girls who experience childhood sexual contacts are at high risk of early and extensive sexual activity during adolescence, which, in turn, increases the likelihood of teenage pregnancy and childbirth (Roosa, 1997; Stock, Bell, Boyer, & Connell, 1997), multiple sexual partnerships (Roosa, 1997), and their associated adverse effects (including sexually transmitted infection), all of which may combine to reduce sexual functioning and the capacity to establish stable sexual partnerships in adulthood. Unequipped to manage the consequences of a sexually charged interaction style (Mausert-Mooney et al., 1995), some girls who have experienced early sex may be vulnerable to sexually aggressive or predatory men. Subsequent forced sexual experiences in adolescence and early adulthood will independently impact sexual adjustment.

For men, more active and less stable sexual careers in adolescence may also reduce the likelihood of maintaining an enduring sexual relationship in adulthood. Indeed, the link between childhood sexual experiences and adverse outcomes in adulthood may, in part, be a function of the fact that men who experience early sexual activity are less likely to be currently enjoying the benefits accruing to men from marriage. Married men are more likely to report high levels of well-being and relationship satisfaction than men in other forms of relationships or single men (Waite & Joyner, 2001). Same-gender sexual tendencies also reduce the chances of marriage and may provoke negative reactions from family members. Finally, active sexual careers also increase the likelihood of sexually transmitted infection for men, which may have long-term implications for adequate sexual functioning.

SOCIAL CONTROLS IN THE AFTERMATH OF CHILDHOOD SEXUAL EXPERIENCES

Sexualized behavior patterns stemming from early sexual experiences may have a cumulative impact on the strength and effectiveness of social controls. Since a majority of children who have early sexual experiences never tell anyone about the event (Laumann, Gagnon, Michael, & Michaels, 1994), sexualized behavior may be perceived as an unprovoked conduct disorder requiring discipline. Attempts to correct the behavior may lead to conflicts with parents or teachers, resulting in "child effects" on the likelihood of negative responses (Lytton, 1990). In one sample of abused children, Gomes-Schwarz et al. (1990) found that conflict with parents and siblings worsened between an initial postabuse evaluation and an 18-month follow-up interview. In cases where the adult-child sexual contact comes to the attention of parents and/or authorities, family relationships and living arrangements may in some instances be disrupted. Widom (1991) has suggested that one mechanism through which adult-child sexual contact may lead to subsequent deviant outcomes is through its effect on environments or family conditions, which, in turn, may later predispose the child to delinquency. In this way, antisocial behavior may result not so much from the abuse or neglect but from the chain of events subsequent to the abuse or neglect. For example, being taken away from one's biological parents and placed in foster care—as a result of abuse or neglect—may be associated with deleterious effects (Widom, 1991).

Widom's example focuses on less typical abuse cases that involve official intervention. Sexually aggressive or age-inappropriate behavior, however, may also challenge or disrupt the parent-child bond. Indeed, these observations point to the potentially significant role of the relationship between the child and the adult perpetrator for the breakdown of social controls. Intrafamilial adult-child sexual relationships—involving fathers or stepfathers specifically—may disrupt an important attachment, leading to attenuated informal social control. Yet fathers or stepfathers who are predisposed to engage in sexual relationships with their children may not be performing an important caretaking role to begin with. In such cases, there may be little prior attachment to threaten through a sexually abusive relationship.

Researchers in human development and criminology have found strong correlations among deviant behaviors in adolescence, including early age at first intercourse, illicit drug use, and delinquency, suggesting that unconventional behaviors tend to cluster together (Elliott & Morse, 1989; Huizinga, Loeber, & Thornberry, 1994; Jessor, Costa, Jessor, & Donovan,

1983). The effects of heightened levels of sexual interest and the attenuation of social controls may lead children who have experienced early sexual contacts to select deviant peer groups. This tendency has been demonstrated among adolescent girls with respect to sexual behavior. Billy, Rodgers, and Udry (1985) found that girls tend to select friends whose sexual behavior is similar to their own, even after controlling for other more visible forms of deviant behavior. Comparable analyses of boys have not yielded evidence that sexual behavior serves as a selection criterion for entry into deviant peer groups. However, the attenuation of social controls may lead boys to engage in nonsexual deviant behaviors (for instance, aggression) that serve as selection criteria.

Cairns and Cairns have noted the mutuality of this process of peer group formation. That is, "bi-selection" operates when peer groups identify and select compatible peers for membership while being concomitantly selected by the targeted adolescent (Cairns & Cairns, 1994). Moreover, even if boys do not directly select sexually active peers for associates, they may be aware of the deviant behavior patterns of others in the social environment who are known to be sexually active (Moffitt, 1997). In this context, the prior and potentially ongoing attenuation of informal social controls may be easily translated into a range of deviant activities. Participation in these activities, in turn, may further contribute to the deterioration of controls (Thornberry, 1987). From this perspective, we would expect early sexual experiences to be associated with a generalized pattern of problem behavior.

Participation in a range of adolescent problem behavior and the network-level anchoring of this behavior can have a cascading effect on long-term well-being, particularly for men. Delinquency, for instance, diminishes the chances of entering or maintaining a successful marriage (Sampson & Laub, 1993). Childhood sexual experiences on nonsexual trajectories may also influence current well-being and sexual adjustment through their effects on the physical health of the men (i.e., through drug and alcohol use or physical injury). Pathways from early childhood sexual experiences to reduced well-being in adulthood, then, are multiple and interdependent over time.

THE COMMUNITY CONTEXT OF ADAPTATION
TO CHILDHOOD SEXUAL EXPERIENCES

Building on the recognition that the strength of social controls during later childhood, adolescence, and even adulthood is an important component of the unfolding consequences of early sexual experiences, the life course perspective highlights the potential role of neighborhood social context in the association between childhood events and later well-being. Is childhood sexual experience more likely to lead to subsequent adverse events like early first intercourse and generalized deviance in contexts that lack adequate extrafamilial social controls?

The emerging literature on the role of neighborhood in regulating problem behavior among adolescents suggests that an exclusive focus on parent-child or peer attachments may neglect the informal social control functions of broader communities of residence. Sampson, Raudenbush, and Earls (1997), for instance, found that structural factors such as poverty, residential instability, and immigrant concentration were associated with perceptions of violence, self-reported victimization, and the homicide rate in Chicago neighborhoods. A substantial proportion of the effect of these structural factors was mediated by neighborhood "collective efficacy" or the combined social cohesion and capacity for informal social control exhibited by Chicago communities. Research on the role of neighborhood in early child development has also indicated that structural features of children's social context may exert independent effects on their well-being (e.g., cognitive development [Brooks-Gunn, Duncan, Klebanov, & Sealand, 1993; Sampson, 1997]).

These and other studies suggest that community context may also have important moderating effects on children's adaptation to sexual abuse. Beyond the social control capacity of the family, communities that exert some measure of informal social control over adolescent sexual behavior (e.g., by regulating access to risky sexual partners or spaces where risky sexual behavior may occur) may diminish the vulnerability of children who have experienced sexual abuse. The protective effects of "socially organized" neighborhoods thus may extend to the cumulative consequences of child sexual abuse, shielding some children from subsequent adverse events that have independent consequences for adult well-being.

Conclusions

Recognizing that sexual abuse can be experienced as a traumatic event, we have argued that explanation of its long-term effects must acknowledge the impact of life course trajectories in the aftermath of early sexual contacts. First, undue reliance on the concept of trauma to account for the range of long-term effects of childhood sexual contacts has obscured the cumulative impact of these experiences. Childhood sexual experiences should be understood as embedded in dynamically unfolding lives. Research efforts that seek to track the consequences of early sexual events through behavioral pathways may prove more fruitful than the continued and restrictive focus on the nature and severity of event-specific trauma. Second, and relatedly, shifting attention away from the direct effects of variably traumatic early sexual experiences to the consequences of behavioral patterns in their aftermath motivates a search for the determinants of the onset and persistence of risky trajectories. More subtle attention to the mechanisms by which consequential sexual trajectories are sustained through adolescence and adulthood may lead to an increased focus on the role of family as well as community in channeling the impact of child sexual experiences (as well as other forms of child maltreatment) over time. Future research may also illuminate the consequences of sexualized behavior for the effectiveness of informal social controls and the potential for a wider range of problem behavior to result as a function of the intervening attenuation of critical social bonds (a pathway which may be particularly relevant for boys).

Finally, the perspective developed here points to the potential efficacy of protective as opposed to palliative intervention strategies. Trauma-based conceptions of the long-term effects of early sex often imply a certain degree of inevitability to negative adult outcomes. Highly traumatic events, in this view, "doom" a child to lingering psychic pain. If the long-term effects of early sexual experiences are cumulative, however, a better understanding of "turning points" away from risky trajectories may aid in the development of mechanisms to shield at-risk youth from the adverse experiences to which they are vulnerable.

Notes

1. The typology is based loosely on Robert Agnew's discussion of types of delinquency that produce strain (Agnew, 1992).

2. Indeed, empirical tests of the dose-response hypothesis are one of the most common applications of the psychogenic perspective more broadly. Other event characteristics that have been examined include the relationship of the child to the adult involved and the age of the child at the time of the event (Rind, Tromovitch, & Bauserman, 1998).

3. The utility of the scripting concept in this context is in its recognition of the learned nature of sexual interaction. The notion of learned interpersonal scripts for sexual communication and their intrapsychic grounding through fantasy can be fruitfully applied to the investigation of the effects of early sexual experiences. This more narrow employment of the scripting framework does not require importing its claim that sexual phenomena are entirely socially constructed.

4. Gagnon and Simon (1973, p. 77) define eroticization as the process by which parts of the body are "given meanings such that when they are touched in appropriate circumstances" an individual is able to report to him- or herself that pleasure is being experienced.

5. "Sexualization" should be distinguished from "eroticization." Sexualization occurs when eroticization is not accompanied by the development of effective internal controls on sexual expression. The connection of the term "sexualization" to Finkelhor's "traumatic sexualization" is deliberate. The emphasis of that particular traumagenic dynamic in Finkelhor's model is on the impact of inappropriately rewarded sexual behavior. The child may learn to use sexuality manipulatively and may "fetishize" sexual parts of his or her body. These consequences conform to the more general processes high-

lighted by the life course approach—reinforcement of both activities as well as interactional dynamics occurring during the early sexual experience.

References

Agnew, R. (1992). Foundation for a general strain theory of crime and delinquency. *Criminology, 30,* 47–87.

Akers, R. L. (1973). *Deviant behavior: A social learning approach.* Belmont, CA: Wadsworth.

American Psychiatric Association. (1994). *Diagnostic and statistical manual of mental disorders* (4th ed.). Washington, DC: Author.

Armstrong, L. (1978). *Kiss Daddy goodnight.* New York: Hawthorn.

Bandura, A. (1973). *Aggression: A social learning analysis.* Englewood Cliffs, NJ: Prentice Hall.

Bandura, A., & Walters, R. (1963). *Social learning and personality development.* New York: Holt, Rinehart and Winston, Inc.

Beitchman, J. H., Zucker, K. J., Hood, J. E., DaCosta, G. A., & Akman, D. (1991). A review of the short-term effects of child sexual abuse. *Child Abuse & Neglect, 15,* 537–556.

Beitchman, J. H., Zucker, K. J., Hood, J. E., DaCosta, G. A., Akman, D., & Cassavia, E. (1992). A review of the long-term effects of child sexual abuse. *Child Abuse & Neglect, 16,* 101–118.

Bem, D. J. (1996). Exotic becomes erotic: A developmental theory of sexual orientation. *Psychological Review, 103,* 320.

Billy, J. O. G., Rodgers, J. L., & Udry, J. R. (1985). Adolescent sexual behavior and friendship choice. *Social Forces, 62,* 653–678.

Briggs, L., & Joyce, P. R. (1997). What determines post-traumatic stress disorder symptomatology for survivors of childhood sexual abuse? *Child Abuse & Neglect, 21,* 575–582.

Brooks-Gunn, J., Duncan, G. J., Klebanov, P. K., & Sealand, N. (1993). Do neighborhoods influence child and adolescent development? *American Journal of Sociology, 99,* 353–395.

Browne, A., & Finkelhor, D. (1986). Impact of child sexual abuse: A review of the research. *Psychological Bulletin, 99,* 66–77.

Browning, C. R. (2003). Trauma or transition: A life course perspective on the link between childhood sexual experience and men's adult well-being. *Social Science Research* (pp. 473–510).

Browning, C. R., & Laumann, E. O. (1997). Sexual contact between children and adults: A life course perspective. *American Sociological Review, 62,* 540–560.

Cairns, R. B., & Cairns, B. D. (1994). *Lifelines and risks.* Cambridge, MA: Cambridge University Press.

Caspi, A. (1987). Personality in the life course. *Journal of Personality and Social Psychology, 53,* 1203–1213.

Deblinger, E., McLeer, S. V., Atkins, M. S., Ralphe, D., & Foa, E. (1989). Post-traumatic stress in sexually abused, physically abused, and nonabused children. *Child Abuse & Neglect, 13,* 403–408.

Elder, G. H., Jr. (1985). Perspectives on the life course. In G. H. Elder, Jr. (Ed.), *Life course dynamics: Trajectories and transitions, 1968–1980.* Ithaca, NY: Cornell University Press.

Elliott, D. S., Huizinga, D., & Ageton, S. S. (1985). *Explaining delinquency and drug use.* Beverly Hills, CA: Sage.

Elliott, D. S., & Morse, B. J. (1989). Delinquency and drug use as factors in teenage sexual activity. *Youth and Society, 21,* 32–60.

Eth, S., & Pynoos, R. S. (1985). *Post-traumatic stress disorder in children.* Washington, DC: American Psychiatric Press.

Felitti, V., Anda, R. F., Nordenberg, D., Williamson, D. F., Spitz, A. M., Edwards, V., et al. (1998). Relationship of childhood abuse and household dysfunction to many of the leading causes of death in adults. *American Journal of Preventive Medicine, 14,* 245–258.

Finkelhor, D. (1988). The trauma of child sexual abuse: Two models. In G. E. Wyatt & G. J. Powell (Eds.), *Lasting effects of child sexual abuse* (pp. 61–84). Newbury Park, CA: Sage.

Finkelhor, D. (1990). Early and long-term effects of child sexual abuse: An update. *Professional Psychology: Research and Practice, 21,* 325–330.

Finkelhor, D., Hotaling, G., Lewis, I. A., & Smith, C. (1990). Sexual abuse in a national survey of adult men and women: Prevalence, characteristics, and risk factors. *Child Abuse & Neglect, 14,* 19–28.

Freud, S. (1955). The aetiology of hysteria. In J. Strachey (Ed. & Trans.), *The standard edition of the complete psychological works of Sigmund Freud* (Vol. 3, pp. 146–158). London: Hogarth. (Originally published 1896.)

Freyd, J. (1996). *Betrayal trauma.* Cambridge, MA: Harvard University Press.

Friedrich, W. N. (1988). Behavior problems in sexually abused children. In G. E. Wyatt & G. J. Powell (Eds.), *Lasting effects of child sexual abuse* (pp. 171–191). Newbury Park, CA: Sage.

Friedrich, W. N., & Luecke, W. J. (1988). Young school-age sexually aggressive children. *Professional Psychology: Research and Practice, 19,* 155–164.

Gagnon, J. H., & Simon, W. (1973). *Sexual conduct: The social sources of human sexuality.* Chicago: Aldine.

Gay, P. (1989). *The Freud reader.* New York: W. W. Norton.

Gelinas, D. J. (1983). The persisting effects of incest. *Psychiatry, 46,* 312–332.

Gomes-Schwarz, B., Horowitz, J., & Cardarelli, A. (1990). *Child sexual abuse: The initial effects.* Newbury Park, CA: Sage.

Gottfredson, M., & Hirschi, T. (1990). *A general theory of crime.* Stanford, NY: Stanford University Press.

Green, A. H. (1992). Applications of psychoanalytic theory in the treatment of the victim and the family. In W. O'Donohue & J. H. Geer (Eds.), *Sexual abuse of children: Vol. 2. Clinical issues* (pp. 285–300). Hillsdale, NJ: Lawrence Erlbaum.

Green, A. H. (1993). Child sexual abuse: Immediate and long-term effects and intervention. *Journal of the American Academy of Child and Adolescent Psychiatry, 32,* 890–902.

Hirschi, T. (1969). *Causes of delinquency.* Berkeley: University of California Press.

Hirschi, T., & Gottfredson, M. R. (1994). *The generality of deviance.* New Brunswick, NJ: Transaction.

Hoier, T. S., Shawchuck, C. R., Pallotta, G. M., Freeman, T., Inderbitzen-Pisaruk, H.,

MacMillan, V. M., et al. (1992). The impact of sexual abuse: A cognitive-behavioral model. In W. O'Donohue & J. H. Geer (Eds.), *Sexual abuse of children: Vol. 2. Clinical issues* (pp. 100–142). Hillsdale, NJ: Lawrence Erlbaum.

Horowitz, M. J. (1976). *Stress response syndromes.* New York: Jason Aronson.

Huizinga, D., Loeber, R., & Thornberry, T. P. (1994). *Urban delinquency and substance abuse: Initial findings.* Washington, DC: U.S. Department of Justice, Office of Juvenile Justice and Delinquency Prevention.

Janoff-Bulman, R. (1985). The aftermath of victimization: Rebuilding shattered assumptions. In C. R. Figley (Ed.), *Trauma and its wake: The study and treatment of post-traumatic stress disorder* (pp. 15–35). New York: Brunner/Mazel.

Jessor, R., Costa, F., Jessor, L., & Donovan, J. E. (1983). Time of first intercourse: A prospective study. *Journal of Personality and Social Psychology, 44,* 608–626.

Knutson, J. F. (1995). Psychological characteristics of maltreated children: Putative risk factors and consequences. *Annual Review of Psychology, 46,* 401–431.

Kornhauser, R. R. (1978). *Social sources of delinquency.* Chicago: University of Chicago Press.

Laumann, E. O., Gagnon, J. H., Michael, R. T., & Michaels, S. (1994). *The social organization of sexuality: Sexual practices in the United States.* Chicago: University of Chicago Press.

Lytton, H. (1990). Child and parent effects in boys' conduct disorder: A reinterpretation. *Developmental Psychology, 26,* 683–697.

Masson, J. M. (1984). *The assault on truth: Freud's suppression of the seduction theory.* New York: Farrar, Straus and Giroux.

Mausert-Mooney, R., Trickett, P. K., & Putnam, F. W. (1995). *Appeal and vulnerability patterns of girl victims of incest.* Unpublished manuscript.

McLeer, S. V., Deblinger, E., Atkins, M., Foa, E., & Ralphe, D. (1988). Post-traumatic stress disorder in sexually abused children. *Journal of the American Academy of Child and Adolescent Psychiatry, 27,* 650–654.

McLeer, S. V., Deblinger, E., Henry, D., & Orvaschel, H. (1992). Sexually abused children at high risk for post-traumatic stress disorder. *Journal of the American Academy of Child and Adolescent Psychiatry, 31,* 875–879.

Moffitt, T. E. (1997). Adolescence-limited and life course persistent offending: A complementary pair of developmental theories. In T. P. Thornberry (Ed.), *Developmental theories of crime and delinquency* (pp. 11–54). New Brunswick, NJ: Transaction.

Rind, B., Tromovitch, P., & Bauserman, R. (1998). A meta-analytic examination of assumed properties of child sexual abuse using college samples. *Psychological Bulletin, 124,* 22–53.

Roosa, M. W. (1997). The relationship of childhood sexual abuse to teenage pregnancy. *Journal of Marriage and the Family, 50,* 119–130.

Rutter, M. (1988). Longitudinal data in the study of causal processes: Some uses and some pitfalls. In M. Rutter (Ed.), *Studies of psychosocial risk: The power of longitudinal data* (pp. 1–28). Cambridge, MA: Cambridge University Press.

Sampson, R. J. (1997). The embeddedness of child and adolescent development: A community-level perspective on urban violence. In J. McCord (Ed.), *Violence and childhood in the inner city* (pp. 31–77). Cambridge: Cambridge University Press.

Sampson, R. J., & Laub, J. H. (1993). *Crime in the making: Pathways and turning points through life*. Cambridge, MA: Harvard University Press.

Sampson, R. J., Raudenbush, S. W., & Earls, R. (1997). Neighborhoods and violent crime: A multilevel study of collective efficacy. *Science, 227*, 918–923.

Stock, J. L., Bell, M. A., Boyer, D. K., & Connell, F. A. (1997). Adolescent pregnancy and sexual risk-taking among sexually abused girls. *Family Planning Perspectives, 29*, 200–203.

Terr, L. C. (1991). Childhood traumas: An outline and overview. *American Journal of Psychiatry, 148*, 10–20.

Thornberry, T. P. (1987). Toward an interactional theory of delinquency. *Criminology, 25*, 863–891.

Urquiza, A. J., & Capra, M. (1990). The impact of sexual abuse: Initial and long-term effects. In M. Hunter (Ed.), *The sexually abused male: Vol. 1. Prevalence, impact, and treatment* (pp. 105–135). Lexington, MA: Lexington.

Waite, L. J., & Joyner, K. (2001). Emotional and physical satisfaction with sex in married, cohabiting, and dating sexual unions: Do men and women differ? In E. O. Laumann & R. T. Michael (Eds.), *Sex, love, and health in America: Private choices and public policies* (pp. 239–269). Chicago: University of Chicago Press.

Widom, C. S. (1989). Child abuse, neglect, and violent criminal behavior. *Criminology, 27*, 251–272.

Widom, C. S. (1991). Childhood victimization: Risk factor for delinquency. In M..E. Colten & S. Gore (Eds.), *Adolescent stress: Causes and consequences* (pp. 201–222). New York: Aldine de Gruyter.

Wood, P. B., Gove, W. R., Wilson, J. A., & Cochran, J. K. (1997). Nonsocial reinforcement and habitual criminal conduct: An extension of learning theory. *Criminology, 35*, 335–366.

Wyatt, G. E., Newcomb, M. D., & Riederle, M. H. (1993). *Sexual abuse and consensual sex: Women's developmental patterns and outcomes*. Newbury Park, CA: Sage.

Childhood Sexuality and Adult Sexual Relationships

How Are They Connected by Data and by Theory?

JULIA R. HEIMAN, JOHAN VERHULST,
AND AMY R. HEARD-DAVISON

Trying to conceptualize the connections between childhood sexuality and adult sexual relationships is an attempt to track developmental cohesiveness and continuity. This task is challenging given the current climate pervading the scholarship in this area, the cultural hesitation to question (nonabused) children about their sexuality, methodological issues, the correlational nature of the data, the preponderance of existing research on sexual abuse rather than normative sexual development, and the relativity of the definitions of healthy childhood sexuality, sexual abuse, sexual adjustment, and relationship quality. What is an appropriate and healthy level of sexuality in a child or in an adult is ultimately a question of what is good sexuality. The answer will be culturally bound. It is no wonder that there is so much disagreement in the research literature about definitions and proper sampling and measurement.

We will first briefly summarize existing data describing correlations between childhood sexual experience and adult sexual relationships. The data are almost exclusively on the topic of childhood sexual abuse (CSA) rather than normative development and biased toward female research participants, at least in the adult literature. We then propose an initial conceptual framework in terms of levels of influence and of redundancies that reduce the variability of developmental outcomes. No single theoretical perspective by itself offers enough detailed mechanisms to account for the pattern of results relating childhood sexual abuse to adult sexual behaviors.

We distinguish childhood sexual abuse from childhood sexual behavior. Childhood sexual abuse is defined according to the key elements identified in research studies. Although a standard definition is lacking, and some researchers have included noncontact sexual activity and verbal comments, the more common elements of CSA are unwanted sexual contact, during the period when a victim is legally considered a child, and the perpetrator is occupying a position of relative power with respect to the child (Paolucci, Genuis, & Violato, 2001; Rind, Tromovitch, & Bauserman, 1998). Childhood sexual behavior is defined as developmentally appropriate (clearly subject to different interpretations), wanted, and noncoercive, between individuals of similar ages, or incidental nudity between family members. However, much of the literature collapses all childhood sexual behavior into "abuse," suspected precursors of abuse, or evidence of abuse proneness (e.g., young children taking showers with adult family members). This is part of the reality of the current epoch of research in this area. Definitional disagreements are reflective of strong personal and cultural opinions regarding what constitutes normative, healthy childhood sexuality. We can expect these definitions to change over time as well as across cultures. Current definitional imprecision limits our ability to form firm conclusions about the universality, pervasiveness, and durability of CSA correlates for women and men.

Correlations between Childhood Sexual Abuse and Sexuality

Summary of CSA and Childhood Sexuality

Researchers comparing sexually abused children to nonabused comparison samples have found that abused children are more symptomatic on many variables, including fear, posttraumatic stress disorder (PTSD), mental illness, cruelty, tantrums, enuresis, encopresis, self-injurious behavior, and inappropriate sexual behavior (Beitchman, Zucker, Hood, DaCosta, & Akman, 1991; Kendall-Tackett, Williams, & Finkelhor, 1993). When comparisons have been made between sexually abused children and other clinical nonabused samples, sexually abused children were often less symptomatic than clinical samples in most of the studies. However, in their review of 45 studies, Kendall-Tackett et al. (1993) found that the abused children were consistently more symptomatic in their sexual behavior and in PTSD symptoms, although there was no specific syndrome and no single traumatizing process. These authors noted that the most commonly studied symptom was sexualized behavior, which accounted for 43% of the variance and, along with aggression, had the highest effect size (to be viewed cautiously, since only 5–6 studies were available for effect size calculations). Sexualized behavior, mostly found in the preschool-aged samples, typically included excessive or public masturbation, seductive behavior, sexualized play with dolls, placing objects in vaginas or anuses, requesting sexual stimulation, and age-inappropriate sexual knowledge (Beitchman et al., 1991). In adolescence, sexualized behavior was expressed in the forms of promiscuity, sexual aggression, and prostitution.

The study of CSA in children is hampered by the lack of consensus regarding definitions of CSA, report reliability checks, and consistent measures of individual and family functioning. With these limitations in mind, we can briefly summarize several patterns noted in the literature (Kendall-Tackett et al., 1993; Rind et al., 1998): (1) Symptoms may be related to the presence of penetration, force, duration and frequency of abuse, the perpetrator's relationship to the child, and maternal support; (2) Inappropriate sexual behavior outcomes occurred in 26–38% of children and adolescents; about two-thirds show no evidence of sexual symptoms; (3) About one-third of victims are generally asymptomatic; (4) About two-thirds of victims show recovery within 12–18 months; approximately 10–25% may get worse; (5) There is no evidence of a specific syndrome or traumatizing process from CSA.

Summary of CSA and Adult Sexuality

Studies examining the sexual correlates of childhood sexual abuse can be divided into two major categories: sexual functioning and satisfaction, and high-risk behaviors for disease and pregnancy.

In examining sexual satisfaction and functioning in victims of CSA, diverse samples have yielded a wide range of results. Studies involving college undergraduates have found few associations between a history of CSA and subsequent sexual satisfaction, adjustment, and functioning (e.g., Alexander & Lupfer, 1987; Fromuth, 1986; Meston, Heiman, & Trapnell, 1999), though Kinzl, Traweger, and Biebl (1995) found associations between a history of CSA, particularly multiple incidents of CSA, and desire and orgasm disorders, and Meston et al. (1999) found a negative relationship to subjective sexual drive in female but not male undergraduates. Studies utilizing clinical and community samples of CSA victims, on the other hand, have more consistently found disrupted sexual patterns. Such studies have revealed that, compared to nonabused individuals, women with a history of CSA experience less frequent orgasm and less sexual responsiveness (Laumann, Paik, & Rosen, 1999; Tsai, Feldman-Summers, & Edgar, 1979; Walker et al., 1999), more sexual aversion, less subjective sexual arousal and fewer signs of physiological arousal (Wenninger & Heiman, 1998), lower levels of sexual satisfaction (Jackson, Calhoun, Amick, Maddever, & Habif, 1990; Tsai et al., 1979), and higher rates of current and past sexual dysfunction (Jackson et al., 1990; Sarwer & Durlak, 1996; Saunders, Villeponteaux, Lipovsky, Kilpatrick, & Veronen, 1992). The more limited data on men show sexual functioning (sexual desire, arousal, orgasm, and pain) may also be more problematic if there is a history of CSA (e.g., Laumann, Gagnon, Michael, & Michaels, 1994).

The prevalence and extent of these findings vary, depending on sample, sexual activity, and relationship between individuals involved. Meta-analyses by Rind and colleagues have calculated small effect sizes on significant sexual problem variables (Rind & Tromovitch, 1997; Rind et al., 1998).

With regard to "high-risk" sexual behaviors, women with a history of CSA have been found to have more lifetime partners or higher rates of multiple sexual partners (Fergusson, Horwood, & Lynskey, 1997; Luster & Small, 1997; Meston et al., 1999; Tsai et al., 1979; Wenninger & Heiman, 1998; Wyatt, Guthrie, & Notgrass, 1992), as well as higher rates of early-onset consensual sexual activity, teenage pregnancy, and unprotected intercourse (Fergusson et al., 1997; Walker et al., 1999) than their non-abused peers. In addition, a history of CSA has also been linked to low self-efficacy concerning condom use (Brown, Kessel, Lourie, Ford, & Lipsitt, 1997), increased rates of abortion and anal sex (Wingood & DiClemente, 1997), higher rates of STDs (Kenney, Reinholtz, & Angelini, 1998; Wingood & DiClemente, 1997) including HIV (Thompson, Potter, Sanderson, & Maibach, 1997; Wyatt, Forge, & Guthrie, 1998; Zierler et al., 1989), and inadequate safe sex decision-making and HIV prevention communication skills (Brown et al., 1997).

The above behaviors are currently commonly grouped under a single label, "high-risk" sexual behavior, since many of them have significant health correlates and consequences. An alternative perspective is that CSA adults tend to relate to others in a more "sexualized" way, meaning that they report a greater variety of sexual activity, have sex more frequently, and have more partners (e.g., Laumann et al., 1994; Meston et al., 1999). In the years before the HIV pandemic, these may have been neutral to positive findings in men, with the exception of the concern with STDs. Greater sexualization was and is more negative for women, who are more readily labeled promiscuous and are subject to the effects of pregnancy and its consequences.

In sum, research to date indicates that women with a history of CSA are not only more likely to experience difficulties in sexual satisfaction and functioning, but are also more likely to engage in a variety of sexual behaviors, some of which are associated with health risks. Among men, the data are less clear on these points, though there are some data to indicate CSA men are also more at risk for sexual dysfunction (Beitchman et al., 1992; Laumann et al., 1999). These findings have important implications for women's health and well-being. In particular, these findings suggest that women with a history of CSA may experience more relationship stress, associated with difficulties in sexual functioning, and may be at greater risk for a variety of diseases and disorders that are often correlated with high-risk sexual behavior, such as cervical cancer (e.g., La Vecchia et al., 1986), sexually transmitted diseases (Fergusson et al., 1997; Walker et al., 1999; Wingood & DiClemente, 1997) and HIV/AIDS (e.g., Grinstead, Faigeles, Binson, & Eversley, 1993).

CSA and Adult Functioning beyond Specifically Sexual Variables

While we will not review these data in detail, nonsexual variables deserve mention since they may impact a person's sexual functioning and relationships.

Frequently noted long-term correlates associated with CSA include depression (e.g., Saunders et al., 1992; Sedney & Brooks, 1984; Wenniger & Heiman, 1998), anxiety (e.g., Bryer, Nelson, Miller, & Krol, 1987; Cole, 1986), posttraumatic stress disorder (e.g., Brewin, Andrews, & Valentine,

2000; Orr et al., 1998; Rowan & Foy, 1993), borderline personality disorder (e.g., Briere & Zaidi, 1989; Shearer, Peters, Quaytman, & Ogden, 1990; Wagner & Linehan, 1997), and self-destructive behavior (e.g., Brown & Anderson, 1991; Herman & Hirschman, 1981; Saunders et al., 1992). Other symptoms have included dissociation, eating disorders, hostility, low self-esteem, somatization, and social maladjustment (see reviews by Bauserman & Rind, 1997; Beitchman et al., 1992; Briere & Runtz, 1993; Rind et al., 1998).

To the extent that CSA is an impactful event, either by itself or in combination with coexisting family environment variables, the above symptoms may indeed influence the ability to form and/or maintain sexual relationships. For example, depression decreases sexual interest, one's sense of self-worth, communication, and positive experiencing. Couples in which one person is depressed report more relationship discord and unhappiness (Fincham, Beach, Harold, & Osborne, 1997; Kurdek, 1998). Depression is highly prevalent and is twice as common in women as men. Far less common is borderline personality disorder, a diagnosis that is marked by features such as volatile instability of interpersonal relationships and body endangerment including sexual impulsivity (e.g., Wagner & Linehan, 1997).

From the meta-analyses of many of these studies, Rind and colleagues concluded the following: (a) the mean effect sizes were small for both men ($r = .07$) and women ($r = .10$) in college and in national probability samples; (b) significantly more college women than men (68% vs. 42%, respectively) reported some type of negative effect at some point after their CSA experience, though the size of this difference was small to medium ($r = .23$); (c) there were often "third variables" that could account for the CSA adult (i.e., college-age) adjustment effects, including family, school, and social disruption and the presence of other forms of abuse or neglect; (d) in college samples, adult adjustment was related to the level of consent for men but not for women, which means that if CSA is restricted to unwanted sex, men and women reported equivalent CSA-adjustment problems; (e) in college samples, self-reports of lasting effect from the CSA were uncommon in both genders, though women were slightly more likely to report lasting negative effects; (f) in college samples, women's current reflections concerning their CSA experiences were significantly more negative than those of males; and (g) in college samples, CSA and family environment were confounded, as students with a CSA history came from more problematic home environments (as indicated by nonsexual abuse and neglect, adaptability, conflict and pathology, family structure, support and bonding, and traditionalism [Rind & Tromovitch, 1997; Rind et al., 1998]). This work, along with the research using statistical controls, calls into question the assumption that CSA is necessarily highly correlated with (not to mention causes) psychological injury, including sexual adjustment problems. When CSA was a continuous (vs. dichotomous) variable, it was relatively unimportant compared to family environment variables (Rind et al., 1998).

Risk Factors, Contextual Variables, and CSA

While there are no comprehensive studies of risk factors for CSA or for predicting outcomes of CSA, several researchers have examined selected variables. In a national probability sample of U.S. women, Vogeltanz et al. (1999) reported three patterns predictive of CSA: respondents reporting (a) their fathers to be rejecting and unloving; (b) their mothers drinking if the parents remained together; and (c) their fathers drinking if, by age 16, the respondent's biologic family was no longer intact.

Rind et al. (1998) found that force and incest were associated with more negative reactions but only incest was associated with more adult symptoms in college students. In addition, they found repeated evidence that CSA men and women come from more troubled home environments. Family environment was found to be a better predictor of adult adjustment (symptoms) than CSA.

In spite of the recognition of different forms of abuse (physical, sexual, emotional, neglect), it is rare for studies to examine separate groups of individuals with physical vs. sexual abuse. It is very likely that most of the data produced to date on the effects of CSA are in fact confounded by childhood physical abuse. We feel that this impairs any conclusions made about CSA and its consequences. Several aspects of this issue have been examined by the senior author and colleagues (e.g., Meston et al., 1999; Schloredt & Heiman, in press). In college students of 466 Asian and 566 non-Asian ethnic backgrounds, we found that, in men, the selected measure of child sexual abuse was not correlated with measures of child physical abuse, emotional abuse, and neglect ($r = .06-.11$). In women, there was only a modest correlation ($r = .16-.23$) (Meston, Heiman, & Trapnell, 1999). This finding suggested sexual abuse might be an independent category of experience. More importantly, the sexual abuse measure was not correlated with any of the adult sexual behavior variables in men but was (again modestly) correlated with all nine variables in women. In men, emotional abuse was correlated with five of the adult sexual behavior/ adjustment variables.

More recently, we compared a volunteer community sample of women with a childhood history of either sexual (SA), sexual plus physical (SPA), or no abuse (C) (Schloredt & Heiman, in press). We found no differences between the groups on sexual desire, arousal/orgasm, or pain, but significantly greater negative affect (fear, anger, disgust) during sexual arousal for the SPA group, followed by the SA and then the C groups. SPA and SA women reported more negative perceptions of their sexuality and had significantly more (2.5–3 times more) lifetime sexual partners than did women with no abuse history. Except for number of partners, SA women typically did not differ significantly from either SPA or C women and were less impacted on the sexual variables measured than were women with a SPA history.

The Puzzle Presented by the CSA Data

If we accept the findings of the meta-analyses and studies that have used modifier variables or statistical controls, we are faced with an interesting pattern of findings: (1) Few people are intensely or pervasively affected by the experience of some type of abusive sexual contact in childhood; (2) Women are more affected than men by CSA, although men who report that force was involved may be similarly negatively affected; (3) CSA samples report adulthood sexuality that is more varied in behavior and fantasy, with more lifetime partners, earlier consensual intercourse, fewer protected sexual contacts, earlier pregnancy, and yet, more negative experiencing of sexual arousal and more frequent sexual desire and response problems; (4) Many clinical samples report higher levels of CSA. How might we understand and begin to conceptualize these results? And what, if anything, might they tell us about the development of nonabusive sexuality from childhood to adulthood?

From Childhood Sexual Experience to Adult Sexuality: Identifying Levels of Influence and Conceptualizing the Developmental Process

The CSA data and findings, summarized above, are often surprising and seem at times to be contradictory. If one accepts the data as real, one can only conclude that the conceptual framework used to interpret them must be inadequate. Unexpected, counterintuitive, and contradictory data suggest that one may need to adopt a new conceptual framework that makes them understandable and resolves the contradictions. We believe that, in order to make sense of these data, one needs to place them in the context of human psychological development. Children develop in time-place contexts. When focusing on the individual and his or her sexual development, one needs to keep in mind that a person is in fact inseparable from the larger contexts to which he or she belongs, and that sexual development involves a continuous process of interaction between genetic, epigenetic, and environmental factors. Family, social milieu, and culture are important environmental contexts of development. Adding to the complexity of the developmental process, and to our difficulties in describing it, is the fact that, as the individual grows and ages, the environmental contexts change and so do the person's perception and interpretation of past events, thoughts, feelings, and behaviors.

Our heritage for conceptualizing the development of human sexuality consists of psychoanalytic theory, evolution theory, systems theory, and, in sexology, scripting theory. Psychoanalytic theory sees psychosexual development as the basis of personality development and describes various paths that can lead to psychopathology. The evolutionary perspective defines outcomes in terms of fitness for survival and reproduction. Systems theory, as applied to family relationships, attends to the effects of recursive interaction patterns. Scripting theory is relativistic, with many outcomes being possible depending on a broad array of social variables. Different interpretations create different realities. From this perspective, biological propensities are assigned a secondary and more incidental role.

Each one of these theories offers a unique, but necessarily limited, perspective on the development from childhood to adult sexuality and on the development of sexual relationships. It may be useful to think in terms of levels of influence as a first step in conceptualizing the developmental pathways of childhood sexuality in a more comprehensive and overarching way.

Levels of Influence

Based upon general system theory (von Bertalanffy, 1968), Figure 1 diagrams the levels of analysis that we believe to be constitutive of an individual person. The level of the person comprises the totality of one's psychological experiences, integrated into a "biographical self" (Damasio, 1999). The drawing shows permeable boundaries between the levels to signify their potential for mutual interaction and influence. The level of the person encompasses the levels of the biological phenotype and the genes. Family context, social milieu, and cultural environment are its superordinate levels.

This model can be used to organize observations and research data from different theoretical perspectives, as well as to suggest potentially fruitful lines of investigation.

For instance, the content of sexual experiences as a child is likely to affect later sexuality. One can examine the child's *physical* experience (body parts involved, arousal, pain), psychological experience (desire for contact, pleasure, fear, disgust), relationship to the person being sexual (self, friend, family, stranger), interpretation and attribution of meaning (exploration, play, love, force, coercion), and immediately experienced consequences (shame, desire, fear, secrecy, closeness, family upset, exposure, embarrassment, punishment). Though we look at them at the level of the person, all these categories are being co-defined and co-interpreted by the family as well as by the social situation and prevalent cultural values. Furthermore, the memories of the events and their meanings and consequences change over time as the child matures. They will be influenced by additional sexual experiences, for example, or by exposure to further interpretations and proscriptions of sexuality. In our opinion, this process of reviewing and reinterpreting experiences has been insufficiently explored, even though it

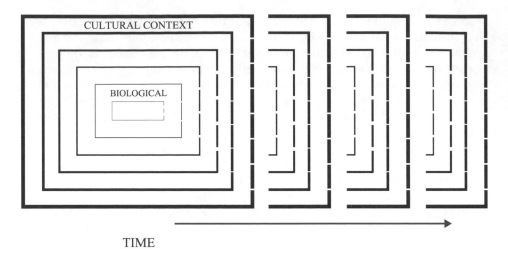

TIME

Figure 1. Levels of Influence

could very well account for the way in which early experiences are incorporated into an adult pattern.

Systems and scripting theories can be helpful, not only in understanding the research results, but also in generating explanatory hypotheses. Systems theory (Howes, Cicchetti, Toth, & Rogosch, 2000; Minuchin, 1985) tries to understand the development and maintenance of interpersonal interaction patterns, and scripting theory (Gagnon, 1990; Gagnon & Simon, 1973) focuses on the power of sociocultural values, expressed as roles and sociosexual scripts that are taken on by an individual. Looking through these lenses, one can assume that the extent to which early sexual experience plays a role in the development of a person's sexuality depends on the emotional intensity of the experience(s) as well as the response from the immediate context, which is usually the family. Aspects of childhood sexual experience are more likely to be incorporated into a sexual learning script if there is a great deal of intensity, either of fear or of pleasure. Similarly, repeated experiences are more likely to be incorporated. Furthermore, the family will shape the meaning of the experiences, especially if the family knows about the sexual incidents. For example, if the family considers any sexual experience of the child to be traumatic and inevitably damaging, then the arousal and pleasure which the child may have experienced will be discounted and even defined as pathological. Alternatively, if the child experiences physical pain from the event, but the family chooses to ignore this or is engaged in a pattern of physical abuse, then the notion that sex is what occurs in a painful, coercive, and threatening context is promoted. Note that social (peer group) and cultural (values, laws) levels may contradict or support such personal and family interpretations.

Bowlby's theory of attachment (Bowlby, 1969, 1970, 1980) has a psychoanalytic and evolutionary (ethological) foundation and systems theory elements. Attachment has begun to be used to examine the connection between CSA and adult sexuality (Fergusson et al., 1997; McCarthy & Taylor, 1999). Bowlby's original construct of attachment described a "biobehavioral safety-regulating system in which the parent is the child's primary protector and haven of safety" (Goldberg, Grusec, & Jenkins, 1999, p. 504). According to attachment theory, children develop cognitive/affective representations or "internal working models" of their experiences in their attachment relationships. These models are hypothesized to form the basis of the quality of later intimate/love relationships. Thus, attachment could support socialization as well as providing a selective advantage for reproductive success (Dickstein, 1999) and individual survival. The attachment literature has focused on child outcomes in many areas, including the quality of adult relationships, interpersonal difficulties, and psychiatric disorders. Attachment style has been shown to be related to levels of satisfaction, commitment, love, and trust in relationships (Davis, Kirkpatrick, Levy, & O'Hearn, 1994). Little empirical research exists on the impact of CSA on adult attachment style. We could locate no studies of attachment style and sexual abuse that excluded other kinds of maltreatment. One recent study of a small sample of U.K. women found that avoidant/ambivalent attachment style, but not child abuse, related to adult relationship difficulties (McCarthy & Taylor, 1999). Thus, though discussed in the literature, the relationship between attachment styles and CSA has not really been researched, in spite of the fact that family variables that might impact attachment have also been found to moderate the effect of CSA. To date, attachment has been used as a heuristic framework for conceptualizing possible roles that internal working models play in mediating continuities in relationship functioning between childhood and adulthood.

Attachment theory is useful to conceptualize early experiences with significant others that include physical closeness, touch, and the teaching of emotion regulation (containing and moderating strong mood states in the presence of another). It is easy to see how a parent who is physically abusive, neglectful in caring and feeding, and very unpredictable in availability will encourage a relationship of insecure attachment. In this situation, a child's working model of intimate attachment, including images and interactions around self and body, may well be biased toward mistrust, aggression, or self-disregard, as he or she grows and associates with other potential intimates. What is less definable is how childhood sexual experience, abusive or nonabusive, will impact the child's working model of (sexual) relationships. If the person who is sexually involved with the child is a family adult, we would expect there to be some impact on the child's attachment experience—most likely greater mistrust and less reliance on the parental system for safety. But a nonfamily adult may have no impact on working models of attachment, especially if the sexual contact is a less physically invasive and incidental occurrence, and/or the family functioning is generally one that provides adequate secure attachment experiences. Once again we see that an understanding of possible impacts of CSA, as well as of consensual and desired sexual activity such as sex play, on attachment and relationship choices requires a consideration of the content of the sexual experience, its frequency, the relationship between the individuals involved, the family context, and the subsequent experiences that have further shaped the child's development.

To understand the findings from CSA research and to generate additional hypotheses, one needs a conceptual framework that connects child and adult sexual relationships. The proposed "levels-of-influence" model could facilitate the design of such a developmental theory. At the same time, it seems to us that recent thinking about evolution and development offers a possible foundation for such a theory (Bronfenbrenner & Ceci, 1994; Griffiths & Gray, 1994).

Evolution and the Developmental Process

We follow Lehrman's (1970) position that evolution selects for outcomes and not for how the outcomes are achieved. Thus, evolution will select for effective sexual functioning as an adaptive outcome because sexual functioning fosters reproduction and may even contribute to stability in the nurturance of the offspring. The question is, what are the means that were selected by evolution to ensure that effective sexual functioning is a likely outcome of sexual development? Indeed, development is the result of extremely complex and continuous interactions between genetic, epigenetic, and environmental factors (see also the "levels of influence" matrix in Figure 1), and there must be numerous pathways and variables that affect the outcome. Should one therefore not expect the outcome of sexual development to be highly variable, with "effective sexual functioning" as a relatively rare occurrence?

Some years ago, Waddington discussed "developmental canalization" to indicate that an evolutionary outcome can be the same in spite of some genetic variation as well as some environmental variation (Waddington, 1959). We have learned that it is not very useful to study the influence of genes on development versus the influence of epigenetic processes or of environmental factors. One has to look at the "developmental system" of genetic, epigenetic, and environmental interactions as a whole (Griffiths & Gray, 1994). Evolution has selected for redundancies in this system that help to reduce the variability of the outcome. More recently, this idea has been further expressed through complexity theory, with the concept of at-

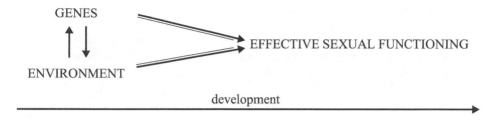

Figure 2. Schematic of Categories for a Selected Developmental Outcome

tractors that promote certain developmental outcomes (Kauffman, 1993). Figure 2 provides a schematic representation of development as a process that reduces the variability of its outcomes.

Reduction of the variability of developmental outcomes can make some research results, such as the finding that CSA often has an unexpectedly small effect upon adult sexual functioning, more understandable. Vulnerabilities can be corrected to achieve the same outcomes. For example, genetic vulnerabilities with respect to sexual functioning might include autonomic hypersensitivity, cardiovascular impairment, dopamine and serotonin impairment, or relative androgen insensitivity. Family physical abuse, mental illness, and alcohol use are examples of environmental vulnerability factors. Yet research consistently shows that the majority of children, growing up with such vulnerabilities, end up with normal functioning, at least if the vulnerabilities are moderate enough to allow correction.

One can use this theoretical insight to look at sex differences, and at the variability of the impact of CSA on adult sexual relationships: (1) As genetically determined propensities, sexual variables such as arousal ease, orgasmic ease, and latency, or sexual desire, are probably distributed according to a bell-shaped curve; (2) The bell-shaped curves, representing male and female populations, are not overlapping: Males typically have more insistent sexual interest than females (e.g., Baumeister, Catanese, & Vohs, 2001); (3) Effective sexual functioning is an outcome which tends to override developmental experiences and cultural proscriptions that interfere with it, for example, the efforts of Victorian culture, confining religious requirements against sexual behavior, or laws prohibiting sexual activities; (4) Given 2 and 3, males might be less vulnerable to the sexual effects of CSA than females, though they may be equally or more vulnerable in nonsexual areas, such as aggression or mood; (5) Also, in women, the multiple pathways of development ensure that sexual abuse will not always lead to impaired sexual functioning and desire in their future relationships.

Summary Remarks

It seems that we know little about how much continuity there is or should be between childhood sexuality, especially as it relates to CSA, and adult sexual relationships. The necessity to locate human sexuality in multiple levels of influence makes it likely that there are many pathways to both sexually functional or satisfying and sexually troubled adult relationships. In addition, evolutionary forces may account for the relative vitality of effective sexual functioning in the face of numerous challenges. Tracking the mechanisms of specific outcomes will require that we pose more balanced and in-depth questions about the emotional processing and meaning of experiences over a person's development. Since all questions are born out of a theoretical orientation, the most prudent course of action would seem not to restrict this search to a single theoretical perspective. As we begin to understand factors impacting sexual development, including CSA, questions that incorporate multiple influences and possible outcomes may provide the most useful information.

References

Alexander, P. C., & Lupfer, S. L. (1987). Family characteristics and long-term consequences associated with sexual abuse. *Archives of Sexual Behavior, 16,* 235–245.

Baumeister, R. F., Catanese, K. R., & Vohs, K. D. (2001). Is there a gender difference in strength of sex drive? Theoretical views, conceptual distinctions, and a review of the relevant evidence. *Personality and Social Psychology Review, 5,* 242–273.

Bauserman, R., & Rind, B. (1997). Psychological correlates of male child and adolescent sexual experiences with adults: A review of the nonclinical literature. *Archives of Sexual Behavior, 26,* 105–141.

Beitchman, J. H., Zucker, K. J., Hood, J. E., DaCosta, G. A., & Akman, D. (1991). A review of the short-term effects of child sexual abuse. *Child Abuse & Neglect, 15,* 537–556.

Beitchman, J. H., Zucker, K. J., Hood, J. E., DaCosta, G. A., Akman, D., & Cassavia, E. (1992). A review of the long-term effects of child sexual abuse. *Child Abuse & Neglect, 16,* 101–118.

Bowlby, J. (1969). Attachment and loss: Vol. 1: Attachment. London: Penguin.

Bowlby, J. (1970). Attachment and loss: Vol. 2: Separation. London: Penguin.

Bowlby, J. (1980). Attachment and loss: Vol. 3: Loss, sadness and depression. New York: Basic Books.

Brewin, C. R., Andrews, B., & Valentine, J. D. (2000). Meta-analysis of risk factors for posttraumatic stress disorder in trauma-exposed adults. *Journal of Consulting and Clinical Psychology, 68,* 748–766.

Briere, J. N., & Runtz, M. (1993). Childhood sexual abuse: Long-term sequelae and implications for psychological assessment. *Journal of Interpersonal Violence, 8,* 312–330.

Briere, J., & Zaidi, L. Y. (1989). Sexual abuse histories and sequelae in female psychiatric emergency room patients. *American Journal of Psychiatry, 146,* 1602–1606.

Bronfenbrenner, U., & Ceci, S. J. (1994). Nature-nurture reconceptualized in developmental perspective: A bioecological model. *Psychological Review, 101,* 568–586.

Brown, G. R., & Anderson, B. (1991). Psychiatric morbidity in adult inpatients with childhood histories of sexual and physical abuse. *American Journal of Psychiatry, 148,* 55–61.

Brown, L. K., Kessel, S. M., Lourie, K. J., Ford, H. H., & Lipsitt, L. P. (1997). Influence of sexual abuse on HIV-related attitudes and behaviors in adolescent psychiatric inpatients. *Journal of the American Academy of Child and Adolescent Psychiatry, 36,* 316–322.

Bryer, J. B., Nelson, B. A., Miller, J. B., & Krol, P. A. (1987). Childhood sexual and physical abuse as factors in adult psychiatric illness. *American Journal of Psychiatry, 144,* 1426–1430.

Cole, C. B. (1986, May). *Differential long-term effects of child sexual and physical abuse.* Paper presented at the Fourth National Conference on the Sexual Victimization of Children, New Orleans, LA.

Damasio, A. (1999). *The feeling of what happens.* New York: Harcourt Brace.

Davis, K., Kirkpatrick, L., Levy, M., & O'Hearn, R. (1994). Stalking the elusive love style: Attachment styles, love styles, and relationship developments. In R. Erber & R. Gilmour (Eds.), *Theoretical frameworks for personal relationships* (pp. 179–210). Hillsdale, NJ: Lawrence Erlbaum.

Dickstein, S. (1999). Confidence in protection: A developmental psychopathology perspective. *Journal of Family Psychology, 13,* 484–487.

Fergusson, D. M., Horwood, L. J., & Lynskey, M. T. (1997). Childhood sexual abuse, adolescent sexual behaviors, and sexual revictimization. *Child Abuse & Neglect, 21,* 789–803.

Fincham, F. D., Beach, S. R. H., Harold, G. T., & Osborne, L. N. (1997). Marital satisfaction and depression: Different causal relationships for men and women? *Psychological Science, 8,* 351–357.

Fromuth, M. E. (1986). The relationship of childhood sexual abuse with later psychological and sexual adjustment in a sample of college women. *Child Abuse & Neglect, 10,* 5–15.

Gagnon, J. H. (1990). The implicit and explicit use of scripts in sex research. *Annual Review of Sex Research, 1,* 1–44.

Gagnon, J. H., & Simon, W. (1973). *Sexual conduct: The social sources of human sexuality.* Chicago: Aldine.

Goldberg, S., Grusec, J. E., & Jenkins, J. M. (1999). Narrow view of attachment or broad view of protection? Rejoinder to the commentaries. *Journal of Family Psychology, 13,* 504–507.

Griffiths, P. E., & Gray, R. D. (1994). Developmental systems and evolutionary explanation. *Journal of Philosophy, 91,* 277–304.

Grinstead, O. A., Faigeles, B., Binson, D., & Eversley, R. (1993). Data from the National AIDS Surveys. I. Sexual risk for human immunodeficiency virus infection among women in high-risk cities. *Family Planning Perspectives, 25,* 252–256, 277.

Herman, J. L., & Hirschman, L. (1981). *Father-daughter incest.* Cambridge, MA: Harvard University Press.

Howes, P. W., Cicchetti, D., Toth, S. L., & Rogosch, F. A. (2000). Affective, organizational, and relational characteristics of maltreating families: A systems perspective. *Journal of Family Psychology, 14,* 95–110.

Jackson, J. L., Calhoun, K. S., Amick, A. A., Maddever, H. M., & Habif, V. L. (1990). Young adult women who report childhood intrafamilial sexual abuse: Subsequent adjustment. *Archives of Sexual Behavior, 19,* 211–221.

Kauffman, S. A. (1993). *The origins of order: Self-organization and selection in evolution.* New York: Oxford University Press.

Kendall-Tackett, K. A., Williams, L. M., & Finkelhor, D. (1993). Impact of sexual abuse on children: A review and synthesis of recent empirical studies. *Psychological Bulletin, 113,* 164–180.

Kenney, J. W., Reinholtz, C., & Angelini, P. J. (1998). Sexual abuse, sex before age 16 and high-risk behaviors of young females with sexually transmitted diseases. *Journal of Obstetric, Gynecologic, and Neonatal Nursing, 27,* 54–63.

Kinzl, J., Traweger, C., & Biebl, W. (1995). Sexual dysfunctions: Relationship to childhood sexual abuse and early family experiences in a nonclinical sample. *Child Abuse & Neglect, 19,* 785–792.

Kurdek, L. A. (1998). The nature and predictors of the trajectory of change in marital quality over the first 4 years of marriage for first-married husbands and wives. *Journal of Family Psychology, 12,* 494–510.

La Vecchia, C., Franceschi, S., Decarli, A., Fasoli, M., Gentile, A., Parazzini, F., et al. (1986). Sexual factors, venereal diseases, and the risk of intraepithelial and invasive cervical neoplasia. *Cancer, 58,* 935–941.

Laumann, E. O., Gagnon, J. H., Michael, R. T., & Michaels, S. (1994). *The social organization of sexuality: Sexual practices in the United States.* Chicago: University of Chicago Press.

Laumann, E. O., Paik, A., & Rosen, R. C. (1999). Sexual dysfunction in the United States: Prevalence and predictors. *Journal of the American Medical Association, 281,* 537–544.

Lehrman, D. S. (1970). Semantic and conceptual issues in the nature-nurture problem. In D. S. Lehrman (Ed.), *Development and evolution of behavior* (pp. 17–52). San Francisco: W. H. Freeman.

Luster, T., & Small, S. A. (1997). Sexual abuse history and number of sex partners among female adolescents. *Family Planning Perspectives, 29,* 204–211.

McCarthy, G., & Taylor, A. (1999). Avoidant-ambivalent attachment style as a mediator between abusive childhood experiences and adult relationship difficulties. *Journal of Child Psychology and Psychiatry and Allied Disciplines, 40,* 465–477.

Meston, C. M., Heiman, J. R., & Trapnell, P. D. (1999). The relation between early abuse and adult sexuality. *Journal of Sex Research, 36,* 385–395.

Minuchin, P. (1985). Families and individual development: Provocations from the field of family therapy. *Child Development, 56,* 289–302.

Orr, S. P., Lasko, N. B., Metzger, L. J., Berry, N.J., Ahern, C. E., & Pittman, R. K. (1998). Psychophysiologic assessment of women with posttraumatic stress disorder resulting from childhood sexual abuse. *Journal of Consulting and Clinical Psychology, 66,* 906–913.

Paolucci, E. O., Genuis, M. L., & Violato, C. (2001). A meta-analysis of the published research on the effects of child sexual abuse. *The Journal of Psychology, 135,* 17–36.

Rind, B., & Tromovitch, P. (1997). A meta-analytic review of findings from national samples on psychological correlates of child sexual abuse. *Journal of Sex Research, 34,* 237–255.

Rind, B., Tromovitch, P., & Bauserman, R. (1998). A meta-analytic examination of assumed properties of child sexual abuse using college samples. *Psychological Bulletin, 124,* 22–53.

Rowan, A. B., & Foy, D. W. (1993). Post-traumatic stress disorder in child sexual abuse survivors: A literature review. *Journal of Traumatic Stress, 6,* 3–20.

Sarwer, D. B., & Durlak, J. A. (1996). Childhood sexual abuse as a predictor of adult female sexual dysfunction: A study of couples seeking sex therapy. *Child Abuse & Neglect, 20,* 963–972.

Saunders, B. E., Villeponteaux, L. A., Lipovsky, J. A., Kilpatrick, D. G., & Veronen, L. J. (1992). Child sexual assault as a risk factor for mental health disorders among women: A community sample. *Journal of Interpersonal Violence, 7,* 189–204.

Schloredt, K. A., & Heiman, J. R. (in press). Perceptions of sexuality as related to sexual functioning and sexual risk in women with different types of childhood abuse histories. *Journal of Traumatic Stress.*

Sedney, M., & Brooks, B. (1984). Factors associated with a history of childhood sexual experience in a nonclinical female population. *Journal of the American Academy of Child Psychiatry, 23,* 215–218.

Shearer, S. L., Peters, C. P., Quaytman, M. S., & Ogden, R. L. (1990). Frequency and correlates of childhood sexual and physical abuse histories in adult female borderline inpatients. *American Journal of Psychiatry, 147,* 214–216.

Thompson, N.J., Potter, J. S., Sanderson, C. A., & Maibach, E. W. (1997). The relationship of sexual abuse and HIV risk behaviors among heterosexual adult female STD patients. *Child Abuse & Neglect, 21,* 149–156.

Tsai, M., Feldman-Summers, S., & Edgar, M. (1979). Childhood molestation: Variables related to differential impacts on psychosexual functioning in adult women. *Journal of Abnormal Psychology, 88,* 407–417.

Vogeltanz, N. D., Wilsnack, S. C., Harris, T. T., Wilsnack, R. W., Wonderlich, S. A., & Kristjanson, A. F. (1999). Prevalence and risk factors for childhood sexual abuse in women: National survey findings. *Child Abuse & Neglect, 23,* 579–592.

von Bertalanffy, L. (1968). *General System Theory: Foundations, development, applications.* New York: George Braziller.

Waddington, C. H. (1959). Canalization of development and the inheritance of acquired characteristics. *Nature, 183,* 1654–1655.

Wagner, A. W., & Linehan, M. M. (1997). Biosocial perspective on the relationship of childhood sexual abuse, suicidal behavior, and borderline personality disorder. In M. C. Zanarini (Ed.), *Role of sexual abuse in the etiology of borderline personality disorder* (pp. 203–223). Washington, DC: American Psychiatric Press.

Walker, E. A., Gelfand, A., Katon, W. J., Koss, M. P., Von Korff, M., Bernstein, D., et al. (1999). Adult heath status of women with histories of childhood abuse and neglect. *American Journal of Medicine, 107,* 332–339.

Wenninger, K., & Heiman, J. R. (1998). Relating body image to psychological and sexual functioning in child sexual abuse survivors. *Journal of Traumatic Stress, 11,* 543–562.

Wingood, G. M., & DiClemente, R. J. (1997). Child sexual abuse, HIV sexual risk, and gender relations of African-American women. *American Journal of Preventive Medicine, 13,* 380–384.

Wyatt, G. E., Forge, N. G., & Guthrie, D. (1998). Family constellation and ethnicity: Current and lifetime HIV-related risk taking. *Journal of Family Psychology, 12,* 93–101.

Wyatt, G. E., Guthrie, D., & Notgrass, C. M. (1992). Differential effects of women's child sexual abuse and subsequent sexual revictimization. *Journal of Consulting and Clinical Psychology, 60,* 167–173.

Zierler, S., Feingold, L., Laufer, D., Velentgas, P., Kantrowitz-Gordon, I., & Mayer, K. (1991). Adult survivors of childhood sexual abuse and subsequent risk of HIV infection. *American Journal of Public Health, 81,* 572–575.

Discussion Paper

CAROL MCCORD

I'm a clinician with the Kinsey Sexual Health Clinic and so come to this discussion with a clinically based perspective and will speak from that, as well as my previous experience from my work as Director of Education, Training, and Counseling at a regional Planned Parenthood clinic, which was in provision of sexuality education to children from a nonclinical population.

I appreciate the focus on the consideration of the issues of childhood sexuality from different methodological perspectives—I think that's important and will become even more so if our understanding of human sexuality is going to deepen. When I sit with a client, what I'm interested in is what meaning their experiences have had for them. In the context of clinical work, it is that with which I have to work. As Julia Heiman just said, such clinical work is based on the assumption that there can be mediating impact from what happens after something has occurred.

The issue of personal understanding, or meaning attribution, is very significant in the clinical setting. Individual differences as they relate to such understanding are important, as each person, each adult and each child, brings to an experience an individual background, including genetic make-up and family and cultural perspectives. So, as we try to work with clients, we need to understand all those different levels of influence that Julia described and what meaning each of those has for the client. If we can't have some understanding of the meaning they attribute to their experiences, we can't join with the client "where they are"—and we can't hope to move them toward improvement of the problem, however they identify improvement.

Obviously, each individual's understanding of the meaning of particular events also varies as they move through developmental stages.

It is also quite clear that the meaning children attribute to a situation will be greatly affected by their parents' views. In teaching sexuality education and in clinical work with children, the role of the impact of adults around them, and parents, in particular, is significant. Such definitions and meanings as "abuse," "coercion," or "sex play" are quickly ascribed to situations experienced by children by the adults around them. In particular, I want to note situations in which children have experienced something that might be a traumatic event, even though it might not have included a physical component, and conversely, situations which might be interpreted by adults as abusive, even if the event might not have held that meaning for the child.

An example is the case of a mother who recognized that there was a problem when her 9-year-old son became extremely upset on the occasion of their purchasing (genital) protective gear for him for the beginning of soccer. She was concerned that he had experienced "sexual abuse," meaning a physical act. He was initially unwilling to talk about it with her or other adults with whom he was familiar. He later wrote it out in a sequence of notes, which he handed over his shoulder to his mother. What he wrote to his mother was that his biological father, who was not in the home, had described sex to him by describing raping his mother. This obviously was a negative experience for him that had some impact on his behavior later but his experience would not be captured in the definition that we've discussed so far today of "sexual abuse." That is a problem for me as a clinician. I also think it is important to consider in terms of research. For example, if this child were included in a study, by our definitions today he could be identified as a "control" subject, and I wonder what effect that might be having on the research data. Likewise, in the case of the opposite scenario: a parent bringing a child to treatment identifying that the child had experienced something traumatic, horrible, awful—"sexual abuse." In that case, even if the child had not defined the experience in that way before it had been so defined by the parent, if he or she were later polled in a survey, he or she might well define that experience as an "abusive" situation.

I note these examples from clinical cases in relation to the discussion of research definitions.

Individuals seeking therapeutic treatment for problems in their adult lives want those problems resolved, whether or not they describe those problems to the clinician as related to previous sexual abuse, or describe them as being related in their own minds, or don't consider abuse as an issue at all. In that way, carefully parsed definitions may not be all that useful clinically. However, accurate predictors of the kinds of situations that can mitigate a response that a child might have to an "abusive" or "coercive" situation are quite helpful to clinical work.

In terms of sexuality education, the presentation of research findings, including definitions, has the potential to have a significant impact on the social and political constraints on the provision of accurate sexuality education in the future.

Discussion Paper

J. MICHAEL BAILEY

The first things I want to talk about are causal models and causal mediation. A very simple causal model is that childhood sexual abuse causes a problem, be it in childhood or adulthood. With a mediational model, childhood sexual abuse causes some mediator, shame or sexualization or whatever, which then causes the problems. Chris Browning was talking about different mediators and he was saying that we should not just think of traumatic mediators, which I agree with. On the other hand, I think we need to step back before we consider mediation at all, because causal mediation requires causes and this leads to one of my goals for you all. Today I have heard all the following phrases in conjunction with childhood sexual abuse: effects, consequences, aftereffects, sequelae, "resulted in," accentuating effects, learning effects, mediating mechanisms, traumatic impact, long-term negative effects. I think we shouldn't talk that way; we haven't earned the right to talk that way yet because we haven't done the right kind of research. And if you do talk that way you should put in the academic provisos, like "putative" causal mechanisms.

So what do we know about the consequences of childhood sexual abuse? This is what I would say we "know" through such work as Rind and colleagues (Rind, Bauserman, & Tromovitch, 2001; Rind, Tromovitch, & Bauserman, 1998). In both of their meta-analyses, on average, the effects of childhood sexual abuse are at most modest. You may disagree with that, but the important thing here is that such data are correlational. Virtually all data in this field are correlational and correlational data do not allow causal inferences. Janet Hyde has already referred to the value of a controlled study; we randomly assign half of a group of 12-year-old girls to be sexually abused and the others not, we follow them up and see how they turn out. Of course, we can't do that. But I don't think we appreciate how much that limits our ability to draw causal inferences. Consider the following gedanken experiment. Suppose that instead of random assignment, I allow 12-year-old girls to choose: You may either be sexually abused or be beaten. Then at age 21 I look at their sexual functioning and I find out that those who were sexually abused have had more sex partners. Do I then conclude that childhood sexual abuse caused that result? I think obviously one would not.

We, including me, have the intuition that child sexual abuse is harmful. But we haven't done the right research to know that it is, because we haven't examined alternatives to the causal model. Let us consider four alternative models. The first is called the genetic or the family environmental model. Would you wager that a father who molests his daughter has average, typical, genes? Would you wager that the kind of environment he provides to his children, other than the fact of molesting them, is completely normal? I wouldn't. I would wager that he has problematic genes and the other environment that he provides is also problematic. This model suggests that it's those genes and environment that leads to the kids' problems and that childhood sexual abuse is only an indicator of the father's or relative's psychopathology. It seems to me a very reasonable alternative model. You can study siblings who are discordant for childhood sexual abuse experience. Look at their adult outcome; if the abused one is still more disturbed as an adult, then it's not just family environment. There have been two such twin studies and both find that with a twin control, the correlation is reduced, and the most recent one, by Kendler and colleagues (2000), did find that differences in outcome were sustained. So the "family environment" model is not sufficient.

The second model is the "development continuity" model. Much of the data that we have discussed here cries out for this model. Child characteristics, because of developmental continuity, are correlated with adult outcome and not all children are at equal risk for childhood sexual abuse. We act as if we think that all 12-year-olds with respect to sex are just alike, that is, they're all inert and some adult picks some of them at random and abuses them sexually; but not all 12-year-olds are alike and some are much more sexual than others. So, given that perhaps the best-established adult outcome or correlate of childhood sexual abuse is so-called "sexualization," it seems an obvious hypothesis that a highly sexual child becomes a highly sexual adult because of developmental continuity. And highly sexual children are more likely to be highly sexual with adults. This model would also account for Ed Laumann's and Jay Paul's data concerning the correlation between homosexual outcome and early experiences with men. At age 12 or 13, many heterosexual boys would love to be seduced by an older woman but this is unlikely to happen. But those who have gay feelings at age 12, and who would become gay anyway, are more likely to find willing partners.

The next model is "systematic reporting bias"; basically the idea that whatever problems one might be having as an adult are related to reports of childhood sexual abuse. One obvious example might be lying; people sometimes lie about sexual abuse. In the *Archives of Sexual Behavior,* Eugene Kanin (1994) published the only study of this I know, showing that in a small town in Indiana, 40% of official rape reports were found to be lies. I don't know why this should be different for childhood sexual abuse retrospectively reported. And I don't think that all women would be equally likely to lie about this. I think there are people wanting to get out of responsibility, wanting to blame others for their problems. It's well known that people high in neuroticism have negative memories, negative reporting biases. And people who are dissatisfied with their lives spend more time listing everything that's ever happened to them and wondering why; they're more likely to summon up memories even if they actually happened.

The last model I'll mention is "iatrogenesis"; this is the idea that when childhood sexual abuse happens, the response to it can exaggerate the problem. So, for example, if a family finds out that their child was touched by a neighbor and takes them right to the doctor and calls the police and so on, it's very plausible that there will be a worse outcome than there might have been otherwise. There are now three studies (Rose, Bisson, & Wessely, 2002) of a therapeutic technique called "trauma debriefing," in which people who have experienced traumas are debriefed by counselors. All three studies have shown that a year later people who received this are worse off than those who didn't. This seems to me to be very analogous to what happens to some children.

Unless we take these models, we can't infer causality from correlational data. We should keep in mind that causal intuitions have been wrong in the past. We used to think that schizophrenia was caused by schizoprenagenic mothers; autism was caused by "refrigerator" mothers. We now know they're not. We used to think that familial environment, that is environmental differences between families, was crucially important for the development of psychological individual differences. That's probably the most surprising and interesting finding in all of behavioral genetics, that the familiar or shared environment tends to have very weak effects.

References

Kanin, E. J. (1994). False rape allegations. *Archives of Sexual Behavior, 23,* 81–92.

Kendler, K. S., Bulik, C. M., Silberg, J., Hettema, J. M., Myers, J., & Prescott, C. A. (2000). Childhood sexual abuse and adult psychiatric and substance use disorders in women: An epidemiological and cotwin control analysis. *Archives of General Psychiatry, 57,* 953–959.

Rind, B., Bauserman, R., & Tromovitch, P. (2001). The condemned meta-analysis on child sexual abuse: Good science and long-overdue skepticism. *Skeptical Inquirer, 25*(4), 68–72.

Rind, B., Tromovitch, P., & Bauserman, R. (1998). A meta-analytic examination of assumed properties of child sexual abuse using college samples. *Psychological Bulletin, 124,* 22–53.

Rose, S., Bisson, J., & Wessely, S. (2002). Psychological debriefing for preventing post traumatic stress disorder (PTSD) (Cochrane Review). *The Cochrane Library,* Issue 4. Oxford: Update Software.

General Discussion

Chris Browning: Carol's highlighting of the distinctions between clinical approaches and some of the work we've been seeing today is important. We need to learn how these types of research findings can be incorporated to improve clinical work. Michael's major concern with this research I wholeheartedly agree with. We are certainly in no position to make any definitive causal statements about the relationship between these experiences and later well-being. On the other hand, I would say, given your concerns about endogeneity, the lack of experimental studies, and problems with observational studies of this type, we would also have to point those criticisms at the vast majority of social science research. We just simply can't do experimental studies in most cases. What we have to do, unless we just abandon the project, is to develop better research designs and go back to my earlier advocacy of well-collected longitudinal data on these experiences. That will get us a bit further toward addressing some of your concerns. Specifically, Michael laid out a number of alternative interpretations of the data that would suggest spurious associations. First, there was a concern with the possibility of intergenerational transmission of a genetic predisposition. That is a possibility, but on the other hand we had only about 4% of our sample where the father was the partner. To the extent that this figure gives us any purchase at all on parental predisposition, it would suggest that genetic transmission may not buy us a lot of explanatory power. Secondly, the concern with children who have an early predisposition toward sexuality or sexual behavior and the likelihood that they will in some way be more likely to become involved in these experiences is something we've also thought. That's certainly a possibility and you might imagine that a child who has a sexual predisposition early on would also then exhibit heightened sexuality later on in adulthood. The continuity there in terms of overall sexual frequency or level of sexual activity could be explained by your selectivity model. On the other hand, we have found a positive association between specific events and behaviors that occurred during childhood sexual events and both the appeal for, and occurrence of, these behaviors in adulthood (Laumann & Michael, 2001). It's hard to make the argument that you have a child that's predisposed to, say, oral sex and seeks it during both childhood and adulthood. I would think it's plausible, rather, to argue that the child is introduced to oral sex and there's a learning effect on adult behavior due to the childhood sexual event. You might consider that it's a reporting issue, but again, in a cross-sectional context, it's hard for me to imagine a process that would result in someone reporting that they have a greater likelihood of engaging in a specific behavior or finding that behavior appealing and then also inaccurately including that behavior as part of a childhood sexual event. Finally, with the lying issue and the fact that adult psychopathology may be associated with a greater likelihood of reporting this event as some sort of excuse for current problems, again, a possibility. What we thought about that was that to some extent the culturally sanctioned excuse is "I was abused," "I had a sexual experience with an older person." However, we do also find virtually the same pattern of association for sexual contacts between peers. Now, recognizing that John has raised some concerns about the measurement of peer sexual contact, I don't think, though, that the peer contacts that we do capture in this survey would serve that same blame-absolving purpose as adult-child contacts. One wouldn't really use that as an excuse. Your current psychopathology probably wouldn't be as effectively attributed to a peer contact. Then there is the likelihood that some event subsequent to the contact, involvement of other parties, could then result in the effect that we're seeing. We did actually look at whether or not the event was disclosed, which presumably would be associated with third-party intervention of the type you're talking about, and we found no association even though we thought we would. There was virtually no difference in the aftermath between people who said that they had told someone about the event and people who didn't. So those are my initial responses. But the general point you're making is well taken. It calls for better research designs.

Julia Heiman: I appreciate, Michael, you bringing up the point of causation. When you're steeped in this literature and keep reading it and nobody mentions this, you slip into a language that presumes causation. What we need to move toward is what kinds of models would we end up recommending, how might this research be done. There are certainly longitudinal studies, but not everybody's going to be able to do longitudinal research. So what other kinds of models could be tested that might be careful about this dimension of causation? In considering your specific examples, I wouldn't combine genetic with parental environment, but make those separate, because parental environment could indeed be very important. But it could be that things have happened to the father or mother together with other behaviors that they have shown toward the child, as opposed to more genetic and biological determinants, because one inherits one's environment also. That would be important to examine more closely than it's been examined so far. It's one of the reasons I'm very interested in this problem of physical abuse, because I think sexual abuse in the context of a family in which there's physical abuse occurring, even if the sexual abuse occurs outside the family, represents something different for the person experiencing it. There's no way for us to find out whether kids are more or less highly sexual and that may be beside the point. The point I would make about that is somewhat indirect, which is that the majority of people with sexual dysfunctions do not have a child sexual abuse history. There's more going on there contributing to a good or bad sexual outcome for people in terms of their ability to form sexual relationships.

Michael Bailey: First, Chris, you're definitely right that causal research is hard and yet I can confidently assert that causal research in this area is retarded relative to research in related areas like psychopathology, depression, and schizophrenia. That may be due in part to the recency of the field, but it's also to do with sensitivity. People are not talking about obvious alternative hypotheses because they're afraid to or, as Julia says, because everybody talks about causality and so everybody gets blinded to alternatives. You both had slight problems with my familial genetic model. Julia, I put "familial" and "genetic" together simply because you can control for both familial environment and genetic effects using the same sibling design. That's why I combined them in the same model. It's the same confound even though they're separable theoretically. And Chris, behavior geneticists think that genes are pleiotropic, that is, they have more than one effect. So a gene that makes somebody molest a child is probably doing other things, like making him impulsive and so on, and it's those other effects that might be transmitted. You would not just want to look to see whether the children of child molesters grow up and be child molesters based on that model. The last thing I want to say is that your design is not especially susceptible to the iatrogenic or the lying phenomena; it's not a clinical setting. Why would these people feel the need to lie in order to escape responsibility? They're doing a paid study.

David Finkelhor: I would broaden Julia's point about the failure to ask about physical abuse. We haven't asked about a whole range of other kinds of victimizations. In the national survey that we did of 2,000 10- to 16-year-olds, we found that the kids who reported sexual victimization were anywhere between two and four times more likely to report having been physically assaulted by their parents, assaulted by peers, witnessing domestic violence, and a variety of other things. It does raise the possibility that reporting a history of sexual abuse is really a marker for being a victim of multiple kinds of victimizations. It may be those other victimizations or the combination of them that are really predicting some of this. We have a new instrument called the Juvenile Victimization Questionnaire, which is a 39-item instrument trying to collect information on the whole spectrum of victimization that kids suffer. This is in parallel to my notion that the juvenile delinquency field has a comprehensive measure of juvenile delinquency and we need one in the victimization area.

This brings me to the second point about a particular kind of victimization that there's very little talked about in which I'm very interested. Carol talked about sexual trauma without contact. This could be called sexual trauma without sex. In this same survey of 10- to 16-year-olds, we found that 9% of the boys said that in the last year someone had hit, kicked, or punched them, or hit them with an object in the genitals, and a quarter of those kids had post-traumatic symptomatology. Close to a third said that they had experienced bleeding or pain that lasted until the next day. You don't have to go very far to get lots of people who can tell you about such experiences, but I could not find a single reference to this phenomenon in the sexological, criminological, or psychiatric literature. It just does not seem to exist and, in fact, it doesn't even really have a name. In the article we wrote, we called it "nonsexual genital assault." But it's really "getting hit in the balls," everyone calls it that, but you can't write an article on the epidemiology of "getting hit in the balls," and it's interesting that this isn't really recognized. I'm not contending that it's necessarily a long-term traumatic event, but it seems to me that for some subgroup of kids it may affect their sexual behavior or sexual feelings. The trauma may primarily result in fear of further violence.

There is research consistent with the fact that some of the outcomes associated with sexual abuse may be a continuation of prior psychological problems (Boney-McCoy & Finkelhor, 1996). We interviewed 10–16-year-old youth at two points over an 18-month period. We found that, of those who were sexually victimized during that 18-month period, 40% were depressed prior to the first interview and hence prior to their victimization. That was three-and-a-half times the rate for the kids who were not victimized. So clearly when we evaluated the youth the second time after their victimization and found out they were depressed (the typical study design), some of that was likely to be the continuity of the depression that they had beforehand. Their prior depression may have been one of the reasons why they were sexually victimized. That is a difficult thing to control for in a retrospective study.

But about the general point from Michael's paper that the evidence for negative impact is not there, I want to part company with him. Using the same logic and critique of the research evidence, one could also say there is no certain evidence that rape is traumatic. This extreme argument would insist: How do we know that women who show post-traumatic stress as a result of rape didn't look that way prior to their being raped?

Part of the problem here is that people get focused exclusively on the issue of long-term effects, of the effect of childhood sexual abuse on adult functioning. That does reflect what is sometimes called an "adultocentric bias." The only outcomes of concern to adults are how something affects adult functioning, not what the immediate subjective experience might be like. There is valid scientific evidence that children who are sexually abused have distress in the aftermath. So we can talk about the strength or certainty of long-term effects, but I don't think that does anything to gainsay the evidence that this is traumatic in the short term for many young people. Some don't show symptoms in the short term, too. But we should not focus so exclusively on the long-term issue as the arbiter of whether or not these are significant experiences. I would contend that even if nobody were traumatized in the long term it would still be a significant personal and mental health problem.

John Bancroft: I agree with David's last point. This was in my mind when there was all the reaction to the Rind paper, that children should be protected from sexual exploitation and other types of exploitation too. There's the question of betrayal of their relationships with adults who should not be exploiting children for their own purposes. Michael has adopted the position of the politically incorrect person here. I know he heard Philip Jenkins and he is basically getting us to revisit some of the ideas that at present are politically unacceptable—that, for example, the child may be in some way seductive or encouraging of the behavior. Even if the child was seductive and encouraging behavior, we don't have to get excited about that. It's still unacceptable on the part of the adult. I was interested in this when we were looking at our data that I reported on yesterday, thinking that early masturbation could be, as I suggested, a marker of some children being more sexual. I was therefore interested to see whether those people would be more likely to experience sexual contact with adults, and our findings showed that they weren't. We found no association between these early indicators of sexuality and whether they had been sexually involved with an older person. It's still possible that the more sexual child may react to the sexual abuse experience differently and I'm interested to know to what extent that might be relevant to the sexualization process, which nobody has begun to explain at this meeting.

Cynthia Graham: One more reaction to the politically incorrect model Michael presented on systematic reporting bias. I think that there is better evidence that could be cited here. In the study that I mentioned by Widom and Morris (1997), looking at substantiated cases of sexual abuse, they found an interesting relationship between current state of depression and how the event was recalled, but no relationship between current depression and whether the event occurred. I would be cautious about using that one study you cited on rape as an example when there are other studies where the data do not support your conclusions.

Michael Bailey: That's a really interesting study but all I can say is that the one study relevant to this which I know about shows what I say it shows, that lying occurs in rape reports (Kanin, 1994).

Cynthia Graham: I wasn't suggesting that it doesn't occur but I think that there is evidence that it's a very small percentage of cases.[1]

John DeLamater: To follow up on Mike's iatrogenic hypothesis, I started thinking about this when Philip Jenkins was presenting because he talked about how in the 1920s there was this movement that has sometimes been referred to in sociology as "child saving," where reformers decide that children are at great risk and need to be saved. Often the effort to save those children probably had more devastating impacts on their lives than if they'd been left wherever they were before the child savers got their hands on them. He did a good job in raising that issue. The really critical question is not did you tell somebody or did somebody find out, but if you told somebody how did they react. One of the things I noticed in the study by Meredith, Deborah, and John is they did ask that. I don't know if you got enough cases there to go back and look at different categories of reactions by whoever was told, but that certainly would be one important thing to look at. Most important, of course, would be looking at cases where some authority was informed in contrast to cases where parents or friends were told. If you tell some social control agent, the sociological criminology literature tells you that you would find that in those circumstances there probably is an independent effect on the subsequent outcomes that would not have occurred if the case had not come to the attention of the authorities.

Carol McCord: When I was at Planned Parenthood I had lots of cases of child sexual abuse reported and they had to be reported to agencies. It was depressing, but almost invariably the kids were in worse shape after the report and after whatever happened, in all kinds of different ways. Families can be taken apart. There's often more public knowledge of the event so there's more experience of shame at a public level. And because authority figures get involved—"it's somebody in a uniform and I'm being asked questions—I'm somehow bad, even though I'm being told I'm not bad." There was even one case in southern Indiana where the person who was investigating actually reabused the child in the course of the investigation. That was one of the worse examples, but it happens.

Anke Ehrhardt: We are now clearly considering the potential effects of childhood sexual abuse long-term and we are a long way away from normal sexual development in children. I agree with John and David. Even if you don't have long-term effects, I think we have a consensus that adults shouldn't have sex with prepubertal children; they should be protected from such experiences. We could expand on that whether we have the evidence or not, but another issue is, do some children sail through that without long-term effects? I think we all can agree that we do have the evidence that that is true. So I would like us to get back to what Elsie was saying earlier; that the issue of differentiating abuse from normal sexual development in children is much more a matter of which kinds of peer sexual behavior in childhood are labeled as sexually abusive, and reportable and punishable. In the arena of peer sexual behavior and expression of childhood sexual behavior, we are much more into the process of deciding what is developmentally appropriate. This afternoon we have only briefly talked about peer sexual relationships. The adult-child issue is relatively straightforward; I think we all would say that shouldn't happen and children should be protected from it.

Gil Herdt: This is a theoretical point that I wanted to pose to Chris. I've been thinking about Ed's interesting claim earlier about immigrant populations in the United States and what that has done. The point is this: Do you have to have a cultural script that says it's legitimate and acceptable to talk about sexual abuse or sexual coercion in order to report it, does there have to be a preceding idea of a cultural story? Ken Plummer's work on telling sexual stories shows rather convincingly that when you have an agreed-upon cultural script it facilitates the person telling the story regardless of the situation. Now with immigrant populations coming into the United States I think there's very, very good evidence about Mexican Americans, about which I know a little bit more. Studies of Raphael Diaz, the anthropologist Joe Carrier, whose work I know quite well, and a woman who has joined our group, Gloria Gonzales, all show a lot of sexual coercion and sexual contact going on; 40% sexual coercion of young immigrant Mexican American women in the group that she's looking at. Feminine Mexican boys in crowded living conditions, particularly sleeping in the same bed, typically report very high levels of sexual interest in them. But this is a culture in which there is very powerful sexual shame and sexual silence. The idea is this is what happens. You don't talk about it. You don't report it to anybody. They come to the United States and then they can talk about it. So at a theoretical level, does there have to be built into a life course perspective the idea that somebody has available to them a cultural script that tells, first of all, this is a phenomenon that exists, it's not just some idiosyncratic or private or accidental thing that happens to me as an individual, and secondly, that gives them permission to perform it, to express it whenever the occasion occurs, including during the survey, when a researcher comes along and says, has this happened to you?

Chris Browning: There are two issues here. One, the issue of disclosure to the interviewer and secondly, in terms of the life course model itself, I'm not sure how this model would be affected by the presence or absence of such a cultural script. Are you implying that that's relevant for the processes that we're referring to in terms of the life course model? I recognize that the reporting issue—whether or not we're going to get differential rates of disclosure by particular groups—is very important. We didn't actually survey non–English speaking populations in this study, but it's clearly an issue. But, regarding your other issue of effects on the life course model itself . . .

Gil Herdt: What if it doesn't count as a phenomenon, that's the point. If it's not regarded as a phenomenon, it doesn't exist. It's like a black hole.

Nobody in the culture has ever said this exists, that it's a phenomenon; it's nothing to count. There's nothing to report. That's how I think it's relevant in how you tap into the person's life experience.

Chris Browning: What you're asking is, I would say, a larger theoretical question about whether or not we need to have cognitive categories for our behavior in order to activate that behavior subsequently. I don't know to what extent such behavior is basically unrecognized within these subpopulations; it's a speculation. To the extent that it is, I'm not sure it would have such an important effect. I would say that there is a direct effect of sexual interest upon later likelihood of such events occurring. I don't think it necessarily needs to have that cognitive mediation, even though at the margin the cognitive mediation may be relevant.

Jay Paul: In terms of wondering whether people would report it, I think that says something more to how we need to ask our questions in these surveys, and how we need to be very conscious of how these experiences may have very different meanings for different people. And how we need to respect the variability of those meanings in asking the questions, getting some general behavioral information without imputing a whole bunch of meanings to it by the way that we phrase the question.

Deborah Tolman: The exchange between Gil and Chris just now was a very good illustration of something that I've been concerned about the entire time that we've been here, which is what our beliefs are about what sexuality is. Now I think yours, Chris, doesn't connect with what Gil was saying, because you're coming from completely different constructions of what sexuality is; it's almost as if you are trying to speak to each other in two separate languages, only no one has mentioned that this is happening and that it might be problematic. What Gil was saying, and because it makes more sense to me I can talk about his view better, is that if there is no cultural script, then the experience was never constructed and doesn't exist. That's his model, his idea about sexuality. You took what he said and put it into your model, which is cognitive mediation, so you're thinking about what he means by cultural stories as "the behavior happens, it gets processed in a certain way and then you can or can't talk about it." I don't think that's what Gil meant.

Gil Herdt: Thank you. That's a nice synopsis.

Chris Browning: It's a disciplinary issue to some extent. To crudely characterize what I think was the underlying assumption, nothing happens without culture. There is no categorization of experience without culture. We can argue about that, but as a sociologist coming out of a structural perspective, I would argue that cultures vary in their strength and that the sexuality itself is not entirely culturally determined.

Deborah Tolman: And I think that's a good articulation of your perspective.

Chris Browning: So we're really addressing things at a higher theoretical level here and we need to, as I think you have effectively done, make some of those assumptions more apparent.

John Bancroft: I don't think it's just a disciplinary issue. Gil is saying it may not exist because there isn't a social script for it. So we then need to ask, does that mean that an unscripted experience which happened is more likely to be forgotten? Is that what you're implying?

Gil Herdt: I was emphasizing the active component is not only the absence of the category, there's also the active silencing and the active shaming that says you do not discuss this in public. So that in a sense there's a voiding of the experience. But there's the more active socially constructive process that says you don't ever talk about this to anybody, even in your family. It's a secret, and this is how in some sexual cultures there is an inherently "conservative" force. You don't talk about these matters with anybody, including yourself; that's what I was trying to get at.

John Bancroft: So you wouldn't have forgotten it, you just wouldn't refer to it.

Gil Herdt: I think now we're getting into individual differences. How would it be processed by particular persons?

Ed Laumann: We were quite aware of the silence about these matters in the Hispanic community when we were designing this survey. We did not deal with this in the national survey because of the cost of developing a bilingual version. But we did cross that bridge in Chicago in the more recent survey. There we had a very large Hispanic sample. We were warned about the lack of knowing the words on the part of women in particular in discussing some of these issues. So we spent a lot of time translating back and forth with native-speaking Spanish folk and we moved very strongly to a behavioral characterization of sexual acts. (That is, we described to every respondent behavioral events, such as oral or anal sex, in everyday words, so that the respondents would better understand what we meant.) There is no question that we are not in the position to reconstruct the *meaning* of these things, but we do know that some events happened and the Hispanic women did describe frequency of sexual activities that were comparable to the men. In fact, the Hispanic group as a whole had higher rates of partnered sexual activity than the white community did. So we did not feel that there was underreporting in this community.

We had an informant who was a clinically trained psychologist who worked at a parish in Pilsen. She came from Peru, was trained as a witch, and had a grandmother who was a witch, and so she discussed with newcomers from Latin America the meanings of sexual transactions of various kinds. Newly arrived immigrants trusted her. The women were complaining that the men never hugged and kissed them. They were married and their husbands would give them money and they really believed that their husbands loved them. She began interviewing the men to try and find out why. Finally a man offered the explanation that *machismo* was very important in this community and penetration was the key part of defining a man's role. There was fear that if they hugged and kissed their women, that this would spoil them for the act that they wanted. It's very clear that the women are, at some level, not seen as sexual objects but at other levels they are very much so. So I think that you're putting your finger on a very important part of this story about what adult-child sexuality would mean in these settings and how would we interpret it, and would there be different consequences that flow from it, because potential trauma would be different. That sensitizes us to how you measure these things and the need for doing good pilot work.

Chris Browning: Can I just add a point about the theoretical issue of the need for a cultural script in order for the life course model to proceed? The discussion of shaming and silence implies some encoding. You can't be silent about something that has not been recognized to some extent.

Bill Friedrich: This is also related to the issue of the parent being comfortable with sexual words. We utilized a number of public day care centers in LA. The sample was two-thirds Hispanic and typically lower income. Including this sample helped to improve the demographic variability of the normative sample. From the outset, we were told that the words in the CSBI were too provocative. Consequently, we had to prepare the day care staff and parents. Before they completed the measure, the parents heard a brief talk about children, behavior, and sexuality. This seemed to ease the way for parents to share this information with us. In fact, we obtained frequencies similar to a sample of Belgian children, but we had to prepare the sample first.

I also have a comment on the issue of normal peer sexuality. This ties into Julia's comments about the persistent neglect of physical abuse. In two studies with European colleagues, the parents were surveyed about their children "playing doctor." The question assessed the frequency of peer sexual interest that involved either exposing genitals or touching a peer's genitals. By combining two items from the CSBI, e.g., exposing sex parts to other children and touching other children's sex parts, we ended up with a fairly similar frequency in terms of "playing doctor" in the 2–5-year-old U.S. sample relative to the Swedish sample. In the U.S. samples, we also had information about concurrent physical abuse. We found a significant and positive relationship between reported physical abuse and the sum of these two peer sexual items.

I am currently doing a study that has enabled me to examine the relationship between emotionally and physically harsh discipline as measured by the Conflict Tactics Scale (CTS) and intrusive sexual behavior as measured by the CSBI. What we're finding with this sample is that emotional abuse is also a significant correlate of elevated levels of peer-peer interaction. I believe that the overall level of family conflict is the key variable, whether it is primarily emotional, physical, or sexual abuse.

This takes me to a study I did looking at the effects of maltreatment experience on mammogram and Pap smear utilization. We hypothesized that sexual abuse would be related to delayed or missing scheduled Pap smears and mammograms. We had Mayo Clinic billing records to validate self-report. While sexual abuse was related to a lower utilization of these screening procedures, the most significant predictor was the patient's report of emotional abuse. Emotional abuse was rated on a six-item measure including such items as "yelled at," "put down," and "made to feel like a bad person," etc. I strongly suggest that other maltreatment experiences be examined simultaneously to understand disturbed behavior.

John DeLamater: Anke raised the issue of getting back to discussing peer sexual context. Were you thinking about identifying what types of peer contacts are normal and whether there is some range of peer sexual contacts that's abnormal, or were you thinking more of distinguishing peer from adult?

Anke Ehrhardt: If we want to reach a consensus on what is normal childhood sexuality in whatever way we define it, then that is the area which we need to debate. I don't think the adult-child issue needs debate. To take something like playing doctor: because it may be increased in cases of sexual abuse or physical abuse doesn't make it itself abnormal. You have beautifully shown that in many of your nonabuse samples you have a variety of sexual behaviors which children show to varying frequencies. Then you add emotional abuse or physical abuse and maybe then some of these behaviors get increased for some of the kids. But the conclusion is that that doesn't make the "playing doctor" itself abnormal. Otherwise, as Elsie has in her records, these children are seen as abnormal because they "play doctor." We need to clearly frame what our position is about childhood sexuality theoretically.

Julia Heiman: It again raises the difficult issue of defining normal sexuality. Does it happen only in normal families that have no abuse? Is a family normal if it has no abuse? I don't mean sexual but all the other types of abuse. This raises a very sticky issue; where do we measure? If we could measure children's sexual behavior, what families would we choose?

Anke Ehrhardt: If our only angle is that intrusive behavior by adults towards children induces or increases sexual behavior in those children, then obviously Bill Friedrich's approach of looking at abusive and nonabusive families is the right one. But we have found that's not true; lots of behaviors which parents endorsed were in children who were not abused. So you find this whole spectrum of childhood sexual behavior which isn't related to abuse. If we want to map what children do developmentally over time, then we need a different kind of design. We do this in all other kinds

of child development behavior. We do it in play behavior. We do it in learning behavior. What toys do kids like, when do they learn to read, how do
they read, what kind of books do they read? We can't say there is no way
to describe children's sexual behavior. I think we step back because we're
so concerned that we might fall into this pathologizing model. We don't
have a really good description of when children do what sexually and what
do girls do and what do boys do and what's the whole spectrum.

David Finkelhor: I'm going to raise the issue about asymmetries, a
very important issue in sexual relationships. Even our moral/ethical context has to do with consent and symmetry and quality. The dilemma is that
in a lot of children's sexual interactions with each other, as in their general
social interaction, there are forms of asymmetry not just in terms of the
power difference between them but in the status difference between them,
the kinds of scripts that they bring to a situation. The question is, in order
for the sexual experience or sexual interaction between children to be
normal or appropriate, what levels of asymmetry are permissible? We're
struggling with this and I don't know what kind of evidence we have to
bear on this. There are some obvious criteria, for example if there's obvious
coercion involved, but suppose that one of the partners is reluctant and
uncomfortable but goes along and then reports ambivalent attitudes about
it later on. Is that something we want to decide is problematic? I think the
genders have very different sexual scripts, even at an early age, that they
may bring to these situations. Girls already have a certain fear of boys and
the physical power that they have even prepubertally, the fact that as they
approach puberty boys begin to see any kind of sexual experience as somehow positive and advantage-building for them, whereas girls are much
more aware of the danger involved. I'd be interested to have some guide to
this kind of thing.

Jany Rademakers: That's not just a sexual issue that you're talking
about. Your child has to develop socially and will interact with other children and sometimes they fight and sometimes there is coercion to do something they don't like, and then your child cries or is upset. Then you teach
him to speak out or be more assertive or you tell the teacher. That's part
of socialization and upbringing. That's not so different when it comes to
soxiosexual encounters. But what happens now is that people treat sexual
play and sexual development as being fundamentally different from other
aspects of child development. I think there are many more similarities than
differences.

David Finkelhor: I agree with that, and was trying to make that point
myself, although I regard it as somewhat of an empirical question as to
whether it is a different realm or not. There are arguments that one could
make that it is a different realm. For example, if there is a strong likelihood
in the sexual realm for there to be "one-trial learning" effects, strong learning that occurs in a single experience; that may not be true in some other

social interactions. One could argue that the sexual realm is different in terms of the things that we are concerned about.

Janet Hyde: Psychologists have studied single-trial learning quite a bit, and it occurs for any kind of behavior or response that's highly conditionable. An example is food aversion; you eat a food once and get sick afterwards and you never want to eat that again. I think that there are a lot of sexual behaviors that are very conditionable and this is probably one of the explanations for fetishes. I think there are lots of examples in sexuality.

Anke Ehrhardt: But what are we talking about in children? They look at each other's genitals, they have some play behavior. We rarely talk about penetrative coital behavior or fetishistic behavior in child-child behavior. What do kids do? Some of them masturbate, they look at each other's genitals, they may touch each other's genitals, they may even play "lovemaking." That's what we're talking about in peer-peer interactions. It's not one-time learning because kids, if they're left alone, do that throughout their childhood. So it's that kind of behavior which Jany is talking about; kids do lots of play behavior, they have to learn about their bodies, they have to learn about those kinds of things.

Jany Rademakers: There can be all kinds of behaviors which are "one-time traumatic." When a child is beaten up by five other children, that's traumatic. So you can think of very bad things happening to children. But in general what Anke is saying is sexual play is play, it's not only playing doctor but also playing Father and Mother, and they play school and they do other kinds of imitation play, and that's what normal sexuality of children is about, rather than the more extreme behavior. We can always go to the extreme examples but I think we have to think more about —normal is a difficult word, but common, ordinary behavior.

Elsie Pinkston: I think I was ruined early in my career because I spent my time teaching young children to do things Piaget said they shouldn't be able to do. But it gave me a clear picture of how divergent each sample is. We should think about whether or not we really want to tie this to developmental stages or whether we want to think of "becoming more sexual" as a process. There are already plenty of charts in the sexual aggression child literature that show you how the child is supposed to behave at this age and that age, and that's exactly how people get in trouble, because most children don't actually follow those lines carefully, precisely. So we need to think about divergent samples and also the issue of developmental delay in children. For instance, with the criteria that I have referred to, if you told the child on three different occasions not to do something and they went ahead and did it, then they were defined as sexually aggressive when, in fact, if you're developmentally delayed that's what happens.

David Finkelhor: The developmental difference between, say, a 6-year-old and a 4-year-old can be much greater than the developmental difference between a 21-year-old and a 14-year-old. Even a small age difference at a young age can have very big consequences. I don't know what that means for sexual interaction between 6-year-olds and 4-year-olds, but we certainly just shouldn't lump everything that children do with one another together without trying to figure out whether there are differences in how their experiences are perceived or described by the children.

Note

1. The statistics on false accusations of rape vary widely, from 2% (a figure that has frequently been cited) to Kanin's (1994) figure of 41%, which derives from a case study of one policy agency in a small metropolitan city in the Midwest. FBI statistics for the annual rate of false reporting of forcible sexual assault across the country have been a consistent 8% (Haws, 1997). A search of the literature on false rape reports revealed two things: Firstly, there appears to be very little research on the rate of false allegations of rape, and secondly, Kanin's (1994) figure of 41% of rapes reported to the police subsequently classified as false is regarded as unusually high.

References

Boney-McCoy, S., & Finkelhor, D. (1996). Is youth victimization related to trauma symptoms and depression after controlling for prior symptoms and family relationships? A longitudinal, prospective study. *Journal of Consulting and Clinical Psychology, 64*, 1406–1416.

Haws, D. (1997). The elusive numbers on false rape. *Columbia Journalism Review, 36*(4), 16.

Kanin, E. J. (1994). False rape allegations. *Archives of Sexual Behavior, 23*, 81–92.

Laumann, E. O., & Michael, R. T. (Eds.). (2001). *Sex, love, and health in America: Private choices and public policies.* Chicago: University of Chicago Press.

Widom, C. S., & Morris, S. (1997). Accuracy of adult recollections of childhood victimization: Part 2. Childhood sexual abuse. *Psychological Assessment, 9*, 34–46.

Part 7.

Toward a Consensus

Conclusions from Research, Policy, and Advocacy Perspectives

DIANE DI MAURO

Introduction

In keeping with the view of research that the inquiry itself is of paramount importance, my conclusions ask or prompt more questions than they answer. I've organized my remarks according to the following categories: the historical context, the research agenda, and research dissemination. Lastly, I will address potential policy-relevant activities and initiatives.

The Historical Context

Today in the United States, we "remain wedded to an ideology of childhood sexual innocence" (Herdt, 2003). In the public sphere, there is typically present an obsessive focus on the trauma of early sexual experiences (ESE) and on the assumed inevitable lifelong negative effects which in turn has "institutionalized" certain aspects of sexual abuse (Jenkins, 2003). Campaigns of victimization infused with moral outrage have become a predominant feature of our social work/foster care/legal system, and very little of this work is informed by scientific understandings of normative childhood sexuality and the complexity and/or significance of ESE, as aptly illustrated by the examples provided—such as the SACY database of children identified as sexually aggressive (Thigpen, Pinkston, & Mayefsky, 2003). Substantiated incidents of sexual abuse have declined yet the demonology continues, alongside an increasing tendency to criminalize child sexual behavior, characterized by the alarming elaborations of sexual abuse in the name of prevention. In the family and educational domain, most parents avoid sexual communication with their children and fail to provide their children with a suitable sexual language; when children reach school-age level, the educational system is as well failing them in this regard. How to move beyond this confining focus is the challenge before us.

The Research Agenda

Gaps in knowledge are considerable. As has been stated here, research is needed to assess both what is known (and this conference has been a very important first step in that direction), and to map what have emerged as key needs for future research identified by many of the papers presented —for we "are looking at childhood sexuality without any standards. We have somehow lost sight of the ranges of normalcy" (Ehrhardt, 2003). We need to define, plan, and enact a research agenda that integrates policy implications, one that tackles this multifaceted topic via a variety of approaches, including a new emphasis on observational work, retrospective techniques, in-person interviews, and focus groups, as well as analytic and theoretical approaches to delineate "the cultural map of childhood sexuality" (Frayser, 2003). The discussions of the first day of this meeting outlined some of the important methodological concerns/issues in this regard. Some promising work is moving forward, making use of culturally sensitive interviews, focus groups with parents and with children (O'Sullivan, 2003), and the CASI computer techniques to obtain explicit information from subjects (Reynolds & Herbenick, 2003).

So what would a preliminary framework/model of normative childhood sexuality that incorporates policy implications look like? Given what has been said in the past two days based on the presentations, an important starting point is the range of behavioral parameters of different populations of children by age, ethnicity, and culture—an outlining of the variability of sexual behavior, of the benchmarks of sexual and gender development over the life course, and of the process of sexual socialization (and here I refer to "purposeful" socialization with specific objectives and guidelines vs. sexual socialization "by default," which is so common in the United States). Moreover, in filling the gap in the knowledge base about normative childhood sexuality, it has been said at this meeting that the research gaze should focus on sexual culture of the family, social/cultural change, the multiplicity of sexuality cultures in the United States, body awareness, experiences with physical intimacy and the acquisition of sexual meaning, and sexual responsivity and awareness in childhood, as well as the impact of environmental factors, changing family structure, and peer group influences. Included in this framework is the needed emphasis on relevant markers of sexual development (e.g., masturbation or first ejaculation).

In addressing the research agenda with regard to ESE, an initial task would be to demarcate what constitutes sexual abuse and coercion, their distinctive features, and the multilayered components that characterize and account for their occurrence and impact within the domain of negative early sexual experiences. This task would inevitably focus on the identification of developmental markers as potential antecedents for such experiences, including familial, religious, and cultural factors. It has also been suggested that it might be more useful to focus on the "sexual trajectory" and the potential consequences of specific behavioral pathways and patterns following ESE over the life course than to focus narrowly on the severity and nature of event-specific trauma (Browning & Laumann,

2003). Included in this framework are the "person-level variables" of child sexual experiences, including their physical and psychological impact, their meanings and interpretations for the individual, and the immediate consequences of such experiences. Likewise, we need to look more closely at ESE as part of an unfolding developmental process involving the family and community in channeling or moderating its cumulative impact over time. Research is needed on the diverse outcomes of ESE and their short-term social and familial consequences; a needed emphasis here is the analysis of ESE within a framework of cultural adaptation. Other important research issues include systematic reporting bias, the validity of self-report sexual coercion and those methods more likely to be successful in obtaining more accurate reports of sexual abuse (Fortenberry & Aalsma, 2003; Reynolds & Herbenick, 2003), approaches that focus on adult pathology, the incorporation of a developmental continuity model, and the impact of iatrogenesis in trauma in which the reaction exacerbates the initial experience.

Lastly, on the topic of the research agenda, I would propose research on the use and development of sexual language and its appropriate use on the part of children as an important potential intervention tool. As a former sexuality educator, I was always impressed by the resolution of educators in assuming that it was possible to empower children by teaching sexual negotiation language in order to be able to respond to an adult's inappropriate sexual overtures. Referring to what is called the NO, GO TELL approach, this technique requires that a child (a) recognize an inappropriate adult overture ("if you feel uncomfortable or confused about how someone is touching or talking to you"), (b) have the ability and courage to say "no" or "stop that," and (c) be able to quickly move away, and accurately represent the offending adult overtures to a trusted adult, a person whom they choose to tell of the incident. This method, while it may have considerable potential, assumes an ability to use sexual language and negotiate such situations in ways most children in the United States are not able to do, for reasons all too familiar to us here.

Research Dissemination

Our dissemination efforts must be guided by the important question of who needs to know what from the research initiative for what purpose, and how that individual can access this information. Answering this question first necessitates identifying the policy/advocacy audience, and second, determining how one takes a pro-active position on this issue. If the mainstay of policy-relevant research is adequate dissemination to those constituencies with a vested interest in the topic, the primary constituency in this case is obviously the professionals in the legal and social welfare system— those at the front line of the child welfare system in the United States working with families and children, such as legal specialists, medical and health care providers, psychologists, and social workers. From there other relevant constituencies would include educators, religious and community leaders, other recognized spokespersons, parents, and caretakers in need of knowledge and guidance regarding what constitutes "normative" child sexuality. Lastly, there is the general public, who need to be engaged in an informed, constructive dialogue on the topic. Given the current U.S. climate, the next important issue is to ask, on what basis and in what context and form can targeted dissemination initiatives/activities occur?

The issue of "accessibility" of research is of paramount importance, and this typically pertains to the act of translating the research finding from the published book or article in order to make it useful for others outside of the research arena. Perhaps what might be considered in this regard is the inclusion of a "policy-relevant" section in the discussion pages of research findings. Yet research translation and dissemination needs to go beyond the printed word as such, and the challenge here is to creatively design and implement a series of dissemination activities appropriate for a variety of constituencies who have different vested interests in the issue. With regard to the topic at hand, research outlining normative sexuality frameworks might be easier to disseminate across different arenas than research on the complexity of ESE and on its confluence of multiple factors and outcomes. It is especially difficult to promote the policy relevance of research challenging trauma-based conceptions of the long-term effects of ESE that imply inevitability and negative adult outcomes. Perhaps an important focus could be the protective intervention strategies (as outlined by Browning & Laumann, 2003) based on a more sophisticated and better understanding of the "turning events," meaning, those events and circumstances that help turn the youth away from a risky trajectory, including a focus on the family and community in their "contradictory" roles of both helping the youth move away from risk and posing obstacles to "turning away." Here, the intent would be to develop mechanisms that can shield at-risk youth from future adverse experiences and to better understand the relationship of abuse to risk behaviors and health-compromising behaviors.

Other Policy-Relevant Activities and Initiatives

An important initial question in thinking about dissemination activities and initiatives would be: What are the parameters, focus, and expected practical outcomes of such discussions, based on what we know?

Access refers not only to the need for researchers to move outside of the science "ghetto" to disseminate their work among other constituencies, but, as well, to the need for them to seek out those arenas in which their research findings can be discussed with the intent of advancing public policy. I offer only a few of the many possibilities.

One category of such arenas includes professional gatherings such as invitational forums and collaborative research initiatives that involve teams of researchers and other practitioner professionals. Researchers could also participate in forums targeting policymakers and community and religious leaders.

Another category is perhaps suggested by my immersion in parenting over the last 14 years. I think parents, representing both the general public and individuals of particular relevance to the topic at hand, constitute a very significant target group. Arenas targeting parents can include parent forums in which parents talk with professionals about normative patterns, benchmarks of development, and the topic of ESE as elucidated by research on these topics. Also, research initiatives involving parents should incorporate specific outreach activities upon conclusion of the research project for purposes of translation and debriefing. In the absence of consistent parent-child sexual communication and an accepting home environment regarding sexuality issues, parents are not likely to be adequate sources of research information; they will not be able to conduct "noninterfering" observation of children's sexual behavior and provide accurate and objective representation of what has been observed. Without such formal opportunities in which parents can become more knowledgeable about childhood sexuality, parents will continue to "traumatically" respond to perceived and actual abuse incidents committed against their children, aiding and abetting the emotionally charged reaction to such events.

In conclusion, the policy challenges for this work are considerable.

References

Browning, C. R., & Laumann, E. O. (2003). The social context of adaptation to childhood sexual maltreatment: A life course perspective. In J. Bancroft (Ed.), *Sexual development in childhood* (pp. 383–403). Bloomington: Indiana University Press.

Ehrhardt, A. (2003). Discussion paper. In J. Bancroft (Ed.), *Sexual development in childhood* (pp. 126–137). Bloomington: Indiana University Press.

Fortenberry, J. D., & Aalsma, M. C. (2003). Abusive sexual experiences before age 12 and adolescent sexual behaviors. In J. Bancroft (Ed.), *Sexual development in childhood* (pp. 359–369). Bloomington: Indiana University Press.

Frayser, S. G. (2003). Cultural dimensions of childhood sexuality in the United States. In J. Bancroft (Ed.), *Sexual development in childhood* (pp. 255–273). Bloomington: Indiana University Press.

Herdt., G. (2003). Discussion paper. In J. Bancroft (Ed.), *Sexual development in childhood* (pp. 274–279). Bloomington: Indiana University Press.

Jenkins, P. (2003). Watching the research pendulum. In J. Bancroft (Ed.), *Sexual development in childhood* (pp. 3–20). Bloomington: Indiana University Press.

O'Sullivan, L. F. (2003). Methodological issues associated with studies of child sexual behavior. In J. Bancroft (Ed.), *Sexual development in childhood* (pp. 23–33). Bloomington: Indiana University Press.

Reynolds, M. A., & Herbenick, D. L. (2003). Using computer-assisted self-interview (CASI) for recall of childhood sexual experiences. In J. Bancroft (Ed.), *Sexual development in childhood* (pp. 77–81). Bloomington: Indiana University Press.

Thigpen, J. W., Pinkston, E. M., & Mayefsky, J. H. (2003). Normative sexual behavior of African American children: Preliminary findings. In J. Bancroft (Ed.), *Sexual development in childhood* (pp. 241–254). Bloomington: Indiana University Press.

Conclusions from a Theoretical Perspective

JOHN BANCROFT

Apart from a general lack of knowledge about sexual development during childhood, two themes emerged during this meeting as clearly needing our attention: methodology and the lack of relevant theory.

Methodology. There was general agreement that we need to address our methods of studying childhood sexuality, whether involving sexual abuse or not, and more research is needed for developing new or better methodologies. Following is a list of the methods that have been used for investigating childhood sexual experiences, most of which were considered at this meeting.

Methods of Investigating Childhood Sexual Experiences

1. Recall by adults/adolescents (Laumann, Browning, van de Rijg, & Gatzeva, 2003)
2. Asking parents (questionnaire/interview) (Friedrich, 2003; Meyer-Bahlburg & Steel, 2003)
3. Training parents as observers (Schuhrke, 2000)
4. Direct observations of children (Langfeldt, 1990)
5. Asking children (O'Sullivan, 2003)
6. Incidents reported to clinics/authorities (Williams, 1994)
7. Using older children as "interviewers" (Borneman, 1990)

There was general agreement that each one of these had fairly major limitations. Some of those limitations could be reduced by improving methodology; some are inevitable. So the priorities in relation to methodology can be stated as follows: (a) What types of question are best answered by each of these different methods, (b) how can each of those methods be improved, and (c) are there other methods of investigating childhood sexual development that we haven't considered that might be developed?

The issue of study design was not considered much, though the importance of longitudinal studies was raised a number of times, however difficult they may be to implement. But an important point that was raised is that longitudinal studies are set up for various reasons and there are opportunities to hook into those and get some questions added that might address "normal" sexual development. The paper by Jack Bates and his colleagues (Bates, Alexander, Oberlander, Dodge, & Pettit, 2003) is an example. David Ferguson and colleagues' study in New Zealand (Fergusson, Horwood, & Lynskey, 1997) is perhaps the best-known example, in which a birth cohort was assessed at intervals until early adulthood. At the age of 18, female subjects were asked about previous experience of CSA. Such experience was associated with a variety of negative sexual outcomes during adolescence. When family and other childhood factors were controlled for, this association was reduced substantially. But there remained evidence of a direct causal link between CSA and early onset of sexual activity, which, in the "life course" perspective, led to other undesirable sexual outcomes. There are also a few longitudinal studies where the children have been followed up after being identified as having experienced sexual abuse (e.g., Widom & Morris, 1997; Williams, 1994), but it would be good to have longitudinal studies looking at normal child development. The Schuhrke (2000) study is a modest example of how you might do this in a qualitative way, having a group of mothers who are trained and then getting them to observe their children and interviewing the mothers over a period of time. More quantitative methods of assessment, for example, Bill Friedrich's type of questionnaire, could be used periodically as well.

Theory. There is a notable lack of theory in this literature, relating to both normal development and the effects of negative experiences. Kendall-Tackett, Williams, and Finkelhor (1993), in their review of child sexual abuse studies, comment on "a nearly universal absence of theoretical underpinnings in the studies conducted to date," and go on to say "researchers evince a great deal of concern about the effects of sexual abuse but disappointingly little concern about why the effects occur." That seems to be partly because of the political incorrectness of paying attention to why or how a child is affected and the need to take for granted that the child has been devastated, as the incredible reaction to the Rind, Tromovitch, and Bauserman (1998) study demonstrated. "Why do you want to ask about how he's been devastated; the fact is he's been devastated." We have apparently been inhibited by this political correctness factor, and that has to change.

Chris Browning, in his presentation, pointed out the heuristic value of separating out "psychogenic" and "life course" factors, but he was very ready to acknowledge that we really need to be looking at both of these approaches and how they interact.

Following is a list of some theoretically relevant issues which we might want to consider.

1. What factors occur during childhood that impact on sexual development?

2. What mechanisms mediate between childhood experiences, both positive and negative, and sexual development?

These two issues were considered by Browning & Laumann (2003) and Heiman, Verhulst, & Heard-Davison (2003).

3. Children vary in their awareness of and responsiveness to sexually relevant stimuli or situations. This issue was raised by the Kinsey Institute researchers (Bancroft, Herbenick, & Reynolds, 2003; Reynolds, Herbenick, & Bancroft, 2003) and it leads to a number of interesting, theoretically relevant questions:
   (a) To what extent is such individual variability learnt (e.g., in the family environment) or innate?
   (b) What are good indicators of this variability (e.g., prepubertal masturbation)?
   (c) Do more sexually aware/responsive children show more positive sexual adjustment in adolescence/adulthood? (We have some evidence to support this.)
   (d) Are more sexually aware/responsive children more likely to be abused by older people? (We found no evidence to support this.)
   (e) Do more sexually aware/responsive children differ from less sexually aware/responsive children in their response to sexual abuse? (There appears to be no evidence on this point.)
   (f) How relevant are the media/Internet/pornography? (We found some evidence; an association between early exposure to pornography and prepubertal onset of masturbation was more marked in the females.) Clearly much more evidence is needed on this crucial topic.

Children vary in their reactions to abusive or exploitative sexual experiences, in terms of both severity and duration. This was addressed at several points in the meeting.

4. What determines the *nonspecific* (i.e., not sexual) reactions to CSA (e.g., PTSD, stigmatization, feelings of betrayal/loss of trust, powerlessness, depression proneness, attachment problems)? To what extent is a negative consequence the result of the sexual experience, the disruptive impact of the sexual abuse on the family, or the traumatic effect of the legal investigation/community reaction to the abuse? We need a theoretical model which would help us predict what "nonspecific" outcome is most likely in which circumstances, taking into account the preabuse characteristics of the child and family as far as possible. This would address most of Michael Bailey's concerns. In terms of depression proneness, we should consider other well-documented examples of how childhood experiences, such as the death of a par-

ent, can be associated with increased likelihood of depressive illness in later life. The important issue of how our propensities for affective reactions are organized during childhood is something we know little about.

5. Why do some children react to child sexual abuse with what is usually described as "traumatic sexualization"? Is there any explanation available? We can consider some possibilities.

    (a) Mood and sexuality. Recent research at The Kinsey Institute (Bancroft, Janssen, Strong, et al., 2003; Bancroft, Janssen, Strong, & Vukadinovic, 2003) shows that adults vary in the relationship between mood and sexuality. Most commonly, in negative mood states sexual interest goes down. But there is an important minority who report an increase of sexual interest in negative mood states, leading to sex being used as a mood regulator, and apparently forming the basis for "compulsive" and high-risk patterns of behavior. These paradoxical mood-sexuality relationships are more common in younger adults. When do they become established? Are they genetically determined? Are they established during childhood? Could they be established prematurely as a result of child sexual abuse? To what extent can childhood sexuality be a mood regulator? To what extent can children develop "compulsive sexual behavior" related to negative mood?

    (b) Sex as a source of pleasure. To what extent can this "sexualized" behavior be understood as a result of discovering sexual pleasure from the CSA?

    (c) Sex as a method of exerting control. There is evidence that some individuals who have been abused become abusers when they are older, and it has been suggested that this may be a way of dealing with the loss of control experienced during the abuse by exerting comparable control over others. How relevant is this to understanding "sexualization"?

    (d) Sex as a means of attracting attention. Many children who have experienced sexual abuse discover that, once the abuse is known about, considerable attention is paid to the incident, and the child in the process. Are further displays of "sexualized" behaviors motivated by a desire for increased parental attention?

We need a theoretical model which would help us predict when "sexualization" is most likely to result.

6. How does sexual abuse as a child lead to specifically sexual consequences in adolescence and later in the "life course"?

    (a) To what extent does "traumatic sexualization," established in childhood, continue into adolescence and adulthood to account for the "life course" consequences? To what extent does it lead to later patterns of "compulsive sexuality," or use of sex as a mood regulator?

(b) To what extent are the long-term consequences of child sexual abuse the result of altered patterns of sexual response, or alternatively of altered patterns of establishing sexual relationships (e.g., impaired "attachment style")? Julia Heiman commented that in comparing the sexuality of abused and nonabused women, she didn't find any difference in sexual responsiveness or arousability but she found differences in numbers of partners. What does this mean? Why are people who have had these early childhood experiences more likely to get involved in sexual relationships later? Is it a sexual issue? Is it an issue about insecurity in relationships? Is it a need for affection? Is it a way of regaining control?

7. Given the traumatic nature of much child sexual abuse, why is there so little evidence in the literature of individuals developing a sexual aversion and avoiding sex as a consequence? Such cases do arise in clinical practice.

Once again we need a theoretical model that adequately captures the complexity of the potential mediating mechanisms.

References

Bancroft, J., Herbenick, D. L., & Reynolds, M. A. (2003). Masturbation as a marker of sexual development: Two studies 50 years apart. In J. Bancroft (Ed.), *Sexual development in childhood* (pp. 156–185). Bloomington: Indiana University Press.

Bancroft, J., Janssen, E., Strong, D., Carnes, L., Vukadinovic, Z., & Long, J. S. (2003). The relation between mood and sexuality in heterosexual men. *Archives of Sexual Behavior, 32,* 217–230.

Bancroft, J., Janssen, E., Strong, D., & Vukadinovic, Z. (2003). The relation between mood and sexuality in gay men. *Archives of Sexual Behavior, 32,* 231–242.

Bates, J. E., Alexander, D., Oberlander, S., Dodge, K. A., & Pettit, G. S. (2003). Antecedents of sexual activity at ages 16 and 17 in a community sample followed from age 5. In J. Bancroft (Ed.), *Sexual development in childhood* (pp. 206–238). Bloomington: Indiana University Press.

Borneman, E. (1990). Progress in empirical research on children's sexuality. In M. E. Perry (Vol. Ed.), *Handbook of sexology: Vol. 7. Childhood and adolescent sexology* (pp. 201–210).

Browning, C. R., & Laumann, E. O. (2003). The social context of adaptation to childhood sexual maltreatment: A life course perspective. In J. Bancroft (Ed.), *Sexual development in childhood* (pp. 383–403). Bloomington: Indiana University Press.

Fergusson, D. M., Horwood, L. J., & Lynskey, M. (1997). Childhood sexual abuse, adolescent sexual behaviors, and sexual revictimization. *Child Abuse & Neglect, 21,* 789–803.

Friedrich, W. N. (2003). Studies of sexuality of nonabused children. In J. Bancroft (Ed.), *Sexual development in childhood* (pp. 107–120). Bloomington: Indiana University Press.

Heiman, J. R., Verhulst, J., & Heard-Davison, A. (2003). Childhood sexuality and adult sexual relationships: How are they connected by data and by theory? In J. Bancroft (Ed.), *Sexual development in childhood* (pp. 404–420). Bloomington: Indiana University Press.

Kendall-Tackett, K., Williams, L. M., & Finkelhor, D. (1993). Impact of sexual abuse on children: A review and synthesis of recent empirical studies. *Psychological Bulletin, 113*(1), 164–180.

Langfeldt, T. (1990). Early childhood and juvenile sexuality, development and problems. In M. E. Perry (Vol. Ed.), *Handbook of sexology: Vol. 7. Childhood and adolescent sexology* (pp. 179–200).

Laumann, E. O., Browning, C. R., van de Rijg, A., & Gatzeva, M. (2003). Sexual contact between children and adults: A life course perspective with special reference to men. In J. Bancroft (Ed.), *Sexual development in childhood* (pp. 293–326). Bloomington: Indiana University Press.

Meyer-Bahlburg, H. F. L., & Steel, J. L. (2003). Using the parents as a source of information about the child, with special emphasis on the sex problems scale of the Child Behavior Checklist. In J. Bancroft (Ed.), *Sexual development in childhood* (pp. 34–53). Bloomington: Indiana University Press.

O'Sullivan, L. F. (2003). Methodological issues associated with studies of child sexual behavior. In J. Bancroft (Ed.), *Sexual development in childhood* (pp. 23–33). Bloomington: Indiana University Press.

Reynolds, M. A., Herbenick, D. L., & Bancroft, J. (2003). The nature of childhood sexual experiences: Two studies 50 years apart. In J. Bancroft (Ed.), *Sexual development in childhood* (pp. 134–155). Bloomington: Indiana University Press.

Rind, B., Tromovitch, P., & Bauserman, R. (1998). A meta-analytic examination of assumed properties of child sexual abuse using college samples. *Psychological Bulletin, 124*(1), 22–53.

Schuhrke, B. (2000). Young children's curiosity about other people's genitals. *Journal of Psychology and Human Sexuality, 12,* 27–48.

Widom, C. S., & Morris, S. (1997). Accuracy of adult recollections of childhood victimization: Part 2. Childhood sexual abuse. *Psychological Assessment, 9*(1), 34–46.

Williams, L. M. (1994). Recall of childhood trauma: A prospective study of women's memories of child sexual abuse. *Journal of Consulting and Clinical Psychology, 62*(6), 1167–1176.

General Discussion

Ed Laumann: We need an assessment of the knowledge base—what we do or don't know about normal childhood sexuality. If we were clearer about what we don't know and why we don't know these things, this would help to motivate methodological inquiries. Clearly the clinical literature, which presumably is referring to kids with problems, is not the best source for assessing normal childhood experiences. The kind of research that Jany Rademakers' (Rademakers, Laan, & Straver, 2003) and Bill Friedrich's (Friedrich, 2003) groups have been working on more directly address these issues. I would like to have more different types of assessment.

In your theoretical discussion you have considered adult-child sexual interaction involving another person visiting on the child some unexpected and often difficult-to-assimilate experience. But there are some other very common childhood experiences that we need to research; one is the very common experience in modern America of the breaking up of a family, with the mother typically beginning a search for a new sexual partner, which does provide modeling for the child of sexual things, making those issues' coming to the fore much more likely. How does this very common pattern, that is part of "normal growing up," impact on the sexual development of the child? This is something that a child has to deal with and may respond to in some more sexual way. We certainly have evidence in our data that children from broken families have earlier ages of first intercourse. Somehow we need to conceptualize a series of collateral events that happen in the life course of children in many cases with considerable frequency. We need to know more about how they characteristically impact the child's sexual development.

John Bancroft: If you remember, we had a discussion of that issue at our theory meeting (Bancroft, 2000): the impact of separation of the parents and the tendency for children of parents who have separated to be more likely to enter sexual relationships early and more likely to separate themselves. There was quite a heated discussion about the number of different explanations for why that should be so. It's an important example of how society is changing and what children are confronted with. In the case of a family breakup, there's emotional trauma. It has to have an impact on how the child deals with attachment as well as confronting the child with the clearly sexual reconnecting of the parent with another partner.

Ed Laumann: There's a lot of literature on the effects of divorce. It seems to me that if we're thinking about the theoretical perspective, we should be considering the social context that the child is experiencing. Sexual abuse is one example, but there are in fact probably more common examples that need to be considered.

John Bancroft: I agree with you. If we start looking at the factors in the environment which confront children with sexuality, we will have quite a number to take into consideration. The number of times I've been sitting with my 6-year-old daughter looking at videos designed for young children, many of them modernized versions of traditional fairy tales, which portray intense romantic relationships, has me wondering what on earth this little 6-year-old girl is thinking about as she watches them. The range of stimuli out there in the environment that confront children with issues related to sex, which they then have to make sense of, is considerable.

Heino Meyer-Bahlburg: This is a useful starting point for considering the theoretical issues, but I am struck by the emphasis on "abuse" and "exploitation." What I would really like to see is a text that is free of "abuse" and "exploitation" and, then, a separate discussion of how the meaning of abuse is acquired by researchers, by the public, and especially by the affected children, adolescents, and adults themselves. I am struck by the way some people seem to reinvent themselves by suspecting that something which happened to them in the past might have been abuse and then start worrying and reinterpreting their life on that basis—something that may have happened but at the time was totally benign or just a minor event. By labeling everything from the outset as "abuse" and "exploitation," we are introducing a marked bias. Especially for the research agenda, we should get rid of this prejudgment of adult-child contact and look at it separately in terms of acquisition of meaning. The same applies to the question of sexuality. When is child sex, sex? How do we conceptualize, even for adolescents and adults, what sex is and what it isn't? I think there needs to be some conceptual work done on these two aspects.

Deborah Tolman: One way to take all of these different specific issues and hold them together theoretically might be to embrace or advocate or explore an ecological model in our approach to normal sexual development. Julia Heiman's model (Heiman, Verhulst, & Heard-Davison, 2003) brought this down even further. Usually, in an ecological model, the center is an individual, but she had ways of breaking that down even further, down to genotypes as the middle point in the concentric circles of her ecological model. Such a model would help us to keep all the many questions in perspective.

Julia Heiman: There's a recent *American Psychologist* article (Thompson & Nelson, 2001) outlining brain development through the age of 18. It summarizes the fact that childhood and adolescence are a period of dramatic brain changes and consolidation. I think it would it be helpful to refer to this as we discuss sexual development. It then makes sense to recognize that this is a time when learning needs to go on, when curiosity in general needs to be stimulated, including curiosity and learning about bodily functions. We need a theory that connects social developmental psychology and brain development. In a sense we know almost more about the brain than we do about sexual development in kids. So the larger concept is the developing child and what he or she needs to function well as an adult. I would also somewhere like to address the issue that the child does need an environment safe from physical as well as sexual abuse, from other traumas to the body.

Philip Jenkins: A couple of moments that have really struck me in this conference have been where someone has made the remark about normal sexual development and somebody else would say yes, but that isn't true for another culture. The more I listen, the more I'm thinking that many people aren't living in the same country I am, because they seem almost in some ways to be in Kinsey's America, which is a country of white people and black people. Within another 40 or 50 years, 25% of America is going to be Latino. There are going to be 50 million Americans of Mexican decent and another 50 million of other Latino descent. Eight percent of the country is going to be Asian American. California just hit majority minority status—that is, non-Latino whites are now the minority. Texas is going to hit that within another five years, and the more I listen to talk about normality the more I'm wondering whose normality. Also in terms of religion, America, contrary to impression, is one of the least religiously diverse countries in the world. It has one of the smallest proportions of non-Christian people of any region. It is a 95% Christian country and it's becoming more so. Religion seems to be a very important factor. Will religion change with big immigrant waves? Yes, it will; it will become more Christian. In fact, America is presently a much less diverse country than say, France, the Netherlands, or, believe it or not, Germany or Britain.

I have two problems with the concept of child abuse; one is the word "child," the other is the word "abuse." One of the things I would most like to see in this document is much more emphasis on the gradation of sexual experience by age and some striking back against the tendency to make everyone under 16, or even 18, God forbid, a child, and much more of the "sliding scale" idea. I would also like to see much more sense of the gradation of abuse and exploitation, so that, for example, one experience with an exhibitionist is not expected to be the same as five years of coercive incest.

Heino Meyer-Bahlburg: As a footnote to what Philip just said, this is specifically directed to the anthropologists here. Our field consists mostly of liberal folk, and one consensus we liberals share is respect for other cultures, especially tribal cultures. Given the ongoing discussion in this country and the related battles about sexual matters, it may actually be quite useful to apply our respect for tribal cultures to the fundamentalists and to look at fundamentalist childrearing principles and the like as cultural expressions of their own, from a distance, without immediately resorting to reflexive liberal responses, and to study them in contrast to nonfundamentalist principles. I wonder whether the anthropologists could help us with that?

Suzanne Frayser: When you say "fundamentalists," what do you mean?

Heino Meyer-Bahlburg: What is usually referred to as the Christian Right. Given the presence of anthropologists, who usually teach us respect for others, I think that we have to take a different perspective and look at these "others" in a more detached mode. I have not seen any decent research or even statements outside of the Christian Right about what effects their principles of childrearing actually have on the development of their children. It is usually addressed from a pejorative perspective, and I am troubled by that.

Suzanne Frayser: One of the things that we can learn from that kind of context is that it's a very structured context. So one question is, do you benefit from at least having guidelines to respond to or embrace your behavior? It reminds me somewhat of initiation ceremonies in other cultures, where at least there is some structured sense of meaning that is given to you by your family. People are seeking some kind of structure or some kind of guide to what it means: "How am I supposed to interpret it?" That's one thing that such groups have to be commended on even if it's not something that is congenial with our liberal point of view.

Anke Ehrhardt: We actually have a lot of information on that through the abstinence movement and what the principles are about sexuality training. While I completely agree with you that we should respect the principles of other groups, in this country the problem is that this minority wants to dictate and has successfully dictated what the educational policies should be for the entire country. So they got together five years ago after the welfare bill and abstinence-only education got the increase, as you all know, to $500 million. The problem that comes with it is that there is no mutual tolerance of diversity; that's how everybody should be and that's how federal dollars should be spent. Another example is the Commission against Teenage Pregnancy, which Sarah Brown is running and which was initiated by Clinton. This specifically brings people with differing views to the table with a very noble agenda of hearing each other's concerns, in contrast to the abstinence-only people who are much more fanatic. This group has tried to hammer out some differences in how best to approach childrearing issues.

Janet Hyde: I'm going to go out on a limb and make a radical statement. One of our problems right now is we have too many issues running around in this group and we'd do much better to focus on them sequentially. I'm going to ask us to focus on the issue of normal or normative child development, and I want to make a radical statement: I think that we should and that we can come to a consensus on what looks like relatively "normal-range" sexuality in childhood. All of you sitting around this table, I'm sure, have parents and clergy and other people who come to you and say, "My child is doing X. Is that normal?" Parents around the United States are tortured by that question, and then we have all these people who are incarcerating and labeling kids because they're doing abnormal stuff when they don't know what the normal stuff is. I think we would do a great service to the nation to have a general, broad-based, science-based, well-thought-out statement about what constitutes normal sexual expression in childhood. As many of you know, I'm co-author of an undergraduate sexuality textbook (Hyde & DeLamater, 2000). Since 1977, there's been a chapter in that textbook on sexual development in childhood and adolescence that's about normal sexual development. It is possible to write about this topic. One of the ways you do it is by talking about ranges, which is exactly what developmental psychologists and pediatricians do with everything. When they talk about milestones for a child walking, they don't say all children should walk at 12 months of age, because it doesn't work that way. So one can talk about sexuality in the same kind of general broad range. You can say that some children in infancy and toddlerhood fondle their genitals; it looks like a substantial percentage from surveys, but a large percentage don't. So it's not abnormal if they do or if they don't— some do, some don't. The same approach can be taken with masturbation, perhaps later in childhood. There's an urgent public need for us to do this. If we don't do it, we continue to make sexual development in childhood unmentionable by not being able to state that there is normal sexual development in childhood. So I would really like to see us focus on what we could say based on the data, not making ridiculously refined statements but talking about ranges and giving general guidance.

Erick Janssen: I have some problems, and I'm sure several of us do, with the use of the word "normal," and to what degree it is a statistical or a normative term that we use. I want to make a plea for an additional sort of study, related to what Heino Meyer-Bahlburg said on the values of adults: a study of the sexual values of adults, what we believe as adults to be normal. We should be studying not just sexual development, but also the outcome of sexual development, namely us and our values. And I have two reasons why I think it is important to focus more on that. If you look at sexual abuse in children, the problem with defining it is, to what extent are we talking about aspects of behavior that we would call wrong, the ethical aspects, versus the potential for harm? Harm clearly is something that could be physical or psychological. But it's very hard to talk about sexual abuse without being aware of values. If you just focus on harm, then we don't know much about it. Because we've not done the right re-search, we don't know really how harmful those experiences are. What we can say is that many people think that many of those experiences are wrong, and being wrong in itself can be harmful to a child, the iatrogenic effects of how society responds to abuse, etc. We need to know more about what makes things "wrong" and what creates adults' values about what sexual development should be like and what to expect. What do we think is appropriate and inappropriate, in addition to studying what children ac-tually do. And that is my second point: Sexual development is not some-thing that unfolds in a child without an environment, without a culture. The majority of behaviors reflective of normal are very likely to be behav-iors that reflect the society's values in the first place. Children's behaviors to a large degree will probably reflect a society's values and adults' values. We have to understand more about society's values and adults' values.

John Bancroft: Janet, this is a Kinsey Institute conference. Kinsey had views about the concept of normality which I haven't entirely rejected. Ba-sically, at the bottom line, I'm in agreement with you—it's a question of terminology. The word "normal" almost inevitably tends to be value-laden and that's where we have difficulty, because of the diversity of cultures with which we're dealing. I have the same problem with sexual health. I was struggling with this with the Surgeon General's report, but there was a majority who felt that sexual health should be a concept that was pro-moted. But sexual health has been used in so many ways over history to present different types of value systems about sexuality, and this recent use seems to be another one. The fact is that we have very little evidence on which we can really base our judgments. Insofar as we do have evidence, there seems to be considerable variability. I often find patients asking, "is it normal that I do this?" or "is it normal that my child does this?" and I end up saying, well, it might not be normal but it's not unusual, or it's not very common but it's not something that we should be concerned about. So I'm wondering, because "normal" is such a provocative term, whether there's some way to deal with the same issues without actually using that precise terminology.

Janet Hyde: I don't care really whether we use the term "normal" or "normal range," which I think is a good substitute. As a psychologist I'm well aware of the problems associated with using the term "normal," but I don't think that we should let our aversion to that term and our academic worries about it deter us from addressing what is a real societal problem. So let's settle on some term and move ahead. In most psychology textbooks in which we teach this material to sophomores, we talk about a number of different ways to define "normal." One is in a statistical sense, saying that a normal behavior is one that's common. That might work for us. Another is the sociological deviance model; if something violates the norms of so-ciety, it's not normal. We probably don't want to use that one. Another definition is how the behavior relates to psychological adjustment; we've been dancing around that issue for the last couple of days, and that might be part of an integration. You could integrate a statistical definition with a psychological adjustment definition, but I actually think the simple statistical definition might not work badly. If you provide parents and policy makers with statements such as "the range of kids who masturbate in early childhood is somewhere between 20% and 70%"—scientifically that's a ridiculous statement because the range is so broad—but I actually think it would be very useful for the general public. And it would be very difficult to argue with scientifically if you gave broad ranges that were justified on the basis of studies.

Anke Ehrhardt: In terms of values, or normal unfolding with environmental input, it applies to all of the child development issues. There are values about when kids should be toilet trained, which influence norms. I like Janet's approach very much and I think it would be very important if we replace sexual behavior for a moment with some other developmental issues. It's as if sexual behavior and curiosity of children are so different from play behavior, curiosity about other body parts, etc. If we could anchor ourselves in the developmental unfolding of other behaviors, then we can come to the range of behaviors. I completely agree with Janet: Parents ask you all the time, when is it normal that my child speaks, speaks words, speaks a sentence, is toilet trained, walks? There are huge ranges in behavior but we can say typically that is it between whatever, 2 and 4, or 20% and 70%, and so on. If we could anchor ourselves to a normal developmental behavioral model, it would help us in this.

Lucia O'Sullivan: I was worrying about how we possibly could set some standards without it being a reflection of value, but I'm beginning to feel that there is something we can do here, something very useful. I was thinking of what Pierre Trudeau said when he was asked to defend why he was supporting homosexual rights and he said, "you know, it may be a sin but it's not a crime." There's a way of sticking to the facts. We can do something useful; we can say there are limitations to what we know scientifically but we know more than anyone knows out there. This is a great chance to provide the sex education that is needed and that they're asking for. I know we can never really be value-free in the numbers we provide, in the behaviors that we discuss or put in any kind of statement. Of course it's going to be a reflection of our values at this cultural moment, this snapshot right here. But it's better than nothing, and at the moment there is nothing, and there's a big need for something. It is true, we all have mothers in particular, it seems, who want to know "When should I be scared?" "When should I be alarmed?" I think we could do a great service here if we can summon up some courage and not worry. If it were language development, we would just stomp right through this.

Diane di Mauro: I would like to support our taking on such a task. I'd like to offer a model that many of you might be familiar with: the SIECUS curriculum guidelines. I was very instrumental in the early stages of creating them and much of the discussion here overlaps the discussion we had then. But we focused on being able to have a conceptual framework of a curriculum. If you look at that, there are a lot of benchmarks and a lot of framework and developmental progression that's very clearly outlined. That process brought together a wonderful panel of people that spent two years hammering it out, with very important consideration given to cultural issues. A framework of sexual development that identifies benchmarks, behaviors, and variations with cultural considerations can be done in this kind of way. If you look at that document, it's an incredible achievement in taking a first step of looking at it from a conceptual point of view. But the outcry after that was "why is there no document that specifically identifies development framework?" SIECUS gets these kinds of inquiries all the time as to the limitations of a document that focuses on curriculum. And of course as an educational organization they were neither in the position nor with the intent of providing an authoritative statement on development. But there's a lot of groundwork that's been done, and this discussion is reminiscent of those early discussions.

Jany Rademakers: I think it's perfectly possible to say some things to a wider audience about normal child sexual development. I give presentations about child sexual development and what it is and what to expect and what not to expect. I think that it's true that we know a lot and we can combine it in a sophisticated way, which a lot of people cannot. On the other hand, when giving such presentations you realize how much we don't know. So what are our own priorities with respect to research? We are at present, in the Netherlands, doing an assessment or mapping of research that has been done on normal sexual behavior. There is a large imbalance between the abuse part and the effects of it and the part about normal sexual behavior, which is the area where we are most lacking data and research. What kinds of behaviors are common in childhood; what's the normal variance within several culturally different populations? What meaning do children attribute to their behavior and sexual experiences and are there gender differences in both behavior and meaning? How do children learn to be sexual in knowledge, attitudes, behavior? Which factors in the individual or the family or the peer group or the social and cultural context stimulate or inhibit such learning processes? What are the developmental lines across the life course perspective?

Ed Laumann: I would endorse the need for statements about age-appropriate behaviors. Rather than say "normal," which labels it in a certain way, we can think about the height and weight charts that we have; we have big-boned, middle-boned, and thin-boned people and we have different ranges there. Do we have the data to be able to state the bottom and top quartile of expected ranges for white Americans, black Americans or African Americans, and Hispanics, or various other significant groups, or even religious groups? If we do, we could then talk about acceleration effects that arise because of sexual experiences, or unwanted sexual attention, or adult-child sexual attention, and delayed expression that arises because the community in which the child is growing up in general is not very supportive or encouraging. For example, you get much lower rates of reported masturbatory behavior by African American men. They are also much less likely to be involved in oral sex, and I would trace that to the conservative upbringing that they have with these kinds of women that are being studied by Jeffry and Elsie.

Jay Paul: While I really feel that Janet made some very good points in trying to get us focused, I do have concerns about the language of normative or normal ranges simply because I think that, in terms of sexual behavior, that becomes so much an issue of social normality, and then social deviance gets drawn in. If you think about same-sex sexual play, and later same-sex sexual interest, clearly that is not normative in terms of what you find among the vast majority of children growing up or what you would say is the social norm. It's important to make sure that our language makes room for this variability and perhaps talks about healthy ranges or healthy variability. When parents come and worry about their children's sexual play and say, "is that normal?" it's a very different question to asking, "is the size of my child within the normal range? Is my child's language acquisition within the normal range?" It's embedded in so many cultural values and cultural concerns and worries that it really needs to be treated as a different set of issues.

John DeLamater: I want to say something about the word "normal." One of my complaints in the last few years is that people don't listen to social scientists. That was crystallized when we had this bill passed that gives $750 million a year to abstinence-only sex education when we already know abstinence-only sex education doesn't work, or at least it doesn't produce the outcomes that the people who voted for the legislation say they're trying to achieve. I've talked to some people about that and they tell me that the reason they don't listen to us is that we don't say things in a way that they can understand, and that we don't give answers to the kinds of questions that they ask us. As Diane said, not only parents but also control agents want to know what's normal. That's the question they ask. When the newspaper reporter calls me about a famous politician who is rumored to have extramarital sex and says is that normal, I know exactly what she wants and she wants me to answer it in those terms. So I think we have two choices. One is, if we are really uncomfortable with the contemporary meaning of the word "normal," we could appropriate the term and change the meaning of it, at least in this context. We can essentially redefine it and work hard to communicate that redefinition to parents, politicians, and control agents. Alternatively, if we don't like the word "normal," we should take on the task of educating people that that's not the right word and we should be prepared to tell them what is the right word and view it as an educational challenge for us. Our big mistake would be to ignore the word "normal." I think we need to either appropriate it and redefine it or we need to educate people about why it's not a reasonable term to use in this context.

Bill Friedrich: The way I got around the word "normal," to make the data from the CSBI useful, was to use the term "developmentally related." In order to separate the age-/gender-specific behaviors that were very unusual from those that were more common, I chose the criteria of at least 20% endorsement. This rate is defensible given what we know of normal distributions, with roughly 34% of the area under the normal curve contained within one standard deviation below the mean. Consequently, a 20% endorsement rate or higher would be within one standard deviation of the mean. These behaviors were labeled "developmentally related."

My measure certainly wasn't representative of all sexual behaviors but that was the strategy that I chose and I found it quite useful, at least for that data. Context also has to be a part of it; it's already a complicated enough task, but if we simply say behavior by itself in terms of frequency we're providing useful information, but there should also be some information about context, whether cultural or the immediate context in which the behavior occurs.

Dennis Fortenberry: I'm reminded of a line from a Robert Lowell poem that he wrote about one of his several hospitalizations for manic-depressive disorder. "The resident physicians said, 'We're not deep in knowledge or wisdom; how can we help you?'" and then the irony of the poem as it went on was all the things that they tried to do to help him. I realized that for a group of professionals the temptation to speak with professional authority and wisdom is nearly irresistible and probably not resistible, but I'm not sure that I think it's appropriate to do so on the basis of what we know and how we know it and the likelihood that whatever we say will be wrong. Our history as professionals over the past 100 years has been to be wrong more often than we've been right. I'm just very nervous about succumbing to the temptation to speak as arbiters of normalcy.

Cynthia Graham: I'm going to disagree with Dennis. I've been thinking a lot about the consensus and there are many different kinds of consensus that we could produce. But I agree with Janet that there is an urgent public need. There's a huge amount we don't know about normal childhood sexual behavior but there are some things that we do know; for example, there are some childhood sexual behaviors that don't necessarily indicate that sexual abuse has occurred. Those are the sorts of things that are crucial to get across. I want to make one other point. Jany Rademakers and Anke Ehrhardt have been emphasizing that sexual development shouldn't be treated differently, but it should be looked at in the same way as other kinds of development, and I agree it would be good if this could be done. But much of what happens in early childhood sexual experience or sexual play is unobservable and there's not a lot we can do about that. We can improve the methodology, and use varied methodologies. But a lot of the behavior will remain private and unobservable in children as young as 2 and 3.

Elsie Pinkston: In my particular perspective all sexual behavior is normal because it's reactive to the environment it comes from, so it can't be abnormal. So I'm most concerned with how we're going to deal with children who come from non-normal or serial non-normal environments. If your behavior is not expected, regardless of context or social learning history or cultural context, then you're in trouble if you're in a state agency. We're not just talking to parents who are concerned about their child; we're talking to people who wish to exert control over sexual behavior in a highly structured environment. I'd like to see the values of the culture being more tolerant of a wider range of behavior than they have been heretofore. If you want to look at fundamentalists, study people like me. A lot of us came to the cities. The rural migration to the city provides a wonderful opportunity to see how we turned out. But we didn't know we were part of the far Right at the time, we just thought we were small-town people. By the way, there isn't anything really wrong with trying to structure your child's environment so that you can ensure their safety and pass on your personal set of beliefs to them. It's just wrong when they don't agree with you.

Anke Ehrhardt: I think we have to become more concrete. I usually agree with Dennis Fortenberry, so what he said made me think he is talking about something different than several of the rest of us. Let me see if we can't agree on something. Sexual behavior is a learned behavior. There are stages of learning. Most or many children are interested to learn about bodies or body parts, about the anatomy of girls and boys, and we can talk about that because people are sufficiently insecure right now that they don't know whether that is normal or abnormal. Many children are interested in pregnancy and babies, where babies come from, etc., etc., and we might want to spell that out. I think people would agree we don't want to suppress children's curiosity about the anatomy of girls and boys and about basic reproductive facts. If we can agree on some of those things, then we can move on to the more difficult issues. Maybe masturbation is still something we can agree on. The next thing is peer behavior. Same-sex inspection "doctor play" is quite common in kids. It's not immediately indicating the course to homosexual orientation. So we can then talk about inspection play, doctor play. We have to be concrete in what we say because otherwise we'll be having different notions in our heads about what's normal and what's not normal, without being aware of those differences.

References

Bancroft, J. (Ed.). (2000). *The role of theory in sex research.* Bloomington: Indiana University Press.

Friedrich, W. N. (2003). Studies of sexuality of nonabused children. In J. Bancroft (Ed.), *Sexual development in childhood* (pp. 107–120). Bloomington: Indiana University Press.

Heiman, J. R., Verhulst, J., & Heard-Davison, A. (2003). Childhood sexuality and adult sexual relationships: How are they connected by data and by theory? In J. Bancroft (Ed.), *Sexual development in childhood* (pp. 404–420). Bloomington: Indiana University Press.

Hyde, J. S., & DeLamater, J. (2000). *Understanding human sexuality* (7th Ed.). New York: McGraw-Hill.

Rademakers, J., Laan, M., & Straver, C. J. (2003). Body awareness and physical intimacy: An exploratory study. In J. Bancroft (Ed.), *Sexual development in childhood* (pp. 121–125). Bloomington: Indiana University Press.

Thompson, R. A., & Nelson, C. A. (2001). Developmental science and the media: Early brain development. *American Psychologist, 56,* 5–15.

Conference Participants

Matthew C. Aalsma is currently completing a postdoctoral psychology fellowship in Adolescent Health Behavior within the Section of Adolescent Medicine at the Indiana University School of Medicine. He completed his graduate work at Ball State University and his predoctoral internship at the University of Washington School of Medicine. He has published in the areas of adolescent personality development and delinquency. His current research focus is on the broader social context of adolescent sexuality.

Douglas B. Alexander is Research Associate in Child Social Development and Developmental Pyschopathology at Indiana University.

J. Michael Bailey is Professor of Psychology at Northwestern University, and specializes in the origins and development of atypical sexuality, especially homosexuality. He is author of *The Man Who Would Be Queen* (2003).

John Bancroft has been Director of The Kinsey Institute since 1995 and is the former leader of the Behavioral Research Group at the Medical Research Council's Reproductive Biology Unit in Edinburgh, Scotland. He has published extensively in various aspects of sexuality research and is author of *Human Sexuality and Its Problems* (1989).

John E. Bates is Professor of Psychology at Indiana University, Bloomington.

Christopher R. Browning is Assistant Professor of Sociology at Ohio State University. His research interests include the life-course consequences of childhood maltreatment and the effects of community structural disadvantage and social organization on risk behavior and health. His research has appeared in *American Sociological Review; Journal of Health and Social Behavior;* and *Journal of Marriage and Family*. He is currently principal investigator on a project funded by the National Institute of Mental Health to study the effects of neighborhood characteristics on HIV risk behavior.

Joseph A. Catania has conducted research on the social and psychological basis of human sexual behavior, thoughts, and feelings, with an emphasis on understanding how people change in these areas over the life span. He also has an ongoing interest in methodological issues in these areas of research.

John D. DeLamater has been studying and writing about sexuality for 30 years. He has published works on premarital sexual behavior, contraceptive use, emotional aspects of sexuality, and social control of sexuality. His current project analyzes the impact of life-course transitions, including having a baby, dissolution of a relationship, and aging on sexual attitudes, behaviors, and relationships. He is co-author of the best-selling *Understanding Human Sexuality* (8th ed.) and editor of *Journal of Sex Research*. He is the recipient of the 2002 Alfred C. Kinsey Award, given by the Society for the Scientific Study of Sexuality for contributions to the study of sexuality.

Diane di Mauro is Director of the Sexuality Research Fellowship Program (since 1995) and Director of the Sexuality and Reproductive Health Fellowship Program for Vietnam at the Social Science Research Council. She received her Ph.D. from the Department of Psychology, State University of New York at Stony Brook. She has worked for more than 20 years in the field of human sexuality, specializing in the areas of sexuality research and education. She is author of *Sexuality Research in the United States: An Assessment of the Social and Behavioral Sciences* (1995). During her tenure as Program Director of the Sexuality Information and Education Council of the U.S., she authored *Winning the Battle: Developing Support for Sexuality and HIV Education* and *Communication Strategies for HIV/AIDS and Sexuality: A Workshop for Mental Health and Health Professionals.* She currently serves on the advisory board for the Center for Gender Equality.

Kenneth A. Dodge is William McDougall Professor of Public Policy Studies and Professor of Psychology at Duke University, where he directs the Center for Child and Family Policy. Since 1978, he has studied children's social development, and is particularly interested in how chronic violent behavior develops, how it can be prevented in high-risk children, and how communities can implement policies to prevent violence. He has published more than 175 scientific articles on the topic of children's development, and has received numerous awards for his scholarship, including the Distinguished Scientific Award from the American Psychological Association, the Boyd McCandless Award, and the Research Scientist Award from the National Institute of Mental Health.

Anke A. Ehrhardt received her Ph.D. in psychology from the University of Düsseldorf, Germany, and completed a postgraduate fellowship in the Psycho-hormonal Research Unit at The Johns Hopkins Hospital. Since 1987, she has been Director of the HIV Center for Clinical and Behavioral Studies at the New York State Psychiatric Institute. She is also a tenured professor of Medical Psychology in the Department of Psychiatry at Columbia University. She came to Columbia University from the State University of New York at Buffalo, where she co-directed the Program of Psychoendocrinology at Children's Hospital. She was also President of the International Academy of Sex Research (1981). She is an internationally known researcher in the field of sexual and gender development of children, adolescents, and adults. For the past 30 years, her research has included a wide range of studies on determinants of sexual risk behavior among children, adolescents, heterosexual women and men, and the gay population, and on comprehensive approaches to preventing HIV and STD infection. She was a member of the Office of AIDS Research from 1995 to 1997 and also served from 1995 to 1999 on the Board of Trustees of The Kinsey Institute. She currently serves on The Ford Foundation Board of Trustees.

David Finkelhor is Director of Crimes Against Children Research Center, Co-Director of the Family Research Laboratory, and Professor of Sociology at the University of New Hampshire. He has been studying the problems of child victimization, child maltreatment, and family violence since 1977. He is well known for his conceptual and empirical work on the problem of child sexual abuse, reflected in publications such as *Sourcebook on Child Sexual Abuse* (1986) and *Nursery Crimes* (1988). He has also written about child homicide, missing and abducted children,

children exposed to domestic and peer violence, and other forms of family violence. In his recent work, he has tried to unify and integrate knowledge about all the diverse forms of child victimization in a field he has termed Developmental Victimology. He is editor and author of 10 books and more than 75 articles and chapters. He has received grants from the National Institute of Mental Health, the National Center on Child Abuse and Neglect, and the U.S. Department of Justice, and a variety of other sources. In 1994, he was given the Distinguished Child Abuse Professional Award by the American Professional Society on the Abuse of Children.

J. Dennis Fortenberry is Professor of Pediatrics at Indiana University. He specializes in adolescent medicine, with specific research interests in adolescents' sexual behavior and sexually transmitted diseases. His earlier research includes factors related to care-seeking for sexually transmitted infections, the influence of relationship quality on adolescent sexual behaviors, and the influence of factors such as literacy and stigma on care-seeking for sexually transmitted infections.

Suzanne G. Frayser is a cultural anthropologist who specializes in cross-cultural research and human sexuality. She has taught the interdisciplinary course on human sexuality at The Colorado College since 1981. She is author of *Varieties of Sexual Experience: An Anthropological Perspective on Human Sexuality,* co-author of *Studies in Human Sexuality: A Selected Guide,* and author of many articles on issues in human sexuality (including an overview of normal childhood sexuality for *Annual Review of Sex Research*). She has served as Western Region President and a member of the Board of Directors of the Society for the Scientific Study of Sexuality, as Secretary/Treasurer of the Society for Cross-Cultural Research, and as a contributing editor to *Journal of Sex Research.*

William N. Friedrich is Professor and Consultant in the Department of Psychiatry and Psychology at Mayo Clinic and Mayo Medical School in Rochester, Minnesota. He is the author of several books on the treatment of sexually abused children and has published numerous articles and chapters on the evaluation and treatment of maltreated children and their parents. He is the developer of the Child Sexual Behavior Inventory published by PAR. His most recent book, *Psychological Assessment of Sexually Abused Children and Their Families,* was published in 2001. He is a Diplomate with the American Board of Professional Psychology in both Clinical and Family Psychology.

Mariana Gatzeva is a fourth-year Ph.D. student in sociology at The University of Chicago.

Cynthia A. Graham is currently Clinical Assistant Professor of Gender Studies and Assistant Professor of Psychiatry at Indiana University. She obtained her Ph.D. in clinical psychology from McGill University. Her research interests include the effects of oral contraceptives on sexuality, menstrual synchrony, methodological issues in recall data on sexual behavior, and gender differences in sexuality.

Amy R. Heard-Davison is currently a Senior Postdoctoral Fellow in Reproductive and Sexual Medicine at the University of Washington Medical Center. Her clinical and research interests include sexual risk behavior, adjustment to chronic pain, and relationship and sexual functioning in chronic illness. Her current research is focused on measurement issues in female sexual response and the psychophysiological effects of medications on sexual response.

Julia R. Heiman is Professor of Psychiatry and Behavioral Science at the University of Washington School of Medicine, where she is Director of the Reproductive and Sexual Medicine Clinic. She earned her Ph.D. from the State University of New York at Stony Brook. Her research and clinical work has focused on human sexual response, sexual dysfunction, sexual abuse histories, and psychophysiology. She has published broadly and is currently editor of *Annual Review of Sex Research* (2000–2004) and serves on a variety of medical advisory boards nationally and internationally.

Debra L. Herbenick is a Research Associate at The Kinsey Institute. She has been involved in research related to childhood sexual development, erectile dysfunction, and vulvar health and disease.

Gilbert Herdt is Professor of Human Sexuality and Anthropology, and Director of the Human Sexuality Studies Program and National Sexuality Resource Center at San Francisco State University. He is also founder of the interdisciplinary Institute on Sexuality, Inequality and Health. He has published more than 50 papers and 20 books.

Janet Shibley Hyde is Helen Thompson Woolley Professor of Psychology and Women's Studies at the University of Wisconsin–Madison. Her research focuses on both gender development and sexuality. She is the author of two textbooks, *Half the Human Experience: The Psychology of Women* (6th ed., 2003), and, with John DeLamater, *Understanding Human Sexuality* (8th ed., 2003). She has published numerous meta-analyses of research on psychological gender differences, including gender differences in sexuality and in self-esteem.

Erick Janssen is Associate Scientist at The Kinsey Institute. He received his Ph.D. at the University of Amsterdam, the Netherlands, in 1995. He has published on sexual psychophysiology, cognitive models of sexual arousal, sexual dysfunction, and mood and sexuality. His current research interests include the study of inhibition and activation of sexual arousal, sexual uses of the Internet, and the determinants of high-risk sexual behavior. He is a member of the Editorial Board of *Archives of Sexual Behavior* and *Dutch Journal of Sexology*, and a reviewer for several journals, including *Journal of Sex Research*.

Philip Jenkins is Distinguished Professor of History and Religious Studies at Penn State University. He has published 16 books, including *Moral Panic: Changing Concepts of the Child Molester in Modern America* (1998) and *Beyond Tolerance: Child Pornography on the Internet* (2001).

M. J. C. Laan is a teacher and psychologist, and specializes in supporting youth who are at risk for or who have experienced sexual abuse.

Edward O. Laumann is George Herbert Mead Distinguished Service Professor of Sociology at The University of Chicago. Since joining the University in 1973, he has acted as the editor of *American Journal of Sociology*, chair of the department of sociology, dean of the division of social sciences, and provost of The University of Chicago, and is currently the director of the Ogburn Stouffer Center for Population and Social Organization. His publications include *The Organizational State: Social Choice in National Policy Domains; The Hollow Core: Interest Representation in National Policymaking; The Social Organization of Sexuality; Sex, Love, and Health in America;* and *Sex in the City* (in press).

Jay H. Mayefsky is a graduate of Roosevelt University and Northwestern University Medical School in Chicago. He completed his pediatric residency at Children's Hospital of Michigan in Detroit. Subsequently, he was a Robert Wood Johnson Fellow in the General Pediatrics Academic Fellowship Program at the University of Rochester. He also earned his M.P.H. at the University of Rochester. Upon completion of training he returned to Chicago and joined the Division of Ambulatory Pediatrics at Cook County Hospital and the Department of Pediatrics of Finch University of Health Sciences/The Chicago Medical School. His responsibilities include teaching, patient care, and clinical research. He currently holds the ranks of Senior Attending Physician, Director of Comprehensive Care Clinic, Associate Director of the Center for Pediatric Environmental Health, and Associate Professor of Pediatrics. He is board certified in Pediatrics and Pediatric Emergency Medicine, and a member of the American Academy of Pediatrics, the Ambulatory Pediatric Association, the Midwest Society for Pediatric Research, and the Council on Medical Student Education in Pediatrics. He is the author of several articles and textbook chapters.

Carol McCord is Staff Therapist at The Kinsey Institute Sexual Health Clinic.

Heino F. L. Meyer-Bahlburg is Research Scientist at the New York State Psychiatric Institute and Professor of Clinical Psychology in the Department of Psychiatry at Columbia University. His research focuses on the development and differentiation of gender and sexuality from prenatal life through mid-adulthood, and his clinical work focuses on children and adolescents with sex hormone disorders and/or problems of genital development and on children with atypical gender development.

Susan F. Newcomer is a statistician and demographer at the National Institutes of Health. She holds a 1983 Ph.D. in sociology from the University of North Carolina. From 1984 to 1988, she was Director of Education at Planned Parenthood Federation of America. At NIH she is the project officer on a portfolio of research grants on fertility, HIV risk, contraceptive use, reproductive health, and adolescent risk behaviors, including interventions to reduce risk in youth and adults. Another part of her job is to develop and maintain contacts with behavioral and social science researchers in the United States and in other countries, and to provide assistance to those wishing to apply for funding to the NIH. Her publications have dealt with adolescent sexuality, fertility, and sexuality education.

Sarah E. Oberlander received her Bachelor of Science degree in Psychology from Indiana University in 2001. At the time of publication, she is enrolled in the Community-Social Psychology Ph.D. program at the University of Maryland, Baltimore County.

Lucia F. O'Sullivan is Research Scientist at the HIV Center for Clinical and Behavioral Studies at the New York State Psychiatric Institute, and an assistant professor of Clinical Psychology in the Department of Psychiatry at Columbia University. After receiving her Ph.D. in social psychology, she completed a postdoctoral fellowship at the HIV Center where she has remained. She has been conducting research with inner-city late childhood and early- to mid-adolescent girls in an effort to assess the development of early heterosexual behavior and related social cognitions. Her other research interests and experience include sexual scripts, decision-making, and communication processes in dating relationships. She is the author or co-author of many articles and chapters on these topics, and an active participant in sexuality and interpersonal relationship research societies.

Jay P. Paul has been affiliated with the University of California, San Francisco's Center for AIDS Prevention Studies for a decade, and has been a co-investigator on several large AIDS behavioral surveys as well as a co-investigator and Project Director on an NIAAA-funded AIDS intervention project with gay male substance abusers. He is currently Principal Investigator of a three-year qualitative study on the determinants of smoking among GLB youth. He is also co-Principal Investigator on the Urban Men's Health Study Longitudinal Follow-up Study, which will test an original model that seeks to explain the increased sexual risk-taking of MSM (men who have sex with men) who have a history of childhood sexual coercion. Trained as a clinical psychologist and sexologist, his work has primarily been on gay and bisexual men in the areas of substance use and abuse and sexual risk behavior, development of HIV risk-reduction interventions, and initiation of health care. Most recently, his papers and research have focused on developmental antecedents to risk-taking behavior and mental health issues among gay men. He was recently elected a Fellow of the American Psychological Association.

Gregory S. Pettit is Alumni Professor in the Department of Human Development and Family Studies at the College of Human Sciences, Auburn University. He received his Ph.D. in interdisciplinary child studies at Indiana University. He is a Fellow of the American Psychological Association and past Associate Editor of *Developmental Psychology*. His research interests focus on the development of social competence in childhood and adolescence, with special reference to the role of parents, peers, and the broader social-cultural contexts of neighborhoods, communities, after-school programs, and extra-curricular activities.

Elsie M. Pinkston is Professor at the School of Social Service Administration at The University of Chicago. She received her doctorate in developmental and child psychology from the University of Kansas, Department of Human Development and Family Life. She is one of the innovators of behavioral clinical social work methods, particularly in the treatment of families. She has directed programs in Parent Education, Home-Based Parent Training, the Program Procedures Project, and Parent Partnership. She divides her time equally between research and teaching with occasional community service. She is first author of *Effective Social Work Practice* and *Care of the Elderly: A Family Approach,* and co-editor of *Environment and Behavior.* As a pioneer in behavioral social work practice, she has published in *Journal of Applied Behavioral Analysis; Behavior Therapy; The Gerontologist; Social Service Review;* and *Social Work.* She is currently writing a book on the use of sexual aggression as a category for treatment of children, entitled *Bad Manners, Bad Politics, and Uncaring Hearts.*

Lance M. Pollack is Research Specialist at the Center for AIDS Prevention Studies at the University of California, San Francisco. In November 1986, he was the first data analyst hired for the Center. He also serves as the senior data analyst for the Health Survey Research Unit, which is based at UCSF. He has worked with Dr. Joseph Catania continuously since 1990 on several major studies including the National AIDS Behavioral Surveys, the National AIDS Behavioral Methodology Studies, and the National Sexual Health Survey. For the Urban Men's Health Study, he served as co-investigator, project director, database manager, and senior data analyst. He has co-authored more than a dozen publications based on data from the UMHS.

Jany Rademakers studied Developmental and Clinical Psychology at the University of Utrecht. In 1991, she completed a thesis entitled "Contraception and Interaction: The Prevention of Teenage Pregnancy in the Netherlands" and received a Ph.D. in Social Sciences. From 1985 to 1992, she was Research Coordinator of

Stimezo Nederland, the association of abortion clinics in the Netherlands. During that period she conducted and supervised studies on the epidemiology of abortion in the Netherlands, the quality of abortion care, and the prevention of unwanted pregnancies. Since 1992, she has held the position of Research Coordinator at the Netherlands Institute of Social Sexological Research (NISSO) in Utrecht, the Netherlands. She is responsible for the research program on the sexuality of children and adolescents. Her main fields of expertise are the sexual development of children and adolescents, teenage sexual and contraceptive behavior, unwanted pregnancy and abortion, and AIDS- and STD-prevention.

Meredith A. Reynolds received her Ph.D. in Clinical Psychology from the University of Michigan in 1997. She was a Social Science Research Council, Sexuality Fellowship Program postdoctoral fellow at The Kinsey Institute from 1997 to 1999.

Stephanie A. Sanders is Associate Director at The Kinsey Institute, Associate Professor of Gender Studies, and a Research Fellow of the Rural Center for AIDS Prevention at Indiana University, Bloomington. A biopsychologist by training, she has been involved in research on sex and gender differences in behavior; sexual behavior patterns related to risk for sexually transmitted infections; sexual orientation and sexual behavior; sex hormones and behavior; the effects of prenatal exposures to drugs and hormones on behavioral, cognitive, and social development; women's menstrual cycling; and sexual arousal in women. She is active in the Society for the Scientific Study of Sexuality.

Jennifer Lynne Steel is Assistant Professor in the School of Medicine at the University of Pittsburgh. Her research focuses on determinants of HIV-risk behavior; the relationship between psychosocial factors, immune functioning, and disease progression in HIV and virally related cancers; and quality of life in patients with cancer and HIV. She also works clinically in the area of oncology and HIV/AIDS.

Cornelis J. Straver was Senior Reseacher and afterwards Director (1987–93) of the Netherlands Institute of Social Sexological Research (NISSO) in Utrecht, the Netherlands. He has conducted research and published on sexual development (life course), unmarried cohabitation (social, psychological, and legal aspects), married couples (traditional and modern), and the future of sexology (research, professional help, and education).

Jeffry W. Thigpen is a doctoral student at The University of Chicago's School of Social Service Administration, and Project Director of the Child Sexual Behavior study conducted by the School's Center for Social Work Practice Research. His intellectual and research interests include sexual behavior of African American children and cross-cultural interpretations of illness and disability.

Deborah L. Tolman is Associate Director and Senior Research Scientist at the Center for Research on Women at Wellesley College. She founded and directs the Gender and Sexuality Project, a series of studies of adolescent sexuality development. She has written numerous papers on female psychosocial development, female and male adolescent sexuality, and the integration of qualitative and quantitative measures. Her book *Dilemmas of Desire: Teenage Girls Talk about Sexuality* was published in 2002.

Arnout Van de Rijt is an M.A. student in Sociology at Utrecht University. Since 1998, he has worked on a research project, "The Management of Matches," with principal investigators Werner Raub and Jeroen Weesie. The project investigates the conditions under which trust and cooperation problems are solved in durable relations between two parties. In 2001, he collaborated with Edward Laumann in analyzing the Chicago Health and Social Life Survey at the National Opinion Research Center at The University of Chicago. He has done research on the empirical tenability of the popular claim "once a victim, always a victim," on the explanation of race- and religion-based group differences in marriage chances, and on an application of bargaining theory to intimate relationships. He will continue his graduate studies at Cornell University starting in 2002.

Johan Verhulst is Associate Professor of Psychiatry and Behavioral Sciences at the University of Washington School of Medicine. He obtained his M.D. at the University of Leuven in Belgium and trained in psychiatry at the universities of Leuven and Utrecht. His scholarly work deals with psychiatric education as well as with partner relationship and sex therapy.

Kenneth J. Zucker is Psychologist-in-Chief at the Centre for Addiction and Mental Health in Toronto; head of the Child and Adolescent Gender Identity Clinic, Child Psychiatry Program, at the Centre; and Professor of Psychology and of Psychiatry at the University of Toronto. He has published widely in the area of psychosexual development, including gender identity disorders in children and adolescents. He is the author (with Susan J. Bradley) of *Gender Identity Disorder and Psychosexual Problems in Children and Adolescents* (1995) and editor of *Archives of Sexual Behavior.*

Index

Italicized numbers indicate tables.